Intrinsic
and Extrinsic
Motivation

This is a volume in the Academic Press
EDUCATIONAL PSYCHOLOGY SERIES

Critical comprehensive reviews of research knowledge, theories, principles, and practices

Under the editorship of Gary D. Phye

Intrinsic and Extrinsic Motivation

The Search for Optimal Motivation and Performance

EDITED BY

Carol Sansone
Department of Psychology
University of Utah

Judith M. Harackiewicz
Department of Psychology
University of Wisconsin–Madison

ACADEMIC PRESS

An Imprint of Elsevier

San Diego   San Francisco   New York   Boston   London   Sydney   Tokyo

The sponsoring editor for this book was Nikki Levy, the editorial coordinator was Barbara Makinster, the production editor was Rebecca Orbegoso. The cover was designed by Cathy Reynolds. Composition was done by Hermitage Publishing Services in Briarcliff Manor, New York, and the book was printed and bound by Quinn-Woodbine in Woodbine, New Jersey.

Cover photo credit: Images © 2000 Photodisc, Inc.

Academic Press
An Imprint of Elsevier
525 B Street, Suite 1900, San Diego, California 92101-4495, USA
http://www.academicpress.com

Academic Press
Harcourt Place, 32 Jamestown Road, London NW1 7BY, UK
http://www.academicpress.com

Library of Congress Catalog Card Number: 00-102571

ISBN-13: 978-0-12-619070-0
ISBN-10: 0-12-619070-4

Transferred to Digital Printing 2007

06   07   08   09   QW   9   8   7   6   5   4   3

CS: To my parents, Mary and Tony Sansone, who taught me the importance of working hard *and* having fun.

JMH: To Mary, Katie, and Cliff Thurber for showing me what intrinsic motivation looks like outside my laboratory.

Contents

Are the Costs of Rewards Still Hidden?
A New Look at an Old Debate

3. REWARDS AND CREATIVITY

Beth A. Hennessey

4. REWARDING COMPETENCE: THE IMPORTANCE OF GOALS IN THE STUDY OF INTRINSIC MOTIVATION

Judith M. Harackiewicz and Carol Sansone

5. THE STRUCTURE AND SUBSTANCE
OF INTRINSIC MOTIVATION

James Y. Shah and Arie W. Kruglanski

2

A New Debate

Hidden Costs (and Benefits) of Achievement Goals

6. MEANING AND MOTIVATION

Daniel C. Molden and Carol S. Dweck

7. WHAT LEARNERS WANT TO KNOW: THE ROLE OF ACHIEVEMENT GOALS IN SHAPING INFORMATION SEEKING, LEARNING, AND INTEREST

Ruth Butler

8. MULTIPLE PATHWAYS TO LEARNING AND ACHIEVEMENT: THE ROLE OF GOAL ORIENTATION IN FOSTERING ADAPTIVE MOTIVATION, AFFECT, AND COGNITION

Elizabeth A. Linnenbrink and Paul R. Pintrich

9. ACHIEVEMENT GOALS AND OPTIMAL MOTIVATION: A MULTIPLE GOALS APPROACH

Kenneth E. Barron and Judith M. Harackiewicz

The Role of Interest in Learning and Self-Regulation

"Extrinsic" versus "Intrinsic" Motivation Reconsidered

10. TURNING "PLAY" INTO "WORK" AND "WORK" INTO "PLAY": 25 YEARS OF RESEARCH ON INTRINSIC VERSUS EXTRINSIC MOTIVATION

Mark R. Lepper and Jennifer Henderlong

11. AN INTEREST RESEARCHER'S PERSPECTIVE: THE EFFECTS OF EXTRINSIC AND INTRINSIC FACTORS ON MOTIVATION

Suzanne Hidi

12. INTEREST AND SELF-REGULATION: THE RELATION BETWEEN HAVING TO AND WANTING TO

Carol Sansone and Jessi L. Smith

13. INDIVIDUAL INTEREST AND ITS IMPLICATIONS FOR UNDERSTANDING INTRINSIC MOTIVATION

K. Ann Renninger

14. PARENTS, TASK VALUES, AND REAL-LIFE ACHIEVEMENT-RELATED CHOICES

Janis E. Jacobs and Jacquelynne S. Eccles

4

Conclusion

Contributors

Numbers in parentheses indicate the pages on which the authors' contributions begin.

Kenneth E. Barron (229), Department of Psychology, University of Wisconsin–Madison, Madison, Wisconsin 53706

Ruth Butler (161), School of Education, Hebrew University of Jerusalem, Jerusalem 91905, Israel

Edward L. Deci (13), Human Motivation Program, Department of Clinical and Social Sciences in Psychology, University of Rochester, Rochester, New York 14627

Carol S. Dweck (131), Department of Psychology, Columbia University, New York, New York 10027

Jacquelynne S. Eccles (405), Department of Psychology, University of Michigan, Ann Arbor, Michigan 48109

Judith M. Harackiewicz (1, 79, 229, 443), Department of Psychology, University of Wisconsin–Madison, Madison, Wisconsin 53706

Jennifer Henderlong (257), Department of Psychology, Stanford University, Stanford, California 94305

Beth A. Hennessey (55), Department of Psychology, Wellesley College, Wellesley, Massachusetts 02481

Suzanne Hidi (309), Ontario Institute for Studies in Education, University of Toronto, Toronto M5S 1A1, Canada

Janis E. Jacobs (405), Department of Psychology and Department of Human Development and Family Studies, Pennsylvania State University, University Park, Pennsylvania 16802

Arie W. Kruglanski (105), Department of Psychology, University of Maryland, College Park, Maryland 20742

Mark R. Lepper (257), Department of Psychology, Stanford University, Stanford, California 94305

Elizabeth A. Linnenbrink (195), Combined Program in Education and Psychology, University of Michigan, Ann Arbor, Michigan 48109

Daniel C. Molden (131), Department of Psychology, Columbia University, New York, New York 10027

Paul R. Pintrich (195), Combined Program in Education and Psychology, University of Michigan, Ann Arbor, Michigan 48109

K. Ann Renninger (373), Program in Education, Swarthmore College, Swarthmore, Pennsylvania 19081

Richard M. Ryan (13), Human Motivation Program, Department of Clinical and Social Sciences in Psychology, University of Rochester, Rochester, New York 14627

Carol Sansone (1, 79, 341, 443), Department of Psychology, University of Utah, 390 S. 1530 E., Room 502, Salt Lake City, Utah 84112

James Y. Shah (105), Department of Psychology, University of Wisconsin–Madison, Madison, Wisconsin 53707

Jessi L. Smith (341), Department of Psychology, University of Utah, 390 S. 1530 E., Room 502, Salt Lake City, Utah 84112

Preface

Why do we do the things we do? Psychologists, philosophers, parents, educators and students, and employers and employees (among others) have long tried to understand the answer to this question. Historically, the field of psychology focused on two main types of explanations: basic biological needs or drives connected to survival and procreation (e.g., hunger, thirst, sex), and extrinsic rewards or punishments. According to these perspectives, motivation energizes and guides behavior toward a particular outcome. Researchers also began to recognize, however, that these two types of explanation were not sufficient. Rather, humans (and other animals) sometimes engage in behaviors that seem to be ends in themselves rather than a means to some outcome. Moreover, these behaviors appear to be associated with positive feelings of interest, enjoyment, and satisfaction. Thus, researchers began to develop theories about "intrinsic" rewards and intrinsic motivation, in which the rewards are inherent to the activity.

The distinction between "intrinsic" and "extrinsic" motivation became controversial almost from the first, however. For example, in the early 1970s, several seminal studies were the first to illustrate the paradox that extrinsic rewards can undermine intrinsic motivation, and they generated much excitement. Subsequently, an impressive number of studies suggested that using an extrinsic reward to motivate someone could backfire when it was something that he or she would have done anyway. In particular, the reward could have negative effects on the quality and creativity of performance and on subsequent motivation to perform the activity once the reward was received.

As research in this area burgeoned, more comprehensive theories were developed and these general conclusions were qualified by a number of carefully documented caveats (e.g., for negative effects to occur, individuals must expect the reward). Additional research found that negative effects on intrinsic motivation and performance were not limited to rewards but seemed to be associated with a variety of extrinsic constraints such as deadlines and surveillance. These issues became even further complicated when researchers started to examine the effects of rewards made contingent upon achieving some level of competence. The findings from these studies were mixed, with performance-contingent rewards resulting in negative, positive, or null effects on intrinsic motivation and performance.

During the 1970s and early 1980s, a lively debate emerged as a number of researchers vociferously challenged the studies and conclusions about the negative relation between "extrinsic" constraints and "intrinsic" motivation and performance. The divergent conclusions were left to coexist in a lingering tension. In the "real world," the use of token economies (in which behavior is controlled by rewards) in schools and hospitals was and continues to be widespread. In business, compensation packages continue to be used to motivate workers, and in schools, teachers still use gold stars and stickers to reward children for good work. At the same time, management consultants counsel against using extrinsic incentives to motivate employees, and education consultants counsel against policies and procedures that interfere with intrinsic motivation to learn. Thus, both sides of this ongoing debate have informed policy.

The debate reerupted in 1996 when Eisenberger and Cameron published an article in *American Psychologist* that suggested that detrimental effects of rewards were a "myth." In this article, they presented a review of the literature based primarily on meta-analytical techniques and described research from their own laboratory. They suggested that any negative effects of rewards are limited to extremely rare occasions in the real world and that in fact "extrinsic" motivation is quite beneficial in motivating most behaviors. The publication of this article in the flagship journal of the American Psychological Association signaled that questions first raised in the early-1970s about the use of rewards were still being debated. Moreover, the debate was of great interest to researchers and practitioners in psychology, education, and work settings.

The appearance of this article also highlighted the need to update the discussion beyond the effects of extrinsic rewards per se, to include newer models, approaches, and applications that have emerged since the early 1970s. Subsequently, we (Sansone and Harackiewicz) organized a symposium for the Society of Experimental Social Psychology meeting in October 1997, that included people from multiple positions in the debate. The discussion among the panel members became somewhat heated, given the different approaches and answers presented.

In light of the debate among the symposium panel members and the renewed and continuing interest in understanding "intrinsic" motivation and "extrinsic" motivation, we sought to put together an edited book that would revisit the earlier work and provide an update on what we have learned since then, and what we have still to learn. In this book, we have a mix of chapters. Some chapters revisit the initial seminal work on this topic and examine how well its conclusions have stood the test of time. Other chapters focus on newer issues or approaches that evolved from the earlier work. The chapters also provide a mix of theory, basic research, and applied research, with research conducted both in laboratories and in education settings.

The book has three major sections. In the first section ("Are the Costs of Rewards Still Hidden? A New Look at an Old Debate"), authors review and update the literature on the effects of rewards and other extrinsic incentives or constraints on motivation and creativity. Several chapters address the conflicting conclusions of recent meta-analyses and embed these reviews within broader conceptual frameworks. Other chapters in this section present a conceptual shift to thinking about the effects of "extrinsic" factors in the context of individuals' goals.

The second section ("A New Debate: Hidden Costs (and Benefits) of Achievement Goals") presents chapters that focus specifically on achievement goals. These chapters present differing views on how mastery goals and performance-achievement goals affect learning, performance, and intrinsic motivation. Echoing some of the earlier debate about the effects of extrinsic rewards and intrinsic rewards, these chapters raise the question of whether there are hidden costs *and* hidden benefits associated with different types of achievement goals.

In the third section ("The Role of Interest in Learning and Self-Regulation: 'Extrinsic' versus 'Intrinsic' Motivation Reconsidered"), chapters revisit the question of how extrinsic and intrinsic motivators may work in everyday life. One important difference between the typical laboratory tasks used and real-life activities is that in real life, activities are not always, or continually, "intrinsically" interesting. These chapters thus address the implied tension between "intrinsic" motivation and "extrinsic" motivation and whether either or both are necessary and/or sufficient to sustain effective performance over time. Several chapters also address the developmental nature of intrinsic motivation and extrinsic motivation over time and address the influences that parents, educators, and employers may have in facilitating the motivation process.

At the conclusion of the book, we (the editors) also identify and discuss what we see as the emerging themes, questions, and issues to arise from this collection. We believe that the rich and diverse chapters pose problems and illustrate paradoxes that go beyond simple questions about the effects of rewarding behavior. The chapters discuss issues that researchers, educators, and parents should consider as they try to make sense of human motivation. Because of the widespread interest in this question, this book should be of interest to researchers in psychology, education, and business as well as to the wider academic audience interested in issues of optimal motivation and performance.

Acknowledgments

We thank Irwin Altman, Marty Chemers, Janet Hyde, and John Kihlstrom for their sage advice at critical points throughout this process. Kenneth Barron provided detailed feedback on multiple chapters in the book, and his thoughtful comments were a great help. We also thank Angela Newman and Sandy Kutler at our respective universities for their critical assistance in managing our files, our mail, and much of our work life. Nikki Levy at Academic Press provided the initial enthusiasm for this project and allowed us the freedom to develop the work as we thought best. We are also grateful to her assistant, Barbara Makinster, who has been a very patient and invaluable source of information and feedback as we worked to put the book together. Finally, we thank our families and friends, who helped to sustain our effort on this project during those rare periods when our intrinsic motivation was low.

CHAPTER

1

Looking beyond Rewards:
The Problem and Promise
of Intrinsic Motivation

CAROL SANSONE
Department of Psychology
University of Utah

JUDITH M. HARACKIEWICZ
Department of Psychology
University of Wisconsin

Understanding why we do the things we do has long been a goal of psychologists. From early on, the field focused on two primary types of explanations for behavior: basic biological needs or drives connected to survival and procreation (e.g., hunger, thirst, sex) and extrinsic rewards or punishments. Both types of explanations suggest that behavior is motivated by the need or desire to achieve particular outcomes (e.g., restoring a tissue deficit to equilibrium, acquiring a reward, or avoiding punishment). Motivation thus energizes and guides behavior toward reaching a particular goal.

THE BIRTH OF DEBATE

Eventually, researchers began to recognize that humans and some other animals sometimes engage in behaviors that do not seem to be motivated by either biological needs or the desire to secure an extrinsic

Intrinsic and Extrinsic Motivation

reward or avoid punishment. These behaviors motivated by "something else" seemed to be engaged in as ends in themselves and seemed to be associated with positive feelings of interest, enjoyment and satisfaction. For example, Woodworth (1921, p. 139) referred to this class of activities as "...less concerned with the struggle for existence than with the joy of living." To explain why we do these things, researchers posited new drives (e.g., play instincts, effectance or competence motivation, curiosity, optimal stimulation) and talked about "intrinsic" rewards and intrinsic motivation, in which the rewards were inherent to the activity (e.g., Berlyne, 1960; Hunt, 1965; White, 1959; Woodworth, 1921). These early theorists also tended to see intrinsic motivation as independent of motivation due to biologically based "tissue deficits" and rewards and punishments. In other words, intrinsic rewards were seen to be an additional source of possible reinforcers that could serve to motivate behavior in the absence of or in addition to the motivation to satisfy a biological deficit or to receive an extrinsic reward or to avoid punishment.

In the early 1970s, several researchers began important programs of research that started to question the additive nature of "intrinsic" and "extrinsic" motivation. An early study by Deci (1972) suggested that college students paid to perform an interesting SOMA Cube puzzle became less likely to perform the puzzle on their own during a free-choice period. In 1973, Lepper, Greene, and Nisbett found that nursery school children offered a "good player award" for drawing a picture (something they normally did because they liked it) were less likely to spontaneously draw when back in their regular classrooms, compared with children who had not been rewarded for drawing. In addition, this study was important because it showed that this decrement did not occur if children received the same reward unexpectedly after drawing; that is, the effect depended on their perception that they were drawing in order to receive a reward. Using terminology from self-perception theory, the researchers called this reduction in free-time play the "overjustification effect." They suggested that when individuals have both sufficient extrinsic (the reward) and intrinsic (interest) reasons to perform a behavior, they will discount the intrinsic reason and attribute their behavior to the extrinsic reward. Thus, when the extrinsic reward is no longer available, individuals no longer have sufficient intrinsic reasons to engage in the behavior. Kruglanski, Alon, and Lewis (1972) found that this decremental effect could occur even when the attribution to the extrinsic reward occurred retrospectively.

These seminal studies were the first of many to illustrate the paradox that extrinsic rewards can undermine intrinsic motivation, and they generated much excitement and spawned a large number of research studies and approaches. The early research was presented in a landmark volume edited by Lepper and Greene (1978) called *The Hidden Costs of Rewards*. In that book, chapters by Lepper, Greene, Deci, Kruglanski, and colleagues, as well as chapters by Condry, Csikzentmihalyi, McCullers, and others, documented an impressive number of studies suggesting that using an extrinsic reward to motivate someone to do something that the person would have done anyway could have detrimental effects on the quality and creativity of the person's performance and on the person's subsequent motivation to perform the activity once the extrinsic reward was received.

As research in this area burgeoned, more comprehensive theories were developed and these general conclusions were qualified by a number of carefully documented caveats. For example, the negative effects of extrinsic rewards on subsequent motivation were found only when individuals found the activity initially interesting (e.g., Calder & Staw, 1975; Lepper et al., 1973), and when the reward was seen as external to the activity (Kruglanski, 1975). In addition, the negative effects found for rewards did not seem to be limited to rewards but seemed to be associated with a variety of extrinsic constraints, such as deadlines and surveillance (e.g., Amabile, DeJong, & Lepper, 1976; Lepper & Greene, 1975). Thus, the field shifted to trying to understand the underlying process rather than focusing on reward effects per se. For example, Deci and Ryan's (1985) cognitive evaluation theory suggested that rather than focusing on a particular external event, we need to understand its functional significance. They proposed that any event can have both informational and controlling properties. If the informational aspect is more salient and positive (i.e., the primary significance of that event for me is that it conveys that I am competent), then it may enhance my subsequent motivation. However, if the controlling aspect is more salient (i.e., the primary significance of that event for me is that it conveys that I am being controlled), then it will decrease my subsequent motivation.

These issues became particularly salient when researchers turned their attention to a different type of reward—a reward offered for achieving a certain level of competence at an activity. These performance-contingent rewards had the potential to be perceived as extremely controlling but also had the potential to communicate positive competence feedback. The effects of these types of rewards were mixed. Sometimes receiving a reward that signified competence at the task appeared to enhance subsequent motivation (Karniol & Ross, 1977), sometimes it seemed to decrease subsequent motivation (Harackiewicz, 1979), and sometimes it seemed to have no effect (Boggiano & Ruble, 1979). These findings highlighted the important role of competence information in intrinsic motivation and the need to develop models that could account for both positive and negative effects on intrinsic motivation. The first chapters in this book review some of these efforts.

During the 1970s and early 1980s, a number of researchers vociferously challenged and questioned these studies and conclusions, sparking a lively debate (e.g., Arnold, 1976; Feingold & Mahoney, 1975; Reiss & Sushinsky,

1975; Vasta and Stirpe, 1979). Many of the vocal critics came from behaviorist backgrounds. These researchers suggested that the "negative" effects were due to poor operationalizations of the reward as a reinforcer, a focus on short-term effects without consideration of overall reinforcement history, and neglect of the enormous amount of research showing that reinforcement makes behavior more, and not less, likely to occur (e.g., Flora, 1990; Mawhinney, 1990).

The divergent conclusions of these different literatures were left to coexist in a lingering tension. In the "real world," the use of token economies (in which behavior is controlled by rewards) in schools and hospitals was and continues to be widespread. In business, compensation packages continue to be used to motivate workers, and in schools, teachers still use gold stars and stickers to reward children for good work. At the same time, management consultants counsel against using extrinsic incentives to motivate employees, and education consultants counsel against policies and procedures which interfere with intrinsic motivation to learn (Kohn, 1993). Thus, both sides of this ongoing debate have informed policy.

THIS BOOK

The debate reerupted in 1996 when Eisenberger and Cameron published an article in *American Psychologist* entitled "Detrimental Effects of Reward: Reality or Myth?" In that article, they presented a review of the literature based primarily on meta-analytic techniques and described research from their own laboratory. On the basis of an earlier meta-analysis (Cameron & Pierce, 1994), they suggested that detrimental effects of rewards on motivation occur only when the reward is tangible (as opposed to verbal), expected (as opposed to unexpected), and not contingent on performance level (as opposed to contingent on meeting some performance standard). They further suggested, on the basis of their laboratory research, that rewards can in fact increase the incidence of creative performance (i.e., "reinforce" creativity) when the criteria for being creative (e.g., coming up with many different uses for an object) are clearly explained to an individual prior to performance. Their conclusions, as summarized in the abstract of the article, were that

> a) detrimental effects of reward occur under highly restricted, easily avoidable conditions; b) mechanisms of instrumental and classical conditioning are basic for understanding incremental and decremental effects of reward on task motivation; and c) positive effects of reward on generalized creativity are easily attainable using procedures derived from behavior theory. (p. 1153)

The publication of that article in the flagship journal of the American Psychological Association signaled that questions first raised in the early 1970s about the use of rewards were still being debated and that the debate was of great interest in psychology. The appearance of the article also highlighted the need to update the discussion beyond the effects of extrinsic rewards per se, to include newer models, approaches, and applications that have emerged since the early 1970s. Subsequently, we (Sansone and Harackiewicz) organized a symposium for the Society of Experimental Social Psychology, meeting in October 1997. As a starting point, we used the recent reemergence of the debate about the effects of rewards and other extrinsic incentives on motivation and creativity to frame the symposium, but we also extended the panel to include new theoretical approaches to the field. Participants in the symposium were Robert Eisenberger and Judy Cameron, Teresa Amabile and Beth Hennessey, Mark Lepper, Ed Deci and Rich Ryan, Tory Higgins, Arie Kruglanski and James Shah, and Judith Harackiewicz and Carol Sansone. The debate became somewhat heated, given the different approaches and answers given.

In light of the debate among the symposium panel members and the renewed and continuing interest in understanding "intrinsic" and "extrinsic" motivation (as evidenced by a 1999 special issue of the *Journal of Experimental Social Psychology*, commentaries in the *American Psychologist* (1998), subsequent meta-analytical reviews and responses published in the *Psychological Bulletin* [1999], etc.), we decided that it was time for a volume to revisit the earlier work and provide an update both on what we have learned since then and on what we have still to learn. Some chapters in this book revisit the initial seminal work on this topic and examine how well its conclusions have stood the test of time. Other chapters focus on newer issues or approaches that evolved from the earlier work. The chapters also provide a mix of theory and basic and applied research, with research conducted both in laboratories and educational settings.

Robert Eisenberger and Judy Cameron were invited to contribute a chapter to this book, but they declined the opportunity. However, most of the other participants in the symposium have contributed chapters. In addition, we have included chapters by other researchers whose work we believe represents important and groundbreaking contributions that attempt to integrate the role of interest and intrinsic motivation into the examination of whether and how people learn and perform.

The book has three major sections. In Part I ("Are the Costs of Rewards Still Hidden? A New Look at an Old Debate"), authors review and update the literature on the effects of rewards and other extrinsic incentives or constraints on motivation and creativity. Thus, Richard Ryan and Edward Deci discuss the results from their meta-analytical review of the rewards literature (Deci, Koestner, & Ryan, 1999) in terms of support for the predictions made by cognitive evaluation theory and their broader self-determination theory. They suggest that individuals have innate needs for competence and control, and that rather than focus on the effects of any particular "extrinsic" event, one must consider the meaning of the event in light of these needs. They then review more recent extensions of this work into other domains such as self-regulation of preventive health behaviors and prosocial motivation.

In earlier work with Amabile and subsequent independent work, Beth Hennessey extended the examination of potentially negative reward effects to the study of creativity, suggesting that individuals must be intrinsically motivated for creativity to occur. In the present book, she presents an overview of this research program and charts progress made in this area, including ways to "immunize" people against potential negative effects of rewards.

The next two chapters in Part I present a conceptual shift to thinking about the effects of "extrinsic" factors in the context of individuals' goals. Thus, Judith Harackiewicz and Carol Sansone review their earlier research on the simultaneous positive and negative effects associated with rewarding competence and discuss their subsequent transition to goal-based models of intrinsic motivation. They suggest that the same "extrinsic" events may affect the motivational process differently as a function of individuals' goals at a particular point in time.

James Shah and Arie Kruglanski present a new model that attempts to identify two distinct definitions of "intrinsic" motivation, one substantive and one structural. The structural definition is based on the degree to which a given activity is associated with unique or common goals in an individual's goal network. They then discuss the implications of this redefinition for the interpretation of the classic findings as well as present new data based on this redefinition.

Part II presents chapters that focus specifically on achievement goals ("A New Debate: The Hidden Costs [and Benefits] of Achievement Goals"). These chapters present differing views on how mastery and performance achievement goals affect learning, performance, and intrinsic motivation. Echoing some of the earlier debate about the effects of extrinsic and intrinsic rewards, these chapters raise the question of whether there are hidden costs and hidden benefits associated with both types of achievement goal.

In line with this question, Daniel Molden and Carol Dweck suggest that there may be hidden costs to performance goals (considered by some to be "extrinsic" goals), particularly when individuals encounter difficulties and setbacks. They discuss data from a program of research in support of this thesis and argue that it is critical to consider the meaning of individuals' goals to understand the costs and benefits of performance and mastery goals.

Ruth Butler proposes that by looking at only the *type* of achievement goal, we miss the possibility that both performance and mastery goals can be focused on acquiring competence or on assessing competence. She outlines the implications of these four distinct patterns for the type of competence information sought while engaged in the task and the impact on intrinsic motivation and learning. Thus, she suggests that some of the primary benefits of mastery goals and primary costs of performance goals may be hidden in the *process* of learning and motivation.

In contrast, Elizabeth Linnenbrink and Paul Pintrich suggest that some performance goals can have positive as well as the more typically cited negative effects on learning and motivation. They present a model that attempts to integrate both patterns within a self-regulatory system, one that includes affective, cognitive, and motivational processes.

Finally, Kenneth Barron and Judith Harackiewicz also suggest that there may be some hidden benefits to performance goals. In particular, they discuss research showing positive effects of performance goals on intrinsic motivation and performance and present a multiple-goals model that examines how pursuing *both* performance and mastery goals can optimize intrinsic motivation and performance.

In Part III ("The Role of Interest in Learning and Self-Regulation: 'Extrinsic' versus 'Intrinsic' Motivation Reconsidered"), chapters revisit the question of how extrinsic and intrinsic motivators may work when we examine motivation as it can occur in real life over time. One important difference between the typical laboratory tasks used and real-life activities is that in real life, activities are not always, or continually, "intrinsically" interesting. These chapters thus address the implied tension between "intrinsic" and "extrinsic" motivation and whether either or both are necessary and/or sufficient to sustain effective performance over time.

To begin, Mark Lepper and Jennifer Henderlong review the rewards literature and conclude that this research unambiguously shows that intrinsic and extrinsic motivation can be in conflict (i.e., they arrive at the same conclusion as Ryan and Deci). However, they further suggest that this is just one way that intrinsic and extrinsic motivation may be related, and they review more recent research suggesting that intrinsic and extrinsic motivation can also work orthogonally or in tandem to affect behavior. They argue that to understand motivation as it works in such real-life contexts as education, one must begin by acknowledging these multiple and complex relationships.

Starting from a different perspective, Suzanne Hidi argues that previous analyses of the effects of rewards and other external factors on intrinsic motivation have not distinguished between interest that arises because of momentary situationally created factors (situational interest) or interest that is more stable and integrated into individuals' self-concept and values (individual interest). She suggests that extrinsic factors might have negative effects only on situational interest and that in fact, these extrinsic factors may have positive effects when individual interest is involved.

Rather than being necessarily antagonistic, Carol Sansone and Jessi Smith suggest that the motivation to experience interest (what they term intrinsic motivation) and the motivation to reach some outcome (what some consider extrinsic motivation) can work sequentially over time in a self-regulatory system. They review a model and discuss research showing that extrinsic factors can increase the likelihood that individuals will attempt to self-regulate interest (i.e., purposely try to make an uninteresting activity more interesting). Furthermore, it is the use of these interest-enhancing strategies (and not the extrinsic factors) that predicts persistence or resumption of the activity. They thus suggest that "intrinsic" and "extrinsic" motivation might be best understood in the context of individuals' goal striving over time.

K. Ann Renninger suggests that to understand individuals' motivation to learn about and engage in a particular activity on their own initiative (i.e., presumably intrinsically motivated behavior), one must focus on individual interest. Individual interest increases as knowledge and the accompanying value of the subject increases, and she suggests that it is individual interest that sustains attention and effort. She discusses how individual interest may develop over time, how this development can be supported by a child's environment, and how individual interest may vary both within and across individuals as a function of gender, age, and atypical development (e.g., particular learning disabilities or syndromes).

Finally, Janis Jacobs and Jacquelynne Eccles review research illustrating the critical role that task value plays in activity choices, and they discuss how interest in an activity is one source of value that combines with more "extrinsic" sources (e.g., what doing this will get me). They trace how interest and other sources of values reflect socialization processes, which may help to explain systematic gender, ethnic, and cultural differences in motivation.

At the conclusion of the book, we (the editors) also identify and discuss what we see as the emerging questions and issues to arise from this collection. We believe that the rich and diverse chapters pose problems and illustrate paradoxes that go beyond simple questions about the effects of rewarding behavior. Rather, they present questions that researchers, educators, parents, and individuals must continue to try to grapple with if they wish to understand motivation based not on the "struggle for existence" but on the "joy of living" (Woodworth, 1921). This understanding is the promise that motivated this book. We leave it ultimately to the reader to decide how well that promise has been fulfilled.

References

Amabile, T. M., DeJong, W., & Lepper, M. R. (1976). Effects of externally imposed deadlines on subsequent intrinsic motivation. *Journal of Personality and Social Psychology, 34,* 92–98.

Arnold, H. J. (1976). Effects of performance feedback and extrinsic reward upon high intrinsic motivation. *Organizational Behavior and Human Performance, 17,* 275–288.

Berlyne, D. E. (1960). *Conflict, arousal and curiosity.* New York: McGraw-Hill.

Boggiano, A. K., & Ruble, D. N. (1979). Competence and the overjustification effect: A developmental study. *Journal of Personality and Social Psychology, 37,* 1462–1468.

Calder, B. J., & Staw, B. M. (1975). Self-perception of intrinsic and extrinsic motivation. *Journal of Personality and Social Psychology, 31,* 599–605.

Cameron, J., & Pierce, W. D. (1994). Reinforcement, reward, and intrinsic motivation: A meta-analysis. *Review of Educational Research, 64,* 363–423.

Deci, E. L. (1972). The effects of contingent and non-contingent rewards and controls on intrinsic motivation. *Organizational Behavior and Human Performance, 8,* 217–229.

Deci, E. L., Koestner, R., & Ryan, R. M. (1999). A meta-analytic review of experiments examining the effects of extrinsic rewards on intrinsic motivation. *Psychological Bulletin, 125,* 627–668.

Deci, E. L., & Ryan, R. M. (1985). *Intrinsic motivation and self-determination in human behavior.* New York: Plenum Press.

Eisenberger, R., & Cameron, J. (1996). Detrimental effects of reward: Reality or myth? *American Psychologist, 51,* 1153–1166.

Feingold, B. D., & Mahoney, M. J. (1975). Reinforcement effects on intrinsic interest: Undermining the overjustification hypothesis. *Behavior Therapy, 6,* 357–377.

Flora, S. R. (1990). Undermining intrinsic interest from the standpoint of a behaviorist. *The Psychological Record, 40,* 323–346.

Harackiewicz, J. M. (1979). The effects of reward contingency and performance feedback on intrinsic motivation. *Journal of Personality and Social Psychology, 37,* 1352–1363.

Hunt, J. M. V. (1965). Intrinsic motivation and its role in psychological development. In D. Levine (Ed.), *Nebraska Symposium on Motivation* (vol. 13, pp. 189–282). Lincoln, NE: University of Nebraska Press.

Karniol, R., & Ross, M. (1977). The effect of performance relevant and performance irrelevant rewards on children's intrinsic motivation. *Child Development, 48,* 482–487.

Kohn, A. (1993). *Punished by rewards: The trouble with gold stars, incentive plans, A's, praise, and other bribes.* Boston: Houghton Mifflin.

Kruglanski, A. W. (1975). The endogenous–exogenous partition in attribution theory. *Psychological Review, 82,* 387–406.

Kruglanski, A. W., Alon, S., & Lewis, T. (1972). Retrospective misattribution and task enjoyment. *Journal of Experimental Social Psychology, 8,* 493–501.

Lepper, M. R., & Greene, D. (1975). Turning play into work: The effects of adult surveillance and extrinsic rewards on children's intrinsic motivation. *Journal of Personality and Social Psychology, 31,* 479–486.

Lepper, M. R., & Greene, D. (Eds.). (1978). *The Hidden Costs of Rewards: New Perspectives on the Psychology of Human Motivation.* Hillsdale, NJ: Erlbaum.

Lepper, M. R., Greene, D., & Nisbett, R. E. (1973). Undermining children's intrinsic interest with extrinsic rewards: A test of the "overjustification" hypothesis. *Journal of Personality and Social Psychology, 28,* 129–137.

Mawhinney, T. C. (1990). Decreasing intrinsic "motivation" with extrinsic rewards: Easier said than done. *Journal of Organizational Behavior Management, 11,* 175–191.

Reiss, S., & Sushinsky, L. W. (1975). Overjustification, competing responses, and the acquisition of intrinsic interest. *Journal of Personality and Social Psychology, 31,* 1116–1125.

Vasta, R., & Stirpe, L. A. (1979). Reinforcement effects on three measures of children's interest in math. *Behavior Modification, 3,* 223–244.

White, R. W. (1959). Motivation reconsidered: The concept of competence. *Psychological Review, 66,* 297–333.

Woodworth, R. S. (1921). *Psychology: A study of mental life.* New York: Henry Holt.

PART

I

Are the Costs of Rewards Still Hidden?

A New Look at an Old Debate

CHAPTER 2

When Rewards Compete with Nature: The Undermining of Intrinsic Motivation and Self-Regulation

RICHARD M. RYAN
EDWARD L. DECI
Department of Clinical and Social Sciences in Psychology
University of Rochester

There once was a rat who loved rewards. He would do anything for an extra pellet or a sugared drink. Quick to learn and easily trained, he was the pride of his experimenters, who chose him for the ultimate reward experiment. They connected him to a device that electrically stimulated an area of the brain that produced an intense pleasurable feeling. All he had to do was press a bar. So powerful was this reward that he threw himself into his work. Hour after hour, day after day, he pressed on, to the neglect of other needs, both physical and social. He neglected his relationships, his exploratory interests, even his health. Yet he persisted, establishing himself as the number-one bar presser, admired by his keepers for his outstanding behavioral efficacy. Sadly, one morning he was discovered by the lab staff, disoriented and near death from starvation, dehydration, and fatigue. The only sign of life remaining was a weakened paw, still reaching for the bar, trying to obtain yet one more dose of the "reward."

Although fictitious, this little animal story is based upon actual experiments. Stripped of its anthropomorphic features, it could be the tale of a rat in a classic Olds (1958) experiment showing the powerful rewarding effects of stimulating pleasure centers in the brain. Rats violated their own natural needs, ignoring available food and opportunities for rest in order to obtain rewards. This and similar studies with other animals (see, e.g. Routtenberg & Lindy, 1965) have long suggested that arbitrary, contingent rewards can direct organisms away from behaviors that are inherent in their organismic nature and would represent healthy self-regulation. Quite simply, it indicates that organisms can become focused on behaviors that yield non–need-satisfying rewards (namely, electrical brain stimulation) at the costs of basic need satisfaction and a decreased sensitivity to cues that would normally guide them toward health.

The important question for us is whether the fable is applicable only to rats or might in fact be a parable for contemporary human behavior. The successful executive who makes hundreds of thousands, maybe millions, of dollars a year while working endless hours to the neglect of family and health might not be so different from our mythic rat. Humans, too, it seems, can have their behavior entrained by external rewards. Indeed, there is little doubt that contingent rewards can be powerful motivators, but the important issue that is all too often ignored, yet that is the central theme of this chapter, is the potential costs to individuals of being subjected to those powerful motivators.

THE INTERPLAY OF REWARDS AND NATURE

Self-determination theory (SDT; Deci & Ryan, 1985b, 1991; Ryan & Deci, 2000) assumes that humans have inherent propensities to be intrinsically motivated, to assimilate their social and physical worlds, to integrate external regulations into self-regulations, and in so doing integrate themselves into a larger social whole. This assumption of active, integrative tendencies in development is not unique to SDT and, indeed, is an assumption shared by numerous theories across the history of psychology (Ryan, 1995). However, specific to SDT is the proposition that these evolved integrative or actualizing tendencies operate in conjunction with basic psychological needs for autonomy, competence, and relatedness. In other words, human development is naturally inclined toward intrapsychic and interpersonal integration—what Angyal (1965) called autonomy and homonomy—yet these propensities must be nurtured by experiences of autonomy, competence, and relatedness to operate effectively. Insofar as the social world allows satisfaction of these basic psychological needs, people move toward greater autonomy and homonomy and, accordingly, experience lessened alienation and greater well-being.

The fundamental question addressed in this chapter concerns the relation of imposed rewards to these evolved propensities toward autonomy and homonomy (Ryan, Kuhl, & Deci, 1997). It is a critical question because there is growing evidence that the use of rewards as a strategy for externally regulating behavior can undermine natural organismic processes that evolved to keep organisms in touch with their needs and responsive to their surroundings. It is because arbitrary reward contingencies can powerfully activate approach behaviors that they are so often used to elicit rewarder-desired behaviors. In fact, in many cases rewards are used explicitly to try to get individuals to do what does not come naturally—for example, work absurdly long hours, ignore their interests and relationships, or engage in nonvalued behaviors—and this in itself represents cause for concern. It turns out, however, that the power of rewards creates an even more serious and long-lasting problem; specifically, the use of arbitrary reward contingencies can undermine intrinsic motivation and override inherent tendencies to integrate the value and meaning of actions, tendencies that form the structural basis for the self-regulation of action. Thus, in this chapter, we examine evidence concerning the potential of contingent rewards to undermine self-regulatory propensities, desensitize individuals to their basic needs, and disrupt awareness and choice, all to the detriment of healthy development.

THE AGE OF REWARDS

Unarguably, our age is the age of rewards. The regulation of behavior by consciously constructed and socially imposed reward contingencies, whether blatant or subtle, is ubiquitous within contemporary Western-oriented societies. To a significant degree this is implicit in the evolution of capitalistic economies wherein corporations compete for scarce resources and for customers (Frey, 1997). One sees it in such practices as giving huge bonuses to professional athletes and enormous stock options to corporate executives, as well as in the operation of the advertising industry, which has the explicit agenda of manipulating appetites and behaviors by subtly promising rewards for people who have the right look or consume the right products. The attention given to wealth and image by the modern media also contributes to our society's reward orientation.

The pervasive use of rewards goes beyond economics and the media, however, for many practitioners and behavior change specialists actively advocate the use of rewards for reinforcing good behavior in homes and in schools as well as for promoting good performance on tests, in concert halls, on ball fields, and in countless other settings. Quite simply, the strong focus on rewards seems to be stitched into the fabric of modern society.

Nonetheless, this strong reward focus is, from a historical viewpoint, a relatively recent phenomenon. Although reward contingencies and natural consequences have always been an implicit feature of life, the difference today is that we now have a highly developed technology of rewards and a self-conscious use of rewards to harness human capital. Imposed reward contingencies are, to a increasing extent, replacing other forces, such as community, tradition, internalized values, and natural consequences, as the central regulators of behavior (Goodenow, 1997; Schwartz & Lacey, 1982). Increasingly, as this is happening worldwide, the evolving global culture seems to be fulfilling Skinner's vision (1971) of shaping social behavior with the use of contingent rewards.

Rewards can, undeniably, be an effective means of controlling behavior, and perhaps that is why their use has become pervasive at every level of society. For us, however, that raises the question of what the empirical evidence says about possible negative, and presumably unintended, consequences of this ubiquitous use of rewards. How do rewards affect natural organismic processes, and are there ways of minimizing or ameliorating whatever negative effects they might have?

We turn now to an examination of the effects of rewards on organismic processes, interpreting the results in terms of the interface between rewards and basic psychological needs. We begin with a consideration of the effects of rewards on intrinsic motivation. Because intrinsic motivation is the focus of this book and the effects of rewards on intrinsic motivation have been extensively studied, that issue, along with its real-world implications, receives the greatest attention in our review. We then move on to a briefer consideration of reward effects on other organismic processes, such as prosocial behavior, and to a discussion of real-world implications. Finally, we consider the general issue of reward effects from the personality perspective of individual differences in motivational orientations and life goals.

REWARDS AND INTRINSIC MOTIVATION

The initial—and still controversial—finding that raised the possibility that rewards have negative effects on natural regulatory processes was the demonstration that rewards could undermine intrinsic motivation (Deci, 1971). The phenomenon of *intrinsic motivation* reflects the primary propensity of organisms to engage in activities that interest them and, in so doing, to learn, develop, and expand their capacities. Intrinsic motivation is entailed whenever people behave for the satisfaction inherent in the behavior itself. These satisfactions typically concern the positive feelings of being effective (White, 1959) and being the origin of behavior (deCharms, 1968), and they often result from engaging in novel and challenging activities (Berlyne, 1971; Csikszentmihalyi, 1975; Deci, 1975). The natural inclination toward intrinsically motivated behavior is a significant feature of human nature and plays an important role in development (Elkind, 1971; Ryan, 1993), high-quality performance (Utman, 1997), and well-being (Deci & Ryan, 1991).

The initial finding of decreased intrinsic motivation for an interesting activity following the experience of being rewarded for doing it has been referred to as the *undermining effect* (Deci & Ryan, 1980; 1985b). The phenomena was first demonstrated by Deci (1971), using monetary rewards with college students, and subsequently by Lepper, Greene, and Nisbett (1973), using symbolic rewards with preschool children. Following these studies, numerous experiments replicated and extended the finding and highlighted its limiting conditions.

To integrate the results of what became a very large body of research, Deci and Ryan (1980) outlined cognitive evaluation theory (CET). That theory, which was later incorporated as part of the larger SDT (Deci & Ryan, 1985b), takes as its specific focus the conditions that *diminish* versus *enhance* intrinsic motivation. In its most general form, CET argues that events that negatively affect a person's experience of autonomy or competence diminish intrinsic motivation, whereas events that support perceived autonomy and competence enhance intrinsic motivation.

Regarding the issue of rewards, CET has been very explicit in its position. It specifies that rewards can have two quite different meanings, and the effects of rewards on intrinsic motivation will depend on which aspect people experience as more salient. On the one hand, rewards are a vehicle for controlling people's behavior, and to the degree that this *controlling aspect* of rewards is salient, CET predicts that rewards will undermine intrinsic motivation. In attributional terms, this controlling aspect of rewards can be understood as conducing toward an external perceived locus of causality (deCharms, 1968; Heider, 1958), which is the sense that the behavior stems from a source outside the self. On the other hand, rewards can also convey information or feedback that affirms or supports people's competence, and to the degree that this *informational aspect* of rewards is more salient, the theory predicts that rewards will maintain or enhance intrinsic motivation. However, according to CET, the informational aspect of rewards will be salient only if people feel a sense of autonomy with respect to the activity and/or its outcomes.

As discussed below, the CET framework has been used to make predictions about the effects on intrinsic motivation of different types of rewards and different reward contingencies in accord with the likely salience of the controlling and informational aspects of the various rewards and contingencies. It has also been used to make prediction about threats, deadlines, communication styles, levels of challenge, goal structures, ego involvement, and other external conditions. Although our focus herein is on the literature related to rewards, we cite some of the other work in passing.

Controversies Concerning Reward Effects
and Cognitive Evaluation Theory

In the years since the publication of the first experiment examining reward effects on intrinsic motivation, the field has not only continued to yield empirical investigations and narrative reviews (Condry, 1977; Deci, 1975; Lepper & Greene, 1978; Ryan, Mims, & Koestner, 1983, among many others) but has also received vigorous criticisms from behaviorist researchers (e.g., Calder & Staw, 1975b; Carton, 1996; Flora, 1990; Reiss & Sushinsky, 1976; Scott, 1976). With more than 100 empirical articles having been published, with the controversial nature of the topic, and with the advent of meta-analytic techniques as a way of systematically synthesizing areas of research, it is hardly surprising that meta-analyses dealing with the effects of extrinsic rewards on intrinsic motivation would begin to appear. To date, there have been five, each of which has dealt with somewhat different issues within the scope of the relation between extrinsic rewards and intrinsic motivation.

The first to appear tested the CET hypothesis that extrinsic rewards with a salient controlling aspect would undermine intrinsic motivation (Rummel & Feinberg, 1988). The authors reviewed 45 published studies in which the rewards were specifically expected to be controlling. They included verbal as well as tangible rewards and expected as well as unexpected rewards, and they reported very strong support for the hypothesis, thus concluding that "this meta-analysis lends support to the adequacy of [CET]" (1988, p. 160).

The second of the meta-analyses limited its analysis to 16 studies that tested whether tangible rewards would undermine the free-choice behavioral measure of intrinsic motivation (Wiersma, 1992). Like Rummel and Feinberg, Wiersma found strong support for undermining. The third meta-analysis reviewed 50 published studies and combined the behavioral and self-report measures into one analysis. It, too, reported strong support for the hypothesized undermining of intrinsic motivation by tangible rewards (Tang & Hall, 1995). These authors also reported that various of the reward contingencies, which are to be discussed in the following section of this chapter, led to reliable undermining, and they found indication that positive feedback (i.e., verbal rewards) enhanced intrinsic motivation.

Cameron and Pierce (1994) presented the fourth meta-analysis of reward effects, which was subsequently republished by Eisenberger and Cameron (1996). They reviewed 96 experiments and reported enhancement of intrinsic motivation by verbal rewards on both behavioral and self-report measures, and undermining of intrinsic motivation by tangible rewards on the behavioral measure but not on the self-report measure. When they analyzed the reward contingencies separately, they reported no undermining by most contingencies, so they concluded that there is no reason not to use reward systems, particularly as a motivational strategy in educational settings, and they called for "abandoning cognitive evaluation theory" (1994, p. 396).

Because there was considerable variability in the methods, approaches, inclusion criteria, and reported results of the four previous meta-analyses, Deci, Koestner, and Ryan (1999) performed a new one to correct errors in the previous meta-analyses and to include all eligible studies. In what follows, we report the results of the new meta-analysis, and detail why Eisenberger, Cameron, and Pierce's results were discrepant from those of the other meta-analyses.

A NEW META-ANALYSIS OF REWARD EFFECTS

The Deci et al. (1999) meta-analysis used a hierarchical approach, first, to analyze studies that used the free-choice behavioral measure of intrinsic motivation as the dependent variable, and second, to analyze those that used self-reported interest as the dependent variable. Both parts began with a calculation of the effects of all rewards on intrinsic motivation and then systematically differentiated the reward conditions. This differentiating of rewards types and reward contingencies in the meta-analysis was essential to test CET because of its assertions that the effects of extrinsic rewards will depend on people's interpretation of the rewards as controlling versus informational and that their interpretation will be affected by the type and contingency of rewards.

First, CET takes account of whether the reward is verbal or tangible, with verbal rewards (i.e., positive feedback) predicted to be more informational and tangible rewards predicted to be more controlling. Second, the theory distinguishes between whether or not the tangible rewards are expected while people are doing the task, predicting that expected rewards will show undermining whereas unexpected rewards will not. Third, CET distinguishes among the specific behaviors on which the expected rewards are made contingent.

Ryan et al. (1983) introduced the following typology of reward contingencies: *task-noncontingent* rewards, which are given for something other than engaging in the target activity, such as simply participating in the study; *task-contingent* rewards, which are given for doing or completing the target activity; and *performance-contingent* rewards, which are given specifically for performing the activity well, matching some standard of excellence, or surpassing some specified criterion (e.g., better than 80% of the other participants). Deci et al. (1999), like Eisenberger and Cameron (1996), made a further distinction between task-contingent rewards that are explicitly dependent on completing the target task (referred to as *completion-contingent*) and those that are dependent on engaging in the activity but do not require completing it (referred to as *engagement-contingent*).

Because task-noncontingent rewards do not require doing the task, there is no reason to expect that they would be experienced as either informational or controlling with respect to the *task*, so intrinsic motivation is predicted not to be affected. With engagement-contingent rewards, people have to work on the task to get the reward, so the reward is likely to be experienced as controlling, and because the reward carries little or no competence affirmation, it is unlikely to increase perceived competence, so there would be nothing to counteract the negative effects of the control. Thus, engagement-contingent rewards are predicted to undermine intrinsic motivation. With completion-contingent rewards, people have to complete the task to get the rewards, so the rewards are likely to be experienced as even more controlling; however, these rewards provide some competence affirmation if the task requires skill, so that implicit positive feedback could offset some of the control. Still, the competence-affirming aspect of these rewards is not expected to be strong relative to the controlling aspect, so completion-contingent rewards are expected, on average, to be undermining of intrinsic motivation.

Finally, with performance-contingent rewards, where rewards are linked to people's performance, there is even stronger control—people have to meet some standard to maximize rewards—so there is a strong tendency for these rewards to undermine intrinsic motivation. However, performance-contingent rewards can also convey substantial positive competence information in cases in which the person does well enough to get a level of reward that signifies excellent performance. In those cases, there would be a significant tendency for performance-contingent rewards to affirm competence and, accordingly, to offset some of the negative effects of control. Because of the strong competing tendencies of the controlling and competence-affirmation aspects of performance-contingent rewards, CET suggests that other factors need to be taken into account in making predictions. Such factors include whether the interpersonal climate within which the performance-contingent rewards are administered is demanding and controlling and whether the level of reward implies excellent performance. Consider each briefly.

The term *interpersonal context* refers to the social ambience of such settings as homes, classrooms, or work groups as they influence people's experience of autonomy, competence, and relatedness (Deci & Ryan, 1991). With respect to the interpersonal context within which rewards are administered, the most important issue is the extent to which the ambience is controlling versus noncontrolling—in other words, the extent to which people within the context feel pressured to think, feel, or behave in particular ways (e.g., Deci, Connell, & Ryan, 1989; Deci, Schwartz, Sheinman, & Ryan, 1981). When examined in the laboratory, interpersonal climate is usually manipulated as the interpersonal style used by the experimenter to administer rewards or feedback (e.g., Ryan, 1982; Ryan et al., 1983). CET predicts that when the interpersonal style of administering performance-contingent rewards is relatively pressuring, the rewards will tend to be experienced as more controlling, leading to more diminishment of intrinsic motivation, whereas when the interpersonal style is relatively noncontrolling, the rewards will tend to be experienced as more informational, leading to less diminishment or possible enhancement of intrinsic motivation. Parenthetically, according to CET, this prediction applies to all rewards, including verbal rewards. Thus, we would expect controllingly administered verbal rewards to be undermining of intrinsic motivation, whereas we would expect informationally administered verbal rewards to be enhancing.

In most studies of performance-contingent rewards, all participants get rewards conveying that they performed very well. But a performance-contingent reward could also convey poor performance if, for example, people were offered, say, $1 for being in the bottom quartile, $2 for being in the 2nd quartile, and so on. Those who got $1 would be getting a performance-contingent reward signifying poor performance. If an experiment compared such individuals to others who were told they were in the bottom quartile but did not get a reward, we would expect that the strong negative feedback would be sufficiently undermining of intrinsic motivation that there would be little left to be affected by the reward. Thus, although we expect substantial undermining for individuals who receive performance-contingent rewards that signify excellence relative to individuals who receive only the feedback signifying excellence, we do not expect much difference between individuals who receive performance-contingent rewards that signify poor performance relative to those who receive only the negative information. Both should lead to a low level of intrinsic motivation.

In the Deci et al. (1999) meta-analysis, studies were included if they appeared between 1971 and 1996 as published articles or unpublished dissertations and also satisfied the following criteria. First, we included only well-controlled laboratory experiments. Second, because intrinsic motivation is pertinent to tasks that people experience as interesting, the issue of reward effects on intrinsic motivation is relevant only when the reward is added to an activity for which there is intrinsic motivation to begin with. Accordingly, studies or conditions within studies were included only if the target task was at least moderately interesting, (i.e., was not defined a priori by the experimenters as an uninteresting task and/or did not have an interest rating in the control condition that was below the midpoint of the scale). Third, the analyses included only studies that assessed intrinsic motivation after the reward had been clearly terminated, because while a reward is in effect, one's behavior reflects a mix of intrinsic and extrinsic motivation. And fourth, studies were included only if they had an appropriate no-reward control group. With these criteria, 128 studies were included; 101 of them used the free-choice measure and 84 used the self-report measure. Two meta-analyses were done, one for the studies with the free-choice measure and one for the studies with the self-report measure.

The Effects of All Rewards

Although the initial discussion of extrinsic-reward effects on intrinsic motivation (deCharms, 1968) considered extrinsic rewards as a unitary concept, even the very earliest investigations of this issue differentiated the concept, finding different results in different categories (Deci, 1971, 1972a; Lepper et al., 1973). Accordingly, aggregating across all types of rewards is not a conceptually meaningful endeavor, for its outcome will depend primarily on how many studies of each type of reward or reward contingency are included in the analyses (Ryan & Deci, 1996). Even so, to be able to compare our results to those of earlier meta-analyses, we examined the overall effect of rewards on intrinsic motivation and found significant undermining for the free-choice measure of intrinsic motivation (with a Cohen composite effect size of $d = -0.24$). The overall effect for the self-report measure was not significant.

In an hierarchical meta-analysis, one begins with the most general category, and if that set of effects is heterogeneous, one proceeds to differentiate the category into meaningful subcategories in an attempt to achieve homogeneity of effects within subcategories. As already mentioned, because there was indication from the earliest studies that all rewards do not affect intrinsic motivation in a uniform way, we both expected and found that the set of effect sizes for all rewards was heterogeneous. Thus, we proceeded with the differentiation, and only after we had exhausted all possible moderator variables within a category did we resort to removing outliers to achieve homogeneity.

Positive Feedback (Verbal Rewards)

In the literature on intrinsic motivation, it is generally predicted that positive feedback will enhance intrinsic motivation. In part this is because verbal rewards are usually unexpected, and as we show in the following section, even tangible rewards that are unexpected do not have a negative effect on intrinsic motivation. However, the prediction of a positive effect for verbal rewards is based on more than that; specifically, verbal rewards tend to enhance people's feelings of competence. Thus, the informational aspect is expected to be salient, assuming the individuals also experience some feelings of autonomy. What is called positive feedback within CET is labeled verbal rewards by behaviorists, so herein we use the two terms interchangeably, despite their divergent metatheoretical underpinnings.

Twenty-one studies examined the effects of positive feedback on free-choice intrinsic motivation and 21 examined its effects on self-reports of interest. Results indicated that positive feedback significantly enhances intrinsic motivation: For the behavioral measure the composite effect was 0.33; for self-report it was 0.31. In spite of the similarity of results, the effects for free-choice behavior were not homogeneous. Thus, in an attempt to achieve homogeneity, we separated the studies into those in which the participants were children and those in which they were college students, finding a significant difference between the two. When we examined the effect size for the two groups separately, we found that with 14 studies employing college students, there was a significant increase in intrinsic motivation with an effect size of 0.41, but with 7 studies employing children, there was not a significant increase in intrinsic motivation. Thus, it appears that the enhancement effect was carried by the college students and that verbal rewards do not reliably enhance intrinsic motivation for children.

A supplemental meta-analysis was performed to test the CET prediction that although verbal rewards tend to enhance intrinsic motivation (at least for college students), they will undermine intrinsic motivation if administered with a controlling interpersonal style. Four studies included informational versus controlling verbal rewards and the results did indeed show that controllingly administered verbal rewards decrease intrinsic motivation.

A few studies have identified four other important caveats to this general finding of enhancement of intrinsic motivation by verbal rewards. Although these effects were not examined in enough studies to test them meta-analytically, the caveats are worth noting briefly. First, according to CET, perceived competence can enhance both intrinsic and extrinsic motivation, but it is only when individuals perceive an internal locus of causality for the efficacious behavior that it will enhance intrinsic motivation. Thus, CET has emphasized that individuals must experience some degree of perceived autonomy for the perceived competence to have a positive effect on intrinsic motivation, and two experiments have tested this. Ryan (1982) found that positive feedback in interpersonal contexts designed to be controlling led to significantly less intrinsic motivation than did positive feedback in interpersonal contexts designed to be noncontrolling (i.e., to be informational). Further, Fisher (1978) reported that positive feedback for which people did not feel responsible had no effect on intrinsic motivation, whereas positive feedback for which they did feel responsible enhanced it. Second, gender differences have appeared in the effects of positive feedback in at least three studies. Deci, Cascio, and Krusell (1975) reported that although positive feedback enhanced the intrinsic motivation of male college students, it undermined the intrinsic motivation of female students, and studies by Kast and Connor (1988) and Koestner, Zuckerman, and Koestner (1987) replicated this finding. On the other hand, Blanck, Reis, & Jackson (1984) did not find this gender difference, but there is nonetheless reason to be cautious about the use of positive feedback with females.

Harackiewicz, Manderlink, and Sansone (1984) highlighted a third caveat about the use of positive feedback when they reported that *expecting* feedback even when it turns out to be positive tends to undermine intrinsic motivation, thus supporting the view that part of the reason verbal rewards often have a positive effect is that they are unexpected during task performance. In the 1984 study by Harackiewicz et al., participants were told before they began an activity that they would, when finished, be told whether they had done well. Subsequently, all participants were told they had done well, but they displayed decreased intrinsic motivation relative to others who got positive feedback unexpectedly after completing the task. It appears that when people know while working on a task that they will be getting feedback about their performance they feel evaluated and that has a negative effect on their intrinsic motivation. The fourth caveat is that the enhancing effect of positive feedback on intrinsic motivation appears to be strong primarily when recipients' goal while engaging the activity is to perform well (Sansone, 1986, 1989; Sansone & Morgan, 1992). When performing well is not important to them, the positive feedback tends not to have its enhancing effect.

To summarize, the meta-analysis of verbal-reward studies indicated that positive feedback tends to have an enhancing effect on intrinsic motivation; however, it also suggested that the enhancement occurred primarily with adults (i.e., college students). In fact, verbal rewards did not enhance the behavioral measure of intrinsic motivation for children. Further, they undermined intrinsic motivation if they were administered controllingly. Narrative accounts that have not been confirmed by meta-analyses also identified four other caveats—namely, that positive feedback (1) is likely to have the enhancing effect only when individuals also feel autonomous, (2) may have a negative effect for women even when it is enhancing for men, (3) is likely to be undermining when it is expected while performing the activity, and (4) is most likely to bolster intrinsic motivation when it is important to the recipients to perform well.

Tangible Rewards

In many life situations, tangible rewards are used to try to get people do things they might not otherwise do. That is, rewards are often used to control behavior. This is especially true of material rewards such as money and prizes, but is also true for symbolic rewards such as trophies or good-player awards. So used, rewards typically promote an external perceived locus of causality for the rewarded behavior, and insofar as they do, they are predicted by CET to undermine intrinsic motivation.

The meta-analysis examined 92 tangible-reward studies with a free-choice measure and 70 with a self-report measure. As predicted by CET, the results showed that on average, tangible rewards significantly undermined both free-choice intrinsic motivation ($d = -0.36$) and self-reported interest ($d = -0.10$). Of course, we have regularly argued that a full understanding of the effects of tangible rewards requires a consideration of additional factors, such as the reward contingency, but the overall tangible-rewards results highlight the risks associated with these rewards.

A comparison of studies of children versus college students revealed that the effects of rewards were significantly more negative for children on both the behavioral and self-report measures of intrinsic motivation. The real-world implications of this pattern of results is extremely important. There is great concern about children's motivation for schoolwork, as well as for other behaviors such as sports, art, and prosocial activities. Using rewards to motivate children may indeed control their behavior in some immediate sense, but these findings suggest that they are likely to have negative consequences in terms of the children's subsequent interest, persistence, and preferences for challenge.

Unexpected Rewards and Task-Noncontingent Rewards

Early studies indicated that rewards not introduced until after a task was completed—so that they were not expected while participants were working on the target task—did not affect intrinsic motivation for that task (Lepper et al., 1973). This is to be expected, for if people are not doing a task to get a reward, they are not likely to experience their task behavior as being controlled by the reward. Similarly, early studies also indicated that rewards not requiring task engagement were unlikely to negatively affect intrinsic motivation for the task (Deci, 1972b). Although relatively few studies of unexpected rewards and task-noncontingent rewards exist, the meta-analysis revealed no evidence that either reward type significantly affected intrinsic motivation, findings that are explicitly consistent with the tenets of CET (Deci & Ryan, 1980; Ryan et al., 1983).

Engagement-Contingent Rewards

Within the category of engagement-contingent rewards, rewards are offered simply for working on the target activity. When children were told they would get an award for doing an art activity (Lepper et al., 1973) and when college students were told that they would receive payment if they performed a hidden-figures activity (Ryan et al., 1983), the rewards were engagement contingent. In both cases, there were no specific performance requirements. They did not have to finish or do well at the task; they simply had to work on it. More studies have used engagement-contingent rewards than any other contingency, and that was particularly true for children. In all, there were 61 experiments investigating the effects of engagement-contingent rewards, 55 of which used the behavioral measure and 35 of which used self-reported interest.

Results of the analyses confirmed that engagement-contingent rewards significantly diminished intrinsic motivation, with an effect size of $d = -0.40$ on free-choice behavior and $d = -0.15$ for self-reported interest. Further, for the behavioral measure, the undermining was significantly stronger for children than for college students. The finding of negative effects of engagement-contingent rewards is extremely important precisely because engagement-contingent rewards—rewards given simply for doing some task—are quite prevalent in life. For example, most hourly employees get paid for working at their jobs without having the pay tied specifically to the number of tasks completed or to meeting a performance requirement, such as doing better than half the other people doing the same job.

Completion-Contingent Rewards

The first study of rewards on intrinsic motivation in humans (Deci, 1971) employed completion-contingent rewards. In it, participants were offered $1 for each of four puzzles they completed within a specified amount of time. Thus, there was a pressure associated with the reward that was greater than in the engagement-contingent studies, a pressure that from the CET perspective would yield an undermining effect. On the other hand, getting the completion-contingent reward provided some affirmation of competence, which according to CET, can counteract some of the negative effects of the implicit control. However, overall CET predicts an undermining effect for this category of rewards.

We located 27 studies that examined completion-contingent rewards, of which 20 included a behavioral measure and 15 included self-reports. Analyses revealed that completion-contingent rewards undermined intrinsic motivation on both dependent measures: $d = -0.44$ for free choice and $d = -0.17$ for self-reports, with one outlier removed for free choice and two removed for self-reports.

Task-Contingent Rewards

The category of task-contingent rewards has been used in this literature for over two decades and was part of the original Ryan et al. (1983) typology. It is simply the combination of what in the meta-analysis by Deci et al. were referred to as engagement-contingent rewards and completion-contingent rewards. Because of its historical significance in the field, we briefly present the meta-analytic results for this category also.

For 74 studies with a free-choice measure, the composite effect size for task-contingent rewards showed highly significant undermining ($d = -0.39$). Further, the undermining for children was significantly stronger than for college students. For 48 studies with a self-report measure of intrinsic motivation, the homogeneous composite effect size also showed significant undermining ($d = -0.16$) with two outliers removed.

Performance-Contingent Rewards

From the standpoint of CET, performance-contingent rewards are surely the most interesting type of tangible rewards. Performance-contingent rewards were defined by Ryan et al. (1983) as being given explicitly for doing well at a task or for performing up to a specified standard. Examples of performance-contingency studies include the study by Ryan et al., in which participants in the performance-contingent-rewards condition received $3 for "having done well at the activity," and the study by Harackiewicz et al. (1984), in which participants received a reward because they were said to have "performed better than 80% of other participants."

According to CET, performance-contingent rewards have the potential to affect motivation in two ways—one quite positive and one quite negative. Performance-contingent rewards can maintain or enhance intrinsic motivation if the receiver of the reward interprets it as an affirmation of competence. Yet, because performance-contingent rewards can be used as a way to control not only what people do but how well they do it, performance-contingent rewards can also feel very controlling, in which case such rewards would be expected to decrease feelings of autonomy and undermine intrinsic motivation. It is a long-standing tenet of CET that it is the relative salience of the competence-relevant versus controlling aspects of a performance-contingent reward that determines its effect on intrinsic motivation.

With performance-contingent rewards, there is an interesting issue that is not relevant to the other types of contingencies. Specifically, because performance-contingent rewards implicitly convey performance feedback, there is the question of whether the appropriate control group is one that provides feedback comparable to that conveyed by the reward or is one that provides neither the reward nor comparable feedback. To examine the effects of the rewards per se, independent of the feedback conveyed by them, one must compare the rewards condition to a condition in which there are no rewards but there is comparable competence-relevant feedback. On the other hand, to examine the *combined* effects of the rewards and the feedback inherent in them to a complete absence of feedback, one would compare the rewards condition to a no-rewards, no-feedback condition. Some studies have used one type of control group, some have used the other, and some have used both.

In most studies of performance-contingent rewards, all participants receive rewards that signify excellent performance, in accord with how Ryan et al. (1983) defined this reward contingency. The studies were done in that way because it allowed researchers to study the informational versus controlling aspects of that reward contingency. However, in real-world situations, some people typically get either smaller rewards or no rewards because they do not reach the performance standard necessary to get the maximum rewards. Some studies have investigated the ecologically relevant issue of the effects of receiving performance-contingent rewards that are less than the maximum. For example, in a study by Pittman, Cooper, and Smith (1977) that used a no-feedback control group, participants could win between 5 cents and 25 cents on each of 10 trials, depending on how well they did at it. Thus, it is likely that at least some of them experienced the implicit feedback contained within the rewards as "negative." Clearly, such studies are quite different from the more typical studies of performance-contingent rewards in which all participants receive the same maximum rewards for having done well, because the less-than-maximum rewards would likely yield both decreased perceived competence and the feelings of being controlled.

In the meta-analysis, we first combined the effects for all studies of performance-contingent rewards. There were 32 that had a free-choice measure and 29 that had a self-report measure. Performance-contingent rewards significantly undermined free-choice behavior ($d = -0.28$), whereas results for the self-report studies were not significant.

Because the set of effects for free-choice behavior was not homogeneous, we separated the effects into four categories in accordance with whether the studies used no-feedback control groups or feedback control groups and whether rewarded participants received the maximum reward or less than the maximum reward. These were the resulting four categories: effects involving no-feedback control groups where everyone got the maximum possible rewards, effects involving no-feedback control groups where all participants did not get the maximum possible rewards, effects involving comparable-feedback control groups where everyone got positive feedback, and effects involving comparable-feedback control groups where participants got negative feedback.

Eighteen studies had no-feedback control groups where everyone got the maximum possible rewards, and there was significant undermining for this group with a composite effect size of $d = -0.15$. Seven studies had no-feedback control groups where all participants did not get the maximum possible rewards, and for the six that made up a homogeneous group there was also significant undermining, with a composite effect size of $d = -0.88$. Ten studies with comparable-feedback control groups where everyone got positive feedback showed significant undermining, with a composite effect size of $d = -0.20$; and three studies with comparable-feedback control groups where participants got negative feedback did not show undermining.

One of these four performance-contingent reward groups stands out and deserves special mention—namely, the group in which some participants got less than the maximal rewards and were compared to a no-feedback control group. When performance-contingent rewards are used in the real world, they are frequently used in this way—that is, people's rewards vary depending on how well they perform. The meta-analysis showed that this type of reward had a considerably larger negative effect size than did any other category in the meta-analysis, indicating clearly that rewarding people as a function of performance runs a very serious risk of negatively affecting their intrinsic motivation. The type of performance contingency that seems most likely to be used in the real world is the one that was found to be most detrimental.

Eisenberger and Cameron (1998) stated that they had done another meta-analysis in which they compared performance-contingent rewards that had specific performance standards (e.g., rewards for surpassing the 80th percentile) to comparable positive-feedback control groups, indicating that there were four such studies with the free-choice measure and seven with the self-report measure. They reported that in both cases these performance-contingent rewards significantly enhanced intrinsic motivation, although they did not provide any methodological details.

To evaluate their claim, we examined the studies of performance-contingent rewards that met the criteria of specific performance standards and positive feedback control groups. There were 6 such studies with a free-choice measure and 10 with a self-report measure. For the 6 free-choice studies, the effects were homogeneous and the average effect size was $d = -0.21$, indicating nonsignificant undermining, thus contradicting the Eisenberger and Cameron claim that this type of reward significantly enhances free-choice intrinsic motivation. For the 10 studies with a self-report measure, the effects were homogeneous and the average effect size of $d = -0.02$ suggests no effect, which also contradicts the claim by Eisenberger and Cameron that this type of reward enhances self-reported interest.

Delayed versus Immediate Effects of Rewards on Intrinsic Motivation

Some studies have examined the effects of tangible rewards when the measure of intrinsic motivation was taken immediately after the reward period, whereas others have assessed intrinsic motivation after delays of several days or longer. The issue here is whether the undermining effect is simply a transitory phenomenon. We did a meta-analytic comparison, collapsing across all types of tangible rewards, in which we contrasted studies that used delayed assessments with those that used immediate assessments. Because all 24 studies with delayed assessments had used children as participants, we used only studies of children in this comparison. The results showed that the average effect size for the 24 studies with delayed assessments was nearly identical to the effect size for the 30 studies in which assessments were done immediately after rewarded behavior.

Summary of the Effects of Rewards
on Intrinsic Motivation

The findings concerning the primary behavioral measure of intrinsic motivation are summarized in Table 2.1. As shown, results reveal that positive
feedback generally enhanced intrinsic motivation whereas tangible rewards
undermined it. Further, in accord with distinctions and predictions explicitly
offered by CET, the results showed that unexpected tangible rewards and
task-noncontingent rewards had no effect on intrinsic motivation, whereas
each of the specific contingencies that require involvement with the target
activity were detrimental to intrinsic motivation. Thus, rewards that were
engagement contingent, completion contingent, performance contingent,
and of course task contingent (which is simply the aggregate of engagement
contingent and completion contingent) all undermined intrinsic motivation.
Further, there were noteworthy age effects such that positive feedback had a
less positive effect on children than on college students and tangible
rewards had a more negative effect on children than on college students.

TABLE 2.1

**Summary of the Meta-analytic Results of the Effects of Extrinsic Rewards on Free-Choice
Intrinsic Motivation, Shown as Cohen's Composite d**

	d	k
All rewards	−0.24[a]	(101)
Verbal rewards	0.33[a]	(21)
College	0.43[a]	(14)[b]
Children	0.11	(7)[b]
Tangible	−0.34[a]	(92)
Unexpected	0.01	(9)[b]
Expected	−0.36[a]	(92)
Task noncontingent	−0.14	(7)[b]
Engagement contingent	−0.40[a]	(55)
College	−0.21[a]	(12)[b]
Children	−0.43[a]	(39)[b]
Completion contingent	−0.44[a]	(19)[b]
Performance contingent	−0.28[a]	(32)
Maximum reward	−0.15[a]	(18)[b]
Not maximum reward	−0.88[a]	(6)[b]
Positive feedback control	−0.20[a]	(10)[b]
Negative feedback control	−0.03	(3)[b]

[a] Significant at $p < .05$ or greater.

[b] These effect sizes are for the most differentiated categories used in the meta-analysis and
each is homogeneous. Some of the 101 studies with a free-choice measure used to determine
the overall effect size had multiple reward conditions, so the total number of effect sizes in
the most differentiated categories was 150. Of those, a total of 6 were removed as outliers to
create homogeneity in the most differentiated categories.

And finally, within the performance-contingent category, the type of rewards that was most detrimental was the most ecologically relevant type—namely, the one in which people's rewards are provided as a direct function of their performance. The results confirmed that controlling people's behavior with reward contingencies undermines their intrinsic motivation, even when the rewards are appetitively and efficaciously pursued.

Squaring our Results with Those
of the Previous Meta-analyses

As already mentioned, four previous meta-analyses examined reward effects. Rummel and Feinberg (1988), Wiersma (1992), and Tang and Hall (1995) all concluded that tangible rewards (especially task-contingent rewards) undermine intrinsic motivation. A meta-analysis reported by Cameron and Pierce (1994) and again by Eisenberger and Cameron (1996) found enhancement of intrinsic motivation by verbal rewards and undermining by tangible rewards. However, the Eisenberger, Cameron, and Pierce group then analyzed the contingencies separately and reported no undermining by either completion-contingent or performance-contingent rewards. Thus, their highly publicized analysis is anomalous compared with both our results and those of three prior meta-analyses.

Because reports of meta-analyses provide substantial information about specific studies used in the analyses, we were able to examine the procedures and calculations used by Eisenberger, Cameron, and Pierce and to identify numerous errors and inappropriate procedures. Presented in detail in Deci et al. (1999), we briefly summarize them here. First, the researchers included conditions that were specifically designed by experimenters to be dull and boring so there would have been no initial intrinsic motivation to undermine, and the researchers then collapsed the effects of rewards across interesting and uninteresting tasks within studies. Because the field of inquiry has always been defined in terms of intrinsic motivation for interesting tasks, because the undermining phenomenon has always been specified as applying to interesting tasks, and because the use of dull tasks in a few experiments was done specifically to isolate limiting conditions to the undermining effect, the inclusion of the dull-task conditions by Eisenberger, Cameron, and Pierce meant that they were not evaluating the field of inquiry as it has traditionally been defined. Furthermore, from the earliest studies conducted using both interesting and uninteresting tasks, the results have shown an interaction, with rewards tending to decrease intrinsic motivation for interesting tasks but not for dull tasks (e.g., Calder & Staw, 1975a; Hamner & Foster, 1975), so by collapsing across tasks, Eisenberger, Cameron, and Pierce managed to obscure the important findings (Lepper, 1998).

Deci et al. (in press) did a meta-analysis of 11 studies with the free-choice measure and 5 with the self-report measure in which both an interesting and a dull task were used. For the 11 studies with a free-choice measure, the composite effect for interesting tasks showed significant undermining ($d = -0.68$), but for uninteresting tasks, there was not a significant effect ($d = 0.18$). For the 5 studies with a self-report measure, the composite reward effect for interesting tasks was $d = -0.37$, thus showing significant undermining, but for uninteresting tasks there was not a significant effect, ($d = 0.10$). Thus, it is clear that the effects of tangible rewards are different when the tasks are interesting versus dull and that the reliable undermining of intrinsic motivation by tangible rewards does not extend to dull, boring tasks. Thus, according to the principles of meta-analysis, these should not be collapsed unless there is also an analysis for the moderating effects of tasks.

Second, Eisenberger, Cameron, and Pierce reported several effects that were calculated using inappropriate control groups. For example, in Swann and Pittman (1977, Experiment 2) an engagement-contingent rewards group that got positive feedback was combined with engagement-contingent rewards groups that got no feedback, and these were then compared to control groups that got no feedback. Clearly, the rewards-plus-feedback group should not have been included unless there was a comparable control group with positive feedback but without tangible rewards. Including the rewards-plus-feedback group without a proper control group confounded the effects of tangible rewards (which tend to be negative) with the effects of positive feedback ((which tend to be positive). Third, their meta-analyses misclassified several studies. For example, in a study by Porac and Meindl (1982), participants received $1.50 for each problem solved, yet that study was classified as engagement contingent instead of completion contingent. Fourth, some studies published during the period covered by the meta-analysis by Eisenberger, Cameron, and Pierce were omitted, and several relevant conditions were omitted from studies in which other conditions were included. For example, although the meta-analyses by Eisenberger, Cameron, and Pierce included the unexpected and engagement-contingent rewards conditions from a study by Greene and Lepper (1974), they did not include the performance-contingent rewards condition. Finally, we identified additional errors, including the use of incorrect effect sizes. These troubling methodological errors call into question their conclusion that there is no meaningful evidence for the undermining of intrinsic motivation by tangible rewards that are performance contingent or completion contingent. In fact, the meta-analysis by Deci et al. 1999 demonstrated that their conclusion was largely unreliable and inappropriate.

Must Rewards Always Be Detrimental to Intrinsic Motivation?

It is clear from the meta-analyses that tangible rewards made contingent on task behavior tend to be experienced as controlling and to undermine intrinsic motivation, which raises the question of whether that is inevitably the case. Is it possible to give rewards in a way that does not decrease intrinsic motivation? As a start to answering this question, consider cases from the meta-analysis in which rewards were found not to have a negative effect. They were verbal rewards, unexpected rewards, and task-noncontingent rewards, and the common element that runs through these types of rewards is that they are not offered to motivate performance before the performance begins. They are either given unexpectedly after task engagement or divorced from the task itself. This suggests, then, that one component of administering rewards so they will not have a negative effect is to make them noncontrolling—to not use them in a salient way or in an attempt to motivate behavior.

In our discussion of verbal rewards, we reported a meta-analysis showing that although positive feedback tends to enhance intrinsic motivation, its effect tends to be negative when administered within a controlling interpersonal context. This important point is relevant to the issue of giving tangible rewards in a way that is not detrimental because it raises the possibility that when tangible rewards (which tend to be controlling) are given within a noncontrolling or autonomy-supportive context, their controlling significance may be ameliorated. Indeed, CET predicts that whereas a controlling interpersonal style of administering contingent tangible rewards will make the controlling aspect of the rewards particularly salient and thus undermine intrinsic motivation, an autonomy-supportive interpersonal style will make the informational aspect of the rewards more salient and thus have a positive effect on intrinsic motivation relative to no rewards and no feedback.

A study by Ryan et al. (1983) illustrated this point. It included two performance-contingent rewards conditions in which all participants were given a $3 reward for doing well on a puzzle activity. The style of administering the rewards was noncontrolling (i.e., informational) in one of the conditions and controlling in the other. Further, it included a no-rewards, no-feedback group. And finally, it included two other no-reward conditions in which participants were given the same positive feedback contained within the performance-contingent rewards; specifically, they were told that they had done well on the puzzle activity. However, this positive feedback was administered informationally in one condition and controllingly in the other. Thus, these two conditions paralleled exactly the two performance-contingent rewards conditions in terms of the feedback conveyed and the style in which it was conveyed. The only difference was the presence versus the absence of the reward itself.

In line with our predictions, the informationally administered performance-contingent rewards led to a higher level of intrinsic motivation than in the no-rewards, no-feedback control group, whereas, of course, the controllingly administered performance-contingent rewards led to a lower level of intrinsic motivation than in the no-rewards, no-feedback control group. Thus, although contingent rewards generally tend to undermine intrinsic motivation, this study showed that relative to no rewards and no feedback, it is possible to give tangible rewards in a way that does not diminish intrinsic motivation if one takes pains to make the interpersonal context noncontrolling.

There was, however, another important finding in this study. Specifically, intrinsic motivation under the informationally administered performance-contingent rewards condition was lower than under the informational–positive feedback condition; and further, intrinsic motivation under the controllingly administered performance-contingent rewards condition was lower than under the controlling–positive feedback condition. Thus, although the condition with performance-contingent rewards, informationally administered, led to more intrinsic motivation than in the no-rewards, no-feedback control group, it led to less intrinsic motivation than under the no-rewards condition that had the noncontrolling positive feedback. It seems that although the information contained within a performance-contingent reward may have a positive effect, the reward itself will often be working against the positive effect of the information.

Harackiewicz et al. (1984) did a study that compared a performance-contingent rewards condition to a condition they called "evaluation," in which participants were told before they began a task that they would get information after finishing it about whether they had reached the performance standard. Subsequently they were told that they had done well and reached the standard. The condition that the researchers called an evaluation condition because participants were told that their performance would be evaluated was essentially an expected verbal-rewards condition. The researchers found that these "expected verbal rewards" without tangible rewards led to a lower level of intrinsic motivation than did the performance-contingent rewards condition, which of necessity also required evaluation of performance. The researchers interpreted the result by suggesting that the expected tangible rewards (relative to the expected verbal rewards) had a *cue value* that sensitized individuals to the competence information in the situation and thus highlighted the competence affirmation contained within performance-contingent rewards that were given for having done well. In essence, cue value is theorized to emphasize the informational aspect of performance-contingent rewards and offset their controlling aspect. A subsequent study by Harackiewicz, Abrahams, and Wageman (1987) showed that cue value functioned most strongly for individuals high in achievement motivation.

To summarize, the evidence, when taken together, indicates that contingent tangible rewards can have a positive effect on intrinsic motivation if one is very careful to minimize the control in the situation by making the rewards nonsalient, by using an autonomy-supportive interpersonal style, and by highlighting competence cues. Even then, the effects of contingent tangible rewards will likely be less positive than the effects of unexpected positive feedback without an accompanying reward. In short, the undermining of intrinsic motivation by tangible extrinsic rewards is strong and pervasive, and attempts to counteract this effect will require careful and diligent attention to making the rewards nonsalient, nonevaluative, and nonpressuring.

The Undermining of Other Important Variables

Thus far we have focused on the effects of extrinsic rewards on intrinsic motivation, viewing intrinsic motivation as important because it is the motivational embodiment of the activity, curiosity, and natural growth orientation of the human organism. And indeed, much of the relevant research on reward effects has used intrinsic motivation as the dependent variable. There are, however, other dependent variables that have been used in some studies and we briefly mention those here. They include learning, creativity, and prosocial behavior—all variables that relate to the proactive qualities of human motivation and behavior.

Learning and Problem Solving

Although one need only look at young children to know that learning is intrinsically motivated, parents and teachers alike frequently fall into the practice of using rewards to promote children's learning, thus raising the question of what effects those rewards might have on learning. Several early studies examining the effects of rewards on learning found that children who were rewarded for doing discrimination-learning tasks learned less well and made more errors than did children who were not rewarded (Miller & Estes, 1961; Spence, 1970; Spence & Dunton, 1967). This set of findings was consistent with the idea that rewards can interfere with intrinsic motivation for learning, although studies examining the effects of rewards on conceptual or rote learning in more ecologically valid settings still need to be conducted.

Other researchers have examined the efficacy of using rewards to promote flexible problem solving. For example, McGraw and McCullers (1979) did a study in which half the participants were offered financial rewards for solving a series of problems and the other half were not. The structure of the task was such that the key to success was being able to engage each new problem flexibly. Results indicated that participants who were rewarded had a harder time thinking flexibly than did those who were not offered a reward. In fact, McGraw (1978) reviewed several studies of reward effects and concluded that tangible rewards do impair performance on interesting, complex activities such as problem solving, although they do not have such an effect on dull, uninteresting tasks.

Creativity

Amabile, Hennessey, and Grossman (1986) employed Amabile's consensual assessment method (1982) for measuring creativity in three studies examining the effects of rewards on people's creative pursuits. Using both children and adults who made paper collages, Amabile et al. (1986) found that when rewards were made salient by having participants contract to produce collages in exchange for rewards, the participants' collages were later judged to be less creative than those made by participants who got no rewards or less salient rewards.

Prosocial Behavior

Many, though by no means all, behavioral scientists believe that empathy and care for others is a natural human propensity (Wilson, 1993), one that is an intrinsic aspect of people's need for relatedness. Still, there seems to be an increasing trend toward using rewards to foster prosocial behavior. As with the issues of reward effects on learning and creativity, the use of rewards for motivating prosocial behavior raises the question of whether such approaches are effective. The relevant evidence is not encouraging.

Indeed, several studies of prosocial or helping behaviors appear to parallel the general findings of reward effects on intrinsic motivation. A study by Fabes, Fultz, Eisenberg, May-Plumlee, and Christopher (1989) indicated that elementary school children whose mothers were prone to use rewards to motivate them were less likely than were other children to care and share at home and, further, that these children were more susceptible to having their prosocial behavior undermined by rewards within a laboratory setting. Grusec (1991) found that children of parents who used verbal rewards to promote prosocial acts were less likely to engage in such behaviors than were children whose parents were less rewarding of those acts. Batson, Coke, Jasnoski, and Hanson (1978), using adults, and Smith, Gelfand, Hartmann, and Partlow (1979), using children, found that those who were rewarded for helping behavior viewed themselves as less altruistic than did those who were not rewarded, and Kunda and Schwartz (1983) found that those who had been paid to help others reported less motivation to behave morally. Batson et al., in summarizing their study, concluded that "extrinsic incentives can, by undermining self-perceived altruism, decrease intrinsic motivation to help others" (p. 90).

Studies of blood donations also revealed that offering rewards to enhance blood donations *decreased* net blood giving and left people feeling less subsequent altruistic motivation for giving (Titmuss, 1970). Similarly, Paulhus, Shaffer, and Downing (1977) found that blood donors who were reminded of the benefits to themselves of giving indicated *less* subsequent willingness to give than did those reminded of altruistic reasons.

Frey (1997) argued that although the use of incentives to motivate environment-friendly behavior can lead to behavioral improvement in discrete areas where the incentives are applied and the behavior is closely monitored, overall environment care appears to be lowered by such programs. Echoing that point, Pelletier, Dion, Tuson, and Green-Demers (1999) suggested that reward strategies have systematically failed to promote enduring environmentally friendly behaviors, as reward–behavior dependencies have been ineffective in producing maintenance and generalization of behaviors in this sphere. In fact, Pelletier et al. found that persistent environment-care behaviors were more likely to occur when people had developed autonomous, value-based motivations for such behaviors rather than external, reward-based motivations.

To summarize, not only have studies shown that tangible rewards tend to undermine intrinsic motivation but they have also shown that these rewards have negative effects on other important variables, including learning, creativity, and prosocial or generative behaviors.

The Significance of the Undermining Phenomenon: Autonomy versus Control

Aside from its obvious practical implications, the clear and undeniable existence of the undermining effect of contingent extrinsic rewards on intrinsic motivation and related variables is of great theoretical importance. It demonstrates that the activation of reward-based goals can displace other regulatory phenomena that might otherwise occur. Specifically, rewards can lead people away from their interests and their inner desire for challenge, instead prompting a more narrow instrumental focus. Indeed, among the greatest hazards of a reward-focused environment may be that people lose touch with their natural interests, psychological needs, and intrinsic satisfactions.

From the perspective of CET, and, more broadly, SDT, reward effects on intrinsic motivation, learning, and creativity are merely special cases of a more general issue concerning autonomy versus control of human behavior in social contexts. Many aspects of the interpersonal environment have been studied with respect to the issue of control and its effects on intrinsic motivation. For instance, studies have examined the effects of controlling language (Ryan et al., 1983), evaluations (Harackiewicz et al., 1984; Ryan, 1982), grades (Grolnick & Ryan, 1987), threats of punishment (Deci & Cascio, 1972), imposed deadlines (Amabile, DeJong, & Lepper, 1976), and competition (Deci, Betley, Kahle, Abrams, & Porac, 1981), all of which were found to decrease intrinsic motivation because the controlling rather than informational aspect was experienced as more salient. Thus, the reward–effect results fit within a larger network of observations concerning how a wide range of factors that decrease perceived autonomy can derail an inherent source of learning and growth. Rewards are one important means through which people attempt to control others, but there are numerous other means of control and all of them appear to run the serious risk of undermining people's intrinsic motivation, conceptual learning, problem solving, creativity, and generosity toward others.

Thwarting Internalization

Just as rewards are merely one type of controlling event that can undermine intrinsic motivation, intrinsic motivation is just one case of natural motivational processes that can be affected by controls. Although less extensively studies, evidence does indicate that the use of controlling motivational practices can interfere with other natural processes and sensibilities, such as the internalization and integration of the meaning and value of many socially prescribed behaviors. For example, Grolnick and Ryan (1989), in a parent-interview study, found that children of parents who emphasized controlling motivational strategies evidenced less internalization and lower self-motivation for doing schoolwork than children of autonomy-supportive parents. The children of controlling parents were also more likely to be rated by teachers as having behavioral problems.

The Detrimental Effects of Controlling Behavior in the Real World

Demonstrations of how the imposition of reward contingencies and the use of other controlling strategies have hidden costs and distract people from other inherent and positive motivational tendencies go well beyond the laboratory experiments already reviewed. We thus turn to a consideration of some important disregulating effects of rewards and controls in the life domains of school and work.

Motivation in Schools. One of the obvious places to observe the negative effects of rewards on intrinsic motivation and autonomous initiative is in schools (Ryan & Stiller, 1991). Researchers have documented a progressive loss of intrinsic motivation over the first 8 years of school (e.g., Harter, 1981). Given the rich literature showing how greater intrinsic motivation is associated with better performance, more positive attitudes, and greater creativity, this decline is indeed a significant problem. However, in systems where teachers are themselves often feeling pressured and controlled by performance contingencies, there remains a widely entrenched practice of using rewards and evaluations—grades, gold stars, contingent privileges, and approval—in an attempt to enhance student performance. Despite the widely held belief in the efficacy of rewards, reward interventions are likely to yield very disappointing results (Ryan & La Guardia, 1999).

It even appears that just holding a strong belief in the efficacy of rewards and controls is predictive of negative effects on children's intrinsic motivation. Deci, Schwartz, Sheinman, and Ryan (1981) compared teachers whom they had preclassified in accord with whether the teachers had espoused a more controlling or a more autonomy-supportive philosophy of motivation. Those who endorsed the use of rewards and punishments were classified as *controlling*, whereas those who eschewed the use of external controls and were oriented toward working from the children's internal perspective were classified as *autonomy supportive*. Results showed that controlling versus autonomy-supportive teachers had dramatically different effects on the motivation of the children in their classrooms. Within a few weeks of the beginning of a school year, children of controlling teachers were already significantly less intrinsically motivated for school—less curious, less desirous of challenge, less self-initiating and mastery oriented. Further, children of the teachers with controlling orientations had lower perceived competence at school and lower feelings of self-worth.

Evaluations and the contingent administration of grades are perhaps the controlling methods of motivation that are most prominently used is schools, and evidence suggests that they can be highly detrimental to both self-motivation and the quality of learning. As already noted, the study by Harackiewicz et al. (1984) showed that when participants were told that their performance would be evaluated and they were then given positive evaluations after they finished the task, they displayed significantly less intrinsic motivation than did others who were not told that they would be evaluated but got the same positive feedback. Smith (1975) reported similar results.

Grolnick and Ryan (1987) did an experiment to examine the effects of telling children their learning would be graded and found that the use of a grade contingency to motivate learning resulted in less conceptual understanding and less well maintained learning than did a nongraded approach to motivating engagement with the material. Butler and Nissen (1986), in a study of sixth graders, found that normative grades produced diminished interest and performance, and Benware and Deci (1984) found that telling college students their learning would be graded also resulted in impairment of intrinsic interest and conceptual understanding. Such findings are consistent with a meta-analysis by Utman (1997) that showed negative effects of external regulation on complex, creative, performances.

Some educators consider grades to be contingent rewards par excellence. Better performance is rewarded with higher grades. Although grades do indeed motivate, what they motivate is not always the type of behavior one might hope to promote when applying them. For example, at least in some students, grades motivate behavior directed toward getting the grade rather than mastering the material (Kellaghan, Madaus, & Raczek, 1996). In other students, as predicted by both CET and related approaches such as

Nicholl's achievement motivation theory (1984), grading systems motivate people to withdraw effort so as to guard themselves against the painful diagnostic information associated with failing at a task at which they tried to succeed. These counterproductive behaviors represent yet other hidden costs of the widely advocated contingent-reward approach (e.g., Eisenberger & Cameron, 1996).

Of course, like other rewards, grades have a feedback component. Grades are an efficient way of conveying information about how well students are doing, and many students claim to want grades so they will know how well they stack up in a system that requires good grades for college admission and other such opportunities. But it seems clear that using grades, like using contingent rewards more generally, is a risky business. Using grades in a way that is likely to be experienced as informational rather than controlling requires astute administration by sensitive teachers whose approach to education is autonomy supportive, and even then it may be hard for students not to get caught up in the control.

Yet another potential problem with the use of rewards in schools concerns their impact on teachers' self-reflective activities. As long as motivational problems are located in reward contingencies that are not strong enough, attention will not be directed to other factors that may hinder motivation, such as unstimulating lessons, lack of optimal challenge, poor communications, and low teacher enthusiasm. By focusing on extrinsic factors as the key to motivation, practitioners are apt to turn inadequate attention to where the real problems may lie: in the process and content of the lessons themselves and in the lack of supportive relationships between school personnel and students.

Motivating Performance in the Workplace.   The very concept of work seems to imply something that is not play, something we do for extrinsic rewards rather than for intrinsic enjoyment (Lepper & Greene, 1975). For many people, work is, and indeed feels like, a *have-to*, an aspect of life they would gladly forgo if they could. Yet, the picture is not as simple as that. Indeed, some evidence suggests that people find tremendous natural challenge at work—opportunities to be agentic, to feel competent, to be creative, and to feel generative. That is, so-called work is not always a passively suffered human experience; for some it is instead a true expression of the self—a sphere of action that can be fully self-endorsed. People work not only for extrinsic rewards but also for intrinsic satisfactions.

Frey (1997), in a recent discussion of the workplace, pointed out that many committed, inspired, and involved workers derive substantial satisfactions by realizing their natural desires to be effective and make contributions. Nonetheless, he argued, many other people appear to be "in it only for the money," a state that results when the use of pay-for-performance strategies crowd out intrinsic motivation and the psychological satisfactions that accrue from productive work. Of course, when employers rely on pay-for-performance as a primary motivational strategy, they typically also use other controls such as surveillance, evaluation, and competition, all of which have also been found to undermine intrinsic motivation and internalization of values (Deci & Ryan, 1985b; Kohn, 1993). The key point, once again, is that the use of rewards and other controls can interfere with the self-motivation and natural sensibilities that could be more prevalent in the workplace if the motivational focus were not so oriented toward control.

Schwartz (1994) argued that a focus on rewards and controls as the principal motivators may also detract from workers' loyalty and honesty. He stated, "When work comes to be defined or framed strictly in terms of the making of money, ... then the sources of satisfaction with a job well done, a product well made, a customer well served erode" (p. 245). He further stated, "the pay structure in many retail trades establishes incentives for salespeople to sell as much as they possibly can without concern for method" (p. 35), thus suggesting that incentive programs for both workers and corporate leaders may encourage dishonest or deceitful behaviors. Similarly, Blumberg (1991) reported that workers who engaged in deceptive practices typically said that it was the structure of rewards that compelled them to behave in ways that were against their values or that they did not personally endorse. From the fudging of quarterly reports to the release of defective products to the use of unscrupulous competitive methods to a lack of concern with worker welfare and loyalty, corporate officers also frequently reported doing "what is required" in today's profit-oriented markets as a behavioral justification. Repeatedly, it appears, the pursuit of rewards overrides values for morality and fairness (Wilson, 1993).

In spite of the negative consequences of contingent extrinsic rewards in the workplace, not only for intrinsic motivation but also for performance and morality, we must keep in mind that rewards are a natural outcome of work. Even people who enjoy the process of their work still typically need their labors to yield resources for living. So the issue here is not whether rewards should be eliminated from the workplace but instead how rewards can be distributed so as not to be seriously damaging to intrinsic motivation, loyalty to the organization, and the satisfactions of quality performance. And again, this is an issue to which the meta-analysis is directly relevant. We have already argued that although tangible rewards have a strong tendency to undermine self-motivation, they will be less detrimental if they are not used as a salient technique for controlling employees and if the interpersonal context within which they are administered is oriented toward autonomy support.

The preceding discussion about the negative effects of rewards in the workplace pertained largely to the point that many work settings use reward systems that are highly salient, that make people's pay dependent on their narrowly defined performance, and that therefore tend to be experienced as coercive and alienating, leading to a range of unfortunate consequences. Another point concerns whether the interpersonal context of a work setting being controlling versus informational (i.e., autonomy supportive) differentially affects the motivation and performance of individuals within it, even coloring the effects of the rewards that are a necessary part of the ecology. In that regard, Deci et al. (1989) found that managers who tended to be more controlling had employees who were less motivated and less trusting than did the employees of managers who were more autonomy supportive. Those who worked for controlling managers also tended to place greater importance on making money and less importance on having satisfying work.

Internalizing the Reward Culture: Individual Differences in Reward Orientations

In a culture that places strong emphasis on rewards, there will be an enticing pull to orient toward external rather than internal cues and to internalize the importance of rewards and their accompaniments. In other words, within a reward-oriented culture such as ours, there will be a tendency for people to accept the importance of trying to attain rewards and of regulating themselves by orienting to the relevant external contingencies. Nonetheless, people display substantial individual differences in the extent to which they value rewards and are regulated by reward contingencies. These individual differences, which are theorized to result from people's experiences with their own socializing agents, have been studied in two ways: first, through causality orientations, and second, through people's predominant aspirations or life goals. We briefly touch on each of these lines of research.

Causality Orientations

People differ in the strength of their causality orientations—that is, in the factors they orient toward when initiating and regulating their behavior (Deci & Ryan, 1985a). Two of the three causality orientations—autonomous and controlled—are particularly relevant to the current discussion. Some individuals, being strongly *autonomy oriented*, are inclined to base their regulation on internal awareness of interests and needs, whereas others, being more strongly *control oriented*, are prone to initiate and regulate behavior by looking outward, by evaluating reward and punishment contingencies that are in their social contexts or have been introjected (Ryan & Connell, 1989). Research findings suggest that the relative predominance of this self-regulation versus contingency-focused regulation is a meaningful personality construct with important consequences.

Research on causality orientations has investigated a variety of issues. For instance, whereas the autonomy orientation was found to be positively associated with ego development, self-actualization, self-esteem, and other indicators of well-being, the control orientation was found to be associated with public self-consciousness, anxiety, and the coronary-prone behavior pattern. Relative to people high on the control orientation, people high on the autonomy orientation also displayed greater personal integration as reflected in more consistency among behavior, attitudes, and motivation (Koestner, Bernieri, & Zuckerman, 1992). Further, additional studies showed the control orientation to be related to placing high importance on extrinsic goals such as wealth and fame (Kasser & Ryan, 1996), to being susceptible to image-based (as opposed to content-based) advertising (Zuckerman, Gioioso, & Tellini, 1988), and having more defensive personal relationships (Hodgins, Koestner, & Duncan, 1996).

It seems clear, then, that being more focused on external cues and contingencies and less aware of one's internal needs and feelings as the basis for regulating one's day-to-day life does indeed have significant costs, both personal and interpersonal.

Intrinsic versus Extrinsic Aspirations

Another line of relevant individual-difference research within the SDT framework has examined the correlates of people's salient aspirations or life goals. Specifically, some people's life goals are concerned primarily with the attainment of outcomes such as money, image, and fame that hold promise of extrinsic satisfaction. Presumably, many people assume that the accumulation of money, the projection of an attractive image, and the attainment of fame can be cashed in for a happy and fulfilled life. This focus on extrinsic aspirations has been contrasted with a more intrinsic focus on the importance of awareness and growth, meaningful relationships, and generativity—aspirations that themselves yield intrinsic satisfactions independent of any instrumental value they might also hold.

In popular literature, the attainment of extrinsic aspirations is portrayed as fulfillment of the "American dream," within which wealth and fame are believed to produce happiness and well-being. Yet, many commentators have questioned whether the pursuit of the American dream does in fact enhance people's quality of life. For example, Schwartz (1994) argued that the values of the market economy erode the "best things in life," and Frank and Cook (1995) suggested that the competitive structures of market economies generally impoverish the life experiences of people who live in them. Schor (1991) further described how the pressures to work, acquire, and consume lead to an unwitting expenditure of personal energies. These commentaries all point to the hypothesis that an overinvestment in the extrinsic "having" goals may be harmful to, rather than the foundation for, well-being and life satisfaction.

In fact, recent research has confirmed the potential harm that can be associated with a strong focus on extrinsic rather than intrinsic goals. Kasser and Ryan (1993) found that mental health and well-being were negatively associated with a strong investment in financial success, relative to the intrinsic goals of personal growth, relatedness, and community. Subsequently, Kasser and Ryan (1996, 1998) showed that the more individuals placed a strong emphasis on the extrinsic goals of wealth, fame, and image, the lower their well-being and the poorer their personal relationships. Ryan et al. (1999) reported some cross-cultural generalizability to this pattern, showing similar effects in Russian as well as U.S. samples. It is noteworthy that in each of these studies, the negative effects of extrinsic aspirations obtained even for people who felt quite confident about achieving their extrinsic aspirations, so the negative effect of strongly valuing extrinsic goals was not a function of holding unrealistic aspirations that were unlikely to be satisfied.

Sheldon and Kasser (1995) found that having short-term personal strivings (Emmons, 1986) linked to longer-term intrinsic aspirations was predictive of greater life satisfaction and positive affect, whereas having strivings linked to extrinsic aspirations was more predictive of negative outcomes. Studies have also shown that whereas perceived *attainment* of intrinsic aspirations is positively associated with well-being, perceived attainment of extrinsic aspirations is not (Kasser & Ryan, 1998). Further, attainment of personal strivings that are linked to intrinsic aspirations were found to have a more positive effect on well-being than were strivings linked to extrinsic aspirations (Sheldon & Kasser, 1998). Research by Richins and Dawson (1992) yielded similar conclusions. They measured people's materialistic orientation and found it to be negatively associated with life satisfaction and prosocial activity. In a related vein, Cantor et al. (1991) showed that sorority women whose appraisal of life tasks was more outcome focused (i.e., more extrinsic) reported less positive affect and emotional involvement in daily life. As with the research by Kasser, Ryan, and colleagues, these findings suggest that a strong emphasis on extrinsic goals may result in a lower level of well-being.

Self-determination theory offers an integrated perspective on these findings, a perspective informed by what we have learned about the effects of rewards on people's motivation (Ryan, Sheldon, Kasser, & Deci, 1996). From this perspective, intrinsic pursuits such as relatedness, growth, and community are likely to directly satisfy basic psychological needs for autonomy, relatedness, and competence (Deci & Ryan, 1991; Ryan, 1995). These innate psychological needs are the presumed source of a true sense of personal well-being or eudaimonia (Deci & Ryan, 1995; From, 1976; Ryff, 1995; Waterman, 1993). In contrast, placing heavy emphasis on pursuit of extrinsic goals and rewards such as money, social recognition, and appearance can provide only indirect satisfaction of these basic needs and may actually distract from or interfere with their fulfillment. Furthermore, extrinsic pursuits, when they are a predominant concern, may entail an ego-involved engagement in the target activities, with its accompanying pressure and stress (Ryan, 1982; Ryan, Koestner, & Deci, 1991), which other research has shown to be associated with less vitality and eudaimonia than self-determined engagement with the activities (Nix, Ryan, Manly, & Deci, 1999).

The Basis for Strong Extrinsic Aspirations

We argue that Western culture has become strongly reward oriented, and evidence reported by Schor (1991) suggests that this focus has had an important influence on people's behavior. For example, Americans—both men and women, laborers and professionals—work longer and harder than ever before. According to Schor, given current productivity rates, American workers could produce the 1948 standard of living in less than half the time it took in that year. But instead, people have sacrificed leisure and family time to work harder and have a much higher standard of living. Unfortunately, the yield of their consumption appears to be stress and ill-being rather than satisfaction and well-being (Richins, 1994).

   The strong cultural emphasis on extrinsic values has had a general effect on Americans, but that still leaves the question of why those values have become more strongly implanted in some Americans than in others, when they surround us all. Recent developmental research suggests that people may acquire overly strong extrinsic goals and expectations when they have experienced deficits in the fulfillment of the basic psychological needs. To the extent that individuals have had inadequate experiences of autonomy and relatedness, they may defensively lose awareness of their basic needs and thus look for external direction. In other words, they may develop stronger culturally sanctioned extrinsic life goals for wealth, fame, and image that represent visible signs of "worth." In line with this, studies by Kasser, Ryan, Zax, and Sameroff (1995) and Williams, Cox, Hedberg, and Deci (in press) have confirmed that adolescents whose parental care was more cold and controlling placed greater value on extrinsic, materialistic goals, consistent with the suggestion that strong extrinsic goals become more important in contexts that thwart basic need satisfaction. It thus seems that the same social contextual factors that undermine intrinsic motivation (Ryan et al., 1983), hinder internalization (Grolnick & Ryan, 1989), and result in more controlled regulation (Deci, Eghrari, Patrick, & Leone, 1994) also promote a strong orientation toward extrinsic life goals, with the resulting costs to well-being.

Self-Regulation versus Regulation by Rewards:
Two Types of Behavioral Activation Systems

Within SDT, tangible contingent rewards are typically expected to have negative effects on intrinsic motivation and self-regulation because they are experienced as controlling and thus thwart satisfaction of people's need for autonomy. Carver and Scheier (1998) discussed the negative effects of control from a different perspective. Following the work of Gray (1990) that distinguished two behavioral systems in the brain—the behavioral activation system (BAS) and the behavioral inhibition system (BIS)—Carver and Scheier's analysis focused on approach (BAS) versus avoidance (BIS) motivation. They made the general points that (1) approach motivation (aimed at attaining outcomes) tends to be associated with more positive outcomes than does avoidance motivation (aimed at escaping outcomes), and that (2) the negative effects of controlled regulation can be accounted for by the fact that it is based on avoidance rather than approach motivation.

We agree that avoidance motivation does often have more negative consequences than does approach motivation (e.g., Elliot and Church, 1997); that some controlled behavior (e.g., behaving to escape punishment or guilt) is representative of avoidance responding; and that people prone to avoidance motivation are especially vulnerable to being controlled and not getting their needs met (Elliot & Sheldon, 1998). However, despite the value of the approach–avoidance distinction, the readiness to embrace approach motivation is, from the self-determination theory perspective, theoretically regressive (Ryan & Deci, 1999). Specifically, among the important conclusions to be drawn from the numerous and varied studies and commentaries reviewed in this chapter is that some of people's controlled behavior—namely, their controlled pursuit of rewards—is indeed appetitive and approach oriented, yet this approach motivation can have a variety of negative consequences. Furthermore, Assor and Kaplan (1999) used a questionnaire format to examine controlled-approach motivation and, as predicted, found such motivation to be lower on the autonomy continuum than the types of motivation theorized to be autonomous, and they also found this controlled-approach motivation to have less positive correlates than did the autonomous types of motivation. This indicates, then, that not all approach motivation has positive consequences and that the negative effects of control do not all come from avoidance motivation. Indeed, like avoidance motivation, some approach motives—such as the vigorous pursuit of rewards—can be problematic, dominating over more integrated self-regulation.

SDT accepts the premise advocated by behaviorists that rewards can be powerful controllers of behavior, and we believe that this occurs at least in part by activating appetitive motivational systems (Gray, 1990). The point, however, is that this reward-based motivation can at times displace the autonomous regulation that might otherwise occur, regulation that would be both based in and supportive of basic psychological needs. Stated differently, regulation by rewards can supplant important innate or intrinsic regulators of behavior, leading to an atrophy of self-regulation strategies and capacities. In short, people, like the rats in the classic Olds (1958) experiments, can be neglecting important needs as they eagerly approach rewards.

Natural and Not-So-Natural Reward Contingencies

What is it, then, that we refer to as self-regulatory processes? According to SDT, self-regulation is the energization and guidance of behavior on the basis of integrated awareness, informed by basic needs. That is, when people are truly self-regulating, they are able to freely process current needs and demands and spontaneously generate actions based on the match between available behaviors and current needs. Sheldon and Elliot (1999) referred to this as self-concordance, which is a state of congruent self-organization. Under most natural circumstance, SDT suggests, people display an evolved, efficient tendency to construct meaningful goals that are fully endorsed by the self to meet basic needs and energize effective action. This natural tendency depends on being receptive to all need-related thoughts and feelings and being authentically sensitive to external circumstances.

Throughout most of human history, reward contingencies in the environment have typically represented informational inputs to effective self-regulation, conveying important facts about what outcomes were truly need satisfying and how to obtain those outcomes efficiently. Natural reward contingencies, such as those that yielded food, were an important aid to self-regulation, for they conveyed crucial information about the behaviors that lead to physiological need fulfillment. Similarly, experiencing the intrinsic rewards of feeling competent, related, and autonomous and learning how to achieve those satisfactions have been important for guiding behavior in directions that typically ensure both personal growth and investment in community. Accordingly, the attainment of need-satisfying rewards that occurred naturally in the world have traditionally been the basis for self-regulation, health, and well-being.

Increasingly, however, arbitrary reward contingencies and the non-natural pairings of certain behaviors with reward sensations have been created within the social world to control behavior, and with that, the gyroscope of natural self-regulation has become more vulnerable. The BAS system, so readily activated by stimulating rewards, has become likely prey for external agents attempting to stimulate and hook this regulatory system. Indeed, because exogenously incited appetitiveness can short-circuit self-regulation, it allows external forces to harness people's energies and appetites for purposes that are not in the best interests of the people or their collectives.

CONCLUSIONS

A meta-analysis (Deci et al., 1999) of experiments examining the effects of rewards on intrinsic motivation (using both free-choice behavior and self-reported interest) revealed significant undermining by tangible rewards on both measures, providing compelling evidence that the imposition of extrinsic rewards can significantly interfere with aspects of natural human self-regulation. Research has also revealed that these rewards can negatively affect conceptual learning, creativity, prosocial behavior, and the assimilation and integration of human values and meaning. SDT interprets these effects as indicating that rewards, which are effective external regulators of action, can circumvent such considerations as personal interests, innate psychological needs, and other social values and sensibilities that are the basis for autonomous self-regulation. However, although tangible rewards have a very strong tendency to impair intrinsic motivation and related processes, they are less detrimental if they are not used contingently or saliently and if the social context within which they are offered is more oriented toward autonomy support than control.

We reviewed two sets of individual difference studies showing first that when people are more oriented toward external rewards and controls than internal needs and cues, there are a variety of negative consequences, including poorer mental health, and second that when people place strong importance on the extrinsic life goals of wealth, fame, and image relative to the intrinsic life goals of growth, relationships, and community, they exhibit poorer well-being. We also argued that regulation by rewards, although it has a variety of negative consequences, often represents approach motivation, so the negative effects of control are not merely restricted to its linkage to avoidance motivation.

True self-regulation represents the integrated endorsement of an activity, considered with respect to people's needs, values, and judgments. Although pursuit of rewards can be consistent with self-regulation, it all too rarely is. Increasingly, and especially within market-based societies, rewards are used in ways that override self-regulation, with the apparent intent of fostering more work and more consumption. The current review makes clear that serious costs to the human personality and community may be linked to this trend. It appears that with such a strong emphasis on rewards, the evolved basis by which individuals regulated and maintained their growth and sense of connectedness is being unwittingly supplanting by a reliance on externally imposed incentives to act in ways that may not be congruent with their needs and self-regulatory tendencies. Motivational researchers, by attending to truly basic human needs and to the conditions that facilitate the expression of people's innate tendencies toward autonomy and homonomy, will be able to gauge both the promise and the perils of this increasing reliance on the use of rewards.

Acknowlegment

Preparation of this chapter was supported in part by grant MH53385 from the National Institute of Mental Health.

References

Amabile, T. M. (1982). Social psychology of creativity: A consensual assessment technique. *Journal of Personality and Social Psychology, 43*, 997–1013.

Amabile, T. M., DeJong, W., & Lepper, M. R. (1976). Effects of externally imposed deadlines on subsequent intrinsic motivation. *Journal of Personality and Social Psychology, 34*, 92–98.

Amabile, T. M., Hennessey, B. A., & Grossman, B. S. (1986). Social influences on creativity: The effects of contracted-for rewards. *Journal of Personality and Social Psychology, 50*, 14–23.

Angyal, A. (1965). *Neurosis and treatment: A holistic theory.* New York: Wiley.

Assor, A., & Kaplan, A. (1999, April). *Introjected-approach as compared to introjected-avoidance motivation: A desirable alternative or the least of two perils?* Paper presented at the annual meeting of the American Education Research Association, Montreal, Canada.

Batson, C. D., Coke, J. S., Jasnoski, M. L., & Hanson, M. (1978). Buying kindness: Effect of an extrinsic incentive for helping on perceived altruism. *Personality and Social Psychology Bulletin, 4*, 86–91.

Benware, C. & Deci, E. L. (1984). Quality of learning with an active versus passive motivational set. *American Educational Research Journal, 21*, 755–765.

Berlyne, D. E. (1971). *Aesthetics and psychobiology.* New York: Appleton-Century-Crofts.

Blanck, P. D., Reis, H. T., & Jackson, L. (1984). The effects of verbal reinforcements on intrinsic motivation for sex-linked tasks. *Sex Roles, 10*, 369–387.

Blumberg, P. (1991). *The predatory society.* New York: Oxford University Press.

Butler, R., & Nissen, M. (1986). Effects of no feedback, task-related comments, and grades on intrinsic motivation and performance. *Journal of Educational Psychology, 78*, 210–216.

Calder, B. J., & Staw, B. M. (1975a). Self-perception of intrinsic and extrinsic motivation. *Journal of Personality and Social Psychology, 31*, 599–605.

Calder, B. J., & Staw, B. M. (1975b). The interaction of intrinsic and extrinsic motivation: Some methodological notes. *Journal of Personality and Social Psychology, 31*, 76–80.

Cameron, J., & Pierce, W. D. (1994). Reinforcement, reward, and intrinsic motivation: A meta-analysis. *Review of Educational Research, 64*, 363–423.

Cantor, N., Norem, J. K., Langston, C. A., Zirkel, S., Fleeson, W., & Cook-Flanagan, C. (1991). Life tasks and daily life experience. *Journal of Personality, 59*, 425–451.

Carton, J. S. (1996). The differential effects of tangible rewards and praise on intrinsic motivation: A comparison of cognitive evaluation theory and operant theory. *The Behavior Analyst, 19*, 237–255.

Carver, C. S., & Scheier, M. F. (1998). *On the self-regulation of behavior.* New York: Cambridge University Press.

Condry, J. (1977). Enemies of exploration: Self-initiated versus other-initiated learning. *Journal of Personality and Social Psychology, 35*, 459–477.

Csikszentmihalyi, M. (1975). *Beyond boredom and anxiety.* San Francisco: Jossey-Bass.

deCharms, R. (1968). *Personal causation: The internal affective determinants of behavior.* New York: Academic Press.

Deci, E. L. (1971). Effects of externally mediated rewards on intrinsic motivation. *Journal of Personality and Social Psychology, 18*, 105–115.

Deci, E. L. (1972a). Intrinsic motivation, extrinsic reinforcement, and inequity. *Journal of Personality and Social Psychology, 22*, 113–120.

Deci, E. L. (1972b). The effects of contingent and non-contingent rewards and controls on intrinsic motivation. *Organizational Behavior and Human Performance, 8*, 217–229.

Deci, E. L. (1975). *Intrinsic motivation*. New York: Plenum.

Deci, E. L., Betley, G., Kahle, J., Abrams, L., & Porac, J. (1981). When trying to win: Competition and intrinsic motivation. *Personality and Social Psychology Bulletin, 7*, 79–83.

Deci, E. L, & Cascio, W. F. (1972, April). *Changes in intrinsic motivation as a function of negative feedback and threats*. Paper presented at the meeting of the Eastern Psychological Association, Boston.

Deci, E. L., Cascio, W. F., & Krusell, J. (1975). Cognitive evaluation theory and some comments on the Calder and Staw critique. *Journal of Personality and Social Psychology, 31*, 81–85.

Deci, E. L., Connell, J. P., & Ryan, R. M. (1989). Self-determination in a work organization. *Journal of Applied Psychology, 74*, 580–590.

Deci, E. L., Eghrari, H., Patrick, B. C., & Leone, D. R. (1994). Facilitating internalization: The self-determination theory perspective. *Journal of Personality, 62*, 119–142.

Deci, E. L., Koestner, R., & Ryan, R. M. (1999). A meta-analytic review of experiments examining the effects of extrinsic rewards on intrinsic motivation. *Psychological Bulletin. 125*, 627–668.

Deci, E. L., & Ryan, R. M. (1980). Self-determination theory: When mind mediates behavior. *Journal of Mind and Behavior, 1*, 33–43.

Deci, E. L., & Ryan, R. M. (1985a). The general causality orientations scale: Self-determination in personality. *Journal of Research in Personality, 19*, 109–134.

Deci, E. L., & Ryan, R. M. (1985b). *Intrinsic motivation and self-determination in human behavior.* New York: Plenum.

Deci, E. L., & Ryan, R. M. (1991). A motivational approach to self: Integration in personality. In R. Dienstbier (Ed.), *Nebraska Symposium on Motivation Vol. 38. Perspectives on motivation:* (pp. 237–288). Lincoln, NE: University of Nebraska Press.

Deci, E. L., & Ryan, R. M. (1995). Human autonomy: The basis for true self-esteem. In M. Kernis (Ed.), *Efficacy, agency, and self-esteem* (pp. 31–49). New York: Plenum.

Deci, E. L., Schwartz, A. J., Sheinman, L., & Ryan, R. M. (1981). An instrument to assess adults' orientations toward control versus autonomy with children: Reflections on intrinsic motivation and perceived competence. *Journal of Educational Psychology, 73*, 642–650.

Eisenberger, R., & Cameron, J. (1996). Detrimental effects of reward: Reality of myth? *American Psychologist, 51*, 1153–1166.

Eisenberger, R., & Cameron, J. (1998). Reward, intrinsic interest, and creativity: New findings. *American Psychologist, 53*, 676–679.

Elkind, D. (1971). Cognitive growth cycles in mental development. In J. K. Cole (Ed.), *Nebraska Symposium on Motivation: Vol. 19.* (pp. 1–31). Lincoln, NE: University of Nebraska Press.

Elliot, A. J., & Church, M. A. (1997). A hierarchical model of approach and avoidance achievement motivation. *Journal of Personality and Social Psychology, 72*, 218–232.

Elliot, A. J., & Sheldon, K. M. (1998). Avoidance personal goals and the personality–illness relationship. *Journal of Personality and Social Psychology, 75*, 1282–1299.

Emmons, R. A. (1986). Personal strivings: An approach to personality and subjective well-being. *Journal of Personality and Social Psychology, 51*, 1058–1068.

Fabes, R. A., Fultz, J., Eisenberg, N., & May-Plumlee, T., & Christopher, F. S. (1989). Effects of rewards on children's prosocial motivational: A socialization study. *Developmental Psychology, 25*, 509–515.

Fisher, C. D. (1978). The effects of personal control, competence, and extrinsic reward systems on intrinsic motivation. *Organizational Behavior and Human Performance, 21*, 273–288.

Flora, S. R. (1990). Undermining intrinsic interest from the standpoint of a behaviorist. *The Psychological Record, 40*, 323–346.

Frank, R. H., & Cook, P. J. (1995). *The winner-take-all society.* New York: Free Press.

Frey, B. S. (1997). *Not just for the money.* Brookfield, VT: Edward Elgar Publishing.

Fromm, E. (1976). *To have or to be?* New York: Harper & Row.

Goodenow, J. J. (1997). Parenting and the transmission and internalization of values: From social-cultural perspectives to within-family analyses. In J. E. Grusec & L. Kuczynski (Eds.), *Parenting and children's internalization of values* (pp. 333–361). New York: Wiley.

Gray, J. A. (1990). Brain systems that mediate both emotion and cognition. *Cognition and Emotion*, 4, 269–288.

Greene, D., & Lepper, M. R. (1974). Effects of extrinsic rewards on children's subsequent intrinsic interest. *Child Development*, 45, 1141–1145.

Grolnick, W. S., & Ryan, R. M. (1987). Autonomy in children's learning: An experimental and individual difference investigation. *Journal of Personality and Social Psychology*, 52, 890–898.

Grolnick, W. S., & Ryan, R. M. (1989). Parent styles associated with children's self-regulation and competence in school. *Journal of Education Psychology*, 81, 143–154.

Grusec, J. E. (1991). Socializing concern for other in the home. *Developmental Psychology*, 27, 338–342.

Hamner, W. C., & Foster, L. W. (1975). Are intrinsic and extrinsic rewards additive: A test of Deci's cognitive evaluation theory of task motivation. *Organizational Behavior and Human Performance*, 14, 398–415.

Harackiewicz, J. M., Abrahams, S., & Wageman, R. (1987). Performance evaluation and intrinsic motivation: The effects of evaluative focus, rewards, and achievement orientation. *Journal of Personality and Social Psychology*, 53, 1015–1023.

Harackiewicz, J. M., Manderlink, G., & Sansone, C. (1984). Rewarding pinball wizardry: The effects of evaluation on intrinsic interest. *Journal of Personality and Social Psychology*, 47, 287–300.

Harter, S. (1981). A new self-report scale of intrinsic versus extrinsic orientation in the classroom: Motivational and informational components. *Developmental Psychology*, 17, 300–312.

Heider, F. (1958). *The psychology of interpersonal relations*. New York: Wiley.

Hodgins, H. S., Koestner, R., & Duncan, N. (1996). On the compatibility of autonomy and relatedness. *Personality and Social Psychology Bulletin*, 22, 227–237.

Kasser, T., & Ryan, R. M. (1993). A dark side of the American dream: Correlates of financial success as a central life aspiration. *Journal of Personality and Social Psychology*, 65, 410–422.

Kasser, T., & Ryan, R. M. (1996). Further examining the American dream: Differential correlates of intrinsic and extrinsic goals. *Personality and Social Psychology Bulletin*, 22, 80–87.

Kasser, T., & Ryan, R. M. (1998). Be careful what you wish for: Optimal functioning and the relative attainment of intrinsic and extrinsic goals. Unpublished manuscript, University of Rochester, Rochester, NY.

Kasser, T., Ryan, R. M., Zax, M., & Sameroff, A. J. (1995). The relations of maternal and social environments to late adolescents' materialistic and prosocial values. *Developmental Psychology*, 31, 907–914.

Kast, A., & Connor, K. (1988). Sex and age differences in response to informational and controlling feedback. *Personality and Social Psychology Bulletin*, 14, 514–523.

Kellaghan, T., Madaus, G. F., & Raczek, A. (1996). *The use of external examinations to improve student motivation*. Washington, DC: American Educational Research Association.

Koestner, R., Bernieri, F., & Zuckerman, M. (1992). Self-determination and consistency between attitudes, traits, and behaviors. *Personality and Social Psychology Bulletin*, 18, 52–59.

Koestner, R., Zuckerman, M., & Koestner, J. (1987). Praise, involvement, and intrinsic motivation. *Journal of Personality and Social Psychology*, 53, 383–390.

Kohn, A. (1993). *Punished by rewards*. Boston: Houghton Mifflin.

Kunda, Z., & Schwartz, S. H. (1983). Undermining intrinsic moral motivation: External reward and self-presenation. *Journal of Personality and Social Psychology*, 45, 763–771.

Lepper, M. R. (1998). A whole much less than the sum of its parts. *American Psychologist*, 53, 675–676.

Lepper, M. R., & Greene, D. (1975). Turning play into work: The effects of adult surveillance and extrinsic rewards on children's intrinsic motivation. *Journal of Personality and Social Psychology*, 31, 479–486.

Lepper, M. R., & Greene, D. (1978). *The hidden costs of reward*. Hillsdale, NJ: Erlbaum.

Lepper, M. R., Greene, D., & Nisbett, R. E. (1973). Undermining children's intrinsic interest with extrinsic rewards: A test of the "overjustification" hypothesis. *Journal of Personality and Social Psychology*, 28, 129–137.

McGraw, K. O. (1978). The detrimental effects of reward on performance: A literature review and a prediction model. In M. R. Lepper & D. Greene (Eds.), *The hidden costs of reward* (pp. 33–60). Hillsdale, NJ: Erlbaum.

McGraw, K. O., & McCullers, J. C. (1979). Evidence of a detrimental effect of extrinsic incentives on breaking a mental set. *Journal of Experimental Social Psychology*, 15, 285–294.

Miller, L. B., & Estes, B. W. (1961). Monetary reward and motivation in discrimination learning. *Journal of Experimental Psychology*, 61, 501–504.

Nicholls, J. G. (1984). Achievement motivation: Conceptions of ability, subjective experience, task choice, and performance. *Psychological Review*, 91, 328–346.

Nix, G. A., Ryan, R. M., Manly, J. B., & Deci, E. L. (1999). Revitalization through self-regulation: The effects of autonomous and controlled motivation on happiness and vitality. *Journal of Experimental Social Psychology*, 35, 266–284.

Olds, J. (1958). Satiation effects in self-stimulation of the brain. *Journal of Comparative Physiological Psychology*, 51, 675–678.

Paulhus, D. L., Shaffer, D. R., & Downing, L. L. (1977). Effects of making blood donor motives salient upon donor retention: A field experiment. *Personality and Social Psychology Bulletin*, 3, 99–102.

Pelletier, L. G., Dion, S., Tuson, K., & Green-Demers, I. (1999). Why do people fail to adopt environmental behaviors? Towards a taxonomy of environmental amotivation. *Journal of Applied Social Psychology*, 29, 2481–2504.

Pittman, T. S., Cooper, E. E., & Smith, T. W. (1977). Attribution of causality and the overjustification effect. *Personality and Social Psychology Bulletin*, 3, 280–283.

Porac, J. F., & Meindl, J. (1982). Undermining overjustification: Inducing intrinsic and extrinsic task representations. *Organizational Behavior and Human Performance*, 29, 208–226.

Reiss, S., & Sushinsky, L. W. (1976). The competing response hypothesis of decreased play effects: A reply to Lepper and Greene. *Journal of Personality and Social Psychology*, 33, 233–245.

Richins, M. L. (1994). Valuing things: The public and private meanings of possessions. *Journal of Consumer Research*, 21, 504–521.

Richins, M. L., & Dawson, S. (1992). A consumer values orientation for materialism and its measurement: Scale development and validation. *Journal of Consumer Research*, 19, 303–316.

Routtenberg, A., & Lindy, J. (1965). Effects on the availability of rewarding septal and hypothalamic stimulation on bar pressing for food under conditions of deprivation. *Journal of Comparative and Physiological Psychology*, 60, 158–161.

Rummel, A., & Feinberg, R. (1988). Cognitive evaluation theory: A meta-analytic review of the literature. *Social Behavior and Personality*, 16, 147–164.

Ryan, R. M. (1982). Control and information in the intrapersonal sphere: An extension of cognitive evaluation theory. *Journal of Personality and Social Psychology*, 43, 450–461.

Ryan, R. M. (1993). Agency and organization: Intrinsic motivation, autonomy and the self in psychological development. In J. Jacobs (Ed.), *Nebraska symposium on motivation: Developmental perspectives on motivation* (vol. 40, pp. 1–56). Lincoln, NE: University of Nebraska Press.

Ryan, R. M. (1995). Psychological needs and the facilitation of integrative processes. *Journal of Personality*, 63, 397–427.

Ryan, R. M., Chirkov, V. I., Little, T. D., Sheldon, K. M., Timoshina, E., & Deci, E. L. (1999). The American dream in Russia: Extrinsic aspirations and well-being in two cultures. *Personality and Social Psychology Bulletin*, 25, 1509–1524.

Ryan, R. M., & Connell, J. P. (1989). Perceived locus of causality and internalization: Examining reasons for acting in two domains. *Journal of Personality and Social Psychology*, 57, 749–761.

Ryan, R. M., & Deci, E. L. (1996). When paradigms clash: Comments on Cameron and Pierce's claim that rewards do not undermine intrinsic motivation. *Review of Educational Research*, 66, 33–38.

Ryan, R. M., & Deci, E. L. (1999). Approaching and avoiding self-determination: Comparing cybernetic and organismic paradigms of motivation. *Advances in Social Cognition*. Vol XII (pp. 193–215). Mahwah, N.J.: Erlbaum.

Ryan, R. M., & Deci, E. L. (2000). Self-determination theory and the facilitation of intrinsic motivation, social development, and well-being. *American Psychologist*, 55, 68–78.

Ryan, R. M., Koestner, R., & Deci, E. L. (1991). Varied forms of persistence: When free-choice behavior is not intrinsically motivated. *Motivation and Emotion*, 15, 185–205.

Ryan, R. M., Kuhl, J., & Deci, E. L. (1997). Nature and autonomy: An organizational view on the social and neurobiological aspects of self-regulation in behavior and development. *Development and Psychopathology*, 9, 701–728.

Ryan, R. M., & La Guardia, J. G. (1999). Achievement motivation within a pressured society: Intrinsic and extrinsic motivations to learn and the politics of school reform. In T. Urdan (Ed.), *Advances in motivation and achievement. Vol. II (pp. 45–86)*. Greenwich, CT: JAI Press.

Ryan, R. M., Mims, V., & Koestner, R. (1983). Relation of reward contingency and interpersonal context to intrinsic motivation: A review and test using cognitive evaluation theory. *Journal of Personality and Social Psychology*, 45, 736–750. (Reprinted in Vroom, V. H., & Deci, E. L. [Eds.] 1992. *Management and motivation* (2nd ed.). London and Baltimore: Penguin.)

Ryan, R. M., Sheldon, K. M., Kasser, T., & Deci, E. L. (1996). All goals are not created equal: An organismic perspective on the nature of goals and their regulation. In P. M. Gollwitzer & J. A. Bargh (Eds.), *The psychology of action: Linking cognition and motivation to behavior* (pp. 7–26). New York: Guilford.

Ryan, R. M., & Stiller, J. (1991). The social contexts of internalization: Parent and teacher influences on autonomy, motivation and learning. In P. R. Pintrich & M. L. Maehr (Eds.), *Advances in motivation and achievement: Vol. 7. Goals and self-regulatory processes* (pp. 115–149). Greenwich, CT: JAI Press.

Ryff, C. D. (1995). Psychological well-being in adult life. *Current Directions in Psychological Science*, 4(4), 99–104.

Sansone, C. (1986). A question of competence: The effects of competence and task feedback on intrinsic interest. *Journal of Personality and Social Psychology*, 51, 918–931.

Sansone, C., & Morgan, C. (1992). Intrinsic motivation and education: Competence in context. *Motivation and Emotion*, 16, 249–270.

Schor, J. B. (1991). *The overworked American*. New York: Basic Books.

Schwartz, B. (1994). *The costs of living*. New York: Norton.

Schwartz, B., & Lacey, M. (1982). *Behaviorism, science, and human nature*. New York: Norton.

Scott, W. E., Jr. (1976). The effects of extrinsic rewards on "intrinsic motivation": A critique. *Organizational Behavior and Human Performance*, 15, 117–129.

Sheldon, K. M., & Elliot, A. J. (1999). Goal striving, need satisfaction, and longitudinal well-being: The self-concordance model. *Journal of Personality and Social Psychology*, 76, 482–497.

Sheldon, K. M., & Kasser, T. (1995). Coherence and congruence: Two aspects of personality integration. *Journal of Personality and Social Psychology*, 68, 531–543.

Sheldon, K. M., & Kasser, T. (1998). Pursuing personal goals: Skills enable progress but not all progress is beneficial. *Personality and Social Psychology Bulletin*, 24, 1319–1331.

Skinner, B. F. (1971). *Beyond freedom and dignity*. New York: Knopf.

Smith, C. L., Gelfand, D. M., Hartmann, D. P., & Partlow, M. E. Y. (1979). Children's causal attributions regarding help giving. *Child Development*, 50, 203–210.

Smith, W. E. (1975). *The effect of anticipated vs. unanticipated social reward on subsequent intrinsic motivation*. Unpublished dissertation, Cornell University, Ithaca, NY.

Spence, J. T. (1970). The distracting effect of material reinforcers in the discrimination learning of lower- and middle-class children. *Child Development*, 41, 103–111.

Spence, J. T., & Dunton, M. C. (1967). The influence of verbal and nonverbal reinforcement combinations in the discrimination learning of middle- and lower-class preschool children. *Child Development*, 38, 1177–1186.

Swann, W. B., & Pittman, T. S. (1977). Initiating play activity of children: The moderating influence of verbal cues on intrinsic motivation. *Child Development*, 48, 1128–1132.

Tang, S-H, & Hall, V. C. (1995). The overjustification effect: A meta-analysis. *Applied Cognitive Psychology*, 9, 365–404.

Titmuss, R. M. (1970). *The gift relationship*. London: Allen and Unwin.

Utman, C. H. (1997). Performance effects of motivational state: A meta-analysis. *Personality and Social Psychology Review*, 1, 170–182.

Waterman, A. S. (1993). Two conceptions of happiness: Contrasts of personal expressiveness (eudaimonia) and hedonic enjoyment. *Journal of Personality and Social Psychology*, 64, 678–691.

White, R. W. (1959). Motivation reconsidered: The concept of competence. *Psychological Review*, 66, 297–333.

Wiersma, U. J. (1992). The effects of extrinsic rewards in intrinsic motivation: A meta-analysis. *Journal of Occupational and Organiational Psychology*, 65, 101–114.

Williams, G. C., Cox, E. M., Hedberg, V. A., & Deci, E. L. (in press). Extrinsic life goals and health risk behaviors in adolescents. *Journal of Applied Social Psychology*.

Wilson, J. Q. (1993). *The moral sense*. New York: Free Press.

Zuckerman, M., Gioioso, C., & Tellini, S. (1988). Control orientation, self-monitoring, and preference for image versus quality approach to advertising. *Journal of Research in Personality*, 22, 89–100.

Rewards and Creativity

BETH A. HENNESSEY

Department of Psychology
Wellesley College

Extrinsic incentives can increase interest in activities, reduce interest, or have no effect.
— Albert Bandura (1981)

In the November 1996 volume of the *American Psychologist*, there appeared a provocative article authored by Eisenberger and Cameron dedicated to the proposition that detrimental effects of reward occur only "under limited conditions that are easily avoided" (p. 1164). The data on which the authors based their conclusions came primarily from a previously reported meta-analysis (Cameron & Pierce, 1994). Taken together, these two articles have generated a great deal of interest—and, on occasion, some heated exchanges. Two major aspects of the controversy regarding their conclusions have been the criteria for study selection and the method used to combine investigations. The investigations entered into the analysis were often aggregated without regard for crucial factors such as task or reward type, interpersonal context, or intrinsic motivation measure. In addition, many carefully executed and well-known studies were excluded, and an explicit decision was made *not* to procure unpublished data from individuals known to be doing work on intrinsic motivation/overjustification. Termed the *file drawer problem* (Rosenthal, 1984), this failure to look beyond published materials poses an important threat to the validity of meta-analytical research.

Intrinsic and Extrinsic Motivation

In essence, the controversy boils down to a conflict between researchers and theorists trained in the behaviorist tradition (Eisenberger, Cameron, and colleagues) and those espousing a more social psychological viewpoint. In October 1997, Eisenberger had the opportunity to debate the issues with some social psychologists at the annual meeting of the Society for Experimental Social Psychology in Toronto. Seemingly overnight, there was in the academic community renewed interest in the reward literature. Published in the June 1998 volume of the *American Psychologist* were three comments (authored by Hennessey and Amabile, by Lepper, and by Sansone and Harackiewicz) on the Eisenberger and Cameron (1996) piece. Also in that same issue, there appeared a response from the authors (Eisenberger and Cameron, 1998).

This chapter expands on some of the issues raised in these exchanges and focuses, in particular, on the impact of reward on creativity. Eisenberger and Cameron (1996, 1998) claimed that any detrimental effects of reward on creativity can be avoided. In fact, it has been their contention that creativity can be easily *increased* by the use of rewards (1996). However, these authors overlooked or failed to adequately explain numerous demonstrations of lowered creativity on rewarded activities as compared with nonrewarded activities.

The social psychological study of the impact of expected reward has a long and well-established tradition. The first published studies of this genre appeared in the 1970s (e.g., Deci, 1971, 1972; Kruglanski, Friedman, & Zeevi, 1971; Lepper, Greene, & Nisbett, 1973). Experimental subjects who had been promised a reward for their participation typically worked at an interesting and fairly complex task such as the SOMA Cube or hidden-figures puzzles, whereas control subjects performed in the absence of any reward expectation. To obtain the dependent measure of intrinsic motivation, experimenters then unobtrusively monitored study participants during a subsequent free-choice period in which they were alone and had no extrinsic reasons for working on the experimental task for which they had earlier been rewarded. Because participants were unaware that they were being observed and because they had a variety of interesting activities from which they could choose, the time they spent with the target activity was used as the measure of their intrinsic motivation.

Employing this and similar research approaches, investigators have gone on to conduct hundreds of studies of the effects of expected reward on intrinsic interest. Although over the years the experimental paradigms have become increasingly complex, the basic message has remained the same: The promise of a reward made contingent on task engagement can often serve to undermine intrinsic task motivation. This effect is so robust, in fact, that it has been found to occur across the entire life span, with preschoolers and seasoned professionals experiencing the same negative consequences.

Importantly, this powerful undermining effect has been found to obtain when what have come to be termed *task-contingent* rewards have been promised. Task-contingent rewards are rewards made conditional simply on task completion. The impact of so-called performance-contingent rewards, rewards promised and delivered only if a certain level of competency or proficiency is reached, has been found to be far more complex. Under certain specific circumstances, in fact, the informational value implicit in performance-contingent rewards has been shown to *augment* feelings of self-efficacy, intrinsic task interest, and qualitative aspects of performance (e.g., Deci, 1975; Deci & Ryan, 1980, 1985b; Harackiewicz, Manderlink, & Sansone, 1984).

Had Eisenberger and colleagues chosen to focus their attention solely on these informationally laden rewards, their conclusion that rewards can sometimes boost both intrinsic task motivation and qualitative aspects of performance, including creativity of performance, would have surprised and angered no one. The problem is that their analyses and subsequent conclusions cut across reward categories and, in so doing, ignored and negated many important and carefully validated discoveries about the significant differences between task-contingent and performance-contingent reward types.

TASK-CONTINGENT REWARD STUDIES

Within the task-contingent reward literature, the impact of monetary rewards has received perhaps the greatest amount of research attention (e.g., Calder & Staw, 1975; Deci, 1972; Pinder, 1976; Pritchard, Campbell, & Campbell, 1977), yet money is not the only type of reward that has been observed to have deleterious effects. Widely ranging varieties of reward forms have now been tested, with everything from having the opportunity to use an instant camera to receiving marshmallows producing decrements in intrinsic motivation (e.g., Amabile, Hennessey, & Grossman, 1986; Greene & Lepper, 1974; Harackiewicz, 1979; Kernoodle-Loveland & Olley, 1979; Ross, 1975).

As this body of literature establishing the undermining effects of expected reward on intrinsic interest continued to grow, so, too, did the understanding that the negative impact of reward can reach well beyond the issue of task motivation. In an early study of the effect of reward on children's artistic creativity, Lepper et al. (1973) found that for preschoolers who initially displayed a high level of intrinsic motivation for drawing with felt-tip markers, working for an expected "good player award" decreased both their task interest and the globally assessed quality (as rated by teachers) of their drawings. It was not long before other researchers also began to find decrements in performance quality under reward conditions (Garbarino,

1975; Greene & Lepper, 1974; Kernoodle-Loveland & Olley, 1979; Kruglanski et al., 1971; McGraw & McCullers, 1979). And Pittman, Emery, and Boggiano (1982) and Shapira (1976) reported that nonrewarded participants showed a subsequent preference for complex versions of a game or puzzle, whereas rewarded participants chose simpler versions.

Taken together, these studies point to the same conclusions as did the original findings of Lepper et al. in 1973. For people who initially display a high level of interest in a task, working for an expected reward both decreases their motivation and undermines the globally assessed quality of their performance.

THE IMPACT OF TASK-CONTINGENT REWARD ON CREATIVITY OF PERFORMANCE

Intrigued by these research findings, a small group of investigators and theorists who had been trained primarily as social psychologists began to explore the impact of expected reward on creative aspects of performance. Over the years, the research evidence has grown to reveal a direct link between the motivational orientation brought by an individual to a task and creativity of performance on that task. Whether they are 3 or 83 years of age, if individuals are to reach their creative potential, they must engage in an activity for the sheer pleasure and enjoyment of the task itself rather than for some extrinsic goal (such as reward). So certain were researchers about the crucial role played by intrinsic interest in the creative process that they came to subscribe to what Amabile termed the "intrinsic motivation principle of creativity" (Amabile, 1983, 1996): Intrinsic motivation is conducive to creativity and extrinsic motivation is almost always detrimental to it.

Researchers have found not only that this construct we call intrinsic motivation is essential for creativity but also that it is especially ephemeral. In other words, although an individual's creativity skills (e.g., familiarity with brainstorming and related techniques or the ability to temporarily suspend judgment) or domain skills (e.g., knowledge of chemistry, physics, or engineering or facility with a paintbrush) may be fairly stable, motivational orientation is highly variable and largely situation dependent. None of us is always intrinsically motivated under all conditions, and there are few social conditions more damaging to intrinsic interest than situations in which rewards have been promised for task completion.

In a typical experiment, investigators working in this area will randomly assign people to expected reward or control (no-reward) conditions and then go on to assess their task motivation and creativity of performance. In one study of this sort (Amabile et al. 1986), the reward offered to elementary school children was not a tangible gift to be delivered afterward. Instead, it was an attractive activity—playing with a Polaroid camera—that the children were allowed to engage in before completing the target experimental task. In other words, children assigned to the reward condition signed a contract and promised to later tell a story in order to first have a chance to use the camera. Children in the no-reward condition were simply allowed to use the camera and then were presented with the storytelling instructions; there was no contingency established between the two tasks.

In order that the impact of reward expectation on children's verbal creativity could be examined, the children in this study were asked to tell a story into a tape recorder to accompany a set of illustrations in a book with no words (see Hennessey & Amabile, 1988). This storytelling activity was designed with three specific goals in mind. First, it was necessary that individual differences in verbal fluency be minimized because these differences could lead to high variability in baseline performances. In the case of this storytelling task, this was accomplished with the stipulation that children say only "one thing" about each page. Second, to be appropriate for testing hypotheses about creativity, the task had to allow for a wide variety of responses. In other words, the target activity had to be an open-ended one for which a wide variety of responses were possible (Amabile, 1982; Hennessey & Amabile, 1999; McGraw, 1978). Finally, like all the creativity tasks used in research of this type, it was important that the storytelling procedure be pretested to ensure that children of this age group did, in fact, find it to be intrinsically interesting.

In an application of the consensual creativity assessment technique (Amabile, 1982; Hennessey & Amabile, 1999; McGraw, 1978), elementary school teachers familiar with children's writing later rated the stories relative to one another on creativity and a variety of other dimensions. These judges were instructed to use their own subjective definitions of creativity. They were not trained in any way, nor were they permitted to confer with one another. A high level of interrater reliability was reached, and results indicated that overall, stories produced by children in the no-reward condition were judged to be more creative than were stories produced by children in the reward condition. This main effect of reward was, in fact, statistically significant. Importantly, the only difference in the experience of the rewarded and nonrewarded children in this paradigm was their *perception* of the picture-taking reward as contingent or not contingent on the target storytelling activity.

Research evidence from this and other similar investigations of the impact of expected reward have led to the understanding that it is the perception of a task as the means to an end that is the crucial element for creativity decrements in task engagement. Whether they were asked to title a paragraph and write a story (Kruglanski et al., 1971), solve Duncker's set-breaking candle problem (Glucksberg, 1962, 1964), or attempt Luchin's water jar problems

(McGraw & McCullers, 1979), people expecting a reward for their task participation were significantly less creative than were their nonrewarded counterparts. Rewards "promised" and "delivered" by a computer have also been found to negatively affect the creativity of children performing a creative line-drawing task (Hennessey, 1989). So robust is this finding that expected reward undermines intrinsic interest and creativity, in fact, that one group of researchers (Lepper, Sagotsky, Dafoe, & Greene, 1982) was able to demonstrate that when children engaged in one intrinsically interesting activity in order to have a chance to engage in another, their interest in the first activity plummeted as well. This effect held regardless of which task was presented as the means and which task was presented as the reward. Thus, rewards will undermine intrinsic interest even if they are no more "reward-like" than the tasks upon which they have been made contingent.

Over the years, investigators employing variations on this same basic research methodology have found that the promise of reward is not the only extrinsic constraint that can undermine intrinsic task motivation and, as a consequence, creativity of performance. In fact, a number of environmental factors can often lead to decrements in intrinsic motivation. Expected reward, expected evaluation, competition, restricted choice, surveillance, and time limits have each been demonstrated to decrease intrinsic interest and creativity. Yet of all the killers of motivation on this list, none has received more research attention than expected reward. Perhaps this is because the proposition that the promise of reward can bring seriously negative consequences is so counterintuitive. The behaviorists, among others, have been telling us for years that reward is a good thing. Teachers learn that if they want their third graders to continue with their efforts to master the multiplication tables, they should reward them for their progress. And employers believe that incentive systems that dole out everything from monetary bonuses to trophies are a necessary component of a productive work environment.

THE BEHAVIORIST POSITION: A RESOLUTION OF CONTRADICTORY FINDINGS

According to the classical Skinnerian model (e.g., Skinner, 1938), reinforcement is the key to behavioral control. A wealth of research evidence gathered over more than 60 years supports the proposition that if desired behaviors (or successive approximations to them) are rewarded, the likelihood that those behaviors will be repeated will increase. Animal researchers and trainers, educators (particularly those involved in special education), and professionals who work with clinical populations in institutional settings have long employed positive reinforcement systems and can attest to their success.

The question to be addressed is how these findings, which stand in apparent direct contradiction to the data presented earlier, can be explained. How can these two bodies of work, these two traditions, be reconciled? The answer lies in the fact that the behaviorist and the social psychologist are concerned with different processes, different types of tasks, and, in some cases, different types of rewards as well. It is their unwillingness to acknowledge these differences that has caused Eisenberger and Cameron to come under fire.

Generally speaking, studies designed in the behavior modification tradition do in fact show *positive* effects of reward on creative performance. Importantly, however, in virtually every one of these creativity-enhancement demonstrations, creative performance is operationalized in terms of scores on a standard creativity test. Research reported by Glover and Gary (1976), for example, demonstrates that children expecting a reward for high scores on a particular dimension of Guilford's Unusual Uses Test (1967) were actually able to improve their performance over baseline levels. Similarly, subjects offered a reward for doing well on the Torrance Tests of Creative Thinking (Torrance, 1962) have shown significantly higher scores than have nonrewarded groups (e.g., Halpin & Halpin, 1973; Raina, 1968). Fluency on the Wallach and Kogan Tests has also been increased by both tangible and verbal rewards (Milgram & Feingold, 1977; Ward, Kogan, & Pankove, 1972), but as Hocevar and Bachelor (1989) rightly pointed out, these creativity tests may not be appropriate for investigations of the impact of situational variables on intrinsic motivation and creativity of performance on specific real-life tasks.

The tests developed by Torrance, by Guilford, and by Wallach and Kogan were primarily designed to serve as measures of creative "personality" factors, divergent thinking abilities, or other particular cognitive styles, skills, or processes that are conducive to creativity. In short, these measures are based on the operationalization of creativity as a relatively enduring personal trait, and they were intended to give a global indication of a test taker's overall creativity. Experimenters interested in the impact of expected reward on motivation and creativity are not interested in identifying such enduring individual differences. Instead, they must rely on measurement techniques, like the consensual assessment of products, that focus on an individual's motivational state and his or her resulting creativity of performance in a particular place and time.

As noted earlier, rewards that convey competence information may not undermine intrinsic motivation (and creativity of performance) as much as rewards that convey only controlling information. In fact, when compared with no-reward controls, people receiving informational rewards have under certain circumstances been shown to experience enhanced intrinsic motivation (Deci, 1975; Deci & Ryan, 1980, 1985b). Unlike the "picture taking" study (Amabile et al., 1986) and other similar social psychological investigations of the impact of reward described earlier, in many of the "token economy" studies cited by Eisenberger and Cameron (1996, 1998), subjects received almost continuous information about their performance as they were contingently rewarded over long periods of time. Thus, the informative aspect of reward became more salient, more important, than did the controlling aspect, and subjects were far less likely to demonstrate decreased intrinsic motivation.

The nature of the experimental tasks used in these behavior modification studies can also account for the apparently contradictory findings on the effects of reward. Intrinsic-motivation theorists have long emphasized that it makes sense to expect an undermining of intrinsic motivation only when the target task is initially intrinsically interesting to study participants (e.g., Deci & Ryan, 1980; Lepper & Greene, 1978). If there is no intrinsic interest to begin with, there obviously can be no decrease after rewards are promised and delivered. Similarly, McGraw (1978) pointed out that rewards will undermine task performance only when the individual's own interest in those tasks is enough to motivate engagement. Although there is some evidence that shows that study participants find open-ended tasks such as story-telling, problem solving, and drawing intrinsically interesting, there are no data on participants' initial feelings about standard creativity tests like the Torrance or Guilford measures. Innate levels of interest in the target creativity task is one important difference between empirical studies showing negative and positive effects of reward. The fact that the promise of reward has been found to enhance performance on these standardized measures is not surprising, given that intrinsic task interest may be initially low.

Clearly, there are many important distinctions to be made between these two opposing traditions. Most important of all may be the differences in the definitions of creativity driving investigations and the algorithmic or heuristic nature of the experimental tasks employed (cf. McGraw, 1978). Eisenberger and colleagues relied on dependent measures that equate creativity with novelty, yet theorists working from a social psychological perspective contend that this criterion is not sufficient. These researchers point out that even though an idea or product may be novel, it is not always creative (Amabile, 1983, 1996; Stein, 1974). For this reason, most social psychologists have come to define creativity in terms of both novelty and appropriateness (Amabile, 1983, 1996). In addition, theorists trained in a social psychological tradition argue that performance on a task can be considered creative only if that task is heuristic (Amabile, 1996). In other words, the task presented to participants must be fairly open ended. There must be a variety of possible solutions, some more creative or elegant than others, and there must be no one clear or straightforward path to solution.

Importantly, the overwhelming majority of tasks used in the behavior modification literature *do* have relatively clear and straightforward paths to solution. The difficulty lies in the fact that in many of these investigations, subjects were purposefully told *exactly* what kinds of responses would be deemed creative, and in other investigations, creativity was operationalized as the simple statistical infrequency of responses. For example, in one series of investigations on the impact of reward carried out by Eisenberger and Selbst (1994), children performed two target tasks. They were asked to make as many new words as they could using the letters from a target word presented on a card, and they drew pictures incorporating circles printed on a sheet.

Although these simple measures might be legitimately termed "original-ity" or "divergent thinking," they do not adequately capture the elements of creativity as it is generally defined in the literature: novelty combined with appropriateness, value, or usefulness. In addition, because the children were shown examples of appropriate responses, the target experimental tasks were rendered algorithmic rather than heuristic. By definition, these solutions should not be considered creative.

It is not really surprising that when it was explained to subjects exactly what they needed to do to make a "creative" product, external reward was linked to improved performance. Previous work coming from a social psy-chological tradition (e.g., Amabile, 1979) supports this argument, and a close examination of the results reported in the behavior modification lit-erature reveals that in the majority of cases, it was the more algorithmic aspects of assessed creativity (sheer quantity and variety of responses) that were most strongly bolstered by the promise of a reward. Originality (statistical infrequency of responses) was often not enhanced; when it was, participants had usually been explicitly told that they should give unusual responses.

In sum, many of the studies reported by Eisenberger and colleagues do not really examine creativity, as it has come to be defined in the mainstream literature (e.g., Amabile, 1983, 1996; Stein, 1974; Torrance, 1962). In fact, the behaviorist model was never intended to account for the complexities of human creative performance. Indeed, B. F. Skinner himself often proclaimed that "subjective entities" such as mind, thought, and creativity do not exist but are only "verbal constructs, grammatical traps ... explanatory entities" that themselves are inexplicable (Skinner, 1979). It was Skinner's contention that all attention must be paid to outward, observable actions. To speculate about or try to model the inner workings of the mind, he argued, would sim-ply serve to confuse the issues and muddy our understanding.

Eisenberger and Cameron (1996) presented only a very narrow slice of the creativity literature. The evidence that they provided of increased cre-ativity under reward is more informative about relatively simple human behaviors such as filling in circles or word generation than it is about intrin-sically interesting tasks that allow for complex creative performance. They operationalize creativity almost solely in terms of statistical infrequency and choose to cite only studies that present subjects with somewhat contrived paper-and-pencil activities that require relatively low levels of innovation. Missing from their discussion are a number of published reports on experiments (e.g., Amabile et al., 1986; Garbarino, 1975; Greene & Lepper, 1974; Harackiewicz, 1979; Kernoodle-Loveland & Olley, 1979; Ross, 1975) that reveal that across a wide variety of domains and tasks, real-world products made by participants working for reward are reliably assessed by judges who are experts in the domain being examined as less creative than products made by participants not working for reward.

INTERNAL MECHANISMS

Those trained in the behaviorist tradition focus on straightforward, sometimes even rote, *behaviors*. Creative performance, on the other hand, results from a highly complex combination of past experience, accumulated knowledge, and *internal* processes and cognitions. Oftentimes, in fact, a creative idea or response to a problem can be generated without the help of any outwardly observable behavior whatsoever.

Investigators seeking an understanding of creative performance must concentrate their attention on the cognitive and perhaps even the affective processes that make creativity possible, as well as on the overt behaviors. Yet Eisenberger and Cameron failed to address these internal cognitive, emotional, and affective components of the creative process.

Researchers have found it all too easy to undermine task motivation and creativity of performance with the promise of a reward. Demonstrating how to kill motivation and creativity has been the straightforward part. What has not been as easy is understanding why reward can have such a negative impact. What are the internal mechanisms that bring about the undermining effects of reward?

What we have come to learn is that most of us are not all that in touch with our own motivations. We do not always know why it is that we do the things we do. Almost as if we were outside observers of even our own actions, we seem to use essentially the same rubrics for explaining our own behaviors as we do for explaining why others behave in the ways that they do. In situations where both a plausible internal and external (intrinsic and extrinsic) cause of behavior are present, we tend to *discount* the internal cause in favor of the external cause. A preschooler in the seminal Magic Marker study (Lepper et al., 1973) thinks to herself: "I must be making this picture not because it's fun and I love using markers but because this man has told me that I will get a good player award." And a research and development scientist reasons: "I am working night and day on this project not because I was intrigued by the assignment and excited about the potential applications of this new technology but because I know that the group that comes up with the most marketable product will receive a substantial bonus."

In these examples, when multiple explanations for their behavior are available, the scientist and the preschooler discount their own intrinsic interest in favor of a purely external explanation for their task engagement; in fact, some social psychologists have come to refer to this process as the "discounting principle" (e.g., Kelley, 1973). Other theorists propose a related explanation termed the "overjustification" hypothesis, a formulation derived from the attribution theories of Bem (1972), Kelley (1967, 1973), and deCharms (1968). According to this model, when a behavior is overjustified (when there exists both a possible internal and external cause for one's own or another's behavior), each of us will tend to overlook the internal cause (the presence of intrinsic task motivation) in favor of the external cause (a reward was at stake). In effect, we discount the excess justification for explaining why we did something.

Whatever the particulars of the theoretical explanation evoked, the fact remains that in the face of expected task-contingent reward, intrinsic motivation is bound to suffer. And without high levels of intrinsic motivation, creative performance is highly unlikely. Why is intrinsic motivation so necessary to creative performance?

Researchers in the area of cognitive psychology offer empirical evidence and models that have proven useful in understanding how the type of motivation brought to a task can influence performance on that task. Simon (1967) proposed that the most important function of task motivation is the control of attention. He postulated that task motivation determines which of many goal hierarchies will be activated and went on to suggest that the more intense the motivation to achieve a goal, the less attention will be paid to environmental aspects that are seemingly irrelevant to achieving that goal. This formulation can be used to explain the widely reported finding that incidental or latent learning is impaired when a reward is promised for task completion (e.g., Kimble, 1961; Spence, 1956). It can also help to explain the negative effects of reward on creativity.

Amabile has offered a maze metaphor that is helpful in illustrating these undermining effects of reward. She asked that we think of an open-ended "creativity-type" task as a maze. There is one starting point, one entrance, into this maze, but there are a variety of exit points and many different paths to those exits. Most importantly, some of those exits, or solutions, are more "elegant" or creative than others. In the face of an expected task-contingent reward, the goal is to get in and out of the maze as quickly as possible. The "safest," most straightforward path will be chosen, as all behavior is narrowly directed toward attaining the reward. For a creative idea to be generated, however, it is often necessary to temporarily "step away" from the reward (Newell, Shaw, & Simon, 1962), to become immersed in the maze itself, to experiment with alternative pathways, and to direct attention toward more seemingly incidental aspects of the task and the environment. The more focused an individual is about a promised reward, the less likely it is that risks will be taken and that these alternative paths to solution will be explored.

Many theorists, including Eisenberger and Cameron, have suggested that this undermining effect of reward on intrinsic motivation and creativity of performance, this unwillingness or inability to experiment within the maze, can be explained by a simple "diffusion of attention" or "competing response" model (e.g., Reiss & Sushinsky, 1975). In other words, individuals who are promised a reward are distracted by their excitement about a soon-to-be-delivered prize or gift. Their intrinsic motivation and enjoyment of the task at hand are directly blocked by the competing response of reward anticipation, and they rush through their work as quickly as possible.

Importantly, although this diffusion of attention or competing response hypothesis may explain the undermining impact of reward under some circumstances, these models fail to adequately explain the negative effects of rewards in all situations. Recall the "picture taking" study described earlier (Amabile et al., 1986). In that investigation, even a reward promised and delivered *prior* to task engagement was found to undermine subjects' interest and performance. The mere labeling of the opportunity to use a camera as a reward contingency was enough to kill intrinsic motivation and creativity, whereas children in a control condition who also participated in the picture taking but believed this was just one in a series of "things to do" suffered no such decrements. Furthermore, investigations examining the interactive effects of reward and choice (e.g., Amabile, Goldberg, & Capotosto, 1982) also call into question the diffusion-of-attention explanation. These studies reveal that when subjects who perceive they have no choice but to participate in an investigation are offered a reward, their task motivation and creativity do not suffer the usual decrements.

When working under the expectation of reward, people may indeed pay less attention to a task or less attention to aspects of their environment that might prove useful in generating a response to that task. However, this shift in focus need not always occur simply because they are distracted by the reward they are to receive or by their worries about what they have to do to attain that reward. Under reward conditions, people may simply *feel* less intrinsically involved. They may feel less positively toward the task and less inclined to devote their energy and attention to it.

There is good reason to believe, in fact, that affective processes can and do play an important role in the mediation of the impact of reward on interest and creativity. Earlier in this chapter, explanations of cognitive mechanisms such as discounting and overjustification were offered. Although these models have proven useful for understanding the negative effects of reward in adults, they fail to adequately explain why young children have also been observed to suffer decreases in intrinsic motivation and creativity. Simply stated, children younger than the age of 7 or 8 years have consistently been shown to lack the cognitive capabilities necessary for weighing multiple sufficient causes and employing discounting (e.g., Shultz, Butkowsky, Pearce, & Shanfield, 1975; Smith, 1975). In fact, some studies have indicated that many young children seem to employ an additive algorithm and interpret the expectation of reward as an *augmentation* of intrinsic interest (e.g., DiVitto & McArthur, 1978; Morgan, 1981). How is it that when working under the expectation of reward, young children frequently demonstrate decreases in intrinsic motivation and creativity of performance yet they seem cognitively incapable of engaging in the thought processes that underlie the overjustification paradigm?

One viable alternative to the discounting explanation is that the reduction of intrinsic interest in young children (and perhaps all of us) is driven primarily by the learned expectation that rewards are usually paired with activities that need to be done—activities that are often not fun and sometimes are even aversive. The undermining of intrinsic interest may result as much from emotion or affect as it does from thoughts or cognitive analysis. Children may learn to react negatively to a task as "work" when their behavior is controlled by socially imposed factors (such as rewards), and they may react positively to a task as "play" when there are no constraints imposed. Negative affect resulting from socially learned stereotypes or scripts of work (see Lepper et al., 1982; Morgan, 1981; Ransen, 1980) may be what leads to decrements in intrinsic interest (see Hennessey, 1999).

REFINING THE MODEL

Must intrinsic motivation and creativity always suffer when task-contingent rewards are promised? Not necessarily. When investigations into what has come to be known as the "social psychology of creativity" were begun in the mid-1970s, it was thought that the determinants of motivational orientation were pretty much the same for everyone. Intrinsic and extrinsic motivation were believed to combine in a sort of hydraulic fashion. In other words, high levels of extrinsic motivation were thought to preclude high levels of intrinsic motivation—as rewards were imposed, intrinsic motivation (and creativity) would necessarily be decreased.

Now, a good many years and over 100 investigations later, most researchers taking a social psychological approach to the study of creativity have come to appreciate the many complexities of both motivational orientation and the reward process. They have come to supplement their original hydraulic conceptualization with an additive model that recognizes that under certain specific conditions, the expectation of reward can sometimes increase levels of extrinsic motivation without having any negative impact on intrinsic motivation or performance. In fact, some types of extrinsic motivation can actually enhance creativity of performance.

As early as 1983, the experimental evidence that would eventually mandate the reconceptualization of the hydraulic model had begun to mount. In a study that crossed the expectation of reward with choice about task engagement, participants who perceived their receipt of a reward as a kind of bonus were the most creative and most intrinsically motivated of any of the design groups, including a no-reward control condition (Amabile et al., 1986). Researchers have since discovered an additive effect of intrinsic and extrinsic motivation in a variety of circumstances. Probably none of those experimental demonstrations has been more striking than the "immunization" studies (Hennessey, Amabile, & Martinage, 1989; Hennessey & Zbikowski, 1993).

THE "IMMUNIZATION" STUDIES

In a series of investigations, rather than demonstrate how motivation can be killed, my colleagues and I set out to study whether creativity and motivation might be maintained even in the face of reward. In our design of these experiments, we were guided by a medical metaphor. We decided to look at the extrinsic constraint of an expected reward as a kind of germ or virus and wondered whether it might be possible to "immunize" people against its usually negative effects on intrinsic motivation and creativity. Again drawing on a biological analogy, our goal was twofold: (1) to strengthen intrinsic motivation and (2) to provide antibodies (techniques) for fighting extrinsic motivation.

In the first of these research attempts (Hennessey et al., 1989, Study 1), elementary school students (aged 7 to 11 years) were randomly assigned to intrinsic motivation focus or control groups and met with an experimenter over 2 consecutive days for the purpose of viewing videos and engaging in directed discussion. The tapes shown to students in the intrinsic motivation focus condition depicted two 11-year-olds talking with an adult about various aspects of their schoolwork. Scripts for this condition were constructed so as to help children focus on the intrinsically interesting, fun, and playful aspects of a task. Ways to make even the most routine assignment exciting were suggested and participants were helped to distance themselves from socially imposed extrinsic constraints, such as rewards. Tapes shown to students in the control condition featured the same two young actors talking about some of their favorite things, including foods, music groups, movies, and seasons.

Following this training procedure, all students met individually with a second adult for testing. Half the children in each of the training conditions were told that they could take two pictures with an instant camera only if they promised to tell a story later for the experimenter. For children in the no-reward conditions, this picture taking was presented simply as the first in a series of "things to do."

In this 2 × 2 factorial design, presentation of reward was crossed with type of training received. It was expected that only those participants who had been specifically instructed in ways to overcome the usual deleterious effects of extrinsic constraints would maintain baseline levels of intrinsic motivation and creativity in situations of expected reward (i.e., they would be immunized against the effects of extrinsic constraints). The data from this initial investigation not only confirmed these expectations but also gave us reason to believe that our intervention had much more of an impact than we had expected. Intrinsic-motivation–trained children tended to report higher levels of intrinsic motivation on a paper-and-pencil assessment than did children in the control (no-training) condition; in addition, we found that the offer of reward actually augmented the creativity of the trained group. This additive effect of intrinsic motivation and extrinsic motivation was quite robust. In fact, the creativity of children who received intrinsic-motivation training and expected a reward was significantly higher than that of any other design group.

In our initial discussion of these immunization study results, we conjectured that children who entered the creativity testing situation after having undergone intrinsic-motivation training would have a much more acute awareness of their own intrinsic interest in school-type tasks. Thus, the reward may have served to heighten their already positive feelings about the tasks they were doing.

Two follow-up investigations of our intrinsic-motivation focus techniques (Hennessey et al., 1989, Study 2; Hennessey & Zbikowski, 1993) were subsequently carried out. Each was designed as a conceptual replication of Study 1. Essentially the same experimental design was employed, and it was again the children who had received immunization training and who were expecting a reward who produced the most creative products. Yet in these subsequent two studies, the effect of training was far less dramatic. In Study 2, statistical comparisons revealed that the creativity of those children receiving training and expecting a reward for their performance was significantly different from only one of the other three design groups, and in Study 3, although children assigned to the intrinsic-motivation focus–reward condition again produced the most creative products, their performance was only significantly different from that of the no-training–reward group. Taken together, the results of Studies 2 and 3 indicate that we cannot expect that children exposed to our intrinsic-motivation training and offered a reward for their performance will demonstrate unusually high levels of creativity. We can expect, however, that these children will be able to maintain baseline levels of intrinsic motivation and creativity under reward conditions.

What is it about our immunization procedures that allow children to maintain their creativity even when they expect a reward? It appears that our efforts to help them learn to de-emphasize the importance of extrinsic incentives and concentrate instead on their own intrinsic interest and task enjoyment paid off. Even in the face of reward, the children were able to maintain a positive, intrinsically motivated approach. They brought to our experimental tasks a playfulness and a willingness to take risks that many researchers believe are crucial to creativity (Amabile, 1983, 1996; Barron, 1968; Campbell, 1960; Crutchfield, 1962; Dansky & Silverman, 1975; Lieberman, 1965; Stein, 1974).

Evidence from nonexperimental studies coupled with observations of and interviews with artists and other people who rely on their creativity for their life's work echo our "immunization" results. Although many of the "killers" of motivation and creativity that have been isolated experimentally have also been found to be detrimental in the "real world" of work, these negative effects have not proven universal. For some people, certain extrinsic motivators have been shown to have either no effects or even a positive effect on task interest and creativity of performance. For example, in a study of commissioned and noncommissioned works done by professional artists, the extrinsic incentive of a commission was seen by some artists as a highly controlling constraint and the creativity of their work plummeted. Yet for those who looked at the commission as an opportunity to achieve recognition or a confirmation of their competence by respected others, creativity was enhanced (Amabile, Phillips, & Collins, 1994).

How can these individual differences be explained? Our data on these professional artists and the children taking part in our immunization studies parallel nicely earlier work exploring the relevance of self-perception processes to the overjustification effect. In a 1981 investigation carried out by Fazio, the negative impact of expected reward was also mitigated in young children for whom initial intrinsic interest in the target activity had been made salient. In other words, it may not be the expectation of reward per se that undermines intrinsic motivation; rather, it may be the individual's interpretation of that reward and his or her role in the reward process that in large part determines whether task motivation will be undermined, be enhanced, or remain unchanged.

Work done by Deci and Ryan has further demonstrated that extrinsic motivation must not be automatically equated with perceptions of constraint. Their research again makes clear that although rewards are often experienced as externally controlling, they can under some circumstances serve to heighten feelings of competence or support autonomy. Rewards and other environmental inputs found to have these facilitative effects are often termed "informational" and have been shown to maintain or even enhance intrinsic motivation (Deci & Ryan, 1985b).

Although this informational aspect of reward may help to explain how professional artists working for a large commission were able to sustain task motivation, this formulation is not easily applied to the immunization study findings. Children in those investigations were promised a reward simply for task completion. The opportunity to take pictures with an instant camera (Studies 1 and 2) or to paint a T-shirt (Study 3) was not made contingent on quality of performance, and it is unlikely that study participants viewed these activities as a confirmation of their competence.

Amabile's 1993 discussion of "motivational synergy" has proven somewhat helpful in reconciling the training study results with the findings reported in the earlier task-contingent and performance-contingent reward literature. This model proposes that rewards can sometimes serve as "synergistic extrinsic motivators." In other words, rather than detract from initial interest, they can, under certain specific circumstances, combine in an *additive* fashion with intrinsic motivation and actually enhance task enjoyment and involvement. A revision of the intrinsic motivation principle of creativity (Amabile, 1996) explained the process this way:

> Intrinsic motivation is conducive to creativity; controlling extrinsic motivation is detrimental to creativity, but informational or enabling extrinsic motivation can be conductive, particularly if initial levels of intrinsic motivation are high. (p. 119)

The important element here seems to be the preservation of a sense of self-determination (Deci & Ryan, 1985b). Any extrinsic factors that support a sense of competence without undermining self-determination should positively contribute to intrinsic motivation. Thus, rewards that are perceived as bonuses rather than as instruments of coercion can serve to increase involvement in the task at hand and should not be expected to have detrimental effects.

In keeping with Bem's suggestion (1972) that individuals' internal attitudes and states will be most subject to external influences when their initial internal states are vague or ambiguous, this synergistic effect has been found to occur only under circumstances in which initial task intrinsic motivation is especially strong and salient. For elementary school students who had undergone our intrinsic-motivation training, their enjoyment of school-related work was exactly that. In each of the three immunization investigations, the data showed that children in the intrinsic-motivation training condition scored significantly higher than did their nontrained peers on a questionnaire designed to tap motivation for learning.

In training Study 1, this high degree of intrinsic interest demonstrated by the children in the intrinsic-motivation training condition appears to have allowed them to view our offer of reward as an added bonus, rather than as a source of external control. The creativity of the products they produced was judged to be significantly higher than that of any of the other design groups. In what can be seen as an "extrinsics in service of intrinsics cycle" (Amabile, 1993, p. 194), the offer of a reward combined positively with intrinsic motivation and enabled these children to do exciting work.

In Studies 2 and 3, the impact of our training, although still significant, was not as dramatic. In these investigations, no synergistic effect was found.

Children who had undergone intrinsic-motivation training and were promised a reward did not demonstrate the highest levels of creativity. Unlike their peers in the control condition, they were, however, able to maintain baseline levels of performance even in the face of expected reward.

Importantly, the motivational synergy model (Amabile, 1993) fails to account for such outcomes as were shown in the last two immunization attempts. Rather than experiencing a true additive effect of intrinsic and extrinsic motivation, these children instead evidenced an immunity to the effects of reward but no enhanced intrinsic motivation. They were deeply involved in their work and their intrinsic motivation appears to have been relatively impervious to the negative effects of extrinsic motivators.

How can we predict whether an individual's motivation and creativity of performance will be undermined, enhanced, or relatively impervious to the promise of a reward? Although a single model or theory accounting for all of these various outcomes has yet to be advanced, in recent years, some researchers have added to our understanding with the introduction of what they have termed *expectancy-value theory* (Eccles, 1983; Eccles, Wigfield, & Schiefele, 1998). According to this model, the offer of a reward can, under specific circumstances, cause the individual to place increased value on performance, leading to deeper task involvement and interest. Although many of the investigators subscribing to this view have tended to focus on the self-regulation of behavior rather than intrinsic motivation per se, others have worked to bridge the intrinsic-motivation and expectancy-value approaches with a focus on the individual's phenomenal experience while working toward a goal.

In an exploration of the role played by affect in the regulation of behavior, Sansone and Harackiewicz (1996) contended that we must think about intrinsic motivation or extrinsic motivation not only as an end state but also as a process. In other words, whereas outcome-derived motivation resulting from the promise of a reward may pull one into an activity, a self-regulated, process-derived motivation (e.g., cognitive and affective absorption in the task) may be necessary to maintain performance over time. Sansone and Harackiewicz have stated that they believe that this self-regulation of behavior requires that the individual actively maintain both internal and external sources of motivation. If a task is to be brought to successful completion, expectancy and valuation processes must be oriented at compatible outcomes. In other words, like Amabile, they have argued that extrinsic incentives and task motivation must combine in a synergistic, additive, or complementary fashion.

This melding of the these two goal types, the individual's own goals for task engagement and the incentives introduced into the environment, is critical to the self-regulatory process. External intervention has, under certain circumstances, proven effective in helping individuals to make this match and change their phenomenal experience from neutral or negative to a more positive state. Additionally, some people have themselves been found to intervene and transform a task into something more positive to perform (Sansone & Harackiewicz, 1996).

CONCLUSIONS AND FUTURE DIRECTIONS

Research evidence obtained since the mid-1980s has led investigators to stand firm in their support of the intrinsic motivation principle of creativity (Amabile, 1983, 1996). Whatever an individual's particular talents, domain skills, and creative thinking abilities, the conditions under which he or she works can significantly affect the level of creativity produced. Intrinsic motivation is still believed to be a primary driving force behind the creative process, and it is the social environment that in large part is credited with determining this motivational orientation.

Investigators interested in specifying this link between motivation and creativity initially focused on experimental settings. They directly manipulated aspects of the social environment and looked for accompanying changes in the creativity of the ideas and products produced. More recent investigations have also included nonexperimental methods such as surveys, interviews, and an examination of archival sources. This broadening of focus convinced researchers that the original intrinsic motivation principle of creativity and related models had to be revised to reflect a more comprehensive "systems" approach. The impact of expected reward is far too complex to be summarized in terms of absolutes. Individual difference variables must also be considered.

Many theorists and researchers have come to believe that motivation can no longer be conceptualized simply in terms of a transitory and very much situation-specific state. They argue instead for a consideration of both environmentally induced states and enduring motivational orientations or "traits." Deci and Ryan (1985a), for example, used the concept of causality orientations, or characteristic ways that each of us develops for understanding and orienting to inputs. More specifically, they hypothesized that individuals vary in the degree to which they exhibit three such orientations ("autonomy," "control," and "impersonal"), and they argued that these individual differences have important implications for a variety of motivationally involved processes.

Amabile, Hill, Hennessey, and Tighe (1994) also advocated for the examination of stable traitlike motivational orientations. Toward this end, they developed a personality inventory designed to assess intrinsic and extrinsic motivational tendencies in adults. The Work Preference Inventory has been administered to hundreds of college students and working adults, and a number of important differences between respondents have been revealed. Although there has consistently emerged a positive relation between intrinsic motivation and creativity, it is clear that for some people certain reward types and other extrinsic forces in the workplace can serve as positive motivators that provide information value or facilitate task engagement. Not all of us define the optimal work environment in the same way.

In their initial form, investigations into the social psychology of creativity were carried out in an effort to move beyond the framework of personality psychology, a discipline that at one time completely dominated the creativity literature. During the 1980s and 1990s, the focus was placed entirely on situational factors, but now measures of personality, cognition, and other individual difference variables are being infused back into the field. Social psychology researchers have come to understand that no one theoretical approach can carry the day. Only through an integration of the disciplines can we hope to ever have a detailed understanding of the creative process.

Investigators and theorists trained in the behaviorist tradition should now join in that integration. Even though it may make some sense to adopt a rigid stance or think only in narrow terms at the beginning stages of theory building, behaviorism has grown to be a well-established and highly respected tradition. It is time to refine the reinforcement model and abandon all sweeping claims about the inherent benefits of reward.

This chapter began with a quotation from a 1981 chapter authored by Albert Bandura. Although the development of social learning theory might have been greatly influenced by his training in behaviorism, Bandura recognized the complexities of the reward dynamic. Long before most of us, he took the view that extrinsic incentives [rewards] can increase interest in activities, reduce interest, or have no effect. Social psychologists, too, have come to recognize those complexities. We have come to realize that rewards are not delivered in a vacuum. Perhaps if there were no learning effects, no past experience with rewards, no individual differences in terms of self-esteem, self-efficacy, or personality ... maybe then it might make sense to make sweeping statements claiming that reward always (or never) has a negative impact on the intrinsic-motivation and creative aspects of performance. People are highly complex organisms and rewards are not delivered in vacuums, however. As a group social psychologists have come to realize these facts. Under the direction of people like Bandura, researchers trained in behaviorism were also at one time attempting to incorporate the complexities of the human condition into their model. It is time that contemporary behaviorists renew the effort to move in this direction.

References

Amabile, T. M. (1979). Effects of external evaluation on artistic creativity. *Journal of Personality and Social Psychology*, 37, 221–233.
Amabile, T. M. (1983). *The social psychology of creativity*. New York: Springer-Verlag.

Amabile, T. M. (1993). Motivational synergy: Toward new conceptualizations of intrinsic and extrinsic motivation in the workplace. *Human Resource Management Review*, 3, 185–201.

Amabile, T. M. (1996). *Creativity in context*. Boulder, CO: Westview.

Amabile, T. M., Goldberg, N., & Capotosto, D. (1982). *Effects of reward and choice on adults' artistic creativity*. Unpublished manuscript, Brandeis University, Waltham, MA.

Amabile, T. M., Hennessey, B. A., & Grossman, B. (1986). Social influences on creativity: The effects of contracted-for reward. *Journal of Personality and Social Psychology*, 50, 14–23.

Amabile, T. M., Hill, K., Hennessey, B. A., & Tighe, E. (1994). The Work Preference Inventory: Assessing intrinsic and extrinsic motivational orientations. *Journal of Personality and Social Psychology*, 66, 950–967.

Amabile, T. M., Phillips, E. D., Collins, M. A. (1993). *Creativity by contract: Social influences on the creativity of professional artists*. Unpublished manuscript, Brandeis University, Waltham, MA.

Bandura, A. (1981). Self-referent thought: A developmental analysis of self-efficacy. In J. Flavell & L. Ross (Eds.), *Social cognitive development* (pp. 200–239). New York: Cambridge University Press.

Barron, F. (1968). *Creativity and personal freedom*. New York: Van Nostrand.

Bem, D. (1972). Self-perception theory. In L. Berkowitz (ed.), *Advances in experimental social psychology* (pp. 1–62). New York: Academic Press.

Calder, B., & Staw, B. (1975). Self-perception of intrinsic and extrinsic motivation. *Journal of Personality and Social Psychology*, 31, 599–605.

Cameron, J., & Pierce, W. (1994). Reinforcement, reward, and intrinsic motivation: A meta-analysis. *Review of Educational Research*, 64, 363–423.

Campbell, D. (1960). Blind variation and selective retention in creative thought as in other knowledge processes. *Psychological Review*, 67, 380–400.

Crutchfield, R. (1962). Conformity and creative thinking. In H. Gruber, G. Terrell, & M. Wertheimer (Eds.), *Contemporary approaches to creative thinking* (pp. 120–140). New York: Atherton Press.

Dansky, J., & Silverman, I. (1975). Play: A general facilitator of fluency. *Developmental Psychology*, 11, 104.

deCharms, R. (1968). *Personal causation*. New York: Academic Press.

Deci, E. L. (1971). Effects of externally mediated rewards on intrinsic motivation. *Journal of Personality and Social Psychology*, 18, 105–115.

Deci, E. L. (1972). Intrinsic motivation, extrinsic reinforcement, and inequity. *Journal of Personality and Social Psychology*, 22, 113–120.

Deci, E. L. (1975). *Intrinsic motivation*. New York: Plenum.

Deci, E. L., & Ryan, R. M. (1980). The empirical exploration of intrinsic motivational processes. In L. Berkowitz (Ed.), *Advances in experimental social psychology* (pp. 39–80). New York: Academic Press.

Deci, E. L., & Ryan, R. M. (1985a). The general causality orientations scale: Self-determination in personality. *Journal of Personality and Social Psychology*, 19, 109–134.

Deci, E. L., & Ryan, R. M. (1985b). *Intrinsic motivation and self-determination in human behavior*. New York: Plenum.

DiVitto, B., & McArthur, L. Z. (1978). Developmental differences in the use of distinctiveness, consensus, and consistency information for making causal attributions. *Developmental Psychology*, 14, 474–482.

Eccles, J. (1983). Expectancies, values and academic behaviors. In J. T. Spence (Ed.), *Achievement and achievement motives: Psychological and sociological approaches* (pp. 75–146). San Francisco: W. H. Freeman.

Eccles, J., Wigfield, A., & Schiefele, U. (1998). Motivation to succeed. In W. Damon (Series Ed.) & N. Eisenberg (Vol. Ed.), *Handbook of child psychology: Vol. 3. Social, emotional, and personality development* (5th ed., pp. 1017–1096). New York: Wiley.

Eisenberger, R., & Cameron, J. (1996). Detrimental effects of reward: Reality or myth? *American Psychologist*, 51, 1153–1166.

Eisenberger, R., & Cameron, J. (1998). Reward, intrinsic interest, and creativity: New findings. *American Psychologist, 53*, 676–679.

Eisenberger, R., & Selbst, M. (1994). Does reward increase or decrease creativity? *Journal of Personality and Social Psychology, 66*, 1116–1127.

Fazio, R. H. (1981). On the self-perception explanation of the overjustification effect: The role of the salience of initial attitude. *Journal of Experimental Social Psychology, 17*, 417–426.

Garbarino, J. (1975). The impact of anticipated reward upon cross-age tutoring. *Journal of Personality and Social Psychology, 32*, 421–428.

Glover, J., & Gary, A. L. (1976). Procedures to increase some aspects of creativity. *Journal of Applied Behavioral Analysis, 9*, 79–84.

Glucksberg, S. (1962). The influence of strength of drive on functional fixedness and perceptual recognition. *Journal of Experimental Psychology, 63*, 36–41.

Glucksberg, S. (1964). Problem-solving: Response competition and the influence of drive. *Psychological Reports, 15*, 939–942.

Greene, D., & Lepper, M. (1974). Effects of extrinsic rewards on children's subsequent interest. *Child Development, 45*, 1141–1145.

Guilford, J. P. (1967). *The nature of human intelligence.* New York: McGraw-Hill.

Halpin, G., & Halpin, G. (1973). The effect of motivation on creative thinking abilities. *Journal of Creative Behavior, 7*, 51–53.

Harackiewicz, J. M. (1979). The effects of reward contingency and performance feedback on intrinsic motivation. *Journal of Personality and Social Psychology, 37*, 1352–1363.

Harackiewicz, J. M., Manderlink, G., & Sansone, C. (1984). Rewarding pinball wizardry: The effects of evaluation on intrinsic interest. *Journal of Personality and Social Psychology, 47*, 287–300.

Hennessey, B. A. (1999). Intrinsic motivation, affect and creativity. In S. Russ (Ed.), *Affect, creative experience and psychological adjustment* (pp. 77–90). Philadelphia: Taylor & Francis.

Hennessey, B. A. (1989). The effect of extrinsic constraint on children's creativity while using a computer. *Creativity Research Journal, 2*, 151–168.

Hennessey, B. A., & Amabile, T. M. (1999). Consensual assessment. In M. Runco & S. Pritzker (Eds.), *Encyclopedia of creativity.* (pp. 347–359). New York: Academic Press.

Hennessey, B. A., & Amabile, T. M. (1988). Story-telling: A method for assessing children's creativity. *Journal of Creative Behavior, 22*, 235–246.

Hennessey, B. A., & Amabile, T. M. (1998). Reward, intrinsic motivation, and creativity. *American Psychologist, 53*, 674–675.

Hennessey, B. A., Amabile, T. M., & Martinage, M. (1989). Immunizing children against the negative effects of reward. *Contemporary Educational Psychology, 14*, 212–227.

Hennessey, B. A., & Zbikowski, S. (1993). Immunizing children against the negative effects of reward: A further examination of intrinsic motivation training techniques. *Creativity Research Journal, 6*, 297–307.

Hocevar, D., & Bachelor, P. (1989). A taxonomy and critique of measurements used in the study of creativity. In J. Glover, R. Ronning, & C. Reynolds (Eds.), *Handbook of creativity.* New York: Plenum.

Kelley, H. (1967). Attribution theory in social psychology. In D. Levine (Ed.), *Nebraska Symposium on Motivation: Vol. 15* (pp. 192–240). Lincoln: University of Nebraska Press.

Kelley, H. (1973). The processes of causal attribution. *American Psychologist, 28*, 107–128.

Kernoodle-Loveland, K., & Olley, J. (1979). The effect of external reward on interest and quality of task performance in children of high and low intrinsic motivation. *Child Development, 50*, 1207–1210.

Kimble, G. (1961). *Hilgard and Marquis' conditioning and learning* (2nd ed.). New York: Appleton-Century-Crofts.

Kruglanski, A. W., Friedman, I., & Zeevi, G. (1971). The effects of extrinsic incentive on some qualitative aspects of task performance. *Journal of Personality, 39*, 606–617.

Lepper, M., & Greene, D. (Eds.). (1978). *The hidden costs of reward*. Hillsdale, NJ: Erlbaum.

Lepper, M., Greene, D., & Nisbett, R. (1973). Undermining children's intrinsic interest with extrinsic rewards: A test of the "overjustification" hypothesis. *Journal of Personality and Social Psychology*, 28, 129–137.

Lepper, M., Sagotsky, G., Dafoe, J. L., & Greene, D. (1982). Consequences of superfluous social constraints: Effects on young children's social inferences and subsequent intrinsic motivation. *Journal of Personality and Social Psychology*, 42, 51–65.

Lieberman, J. N. (1965). Playfulness and divergent thinking: An investigation of their relationship at the kindergarten level. *Journal of Genetic Psychology*, 107, 219–224.

McGraw, K. (1978). The detrimental effects of reward on performance: A literature review and a prediction model. In M. Lepper, & D. Greene (Eds.), *The hidden costs of reward*. Hillsdale, NJ: Erlbaum.

McGraw, K., & McCullers, J. (1979). Evidence of a detrimental effect of extrinsic incentives on breaking a mental set. *Journal of Experimental Social Psychology*, 15, 285–294.

Milgram, R. M., & Feingold, S. (1977). Concrete and verbal reinforcement in creative thinking of disadvantaged children. *Perceptual and Motor Skills*, 45, 675–678.

Morgan, M. (1981). The overjustification effect: A developmental test of self-perception interpretations. *Journal of Personality and Social Psychology*, 40, 809–821.

Newell, A., Shaw, J., & Simon, H. (1962). The processes of creative thinking. In H. Gruber, G. Terrell, & M. Wertheimer (Eds.), *Contemporary approaches to creative thinking* (pp. 63–119). New York: Atherton.

Pinder, C. (1976). Additivity versus non-additivity of intrinsic and extrinsic incentives: Implications for theory and practice. *Journal of Applied Psychology*, 61, 693–700.

Pittman, T. S., Emery, J., & Boggiano, A. K., (1982). Intrinsic and extrinsic motivational orientations: Reward-induced changes in preference for complexity. *Journal of Personality and Social Psychology*, 42, 789–797.

Pritchard, R., Campbell, K., & Campbell, D. (1977). Effects of extrinsic financial rewards on intrinsic motivation. *Journal of Applied Psychology*, 62, 9–15.

Raina, M. K. (1968). A study into the effect of competition on creativity. *Gifted Child Quarterly*, 12, 217–220.

Ransen, D. (1980). The mediation of reward-induced motivation decrements in early and middle childhood: A template matching approach. *Journal of Personality and Social Psychology*, 35, 49–55.

Reiss, S., & Sushinsky, L. W. (1975). Overjustification, competing responses, and the acquisition of intrinsic interest. *Journal of Personality and Social Psychology*, 31, 1116–1125.

Rosenthal, R. (1984). *Meta-analytic procedures for social and behavioral research*. Beverly Hills, CA: Sage.

Ross, M. (1975). Salience of reward and intrinsic motivation. *Journal of Personality and Social Psychology*, 32, 245–254.

Sansone, C., & Harackiewicz, J. M. (1996). "I don't feel like it": The function of interest in self-regulation. In L. Martin & A. Tesser (Eds.) *Striving and feeling: Interactions among goals, affect and self-regulation* (pp. 203–228). Mahwah, NJ: Erlbaum

Sansone, C. & Harackiewicz, J. M. (1998). Reality is complicated. *American Psychologist*, 53, 673–674.

Shapira, Z. (1976). Expectancy determinants of intrinsically motivated behavior. *Journal of Personality and Social Psychology*, 39, 1235–1244.

Shultz, T., Butkowsky, I., Pearce, J., & Shanfield, H. (1975). The development of schemes for the attribution of multiple psychological causes. *Developmental Psychology*, 11, 502–510.

Simon, H. (1967). Motivational and emotional controls of cognition. *Psychological Review*, 74, 29–39.

Skinner, B. F. (1979). *The shaping of a behaviorist*. New York: Knopf.

Skinner, B. F. (1938). *The behavior of organisms: An experimental analysis*. New York: Appleton-Century-Crofts.

Smith, M. C. (1975). Children's use of the multiple sufficient cause schema in social perception. *Journal of Personality and Social Psychology, 32*, 737–747.

Spence, K. (1956). *Behavior theory and conditioning*. New Haven, CT: Yale University Press.

Stein, M. I. (1974). *Stimulating creativity* (vols. 1 and 2). New York: Academic Press.

Torrance, E. P. (1962). *Guiding creative talent*. Englewood Cliffs, NJ: Prentice-Hall.

Ward, W. C., Kogan, N., & Pankove, E. (1972). Incentive effects in children's creativity. *Child Development, 43*, 669–676.

CHAPTER

4

Rewarding Competence: The Importance of Goals in the Study of Intrinsic Motivation

JUDITH M. HARACKIEWICZ

Department of Psychology
University of Wisconsin

CAROL SANSONE

Department of Psychology
University of Utah

Some people are lucky enough to make a living doing things they love. Kids who enjoy basketball and play the game during every free minute discover when they grow up (if they grow enough) that they can obtain college scholarships and lucrative NBA or semilucrative WNBA contracts for playing the game they love. Academically inclined students who love reading and learning and who freely choose to remain in school long after their peers are earning salaries and starting families can end up with nonlucrative academic contracts and remain at school forever. Of course, these monetary rewards require a certain level of competence at the beloved activity, a competence that is often acquired and nurtured in the absence of salient external rewards. Thus, even when activities begin as their own reward, they can end up being externally rewarded.

When individuals freely engage in an activity for its own sake, their behavior is considered intrinsically motivated. In reality, however, very few behaviors occur in a social vacuum, and most people eventually encounter external constraints on their favorite activities. For example, young basket-ball players may find that their parents reward them when they make the basketball team, or students may be required by teachers to read interesting books. Parents and teachers often have vested interests in directing, encour-aging, or controlling the behavior of their children and students, even when those behaviors are intrinsically motivated. To shape behavior, they may offer rewards, set requirements, suggest goals, evaluate performance, or provide feedback. These interventions, communications, and incentives rep-resent extrinsic intrusions that can affect subsequent intrinsic motivation.

As reviewed by Lepper and Henderlong (chapter 10, this book) and Ryan and Deci (chapter 2, this book), previous theory and research indi-cates that intrinsic motivation can suffer when task participation is extrinsically constrained. In the first studies to demonstrate this effect, people were offered rewards simply for doing an interesting activity, with-out regard for the quality of task performance (Deci, 1972; Lepper, Greene, & Nisbett, 1973). These *task-contingent* rewards proved to under-mine subsequent interest in the activity, compared with groups not promised rewards, and this result is often referred to as the overjustifica-tion or undermining effect. This effect has been replicated many times across a wide range of research participants, activities, and constraints. Despite the controversy engendered by dueling meta-analyses and responses (e.g., Eisenberger & Cameron, 1996; Lepper, Henderlong, & Gingras, 1999; Lepper, Keavney, & Drake, 1996; Ryan & Deci, 1996; San-sone & Harackiewicz, 1998), there is little doubt that task-contingent rewards can undermine intrinsic motivation (Deci, Koestner, & Ryan, 1999a). This effect has been explained in terms of changes in the per-ceived locus of causality for behavior (Deci & Ryan, 1985; Lepper et al., 1973). Rewards are assumed to promote perceptions of external control and to induce extrinsic attributions for task engagement ("I am doing this to get a reward"), and this reduces subsequent intrinsic motivation, mea-sured in situations in which rewards are no longer available or expected.

In this chapter, we hope to move beyond controversies about meta-analy-ses to consider one specific type of reward structure in detail. People rarely receive external rewards simply for participating in enjoyable activities. Rather, rewards in real life usually depend on the quality of a person's task performance. When a reward depends on attaining a certain level of perfor-mance (e.g., outperforming 80% of peers), the reward is considered *perfor-mance-contingent*. Rather than debate whether these quality-dependent rewards have negative, positive, or null effects, we consider the different processes through which performance-contingent rewards can both enhance and undermine intrinsic motivation. We believe that this analysis can contribute to a more general understanding of intrinsic motivation. In fact, our earlier work with performance-continent rewards led to the devel-opment of a process model of intrinsic motivation that has guided our more recent work on goals and self-regulation (to be discussed in later chapters). In this chapter, we describe the evolution of this model (Harackiewicz & Sansone, 1991; Sansone & Harackiewicz, 1996).

Performance-contingent rewards may reduce interest for the same reasons that task-contingent rewards do. A performance-contingent reward may be perceived as controlling behavior or may engender external attributions for task engagement. In fact, performance-contingent rewards may be perceived as even more externally controlling than task-contingent rewards (Deci & Ryan, 1985; Harackiewicz, 1979). Under a task contingency, people know that they will receive a reward at task conclusion, regardless of the quality of their performance. A performance contingency is more demanding—it assumes participation but also requires a particular level of performance. Thus, performance contingencies are more constraining, and individuals may experience greater pressure than under task contingencies, leading to even larger decrements in intrinsic motivation.

The behaviors controlled by task contingencies and performance contingencies are different, however, which complicates a simple attributional analysis. Task-contingent rewards for enjoyable activities mandate participation in an activity that people would engage in without rewards and are therefore functionally superfluous (i.e., the reason the behavior is considered "overjustified"). Performance-contingent rewards offered for an enjoyable activity are equally superfluous regarding participation, but they are not necessarily superfluous in the case of performance quality. A performance contingency may motivate individuals to exert more effort and work harder than they would otherwise. Performance-contingent rewards may therefore serve an effective incentive function with respect to performance quality and promote higher levels of performance (Lepper, 1981).

Performance contingencies can also change the way a person defines a task. The promise of a reward for doing well may signify that performance quality is a central issue, and such rewards can influence an individual's motivational orientation going into a task. As a result of being offered a performance-contingent reward, people may define an activity as an achievement task in which they are motivated to develop and demonstrate competence (Dweck, 1986; Harackiewicz, Abrahams, & Wageman, 1987; Nicholls, 1984). If they come to view the rewarded activity as a challenge or as an opportunity to assess their abilities or demonstrate their skills, they may be more responsive to performance feedback (Harackiewicz & Manderlink, 1984; Harackiewicz, Manderlink & Sansone, 1984). In sum, performance-contingent rewards may lead individuals to define, approach, and perform tasks differently than they would in the absence of rewards, *and* differently than when offered task-contingent rewards. This difference in approach may be critical in determining how individuals experience activities and whether they continue to enjoy them after rewards are no longer available.

Performance-contingent rewards also provide feedback about performance quality. When individuals receive (or fail to receive) a reward, they learn whether they have attained a performance criterion and satisfied the reward contingency. This feedback may affect their perceptions of competence, which can influence intrinsic motivation directly. Many theorists argue that perceived competence is a primary determinant of intrinsic motivation (Bandura, 1986; Deci & Ryan, 1985; Harter, 1981; Lepper & Henderlong, chapter 10, this book; White, 1959). According to these formulations, individuals should enjoy activities that afford a sense of mastery or efficacy. The development of competence can be intrinsically rewarding and foster continuing interest in an activity. For example, the mastery of a new shot or defensive technique may make basketball even more enjoyable for young players. If performance contingencies make individuals feel more or less competent at an activity, they can affect subsequent intrinsic motivation through this mastery process.

Because performance-contingent rewards constrain behavior, influence a person's approach to a task, and provide competence feedback, they invoke several motivational processes that may have contradictory implications for intrinsic motivation. There have been relatively few studies of performance-contingent rewards, compared with task-contingent rewards, and these studies vary widely in the nature of the performance contingency employed, the level of performance feedback provided, and the control groups employed. Given the complexity of this reward structure and the differences between studies, it is perhaps not surprising that meta-analyses for this particular type of reward reveal inconsistent and inconclusive results. For example, Deci et al.'s (1999a) meta-analysis of reward effects revealed an overall tendency of performance-contingent rewards to undermine intrinsic motivation when measured behaviorally but found no reliable effects of these rewards on self-report measures of interest (see also Deci, Koestner, & Ryan, 1999b). In contrast, Eisenberger, Pierce, and Cameron's (1999) meta-analysis of performance-contingent reward effects revealed null and positive effects on behavioral measures and positive effects on self-report measures.

OUR MODEL OF
PERFORMANCE-CONTINGENT REWARDS

We believe that an understanding of performance-contingent reward effects will benefit more from careful theoretical analysis than it will from meta-analysis. Our model (Harackiewicz, 1989; Harackiewicz et al., 1984) builds on earlier work that documented the negative effects of task-contingent rewards and the positive effects of competence information on intrinsic motivation (Deci & Ryan, 1985; Lepper, 1981). In our model, we identify the functional properties of extrinsic constraints and specify how these properties influence intrinsic motivation. We first describe the model as it applies to performance-contingent reward structures and later discuss its broader implications.

A critical feature of our model is the analysis of reward effects over time, and we consider the motivational processes initiated at different times over the course of an individual's engagement in a task. In particular, we believe that it is essential to separate the effects of a reward *offer* from the effects of the reward *outcome*. Figure 4.1 presents a schematic model of the processes initiated over time by the offer and receipt of a performance-contingent reward. The offer of a performance-contingent reward may cause individuals to approach tasks differently, with a greater emphasis on performing well and demonstrating competence. An individual's motivational orientation while striving for competence (but before receiving any feedback) should influence reactions to the activity during performance, as well as subsequent intrinsic motivation. Motivational orientation can also amplify reactions to the feedback eventually received (represented by the dashed path in Figure 4.1). Finally, at task conclusion, individuals learn whether they have earned the reward (the reward outcome). The receipt (or nonreceipt) of a reward can influence perceived competence and in turn influence subsequent intrinsic motivation.

The offer of a performance-contingent reward means that performance will be evaluated, and it also means that some type of feedback will be provided. However, the actual evaluation and resultant feedback come much later in the process. For example, as soon as basketball players are promised a reward for making more free throws than 80% of their peers, they know that their performance will be evaluated, and they know that they will eventually receive some feedback. If they receive the reward, they know that they have scored in the top 20%. However, the reward adds something to this competence information—it *symbolizes* their competence at the activity. As such, the reward may motivate players to care more about the quality of their performance as soon as the offer is made as well as when they actually receive (or fail to receive) this symbolic reward. The offer of a performance-contingent reward makes the possibility of attaining competence immediately salient, whereas the receipt of the reward symbolizes the competence attained.

Our model identifies three distinct properties of performance-contingent rewards: *evaluative threat, competence feedback*, and *symbolic cue value*. Evaluative threat and cue value can influence how individuals approach and experience an activity during task performance, and competence feedback and cue value can influence how individuals perceive and react to their level of performance at task conclusion. All three factors can independently influence intrinsic motivation, but they have their effects at different points in the process of task engagement. We refer to three stages in the reward process:

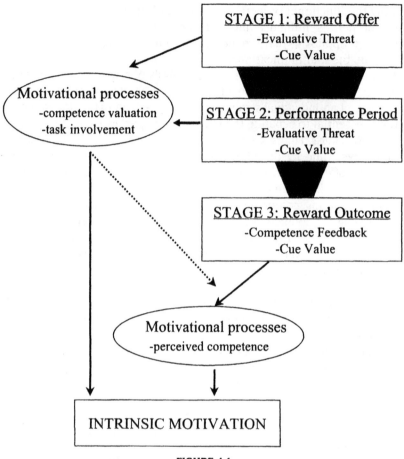

FIGURE 4.1
A schematic model of the reward process over time.

(1) before the start of the task, when a reward is promised, contingent on the quality of performance (the reward offer); (2) during task performance (the performance period); and (3) at task conclusion, when participants receive feedback and learn if they earned the reward (the reward outcome). We discuss how each of the three reward properties affects motivational processes over this time course.

Evaluative Threat: The Reward Offer

When individuals learn that rewards are dependent on the quality of their performance, they know they will be evaluated. The anticipation of evaluation may affect individuals' experience during the performance period

(Harackiewicz, Manderlink, & Sansone, 1992). Evaluation is usually conducted by the person offering the performance-contingent reward, although people may sometimes receive enough information to evaluate their own performance as they work. In either case, individuals are aware of evaluation during the performance period, and they may feel pressured or controlled by it (Deci & Ryan, 1985; Ryan, 1982).

The effects of evaluative threat have been examined extensively in the area of test anxiety (cf. Sarason, 1980). Although theorists and researchers in this area are primarily concerned with identifying the processes that interfere with performance and academic achievement, much of the work is also relevant to intrinsic motivation. Factors that debilitate ongoing performance may also affect task involvement and influence how an individual feels about an activity. The test-anxiety literature suggests that people anticipating evaluation can become anxious about their performance (Geen, 1980) and that they may become distracted from the task if they ruminate about their inadequacies (Wine, 1971). These findings come from studies conducted in academic testing situations, where performance evaluation can be quite stressful, and we would not expect individuals to become highly anxious in situations where their performance on an enjoyable game is evaluated. However, milder levels of evaluation may still produce cognitive interference (Wine, 1971), which could disrupt task involvement and interest during performance (Harackiewicz et al., 1984). In other words, the expectation of evaluation can disrupt the positive state of task involvement even when it does not directly create a negative state such as anxiety or worry.

We consider the evaluative threat inherent in performance contingencies to be one property responsible for decrements in interest. Studies have shown that the anticipation of performance evaluation in nonreward contexts undermines intrinsic interest in an activity (Amabile, 1979; Harackiewicz et al., 1984, 1987), and we believe that it should have similar effects in the context of performance-contingent rewards. Our model predicts that evaluative threat distracts people from the task they are working on and produces cognitive interference. Without something to counter this effect, individuals are likely to become less involved in the activity and to enjoy it less. Even if these individuals eventually learn that they did well, the positive experience of working on an interesting and challenging activity will have been clouded by disruptive cognition and distraction.

Competence Feedback: The Reward Outcome

The competence feedback inherent in performance contingencies, when positive, may repair some of the damage inflicted by the evaluative threat at the outset of task engagement. People may begin to feel more competent as they work on the task (especially if they are working harder or more effectively), but the full effect of competence feedback does not typically occur until rewards are awarded (or not). Perceived competence is an important determinant of subsequent interest in an activity (Bandura, 1986; Deci & Ryan, 1985). If reward attainment leads individuals to perceive themselves as competent, they may become more interested in the activity. Numerous studies have documented the positive effects of competence feedback on intrinsic motivation for skill-based activities (Deci, 1971; Fisher, 1978; Harackiewicz, 1979; Ryan, 1982), presumably due to enhanced feelings of competence. Some studies have shown that the receipt of performance-contingent rewards can in fact enhance perceived competence relative to no-reward, no-feedback controls (Boggiano & Ruble, 1979; Harackiewicz, 1979; Karniol & Ross, 1977).

Of course, the offer of a performance-contingent reward does not guarantee positive performance feedback, and this is one of the serious problems with using these rewards in the real world (Deci et al., 1999b; Kohn, 1996; Ryan & Deci, chapter 2, this book). When people do not perform up to the standards stipulated by a reward contingency, not only do they fail to receive the reward but they also receive negative performance feedback that can undermine interest in an activity. In fact, Deci et al. (1999a) conducted some of their meta-analyses of performance-contingent rewards separately as a function of whether participants received maximal rewards (i.e., all participants received the performance-contingent reward offered) or received less-than-maximal rewards (i.e., participants were offered performance-contingent rewards over a series of trials and failed to earn the maximum rewards). Deci et al. (1999a) found the largest decrements in intrinsic motivation when participants received less than maximal rewards, suggesting that the combination of evaluative rewards and negative feedback can have deleterious effects.

Our model assumes that the effects of evaluative threat, which are initiated early in the reward process, and the effects of competence feedback, which come later, are additive with respect to their combined effect on subsequent interest. Thus, positive competence feedback may effectively offset the negative effects of evaluative threat on intrinsic motivation, producing a null effect relative to a no-reward, no-feedback control group. In contrast, negative feedback (and reward nonattainment) could exacerbate the negative effects of evaluative threat and undermine intrinsic motivation relative to no-reward controls. Rather than describe a reward structure as either controlling (i.e., evaluative) or informational (because it provides competence feedback), we assume that both properties operate over the course of time, and we examine how they combine to influence interest.

Symbolic Cue Value

Evaluative threat and competence feedback are two important reward properties, but they are not sufficient to explain the effects of performance-contingent rewards on intrinsic motivation. Neither property captures the positive motivational processes that may be invoked by rewards for competence. The feature that distinguishes a performance-contingent reward from evaluative situations in general is that individuals have the opportunity to earn a reward as a consequence of a positive evaluation. The meaning, or symbolic cue value, of that reward may influence interest independently of evaluative threat and feedback (Harackiewicz et al., 1984). Cue value can influence intrinsic motivation throughout the reward process. The initial offer of a performance-contingent reward may generate positive motivational processes as individuals approach and perform activities eager to attain competence. In turn, the receipt of a performance-contingent reward can symbolize that competence and instill feelings of accomplishment and pride.

A reward has meaning in terms of the level of competence it represents (the "cue") and with respect to the value of competence in the situation. Cue value should be greater when rewards symbolize higher levels of achievement. For example, a reward for finishing first in a free-throw shooting contest symbolizes a higher level of competence than a reward for finishing in the top three (the cue), and the same reward will have greater value at a state tournament than it would in gym class.

The Reward Offer

A reward offer provides an opportunity to earn something that symbolizes competence at the activity, and it can motivate individuals to care more about doing well (Harackiewicz & Manderlink, 1984). Performance-contingent rewards can therefore influence the way individuals approach a task and their motivation during the performance period. Of course, some of these effects may be due to the incentive function of the reward—people want to do well because they want the tangible reward. Even when the reward serves an incentive function, however, it also serves to sensitize individuals to the competence information available in the situation. Earlier, we suggested that evaluative threat could interfere with attention to the activity by inducing disruptive thoughts about the upcoming performance evaluation. We are now suggesting that cue value can reorient the individual to the activity at hand because rewards can make doing well more personally important. Rewards may thus help people focus on attaining competence and keep them focused on their performance of the task.

The Reward Outcome

In addition to supplying a desired material outcome, the receipt of a performance-contingent reward supplies tangible evidence of excellence, which can enhance the emotional significance of the competence information provided. The cue value of a reward may increase subsequent interest by enhancing feelings of accomplishment, pride, and satisfaction beyond those produced by the competence feedback alone. Thus, cue value can affect motivation throughout the three stages of the reward process.

The positive effects of symbolic cue value should be mediated by affective processes related to the pursuit and attainment of competence. These effects may combine with the effects of competence feedback such that when rewards are attained, symbolic cue value and competence feedback each have positive effects that together outweigh the negative effects of evaluative threat. Because evaluative threat, cue value, and competence feedback can have simultaneously positive and negative effects, the net effect of performance-contingent rewards on intrinsic motivation compared to no rewards will depend on the relative weighting of each reward property in a situation. When the positive effects of cue value and feedback outweigh the negative effect of evaluative threat, performance-contingent rewards can actually enhance intrinsic motivation. Later in this chapter, we discuss factors that can affect the weighting of these properties.

EMPIRICAL SUPPORT FOR THE MODEL

Although the three properties identified here are interrelated, it should be possible to identify their individual contributions under appropriate experimental conditions. To simplify the simultaneous consideration of these three properties, we contrast performance-contingent rewards with two comparison groups. First, we compare them with no-reward control groups receiving comparable competence feedback (feedback controls), thereby controlling for the effects of performance feedback. Another critical comparison group is one exposed to the same evaluative contingency and receiving the same feedback, but without the promise or receipt of a reward (evaluation-only groups). Inclusion of this condition controls for both evaluation and feedback. Table 4.1 summarizes the relation of the three reward properties to their predicted effects on intrinsic motivation under three experimental conditions: performance-contingent rewards, evaluation-only groups, and feedback controls. Of course, a third comparison group that is not promised rewards, does not expect evaluation, and does not receive feedback (i.e., a baseline control) could also be employed to evaluate the net effects of performance-contingent rewards. However, comparisons with this group would provide the least information about reward dynamics because evaluation, cue value, and feedback would all be uncontrolled.

When performance-contingent reward conditions are compared with feedback controls, any reward effects will be due to the opposing effects of evaluative threat and symbolic cue value, which are predicted to work simultaneously. If the effects of evaluative threat and cue value are equal in magnitude, they should produce a net effect of no difference between rewards and feedback controls. In contrast, the comparison of evaluation-only

TABLE 4.1
A Model of Performance-Contingent Rewards Relating Reward Properties to Predicted Effects on Intrinsic Motivation

	Experimental conditions		
Reward properties	Feedback only	Evaluation with feedback	Performance-contingent reward
Evaluative threat		−	−
Competence feedback	+	+	+
Cue value			+
Net effect on intrinsic motivation	+	0	+

+ = increment in interest; − = reduction in interest; 0 = no change in interest.

groups with feedback controls should demonstrate the negative effect of evaluative threat. In turn, the comparison of performance-contingent reward groups with evaluation-only groups should demonstrate the positive effect of symbolic cue value, because both groups are exposed to the same evaluative threat and receive identical competence feedback. This comparison is a critical one, because it unconfounds the expectation of evaluation and cue value. Only by employing both comparison groups can one document the opposing effects of evaluative threat and cue value.

To test these hypotheses, we have conducted several experiments examining the effects of performance evaluation by itself and when paired with a performance-contingent reward (Harackiewicz et al., 1984, 1987). In one study (Harackiewicz et al., 1984, Study 1), participants in performance-contingent reward groups were promised a reward (a movie pass) if their performance on a pinball game surpassed the 80th percentile criterion. At task conclusion, they learned that they had surpassed the criterion and received the movie pass. Evaluation-only groups were told that their performance would be evaluated against the same criterion and then learned they had surpassed it but were not promised (nor did they receive) a reward for their accomplishment. Feedback-control groups received unanticipated feedback at task conclusion that they had scored above the 80th percentile. Thus, all participants received the same positive feedback about their performance on the pinball game.

We found that the combination of evaluative threat and positive feedback reduced intrinsic motivation (measured behaviorally and with self-report) compared with the feedback control group, demonstrating the negative effect of anticipated evaluation. Table 4.2 presents the behavioral results from Study 1 (Harackiewicz et al., 1984). The evaluative contingency employed in the evaluation-only group was identical to that embodied in the reward contingency, suggesting that the evaluative-threat property of performance-contingent rewards may be responsible for negative effects on

TABLE 4.2
Means for Balls Played by Reward Condition (Harackiewicz et al., 1984)

Experimental Conditions		
Feedback only	Evaluation with feedback	Performance-contingent reward
7.56^a	3.06^b	8.13^a

Balls played was the number of additional balls played on a pinball machine during a free-choice period. M values not sharing a superscript differ at $p < .05$.

intrinsic motivation. However, we also found that the performance-contingent reward *enhanced* intrinsic motivation compared with the evaluation-only group. The only difference between these two groups was the availability of a reward for surpassing the performance criterion, and this finding therefore demonstrates the positive effect of cue value. This result reveals that symbolic rewards can enhance interest independently of their informational properties. In other words, the positive effects of performance-contingent rewards documented here cannot be attributed to the positive feedback they conveyed (because all participants received the same information about their performance). Rather, these effects reflect differences in the way participants approached the task when offered a reward and differences in the way they responded to the identical performance feedback. In sum, by employing two comparison groups, we were able to isolate both positive and negative reward effects in the same study. Moreover, we have replicated these effects in several subsequent studies (Harackiewicz et al., 1984, Studies 2 and 3; Harackiewicz et al., 1987).

It is important to note, however, that the reward groups did not differ from the feedback-only groups, demonstrating the null effect that resulted from the opposing effects of evaluative threat and cue value. Clearly, then, we are not arguing that performance-contingent rewards have only positive effects or that they will always have positive effects. Rather, we believe that our results demonstrate the complexity of performance-contingent reward effects and reveal the potential for simultaneously positive and negative effects. Our methodology and our results force us to move beyond simplistic questions about whether rewards are good or bad and ask more focused questions about the properties of performance-contingent rewards that produce these positive and negative effects and more complex questions about how the properties combine to influence intrinsic motivation.

META-ANALYSES REVISITED

Reward effects may be defined in relation to no-reward, no-feedback controls; feedback controls; or evaluation-only groups. Each comparison may be important for different theoretical and applied questions: What is the net effect of these rewards, compared with no-reward, no feedback conditions? How do performance-contingent rewards affect interest independently of the competence information they provide? What is the effect of rewarding competence in an evaluative context? Do reward effects depend on the feedback provided? From an applied perspective, our results suggest that it is particularly important to consider the *context* in which rewards will be offered. Our recommendations would differ according to the degree of evaluative threat already present in the context. Careful consideration of these questions requires the use of different comparison groups, and our results suggest that it will take more than one comparison group in any study to address these questions. In sum, we will draw overly simplistic conclusions about reward effects if we focus on just one control group or just one of these questions.

Deci et al. (1999a) have also discussed the importance of different comparison groups. For example, they conducted some of their meta-analyses of performance-contingent rewards separately as a function of whether no-reward control groups included performance feedback. Results across these subcategories varied considerably, indicating that performance feedback is an important moderator of reward effects. It is important to note that the number of studies in these subcategories was rather small (as few as three in one category). In fact, the largest number of studies have been conducted with the least informative no-reward, no-feedback control condition, and a smaller number have been conducted with feedback controls. However, Deci et al. reported no meta-analyses of studies comparing performance-contingent rewards with no-reward groups exposed to the same evaluation and receiving the same feedback, yet our results suggest that this comparison provides particularly valuable information about reward dynamics (cf. Eisenberger et al., 1999). In sum, given the relative paucity of studies employing multiple control groups, we do not believe that any meta-analysis of the extant literature can yield definitive conclusions about the effects of performance-contingent rewards.

MODERATORS OF REWARD PROPERTIES

In Table 4.1, the reward properties are assumed to carry equal weight in determining subsequent intrinsic motivation, but this may not always be the case. Other situational factors may lead to one reward property's being more heavily weighted in affecting intrinsic motivation. One factor that may moderate the effects of cue value is the difficulty of a reward contingency. Rewards that symbolize higher levels of achievement may have greater affective significance and enhance interest to a greater degree than rewards less indicative of competence, under conditions of positive feedback and reward attainment. For example, a prize for writing the best poem in a city-wide competition may have more value and impact than a gold star pasted on a student's poem in the classroom.

However, higher levels of cue value are often associated with more intense evaluative threat. When reward contingencies are difficult to satisfy, this evaluative pressure may result in more cognitive interference. For example, students may become more distracted while writing a poem when they know that the poem is going to be read and evaluated by the mayor's select committee than when they know that the poem is going to be read and evaluated by their teacher. As performance criteria become increasingly difficult to attain, the evaluative pressure may actually create negative states of anxiety and worry and not just interfere with attention to the task (Sarason, 1980). In support of this analysis, Harackiewicz et al. (1984) found that evaluative threat was more detrimental to task interest when performance was evaluated with respect to more challenging criteria (e.g., the 80th as opposed to 50th percentile criterion) and that the counteracting effect of cue value increased. Thus, both the negative effects of evaluative threat and the positive effects of cue value may be more pronounced under more stringent performance contingencies. Furthermore, because the *tangible* reward was the same across levels of difficulty in this study (a movie pass), this pattern of results confirms that it is the level of competence *symbolized* by the reward that is responsible for these reward effects.

There are also factors that may reduce the degree of evaluative threat conveyed in a reward contingency. For example, if individuals are able to evaluate their own performance instead of relying on external evaluation by others, they may remain focused on the task, with less cognitive interference. In Study 3 of Harackiewicz et al. (1984), some participants were provided with an objective standard (i.e., the score representing the 80th percentile) that allowed them to monitor and judge their own performance in the pinball game. The negative effects of evaluative threat on intrinsic motivation were attenuated in this evaluation-only condition. This suggests that we may be able to counteract the principal negative property of performance-contingent rewards (evaluative threat) by introducing factors that will moderate the negative impact of evaluation on mediating processes (such as task involvement).

THE POWER OF PROCESS ANALYSIS

Another important test of our model lies in the analysis of processes assumed to mediate the effects of reward properties. Our model predicts that evaluative threat, cue value, and competence feedback all operate in performance-contingent reward structures, but their independent effects may be difficult to identify. These properties have opposing effects on intrinsic motivation and they tend to counteract one another. If we examined only intrinsic motivation outcomes, we would not always find interpretable differences between experimental conditions, and we might find ourselves overinterpreting null effects. In contrast, a careful analysis of the processes assumed to mediate reward property effects allows us to examine *how* the three properties work over time. In particular, we have argued that performance-contingent rewards change the way that individuals approach tasks, and a process analysis should be particularly valuable in documenting differences in approach before feedback is received.

Effects on Hypothesized Mediators: Task Involvement

Our model suggests that the negative effects of evaluative threat are due to cognitive interference and task disruption. We have successfully documented the negative effects of evaluative threat in several studies (Harackiewicz et al., 1984, 1987) and have collected some process data relevant to this issue. In Study 3 of Harackiewicz et al. (1984), participants completed questionnaires about their cognitive activity while playing pinball. The measure was based loosely on Sarason's (1980) Cognitive Interference Questionnaire and included items about distraction and thoughts about the game. We constructed a measure of task involvement based on thoughts about the game itself (e.g., "I thought about keeping the ball in play or manipulating the flippers"). The results indicated that participants in evaluation-only conditions concentrated less on the pinball game than did those in feedback control conditions, supporting our prediction.

However, reward participants exposed to comparable evaluative threat did not show the same impairment in task involvement. Their level of task involvement was virtually identical to that of participants in feedback control conditions. This suggests that cue value may counteract the negative effects of evaluative threat during the course of performance.

We argued earlier that rewards make individuals more concerned about their performance, which might lead to a greater focus on and involvement in task performance. The task involvement results from the Harackiewicz et al. (1984) study offer indirect support for this hypothesis. Results reported by Harackiewicz et al. (1987) provide some additional support for this interpretation. A second measure from the cognitive activity questionnaire concerned thoughts about competence (e.g., "I thought about how well I was doing"). Participants offered performance-contingent rewards thought more about the quality of their performance than did those in evaluation-only and feedback control conditions. This suggests that participants in reward conditions might have remained task involved because they were concerned about doing well. Considered together, the results on the cognitive activity measures support our assertion that evaluative threat undermines task involvement and suggest that the cue value of performance-contingent rewards can counteract this distraction effect and actually promote task involvement.

Effects on Hypothesized Mediators: Competence Valuation

Our model suggests that symbolic cue value enhances interest because rewards motivate individuals to care more about competence and react more strongly to competence feedback. In addition to documenting the positive effects of cue value on intrinsic motivation in the experiments described earlier, we have examined the processes that mediate symbolic cue value in detail. We have identified a motivational process—competence valuation—that affects intrinsic motivation in evaluative situations (Harackiewicz & Manderlink, 1984; Harackiewicz, Sansone, & Manderlink, 1985). Competence valuation reflects both an emotional involvement in attaining competence and responsivity to competence information. This is measured by the personal importance that an individual attaches to competent performance on the evaluated task.

Performance-contingent rewards may enhance subsequent interest through this competence valuation process. We have collected measures concerning participants' attitudes and feelings about task competence, measured before they begin a task, during task engagement, and again after receiving rewards and feedback. In Harackiewicz et al. (1984), preperformance measures revealed that reward participants felt it was more important to do well ("How important is it to you to do well at this game today?") than did than either evaluation-only or feedback control participants. This suggests that participants offered rewards cared more about doing well before they started the task. A measure collected at task conclusion assessed concern about performance ("I cared very much about how well I did", "I tried very hard at this game") and showed the same pattern of effects: participants who received rewards were more concerned about performance than either evaluation-only or feedback control participants. These results suggest that rewards, unlike performance evaluation alone, led individuals to value competence and to care about doing well. Specifically, symbolic rewards affect how people approach, experience, and respond to the competence information they receive (Harackiewicz, 1989; Harackiewicz & Manderlink, 1984; Harackiewicz et al., 1984, 1987).

The findings discussed above suggest that rewards do enhance competence valuation. Two studies have also documented the role of competence valuation as a mediator of reward effects on interest, using path analytic techniques for process analysis (Judd & Kenny, 1981). Harackiewicz and Manderlink (1984) found that performance-contingent rewards raised competence valuation before participants began the task (relative to feedback controls) and that performance-contingent rewards enhanced interest most for individuals who valued competence. Harackiewicz et al. (1987) found that performance-contingent rewards enhanced competence valuation relative to both feedback controls and evaluation-only groups and replicated the mediational results of Harackiewicz and Manderlink (1984). These results indicate that performance-contingent rewards can enhance intrinsic motivation by leading individuals to care more about doing well on a task.

Finally, although external factors can influence how much an individual values competence in evaluative situations, some individuals may characteristically value competence across a wider range of situations. Highly achievement oriented individuals typically desire objective ability feedback (McClelland, 1961), show strong interest in diagnostic ability assessment (Trope, 1975), and become involved in activities that afford self-evaluation (Greenwald, 1982). In contrast, those who are less oriented toward achievement tend to avoid ability assessment when possible and are less likely to value competence (Heckhausen, 1968).

Relative to individuals who are not achievement oriented, achievement-oriented individuals should therefore care more about doing well in any situation in which performance is evaluated (Harackiewicz & Manderlink, 1984). In addition, achievement-oriented individuals should be most responsive to the competence information in evaluative situations and show higher levels of intrinsic motivation when performance feedback is positive (Harackiewicz et al., 1985; Sansone, 1986). We have included measures of achievement orientation in most of our reward studies, and we found support for these predictions, independent of reward effects. For example, Harackiewicz et al. (1987) found that performance-contingent rewards and individual differences in achievement orientation had independent positive effects on competence valuation, measured at the outset of task engagement.

Although these personality effects may occur independently of reward effects, it is also possible that achievement orientation could moderate the effects of reward properties. Just as some situational factors can weight some reward properties more heavily (as discussed earlier), so, too, can personality variables be associated with differential weightings. For example, symbolic rewards might have a greater impact on competence valuation for individuals low in achievement orientation, because they do not characteristically value competence, and we have found some supportive evidence of this (Harackiewicz & Manderlink, 1984). Individual differences in achievement motivation might also moderate the effects of evaluative threat. For example, achievement-oriented individuals may not respond as negatively to evaluative "threat" because they view impending performance evaluation as a challenge rather than a threat. (See Barron & Harackiewicz [chapter 9, this book] and Tauer & Harackiewicz [1999] for discussion of achievement motivation differences in reaction to other types of performance evaluation.)

SUMMARY

We have obtained extensive support for our model of performance-contingent rewards, both in terms of the predicted effects on intrinsic motivation and in terms of the motivational dynamics underlying these reward effects. We have demonstrated that the evaluative properties of performance contingencies can be quite detrimental to interest, even when individuals ultimately receive positive competence feedback. These effects and our analysis are generally consistent with those of other theorists (Amabile, 1983; Deci & Ryan, 1985; Lepper, 1981). Where we differ from other theorists, however, is in our recognition of the positive potential of performance-contingent rewards to *enhance* intrinsic motivation in some circumstances (cf. Hidi, chapter 11, this book). We have demonstrated that the symbolic properties of rewards can increase intrinsic motivation, and we have documented the motivational processes that mediate these effects. Our theoretical analysis and our results highlight the potential of external interventions to make competence salient and lead individuals to become more involved in the pursuit of competence (Hidi & Harackiewicz, 2000). It is important to note, however, that the success of these interventions depends on the ultimate attainment of competence, and we recognize that we have tested performance-contingent rewards (to date) under only the most optimal conditions: all participants attained competence and received positive feedback and the promised rewards. It seemed reasonable to begin our research program by studying the effects of rewards when they were actually attained (which should be the strictest test of negative reward effects). It will be critically important in the future, however, to study the effects of rewards when they are offered but not awarded (which will be the strictest test of any positive reward effects).

BACK TO THE FUTURE

The careful reader may have noticed that the empirical work discussed here was all published in the 1980s and may wonder whether we stopped doing research or why we abandoned the study of reward effects. Although our attention to rewards waned, our interest in more general models of intrinsic motivation grew. Armed with an appreciation of process analysis, we sought to apply the insights gained from our analyses of reward effects to more general questions about intrinsic motivation and self-regulation.

Our rewards research revealed the importance of examining how external factors affect individuals' approach to an activity, their experience during task performance, and their reaction to outcomes. Moreover, we found that reactions to events that occurred later in the process (e.g., reward outcomes) could vary as a function of reactions to events initiated earlier in the process (e.g., reward offers). For example, positive competence feedback (scoring better than 80% of peers) might have different effects depending on whether individuals anticipate evaluation as they perform an activity or whether that same feedback is unexpected (e.g., Harackiewicz et al., 1984). Similarly, competence feedback seems to have more significance when associated with symbolic rewards. These results highlighted the importance of studying how different external conditions create a context for task engagement and how that context impacts reactions to feedback.

For example, if contextual factors such as the offer of a performance-contingent reward could make positive competence feedback more critical for interest and enjoyment, we reasoned that contextual factors could also make positive competence feedback *less* critical. To test this possibility, Sansone (1986, 1989) sought to develop an activity that might be interesting even in the absence of competence feedback. She created a trivia game in which people had to name obscure parts of objects. This engaging and unusual activity aroused curiosity about the correct answers as well as uncertainty about individual performance. She then compared the effects of feedback indicating that participants had performed better than 80% of their peers to feedback that satisfied curiosity (i.e., the correct names), but was silent as to individual competence. As expected, the positive competence feedback enhanced perceived competence compared with the curiosity feedback. However, both types of feedback were equally effective in enhancing interest compared with no-feedback controls (Sansone, 1986, 1989). These results suggest that when characteristics of the activity (a contextual factor) allow for multiple routes to interest (e.g., satisfying curiosity, mastering a skill), feedback does not have to convey positive competence information to enhance intrinsic motivation.

On the other hand, even when task characteristics de-emphasize individual competence, other contextual factors can make competence-related feedback more important (Sansone, Sachau, & Weir, 1989). For example, when an added contextual cue (an ego-involvement manipulation) made competence more salient at the outset of the trivia task, positive competence feedback did enhance subsequent interest relative to curiosity feedback (Sansone, 1986). Moreover, perceived competence mediated the effects of feedback on interest, but only when this contextual cue made competence salient.

This research challenged the assumptions that competence feedback is the only type of feedback relevant to intrinsic motivation and that perceived competence is the only mediator of feedback effects on intrinsic motivation. Instead, as we found with performance-contingent rewards, the effect of competence feedback (or what Deci et al. [1999a] and Eisenberger and Cameron [1996] termed *verbal rewards*) depended on individuals' orientation toward the task at the outset of task performance, and this orientation, in turn, was affected by situational factors.

Our empirical work, which began with the examination of reward effects, thus expanded to include a wider array of contextual features and individual differences. As our work did so, our conceptual approach shifted to an even greater emphasis on underlying processes and on how these processes simultaneously affect intrinsic motivation in both positive and negative ways. We subsequently extended and formalized this approach into a model of intrinsic motivation that gave individuals' goals a central role in the motivational dynamics. We proposed that contextual and individual characteristics influence individuals' approach to a particular activity through their effects on individuals' goals when individuals begin a task. Moreover, we proposed that these goals serve to direct attention and define what is important about engagement, which can then influence processes such as competence valuation, task involvement, and perceived competence, as well as influence how these processes are related to intrinsic motivation.

In 1991, we formalized a process model of intrinsic motivation that emphasized the role of goals in intrinsic motivation (Harackiewicz & Sansone, 1991; Sansone & Harackiewicz, 1996). Because intrinsically motivated activities had been defined as autotelic (Csikszentmihalyi, 1975), the importance of individuals' goals as individuals engage in an activity had been overlooked in the early research. Our empirical work suggested, in contrast, that individuals approach and begin to perform activities with some idea about what they want to accomplish, and we refer to these ideas as perceived goals. Goals can be pursued at a number of levels of abstraction, ranging from lower-order goals that are concrete and situationally specific (e.g., "I want to read a chapter of my psychology text tonight") to higher-order goals that are broad, cross-situational, and consistent over time (e.g., personal strivings, possible selves). However, we believe that intrinsic motivation is best construed as specific to a particular activity at a particular point in time. We therefore focused on two levels of goals at the lower end of the goal continuum, which we labeled purpose and target goals (Figure 4.2).

Purpose goals reflect the reasons for engaging in a task. For example, when offered rewards are contingent on performing well, individuals are likely to hold achievement-purpose goals (i.e., the desire to develop or demonstrate one's competence). However, purpose goals can also encompass other reasons for engaging in an activity that do not involve competence (e.g., to have fun, to relax, to socialize; see Sansone & Smith, chapter 12, this book). Purpose goals help establish the motivational context that influences how an individual approaches and experiences an activity (a C path in Figure 4.2). Target goals, on the other hand, reflect more specific guidelines for what individuals need to do to achieve their overarching purpose goal (Bandura, 1986; Locke & Latham, 1990). For example, when offered performance-contingent rewards, individuals are likely to

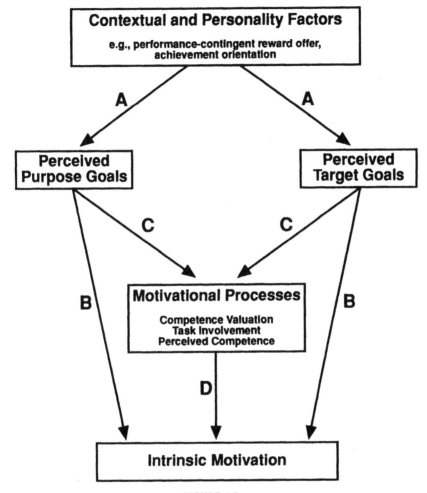

FIGURE 4.2

A schematic model of the Harackiewicz and Sansone (1991) process model of intrinsic motivation. See text for explanation of paths A through D.

hold target goals that reflect the specific standard of performance (e.g., scoring more than 20,000 points) that meets the performance contingency. Target goals thus reflect a more specific idea of *what* individuals are trying to accomplish while performing an activity, whereas purpose goals reflect *why* they are engaging in the activity.

We also recognized that purpose and target goals are, in turn, embedded in a hierarchy of individual and situational factors. We thus drew an important distinction between the goals that are suggested or implied by external factors and the goals that are actually adopted by an individual in a particular situation (the perceived purpose and target goal; see Figure 4.2).[1] The goals an individual adopts in a given situation can have multiple determinants, and these effects are represented as A paths in Figure 4.2. One class of determinants involves contextual factors, such as the offer of a performance-contingent reward. A second important class of determinants involves personality factors, such as individual differences in achievement orientation. This distinction between situational goals and their determinants implies that there can be characteristic differences between people in the goals they pursue but also that goals can differ across situations and over time.

Our initial transition to a goal-based model of intrinsic motivation has subsequently evolved in different directions for each of us as we have focused on different motivational questions. For example, Barron and Harackiewicz (chapter 9, this book) present and discuss a more recent model in which some of the initial distinctions made by Harackiewicz and Sansone (1991) have been elaborated and developed more systematically in the context of achievement goals (see also Harackiewicz, Barron, & Elliot, 1998). The nature of the relationships are addressed in greater detail, the effects on relevant mediating processes are further elaborated, and the role of individual differences in achievement motivation has been more fully incorporated into their model. Barron and Harackiewicz extend this work to college classrooms and discuss how the pursuit of multiple goals can optimize motivation and performance in education.

In contrast, Sansone and Smith (chapter 12, this book) elaborate and incorporate this goal-based approach to intrinsic motivation with the more typical goal-based approach to self-regulation of behavior (see also Sansone & Harackiewicz, 1996; Sansone, Weir, Harpster, & Morgan, 1992). They suggest that the positive phenomenological experience of interest and involvement may serve as the most proximal motivator for many goal-relevant behaviors, particularly when the goal is higher level and longer term (e.g., a career goal). As a consequence, they argue that self-regulation of behavior over time must include the regulation of motivation to reach goals as well as motivation to experience interest, and they argue that these two kinds of motivation may work together or in opposing ways to determine behavior.

---

[1] In Harackiewicz and Sansone (1991), we also noted and discussed the possibility that purpose goals and individual differences can moderate the paths shown in Figure 4.2. For example, the effect of an experimental manipulation on motivational processes (a C path in Figure 4.2) could vary as a function of individual differences. Similarly, the effect of motivational processes on intrinsic motivation (a D path in Figure 4.2) could vary as a function of purpose goals or personality. For the purpose of clarity in the current presentation, however, we have omitted these moderating paths from the figure (cf. Harackiewicz, Barron, & Elliot, 1998; Sansone & Smith, chapter 12, this book).

In sum, our current research on intrinsic motivation has been enriched by our earlier examination of performance-contingent reward processes. On the basis of this initial work, we recognized that individuals' engagement with an activity involves cognitive and affective processes over time and that as a consequence, the same external factors can have positive *and* negative effects at different points in the process and over time. From this earlier work driven by the question of rewards, therefore, we have developed increasingly more complex and richer models of the motivation process in particular domains (e.g., achievement domains) and as they fit within broader human functioning. As we develop more complex models of intrinsic motivation and self-regulation, our results sections get longer, our path models get messier, and we move farther from any findings that could be easily cataloged in current meta-analytic approaches. It is too early to know whether we are any closer to the truth about human motivation, but we certainly have a greater appreciation of the complexity of motivational dynamics and of the challenge of understanding intrinsic motivation.

Acknowledgments

We thank Kenn Barron, Robert Krauss, and John Tauer for helpful comments on earlier drafts of this chapter.

References

Amabile, T. M. (1979). Effects of external evaluation on artistic creativity. *Journal of Personality and Social Psychology, 37*, 221–223.

Amabile, T. M. (1983). *The social psychology of creativity.* New York: Springer-Verlag.

Bandura, A. (1986). *Social foundations of thought and action: A social cognitive theory.* Englewood Cliffs, NJ: Prentice-Hall.

Boggiano, A. K., & Ruble, D. N. (1979). Competence and the overjustification effect: A developmental study. *Journal of Personality and Social Psychology, 37*, 1462–1468.

Csikszentmihalyi, M. (1975). *Beyond boredom and anxiety.* San Francisco: Jossey-Bass.

Deci, E. L. (1971). Effects of externally mediated rewards on intrinsic motivation. *Journal of Personality and Social Psychology, 18*, 105–115.

Deci, E. L. (1972). Intrinsic motivation, extrinsic reinforcement, and inequity. *Journal of Personality and Social Psychology, 22*, 113–120.

Deci, E. L., Koestner, R., & Ryan, R. M. (1999a). A meta-analytic review of experiments examining the effects of extrinsic rewards on intrinsic motivation. *Psychological Bulletin, 125*, 627–668.

Deci, E. L., Koestner, R., & Ryan, R. M. (1999b). The undermining effect is a reality after all—extrinsic rewards, task interest, and self-determination: Reply to Eisenberger, Pierce, and Cameron (1999) and Lepper, Henderlong, and Gingras (1999). *Psychological Bulletin, 125*, 692–200.

Deci, E. L., & Ryan, R. M. (1985). *Intrinsic motivation and self-determination in human behavior.* New York: Plenum.

Dweck, C. S. (1986). Motivational processes affecting learning. *American Psychologist, 41*, 1040–1048.

Eisenberger, R., & Cameron, J. (1996). Detrimental effects of reward: Reality or myth? *American Psychologist, 51*, 1153–1166.

Eisenberger, R., Pierce, W. D., & Cameron, J. (1999). Effects of reward on intrinsic motivation—negative, neutral and positive: Comment on Deci, Koestner, and Ryan (1999). *Psychological Bulletin*, 125, 677–691.

Fisher, C. D. (1978). The effects of personal control, competence, and extrinsic reward systems on intrinsic motivation. *Organizational Behavior and Human Performance*, 21, 273–288.

Geen, R. G. (1980). Test anxiety and cue utilization. In I. G. Sarason (Ed.), *Test anxiety: Theory, research, and applications* (pp. 253–259). Hillsdale, NJ: Erlbaum.

Greenwald, A. G. (1982). Ego task analysis: An integration of research on ego involvement and self-awareness. In A. H. Hastorf & A. M. Isen (Eds.), *Cognitive social psychology* (pp. 109–147). New York: Elsevier North Holland.

Harackiewicz. J. M. (1979). The effects of reward contingency and performance feedback on intrinsic motivation. *Journal of Personality and Social Psychology*, 37, 1352–1363.

Harackiewicz. J. M. (1989). Performance evaluation and intrinsic motivation processes: The effects of achievement orientation and rewards. In D. M. Buss & N. Cantor (Eds.), *Personality psychology: Recent trends and emerging directions* (pp. 128–137). New York: Springer-Verlag.

Harackiewicz, J. M., Abrahams, S., & Wageman, R. (1987). Performance evaluation and intrinsic motivation: The effects of evaluative focus, rewards, and achievement orientation. *Journal of Personality and Social Psychology*, 53, 1015–1023.

Harackiewicz, J. M., Barron, K. E., & Elliot, A. J. (1998). Rethinking achievement goals: When are they adaptive for college students and why? *Educational Psychologist*, 33, 1–21.

Harackiewicz, J. M., & Manderlink, G. (1984). A process analysis of the effects of performance-contingent rewards on intrinsic motivation. *Journal of Experimental Social Psychology*, 20, 531–551.

Harackiewicz, J. M., Manderlink, G., & Sansone, C. (1984). Rewarding pinball wizardry: Effects of evaluation and cue value on intrinsic interest. *Journal of Personality and Social Psychology*, 47, 287–300.

Harackiewicz. J. M., Manderlink, G., & Sansone, C. (1992). Competence processes and achievement orientation: Implications for intrinsic motivation. In A. K. Boggiano & T. S. Pittman (Eds.), *Achievement and motivation: A social-developmental analysis* (pp. 115–137). New York: Cambridge University Press.

Harackiewicz, J. M., & Sansone, C. (1991). Goals and intrinsic motivation: You can get there from here. In M. L. Maehr, & P. R. Pintrich (Eds.), *Advances in motivation and achievement* (vol. 7, pp. 21–49). Greenwich, CT: JAI Press.

Harackiewicz, J. M., Sansone, C., & Manderlink, G. (1985). Competence, achievement orientation, and intrinsic motivation: A process analysis. *Journal of Personality and Social Psychology*, 48, 493–508.

Harter, S. (1981). A new self-report scale of intrinsic versus extrinsic orientation in the classroom: Motivational and informational components. *Developmental Psychology*, 17, 300–312.

Heckhausen, H. (1968). Achievement motive research: Current problems and some contributions towards a general theory of motivation. In W. J. Arnold (Ed.), *Nebraska Symposium on Motivation: Vol.* (pp. 103–174). Lincoln: University of Nebraska Press.

Hidi, S., & Harackiewicz, J. M. (2000). Motivating the academically unmotivated: A critical issue for the 21st century. *Review of Educational Research*.

Judd, C. M., & Kenny, D. A. (1981). Process analysis: Estimating mediation in treatment evaluations. *Evaluation Review*, 5, 602–619.

Karniol, R., & Ross, M. (1977). The effect of performance-relevant and performance-irrelevant rewards on children's intrinsic motivation. *Child Development*, 48, 482–487.

Kohn, A. (1996). By all available means: Cameron and Pierce's defense of extrinsic motivators. *Review of Educational Research*, 66, 1–4.

Lepper, M. R. (1981). Intrinsic and extrinsic motivation in children: Detrimental effects of superfluous social controls. In W. A. Collins (Ed.), *The Minnesota Symposiam on Child Psychology: Vol. 14. Aspects of the development of competence* (pp. 155–214). Hillsdale, NJ: Erlbaum.

Lepper, M. R., Greene, D., & Nisbett, R. E. (1973). Undermining children's intrinsic interest with extrinsic rewards: A test of the "overjustification" hypothesis. *Journal of Personality and Social Psychology, 28*, 129–137.

Lepper, M. R., Henderlong, J., & Gingras, I. (1999). Understanding the effects of extrinsic rewards on intrinsic motivation—uses and abuses of meta-analysis: Comment on Deci, Koestner, and Ryan (1999). *Psychological Bulletin, 125*, 669–676.

Lepper, M. R., Keavney, M., & Drake, M. (1996). Intrinsic motivation and extrinsic rewards: A commentary on Cameron and Pierce's meta-analysis. *Review of Educational Research, 66*, 5–32.

Locke, E. A., & Latham, G. P. (1990). *A theory of goal setting and task performance.* Englewood Cliffs, NJ: Prentice-Hall.

McClelland, D. C. (1961). *The achieving society.* Princeton, NJ: Van Nostrand.

Nicholls, J. G. (1984). Achievement motivation: Conceptions of ability, subjective experience, task choice, and performance. *Psychological Review, 91*, 328–346.

Ryan, R. M. (1982). Control and information in the intrapersonal sphere: An extension of cognitive evaluation theory. *Journal of Personality and Social Psychology, 43*, 450–461.

Ryan, R. M., & Deci, E. L. (1996). When paradigms clash: Comments on Cameron and Pierce's claim that rewards do not undermine intrinsic motivation. *Review of Educational Research, 66*, 33–38.

Sansone, C. (1986). A question of competence: The effects of competence and task feedback on intrinsic interest. *Journal of Personality and Social Psychology, 51*, 918–931.

Sansone, C. (1989). Competence feedback, task feedback, and intrinsic interest: An examination of process and context. *Journal of Experimental Social Psychology, 25*, 343–361.

Sansone, C., & Harackiewicz, J. M. (1996). "I don't feel like it": The function of interest in self-regulation. In Martin, L. L. & Tesser, A. (Eds.), *Striving and feeling: Interactions among goals, affect, and self-regulation* (pp. 203–228). Mahwah, NJ: Erlbaum.

Sansone, C., & Harackiewicz, J. M. (1998). "Reality" is complicated. Comment on Eisenberger & Cameron. *American Psychologist, 53*, 673–674.

Sansone, C., Sachau, D. A., & Weir, C. (1989). The effects of instruction on intrinsic interest: The importance of context. *Journal of Personality and Social Psychology, 57*, 819–829.

Sansone, C., Weir, C., Harpster, L., & Morgan, C. (1992). Once a boring task always a boring task? Interest as a self-regulatory mechanism. *Journal of Personality and Social Psychology, 63*, 379–390.

Sarason, I. G. (1980). Introduction to the study of test anxiety. In I. G. Sarason (Ed.), *Test anxiety: Theory, research, and applications* (pp. 3–14). Hillsdale, NJ: Erlbaum.

Tauer, J. M., & Harackiewicz, J. M. (1999). Winning isn't everything: Competition, achievement orientation, and intrinsic motivation. *Journal of Experimental Social Psychology, 35*, 209–238.

Trope, Y. (1975). Seeking information about one's own ability as a determinant of choice among tasks. *Journal of Personality and Social Psychology, 32*, 1004–1013.

White, R. W. (1959). Motivation reconsidered: The concept of competence. *Psychological Review, 66*, 297–333.

Wine, J. D. (1971). Test anxiety and direction of attention. *Psychological Bulletin, 76*, 92–104.

The Structure and Substance
of Intrinsic Motivation

JAMES Y. SHAH
Department of Psychology
University of Wisconsin

ARIE W. KRUGLANSKI
Department of Psychology
University of Maryland

Scientific research programs often pass through dialectic cycles. Typically, a cycle is initiated by a relatively simple hypothesis, but as the work progresses, various boundary conditions are identified and the picture gets increasingly murky. At a critical juncture a new cycle may commence, promoting a new simplification—stated, one hopes, at a higher level of generality and informed by what has been learned to that point. Intrinsic motivation research seems to have followed such a history, at least until now. Whereas back in the early 1970s researchers started with a few fundamental ideas, subsequent work has uncovered numerous qualifications and caveats. Perhaps this book provides an opportunity to start a new simplifying cycle. In Albert Einstein's immortal phrase, "things should be as simple as possible, but no simpler." The following "simplifying" notions are based on a goal-structure perspective that we have been recently developing.

As a preview of what is to come, we first discuss the language that has evolved for exploring the intrinsic-motivation phenomena and then go on to propose a theoretical perspective phrased in terms of this language.

THE LANGUAGE OF INTRINSIC MOTIVATION

The language issue arises because the discourse of the field thus far has meandered between two different languages: that of "rewards" and that of "goals." Undoubtedly, the rewards language has much to recommend it. It maintains continuity with the rich behaviorist tradition and the powerful notion of reinforcement. Besides, it feels comfortable to many potential consumers of our theories, such as parents, educators, and business managers.

However, the rewards language has its limitations. It essentially refers to external events outside the "black box." As such, it has obvious problems explaining the phenomenological experiences that accompany motivations, such as the perceptions, feelings, and actions of complex human beings. Indeed, one lesson of research in this area has been that no simple notions about reward will suffice and that our initial proposals need to be buttressed by an ever-expanding array of provisos. Already the early work by Deci, Lepper, and others distinguished between verbal and tangible rewards and between expected and unexpected rewards (Deci, 1975; Deci & Ryan, 1985; Lepper, Greene, & Nisbett, 1973). But soon it became apparent that we also needed to distinguish between salient and nonsalient rewards; among quality-contingent, completion-contingent, and performance-independent rewards; between multiple-versus single-trial rewards, and so on. (For reviews, see Deci & Ryan, 1985; Eisenberger & Cameron, 1996; Pittman & Heller, 1987; Tang & Hall, 1995.) It is doubtful that even this increasingly complex matrix of reward properties would suffice. People vary considerably in their personality characteristics and cultural backgrounds and may find themselves in a plethora of diverse situations. What may constitute a reward for one person in one situation may constitute a punishment for another person in another situation. In recognition of these difficulties with how rewards are interpreted, a growing number of researchers have substituted the language of goals for that of rewards. (See, for instance, Harackiewicz & Elliot, 1993; Ryan, Sheldon, Kasser, & Deci, 1996; Sansone & Harackiewicz, 1996.)

THE LANGUAGE OF GOALS

The big advantage of the goal language is that it refers to "internal" events or "mental representations," highly appealing in this "age of cognition" where the person is portrayed as the processor of symbolic information and the constructor of meaning. It is also compatible with the presumed flexibility of our cognitive system, affording a wide heterogeneity of possible goals that depend on culture, personality, and context. From this perspective, rewards, contingencies, and other external events represent concrete operations whose ultimate psychological effects entirely depend on the goals they serve to institute. Framing questions in the reward language (e.g., asking whether or what kind of rewards undermine or enhance intrinsic motivation), then, is inappropriate from this perspective because, strictly speaking, rewards are now assumed to have merely operational and highly contextualized significance rather than a general utility. In short, the question has become not what the rewards can do to you, but rather what you are willing to do for the rewards—that is, what goals do the reward operations set in place?

But the choice of language is only the beginning, for language is a mere tool for theory construction. And it is in regard to theory that another simplification may be possible. It relates to the structural and substantive senses of intrinsic motivation that are well worth distinguishing from each other.

The structural sense refers to the relation between the activity and its goal. In this vein, intrinsic motivation exists where the activity is perceived as its own end (cf Kruglanski, 1975). The substantive sense concerns the type of goal the activity is meant to attain; that is, it concerns the specific need fulfilled by the goal. Self-determination, competence, and mastery are examples of goals that have been typically regarded as fulfilling intrinsic needs (see Ryan et al., 1996), whereas goals pursued for tangible rewards or evaluative pressures have typically been regarded as extrinsic. However, as we explain later in greater detail, these structural and substantive senses of intrinsicality are conceptually independent; in many cases, they simply do not refer to the same thing.

Consider activities such as lying on the beach or smoking a cigar. These activities may be experienced as intrinsic in the sense that they are performed as ends in and of themselves. That is, the activity is phenomenologically inseparable from the goal. But such activities may not be "intrinsically" motivated in the substantive sense; that is, they may not necessarily be performed for reasons of self-determination, competence, or mastery.

Furthermore, goals "intrinsic" in the substantive sense could still be structurally "extrinsic" to some activities. That is, an activity could be experienced as a means to an intrinsic end because the activity is separable from the goal. A teenager, for instance, may lie on the beach as a means for asserting his or her autonomy over school requirements or the wishes of parents (i.e., the teenager may be extrinsically motivated by the goal of self-determination). In short, any activity may be intrinsically motivated in the structural sense if it constitutes its own end, but only a subset of activities, by definition, are also intrinsically motivated in the substantive sense (e.g., activities pursued for autonomy or for self-determination).

Possibly, our failure to draw this distinction between structure and substance has occurred because substantive intrinsicality assumes at least a minimal structural relation between goal and means. Indeed, a minimal structural relation may be required for substantive intrinsicality to emerge.

We may also have ignored the distinction because our *real* interest has been in educational or work-related activities (e.g., learning or problem solving), to which mastery and competence goals may well be intrinsic in both senses. Yet, we would argue that to better understand even these activities, it is best to treat structure and substance separately to clearly see what part of the variance in motivational phenomena each accounts for.

Yet the relation of goals to means does not occur in a self-regulatory vacuum. Whether goals are structurally intrinsic to an activity may depend not only on their direct relation to each other but also on their relation to other goals and means. Thus, before we proceed further, let us first discuss other facets of goal–means structure that indirectly effect the goal–means relation and thus relate to intrinsic motivation phenomena

A STRUCTURAL ANALYSIS OF GOALS AND MEANS

By *goal–means structure* we mean all those properties of a goal that concern how it relates to other goals, and to specific activities or behaviors. These structural properties can be considered independently of goal substance and therefore are applicable to any given goal and activity, regardless of its specific content. In defining these parameters, we start from the assumption that our goals and activities (or behaviors) are mentally represented as distinct knowledge structures (Kruglanski, 1989, 1996). Indeed, although activities are often identified in terms of the goals they are currently serving, these identifications are often quite malleable. (See, for instance, Higgins & Trope, 1990; Sansone, Weir, Harpster, & Morgan, 1992.) We therefore assume that although activities are typically associated with goals, they nevertheless can be represented separately (i.e., without explicit reference to any particular goal they serve). Furthermore, as knowledge structures, these representations should follow similar principles of activation, change, and organization that have been articulated in reference to all knowledge representations (e.g., Higgins, 1996).

In terms of the mental organization of goals and attainment behaviors, associative network models (e.g., Anderson & Bower, 1973; Srull, 1981) assume that knowledge constructs can be represented as interconnected "nodes" where activation of any one node will spread to others if an associative link has been formed. The strength of this associative link determines the amount and speed of spreading activation. Like other knowledge constructs, goals can vary in the number and strength of their connection to other representations. Yet because goals represent a specific type of knowledge construct, one that defines a future state to approach or avoid, they should come to be particularly associated with representations of those activities or behaviors that help bring about their attainment (i.e., attainment means).

For this reason, needs, goals, and attainment means are commonly thought to be cognitively organized hierarchically, with a general need being served by relatively few abstract goals, which in turn are served by a larger number of concrete activities, or means (Miller, Galanter, & Pribram, 1960; Powers, 1973, 1989).

With this organization in mind, consider the hypothetical goal network depicted in Figure 5.1. Here Goals 1 and 2 (e.g., doing well in school; getting a job) serve a specific general need (e.g., autonomy) and are themselves served by more concrete means (studying; reading the classifieds). Activation within this network can spread *downward* from higher-order goal to the lower-order means, especially to address the issue of *how* a goal should be completed. Activation can also spread *upward* from means to goal, especially to address *why* an activity should be engaged in.

The strength of the association between a given goal and means is defined as the likelihood that activation of the given goal will result in the activation of a given means, which increases the likelihood of it being used. We also assume that the association between a goal and a means is proportional to the degree to which the means has led to goal attainment on prior occasions.

We have recently tested the associative link of goals to attainment means through the use of a supraliminal sequential priming procedure

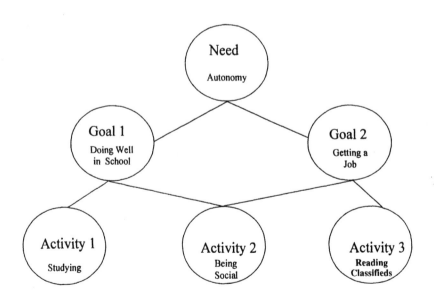

FIGURE 5.1
System of goals and means.

designed to measure cognitive associations between knowledge constructs more generally (Shah & Kruglanski, 2000a). Our technique requires participants to observe the presentation of a prime stimulus before responding to a target word, and it assumes that responses will be quicker when the prime is cognitively associated with the target. This follows from classic studies in cognitive psychology wherein responses to a target word (e.g., *nurse*) were faster if a semantically associated word (e.g., *doctor*) had preceded it rather than an unrelated word. (See, for instance, Meyer & Schvaneveldt, 1976.) In our study, a computer program asked participants to describe a number of different attributes that they desired to possess. We regarded these attributes as abstract goals to which our participants aspired. The participants were also asked to list one activity they could perform to attain each of the attributes. We regarded these as means to those particular goals. After participants completed the initial procedure, the computer prompted them to list all the activities they could think of that would help them possess each of the attribute goals. Finally, participants completed a reaction-time procedure in which they were asked to determine whether a target word was an attribute or activity or it was not. Before making each determination, participants first saw a prime word for 3 seconds. The attributes listed by the participant and the first attainment means listed for each attribute were randomly included in the presented set of prime and target words. The link between attributes and means could be assessed, then, by examining reaction times when the attribute was the prime for an activity that constituted its means versus an activity to which it was not related. We found that reactions to activity words were significantly faster when the prime stimulus was the corresponding attribute goal than when it was an unrelated attribute goal to which the activity did *not* constitute a means.

This finding is consistent with the notion that goals and means form significant cognitive associations. But might the strength of these associations vary for different goals and behaviors? If so, what are some of the factors that might affect such a relation? Certainly differences in goal content may affect this relation. Goals relating to autonomy or competence, for instance, may be inherently more or less linked to specific behaviors than are goals relating to more extrinsic needs, such as self-presentation. Similarly, some activities may be inherently less associated with an individual's important or "intrinsic" goals or, conversely, may be associated with numerous goals (and presumably with none very strongly). But the strength of associations between goals and means may differ even when the substantive nature of goals and activities remains constant. That is, the association of specific goals to specific behaviors may differ across different situations and for different individuals. In the following section, we consider some possible determinants of the strength of these associations.

Equifinality and the Association of Goals to Means

Psychologists have long assumed that most goals have the property of equifinality whereby they can be attained through a number of different routes (see McDougal, 1923; Heider, 1958; Lewin, 1935). For instance, the work of Steele and Lui (1983) and that of Tesser, Martin, and Cornell (1996) has suggested that various psychological phenomena, such as dissonance and self-affirmation, are in fact substitutable means for attaining or maintaining self-esteem. (See also Solomon, Greenberg, & Pyszczynski, 1991.) Consider another example: the many possible ways one might choose to get in shape. Certainly the manner in which we pursue this goal may vary across different individuals and different situations. One individual, for instance, may generally consider a single means for exercising (e.g., running), whereas another may weigh many different activity options (e.g., running, lifting weights, playing basketball). Moreover, the consideration of means may vary across different situations. For instance, one may choose to run in certain situations (e.g., when the weather is pleasant) and play basketball at other times (e.g., when it is raining or when the team is available).

As noted above, however, goals may vary not only in the number of different ways they can be attained but also in how strongly they invoke a particular activity (i.e., the strength of their association with each available means). Yet if one assumes that each means or activity is sufficient to attain the superordinate goal, the strength of the association between a goal and an activity should decrease as more alternative activities become available, holding other determinants of this association strength constant. We refer to this phenomenon as *means dissociation* because it suggests that a goal's association with a single means is weakened by the presence of other available means.

Indeed, in the study described earlier, the attribute–activity link was also found to be significantly negatively related to the average number of activities listed for possessing each attribute. Therefore, the more subsequent attainment means listed for each attribute, the weaker the association between the attribute and the first means listed.

In another study, Shah (1998) asked university students to write an attribute of the type of person it was their goal to be. Participants listed attributes such as *educated* or *moral* After listing the attribute, participants were randomly asked to list either one or two activities that they could perform in order to possess this attribute. After listing the activity or activities, participants rated how involved they were in doing the *first* activity they listed. Participants subsequently rated themselves as having less commitment to the first activity they listed when they were also asked to list another activity. One explanation for this finding would be that the momentary strength of the goals' association to either activity was lessened by the "presence" of the other. The structural nature of equifinality is represented in Figure 5.2.

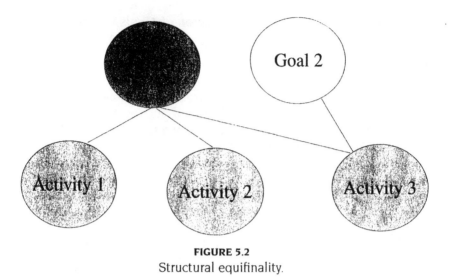

FIGURE 5.2
Structural equifinality.

Multifinality and the Association of Means to Goals

But just as goals can have more than one means of attainment, any one means may serve more than one goal. We refer to this property as *multifinality*. Like equifinality, this property can vary as a function of differences in goal contents and of one's past experiences with specific goals. The simple act of walking, for instance, can be viewed as a means of transportation in one context and a means of exercising in another. Alternatively, consider the significant psychological phenomenon of in-group bias. Although many researchers have viewed this bias as a means for attaining self-esteem, Shah, Kruglanski, and Thompson (1998) found that it may also serve as a means for attaining cognitive closure. That is, in addition to boosting one's self-esteem, a favorable appreciation of one's own group may uphold the shared social reality that is created by its members, which promotes cognitive closure by increasing one's general sense of certainty of one's understanding of the world. Figure 5.3 illustrates the structural nature of multifinality.

Just as with the association of a single goal to several activities, the number of associations between a single activity and several goals should be negatively related to the strength of any single goal–activity association. So if one strongly associates the act of jogging with the goal of getting in shape, one may be less likely to consider it as a means for getting to school. This notion of goal dissociation refers to the weakening of association between an activity and a given goal owing to its association with other goals. As an example from the intrinsic-motivation literature, consider the well-studied phenomenon that offering a reward for engaging in an interest-

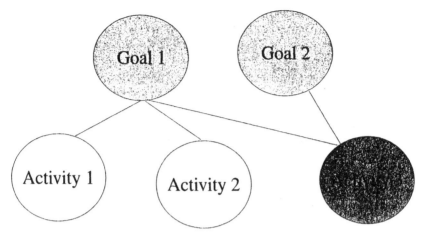

FIGURE 5.3
Structural multifinality.

ing activity can undermine subsequent motivation when the reward is removed. (For reviews, see Deci, 1975; Deci & Ryan, 1985; Kruglanski, Friedman, & Zeevi, 1971; Lepper et al., 1973.)

From our structural perspective, linking an activity with a tangible reward may create an association between the activity and an extrinsic goal (e.g., a tangible reward) to the detriment of any prior association of the activity to other intrinsic goals, such as mastery or competence. When the tangible reward is ultimately withdrawn, the tendency to engage in the activity is reduced because the activity's original association with a given goal has been diminished. Given that such reward has come to be seen as the activity's goal, its dissociation from the activity leaves it goal-less and hence less likely to be performed. Of course, it may not be as easy to dissolve the contingency between an activity and an intrinsic goal as it is to dissolve the contingency between an activity and an extrinsic goal. Indeed, a straightforward implication of our structural analysis is that intrinsic goals are inherently more difficult to dissociate from activities. But note that this is a strictly structural implication, unrelated to goal substance. It is not restricted, in other words, to the removal of tangible goal objects. For instance, two substantively intrinsic goals may nevertheless differ in their structural association to an activity. If a rebellious teenager's cigarette smoking was performed for a goal of autonomy, which is structurally extrinsic in this case, it should be easier to dissolve this contingency (e.g., by providing information that her parents actually approve of smoking) than to dissolve the contingency between smoking and goals of experiencing the tobacco flavor or experiencing relaxation, both of which would be structurally intrinsic.

Here is one final example: Deci, Koestner, & Ryan (1999) concluded from their meta-analysis that although self-reported interest in an activity may be undermined by the use of performance-independent rewards, it may not be significantly hindered by the use of performance-contingent rewards (see also Eisenberger & Cameron, 1996; Ryan & Deci, 1996). This distinction could arise because performance-contingent rewards, in addition to introducing an extrinsic reward goal, reinforce mastery and competence goals that are intrinsic and hence difficult to dissociate from those specific activities. By contrast, performance-independent rewards make salient extrinsic, readily dissociable goals, the removal of which renders the activity unlikely to be performed. (See also chapter 9 of this volume.)

The work of Higgins, Lee, Kwon, and Trope (1995) suggests, further, that this goal dissociation is not limited to situations involving the linkage of an activity with a new extrinsic goal. Their results demonstrated that combining activities such as coloring and reading may undermine children's later interest in both traditionally "intrinsic" activities. Goal dissociation, then, may occur even when both the old and the new goals are intrinsic, suggesting that this phenomenon may have as much or more to do with the strength of the association between goals and means than with differences in specific goal contents. (See also Higgins & Trope, 1990.)

A STRUCTURAL PERSPECTIVE
ON INTRINSIC MOTIVATION

On the basis of the model of goal structure outlined above, we assume that a major structural antecedent of intrinsic motivation is the degree of association between an activity and goal attainment. This intrinsic "meshing" of activity to goal is optimized when (1) every time the activity is engaged in the goal is pursued, (2) the activity is not associated with attainment of any other goal, and (3) no other activity is associated with attainment of that particular goal. This structural notion of intrinsicality is highlighted in Figure 5.4.

This structural perspective suggests that the goal–activity association can be considered from either a top-down (from goal to activity) or a bottom-up (from activity to goal) standpoint. In fact, the degree to which goals strongly or exclusively bring to mind particular activities may be quite different from the degree to which activities strongly or exclusively bring to mind a goal.

Yet does such a perspective shed any new light on the phenomena traditionally associated with the concept of intrinsic motivation? We now turn to the implications that this perspective may have for how goals and activities are experienced and pursued.

(a) Intrinsic   (b) Extrinsic   (c) Extrinsic
                       Goal Dissociated   Means Dissociated

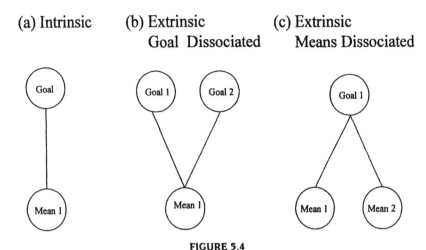

FIGURE 5.4

"Intrinsic" and "extrinsic" associations: (a) intrinsic; (b) extrinsic goal dissociated; (c) extrinsic means dissociated.

Goal Commitment

Clearly, one aspect of intrinsic motivation is commitment. From our structural perspective, commitment can be viewed at two different levels of abstraction: commitment to the goals and commitment to activities associated with goal attainment. In one sense, commitment to a goal represents the purest structural form of intrinsic motivation by defining an activity in terms of its goal (e.g., defining *studying* solely in terms of self-improvement brands it as intrinsically motivated in the structural sense). As suggested earlier, the association of goals to means may be a particularly important determinant of goal commitment. Indeed, the work of Gollwitzer and Brandstatter (1997) has shown that accessibility of attainment means is a crucial determinant of whether one follows through with goal attainment.

To test this notion more precisely, we (Shah & Kruglanski, 2000b) had participants interact with a computer program, very similar to the one described earlier, that asked them to perform a lexical decision task by determining whether a presented letter string was a word after first seeing a prime word. Randomly distributed among the set of prime and target words, participants were presented with common attribute goals—that is, goals most people in American culture may subscribe to (e.g., being educated, caring, strong, and outgoing) and activities that represented attainment means for these attributes (e.g., study, volunteer, exercise, and socialize). All possible combinations of activities and attributes as primes and targets were presented.

After completing the word-recognition task, individuals rated the degree to which possessing each attribute represented one of their goals. This constituted our measure of goal commitment. The goal–means association was calculated by summing the times to identify an activity as a word or not when the prime word was an attribute that, a priori, had been considered attainable through this activity. The goal–nonmeans association was calculated by summing the times to identify an activity as a word or not when the prime word was an attribute that had not been considered related to the activity.

A regression analysis of these variables indicated that overall goal commitment was positively and significantly related to the strength of the goal–means association but not to the goal–nonmeans association. A second study tested this same idea using participants' own idiosyncratic goals and means, rather than the normative set of goals and means used in our previous study. In most other respects, however, the procedure was similar to that of the first study and a regression analysis of the same set of variables again indicated that overall goal commitment was positively related to the strength of the goal–means connection. The results of these two studies are summarized in Table 5.1.

A final study attempted to manipulate the association between goals and means and examined the effect this had on goal commitment and another frequently studies aspect of intrinsic motivation, goal enjoyment. Participants were randomly assigned to one of two experimental conditions. All were asked to provide two attributes, described in one word, that it was their goal to possess. For each attribute, they were also asked to list two activities that they viewed as means for attaining the attribute. After listing these attributes and activities, participants completed a priming task on the computer similar to the one described above, except this time, the prime word was presented subliminally and backward-masked. All participants completed a common set of trials presented in a random order. Participants in the *goal–means* group completed an additional set of trials that presented their attribute goals as the primes and their activity means as the targets. The repeated presentation of these trials was thought to increase the association between attribute goals and activity means. Participants in the *con-*

TABLE 5.1
Partial Correlation of Goal Associations with Goal Commitment
for Normative Goals and Personal Goals

Type of association	Goal commitment	
	Normative goals (n = 47)	Personal goals (n = 49)
Goal to nonmeans	.12	−.21
Goal to means	.33[a]	.35[a]

[a] $p < .05$.

trol–means group completed an additional set of trials in which the control word was the prime and the target word was one of the activity means. After completing the total set of trials (common and unique), all participants then completed a questionnaire that asked them to indicate how committed they were right then to possessing each of the attribute goals they had just listed and how much they enjoyed pursuing these goals. All ratings were provided on a 7-point scale ranging from 1 (not at all) to 7 (extremely). Consistent with the last study, attribute-goal commitment ratings were significantly higher for participants in the goal–means group than for those in the control–means group. In addition, participants in the former group also rated their pursuit of this goal as significantly more enjoyable than did participants in the control–means group. Apparently, goal commitment and enjoyment may depend not only on substantive qualities of the goal itself but also on the strength of its implicit relation to attainment activities. A strong goal–means association increases both one's commitment to goal attainment and the enjoyment one takes in goal pursuit. Furthermore, the use of subliminal priming in this study suggests that strong goal–means association is not dependent on individuals' making an explicit conscious inference about the link between goals and means.

Activity Engagement

Although the top-down association of goals to activities may influence goal commitment, the strength of the bottom-up association of an activity to a goal should also affect the activity's perceived intrinsicality, defined as the attribution that one is performing the activity for its own sake or as an end in itself (see Deci, 1975; Deci & Ryan, 1985; Kruglanski, 1975). The greater the association between an activity and a goal, the more likely engagement in the activity will be seen as the end in itself—that is, the more likely that activity engagement will be experienced as goal fulfillment. This should be especially likely when the activity is not associated with other goals and the goal has no other means of attainment, because, as noted earlier, the more singular the association between an activity and a goal, the stronger should be this connection. In an initial examination of this idea, we explored how the strength of association between means and goals may influence means commitment (Shah & Kruglanski, 2000b). The experimental paradigm for this study was similar to ones described earlier in that we again used a priming procedure to measure the association between means and goals. In this case, however, we sought to examine how the strength of the means–goal association (defined as how strongly an activity identified as a means brings to mind the goal it serves) relates to one's commitment to engaging in the activity in question. We compared this association to the degree to which the means brought to mind unrelated goals (i.e., the means–nongoal association). Consistent with our predictions, we found that the strength of the means–goal association was positively related to such indices of intrinsic motivation as the self-reported frequency in which one engages in the activities and the importance one places in doing so. The strength of individuals' means–nongoal associations, however, was not related to these indices. These findings are summarized in Table 5.2.

The Transfer of Goal Qualities to Activities

According to our model, the degree of perceived association between activity and goal attainment is stronger for intrinsically than for extrinsically moti-vated activities. This should have implications not only for one's overall com-mitment to goals and activities but also for the degree to which the qualities of one's specific goal pursuit are "transferred" to one's engagement with the activity—that is, the degree to which one's general experiences with engag-ing in the activity comes to resemble one's general experiences with pursu-ing the associated goal. Three such transferable qualities are examined here: commitment; affective experiences, and strategic inclinations.

Commitment Transfer

One goal quality that may be readily transferred to an associated activity is goal commitment. Increasing perceived goal value, for instance, should increase more the perceived value of intrinsically than of extrinsically moti-vated activities. Because, by definition, intrinsically motivated activities are more strongly associated with the goals they serve than are extrinsically motivated activities, the transfer of perceived value from goals to activities should be greater for intrinsically versus extrinsically motivated activities.

Thus, the association between an activity and goal attainment is assumed to lend the activity positive value in proportion to goal magnitude and the degree of association. Similarly, association between an activity and attainment failure will lend it negative value, again proportionately to goal magnitude and degree of association. Various statements by intrinsic-moti-vation theorists implicitly support these notions in reference to specific

TABLE 5.2
Partial Correlation of Means Associations with Means
Importance and Means Use

	Means ratings (n = 59)	
Type of association	Importance	Frequency of use
Means to nongoals	−.02	−.08
Means to goals	.27[a]	.29[a]

[a] $p < .05$.

goals. For instance, Deci and Ryan (1985) argued that an activity that promotes self-determination or competence will be liked and engaged in, whereas an activity that undermines these goals will be disliked. Harackiewicz and Sansone (1991) further implied that this should be proportionate to goal magnitude. Specifically, they proposed that tangible rewards may often constitute symbolic cues to goal importance. Such cues increase interest in an activity associated with goal attainment but decrease interest in activity associated with nonattainment.

Indeed, in the study described previously, Shah and Kruglanski (2000b) found that the relation of goal importance to means commitment was moderated by the strength of the means–goal association strength. The stronger the relation between means and goal, the more likely it was that commitment to the goal transferred to a commitment to the associated activity. Therefore, one's commitment to becoming educated, for example, will more likely affect one's commitment to studying when this activity is strongly associated with pursuing one's education goal. Likewise, one's education goal may also determine one's commitment to traveling, but only to the degree that traveling has become associated with education.

Affective Transfer

A related phenomenon that to our knowledge has not been specifically examined is what we have labeled *affective transfer*, whereby intrinsically motivated activities acquire the particular affective flavor of their specific associated goals. Recall that structurally speaking, intrinsically motivated activities constitute their own ends. Their performance, in other words, represents goal attainment, which typically is accompanied by specific affect. Such affective transfer should be less apparent with extrinsically motivated activities that are less isomorphic with goal attainment. If one is painting for intrinsic reasons, for instance, one's emotional reaction to finishing a work would depend solely on how one feels about the result itself rather than encompassing other "extrinsic" considerations such as how much the painting is worth.

The association between goals and means may also influence how an activity is experienced in a number of different ways. The strength of the association between the means and its goal increases the overall emotional positivity of succeeding at the activity and negativity of failing (i.e., how good or bad one feels) if the goal to which it is associated is emotionally significant. The goal will lend the activity positive or negative valence in proportion to the goal's emotional importance and the degree to which the activity is associated with goal attainment or failure. Although the association between goal and means may affect more than the general emotional positivity or negativity of engaging in the means, it may also affect the *type* or *quality* of experienced affect while pursuing the given means. Ryan, Sheldon, Emmons,

& Deci (1996) stressed that "all goals were not created equal," and goals certainly may differ in the regulatory needs they fulfill. In addition to addressing needs for competence and autonomy and control, goals can differ with respect to their focus on promotion and nurturance versus prevention and security (see Higgins, 1997) or on performance versus mastery (Legget & Dweck, 1988). The pursuit of these various types of goals has been shown to have differing emotional consequences, and the distinct types of affect associated with goal pursuit should transfer to activities associated with these diverse goals. Therefore, like goals, *all motivated activities are not created equal*, and a major way in which they are unequal is in terms of their affective qualities, borrowed directly from their associated goals. That is, the specific emotional experiences associated with goal attainment or attainment failure may be transferred to the means that serve these goals.

One example of this "affective transfer" comes from work on the framing of a task goal to relate to different regulatory concerns. Higgins, Shah, and Friedman (1997) demonstrated that the same task—solving anagrams—can relate to different emotional experiences when associated with a promotion goal versus a prevention goal. A memory task was framed to relate to either a goal of promotion or a goal of prevention. In the promotion condition, participants were told that they would receive a payment of $5 for their participation but that they could possibly gain an additional $1. They would receive the extra $1 if their performance exceeded or equaled that of the 70th percentile of students who had participated in the study. In the prevention condition, participants were told that they would receive a payment of $6 for their participation but that they could possibly lose $1. They would not lose the $1 if their performance exceeded or equaled that of the 70th percentile of students who had participated in the study. Participants' levels of happiness, dejection, quiescence, and agitation were measured before participants completed the memory task and after completing the task and randomly receiving either success or failure feedback.

As shown in Table 5.3, success or failure at the anagram task led to more happiness or dejection, respectively, when it was associated with a promotion goal but to more quiescence or agitation, respectively, when the task was associated with a prevention goal. How an activity was experienced, then, was a function of the regulatory qualities of the goal with which it was associated. The same activity (e.g., painting) may result in different emotional experiences depending on the goal with which it is associated in different situations or different individuals. Thus, in situations in which a child associates painting with mastery, he or she may feel quite differently about his or her work and its production than in situations in which he or she is being extrinsically rewarded for the paintings.

So far, we have examined how the strength or existence of associations between activities and goals may have important implications for issues of commitment and subjective experience. A final aspect of transfer involves

TABLE 5.3
Feedback-Consistent Emotional Change as a Function of Regulatory Focus
Framing and Emotion Dimension

Regulatory focus framing	Emotional dimension[a]	
	Cheerfulness–dejection	Quiescence–agitation
Promotion	1.07	−.52
Prevention	.78	.68

[a] The higher the number, the more consistent the change.

the manner in which one pursues a goal (i.e., the tactics one uses). These attainment strategies may also be transferred to associated activities, influencing the manner in which they are engaged. As we discuss in the next section, this notion of strategic transfer might lend new insights to the current debate on how intrinsic motivation relates to creativity.

Strategic Transfer: Implications for Creativity

Classic studies on creativity by Amabile and others (see Amabile, 1979, 1983) have suggested that activities motivated by "intrinsic" concerns are pursued more creatively and that the introduction of an external reward for this pursuit hinders creativity by diverting attention from the task itself and the creative ways it could be accomplished. This view has been challenged by Eisenberger and Cameron (1996), who suggested that rather than hinder creativity, rewards can actually increase creative output in many situations (but see Deci et al., in press; Hennessey & Amabile, 1998; Lepper, 1998; Sansone & Harackiewicz, 1998). Although it is as yet untested, our structural perspective on intrinsic motivation may offer fresh insights into these divergent standpoints.

To explain, we must first return to how goal contents relates to structure. As has already been noted, goals may differ in the regulatory purpose they serve and the emotional experiences that accompany their pursuit, and these differences may affect how associated activities are experienced and the extent to which they are pursued through the process of transfer. But goals may differ in other ways as well, such as the attainment strategies associated with their pursuit. For instance, the goals of mastery and competence for problem-solving activities may quite possibly be typically associated with deliberate and creative exploration, whereas tangible material goals of consumerism may be intimately tied to more routine actions that reflect a general strategy to do only what is necessary to gain reward.

These attainment strategies may be transferred from goal to activity in the same manner as the goal's emotional consequences. The amount of strategic transfer would again depend on the strength of the association between goal and activity. Consider, as one example of how strategic inclinations may transfer from goals to means, the distinction between promotion and prevention (Higgins, 1997). The different types of goals that address these regulatory concerns have been shown to relate to distinct attainment strategies and behaviors (see Crowe & Higgins, 1997; Shah, Higgins, & Friedman, 1998). Goals concerning promotion or nurturance tend to be associated with approach-related behaviors, whereas goals concerning prevention or security become associated with avoidance-related actions. In one study, Higgins, Roney, Crowe, and Hymes (1994) found that participants who viewed friendship in promotion terms used more approach strategies (e.g., being supportive), whereas participants who viewed friendship in prevention terms used more avoidance strategies in pursuing friendship (e.g., do not lose contact). If strategies related to the attainment of specific goals do transfer to associated activities in direct proportion to the degree of goal–activity association, promotion and prevention strategies should similarly transfer and affect how related activities will be performed.

A similar type of strategic transfer could occur between activities and substantively intrinsic or extrinsic goals. Thus, although under certain circumstances creativity could be intensified by linking it to highly significant material (i.e., extrinsic) rewards, as Eisenberger and Cameron (1996) suggested, it might be more efficient to enhance the use of creative strategies by appealing to nonmaterial goals, such as competence or mastery, with which such strategies are more intimately associated (see also Shah & Kruglanski, 2000c). As an illustration, consider how you might get a child to paint more creatively. It might be more efficient to enhance creative painting by showing how the activity may lead to a sense of autonomy or mastery, because such goals are often pursued creatively and thus may induce a similar quality in one's paintings. Linking painting to material reward, on the other hand, may be less effective at inducing creativity because such extrinsic goals are often pursued rather inflexibly.

Enhancing Intrinsic Motivation

Finally, a focus on structure may yield significant approaches to enhancing intrinsic motivation and its consequences. Perhaps the most common method for manipulating the intrinsicality of an activity has been to add or highlight task elements that relate it to the fulfillment of the specific types of goals thought to fulfill intrinsic needs. Malone and Lepper (1987), for instance, identified four such task elements: challenge, control, curiosity, and fantasy (see also chapter 10 of this book). Our structural approach would suggest that increasing an activity's unique association to *any* important goal may have beneficial effects for intrinsic motivation by allowing the activity to cognitively mesh with the goal. Additionally, this meshing may be aided by lessening the association of an activity to other "extrinsic" goals, and lessening the focal goal's association to other activities may also strengthen intrinsic motivation for the activity. As a concrete example, take the activity of running. One may enhance intrinsic motivation for this activity by strengthening its association to an important goal (e.g., getting in shape). This, in turn, may be aided by (1) lessening this goal's association to other activities (e.g., playing tennis) and (2) lessening the activity's association to other goals (e.g., pleasing one's romantic partner). Again, this process of enhancing the association of activities to goals may be inherently easier or harder, depending on the contents of the goal.

Such an enhancement in intrinsic motivation toward an activity may have a number of advantages: It may enhance both activity commitment and enjoyment when these qualities are transferred from the goal, and it may render the activity less vulnerable to association with other extrinsic goals. In many ways this approach is similar to those that attempt to enhance task enjoyment by "redefining" a boring activity into something more appealing (see Higgins & Trope, 1990; Sansone et al., 1992). Our model would suggest that the process of redefining an activity's identification involves linking it to a different desirable goal, optimally one that is substantively intrinsic. It further suggests that the ease at which this redefinition occurs may depend on how strongly it is redefined (i.e., linked to a new goal). This, in turn, may depend on whether the activity has other "definitions" and on whether its new definition is shared with other activities.

CONCLUSION

Finally, it should be noted that our focus on the "cognitive" aspects of intrinsic motivation is not as radical as might initially be supposed. Indeed, although the dominant perspective on distinguishing intrinsic and extrinsic motivation has been in terms of relating these orientations to different needs, Higgins and Trope (1990) noted that intrinsic-motivation researchers have also explored how differences in the *inferences* made about goals can affect whether they are seen as intrinsic or extrinsic. Boggiano and Main (1986), for instance, demonstrated that the intrinsicality of two activities can be changed by manipulating whether completion of one will allow them to do the other. If an "If you do X, then you will get Y" contingency is set up, participants end up preferring Y over X, presumably because they come to see X as a means to attaining Y. In this case, inferences about which activity serves which seems to have influenced the intrinsicality of both, independent of differences in contents (see also Lepper, Sagotsky, Dafoe, & Greene, 1982). Sansone and Harackiewicz (1996) proposed that task interest and commitment results from the *relation* of two types of goals associated with a task or activity: specific *target goals*, which are the task requirements or the guidelines for how to do the activity, and more abstract *purpose goals*, defined as the reasons for performing the task and perhaps other tasks as well. According to this model, it is not the content of the purpose goals that is of primary importance but their match with the task requirements. When specific task requirements (target goals) relate to abstract purpose goals, one is more committed and interested than when the requirements and goals do not align. Their emphasis on the perceived relation of general-purpose goals to concrete target goals and its implications for self-regulation and subjective experience nicely anticipates our present focus on the structure and interrelation of goals and means and the importance of considering goals at varying levels of abstraction.

Indeed, Like Sansone and Harackiewicz, we have examined intrinsic motivation by considering goals at varying levels of abstraction. We have considered both participants' pursuit of situationally specific task goals, such as solving anagrams, as well as their more generalized pursuits that individuals "carry with them" from situation to situation. Although the former task goals represent a traditional focus of the field, the latter "self-guides" have been shown to have significant long-term implications for subjective experience and our day-to-day behavior (Cantor & Langston, 1989; Emmons, 1989; Higgins, 1997; Markus & Ruvulo, 1989). Moreover, we assume that the structural principles outlined here apply to all goals and means, regardless of their particular contents or abstraction.

By distinguishing the structural from the substantive, then, our perspective may help to partition the variance in intrinsic motivation phenomena and suggest new avenues of research involving their intricate interrelation. Although we have emphasized the importance of considering the structural relation of activities to goals generally, our perspective nevertheless incorporates previous findings that emphasize the significance of goal substance by suggesting that the contents of goals may influence their association to specific activities and behaviors. In doing so, it may also simplify our thinking about intrinsic motivation phenomena by offering a unifying language for both its "hot" and "cold" characteristics. Recalling Einstein, we believe such a simplification is not beyond what is possible.

References

Amabile, T. M. (1979). Effects of external evaluation on artistic creativity. *Journal of Personality and Social Psychology*, 37, 221–233.
Amabile, T. M. (1983). *The social psychology of creativity*. New York: Springer-Verlag.
Anderson, J. R., & Bower, G. H. (1973). *Human associative memory*. Washington, DC: V. H. Winston.
Boggiano, A. K., & Main, D. S. (1986). Enhancing children's interest in activities used as rewards: The bonus effect. *Journal of Personality and Social Psychology*, 51, 1116–1126.
Cantor, N., & Langston, C. A. (1989). Ups and downs of life tasks in a life transition. In L. A. Pervin (Ed.), *Goal concepts in personality and social psychology* (pp. 127–168). Hillsdale, NJ: Erlbaum.

Crowe, E., & Higgins, E. T. (1997). Regulatory focus and strategic inclinations: Promotion and prevention in decision-making. *Organizational Behavior and Human Decision Processes, 69,* 117–132.

Deci, E. L. (1975). *Intrinsic motivation.* New York: Plenum.

Deci, E. L., Koestner, R., Ryan, R. M. (1999). A meta analytic review of experiments examining the effects of extrinsic reward on intrinsic motivation. *Psychological Bulletin.* 125, 627–662.

Deci, E. L., & Ryan, R. M. (1985). *Intrinsic motivation and self-determination in human behavior.* New York: Plenum Press.

Eisenberger R., & Cameron, J. (1996). Detrimental effects of reward: Reality or myth? *American Psychologist*, 51, 1153–1166.

Emmons, R. A. (1989). The personal striving approach to personality. In L. A. Pervin (Ed.), *Goal concepts in personality and social psychology* (pp. 87–126). Hillsdale, NJ: Erlbaum.

Emmons, R. A., & King, L. A. (1989). Personal striving complexity and affective reactivity. *Journal of Personality and Social Psychology*, 56, 478–484.

Fein, S., & Spencer, S. J. (1997). Prejudice as self-image maintenance: Affirming the self through derogating others. *Journal of Personality and Social Psychology*, 73, 31–44.

Gollwitzer, P. M., & Brandstatter, V. (1997). Implementation intentions and effective goal pursuit. *Journal of Personality and Social Psychology*, 73, 171–183.

Harackiewicz, J. M., & Elliot, A. J. (1993). Achievement goals and intrinsic motivation. *Journal of Personality and Social Psychology*, 65, 904–915.

Harackiewicz, J. M., Manderlink, G., & Sansone, C. (1984). Rewarding pinabll wizardry: Effects of evaluation and cue value on intrinsic interest. *Journal of Personality and Social Psychology*, 47, 287–300.

Harackiewicz, J. M., & Sansone, C. (1991). Goals and intrinsic motivation: You can't get there from here. In M. L. Maehr & P. R. Pintrich (Eds.), *Advances in motivation and achievement: Goals and self-regulatory processes* (vol. 7, pp. 21–49). Greenwich, CT: JAI Press.

Heider, F. (1958). *The psychology of interpersonal relations.* New York: Wiley.

Hennessey, B. A., & Amabile, T. M. (1998). Reward, intrinsic motivation, and creativity. *American Psychologist*, 53, 674–675.

Higgins, E. T. (1996). Knowledge activation: accessibility, applicability, and salience. In E. T. Higgins & A. W. Kruglanski (Eds.), *Social psychology: Handbook of basic principles.* New York: Guilford Press.

Higgins, E. T. (1997). Beyond pleasure and pain. *American Psychologist*, 52, 1280–1300.

Higgins, E. T., Lee, J., Kwon, J., & Trope, Y. (1995). When combining intrinsic motivations undermines interest: A test of activity engagement theory. *Journal of Personality and Social Psychology,* 68, 749–767.

Higgins, E. T., Roney, C., Crowe, E., & Hymes, C. (1994). Ideal versus ought predilections for approach and aviodance: Distinct self regulatory systems. *Journal of Personality and Social Psychology, 66,* 276–286.

Higgins, E. T., Shah, J. Y., & Friedman, R. (1997). Emotional responses to goal attainment: Strength of regulatory focus as moderator. *Journal of Personality and Social Psychology,* 72, 515–525.

Higgins, E. T., & Trope, Y. (1990). Activity engagement theory: Implications of multiply identifiable input for intrinsic motivation. In E. T. Higgins & R. M. Sorrentino (Eds.), *Handbook of motivation and cognition: Foundations of social behavior* (Vol. 2, pp. 229–264). New York: Guilford Press.

Kruglanski, A. W. (1975). The endogenous–exogenous partition in attribution theory. *Psychological Review,* 82, 387–406.

Kruglanski, A. W. (1989). *Lay epistemics and human knowledge: Cognitive and motivational bases.* New York: Plenum.

Kruglanski, A. W. (1996). Goals as knowledge structures. In P. M. Gollwitzer & J. A. Bargh (Eds.), *The psychology of action: Linking cognition and motivation to behavior* (pp. 599–619). New York: Guilford Press.

Kruglanski, A. W., Friedman, I., & Zeevi, G. (1971). The effects of extrinsic incentive on some qualitative aspects of task performance. *Journal of Personality and Social Psychology*, 39, 606–617.

Legget, E. L., & Dweck C. S. (1988). A social-cognitive approach to motivation and personality. *Psychological Review*, 95, 256–273.

Lepper, M. R., Greene, D., & Nisbett, R. E. (1973). Undermining children's intrinsic interest with extrinsic reward: A test of the overjustification hypothesis. *Journal of Personality and Social Psychology*, 28, 129–137.

Lepper, M. R. (1998). A whole much less than the sum of its parts. *American Psychologist*, 53, 675–676.

Lepper, M. R., Sagotsky, G., Dafoe, J. L., & Greene, D. (1982). Consequences of superfluous social constraints: Effects on young children's social inferences and subsequent intrinsic interest. *Journal of Personality and Social Psychology*, 42, 51–65.

Lewin, K. (1935). *A dynamic theory of personality: Selected papers* (D. E. Adams & K. E. Zener, Trans.). New York: McGraw-Hill.

Malone, T. W., & Lepper (1987). Making learning fun: A taxonomy of intrinsic motivations for learning. In R. E. Snow & M. J. Farr (Eds.), *Aptitude learning and instruction: III. Conative and affective processes analysis* (pp. 255–296). Hillsdale, NJ: Erlbaum.

Markus, H., and Ruvolo, A. (1989). Possible selves: Personalized representations of goals. In L. A. Pervin (Ed.), *Goal concepts in personality and social psychology* (pp. 211–241). Hillsdale, NJ: Erlbaum.

McDougal, W. (1923). *Outline of psychology*. New York: Scribners.

Meyer, D. E., & Schvaneveldt, R. (1976). Meaning, memory structure, and mental processes. *Science*, 192, 27–33.

Miller, G. A., Galanter, E., & Pribram, K. H. (1960). *Plans and the structure of behavior*. New York: Holt.

Niedenthal, P. M., Setterlund, M. B., & Wherry, M. B. (1992). Possible self-complexity and affective reactions to goal-relevant evaluation. *Journal of Personality and Social Psychology*, 63, 5–16.

Pittman, T. S., & Heller, J. F. (1987). Social motivation. *Annual Review of Psychology*, 38, 461–489.

Powers, W. T. (1973). *Behavior: The control of perception*. Chicago: Aldine.

Powers, W. T. (1989). *Living control systems*. Gravel Switch, KY: Control Systems Group.

Ryan, R. M., & Deci, E. L. (1996). When paradigms clash: Comments on Cameron and Pierce's claim that rewards to not undermine intrinsic motivation. *Review of Educational Research*, 66, 33–38.

Ryan, R. M., Sheldon, K. M., Kasser, T., & Deci, E. L. (1996). All goals are not created equal. In P. M. Gollwitzer & J. A. Bargh (Eds.), *The psychology of action: Linking cognition and motivation to behavior* (pp. 7–26). New York: Guilford Press.

Sansone, C., & Harackiewicz, J. (1996). "I don't feel like it": The function of interest in self-regulation. In L. L. Martin & A. Tesser (Eds.), *Striving and feeling: Interactions among goals, affect, and self-regulation* (pp. 11–54). New Jersey: Erlbaum.

Sansone, C., & Harackiewicz, J. M. (1998). "Reality" is complicated. *American Psychologist*, 53, 673–674.

Sansone, C., Weir, C., Harpster, L., & Morgan, C. (1992). Once a boring task always a boring task? Interest as a self-regulatory mechanism. *Journal of Personality and Social Psychology*, 63, 379–390.

Shah, J. Y. (1998). *A study of activity commitment*. Unpublished research data.

Shah, J. Y., Higgins, E. T., & Friedman, R. (1998). Performance incentives and means: How regulatory focus influences goal attainment. *Journal of Personality and Social Psychology*, 74, 285–293.

Shah, J. Y., & Kruglanski, A. W. (2000a). *"Goal pull": How intergoal associations affect goal pursuit*. Manuscript under review.

Shah, J. Y., & Kruglanski, A. W. (2000b). *Goal–means associations and commitment*. Manuscript in preparation.

Shah, J. Y., & Kruglanski, A. W. (2000c). *Regulatory focus and goal structure*. Manuscript in preparation.

Shah, J. Y., Kruglanski, A. W., & Thompson, E. P. (1998). Membership has its (epistemic) rewards: Need for closure effects on ingroup favoritism. *Journal of Personality and Social Psychology, 75*, 383–393.

Somon, S., Greenberg, J., & Pyszczynski, T. (1991). Terror management theory of self-esteem. In C. R. Snyder & O. R. Forsyth (Eds.), *Handbook of social and clinical psychology: the health perspective* (pp. 21–40). New York: Pergamon Press.

Srull, T. K. (1981). Person memory: Some tests of the associative storage and retrieval models. *Journal of Experimental Psychology: Human Learning and Memory, 7*, 440–462.

Steele, C. M., & Liu, T. J. (1983). Dissonance processes as self-affirmation. *Journal of Personality and Social Psychology, 45*, 5–19.

Tang, S., & Hall, V. (1995). The overjustification effect: A meta-analysis. *Applied Cognitive Psychology, 9*, 365–404.

Tesser, A., Martin, L. L., & Cornell, D. P. (1996) On the substitutability of self-protective mechanisms. In P. M. Gollwitzer & J. A. Bargh (Eds.), *The psychology of action: Linking cognition and motivation to behavior* (pp. 48–68). New York: Guilford Press.

PART

II

A New Debate

Hidden Costs (and Benefits)
of Achievement Goals

CHAPTER

6

Meaning and Motivation

DANIEL C. MOLDEN
CAROL S. DWECK
Department of Psychology
Columbia University

What are people really striving for in an achievement situation? What does it promise (or threaten)? What does a failure mean? When will it undermine intrinsic motivation and when might it enhance it? All of these questions are critical ones for the study of motivation, and they are questions of meaning—what the achievement situation, its prospect, and its outcomes mean to the person.

In this chapter, we examine how the meaning that people assign to an achievement situation affects their motivation—how it affects the goals they pursue, the effectiveness with which they pursue them, and the interest and enjoyment that accompanies their pursuit. Moreover, we will show how different people may imbue even the "same" goal with widely different meanings, resulting in widely different motivational patterns. Finally, we will show how this formulation integrates a number of prominent theories within the study of achievement motivation—namely, those theories involving goals, attributions, approach/avoidance motivation, and self-worth.

We begin by providing a brief history of the field of achievement motivation from a "meaning" perspective, illustrating how this critical idea emerged but is now in danger of disappearing from current conceptions.

EARLY ACHIEVEMENT MOTIVATION THEORIES

Early theories of achievement motivation were theories of drives and "action" (Atkinson, 1957; cf. Lewin, Dembo, Festinger, & Sears, 1944). It was believed that people seek achievement because they possess an affective desire, a "need," for it, as they do for food or water (McClelland, Atkinson, Clark, & Lowell, 1953). These drive theories identified two basic motives behind achievement motivation, namely, a "need to achieve" and a "fear of failure" (Atkinson, 1957; McClelland, 1951), and then set out to discover when and how these motives expressed themselves. The picture of motivation that emerged from this endeavor centered around questions of who strives for success, when this striving is initiated, and for what length of time it is sustained. Although Atkinson and many others (see Atkinson & Feather, 1966) did a superb job of addressing these questions, it eventually became apparent that affective mechanisms alone provided an incomplete picture and that more needed to be said about other psychological mechanisms behind achievement motivation. What are the specific goals towards which people's efforts are directed? What meanings do these goals have for the person who has undertaken them, and what does it mean to succeed or fail in the course of pursuit? To address these questions, a new approach and new concepts were needed that would allow researchers to somehow illuminate these additional processes.

ATTRIBUTION THEORY

A major approach that arose to answer this need was Weiner's attributional theory of motivation (Weiner 1985; Weiner & Kukla, 1970). Rooted in the guiding principle of earlier attributional theories—that people possess a strong desire to understand their world (Heider, 1958; Kelley, 1967)—the system of motivation that Weiner created revolved around the fundamental questions that people ask themselves about the causes of success and failure. His demonstration that the different meaning, or attributions, that people assigned to outcomes could create different emotional and behavioral reactions to this outcome (Weiner, 1980a, 1980b) was a large step forward for the field. No longer could achievement be talked about only in terms of when, and how forcefully, certain drives were initiated, but the meanings of the outcomes resulting from these drives had to be considered as well.

Yet, although attribution theory introduced the concept of meaning to achievement motivation and closed some of the psychological gaps associated with drive-based theories, it also overlooked some of the most useful aspects of previous conceptions. Attribution theory explained how individuals' reactions to their outcomes mediated persistence in achievement situations, but it did not address the factors behind the initiation of achievement behavior in the first place. Within this framework, researchers could identify the cognitive, affective, and behavioral consequences of outcomes, but the question that still remained was this: What leads people to seek success? Attempts to create a theory of motivation that could resolve this question and at the same time retain the descriptive and explanatory power of previous approaches led to the introduction of goals to the achievement literature (Dweck & Elliott, 1983; Nicholls, 1984).

GOAL THEORY

The construct of goals, which were loosely defined as the specific *purposes* toward which a person's efforts were directed, was meant to provide a window into the psychological processes involved in *creating* achievement behavior. Individuals entering situations for different reasons could also, in theory, bring with them different means of achieving, different ideas about what causes success and failure, and different concerns about reaching or not reaching their desired outcome. Therefore, considering someone's goal could capture many of the factors involved in the earlier theories. For example, goals could illuminate the initiation of achievement behavior as well as promote an understanding of the generation and impact of subsequent attributions.

Goal theorists proposed that much of achievement motivation could be captured by two qualitatively different categories of goals, one in which people are attempting to validate or demonstrate an ability (or avoid a demonstration of incompetence), and one in which people are attempting to develop or acquire an ability (Dweck & Elliott 1983; Dweck & Leggett, 1988; Nicholls, 1984; see also Maehr, 1989; Spence & Helmreich, 1983). Although different definitions of these goal categories have been used in the literature, we believe, and several reviews have suggested, that the above distinction between a *performance goal* involving the demonstration of ability (also referred to in some literatures as an *ego* or *ability goal*) and a *learning goal* involving the development of ability (also called a *mastery* or *task goal*) is the most fundamental and captures the important features of the other distinctions (Ames, 1992; Ames & Archer, 1988; Utman, 1997).

Thus far, a goals framework has made significant contributions to the achievement literature. Studies that have measured people's naturally occurring goals (e.g., Farrell, 1985; Meece, Blumenfield, & Hoyle, 1988; Nicholls, Cheung, Lauer, & Patashnick, 1989; Nolen, 1988), as well as those that have manipulated goals within a specific situation (e.g., Elliott & Dweck, 1988; Graham & Golan, 1991; see Utman, 1997), have demonstrated that an orientation toward a performance goal over a learning goal can predict vulnerability to a "helpless" response to failure, whereas an orientation toward a learning goal over a performance goal tends to lead to a "mastery-oriented" response to failure. Helpless responses are made up of low ability attributions for failure, negative affect following failure, use of ineffective strategies, and decreases in subsequent performance. Mastery-oriented responses, in contrast, tend to include effort attributions for failure, a maintenance of positive affect, use of effective strategies, and steady or increased task performance (Diener & Dweck, 1978, 1980). In short, it appears that when people are highly concerned with demonstrating their level of ability, they are more likely to see failure as measuring important aspects of themselves and are more likely to experience failure as disheartening. In contrast, when people are highly concerned with increasing their level of ability, setbacks are more likely to be seen as a natural part of learning—as information about their effort or strategy—and as an incentive for greater effort.

In the same vein, performance goals have often been seen to support lower levels of intrinsic motivation than have learning goals (Ames & Archer, 1988; Archer, 1994; Duda & Nicholls, 1992; Harackiewicz, Barron, Carter, Lehto, & Elliot, 1997; Pintrich, 1989; Plant & Ryan, 1985; Ryan, 1982; Ryan, Koestner, & Deci, 1991; for reviews, see also Ames, 1992; Heyman & Dweck, 1992). Although some of these studies do not describe their manipulations in terms of goal theory and instead use the labels *ego involving* versus *task involving*, the particular instructions given to participants (i.e., that a task was designed either to evaluate a person's intellectual ability or not) are inductions conceptually equivalent to those used for performance goals. Specifically, experiments using these and other more explicit goal manipulations have found that lower levels of task enjoyment and a reduced desire to continue with a task exist in people with performance goals when compared to those with learning goals, both when succeeding (e.g., Butler, 1987; Harackiewicz, Abrahams, & Wageman, 1987; Koestner, Zuckerman, & Koestner, 1987; Ryan et al., 1991; but see Rawsthorne & Elliot, 2000) and after encountering setbacks (Mueller & Dweck, 1998). Taken together, these results indicate that people who enter achievement situations with strong performance goals—that is, with a focus on validating or demonstrating their abilities—often fall prey to impairments of performance and intrinsic motivation to a greater degree than those who enter these situations with a desire to learn.

RECENT EXPANSIONS OF GOAL THEORY

Although Dweck and her colleagues took care to stress that they believed performance goals to be a critical component of achievement (Dweck, 1991; Heyman & Dweck, 1992), and although Elliott and Dweck (1988) clearly demonstrated that performance goals could sometimes create a hardy, mastery-oriented response pattern, the overall emphasis in their research was on the vulnerability that performance goals can create. Yet given that in so many settings, such as education, sports, and business, the final result (grades, wins, or dollars) is critical and demonstrations of ability are highly important, it was evident that the potential benefits of adopting performance goals had perhaps not received enough attention.

In an attempt to address this situation and distinguish exactly when performance goals are beneficial versus detrimental, several researchers have reconsidered the past literature and begun to suggest that in the progression from drives to attributions to goals, an important component of achievement motivation has been lost (Elliot, 1997; Elliot & Church, 1997; Elliot & Harackiewicz, 1996). As mentioned previously, in the early theories of Atkinson and McClelland, achievement motivation revolved around *two* motives, one involving the approach-oriented need to achieve and another involving a separate avoidance-oriented fear of failure. However, when the existing goal theories were examined, it was found that the approach-oriented performance goal of seeking to demonstrate competence and the avoidance-oriented performance goal of seeking to not demonstrate incompetence were typically considered together instead of separately (e.g., Dweck & Leggett, 1988; Nicholls et al., 1989). Although both of these forms had been conceptualized and identified (Dweck & Elliott, 1983), the ways in which they might differ were never pursued.

Recently, Elliot (1997) and Skaalvik (1997) have pointed out that combining these approach-oriented and avoidance-oriented forms of performance goals may obscure fundamental differences that exist between the two. Indeed, when Elliot and Harackiewicz (1996) presented a task to participants and framed it as a performance goal cast in approach language, or a performance goal cast in avoidance language, they observed different effects for each of these goals on intrinsic motivation. Building on these findings, Elliot and Church (1997) have proposed a model of achievement motivation based on a return to Atkinson and McClelland's two achievement motives (i.e., to approach success and to avoid failure). These motives are seen as creating distinct approach and avoidance forms of achievement goals, which then are conceived of as the "direct regulators" of achievement behavior.

Learning goals are thought to stem from a pure motive to approach success, and as such, should spur intrinsic motivation and performance (although not necessarily graded performance; see Elliot & Church, 1997). In contrast, what Elliot and Church call "performance avoidance" goals are thought to stem from a pure motive to avoid failure and thus should put performance and intrinsic motivation at risk because of the anxiety and worry this motive manifests (Elliot & McGregor, 1999). Finally, "performance approach" goals are conceived of as arising from both motives to approach success and motives to avoid failure (i.e., as serving a viable function for both motives). They therefore encompass both of these potentially antagonistic forces and may have either positive or negative effects on performance and intrinsic motivation, depending on which predominates. Should a performance-approach goal arise from desires to approach success, positive consequences would be expected, yet should a performance-approach goal arise from desires to avoid failure, negative consequences would be expected. Studies (Elliot & Church, 1997; Elliot & Harackiewicz, 1996) have confirmed that these three separate goals can, in fact, be associated with their hypothesized effects.

This reintroduction of approach/avoidance tendencies within the current goals approach has proven particularly useful. By separating performance goals into approach and avoidance components, this framework provides researchers with a potential way of classifying when performance goals may be beneficial and when they may be detrimental. Although we have thus far focused on the view that performance goals generally have negative consequences, several lines of work have demonstrated that performance goals can, in certain circumstances and for certain people, increase intrinsic motivation (Epstein & Harackiewicz, 1992; Harackiewicz & Elliot, 1993; Koestner et al., 1987; Koestner, Zuckerman, & Olsson, 1990; Sansone, 1986; Sansone, Sachau, & Weir, 1989; see chapters 8 and 9, this book; Harackiewicz, Barron, & Elliot, 1998). The work done by Elliot and others suggests that only when performance goals involve avoidance (i.e., a fear of demonstrating incompetence) should they be associated with decreases in intrinsic motivation. In contrast, performance goals that involve approach (i.e., the desire to demonstrate competence) would not necessarily have these negative consequences and could even increase intrinsic motivation. It is possible, then, that this formulation can illuminate some of the discrepant findings in the larger achievement-goal literature.

Harackiewicz, Sansone, and their colleagues (Harackiewicz et al., 1997; Harackiewicz et al., 1998; Harackiewicz & Elliot, 1993; Harackiewicz & Manderlink, 1984; Harackiewicz & Sansone, 1991; Sansone, 1986) have shed additional light on the issue of when performance goals may have beneficial effects. According to them, achievement situations can be quite enjoyable when people are seeking to demonstrate their competence and are succeeding, because this evokes their feelings of how much they value competence and increases their involvement with a task. This is compatible with the idea that performance approach goals can support intrinsic motivation (Mueller & Dweck, 1998) and with the findings by Elliott and Dweck (1988) that some students with performance goals are able to maintain a vigorous mastery-oriented pattern in the face of failure. However, it also implies that when people are pursuing performance goals and are experiencing themselves as *incompetent*, their failure to perform well may have particularly harsh consequences leading to reduced task involvement and decreased intrinsic motivation (Mueller & Dweck, 1998). Therefore, this formulation offers another perspective on when performance goals should stoke versus dampen motivation.

A MEANING PERSPECTIVE
ON ACHIEVEMENT MOTIVATION

Although these recent expansions of goal theory appear to have potential for clarifying the achievement-goal literature by specifying exactly when performance goals may have positive effects for an individual (e.g., when they are regulated by approach motives or when they result in feelings of competence) versus when they may have negative effects (e.g., when they are regulated by avoidance motives or when they result in feelings of incompetence), we would like to take a different approach to this issue. Just as original drive theories of achievement motivation overlooked the psychological meaning of achievement drives, of the purposes toward which they were aimed, and of the outcomes that ensued, we believe that this reworking of goal-based theories of achievement motivation has also tended to underemphasize these critical issues. It may be true that trying to avoid incompetence can result in decreased task success and reduced intrinsic motivation, whereas trying to approach competence may in some cases actually increase overall task success and intrinsic motivation, but what is it specifically about these two frameworks that creates these differences, and why, psychologically speaking, might someone adopt one or the other? In this chapter, we propose an expansion of current goal theory that we believe can begin to address these additional questions.

Our primary concern is that recent approach/avoidance formulations of goal theories seem to have lost an important feature of Weiner's initial innovations. By de-emphasizing goal meaning and outcome attributions in favor of reexamining different motives, goal theorists may be in danger of losing touch with the psychological core of achievement motivation that was amended to the original drive-based theories. Without considering issues of meaning, one cannot fully address questions such as what *psychological processes* lead some people to fear failure whereas others simply seek to achieve, *why* some people withhold effort from important endeavors or experience debilitation from setbacks whereas others do not, and *why* some people enjoy a task less after encountering difficulty whereas others enjoy it as much or more. We believe that to allow examination of these questions and development of a more complete understanding of the processes involved in achievement motivation, meaning must be returned to a prominent role. The fundamental question that goal-based theories ask—"What is the purpose toward which a person's strivings are directed?"—must be amended by "What *meaning* does this purpose have for the person who has undertaken it?" (See also, Deci & Ryan, 1985, 1987; and Higgins, 1998, for examples of the effects of meaning on achievement.)

In addition to advocating a meaning-based approach to achievement motivation in general, we are also proposing a specific framework through which meaning can moderate achievement. This framework grows out of our work on implicit theories of intelligence and integrates goal theory, Weiner's attribution theory, and approach/avoidance distinctions, as well as Covington's (1992) insights about the role of self-worth concerns in achievement motivation. The remainder of this chapter focuses on a description of, and evidence for, this framework. Specifically, we argue that when a task involving performance goals is believed to measure a global and enduring attribute of the self (as opposed to a specific acquirable skill), individuals (1) will be more likely to adopt risk-avoidant and defensive strategies; (2) will tend to produce more global, stable attributions for the outcomes of their performance; (3) will be more vulnerable to overall impairments in performance and intrinsic interest; and (4) will be more likely to manifest avoidance concerns on encountering setbacks, regardless of whether they begin the task from a stance of approach or one of avoidance.

Indeed, as we will see, recent work from our laboratory (Stone & Dweck, 1998) has demonstrated that people can have markedly different beliefs about the personal qualities that are under evaluation in achievement situations. Some people believe that performance tasks measure their fundamental and permanent intelligence, whereas others see these tasks as providing them with an indication of their current level of a more specific, acquirable skill. (It is important to note that these are not attributions made after a success or failure but are beliefs about the nature of ability, and the way in which future tasks will reflect on that ability, that are brought into a situation.) Although in both instances an individual may be highly committed to the goal of demonstrating his or her ability and performing well, for each individual the effective meaning of the goal differs, the quality of goal pursuit may differ, and the attributions that arise from the outcome should differ. We suggest that these different beliefs form the bases of two different meaning systems that moderate the selection and implementation of both performance and learning goals. We further propose, as suggested above, that our meaning system approach can unite several different approaches in the achievement literature (including goal, attribution, approach/avoidance, and self-worth approaches) to suggest when performance and learning goals will be beneficial or detrimental.

Within our framework, there are several points we would like to emphasize. First, we suggest that concerns with failure and attempts to avoid appearing incompetent grow directly out of the belief that an achievement task measures one's fixed intelligence—and therefore that task performance has implications for self-worth. When people believe that a task simply identifies a current level of an acquirable ability, however, they should be free of these implications and should not display this concern with failure and its avoidance.[1]

Second, we propose that even when individuals are pursuing performance goals within an approach mode, those who are concerned about

---

[1] In some Asian cultures, students may be judged more on their level of effort than on their level of ability (Grant & Dweck, in press). In these cultures, effort may take on some traitlike qualities and become more tied to self-worth. For this situation, concerns with failure and tendencies toward avoidance could perhaps stem from beliefs that one's effort level, as well as one's ability, is fixed.

their fixed intelligence may readily shift into an avoidance mode. Two students may be equally invested in demonstrating their competence in a certain situation, and this may continue as long as both students are succeeding. However, as soon as the specter of failure looms within a task, students whose more global and permanent qualities are invested in this task may suddenly become concerned with avoiding a demonstration of incompetence, whereas those who consider only the immediate implication of that failure for their current skill level may not.

Furthermore, students who tend to feel that their global and stable abilities are being tested may not be able to approach even a learning goal in the same way as students who tend to feel that only a specific skill is at issue. Because developing new skills often involves challenge, people who feel that their more general abilities are being evaluated might be distracted by performance concerns and worries of demonstrating incompetence as they attempt to learn. A person lacking this additional threat of global evaluation would be less likely to have these worries. In this case, only the latter would truly experience the benefits in intrinsic motivation typically found in challenging situations involving learning goals.

Thus, although anyone can enter a task with avoidance as a primary objective, we suggest that a certain subset of people (i.e., those who feel that some global fixed ability is at stake) will have not only a greater tendency to do so but also a greater likelihood to become engulfed in these avoidance concerns under the threat of failure, regardless of their initial orientation toward the task. This means that assessing the impact of performance and learning goals on intrinsic motivation when this element of threat is not present, such as when the task is easy or when individuals are doing well, may obscure the full effects of these goals. To obtain a complete picture of the processes at work in achievement, observations must be made at a point where challenges or setbacks are involved.

Finally, although we would like to underscore the importance of attributions in motivation, we argue that these attributions may not simply "arise" once an outcome is experienced. They can instead be set up beforehand by the meaning system that an individual (or situation) imposes on a task. When a task is seen as measuring an enduring quality of the self, then a global, stable, and internal attribution for failure is more likely to result. When a task is seen as assessing current skills and strategies, however, then a more specific attribution, such as an attribution to effort, strategy, or temporary skill level should be favored. Indeed, our research has demonstrated that these different views of ability play a causal role in creating such attributions (Hong, Chiu, Dweck, Lin, & Wan, 1999).

In short, we are arguing that students' systems of meaning not only orient them toward certain goals within achievement situations but, in addition, alter the way these goals are perceived and pursued. We turn now to research that bears on these issues.

INDIVIDUAL DIFFERENCES IN GOAL MEANING

To begin our discussion of how meaning systems affect achievement motivation, we first consider the chronic beliefs that people may carry with them into particular situations, and how these chronic beliefs can influence the goals that people pursue. Previous research in our laboratory has repeatedly demonstrated that an important factor in predicting behavior in achievement situations is a person's belief about his or her intelligence (Bandura & Dweck, 1985; Dweck & Leggett, 1988; Dweck & Sorich, 1999; Henderson & Dweck, 1990, Hong et al., 1999). These beliefs have been labeled "implicit theories" and represent deeply held, but rarely articulated, thoughts about the nature of intelligence. Specifically, one class of implicit theories refers to people's sense of whether intelligence is an immutable, uncontrollable quality of a person, or a malleable, controllable one. These theories are evaluated by a questionnaire that asks people the extent to which they agree with statements such as "The amount of intelligence that someone has is something very basic about them and it can't be changed very much" and "Everyone can significantly change the amount of intelligence that they have" (Dweck, Chiu, & Hong, 1995; Levy & Dweck, 1997; see Dweck, 1999). Those who believe that intelligence is something that is fixed and cannot be developed over time are labeled *entity theorists*, whereas those who believe that intelligence is malleable and can be changed over time are called *incremental theorists*.

In the past, these implicit theories have been shown to affect achievement motivation by leading people to favor either learning goals or performance goals when they are confronted with an achievement task and asked to choose between these two classes of goals (Bandura & Dweck, 1985; Dweck & Leggett, 1988; see also Dweck, 1999; Dweck & Sorich, 1999; Stone & Dweck, 1998). Individuals who have an entity theory of intelligence (i.e., those who believe that intelligence is fixed) tend to choose performance goals over learning goals, whereas those who have an incremental theory of intelligence (i.e., those who believe that intelligence is malleable) appear to prefer learning goals over performance goals. Explanations for these differences stem directly from the beliefs that separate these two groups. Because they feel that their attributes are fixed, entity theorists embrace performance goals because these goals allow them to document their personal levels of these attributes. They avoid challenging learning goals because they tend to involve the risk of failure at some point and therefore pose the threat of revealing incompetencies. Incremental theorists, however, lean toward learning goals, because this allows them the opportunity to increase their current level of ability. Performance goals (particularly challenge-avoidant ones) are often not as valuable within this framework, because even though they allow incremental theorists to judge their current level of ability, they do not provide the means for developing it. Thus, although everyone pursues both learning and performance goals, and even though it may sometimes be possible for a person to pursue some aspects of both goals simultaneously (see chapter 9, this book), we find that entity theorists may sacrifice a chance to learn if there is the threat of failure whereas incremental theorists may sacrifice a chance to document their abilities if there is an opportunity to learn.[2]

More recently, however, we have begun to think that aside from preferring different goals when they are pitted against each other, entity and incremental theorists may ascribe different meanings to the "same" goal. That is, for entity theorists the belief that intelligence is a fixed trait may lead to beliefs about what it means to evaluate this intelligence as well. Performance situations may become instances in which they are putting their enduring intelligence on display for judgment. In contrast, for incremental theorists who believe that intelligence is dynamic and malleable, performance situations may become instances in which they can receive valuable information about their present proficiency in an area.

Current research in our laboratory designed to explore this possibility has found that implicit theories of intelligence do, in fact, create strikingly different systems of meaning not only for achievement tasks as whole but also for the goals that operate within them. Stone and Dweck (1998) conducted research that explicitly attempted to illuminate these meaning systems. After classifying fifth-grade students as entity or incremental theorists, they asked these students direct questions about tasks representing both performance and learning goals. Performance-goal tasks were presented to the students as ones that "can test how smart you are at these kinds of things," and learning goal tasks were described as ones that "may not make you look very smart, but ... may teach you a skill that can help you with your schoolwork." After the students had selected which type of task they would most like to pursue at a later time, they were questioned about the meaning of the tasks representing both performance and learning goals, regardless of which they preferred.

---

[2] Multiple studies have addressed the possibility of simultaneously pursuing both learning and performance goals (Ames & Archer, 1988; Archer, 1994; Barron & Harackiewicz, chapter 9 in this book; Elliot & Church, 1997; Elliot & McGregor, 1999; Harackiewicz et al., 1997; Meece & Holt, 1993; Pintrich and Garcia, 1991). Some have demonstrated that the greatest levels of engagement and performance occur for people with strong learning goals that are paired with weak performance goals (e.g., Meece & Holt, 1993; Pintrich & Garcia, 1991), whereas others have found greater self-regulation and higher performance when people displayed strong learning and strong performance goals in combination (e.g., Bouffard, Boisvert, Vezeau, & Larouche, 1995). Although we see no obstacles for incremental theorists in flexibly pursuing both goals at once, this may be more difficult for entity theorists. Although Stone and Dweck (1998), as discussed below, clearly showed that entity theorists value both performance and learning, when learning tasks are particularly challenging and concerns about failure may be paramount, these concerns could overwhelm the learning component of the task and allow entity theorists to concentrate on only a performance goal.

For example, students were asked what they thought the performance-goal task actually measured. These questions focused on three possibilities: present skills in the area, global intelligence, and global intelligence in the future. For the first statement, "These problems would show how good I am at these kinds of things," both entity theorists and incremental theorists showed high levels of agreement and, in fact, incremental theorists reported significantly higher ratings of agreement than did entity theorists. However, for the statements "These problems would show how smart a person I am" and "These problems would show how smart a person I'll probably be when I grow up," entity theorists gave significantly and substantially higher ratings of agreement than did incremental theorists, who indicated overall disagreement. Thus, incremental theorists believed that the only thing being measured by tasks involving performance goals was their current ability for that type of task. In contrast, entity theorists were investing these tasks with the power to diagnose their current and their future intelligence.

Clear differences appeared in answers to questions about learning-goal tasks as well. When, in a free-response format, students were asked what it would mean to them if they experienced difficulty and challenge in a learning-goal task, incremental theorists reported a significantly higher number of learning and effort-related explanations, generally indicating that it meant that they needed more practice or hadn't learned the necessary skills yet. Entity theorists, in contrast, displayed strong ability concerns even in a learning context. They reported to a significantly greater extent that difficulty would show that they were not very smart.

When responses for tasks representing both performance and learning goals are taken together, it appears that students who operate within an entity theory tend to see achievement tasks as measuring global and enduring qualities of the self, to the point where they view difficulty, not only on performance-goal tasks but even on learning-goal tasks, as signaling low intelligence. In contrast, students who operate within an incremental theory seem to feel that tasks involving performance goals and learning goals are measuring only their current and specific skills, as reflected in the fact that they did not believe that their performance said much about their level of intelligence either in the present or in the future.

As an aside, it is important to note that both entity theorists and incremental theorists care greatly about both performance and learning goals. In the Stone and Dweck (1998) study, when students were asked how important it would be for them to do well on the problems in the performance-goal task and how important it would be for them to learn something from the problems in the learning-goal task, both groups attached high (and equally high) importance to these goals. This means that when entity and incremental theorists are asked *in the abstract* about the importance that they attach to each goal (as they are in studies that measure performance goals and learning goals via questionnaires), the differences between the two groups may not be apparent. However, as demonstrated in Stone and Dweck (1998), when the two types of goals are pitted against each other and students have to choose between addressing their performance concerns (via a performance-goal task) or addressing their learning objectives (via a learning-goal task), then the groups can differ markedly. In these studies, incremental theorists chose learning goals to a *far* greater extent than did entity theorists. (See also Dweck & Sorich, 1999, for a study in which students' theories of intelligence predicted their goal choices when learning and performance goals were pitted against each other, but not when each goal was assessed separately.)

MEANING SYSTEMS VERSUS ATTRIBUTIONS

The different meanings given to achievement situations by entity theorists versus incremental theorists that we have described are related to, yet distinct from, several constructs that have received attention in the past. To review, entity theorists believe in fixed intelligence and tend to see achievement tasks as having the power to measure this fixed intelligence. In contrast, incremental theorists believe in malleable, acquirable intelligence and see achievement tasks as either vehicles for increasing intellectual skills or as vehicles for assessing their present, task-specific skills. In a related vein, Abramson, Seligman, & Teasdale (1978) addressed the impact of global, stable versus specific, unstable *attributions*. Attributions, however, come into play after an outcome has occurred. The beliefs we are addressing, as noted above, are prior beliefs about the nature of intelligence and about what achievement tasks measure that people carry with them into achievement situations. These prior beliefs, we have shown, affect the goals that people pursue (e.g., Dweck & Leggett, 1988; Dweck & Sorich, 1999; Stone & Dweck, 1998) and *give rise* to the attributions that they make (Hong et al., 1999; see also Zhao, Dweck, & Mueller, 1998). In our formulation, then, global, fixed definitions of ability and more specific, malleable definitions of ability are not explanations of an event that has already occurred but instead are basic beliefs about one's attributes that can generate goals and attributions.

THEORIES OF INTELLIGENCE AND SELF-WORTH

Believing that their abilities are global and enduring should mean that entity theorists have a lot at stake when they are placed under evaluation. Not only will their performance represent a measure of their general potential, but whatever this potential turns out to be is not something that can be altered. Some findings in our laboratory (Kamins & Dweck, 1999b) support this idea and further extend the notion that for entity theorists, achievement situations carry important information about the self. Along these lines, we have become extremely interested in the idea of contingent self-worth (Burhans & Dweck, 1995; Kamins & Dweck, 1999a; see Covington, 1992; see also deCharms, 1968; Plant & Ryan, 1985; Ryan, 1982; and Ryan et al., 1991 for related concepts of ego involvement). This is the idea that one's worth is dependent on one's successes and is undermined by failure. We have suggested that an entity theory, with its belief that one has global, permanent traits that can readily be judged from performance, may set students up for a sense of contingent self-worth (Burhans & Dweck, 1995; Kamins & Dweck, 1999b; Mueller & Dweck, 1998). Kamins and Dweck (1999b) obtained specific evidence to support this hypothesis, and for a college student sample, they found an extremely high correlation ($r = .78$) between holding an entity theory and reporting a sense of contingent self-worth. In other words, the more students believed that their intelligence was a fixed trait, the more they believed that avoiding failures and attaining successes were necessary to maintain their sense of worth.

In summary, our argument so far is that for some individuals, achievement situations have deeper meaning about the self and that one cannot understand the dynamics of achievement motivation without taking this into account.

RELATIONS BETWEEN IMPLICIT THEORY AND APPROACH/AVOIDANCE MOTIVATION

One particular way in which we believe that meaning systems can have a profound influence on individuals' achievement motivation is the selection of approach- versus avoidance-oriented goals. We propose that by identifying someone who has "permanent-ability" concerns, (i.e., who considers his or her fixed and global intelligence to be under evaluation) or someone who has "current-ability" concerns, (i.e., who considers his or her present level of a particular skill to be under evaluation), one can predict who will display approach or avoidance orientations toward performance goals.

Someone who has a performance goal and who also has permanent-ability concerns could easily have serious anxieties about performing poorly because of the highly negative evaluation of the self that this poor performance would imply. These concerns might lead the individual to concentrate his or her efforts on avoiding a demonstration of incompetence rather than achieving a demonstration of competence. This leads us to expect that entity theorists, who are more susceptible to permanent-ability concerns, would be more likely to adopt an avoidance strategy toward performance goals. (See Rhodewalt, 1994, for a demonstration that entity theorists adopt self-handicapping strategies significantly more than do incremental theorists. Self-handicapping represents a willingness to sacrifice success to avoid a demonstration of incompetence; cf. Elliot & McGregor, 1999.) In addition, someone who is involved in a learning-oriented task with these same permanent-ability concerns might continue to worry about performing poorly despite the fact that the ostensible purpose of this task does not involve evaluation. Therefore, even on tasks where they are pursuing learning goals, it is possible that entity theorists might be more likely to focus on avoiding a demonstration of incompetence, such that this goal might overwhelm their original learning goal.

People who possess a different representation of achievement situations and who have only current-ability concerns, however, should follow a different pattern. For someone with this outlook, poor outcomes in either performance or learning goals do not have such dire consequences and therefore would not be expected to inspire avoidance strategies. Incremental theorists, with their greater prevalence of current-ability concerns, should thus be less constrained in their behavior within achievement situations. That is, viewing evaluation as measuring only current skill levels, and further believing that these skill levels may be increased over time, should provide incremental theorists with a certain degree of flexibility. In the absence of serious ties to self-worth, performance goals for incremental theorists can be pursued in the form that seems most appropriate for the situation, and learning goals can be truly approached in terms of developing one's abilities, even when this proves to be challenging.

Is there evidence for this? In one study (Leggett, 1986), students were given a choice between an easy performance-goal task that would let them do "...problems that are fairly easy, so I'll do well," a difficult performance-goal task that would let them do "...problems that are hard enough to show that I'm smart," and a learning-goal task that would let them do "...problems that are hard, new, and different so that I could learn something from them." By defining these three tasks as representing a performance goal with an avoidance strategy, a performance goal with an approach strategy, and a learning goal, respectively, we are able to get an indication of whether entity theorists and incremental theorists have different predilections for approach versus avoidance as well as for performance versus learning. Analyses reported in Dweck and Leggett (1988) collapsed the two types of performance goal into one, but a reanalysis of the data using all three categories showed significant differences as well: χ^2 (2, N = 63) = 15.47; $p < .001$. An equivalent percentage of entity theorists and incremental theorists chose performance-approach goals (31.8% and 29.3%, respectively), but entity theorists were much more likely to choose performance-avoidance goals (50%, vs. 9.8% of incremental theorists) and incremental theorists were much more likely to choose learning goals (61%, vs. 18.2% of entity theorists). Furthermore, when only the students who chose performance goals (either approach or avoidance) were examined, a significant relation-ship with theory of intelligence also emerged: χ^2 (1, N = 34) = 4.48; $p < .05$. When selecting performance goals, entity theorists were more likely to choose the avoidance form (61%) and incremental theorists were much more likely to choose the approach form (75%). Although this is preliminary evidence, it does indicate a relationship between implicit theories and approach- and avoidance-oriented performance goals that may be tested in future studies.

We have argued thus far that implicit theories affect goal choice and goal meaning. We turn now to research suggesting that these meanings have consequences for intrinsic motivation and behavior.

GOAL MEANING, INTRINSIC MOTIVATION, AND PERFORMANCE

A recent set of studies in our laboratory underscores the importance of thinking in terms of the different meaning systems that individuals can use to structure achievement situations. Mueller and Dweck (1998) performed a series of six studies that used different types of praise for performance to directly examine these different meaning systems and their effects. In these studies, after succeeding on an initial set of problems, students received either (1) praise for their intelligence in the area: "Wow, you did very well on these problems. You got [number of problems] right. That's a really high score. You must be smart at these problems"; (2) praise for their effort: "Wow ... that's a really high score. You must have worked hard at these problems"; or (3) simple outcome praise: "Wow ... that's a really high score," which was intended as a control. After this first task, all students were then given a second set of problems that were much more difficult than the first and on which they performed considerably worse. Finally, so it could be seen whether systems created by the different types of praise would affect performance after failure, a third set of problems (equivalent in difficulty to the first set) was administered.

Multiple dependent measures were devised to thoroughly characterize the meaning systems instilled by the three types of praise and to measure their effects. First, in order to examine the creation of these systems by the different forms of praise, after their praise experiences students answered questions about (1) their beliefs about the fixedness or malleability of intelligence, (2) their choice of achievement goal, and (3) what type of information was most important to them (a comparative evaluation of their performance or strategic tips that would help them improve future perfor-mance). Second, to determine whether the meaning systems were carried through to students' construals of their setbacks, failure attributions were assessed after the second (difficult) trial and measures were taken of students' defensive behaviors in relation to their low scores. Finally, in addition to showing that these systems existed and were manifest in students' attributions, Mueller and Dweck also wanted to document whether these systems had important effects on students' levels of intrinsic motivation throughout the experiment or on students' performance on a third, post-failure problem set.

Before we discuss the results of these studies, how do we think that intelligence and effort praise created different meaning systems and what predictions would be generated from these two systems? Students who are praised for their intelligence in an achievement situation are being given clear, although unspoken, information about that situation. One thing that intelligence praise tells them is that their success is directly linked to some internal quality that they possess rather than to any particular thing that they did. An additional message that may come across is that this quality determining success is something deep seated, something that they either possess or do not possess, and not something that is acquirable over time through effort. Finally, intelligence praise makes it clear that this internal quality can be readily measured by their performance (because the evaluator has simply looked at their performance and evaluated their intelligence). Intelligence praise may thus impose a meaning on the achievement situation equivalent to the one that is spontaneously generated by entity theorists and revolves around permanent-ability concerns.

In contrast to this, students who are being praised for their effort in achievement situations are receiving an entirely different set of messages. First of all, by concentrating on something that is a specific behavioral input to the task, effort praise is teaching students that performance is largely a function of the processes involved. They are thus being shown that the things that can be evaluated by a person's performance are the processes that go into it. These processes, in turn, are more likely to be seen as malleable and within a person's control, and therefore performance will not be diagnostic of any permanent qualities. Effort praise may thus create a meaning system much like the one spontaneously generated by incremental theorists that revolves around concerns about process and current ability.

What predictions, then, would be derived from these two different meanings, and how were these predictions borne out by the actual results of the study? First of all, intelligence praise after success on the first set of problems would be expected to lead students to encode the achievement situation as revolving around their own fixed and internal qualities. This type of representation could strengthen the link between success and self-worth and should lead them to choose performance goals that would continue to allow them to demonstrate these successful qualities (or to *avoid* demonstrating deficient qualities). Because of their concern with their level of ability, they should also seek information that allows them to compare their intelligence to that of others (cf. Butler, 1992, and chapter 7, this book).

Furthermore, it would also be expected that intelligence-praised students' internal and fixed encodings would be applied to failure attributions on the second set of problems. These students should then produce more internal-ability attributions as well as defensive behavior in reporting their poor scores following this second set. Finally, the application of this fixed and internal representation to the failure that they experienced on the second trial should lead them to experience deficits in intrinsic motivation and performance after receiving this type of feedback.

Effort praise after success, however, should cause students to encode the situation as concerning malleable and controllable qualities. This type of representation should free students from self-worth concerns and cause them to prefer learning goals to which they can continue to apply their effort, to seek strategic information that can help them most efficiently guide this effort, and to attribute failure to effort versus intelligence, reducing the need for defensive behavior. Finally, the focus on malleable skills and the effort attributions should lead students to frame setbacks as challenges (not threats), leading to maintained or increased intrinsic motivation and performance.

Interestingly, these predictions contradict some of the previous literature that has explored the effects of praise on achievement and intrinsic motivation. This literature suggests that increases in motivation and achievement are best invoked by giving students high *ability*—not effort—feedback (Bandura, 1986; Miller, Brickman, & Bolen, 1975; Schunk, 1996). Yet in all of these cases, the effects of feedback were tested only under conditions of success. We do not dispute the fact that this type of praise can sometimes make people more confident and can boost performance in the short run, but we are concerned with the larger meaning that may accompany it. As we have noted, many of the most fundamental differences between the meaning systems we are proposing, such as a vulnerability to helpless responses, would not be apparent under success conditions and will emerge only when difficulties or setbacks are encountered.

We now turn to the results of the Mueller and Dweck (1998) studies. To begin with, the results from several measures support the notion that the different feedback conditions did indeed create separate systems of meaning. Questions that directly asked students about their beliefs on the fixedness or malleability of their own intelligence revealed significant differences between those receiving intelligence and effort praise (Studies 4 and 6). These differences were apparent both on rating-scale and free-response measures and demonstrated that individuals who received intelligence praise now believed that intelligence was more fixed than did effort-praised individuals. It is important to note that these differences in intelligence beliefs were seen not only after success (where most people would want to say that their apparently high level of intelligence was fixed) but also after failure.

This confirms our proposal that when the achievement situation is defined in terms of intelligence, this creates a system of meaning where performance becomes diagnostic of a fixed ability, whereas when the situation is defined in terms of effort, this creates a system of meaning where performance measures something more malleable and limited in scope. Also, as predicted, feedback created preferences for different types of goals. In three studies, students were allowed to choose between pursuing a performance goal or a learning goal on a task that they were told they would receive at the end of the session. All of these studies revealed that effort praise created a strong preference for adopting learning goals, whereas intelligence praise created a preference for adopting performance goals.

To further test our predictions for meaning systems, we recently reclassified the goal-choice data from several of the Mueller and Dweck (1998) studies into (1) avoidance-oriented performance goals that centered around avoiding demonstrations of incompetence (i.e., choosing "problems that aren't too hard, so I don't get many wrong" and "problems that are pretty easy so I'll do well"), (2) approach-oriented performance goals that centered around demonstrating competence (i.e., choosing "problems that I'm pretty good at, so that I can show that I'm smart"), and (3) learning goals (i.e., choosing "problems that I'll learn a lot from, even if I won't look so smart). In subsequent analyses, we observed significant differences in goal choice for the three feedback groups (intelligence, effort, and control): χ^2 (4, N = 173) = 41.07; $p < .001$. Students in the intelligence-praise and control conditions chose approach-oriented performance goals to an equivalent degree, but students in the intelligence-praise condition were more likely to choose avoidance-oriented performance goals. When given intelligence praise, students chose avoidance-oriented performance goals more than twice as often as they chose approach-oriented performance goals (46% vs. 22%, respectively), whereas in the control condition, students chose the two with roughly equal frequency (29% vs. 21%, respectively). Students in the effort-praise condition, in contrast, chose almost exclusively learning goals.[3]

Once again, these results are directly analogous to those reported earlier for implicit theories, and they indicate that feedback can affect the larger meaning of the situation. For one group, the situation was more about avoiding negative demonstrations of fixed intelligence; for the other group, it was more about increasing their malleable intelligence.

In addition to influencing beliefs about intelligence and choice of goals, feedback in these studies also determined the type of information that stu-

---

[3] Because so few people in the effort-praise condition chose performance goals of any kind, direct comparisons of predilections for approach or avoidance between this and the intelligence-praise condition were not possible.

dents found most important about the task at hand. When given a choice between a folder containing information about where their performance ranked compared to their peers or a folder containing information about strategies that could allow them to improve on the task, intelligence-praised students greatly preferred the folder that told them about their relative performance, whereas effort-praised students greatly preferred the folder that contained strategic information (Study 4). This again is consistent with the notion that the different types of feedback employed in these studies created separate meaning systems. The fact that intelligence praise orients people toward information that provides them with a measure of their intelligence further indicates that, for these people, this is the crucial factor around which the achievement situation is defined. The selection of strategic information by effort-praised people, however, illustrates that they seek opportunities that might enhance learning.

All of these findings indicate that the different types of feedback provided after the initial problem set did indeed create distinctly different representations of the achievement situation. We now examine how they were carried forth and what their effects were.

To determine whether the meaning systems created by praise did in fact shape the interpretation of failure, students' attributions for failure were evaluated after the second, highly difficult, problem set. This was accomplished by asking students to rate various attributions for their poor performance on this set. Those praised for intelligence on the first set of problems were significantly more likely than their peers to endorse lack-of-intelligence and lack-of-ability attributions for their failure. That is, these students now felt that the failure measured their intelligence and meant that they were *not* smart. Those praised for effort, however, instead tended to view the failure as reflecting on their effort (Studies 1, 3, 5, and 6).

The continuation of the meaning systems was also investigated in another way by evaluating the extent to which students felt the need to engage in defensive behavior following failure on the second set of problems. In one study, students were asked to write a description of the problems that they had just worked on for a student in another school, who would be doing these same problems in the future, and to include their own scores on the problem set. When these reported scores were compared to students' actual scores, those who had been praised for intelligence were significantly more likely to misrepresent (i.e., enhance) their score than those who had been praised for effort or received neutral praise (Study 3). Indeed, 38% of them did so as compared with 13% and 14% in the other groups. This means that for the intelligence-praised students, the negative outcome was so meaningful a reflection of the self that they lied about it even to someone that they would never meet.

These findings clearly indicate that the meaning systems that were induced by feedback after the first problem set continued to exist for people, affecting their interpretations of subsequent failure and their reports of their performance. But did these meaning systems translate into differences in individuals' actual performance? As expected, individuals who had received intelligence praise showed clear and significant decrements in performance, whereas those praised for effort showed clear and significant increases in performance (Studies 1, 3, 5, and 6). These results were seen despite the fact that there were no differences in ability between groups on these problems as measured by their performance on the first problem set. Thus, it appears that the meaning system created by praise for intelligence can cause impaired performance. The alternative system created by praise for effort, however, seems to protect students from these effects and may even inspire them to improve their performance after failure.

Finally, Mueller and Dweck (1998) examined the impact of these meaning systems on intrinsic motivation. This was measured by asking questions about students' levels of task enjoyment and their desire to persist on the task after the experiment was over. To assess task enjoyment, students were asked, after completing the difficult second set of problems, how much fun they thought the problems were and how much they liked them. In addition, to assess their desire to persist on the task, they were asked how much they would like to take the problems home to work on them (Studies 1, 3, 5, and 6). Other students were asked these same questions after the first—success—problem set. There were no differences among the groups after the first problem set. Virtually everyone, regardless of the type of praise received, enjoyed the task and wanted to take the problems home. However, after the difficult second problem set, students who had been praised for intelligence enjoyed the task significantly less than did those who had been given effort (or outcome) praise. Indeed, the effort-praise groups showed no falloff in task enjoyment from the success trial to the failure trail, whereas the intelligence-praise groups showed a large decline.

A similar pattern was found for the desire to persist. Again, despite the fact that there were no differences after the first (successful) problem set, those who had been given intelligence praise showed a much lower desire to continue working on these problems after failure than did both the control and the effort-praised groups. Effort-praised students, in contrast, showed no decrease in their desire to continue with the problems despite the "failure." This indicates that the meaning of the achievement situation can have a marked effect on intrinsic motivation by determining what exactly is at stake for the individual. When permanent intelligence is at stake and things do not go well, students show a loss in intrinsic motivation. When only effort (or specific skills) are at stake, setbacks or difficulty can sustain a greater sense of challenge, enjoyment, and persistence.

It is important to emphasize the equivalence among the groups in their intrinsic motivation after success (in contrast to the dramatically different levels of intrinsic motivation after difficulty). Much research on intrinsic motivation assesses the impact of an experience on students' intrinsic motivation under successful or nonevaluative circumstances. Our findings, however, suggest that certain experiences (or certain meaning systems) make intrinsic motivation vulnerable, such that when setbacks occur, intrinsic motivation declines. The durability versus vulnerability of intrinsic motivation within different meaning systems is an important topic for future research.

To summarize, the findings of the Mueller and Dweck studies support our proposal about the importance of meaning in achievement motivation. Situational manipulations of this meaning in the form of different types of praise for success changed the way in which individuals responded in an achievement situation both before and after a failure (influencing their theory of intelligence, goal choice, interest in different types of information, reports of their own score, performance, and intrinsic motivation). Furthermore, the frameworks created by the praise were directly analogous to the chronic frameworks created by implicit theories of intelligence. In general, then, people for whom an achievement task is measuring something permanent behaved markedly different from people for whom an achievement task reveals information only about an immediate process, like effort, or a malleable skill.

RELATING MEANING SYSTEMS TO RESEARCH ON INTRINSIC MOTIVATION

Taken together, our findings can be related to the current intrinsic-motivation literature in several key ways. First, Elliot (Elliot & Church, 1997; Elliot & McGregor, 1999) has suggested that the negative effects of performance goals on intrinsic motivation are directly linked to the anxiety and worry that are generated within the avoidance forms of these goals. Our model and data indicate that a meaning system that raises permanent-ability concerns is the context in which avoidance-oriented performance goals tend to arise. Moreover, several decades' worth of research has shown that the cognitive worry that accompanies anxiety and damages performance involves doubts and ruminations about one's ability (e.g., Wine, 1971). As we have seen, these, too, arise most frequently within a meaning system that puts permanent ability at stake in achievement situations (Mueller & Dweck, 1998; see also Heyman, Dweck, & Cain, 1992; Hong et al., 1999; Kamins & Dweck, 1999b; Zhao et al., 1998).

Furthermore, we have argued that meaning systems that revolve around permanent abilities are not always incompatible with intrinsic motivation but that this intrinsic motivation may be vulnerable in the face of challenge or failure. We have shown it to drop dramatically in the face of failure, but it might also be undermined during a challenging success in which the individual is worried about the outcome and its implications for the self (see Plant & Ryan, 1985; Ryan, 1982; Ryan et al., 1991; see also deCharms, 1968; Deci & Ryan, 1985, 1987). In contrast, a meaning system in which only current ability is in question should reduce implications for the self and protect self-esteem and intrinsic motivation even in the face of a clear failure.

In a related vein, our formulation also suggests that the role of perceived competence may operate differently within the two meaning systems we have described. Low perceived competence within a permanent-ability system may indeed kill one's enjoyment of a task and one's wish to engage with it voluntarily (e.g., Deci, 1975). However, within a system that emphasizes the acquisition of ability and the evaluation of current skill levels, low perceived competence may make a task all the more desirable, and boost one's engagement for the purpose of mastery.

Finally, we suggest that many of the studies that have shown performance goals to have positive effects on intrinsic motivation create conditions that do not invoke evaluation of permanent ability, do not implicate self-worth, and/or do not evoke the specter of failure. These studies have made valuable contributions to our understanding of achievement goals and their impact by suggesting the necessity of performance goals for achievement and by highlighting the beneficial effects they may have (Epstein & Harackiewicz, 1992; Harackiewicz & Elliot, 1993; Koestner et al., 1987; Koestner et al., 1990; Sansone, 1986; Sansone, Sachau, & Weir, 1989; see Harackiewicz et al., 1998). We now propose, however, that we can further understand the conditions under which performance goals will have positive *or* negative effects by considering the meaning system in which they are embedded (cf. Deci & Ryan, 1987; Higgins, 1998).

In this context, we call once more for intrinsic motivation researchers to consider not only the level of intrinsic motivation participants display after a condition is created, but also the hardiness of that intrinsic motivation. Once again, in the Mueller and Dweck (1998) studies, the students who received intelligence praise were delighted by the task and highly desirous of taking it home with them when it symbolized their high intelligence. However, their intrinsic motivation was fragile, such that when the task became harder and their intelligence no longer shone, it seemed to evaporate. Surely intrinsic-motivation researchers are looking for conditions that will build more lasting engagement, not just fair-weather interest.

SUMMARY, IMPLICATIONS, AND CONCLUSIONS

When we consider our findings as a whole, what kind of larger picture are we able to paint of the relation between meaning and motivation? First of all, people approach achievement situations with expectations about what qualities of the self are being evaluated. These expectations can arise from chronic belief systems, such as someone's implicit theory of intelligence, or from situational factors, such as the nature of the feedback that is provided. Regardless of their source, the overall effect is to create frameworks of interpretation centered around what individuals believe is being measured by achievement tasks. Selection of goals, attributions for success and failure, increases or decreases in performance, and intrinsic motivation are then regulated by these frameworks.

By these means, a person who has an entity theory of intelligence or is situationally induced to view an achievement situation in terms of fixed intelligence is highly likely to develop a system of meaning in which tasks measure his or her permanent intelligence. What follows from such a construal of achievement is a vulnerability to investing one's self-worth in success, a tendency to pursue avoidance-oriented goals, and a vulnerability to decreases in performance and intrinsic motivation in the face of setbacks. It is for these people (or under these circumstances) that challenging performance goals will create motivational vulnerability.

In the same vein, we have suggested that when a person has an incremental theory of intelligence or is situationally induced to view achievement situations in terms of specific abilities or effort, that person adopts a system in which tasks are interpreted as reflecting process (e.g., effort, strategies), or only abilities that are specifically related to that task and can be developed over time. This system, then, does not link performance with underlying traits and self-worth. Thus, performance goals, when valued and pursued, can have largely positive consequences and learning goals should foster high levels of intrinsic motivation of the durable variety.

Throughout, we have emphasized the fact that under conditions of success, people who have adopted a system that involves global and permanent abilities may often appear identical to those who have adopted a system that involves current skills. Although we believe that there is a greater likelihood that individuals with permanent-ability concerns will focus on avoiding demonstrations of incompetence, it is also perfectly possible for them to begin a task with intentions to demonstrate competence or to learn. If they do so, then as long as they continue to succeed, they may be indistinguishable from those who have only current-ability concerns. Only when failure looms and poses a threat to self-worth will the problems of global and stable internal-ability attributions, helpless responses, and decreases in intrinsic motivation emerge.

Consideration of the meaning systems within which people interpret achievement situations, we believe, begins to address the questions we posed at the beginning of this chapter concerning when and why performance goals might be beneficial or detrimental. As we have seen, when a person believes that an achievement situation can measure the amount of global, unchangeable intelligence that he or she has, performance goals can turn out to be detrimental. They can be beneficial, however, when people believe that they are evaluating only their current level of an ability. This occurs because when individuals are free from self-worth concerns, performance goals may engage people's concentration and effort toward the desired standards in achievement situations (cf. Harackiewicz et al., 1998) as well as boost their desire to learn. Furthermore, current-ability concerns can act as a buffer for failure. Because only specific skills and one's effort are at stake, enjoyment is still possible even if one has failed to reach the desired standard.

In addition to specifying when and why performance goals should have positive or negative effects, we believe that examining meaning can help specify when learning tasks may not create the expected boosts in performance and intrinsic motivation. We have seen that people who have their permanent global abilities invested in a task are vulnerable to self-worth concerns even in the context of a learning task. When a learning task includes challenge and setbacks, it is likely that this vulnerability will be manifested and that the benefits learning goals usually confer may be offset by these concerns. People who have only their current skills invested in a task, however, should be able to fully embrace learning goals and experience the documented benefits.

In conclusion, in this chapter we introduced the idea of meaning systems and presented a model of achievement motivation that integrates goal theory, approach/avoidance distinctions, attribution theory, and self-worth theory with our notions about people's implicit theories of intelligence. Past models have made great strides in defining situations in which particular achievement goals have positive and negative effects on performance and intrinsic motivation. What we have attempted to add to these models is a method for determining not only when goals will have these effects but *why* they will.

References

Abramson, L. Y., Seligman, M. E. P., & Teasdale, J. D. (1978). Learned helplessness in humans: Critique and reformulation. *Journal of Abnormal Psychology, 87*, 49–74.

Ames, C. (1992). Classrooms: Goals, structures, and student motivation. *Journal of Educational Psychology, 84*, 261–271.

Ames, C., & Archer, J. (1988). Achievement goals in the classroom: Students' learning strategies and motivation processes. *Journal of Educational Psychology, 80*, 260–267.

Archer, J. (1994). Achievement goals as a measure of motivation in university students. *Contemporary Educational Psychology, 19*, 430–446.

Atkinson, J. W. (1957). Motivational determinants of risk-taking behavior. *Psychological Review, 6*, 359–372.

Atkinson, J. W., & Feather, N. (Eds.). (1966). *A theory of achievement motivation*. New York: Wiley.

Bandura, A. (1986). *Social foundations of thought and action*. Englewood Cliffs, NJ: Prentice-Hall.

Bandura, M., & Dweck, C. S. (1985). *The relationship of conceptions of intelligence and achievement goals to achievement-related cognition, affect, and behavior*. Unpublished manuscript, Harvard University, Cambridge, MA.

Bouffard, T., Boisvert, J., Vezeau, C., & Larouche, C. (1995). The impact of goal orientation on self-regulation and performance among college students. *British Journal of Educational Psychology, 65*, 317–329.

Burhans, K., & Dweck, C. S. (1995). Helplessness in early childhood: The role of contingent worth. *Child Development, 66*, 1719–1738.

Butler, R. (1987). Task-involving and ego-involving properties of evaluation: Effects of different feedback conditions on motivational perceptions, interest, and performance. *Journal of Educational Psychology, 79*, 474–482.

Butler, R. (1992). What young people want to know when: Effects of mastery and ability goals on interest in different kinds of social comparison. *Journal of Personality and Social Psychology, 62*, 934–943.

Covington, M. V. (1992). *Making the grade: A self-worth perspective on motivation and school reform.* New York: Cambridge University Press.

deCharms, R. (1968). *Personal causation: The internal affective determinants of behavior.* New York: Academic Press.

Deci, E. L. (1975). *Intrinsic motivation.* New York: Plenum Press.

Deci, E. L., & Ryan, R. M. (1985). *Intrinsic motivation and self determination in human behavior.* New York: Academic Press.

Deci, E. L., & Ryan, R. M. (1987). The support of autonomy and the control of behavior. *Journal of Personality and Social Psychology, 53*, 1024–1037.

Diener, C. I., & Dweck, C. S. (1978). An analysis of learned helplessness: Continuous change in performance and strategy and achievement cognitions following failure. *Journal of Personality and Social Psychology, 36*, 451–462.

Diener, C. I., & Dweck, C. S. (1980). An analysis of learned helplessness II: The processing of success. *Journal of Personality and Social Psychology, 39*, 940–952.

Duda, J. L., & Nicholls, J. G. (1992). Dimensions of achievement motivation in schoolwork and sport. *Journal of Educational Psychology, 84*, 290–299.

Dweck, C. S. (1991). Self-theories and goals: Their role in motivation, personality, and development. Perspectives on motivation. Current theory and research in motivation. In R. A. Dienstbier (Ed.), *Nebraska Symposium on Motivation: Vol. 38*, pp. 199–235. Lincoln: University of Nebraska Press.

Dweck, C. S. (1999). *Self-theories: Their role in motivation, personality, and development.* Philadelphia, PA: Psychology Press.

Dweck, C. S., Chiu, C., & Hong, Y. (1995). Implicit theories and their role in judgments and reactions: A world from two perspectives. *Psychological Inquiry, 6*, 267–285.

Dweck, C. S., & Elliott, E. S. (1983). Achievement motivation. In P. Mussen & E. M. Hetherington (Eds.), *Handbook of child psychology.* New York: Wiley.

Dweck, C. S., & Leggett, E. L. (1988). A social-cognitive approach to motivation and personality. *Psychological Review, 95*, 256–273.

Dweck, C. S., & Sorich, L. A. (1999). Mastery oriented thinking. In C. R. Snyder (Ed.), *Coping: The psychology of what works.* New York: Oxford.

Elliot, A. J. (1997). Integrating the "classic" and the "contemporary" approaches to achievement motivation: A hierarchical model of approach and avoidance achievement motivation. In M. Maehr & P. Pintrich (Eds.), *Advances in motivation and achievement* (vol. 10; pp. 243–279), Greenwich, CT: JAI Press.

Elliot, A. J., & Church, M. A. (1997). A hierarchical model of approach and avoidance achievement motivation. *Journal of Personality and Social Psychology, 72*, 218–232.

Elliot, A. J., & Harackiewicz, J. M. (1996). Approach and avoidance achievement goals and intrinsic motivation: A mediational analysis. *Journal of Personality and Social Psychology, 70*, 461–475.

Elliot, A. J., & McGregor, H. A. (1999). Test anxiety and the hierarchical model of approach and avoidance achievement motivation. *Journal of Personality and Social Psychology, 76*, 628–644.

Elliott, E. S., & Dweck, C. S. (1988). Goals: An approach to motivation and achievement. *Journal of Personality and Social Psychology, 54*, 5–12.

Epstein, J. A., & Harackiewicz, J. M. (1992). Winning is not enough: The effects of competition and achievement orientation on intrinsic interest. *Personality and Social Psychology Bulletin, 18*, 128–139.

Farrell, E. (1985). *The role of motivational processes in the transfer of learning.* Unpublished doctoral dissertation, Harvard University, Cambridge, MA.

Graham, S., & Golan, S. (1991). Motivational influences on cognition: Task involvement, ego-involvement, and depth of processing. *Journal of Educational Psychology, 83,* 187–194.

Grant, H., & Dweck, C. S. (in press). Meaning systems: Attributions, goals, culture, and motivation. In F. Salili, C. Chiu, and Y. Y. Hong (Eds.), *Motivated learners: an international perspective.* Hong Kong: University of Hong Kong Press.

Harackiewicz, J. M., Abrahams, S., & Wageman, R. (1987). Performance evaluation and intrinsic motivation: The effects of evaluative focus, rewards, and achievement orientation. *Journal of Personality and Social Psychology, 53,* 1015–1023.

Harackiewicz, J. M., Barron, K. E., Carter, S. M., Lehto, A. T, & Elliot, A. J. (1997) Predictors and consequences of achievement goals in the college classroom: Maintaining interest and making the grade. *Journal of Personality and Social Psychology, 73,* 1284–1295.

Harackiewicz, J. M., Barron, K. E, & Elliot, A. J. (1998). Rethinking achievement goals: When are they adaptive for college students and why? *Educational Psychologist, 33,* 1–21.

Harackiewicz, J. M., & Elliot, A. J. (1993). Achievement goals and intrinsic motivation. *Journal of Personality and Social Psychology, 65,* 904–915.

Harackiewicz, J. M., & Manderlink, G. (1984). A process analysis of the effects of performance-contingent rewards on intrinsic motivation. *Journal of Experimental Social Psychology, 20,* 531–551.

Harackiewicz, J. M., & Sansone, C. (1991). Goals and intrinsic motivation: You can get there from here. In M. L. Maehr, & P. R. Pintrich (Eds.), *Advances in motivation and achievement* (vol. 7, pp. 21–49). Greenwich, CT: JAI Press.

Heider, F. (1958). *The psychology of interpersonal relations.* New York: Wiley.

Henderson, V., & Dweck, C. S. (1990). Achievement and motivation in adolescence: A new model and data. In S. Feldman and G. Elliot (Eds.), *At the threshold: The developing adolescent* (pp. 308–329). Cambridge, MA: Harvard University Press.

Heyman, G. D., & Dweck, C. S. (1992). Achievement goals and intrinsic motivation: Their relation and their role in adaptive motivation. *Motivation and Emotion, 16,* 231–247.

Heyman, G. D., Dweck, C. S., & Cain, K. M. (1992). Young children's vulnerability to self-blame and helplessness: Relationship to beliefs and goodness. *Child Development, 63,* 401–415.

Higgins, E. T. (1998). Promotion and prevention: Regulatory focus as a motivational principle. In M. P. Zanna (Ed.), *Advances in experimental social psychology* (vol. 30, pp. 1–46). San Diego, CA: Academic Press.

Hong, Y. Y., Chiu, C. Y., Dweck, C. S., Lin, D., & Wan, W. (1999). Implicit theories, attributions and coping: A meaning system approach. *Journal of Personality and Social Psychology, 77,* 588–599.

Kamins, M. L., & Dweck, C. S. (1999a). Person versus process praise and criticism: Implications for contingent self-worth and coping. *Developmental Psychology, 35,* 835–847.

Kamins, M. L., & Dweck, C. S. (1999b). [Self-theories and self-worth]. Unpublished raw data.

Kelley, H. H. (1967). Attribution theory in social psychology. In D. Levine (Ed.), *Nebraska Symposium on Motivation: Vol. 15.* (pp. 192–238). Lincoln: University of Nebraska Press.

Koestner, R., Zuckerman, M., & Koestner, J. (1987). Praise, involvement, and intrinsic motivation. *Journal of Personality and Social Psychology, 53,* 383–390.

Koestner, R., Zuckerman, M., & Olsson, J. (1990). Attributional style, comparison focus of praise, and intrinsic motivation. *Journal of Research in Personality, 24,* 87–100.

Leggett, E. (1986). *Individual differences in effort/ability inference rules and goals: Implications for causal judgments.* Unpublished doctoral dissertation, Harvard University, Cambridge, MA.

Lewin, K., Dembo, T., Festinger, L., & Sears, P. S. (1944) Level of aspiration. In J. McHunt (Ed.), *Personality and the behavior disorders* (vol. 1, pp. 333–378). New York: Ronald Press.

Levy, S., & Dweck, C. S. (1997). *Implicit theory measures: Reliability and validity data for adults and children.* Unpublished manuscript, Columbia University, New York.

Maehr, M. L. (1989). Thoughts about motivation. In C. Ames and R. Ames (Eds.), *Research on motivation in education: Goals and cognitions* (vol. 3, pp. 299–315). New York: Academic Press.

McClelland, D. C. (1951). Measuring motivation in phantasy: The achievement motive. In H. Guetzkow (Ed.), *Groups, leadership, and men* (pp. 191–205). Pittsburgh, PA: Carnegie Press.

McClelland, D. C., Atkinson, J. W., Clark, R. A., & Lowell, E. L. (1953). *The achievement motive.* New York: Appleton-Century-Crofts.

Meece, J. L., Blumenfield, P. C., & Hoyle, R. H. (1988). Students' goal orientations and cognitive engagement in classroom activities. *Journal of Educational Psychology, 80,* 514–523.

Meece, J. L., & Holt, K. (1993). A pattern analysis of students' achievement goals. *Journal of Educational Psychology, 85,* 582–590.

Miller, R. L., Brickman, P., & Bolen, D. (1975). Attribution versus persuasion as a means for modifying behavior. *Journal of Personality and Social Psychology, 31,* 430–441.

Mueller, C. M., & Dweck, C. S. (1998). Praise for intelligence can undermine children's motivation and performance. *Journal of Personality and Social Psychology, 75,* 33–52.

Nicholls, J. G. (1984). Achievement motivation: Conceptions of ability, subjective experience, task choice, and performance. *Psychological Review, 91,* 328–346.

Nicholls, J. G., Cheung, P. C., Lauer, J., & Patashnick, M. (1989). Individual differences in academic motivation: Perceived ability, goals, beliefs, and values. *Learning and Individual Differences, 1,* 63–84.

Nolen, S. B. (1988) Reasons for studying: Motivation orientations and study strategies. *Cognition and Instruction, 5,* 269–287.

Pintrich, P. R. (1989) The dynamic interplay of student motivation and cognition in the college classroom. In M. Maehr and C. Ames (Eds.), *Advances in motivation and achievement* (vol. 6, pp. 117–160). Greenwich, CT: JAI Press.

Pintrich, P. R., & Garcia, T. (1991). Student goal orientation and self-regulation in the college classroom. In M. L. Maehr and P. R. Pintrich (Eds.), *Advances in motivation and achievement* (vol. 7, pp. 371–402). Greenwich, CT: JAI Press.

Plant, R. W., & Ryan, R. M. (1985). Intrinsic motivation and the effects of self-consciousness, self-awareness, and ego-involvement: An investigation of internally controlling styles. *Journal of Personality, 15,* 435–449.

Rawsthorne, L. J., & Elliot, A. J. (2000). Achievement goals and intrinsic motivation: A meta-analytic review. *Personality and Social Psychology Review, 3,* 326–344.

Rhodewalt, F. (1994). Conceptions of ability, achievement goals, and individual differences in self-handicapping behavior: On the application of implicit theories. *Journal of Personality, 62,* 67–85.

Ryan, R. M. (1982). Control and information in the intrapersonal sphere: An extension of cognitive evaluation theory. *Journal of Personality and Social Psychology, 43,* 450–461.

Ryan, R. M., Koestner, R., & Deci, E. L. (1991). Ego-involved persistence: When free-choice behavior is not intrinsically motivated. *Motivation and Emotion, 15,* 185–205.

Sansone, C. (1986). A question of competence: The effects of competence and task feedback on intrinsic interest. *Journal of Personality and Social Psychology, 51,* 918–931.

Sansone, C., Sachau, D. A., & Weir, C. (1989). The effects of instruction on intrinsic interest: The importance of context. *Journal of Personality and Social Psychology, 57,* 819–829.

Schunk, D. H. (April, 1996). *Attributions and the development of self-regulatory competence.* Paper presented at the annual meeting of the American Educational Research Association, New York.

Skaalvik, E. M. (1997). Self-enhancing and self-defeating ego orientations: Relations with task and avoidance orientation, achievement, self-perceptions, and anxiety. *Journal of Educational Psychology, 89,* 71–81.

Spence, J. T., & Helmreich, R. L. (1983). Achievement-related motives and behaviors. In J. T. Spence (Ed.), *Achievement and achievement motives: Psychological and sociological approaches* (pp. 7–74). San Franciso: Freeman.

Stone, J., & Dweck, C. S. (1998). *Theories of intelligence and the meaning of achievement goals.* Unpublished doctoral dissertation, New York University, New York.

Utman, C. H. (1997). Performance effects of motivational state: A meta-analysis. *Personality and Social Psychology Review, 1,* 170–182.

Weiner, B. (1980a). A cognitive (attribution)–emotion–action model of motivated behavior: An analysis of judgments of help-giving. *Journal of Personality and Social Psychology, 39,* 186–200.

Weiner, B. (1980b). May I borrow your class notes? An attributional analysis of judgments of help giving in an achievement-related context. *Journal of Educational Psychology, 72,* 676–681.

Weiner, B. (1985). An attributional theory of achievement motivation and emotion. *Psychological Review, 92,* 548–573.

Weiner, B., & Kukla, A., (1970). An attributional analysis of achievement motivation. *Journal of Personality and Social Psychology, 15,* 1–20.

Wine, J. (1971). Test anxiety and direction of attention. *Psychology Bulletin, 76,* 92–104.

Zhao, W., Dweck, C. S., & Mueller, C. (1998). *Implicit theories and depression-like responses to failure.* Unpublished manuscript, Columbia University, New York.

What Learners Want to Know: The Role of Achievement Goals in Shaping Information Seeking, Learning, and Interest

RUTH BUTLER

School of Education
Hebrew University of Jerusalem

I always return students' work not only with the numerical grade required by university regulations but also with numerous comments and a lengthy summary of the paper's strengths and weaknesses and of points to think about and develop in the future. Therefore, in my early days as a conscientious lecturer, I was quite concerned when students would ask why I had given them that particular grade and when they would submit later papers (or even later versions of the same paper) with the same weaknesses as their earlier ones. Not only did they seem more interested in the grade than in the comments but also, my comments were not serving, as intended, to promote learning and mastery. This was something of a disappointment to a motivational theorist convinced that students can be motivated to learn and to use the informational environment to promote mastery (e.g., Butler, 1987).

Another theoretical puzzle was presented when I had the opportunity of observing my 5-year-old son, who did not speak English, in his first days in an American kindergarten, where children spent most of the day completing worksheets. In those days, the consensus was both that social comparison behaviors are motivated by the drive for self-evaluation (Festinger,

1954) and that young children are not motivated to engage in social comparison because they cannot as yet use yet such comparisons to evaluate their outcomes and abilities (Veroff, 1969). So I was fascinated to see that my son spent most of his time observing other children and comparing his work with theirs. What was this, if not social comparison? And if it was social comparison, was it motivated by strivings for self-evaluation or by something else?

These rather different anecdotes are both relevant to the central questions that I address in this chapter. Why do students seek information during the learning process, what information do they seek or attend to, and how does information seeking both reflect and shape ongoing learning and motivation? I address these questions from a goal-oriented motivational perspective and ask both how theory and research on achievement goals can illuminate students' information seeking and how studies of information seeking can illuminate the quality and consequences of goal-oriented task engagement. I propose that information seeking is motivated and can thus be conceptualized and examined in terms of the motives, or goals, that guide achievement behavior in general. Thus, in the first sections of this chapter I apply concepts and findings from the literature on achievement goals to developing a motivational framework for defining and predicting information seeking and addressing some intriguing theoretical and empirical controversies. In addition, I propose that because informational search is motivated, it can provide a fascinating window on motivational processes, and thus not just on the why but also on the how of motivated activity. In the later sections of this chapter, I analyze what studies of goal-oriented information seeking can teach us about motivational states and processes, including intrinsic motivation.

ACHIEVEMENT GOALS AND FUNCTIONS OF INFORMATION SEEKING IN ACHIEVEMENT SETTINGS

References to information seeking appear frequently in the psychological literature, at least in part because of the centrality accorded to information processing in cognitive theories of human action. Within social psychology, relevant inquiry has focused mainly on how people use the informational environment to gain knowledge about themselves. Moreover, self-knowledge has usually been defined quite specifically as knowledge about one's abilities (e.g., Festinger, 1954; Trope, 1986), or, in other words, knowledge relevant to evaluating how competent one is relative to one or another standard. As a result, research questions and designs have by and large examined informational search and inferences after task completion. There are two limitations of such inquiries for illuminating information seeking in achievement settings. First, task engagement in itself is often treated as a kind of prerequisite, of little interest in itself, whose main function is to prime people to ask questions about their competence. Thus, relatively little is known as to whether learners seek information relevant to assessing their abilities during learning and task engagement, what information they seek, and how information seeking during, and not only after, task engagement affects continuing competence assessment, learning and motivation. (See critiques by Ashford & Cummings, 1983; Butler, 1993; Trope, 1986.) Second, and perhaps more significantly, the theoretical emphasis on self-evaluation has limited inquiry into the reasonable possibility that to maintain effective interactions with the environment, people should be interested not only in evaluating how competent they are but also in ascertaining whether and how they can become more competent. Diverse approaches ranging from constructivist approaches to development (Piaget, 1954) and progressive approaches to education (Dewey, 1938/1963) to more recent social-cognitive theories of self-efficacy (Bandura, 1977), self-regulation (Zimmerman, 1990), and motivation for learning (Deci & Ryan, 1985; Harter, 1981) all assume that people are motivated to acquire and develop more adequate understandings and behaviors. In this case, they should also be motivated to seek information that can promote competence. Theories of self-evaluation also tend to assume that the motivation to reduce uncertainty about ability reflects strivings to act effectively on the environment (Festinger, 1954), but knowing how well one has performed or how competent one is does not necessarily suffice as a guide to learning how one can become more effective.

In contrast with most prior approaches, in this chapter I focus mainly on processes of informational search during ongoing activity. To this end, I distinguish schematically between two main functions of information seeking. First, people may seek information relevant to *competence acquisition*, which includes information relevant to clarifying task instructions, demands, and parameters; to identifying difficulties and alternative possibilities for action and understanding; to setting goals; and to monitoring progress. Second, they may seek information relevant to *competence assessment*. This distinction has affinities with some recent proposals. Some authors (Taylor & Lobel, 1989; Wood, 1989) who have reviewed research on social comparison, the form of information search that has been studied most extensively in achievement settings, have concluded that social comparison can serve multiple functions and can be guided not only by strivings for veridical self-assessment (e.g., Festinger, 1954) and by self-enhancing strivings for favorable self-appraisal (e.g., Goethals, 1986) but also by strivings for self-improvement. In a somewhat similar vein, Ruble & Frey (1991) distinguished between knowledge relevant to assessing one's capacities on the one hand and knowledge relevant to constructing the nature of the task, to forming goals and to monitoring progress on the other. Because we know far more about competence assessment than about competence acquisition, one of the aims of this chapter is to examine information seeking that is relevant to acquiring competence. In addition, recognition that information seeking can be guided by multiple motives implies that rather than ask which goal or function is most salient in driving information seeking, as many researchers have done, it might be more useful to ask when one or another function will be salient.

Achievement Goals

My attempts to address this question have been guided by a simple assumption that has, however, proven, quite useful: The information that students seek depends on what they want to know, and what they want to know depends on what they want to achieve, or, in other words, on their achievement goals. Thus, together with other theorists (e.g., Festinger, 1954; Ruble & Frey, 1991; Taylor, Neter, & Wayment, 1995), I view information seeking as motivated. However, I propose further that motives for information seeking are secondary to, and thus follow from, the perceived purposes, goals, or motives for learning. Other chapters in this book provide extensive and insightful reviews of theory and research on achievement goals, so my initial introduction is brief. As other contributors note, during the 1980s a new language was introduced to the discourse on human motivation in general and to that of motivation for learning and achievement in particular. The language of goals presented learners as continuously endeavoring to make sense of themselves and the world, and thus as actively engaged in constructing and reconstructing the meaning and purposes of learning (e.g., Butler, 1989a; Nicholls, 1989). Moreover, the assumption that achievement behavior is goal-oriented implies that if one wants to understand what people are doing, a fruitful starting point is to understand what they striving to achieve.

What goals may learners construct and adopt? In this chapter, I focus on two classes of goals whose study has dominated the literature on achievement motivation since the 1980s. For example, Nicholls (1984, 1989) distinguished between task and ego orientation; Dweck (1986), between learning and performance goals; and Ames (1992), between mastery and performance goals. Despite some nontrivial theoretical differences, in general these terminologies reflect a conceptually similar distinction between strivings to acquire and improve skills, proficiencies, and understandings on the one hand and strivings to maintain self-worth by demonstrating superior, or masking inferior, ability on the other. I have chosen to highlight this distinction by distinguishing between *mastery goals*, which orient learners to strive to improve over time, to overcome difficulties, and to acquire skills and understandings through effortful learning, versus *ability goals*, which orient them to demonstrate high ability by outperforming others, succeeding with little effort, or avoiding activities in which they expect to do poorly. To facilitate comparison with relevant contributions in the literature and in this volume, one additional clarification is warranted. Some researchers have treated goal orientation mainly as an individual difference variable and have focused on examining the determinants and correlates of, for example, task-versus-ego or learning-versus-performance orientations to schoolwork (e.g., Harackiewicz, Barron, Carter, Lehto, & Elliot, 1997; Nicholls, Cheung, Lauer, & Patashnik, 1989). As one would expect, these general goal orientations predict achievement strivings for specific learning experiences (e.g., Harackiewicz et al., 1997). However, the degree to which one or another achievement goal is salient at any one time depends also on features of the immediate learning context. Thus, some researchers, including me, have focused on comparing attitudes and behaviors in experimental conditions designed to induce salient mastery versus ability goals. (See the review by Jagacinski, 1992.) Typical experimental manipulations involve presenting a target activity either as an opportunity to learn and acquire worthwhile skills and understandings (mastery-goal condition) or as a measure of individual differences in some valued ability (ability-goal condition).

Goal-Oriented Information Seeking

How may the different concerns characteristic of mastery versus ability goals affect information seeking in achievement settings? Most generally, if informational search is guided by what people want to know, it should be guided by different questions when people adopt different achievement goals. I propose that when people strive for mastery and define success in terms of learning and improvement, they should mainly ask themselves whether they need to learn and improve, how they can improve, and whether they are indeed improving. In this case, they should be strongly motivated to seek information relevant to competence acquisition. Students who adopt mastery goals as they work, for example, on algebra problems should seek information that clarifies task demands or analytical principles, that presents appropriate or alternative strategies, or that indicates where they encountered difficulty and how this can be overcome. In other words, they should be motivated to seek information that enables them not only to understand and solve the problems they are working on but also to improve their subsequent independent problem solving and their math proficiency in general. Pupils cannot, however, know whether there is room for improvement and for developing alternative understandings and strategies unless they have some sense of their present capacities. Thus, mastery goals should also orient pupils to seek information relevant to evaluating their current performance and capacity—that is, to competence assessment. Moreover, pupils who adopt mastery goals should be interested mainly in veridical self-appraisal, because this is most useful for regulating activity and setting goals (Bandura, 1977, Trope, 1986).

Information seeking among pupils who adopt ability goals for the same math problems should, however, be guided by quite different concerns and questions. If ability goals focus attention on documenting, rather than on acquiring, competence (Ames, 1992; Dweck & Leggett, 1988), the salient question should be whether one has high ability. In this case, pupils who adopt ability goals should be primarily motivated to seek information relevant to competence assessment. Moreover, they should be particularly interested in information about their performance and outcomes relative to others, because such normative information is most diagnostic for assessing the level of an ability (Masters & Keil, 1987; Nicholls, 1989). Thus, even if a pupil has access to objective information and knows, for example, that she solved 9 of 10 math problems correctly, she will not be able to evaluate how much math ability she has unless she also knows how many problems other classmates solved. It is, however, important to note that the aim of ability goals is not just to evaluate ability but also to prove or demonstrate high, as opposed to low, ability. In this case, information seeking may be guided more by strivings to maintain favorable self-perceptions than by interest in veridical self-appraisal, and people who expect to do well should seek more information relevant to assessing their competence than should people who expect to do poorly (see also Brown, 1990).

At first sight, this analysis seems to imply that ability goals will not stimulate interest in information relevant to competence acquisition. However, when people strive to attain positive outcomes that reflect favorably on their ability, they should be interested in at least one kind of relevant information—the correct answer. Thus, students who adopt ability goals may be quite inclined, when circumstances allow, to look up the right answer at the back of the textbook or to copy someone else's work, not because they are concerned to learn and promote mastery but because they want to expedite successful task completion and ensure positive outcomes and evaluation.

This analysis is schematically presented in Table 7.1, which distinguishes between two classes of achievement goals (mastery vs ability) and two functions of information seeking (competence acquisition vs competence assessment) to yield four conceptually distinct categories of motivated information seeking and several specific predictions. First, people will actively seek information during task engagement in both mastery-goal and ability-goal settings.

Second, these settings should evoke differential interest in information relevant to competence acquisition and to competence assessment, respectively, which can be manifested in two main ways. Different goal settings should be associated with preferences for different kinds of information, because some kinds of information are inherently more relevant to acquiring competence and others are more relevant to competence assessment (see also Taylor et al., 1995). In addition, achievement goals should affect

TABLE 7.1

**Mastery versus Ability-Oriented Informational Search: Functions and Forms
of Information Seeking under Mastery and Ability Goals**

Functions of Information Seeking	Achievement Goal	
	Mastery	Ability
Competence Acquisition		
Motive for information seeking	Learn	Ensure positive outcomes
Informational preferences	Task information: Clarify demands, acquire concepts, strategies	Task information: solution
	Social comparison: observational learning	Social comparison: copy from others
	Help seeking: explanations, hints	Help seeking: solution
Competence assessment		
Motive for Information-Seeking	Accurate self-assessment	Positive self-assessment
Informational Preferences	Objective or normative scores	Objective or normative scores (if expect these to be positive)
	Temporal: scores over time	
	Social comparison: compare to see if need to improve	Social comparison: compare to evaluate ability if expect to do better than others

people's orientation to sources of information, such as social comparison, that can serve multiple goals or functions. Thus, one can predict that people will be more likely to engage in social comparison to learn from others when they adopt mastery goals, and to evaluate themselves relative to others when they adopt ability goals.

Third, my analysis suggests the novel prediction that information seeking under both mastery and ability goals will be guided, at least to some extent, by strivings for both competence assessment and competence acquisition, but the forms and functions of each will differ under salient mastery goals versus ability goals. Vis-à-vis competence acquisition, Table 7.1 suggests that people will seek information relevant to learning when they adopt mastery goals but will be more interested in information relevant to ensuring successful task completion when they adopt ability goals. Vis-à-vis competence assessment, Table 7.1 suggests that contrasting findings as to whether people are motivated primarily by strivings for veridical or self-enhancing self-appraisal may be resolved, at least in part, by considering the possibility that the former are salient when people adopt mastery goals and the latter when they adopt ability goals.

Achievement goals, information seeking, and the adaptivity of task engagement

The foregoing analysis rests on the assumption that people construe goal attainment in different ways when they adopt mastery goals versus ability goals and thus not only define success in different ways (Nicholls, 1984) but also ask themselves different questions and engage in different performance-related strategies, including information seeking, as they strive to answer their questions and attain their goals. Mixed findings as to the relations between achievement goals and both performance and intrinsic motivation (see reviews by Harackiewicz, Barron, & Elliot, 1998; Rawsthorne & Elliot, 1999; Utman, 1997) imply that mastery and ability goals are each associated with internally consistent, but different, patterns of performance-related strivings, attitudes, strategies, and behaviors, each of which may be adaptive for promoting different kinds of success and for maintaining interest and task involvement (e.g., chapter 8, this book). Some of the inquiry into mastery-versus ability-oriented activity has, however, been characterized by limitations somewhat similar to those typical of research on information seeking. Early conceptualizations and studies tended to focus on performance and motivational outcomes after task completion and shed less light on the role of achievement goals in shaping and maintaining performance and motivation during task engagement. In addition, even when researchers considered the role of competence-related strivings (e.g., Deci & Ryan, 1985), they tended to focus rather narrowly on ability-oriented strivings to attain favorable outcomes that reflect positively on one's ability (see critique in Butler, 1989a).

In this chapter, I propose (Table 7.2) that distinguishing systematically between strivings to acquire competence and strivings to demonstrate high ability and examining how these strivings are expressed in informational search may help clarify how different constructions of the purposes of activity affect processes of goal-oriented task engagement. In brief, Table 7.2 implies that ongoing information seeking, performance, and interest, or, in other words, task involvement, will depend in large part on the degree to which informational search provides positive or negative answers to the questions people ask themselves. If mastery goals orient people to ask themselves what they can learn and whether they are learning, they should be most beneficial for performance when success depends on acquiring new skills and understandings, as long as the environment provides information relevant to acquiring competence and as long as people infer that they are continuing to learn. In a similar vein, if ability goals orient people to ask whether they already have high ability, they may be more beneficial for performance when success depends on the rapid and persistent application of

TABLE 7.2
Processes of Mastery- and Ability-Oriented Task Engagement

Mastery goal		Ability goal	
Initial stages of task engagement			
Question: What can I learn? Seek information relevant to competence acquisition Seek information relevant to competence assessment		Question: How able am I? Seek information relevant to competence assessment	
Later stages of task engagement			
Question: Am I Learning? Can I learn more?		Question: Do I have high ability?	
Yes	No	Yes	No
Recurring cycles of information seeking	Cease information seeking	Continued competence assessment	Cease competence assessment; covert search for solutions if possible
Improve performance in keeping with information received	Performance stable or declines	Performance high and stable (if task does not require new learning)	Performance low and declining (unless receive solutions)
High and possibly increasing interest in activity	Reduced interest; disengage from activity	High interest	Low interest; disengage from activity

well-learned procedures and strategies, as long as the environment provides information relevant to competence assessment and as long as people infer that they are demonstrating high ability.

Although there is empirical support for claims that ability goals undermine both performance (Utman, 1997) and intrinsic motivation (Rawsthorne & Elliot, 1999) relative to mastery goals, the present analysis suggests that this will be the case mainly when task engagement indicates low but not high ability (see also Dweck & Leggett, 1988; chapter 6, this book). However, the present analysis implies further that initial mastery strivings may not in themselves suffice to maintain intrinsic motivation over time. Rather, continuing interest and task involvement should depend on the degree to which people continue to experience task engagement as promoting competence acquisition. Indeed, a further implication of Table 7.2 is that the degree to which people continue to seek goal-relevant information can serve as a measure of their ongoing goal-oriented motivation. If experiences during task engagement indicate that one is not attaining one's goals, declining levels of achievement motivation should be reflected in reduced information seeking. Conversely, continuing information seeking should reflect continuing achievement motivation and should be associated with continuing performance and interest in both mastery and ability goal conditions. These predictions all rest, however, on the assumption that information seeking is a central manifestation of goal-oriented task engagement. Thus, it is first important to examine whether people actively seek information and whether their informational search does indeed differ in mastery versus ability goal settings as predicted in Table 7.1.

ACHIEVEMENT GOALS AND INFORMATIONAL PREFERENCES: EMPIRICAL EVIDENCE

Competence Acquisition versus Competence Assessment

As noted earlier, most prior studies are not directly relevant to examining my predictions concerning the role of achievement goals in shaping information seeking because they examined responses to or preferences for information after, rather than during, task engagement, did not enable participants to decline to receive information, and did not provide them with information relevant to acquiring, as distinct from evaluating, competence (see review in Butler, 1993). In one series of studies that attempted to address these lacunae, college students (Butler, 1993) and junior high school students (Butler, 1999) worked on 10 computer-delivered water jar problems. The aim was to fill a target container (t) using three other containers (a, b, c,) in as few moves as possible. Problems were designed such that each had several solutions; the best (shortest) solution required students to transfer quantities between a, b, and c before making transfers to t, and longer solutions depended on making direct transfers to t. Thus, in principle, the activity primed interest in information relevant both to competence assessment, because the task did not in itself provide complete information as to the quality of a particular solution, and to competence acquisition, because participants could improve their performance if they acquired more effective strategies. Mastery goals versus ability goals were evoked prior to task engagement by instructions that presented the problems either as an opportunity to develop problem-solving skills and strategies or as a test of analytical ability on which students should score high.

After each problem, students could either continue directly to the next one or ask first for one of three kinds of information. They could request the best solution to the problem, which was relevant to acquiring competence because it rested on effective strategies that could then be applied to subsequent problems. Alternatively, they could ask for information relevant to assessing competence—either their score on the problem (objective information) or their percentile score (normative information). Table 7.3 presents mean requests for each kind of information over all 10 problems from one representative study (Butler, 1993, Study 1). Findings confirmed first that overall, participants requested information after most problems, even though this left them with less time for working on the problems themselves. In other words, participants were motivated to seek information in both mastery and ability goal conditions. However, as expected, pupils in the mastery goal condition asked most often for optimal solutions, the only kind of information that could foster learning. In contrast, pupils in the ability goal condition asked most often for normative or objective information, and rarely requested optimal solutions. Further support for the proposal that mastery goals promote interest in acquiring competence is provided in Table 7.3 by the findings that in the mastery condition, students who did poorly on a number of practice problems, and thus had most to learn, requested optimal solutions more frequently than did students who initially scored high. However, when experimental problems were difficult for most participants (Butler, 1993, Study 2), requests for optimal solutions were frequent not only among students who initially scored low on easier practice tasks (M = 4.4) but also among those who scored high (M = 3.6). In contrast, in the ability-goal condition, requests for optimal solutions were rare at both low (M = 1.5) and high (M = 1.1) levels of initial competence.

These findings, which were replicated among junior high school students (Butler, 1999), confirmed that experimental framings that emphasized

TABLE 7.3
Information Seeking in Mastery-Goal versus Ability-Goal Conditions at Low versus High Levels of Attainment

		Mastery		Ability	
		Low	High	Low	High
Water jar study—mean requests for information					
Competence acquisition	Best solution	3.8	2.2	1.5	1.4
Competence assessment	Objective score	2.4	3.5	2.6	3.6
	Percentile score	2.0	1.4	1.4	3.1
	Total Comp. Ass.	4.4	4.9	4.0	6.7
Avoidance of information	Problems for which did not request information	1.8	2.8	4.5	1.9
Tables Study—mean seconds at tables					
Competence acquisition	Creative ideas table	132	115	68	61
Competence assessment	Creative ability table	144	139	111	172
Avoidance of information	Magazines table	24	46	131	77

Source: Water jars: Butler (1993, Study 1); tables: Butler (1995).

mastery goals versus ability goals affected people's preferences for information relevant to acquiring versus assessing competence. A further implication of my framework (see Table 7.1) is that achievement goals will affect people's orientation to certain kinds of information, such as social comparison, that can serve multiple goals or functions. The first indications from my research that social comparison can serve multiple functions in achievement settings were provided by several studies in which we simply observed the frequency with which children at between the ages of 5 and 10 years looked at others' work as each worked on an art project (e.g., creating flowers using colored stickers) and then asked them why they had done so (e.g., Butler, 1989c; Butler & Ruzani, 1993; Butler, 1996). Overall, about half of the participants explained their glances in terms of strivings to acquire competence ("My ground came out crooked so I wanted to see how to do it straight" or "I didn't know how to do petals") and about half did so in terms of strivings to assess competence ("I wanted to see whether my picture was good"; "I wanted to see whose design was best"). Although this chapter does not focus on the development of information seeking, it is interesting to note that before age 7 years, more than 80% of children explained social comparison interest in terms of competence acquisition. Distinguishing between competence acquisition and competence assessment functions of social comparison can thus explain why not only my son but also children in empirical studies (Mosatche & Bragonier, 1981; Pepitone, 1980) engaged in spontaneous social comparison before they acquired the capacity to use such comparisons for self-appraisal.

There is other evidence that people engage in social comparison not only to assess but also to acquire competence (Taylor and Lobel, 1989; Wood, 1989), but the present framework suggests further that these different strivings depend importantly on people's salient achievement goals. This prediction can be addressed by examining explanations for social comparison interest after about age 6 to 7 years, when children have acquired the understanding that others' outcomes are diagnostic for self-appraisal (Nicholls & Miller, 1983), or, in other words, among children who in principle can engage in social comparison both to acquire and to assess competence. Table 7.4 first presents results from children between the ages of 7 and 10 years who worked on an art task in either a mastery goal condition or a competitive condition that focused attention on outperforming others (Butler, 1989b); as expected, children in the mastery condition tended to give competence-acquisition explanations and more children in the competitive condition gave competence-assessment explanations. In this case, motives for social comparison should also be affected by the degree to which natural learning environments foster mastery or ability goal orientations. In one study we compared motives for social comparison among 6- to 8-year-old urban and kibbutz children in Israel (Butler & Ruzani, 1993). In common with typical U.S. schools, classroom practices in the urban schools sampled emphasized

TABLE 7.4
Children's Explanations for Looking at Peers' Work
in Mastery-Goal versus Ability-Goal Contexts

	Experimental manipulations		Natural learning environments	
	Mastery	Ability	Kibbutz	Urban
Competence acquisition: learn from others	54	7	85	0
Competence assessment: evaluate self relative to others	41	83	5	86
Unscorable	5	10	10	14

Source: Butler (1989c): Children between the ages of 8 and 10 years; Butler and Ruzani (1993): Children between the ages of 7 and 9 years who had acquired the understanding that social comparison is diagnostic for self-appraisal.

teacher-led presentation-recitation or individual seatwork and normative evaluation. In contrast, because the kibbutz espouses a collectivist and egalitarian social philosophy, children work mainly on personal projects or in cooperative work groups and receive individual, rather than normative, evaluations of their mastery and progress. These contrasting features have been shown to promote ability- and mastery-achievement orientations, respectively (Ames 1992). Table 7.4 confirms that when we compared those children in both frameworks who had attained the understanding that normative outcomes are diagnostic of ability, we found that more kibbutz children gave competence-acquisition explanations and more urban children competence-assessment explanations for their interest in peers' work.

In another study (Butler, 1995), we combined the logic of the water jar and glances studies and examined preferences for different kinds of social information, which were relevant mainly to acquiring competence on the one hand or to assessing competence on the other. Children worked on a divergent thinking task (creating drawings out of circles) in either a mastery-goal or an ability-goal condition. They were then told that the experimenter needed a few minutes to prepare some materials for a similar task she wanted to give them. These instructions were designed to increase the relevance of current for future activity. Pupils could pass the time by looking at materials set out on tables. One table, labeled "Creative Ideas," presented a pile of drawings made by other pupils, information relevant mainly to acquiring competence by learning from others. Another table, labeled "Creative Ability," provided criteria for computing a total score and determining whether this indicated excellent, good, medium, or poor creative ability relative to others (normative competence assessment). Finally, popular children's magazines set out on a third table gave children the opportunity to curtail or avoid information seeking. The time pupils spent at each table was unobtrusively recorded (see Table 7.3). Although computing scores took longer than looking through peers' work, the effects for achievement goals paralleled those in the water jar studies. Pupils in the mastery-goal condition spent more time at the "Creative Ideas" table and less time at the "Creative Ability" table than did pupils in the ability-goal condition. In addition, pupils who did poorly, and thus had most to learn, spent more time at the "Creative Ideas" table if they had worked on the task in the mastery-goal condition and spent more time avoiding information by reading magazines if they had worked in the ability-goal condition.

Mastery goals thus promoted more interest in competence acquisition than in competence assessment, and ability-goals conditions promoted far more interest in competence assessment. However, Table 7.1 implied further that mastery goals will also promote some interest in competence assessment and that ability goals will also promote some interest in competence acquisition, but the forms and functions of both kinds of information searches will differ depending on whether learners are guided by mastery goals or ability goals. I address this claim in the following sections.

Competence Assessment under Mastery versus Ability Goals

Veridical versus Self-Enhancing Competence-Assessment

The results presented in Table 7.3 confirmed that participants sought information relevant to competence assessment not only in ability but also in mastery-goal conditions. In contrast with the paucity of studies that have examined information seeking relevant to competence acquisition, many have examined competence assessment. A central question addressed by such studies is whether people are motivated mainly to reduce uncertainty about their abilities or to maintain favorable perceptions of their ability. Self-assessment theorists (e.g., Trope 1986) predict that people will seek diagnostic information about their abilities, whether or not they expect it to be favorable. In other words, they expect motivation to seek information to depend mainly on the level of self-evaluative uncertainty, which tends to be greater at lower levels of ability or attainment (Strube, Lott, Le-Xuan-Hy, Oxenberg, Deichman, 1992). However, people do not always prefer to compare themselves with similar others, whose outcomes are most diagnostic for self-assessment and frequently distort or avoid relevant information if this is likely to reflect unfavorably on their abilities (Brown, 1990; Taylor & Lobel, 1989). Thus, self-enhancement theorists (Brown, 1990; Goethals, 1986) propose that people seek information that reflects favorably on the self and they predict that motivation to seek information will depend on expected outcome more than on uncertainty about ability. In this case, information seeking should be greater at high than at low levels of attainment or ability.

The present framework suggests that these conflicting approaches and predictions can be resolved, at least in part, by considering the role of achievement goals. According to Table 7.3, mastery goals should promote strivings for accurate competence assessment, in which case information seeking should be congruent with the predictions of self-assessment theorists. In contrast, ability goals should promote strivings for self-enhancing competence assessment, in which case information seeking should be congruent with the predictions of self-enhancement theorists. The results from my studies (see Table 7.3) confirmed that in mastery-goal conditions, interest in information relevant to assessing competence did not differ among students who performed poorly and received unfavorable feedback relative to those who performed well and received positive feedback. Indeed, students who did poorly tended to seek more information relevant not only to acquiring but also to assessing competence. In contrast, in ability-goal conditions, students who did well sought far more information relevant to assessing competence than did students who did poorly. This was the case even in the water jar studies, when the performance of high scorers was quite stable and a single normative request was often sufficient to establish high ability and reduce self-evaluative uncertainty. The interpretation that achievement strivings affect the degree to which people strive for favorable or veridical self-appraisal is consistent with evidence that biased and self-serving self-appraisal and attributions tend to be greater for ego-central than for non–ego-central activities, especially when potential ego threat is enhanced by low self-esteem or prior failure (see review in Brown, 1990).

Another Form of Competence Assessment: Assessing Competence versus Assessing Acquisition of Competence

A central premise of achievement-goal theory is that ability goals focus attention on evaluating and documenting ability and that mastery goals focus attention on acquiring competence and mastery (Dweck & Leggett, 1988). The results described above confirmed that people were motivated to evaluate their competence also when they strove to acquire competence. However, the competence-assessment information provided in both the water jar studies and the tables studies was more diagnostic for evaluating the level of a particular outcome or ability than for assessing the acquisition of competence and ability and for monitoring progress. To this end, information as to whether one has learned and improved would seem more useful. In this case, one can venture that people who adopt mastery goals should be more likely than people who adopt ability goals to seek and attend to temporal feedback that provides information about their performance and outcomes over time.

Few studies have examined interest in temporal self-evaluation. Indeed, several authors have made the pertinent point that lives are lived through time and it is thus strange that psychologists have paid little theoretical attention to how, when, and why people attend to changes in their outcomes, abilities, and interests and how they incorporate such changes into their self-images and self-narratives (Albert, 1977; Gergen & Gergen, 1997). I am currently applying the framework described here also to examining this relatively neglected kind of information seeking and self-evaluation. Preliminary findings from one study that examined preferences for temporal versus normative feedback are particularly relevant to the present discussion. Junior high school students worked on pencil-and-paper versions of the water jar problems under conditions that emphasized either mastery or ability goals. They also completed a measure of perceived math competence. Students read that their work would be returned with their total score over all problems (objective information). They could also request either their percentile score relative to other students or their own scores for each of the experimental problems, in order of presentation. They could also choose not to receive any additional information. The results, which are presented in Table 7.5, were clear. In the ability condition, more students requested normative than temporal information. Moreover, as one would expect on the basis of the findings reviewed above, information seeking was moderated by self-enhancing biases such that more children with high than low perceived math competence requested normative information, and more children with low perceived competence chose not to receive any feedback. In contrast, in the mastery-goal condition, almost all students requested additional information, most chose temporal information, and choices were not significantly moderated by perceived competence. Few published studies have addressed the possibility that mastery goals orient people to assessing not only the level of an ability but also the degree to which they succeed in acquiring ability over time. However, one study found that self-evaluative inferences and affect were affected only by normative outcome in a competitive condition but were affected also by performance trends in a noncompetitive condition (Ames & Ames, 1984).

TABLE 7.5
Percentages of Children who Requested Normative, Temporal, or No Information by Goal Condition and Perceived Competence in Math

	Mastery condition		Ability condition	
	Low	High	Low	High
Information request				
Normative	30	40	30	62
Temporal	60	55	35	33
Neither	10	5	35	5

Source: Butler (1999), unpublished data.

Competence Acquisition under Mastery Goals versus Ability Goals

Results from studies that used different experimental designs, different kinds of information, and different measures of information seeking provided consistent and converging evidence that forms and functions of competence assessment differ under mastery goals versus ability goals. An additional—and recurring—finding was that interest in information relevant to competence acquisition was marked in mastery-goal settings but seemed to be virtually nonexistent in ability-goal settings. On the surface, this finding seems to cast doubt on my proposal that there are grounds for distinguishing not only between mastery- versus ability-oriented competence assessment but also between mastery- and ability-oriented competence acquisition. Thus, in Table 7.1, I distinguish between information seeking that is guided by strivings to acquire skills and understandings through effortful learning and information seeking that is guided by strivings to expedite successful task completion and to attain outcomes that reflect positively on one's ability. However, in some of the studies reported above, the information relevant to competence acquisition was relevant only to mastery-oriented competence acquisition. For example, viewing optimal solutions for one water jar problem did not automatically provide participants with the best solution for the next problem; instead, they needed to invest thought and effort first to identify and then to apply optimal problem-solving strategies.

If the environment did not provide information relevant to expediting successful task completion, it is not surprising that we found no indications of ability-based competence acquisition. In contrast, in one of the studies that examined children's explanations for looking at peers' work (Butler, 1996), I distinguished between explanations that reflected mastery-based competence acquisition (e.g., "I wanted to have fire coming out of my spaceship and I wasn't sure how to do it") and explanations that reflected ability-oriented competence acquisition (e.g., "I wanted to do a sunshade like hers so my picture would win"; "I didn't want my page to be emptiest, so I copied what he did"). In another study (Butler, 1995), children rated the degree to which each kind of reason explained why they had looked at peers' work. Results confirmed that when the environment enabled children to use others both to learn and to attain positive outcomes without learning, the degree to which informational search was guided by one or the other kind of striving for competence acquisition differed both in mastery-goal versus ability-goal conditions (Butler, 1995, 1996) and among kibbutz versus urban children (Butler, 1996).

These indications that ability goals encouraged children to copy rather than to learn from others imply further that they may encourage at least some students to view cheating as an effective way of succeeding in school.

I explored this possibility further in a study of help seeking, which can be viewed as a particular form of social information seeking (Butler, 1998). Children in late elementary school who were previously identified as endorsing a predominantly mastery orientation or ability orientation to classroom mathematics worked individually on difficult math problems. For each problem, they could request either a hint that clarified strategies or the solution; they could also check their answers against an answer sheet but were expressly instructed not to do so before they had recorded an answer of their own, and not to simply copy the correct answer. Infringement of these instructions provided a behavioral measure of cheating.

In general, children who endorsed a mastery orientation displayed an autonomous style of help seeking, similar to the patterns of information seeking in mastery-goal conditions described earlier. When they encountered difficulty, they did not "cheat" or ask for the answer but requested hints relevant to promoting learning and subsequent independent mastery. In contrast, children who endorsed an ability-goal orientation displayed an avoidant-covert style. They refrained from requesting overt help, even help that would provide them with the correct answer, and were far more likely than their mastery-oriented counterparts to cheat. This pattern makes sense if we consider that although ability-oriented students do not seem motivated to learn, they are certainly not indifferent to their learning outcomes. When they encounter difficulty, they are thus caught in a dilemma between exposing inadequate capacity by requesting help or seeking information and exposing inadequate ability by failing (Butler, 1998). The implication that they may be tempted to resolve this dilemma by cheating is supported by other evidence that ability goals undermine help seeking and question asking and encourage cheating in both experimental and classroom settings (Anderman, Griesinger, & Westerfield, 1998; Butler & Neuman, 1995; Karabenick, 1994; Newstead, Franklin-Stokes, & Armstead, 1996; Ryan & Pintrich, 1997). More generally, our findings for information seeking and help seeking confirm and extend prior claims (Dweck & Leggett, 1988) that failure evokes strivings to learn and overcome difficulty in mastery-goal settings and strivings to salvage self-esteem by masking inadequacy or discontinuing task engagement in ability goal settings.

Taken together, the evidence reviewed here confirms that conceptualizing information seeking as a particular form of goal-oriented behavior and distinguishing systematically between motives to acquire competence versus motives to attain positive outcomes provides a fruitful framework for studying informational search and for resolving debates as to whether people actively seek information during activity, why they do so, and what information they seek. First, although some authors have questioned whether people seek information to the extent that social psychologists assume (Ross, Eyman, & Kishchuk, 1986), in all of our studies students sought information in both mastery and ability settings, even though the experimental designs enabled them to avoid information seeking altogether. Second, the degree to which people engaged in mastery-oriented versus ability-oriented information seeking differed consistently and quite dramatically in different goal conditions in accordance with the predictions presented in Table 7.1. Most generally, informational search seemed to be guided by different questions in different goal conditions. In mastery-goal conditions, people seemed to ask themselves whether they needed to learn and improve, how they could improve, and whether they were indeed improving. In contrast, in ability goal conditions, people seemed mainly to be asking themselves whether they had high ability. I now address the further proposal, presented in Table 7.2, that continuing task involvement—and thus ongoing information seeking, performance, and interest—depends not only on the questions people ask but also on their inferences, or in other words, on the degree to which informational search confirms that task engagement is relevant for attaining their goals.

WHICH GOALS ARE MORE ADAPTIVE? PROCESSES AND CONSEQUENCES OF MASTERY VERSUS ABILITY-ORIENTED INFORMATION SEEKING AND TASK ENGAGEMENT

Continuing Informational Search

In an interesting theoretical analysis of informational search during activity, Ruble and Frey (1991) proposed that the standards people use to assess competence, and thus the information they seek, depend importantly on shifts in skill level during activity. They proposed that at initial stages of engagement on novel tasks, people will first seek information relevant to learning about the activity and acquiring skills; will then assess their current proficiency—for example, by comparing themselves with others; and will continue to repeat this sequence until they have achieved mastery. However, the proposal that information seeking is guided both by the questions people ask as they embark on an activity and by the answers they give themselves suggests that patterns of information seeking over time will differ depending on whether people initially adopt mastery or ability goals. The recurring cycles of competence acquisition and competence assessment described by Ruble & Frey should indeed characterize informational search when people pursue mastery goals, and continuing information seeking should depend on the degree to which people experience themselves as continuing to learn and improve. In contrast, when people adopt ability goals, strivings to demonstrate high ability should prime them to seek information relevant to competence assessment immediately, and continuing information seeking should depend on the results of this initial competence assessment. If it is favorable and conveys that one already knows what one needs to succeed, people should not be motivated to seek information relevant to learning but should continue to seek confirmation of their high ability. In contrast, unfavorable competence assessment should convey that task engagement is not likely to promote one's goal of demonstrating high ability and that continuing informational search is likely to provide further confirmation of inadequate ability. In this case, the findings for information seeking and help seeking reviewed above suggest that people will strive to salvage self-esteem by covertly seeking the correct answers or by ceasing informational search altogether.

Several of the studies described earlier incorporated data relevant to examining sequences of information seeking. In the water jar studies (Butler, 1993, 1999) requests were made and recorded after each problem. In one of the glances studies (Butler, 1996), children explained two glances, filmed in the first and last 2 minutes of task engagement, respectively. In the tables studies (Butler, 1992, 1995) I recorded the order in which children approached tables. Despite the differences in tasks and measures, the studies yielded very similar findings. In mastery-goal conditions, students initially sought information relevant to acquiring competence; they requested the best solution for early water jar problems, explained early glances in terms of competence acquisition, and went first to the table that provided examples of peers' work. Later on, they sought more information relevant to competence assessment; they requested more objective and percentile scores for later problems, gave more self-appraisal explanations for later than for earlier glances, and moved from the competence-acquisition to the competence-assessment table. However, they continued to request some optimal solutions or returned to the table presenting examples of others' work, especially if prior competence assessment indicated that they had performed poorly.

In contrast, students in ability-goal conditions requested objective or percentile scores for initial problems, went first to the "Creative Ability" table, and explained early glances in terms of competence assessment. Moreover, continuing information seeking depended as predicted on the results of initial competence assessment. When this indicated high ability, participants continued to request information relevant to competence assessment. Although one might expect people who strive to attain positive outcomes and who are performing poorly to be strongly motivated to seek information that can help them do better, such students did not then turn, as they did in mastery-goal conditions, to information relevant to competence acquisition. Instead, as Table 7.2 suggests, they tended either to copy or cheat or to cease informational search altogether by ceasing to request feedback for the water jar problems or by reading magazines (see also Table 7.3).

Ongoing informational search does indeed seem to depend on the degree to which people continue to experience task engagement as relevant to attaining their goals. My findings are consistent with other evidence that failure undermines persistence, effort, and task engagement when people are guided by ability strivings (Dweck & Leggett, 1988) but suggest further that goal strivings and task involvement may decline over time also in mastery-goal conditions if people do not continue to experience activity as relevant to learning. In this case, there are grounds for addressing my further predictions (see Table 7.2) that continuing performance and interest will also depend not only on the different questions and definitions of success evoked by initial goal constructions but also on the degree to which students' experiences and inferences during activity convey that they are attaining their goals.

Achievement Goals, Information Seeking, and Performance

Recurring cycles of information seeking relevant to competence acquisition and competence assessment certainly seem adaptive when one strives to learn and when task engagement provides opportunities for learning. In a similar vein, seeking information relevant to competence assessment when this reflects favorably on one's capacities and avoiding such information when it does not also seems adaptive, as long as one's main concern is to maintain favorable self-perceptions. At first glance, however, the information search associated with mastery goals would seem more adaptive for attaining the common aim of achievement strivings—to succeed. However, some recent reviews indicate that although ability goals undermined performance relative to mastery goals in many studies, in others they did not undermine, and on occasion even enhanced, performance (Harackiewicz et al., 1998; Utman, 1997).

These mixed findings have been attributed to the differential effects of mastery versus ability goals both in moderating performance for different kinds of activity (Butler, 1988; Amabile, 1982) and in moderating performance at different levels of actual or perceived ability (Elliot & Dweck, 1988). A meta-analytical review (Utman, 1997) supported claims that ability goals undermine performance relative to mastery goals on complex, creative, or heuristic tasks, apparently because they evoke competing responses, such as evaluative anxiety, and orient people to avoid challenge and to focus attention on outomes rather than on processes (Amabile, 1982; Ames, 1992; Butler, 1987). More generally, our framework and findings for informational search suggest that the critical variable may be the degree to which success depends on acquiring new skills, understandings, and ways of thinking. If mastery goals orient people to ask themselves what they can learn and to seek information relevant to acquiring and assessing learning, they should be most beneficial for performance when success requires new learning. Indeed, when participants were explicitly required to learn something new, instructions that focused attention on learning and on identifying and correcting errors resulted in superior final performance on both complex and more routine tasks relative to instructions that emphasized positive outcomes and error avoidance (Nordstrom, Wendland, & Williams, 1998; Schunk, 1996). However, success does not always require heuristic search and new learning. If ability goals orient people to expedite successful task completion and to continue to strive for positive outcomes, they may quite adaptive when success depends on the rapid and efficient application of well-learned skills, strategies, and understandings (Utman, 1997).

The proposal that different achievement goals are associated with different performance-related strategies and behaviors, including information seeking, that may each promote different kinds of success is supported by evidence that both mastery orientation and ability orientation predict strategy use. However, mastery orientation is associated with the use of deep processing strategies that facilitate comprehension and conceptual learning and ability orientation predicts use of surface processing strategies that promote rote learning, recall, and the rapid and efficient completion of routine tasks (Graham & Golan, 1991; Grolnick & Ryan, 1987; Nolen, 1996; Pintrich & DeGroot, 1990). In our studies, we also found that performance on problem-solving and creative-thinking activities was better in mastery-goal than in ability-goal conditions. Moreover, the former yielded superior performance not only because participants were more likely to request information relevant to mastery-oriented competence acquisition but also because they were more likely to use this information to learn. Thus, the degree to which participants in our studies sought information relevant to learning and acquiring competence predicted creative design quality, performance gains, and subsequent independent mastery among children who endorsed a mastery-goal orientation or worked in mastery-goal conditions, but not among their ability-oriented counterparts (Butler, 1989b, 1993, 1998, 1999, Butler & Neuman, 1995). In other words, even if participants in ability-goal conditions did on occasion seek information that could promote learning, they seemed to use it, much as they do when they cheat, copy, or use surface processing strategies, to attain a positive outcome on the problem at hand rather than to acquire competence.

I also found (Butler, 1993, 1999) that ability goals undermined not only information seeking but also performance at low more than at high levels of initial competence. These findings support Dweck & Leggett's proposal (1988) that failure undermines persistence and subsequent performance in ability-goal settings more than in mastery-goal settings, especially at low levels of perceived competence, because ability goals evoke perceptions of failure as diagnostic of inadequate capacity rather than as challenging and diagnostic of the need to learn. By definition, the need to learn arises when current capacities are inadequate for meeting task demands, or, in other words, when people encounter difficulty. In this case, it is not surprising that an ability-goal condition did not undermine performance even for the novel and fairly complex water jars task (Butler, 1993, Study 1; Butler, 1999) when initial competence assessment confirmed that people already knew what they needed to succeed and attain their goals. However, one can venture further that mastery goals will result in superior performance even at high levels of initial competence, when subsequent success depends on acquiring new proficiencies and understandings. Indeed, when I used more difficult experimental problems (Butler, 1993, Study 2), achievement goals moderated performance also among students who performed well on easier practice tasks. In mastery-goal conditions, such students requested optimal solutions and improved their performance during the session, but in ability-goal conditions they did less well because they continued to apply the strategies that had worked for the practice tasks instead of using the informational environment to acquire strategies appropriate for solving more complex problems.

The proposal that demands for new learning are critical in moderating the relations between achievement goals and performance may account for recent evidence that strivings to demonstrate superior ability predicted graded performance among college students (Elliot & Church, 1997; Harackiewicz et al., 1997). In many college courses, grades depend on effective surface processing, or, in other words, on the ability to recall large amounts of information in a short amount of time in a fashion that will promote accurate recognition of the correct alternative on multiple-choice examination items. Moreover, the evidence cited earlier confirms that ability goals, or, in the college context, motivation to compete for high grades, is associated with persistent and effective use of surface strategies. This interpretation (see also Harackiewicz et al., 1997) has affinities with Linnenbrink and Pintrich's proposal in this book (Chapter 8) that mastery goals are more adaptive for conceptual reorganization, which is, however, not always necessary to attaining high grades. Indeed, in such conditions a mastery orientation may put students at a disadvantage. If mastery-oriented students do not experience the material as inherently engaging, challenging, or relevant to acquiring worthwhile competencies and understandings, they may be less motivated to apply effort than are their ability-oriented counterparts, who are more driven to attain high grades. If, however, they do experience the material as potentially relevant to attaining their goals, they may focus during revision on reading extra material, understanding principles and processes, or discussing interesting ideas with their friends, strategies that may be less effective than recalling facts and findings for getting high grades. This interpretation receives some support from evidence that mastery orientation does predict school achievement in elementary school classrooms (Bouffard, Vezeau, & Bordeleau, 1998; Meece & Holt, 1993), which tend to be less competitive than subsequent academic settings and to focus more on processes and personal progress (Anderman & Maehr, 1994).

It is, however, intriguing that perceived competence did not moderate the effects of ability goals on academic achievement in the study conducted by Harackiewicz and her colleagues (1997). One possibility is suggested by our findings that failure undermined subsequent ability-oriented task involvement and performance in ability-goal conditions at all levels of ability. If people strive in general to demonstrate high ability, their motivation in any given context may thus depend not only on their success during task engagement but also on the degree to which prior experiences lead them to expect task engagement to reflect favorably on their ability. Thus, in familiar classroom contexts, perceived competence may moderate motivation and performance earlier, by affecting the degree to which people pursue strivings to demonstrate high ability.

This conjecture is relevant to recent proposals that emphasize the quality of performance (i.e., ability) strivings, rather than of performance level per se, in moderating the effects of ability goals. Several researchers have distinguished between strivings to succeed (performance-approach goals) and strivings to avoid failure (performance-avoidance goals) and have found that academic achievement was positively correlated with approach and negatively correlated with avoidance orientation (Elliot & Church, 1997; Elliot & Harackiewicz, 1996; Skaalvik, 1997). Although these authors tend to treat performance-approach and avoidance as conceptually distinct goal orientations, they seem to be positively intercorrelated (Butler, 1987; Skaalvick, 1997). Moreover, both performance orientations are associated with ability-oriented perceptions and affects such as fear of failure and anxiety, but, as I speculated above, endorsement of a performance-approach orientation and of a performance-avoidance orientation is associated with high versus low expectancy of success and perceived competence, respectively (Elliot & Church, 1997; Skaalvick, 1997). Indeed, when Elliot & Harackiewicz (1996) wanted to manipulate approach and avoidance goals experimentally, they created conditions that focused initial attention on the probability of success versus failure, respectively. In this case, it is not surprising that the effects of performance-approach versus performance-avoidance goals on achievement parallel those for actual and perceived competence in ability-goal settings. Moreover, a recent study found that although a performance-approach orientation predicted examination performance, only mastery orientation predicted long-term retention, which presumably rests on deep processing (Elliot & McGregor, in press). Thus, early results from this line of research seem consistent with the present interpretation that achievement goals affect performance by affecting the kinds of success students strive for, the ways in which they try to succeed, and how they respond both when they infer that they are attaining their goals and when they infer that they are unlikely to do so. In addition, they imply that processes of ability-oriented task involvement are affected not only by experiences during task engagement but also by the degree to which prior experiences orient people to adopt approach or avoidance goals for the activity in question.

Achievement Goals, Information Seeking, and Intrinsic Motivation

Early conceptualizations of intrinsic motivation, broadly defined as engaging and maintaining interest in an activity "for its own sake," attributed central importance to the degree to which people perceive task engagement as freely chosen and as an end in itself, rather than as externally constrained and a means to some other end (e.g., Deci, 1971; Kruglanski, 1978). Against this background, achievement-goal theorists (Butler, 1987; Dweck, 1986, Nicholls, 1989) assumed that ability goals will undermine intrinsic motivation by encouraging perceptions of the activity as a means to the end of demonstrating superior ability (Nicholls, 1989) or by creating a sense of internal constraint that undermines autonomy and evokes evaluation anxiety (Heyman & Dweck, 1992; Ryan, 1982). On the whole, ability-goal settings undermine both self-reported interest and free-choice persistence relative to mastery goal settings (Butler, 1987; Rawsthrone & Elliot, 1999; Ryan, 1982). However, ability-goal instructions and salient ability cues, such as anticipation of normative evaluation, do not always undermine intrinsic motivation (Harackiewicz & Sansone, 1991; Rawsthorne & Elliot, 1999). In addition, the absence of extrinsic or ability cues does not in itself suffice to maintain interest for appealing activities over time (Butler, 1987, 1988). Thus, initial ability goals do not always undermine, nor do mastery strivings always maintain, task involvement and interest.

These findings have lead some researchers to propose that if people strive to attain their goals, and feel satisfied when they do so, both mastery and ability strivings may promote intrinsic motivation as long as the processes and outcomes of achievement behavior are congruent with one's goals (Butler, 1992; Harackiewicz & Sansone, 1991; Higgins & Trope, 1990). Extrapolating from the general proposition that the shared aim of achievement strivings is to succeed, Harackiewicz, Sansone, and their colleagues conducted several studies designed to test the hypothesis that the degree to which people care about doing well on an activity, a motivational process that they termed competence valuation, will enhance intrinsic motivation. Their hypothesis was supported to some extent for both ability and mastery contexts and orientations. However, the relation between competence valuation and intrinsic motivation seemed to hold most strongly when participants scored high on general ability orientation, when they performed an activity in an achievement context that emphasized ability goals, and when they received positive feedback (see review in Harackiewicz & Sansone, 1991).

In present terms, these findings are consistent with the proposal that mastery goals versus ability goals orient people to strive for different kinds of success. In this case, continuing interest in ability-goal contexts should indeed depend on the degree to which people continue to strive for and to demonstrate high ability. Intrinsic motivation in mastery-goal settings should, however, depend more on the degree to which they experience themselves as continuing to learn and improve. Actual and perceived achievement do indeed moderate not only information seeking and performance but also intrinsic motivation, to a greater extent in ability-goal settings than in mastery-goal settings (Butler, 1992, 1993, 1995; Sansone, 1986, 1989). In a similar vein, Rawsthorne & Elliot (1999) concluded that performance-avoidance goal conditions that focused attention on the probability of failure undermined intrinsic motivation relative both to mastery conditions and to performance-approach conditions that oriented people to expect success. These findings confirm further that even though ability goals may maintain task involvement, performance, and interest when people succeed, they are quite maladaptive when people anticipate or encounter difficulty. (See also chapter 6 in this book.) Few studies have examined processes and consequences of competence acquisition. However, evidence that intrinsic motivation was predicted by total scores in an ability-goal condition but by performance gains in a mastery condition (Butler, 1999; Study 1) is consistent with the proposal that initial mastery goals will not suffice to maintain intrinsic motivation unless people continue to experience themselves as acquiring competence.

Distinguishing between strivings to acquire competence and strivings to demonstrate high ability implies further that the intensity of ability-oriented informational search will reflect the degree to which people continue to pursue ability goals over the course of activity and will thus predict continuing interest in ability-goal settings, much as does competence valuation. In contrast, continuing goal-oriented strivings and intrinsic motivation in mastery-goal conditions should be associated instead with the intensity of ongoing mastery-oriented information seeking. I did indeed find that intrinsic motivation in ability-goal conditions was predicted by a continuing ability-oriented informational search, which, as reported above, depends on the results of initial competence assessment (Butler, 1992, 1999). In contrast, intrinsic motivation in mastery-goal conditions was predicted by the intensity of mastery-oriented information seeking (Butler, 1989b; 1999, Study 1), which depends on the degree to which informational search confirms that people are learning and can learn more.

Another implication of these findings is that students may actively seek information not only to evaluate goal attainment but also to maintain achievement motivation. Seeking information relevant to monitoring one's progress or to acquiring new strategies and understandings may help mastery-oriented students to stay on task and to maintain subjective feelings of task involvement, satisfaction, and interest even when they are tired, working on more routine or dull aspects of their assignment, or tempted to go to a movie with a friend. Seeking information about one's ability and potential grade—for example, by comparing one's solutions or progress with that of others—may serve a similar purpose for ability-oriented students. In other words, when students strive to attain a particular outcome, they may engage in a variety of motivation-enhancing strategies, including information seeking, to maintain task involvement. Their strategies should, however, differ as a function of their goals. This conjecture is consistent with evidence (chapter 12, this book) that students employed various strategies to enhance interest during work on a boring task, especially when they had what they perceived to be a good reason for persisting, and that use of such strategies then predicted actual interest for the task.

Another implication is that if both mastery and ability goals orient people to act to attain their goals and to evaluate whether they are attaining them, achievement strivings should wane not only when information seeking indicates that they are not attaining their goals but also when they do not have access to goal-relevant information. In other words, unavailability of information may undermine achievement motivation, performance, and interest in both ability and mastery conditions, by undermining perceptions of the task as relevant to demonstrating high ability or to learning, respectively. This proposal can account for evidence both that interest and performance in ability-goal conditions that provided positive feedback declined when people no longer anticipated feedback (Butler, 1988; Ryan, Koestner, & Deci, 1991) and that negative feedback undermined intrinsic motivation even in mastery settings, when the context did not also provide information relevant to acquiring competence (Deci & Ryan, 1985). More significantly, no-feedback conditions undermined intrinsic motivation relative not only to conditions that provided feedback relevant to learning but also to ones that provided positive normative feedback (Butler, 1987; 1988; Butler & Nisan, 1986; Sansone, 1986, 1989). Moreover, results from two studies (Butler, 1987; Butler & Nisan, 1986) confirmed that during later stages of task engagement, pupils who received normative grades endorsed ability goals and pupils who received comments that noted both an aspect of the task performed well and an aspect that could be improved endorsed mastery goals. In contrast, pupils who repeatedly received no feedback endorsed neither mastery goals nor ability goals. In this case, the finding that their intrinsic motivation, which was high at baseline, declined steadily over trials, further confirms that initial interest is not sufficient to maintain task involvement over time, unless people continue to experience activity as relevant to attaining valued goals.

More generally, the present review has affinities with other proposals that congruence between initial and subsequent goals and between personal goals and contextual emphases is an important determinant of the degree

to which interest is maintained, undermined, or enhanced during activity
(e.g., Harackiewicz & Sansone, 1991). However, it also confirmed the important role of congruence between goal strivings and goal attainment. Thus, as
Table 7.2 suggests, a central and ongoing concern during activity is with
evaluating whether one is progressing toward attaining one's goals. Moreover, progress toward goal attainment seems to maintain task involvement
and interest not only when people strive to attain mastery but also when
they strive to demonstrate high ability and even when they are guided by
interpersonal rather than by clearly achievement strivings (chapter 12, this
book). It remains, however, to be seen whether progress toward attaining
extrinsic goals (e.g., accumulating course credits because one has been
promised a car on graduation) will also maintain not only goal-oriented
behavior but also interest.

CONCLUSIONS AND IMPLICATIONS

Applying goal theory to informational search has proven useful in clarifying why students seek information and what information they seek. Distinguishing systematically between mastery- and ability-oriented informational search shed light on hitherto neglected strivings to acquire, as
distinct from assessing, competence and confirmed that information
seeking is often guided more by strivings to learn than by strivings to
reduce self-evaluative uncertainty or to confirm high ability. Moreover,
treating motives for information seeking as secondary to—and thus following from—the perceived purposes, goals, or motives for learning can
help resolve theoretical and empirical controversies as to the nature of
both self-evaluative strivings and social comparison. Rather than asking
whether people strive mainly for veridical or self-enhancing self-evaluation, or which motive is salient in guiding social comparison, the research
reviewed here confirmed that what people want to know about their
capacities, and whether they treat others as resources for learning, as
sources of information about their proficiency, or as rivals, depends in
large part on what they are striving to achieve.

Examining information searching and related behaviors, such as help
seeking and information processing, also helped clarify the quality,
processes, and consequences of mastery-oriented versus ability-oriented
task engagement and provided a useful framework for addressing mixed
findings as to the relations between achievement goals and both performance and interest. The implications for the study and promotion of interest and continuing motivation are particularly relevant to this book. Most
generally, focusing not only on the antecedents and consequences but also
on the process of motivated task engagement suggests that feelings of interest are not synonymous with intrinsic motivation, as early conceptualiza-

tions assumed. These (e.g., Csikszentmihalyi, 1975; Deci, 1971) tended to treat intrinsic motivation as a motivational state that arises when people perform activities that are appealing and satisfying "in themselves" in conditions under which they focus on the activity alone and do not direct thought or action to other features of the immediate context or to the implications of activity for the self or for future consequences. Moreover, the reasonable assumption that promoting interest is an important and desirable education aim led many researchers to recommend intrinsic motivation is providing the ideal context for school learning.

Against this background, a central challenge in recent years has been to reconcile these conceptualizations with evidence that both initial extrinsic or ability goals or contexts and apparently extraneous behaviors and concerns during task engagement, such as information seeking, do not always undermine and may on occasion even enhance interest. One direction (e.g., chapter 12, this book) has been to question the usefulness of the rigid dichotomy between intrinsic and extrinsic motivation and thus of conceptualizing intrinsic motivation as a distinct and unique motivational state. Another possibility is that feelings of interest and satisfaction, and even willingness to resume an activity, are not limited to intrinsic motivation strivings and conditions but may arise, at least to some extent, as long as activity is experienced as promoting the attainment of valued goals. The research reviewed here provided converging support for the proposed process by which achievement goals evoke activity relevant both to attaining one's goals and to evaluating goal attainment. The inferences people make on the basis of their informational search then affect continuing goal-oriented strivings and task engagement. Moreover, not only achievement strivings and goal-relevant informational search but also interest may change during activity (see also chapter 12, this book), as students either strive to maintain task involvement at a level conducive to attaining their goals or curtail task involvement because they no longer experience activity as relevant to goal attainment (see Table 7.2).

Recognition that different goals can serve to maintain behavior and interest has led some researchers to wonder, in stark contrast to the early intrinsic-motivation literature, whether a wide variety of reasons or purposes for learning may not be equally adaptive in maintaining task involvement (chapter 8, this book; Wentzel, 1991). The research reviewed here did indeed indicate that initial ability goals can serve to maintain performance and interest as long as students already possess relevant skills and understandings and receive goal-relevant information. Thus, ability orientation may indeed be more adaptive than mastery orientation for some people, in some contexts, for some outcomes (Harackiewicz et al., 1997; Harackiewicz & Sansone, 1991; Rawsthorne & Elliot, 1999). However, mastery goals seem to be more adaptive when present capacities are inadequate for meeting task demands, at least in part because they orient people to seek and apply information and help relevant to learning. Thus, the evidence marshalled here confirmed and extended Dweck & Leggett's prediction (1988) that mastery goals are particularly adaptive relative to ability goals for less able students who are more likely to experience failure and difficulty. In addition, my analysis of goal-oriented informational search casts doubt on the degree to which ability goals are adaptive in the long term, even for capable students. First, salient ability strivings orient students at all levels of ability to respond to difficulty by continuing to rely on ineffective strategies, by cheating, or by avoiding information and help that could help them overcome their difficulty. Second, even students who succeed do not seem to maintain motivation and task involvement unless they continue to anticipate positive feedback. Thus, although negative feedback seems to orient students to salvage self-esteem by avoiding further failure and disengaging from informational search and task engagement, positive feedback seems to encourage them to be too satisfied with their current capacity and outcomes, to rest on their laurels, and to give up on opportunities to learn and do even better in the future.

These conclusions support prior recommendations (Ames, 1992, Dweck, 1986; Nicholls, 1989) that educators should try to foster mastery striving rather than ability striving, because the former orients people to strive for more worthwhile kinds of success and to cope more effectively with difficulty and because the latter ensures both that only the more able can attain their goals and that they, too, pay a price for doing so. Moreover, the present review highlights the central role of the information environment in shaping and maintaining goal-oriented task involvement. Although this chapter focuses on the ways in which achievement goals guide informational search and inferences, there is clear evidence that the kind of feedback students receive or anticipate in itself serves as a potent cue as to the purposes or goals of behavior in both experimental (Butler, 1987; Butler & Nisan, 1986) and classroom settings (Ames, 1992). Indeed, evidence that anticipation of normative information affects achievement strivings to the same extent as do apparently stronger ability goal manipulations (Rawsthorne & Elliot, 1999) implies further that students in competitive schools and societies may be particularly prone to attend to and be influenced by ability-goal cues.

Thus, one can venture that my students, who attend a selective and competitive university, are guided more by ability goals than by mastery goals. As a result, they attend more to the grade than to my comments and do not use the comments to acquire competence. Indeed, in one study (Butler, 1988), I found that receipt of both a grade and a comment affected performance and intrinsic motivation just as did receipt of a grade alone, and quite differently from receipt of only a comment. Although pupils who received only a comment recalled their feedback and used it to improve performance over time, pupils who also received a grade recalled only their grade and did not modify their performance. These results confirm that salient goals affect both the information people attend to and the way they use it and imply further that salient ability cues may undermine initial mastery strivings, much as do extrinsic constraints. One of the limitations of this chapter is that it focused on comparing experimental inductions of mastery goals versus ability goals and did not address the possible effects of multiple goals. However, the evidence cited above that continuing mastery- or ability-oriented task involvement depends both on contextual cues and on the degree to which students' experiences continue to match their goal-relevant strivings may be relevant. Thus, the degree to which ability strivings undermine (Meece & Holt, 1993) enhance (Wentzel, 1991) or do not interact with (Harackiewicz et al., 1997) the effects of jointly held mastery strivings may depend on the degree to which contexts and criteria for success emphasize new learning and personal progress or routine skills and procedures and normative attainment. Moreover, refraining from normative evaluation will not in itself ensure continuing mastery-oriented task involvement, even for challenging and personally relevant activities. Rather, teachers need to provide information, such as worked-out solutions (Butler 1993, 1999), constructive help (Butler, 1998) and task-specific feedback (Butler, 1987, 1988), and opportunities to learn from peers (Ames, 1992; Butler, 1995) that will orient students at all ability levels to learn, to evaluate whether they are learning, and to seek continuing opportunities to learn.

Acknowledgments

I thank the editors of this volume for their very helpful comments on an earlier version of this chapter.

References

Albert, S. (1977). Temporal comparison theory. *Psychological Review, 84*, 485–503.

Amabile, T. M. (1982). Children's artistic creativity: Detrimental effects of competition in a field setting. *Personality and Social Psychology Bulletin, 8*, 573–578.

Ames, C. (1992). Goals, structures and student motivation. *Journal of Educational Psychology, 84*, 261–271.

Ames, C., & Ames, R. (1984). Competitive versus individualistic goal structures: The salience of past performance information for causal attributions and affect. *Journal of Educational Psychology, 73*, 411–418.

Anderman, E. M., Griesinger, T., Westerfield, G. (1998). Motivation and cheating during early adolescence. *Journal of Educational Psychology, 90*, 84–93.

Anderman, E. M., & Maehr, M. L. (1994). Motivation and schooling in the middle grades. *Review of Educational Research, 64*, 287–309.

Ashford, S. J., & Cummings, L. L. (1983). Feedback as an individual resource: Personal strategies of creating information. *Organizational Behavior and Human Performance, 32*, 370–398.

Bandura, A. (1977). Self-efficacy: Toward a unifying theory of behavioral change. *Psychological Review, 84*, 191–215.

Bouffard, T., Vezeau, C., & Bordelau, L. (1998). A developmental study of the relation between combined learning and performance goals and students' self-regulated learning. British Journal of Educational Psychology, 68, 309–319.

Brown, J. D. (1990). Evaluating one's abilities: Shortcuts and stumbling blocks on the road to self-knowledge. Journal of Experimental Social Psychology, 26, 149–167.

Butler, R. (1987). Task-involving and ego-involving properties of evaluation: Effects of different feedback conditions on motivational perceptions, interest and performance. Journal of Educational Psychology, 79, 474–482.

Butler, R. (1988). Enhancing and undermining intrinsic motivation: Effects of task-involving and ego-involving evaluation on interest and performance. British Journal of Educational Psychology, 56, 51–63.

Butler, R. (1989a). Determining the psychological meaning of communications about competence: A reply to Ryan & Deci. Journal of Educational Psychology, 81, 269–272.

Butler, R. (1989b). Interest in the task and interest in peers' work: A developmental study. Child Development, 60, 562–570.

Butler, R. (1989c). Mastery versus ability appraisal: A developmental study of children's observations of peers' work. Child Development, 60, 934–943.

Butler, R. (1992). What young people want to know when: The effects of mastery and ability goals on social information-seeking. Journal of Personality and Social Psychology, 62, 934–943.

Butler, R. (1993). Effects of task- and ego- achievement goals on information-seeking during task engagement. Journal of Personality and Social Psychology, 65, 18–31.

Butler, R. (1995). Motivational and informational functions and consequences of children's attention to peers' work. Journal of Educational Psychology, 87, 347–360 (lead article).

Butler, R. (1996). Effects of age and achievement goals on the development of children's motives for attending to peers' work. British Journal of Developmental Psychology, 14, 1–18.

Butler, R. (1998). Determinants of help-seeking: Relations between perceived reasons for classroom help-avoidance and help-seeking behaviors in an experimental context. Journal of Educational Psychology, 90, 630–643.

Butler, R. (1999). Information seeking and achievement motivation in middle childhood and adolescence: The role of conceptions of ability. Developmental Psychology, 35, 146–163.

Butler, R., & Neuman, O. (1995). Effects of task and ego achievement goals on help-seeking behaviors and attitudes. Journal of Educational Psychology, 87, 261–271.

Butler, R., & Nisan, M. (1986). Effects of no feedback, task-related comments and grades on intrinsic motivation and performance. Journal of Educational Psychology, 78, 210–216.

Butler, R., & Ruzani, N. (1993). Age and socialization effects on the development of normative self-appraisal and social comparison motives in kibbutz and urban children. Child Development, 64, 532–543.

Csikszentmihalyi, M. (1975). Beyond boredom and anxiety. San Francisco: Jossey-Bass.

Deci, E. L. (1971). Effects of externally mediated rewards on intrinsic motivation. Journal of Personality and Social Psychology, 18, 105–115.

Deci, E. L., & Ryan. R. M., (1985). Intrinsic motivation and self-determination in human behavior. New York: Plenum.

Dewey, J. (1938/1963). Experience and education. New York: Collier.

Dweck, C. S. (1986). Motivational processes affecting learning. American Psychologist, 41, 1040–1048.

Dweck, C. S., & Leggett, E. (1988). A social cognitive approach to motivation and personality. Psychological Review, 95, 256–273.

Elliot, A. J., & Church, M. A. (1997). A hierarchical model of approach and avoidance achievement motivation. Journal of Personality and Social Psychology, 72, 218–232.

Elliot, A. J., & Harackiewicz, J. M. (1996). Approach and avoidance achievement goals and intrinsic motivation: A mediational analysis. Journal of Personality and Social Psychology, 70, 461–475.

Elliot, A. J., & McGregor, H. (1999). Test anxiety and the hierarchical model of approach and avoidance achievement motivation. Journal of Personality and Social Psychology, 76, 628–644.

Elliot, E. S., & Dweck, C. S. (1988). Goals: An approach to motivation and achievement. *Journal of Personality and Social Psychology*, 54, 5–12.

Festinger, L. (1954). A theory of social comparison processes. *Human Relations*, 7, 117–140.

Gergen, K. J., & Gergen, M. M. (1997). Naratives of the self. In L. W. Hinchman & S. K. Hinchman (Eds.), *Memory, identity, community: The idea of narrative in the human sciences* (pp. 161–184). Albany, NY: State University of New York Press.

Goethals, G. R. (1986). Social comparison theory: Psychology from the lost and found. *Personality and Social Psychology Bulletin*, 12, 261–278.

Graham, S., & Golan, S. (1991). Motivational influences on cognition: Task involvement, ego involvement and depth of information processing. *Journal of Educational Psychology*, 83, 187–194.

Grolnick, W. S., & Ryan, R. M. (1987). Autonomy in children's learning: An experimental and individual differences investigation. *Journal of Personality and Social Psychology*, 52, 890–898.

Harackiewicz, J. M., Barron, K. E., Carter, S. M., Lehto, A. T., & Elliot, A. J. (1997). Predictors and consequences of achievement goals in the college classroom: Maintaining interest and making the grade. *Journal of Personality and Social Psychology*, 73, 1284–1295.

Harackiewicz, J. M., Barron, K. E., & Elliot, A. J. (1998). Rethinking achievement goals: When are they adaptive for college students and why? *Educational Psychologist*, 33, 1–21.

Harackiewicz, J. M., & Sansone, C. (1991). Goals and intrinsic motivation: You can get to there from here. In M. L. Maehr & P. R. Pintrich (Eds.), *Advances in motivation and achievement* (vol. 7, pp 21–49). Greenwich, CT: JAI Press.

Harter, S. (1981). A new self-report scale of intrinsic versus extrinsic orientation in the classroom: Motivational and informational components. *Developmental Psychology*, 17, 300–312.

Heyman, G. D., & Dweck, C. S. (1992). Achievement goals and intrinsic motivation: Their relation and their role in adaptive motivation. *Motivation and Emotion*, 16, 231–247.

Higgins, E. T., & Trope, Y. (1990). Activity identification theory: Implications of multiple identifications for intrinsic motivation. In E. T. Higgins & R. M. Sorrentino (Eds.), *Handbook of motivation and cognition: Foundations of social behavior* (vol. 2, pp. 229–264). New York: Guilford Press.

Jagacinski, C. M. (1992). The effects of task involvement and ego-involvement on achievement-related cognitions and behaviors. In D. H. Schunk & J. L. Meece (Eds.), *Student perceptions in the classroom* (pp. 307–326). Hillsdale, NJ: Erlbaum.

Karabenick, S. A. (1994). Relation of perceived teacher support of student questioning to students beliefs about teacher attributions for questioning and perceived classroom learning environment. *Learning and Individual Differences*, 6, 187–204.

Krunglanski, A. W. (1978). Endogenous attribution and intrinsic motivation. In M. R. Lepper & D. Greene (Eds.), *The hidden costs of reward*, (pp. 19–29). Hillslade, NJ: Erlbaum.

Masters, J. C., & Keil, L. J. (1987). Generic processes in human judgment and behavior. In J. C. Masters & W. P. Smith (Eds.), *Social comparison, social justice and relative deprivation: Theoretical, empirical, and policy perspectives* (pp. 11–54). Hillsdale, NJ: Erlbaum.

Meece, J., & Holt, K. (1993). Variations in students' goal patterns. *Journal of Educational Psychology*, 85, 582–590.

Mosatche, H. S., & Bragonier, P. (1981). An observational study of social comparison in preschoolers. *Child Development*, 52, 376–378.

Newstead, S. E., Franklin-Stokes, A., & Armstead, P. (1996). Individual differences in student cheating. *Journal of Educational Psychology*, 88, 229–241.

Nicholls, J. G. (1984). Achievement motivation: Conceptions of ability, subjective experience, task choice and performance. *Psychological Review*, 91, 328–346.

Nicholls, J. G. (1989). *The competitive ethos and democratic education*. Cambridge, MA: Harvard University Press.

Nicholls, J. G., Cheung, P. C., Laur, J., & Patashnik, M. (1989). Individual differences in academic motivation: Perceived ability, goals, beliefs, and values. *Learning and Individual Differences*, 1, 63–84.

Nicholls, J. G., & Miller, A. T. (1983). The differentiation of the concepts of difficulty and ability. *Child Development*, 54, 951–959.

Nolen, S. B. (1996). Why study? How reasons for learning influence strategy selection. *Educational Psychology Review*, 8, 335–355.

Nordstrom, C. R., Wendland, D., & Williams, K. B. (1998). "To err is human": An examination of the effectiveness of error management training. *Journal of Business and Psychology*, 12, 269–282.

Pepitone, E. A. (Ed.) (1980). *Children in cooperation and competition: Toward a developmental social psychology*. Lexington, MA: Lexington Books.

Piaget, J. (1954). *The construction of reality in the child*. New York: Basic Books.

Pintrich, P. R., & DeGroot, E. V. (1990). Motivational and self-regulated learning components of classroom academic performance. *Journal of Educational Psychology*, 82, 33–40.

Rawsthorne, L. J., & Elliot, A. J. (1999). Achievement goals and intrinsic motivation: A meta-analytic review. *Personality and Social Psychology Review*, 3, 170–182.

Ross, M., Eyman, A., & Kishchuk, N. (1986). Determinants of subjective well-being. In J. M. Olson, C. P. Herman, & M. R. Zanna (Eds.), *Relative deprivation and social comparison: The Ontario Symposium* (vol. 4, pp. 79–93). Hillsdale, NJ: Erlbaum.

Ruble, D. N., & Frey, K. S. (1991). Changing patterns of behavior as skills are acquired: A functional model of self-evaluation. In J. Suls & T. A. Wills (Eds.), *Social comparison: Contemporary theory and research* (pp. 79–113). Hillsdale, NJ: Erlbaum.

Ryan, A. M., & Pintrich, P. R. (1997). "Should I ask for help?" The role of motivation and attitudes in adolescents' help seeking in math class. *Journal of Educational Psychology*, 89, 329–341.

Ryan, R. M. (1982). Control and information in the intrapersonal shere: An extension of cognitive evaluation theory. *Journal of Personality and Social Psychology*, 43, 450–461.

Ryan, R. M., Koestner, R., & Deci, E. L. (1991). Ego-involved persistence: When free-choice behavior is not intrinsically motivated. *Motivation and Emotion*, 15, 185–205.

Sansone, C. (1986). A question of competence: The effects of competence and task feedback on intrinsic interest. *Journal of Personality and Social Psychology*, 51, 918–931.

Sansone, C. (1989). Competence feedback, task feedback, and intrinsic interest: An examination of process and context. *Journal of Experimental Social Psychology*, 25, 343–361.

Schunk, D. H. (1996). Goal and self-evaluative influences during children's cognitive skill learning. *American Education Research Journal*, 33, 359–382.

Skaalvik, E. M. (1997). Self-enhancing and self-defeating ego orientation: Relations with task and avoidance orientation, achievement, self-perceptions, and anxiety. *Journal of Educational Psychology*, 89, 71–81.

Strube, M. J., Lott, C. L., Le-Xuan-Hy, G. M. Oxenberg, J., & Deichman, A. K. (1986). Self-evaluation of abilities: Accurate self-assessment versus biased self-enhancement. *Journal of Personality and Social Psychology*, 51, 16–25.

Taylor, S. E., & Lobel, M. (1989). Social comparison activity under threat: Downward evaluation and upward contacts. *Psychological Review*, 96, 569–575.

Taylor, S. E., Neter, E., & Wayment, H. A. (1995). Self-evaluation processes. *Personality and Social Psychology Bulletin*, 21, 1278–1287.

Trope, Y. (1986). Self-enhancement and self-assessment in achievement behavior. In R. M. Sorrentino & E. T. Higgins (Eds.), *Handbook of motivation and cognition* (pp. 350–378). New York: Guilford Press.

Utman, C. H. (1997). Performance effects of motivational state: A meta-analysis. *Personality and Social Psychology Review*, 1, 170–182.

Veroff, J. (1969). Social comparison and the development of achievement motivation. In C. P. Smith (Ed.) *Achievement-related motives in children* (pp. 46–101). New York: Russell Sage Foundation.

Wentzel, K. R. (1991). Social and academic goals in school: Motivation and achievement in context. In M. L. Maehr & P. R. Pintrich (Eds.), *Advances in motivation and achievement* (vol. 7, pp. 185–212). Greenwich, CT: JAI Press.

Wood, J. V. (1989). Theory and research concerning social comparison of personal attributes. *Psychological Bulletin*, 106, 231–248.

Zimmerman, B. J. (1990). Self-regulating academic learning and achievement: The emergence of a social cognitive perspective. *Educational Psychology Review*, 2, 173–201.

CHAPTER

8

Multiple Pathways to Learning and Achievement: The Role of Goal Orientation in Fostering Adaptive Motivation, Affect, and Cognition

ELIZABETH A. LINNENBRINK
PAUL R. PINTRICH
Combined Program in Education and Psychology
University of Michigan

The investigation of the role of goals and goal orientation has been an important recent development in achievement motivation theory and research. In contrast to motivational theories that propose that needs or drives provide the wellspring for behavior, goal theories suggest that goals are cognitive representations of what individuals are trying to attain and that these goals can guide and direct achievement behavior. In achievement goal models, "intrinsic" motivation is defined not in reference to basic needs to be self-determining or autonomous (e.g., Deci & Ryan, 1985; chapter 2 in this book) but rather in terms of a focus on the task and a goal of mastery, learning, and understanding (see Ames, 1992; Dweck & Leggett, 1988; Pintrich, 2000a, 2000b; Pintrich & Schunk, 1996). This focus on learning and understanding is generally contrasted with a focus on the self and performance, such as goals of outperforming or besting others, or with a focus on obtaining extrinsic rewards, such as grades and approval from others.

Within research on achievement goals, there has been a general tendency to pit these mastery and performance goals against one another in much the same oppositional manner that intrinsic and extrinsic motivation have been traditionally discussed (cf. Cameron & Pierce, 1994; Deci, Koestner, & Ryan, 1999; Eisenberger & Cameron, 1996; Ryan & Deci, 1996). Accordingly, mastery goals are generally seen as adaptive and as associated with a host of positive cognitive, motivational, affective, and behavioral mediators and outcomes, whereas performance goals are generally seen as maladaptive and as associated with negative mediators and outcomes (Ames, 1992; Dweck & Leggett, 1988; Pintrich & Schunk, 1996). However, there has been some emerging evidence (e.g., Elliot & Harackiewicz, 1996; Harackiewicz, Barron, Carter, Lehto, & Elliot, 1997; Wolters, Yu, & Pintrich, 1996) that this simple, dichotomous, and oppositional characterization of mastery and performance goals may be somewhat misleading in terms of the actual complexity of achievement dynamics.

The nature of the discussion regarding the relative adaptiveness of mastery goals and performance goals parallels in some ways the continuing controversy over extrinsic rewards and intrinsic motivation (cf. Cameron & Pierce, 1994; Deci et al., 1999; Eisenberger & Cameron, 1996; Kohn, 1996; Lepper, Keavney, & Drake, 1996; Ryan & Deci, 1996), albeit the discussion within goal theory does not have the long history of heated debate that characterizes the intrinsic-versus-extrinsic motivation literature. Nevertheless, it seems more important in terms of the scientific advancement of goal theory to move beyond a simple and dichotomous perspective on mastery and performance goals to a more differentiated perspective that reflects the possibility that different goals can give rise to multiple pathways or trajectories for achievement.

Accordingly, the purpose of this chapter is to discuss the role of mastery and performance goals in relation to general achievement outcomes, such as learning and performance. First, we develop a general model of achievement goals that distinguishes between approach and avoidance forms of mastery goals and performance goals. Second, we discuss how these different types of goals may give rise to different ways of approaching, engaging, and reacting to achievement tasks. In particular, we discuss how different goals may be differentially related to motivational, affective, cognitive, and behavioral mediators of learning and achievement. These differential relations among goals and the various mediators represent multiple pathways or trajectories that individuals can follow, with concomitant differences in learning and achievement. We conclude with a section on directions for future research.

A MODEL OF ACHIEVEMENT GOALS

In current research on goals, it seems that there are three general perspectives on goals, each reflecting a somewhat different level of analysis of the goal construct. At the most task-specific level is the social cognitive research on individuals' goals for a particular task or problem (see Bandura, 1997; Locke & Latham, 1990), also called target goals (see Harackiewicz & Sansone, 1991). For example, a student playing a pinball game might set a target goal of scoring 20,000 points, or a student taking an examination or quiz might set a target of getting 8 of 10 answers correct, or a businessperson might set a goal of making or selling 20 widgets in a week. These target goals do specify the standards or criteria by which individuals can evaluate their performance, but they do not really address the reasons or purposes for which an individual may be seeking to attain these target goals.

In contrast, a second level of goals concerns more general goals individuals may pursue that address not just the target goal but also the reasons an individual is motivated (Ford, 1992). This goal content approach attempts to specify the range of potential goals that could subserve motivated behavior. Ford (1992) proposed 24 basic categories of goals in his motivation systems taxonomy, including goals of exploration, understanding, superiority, resource acquisition, mastery, creativity, happiness, safety, and belongingness, to name a few. These general goals should apply to all areas of life and serve to characterize what individuals want or are trying to accomplish as well as the reasons they do something (Ford, 1992). At the same time, these general goals do not necessarily have the same level of specificity in terms of standards or criteria for evaluation as target goals.

The third perspective on goals, achievement goals, reflects an intermediate level between the very specific target goals and the more global goal content approach. Achievement goals refer to the purposes or reasons an individual is pursuing an achievement task, most often operationalized in terms of academic learning tasks, although they can be applied to other achievement contexts, such as athletic or business settings (Pintrich & Schunk, 1996). Task-specific goals and the more general goal content approach can be applied to any context or any type of goal (e.g., happiness, safety), but achievement goal constructs were specifically developed to explain achievement motivation and behavior. As Elliot (1997) pointed out, classic achievement motivation research has been concerned with the energization and direction of competence-related behavior, which includes evaluation of competence relative to a standard of excellence. Given this general definition, current achievement goal constructs address the issue of the purpose or reason students are pursuing an achievement task as well as the standards or criteria they construct to evaluate their competence or success on the task. Accordingly, achievement goal constructs represent an integrated and organized pattern of beliefs about not just the general purposes or reasons for achievement but also the standards or criteria (the "target") that will be used to judge successful performance (Urdan, 1997).

In this sense, achievement goal constructs represent a combination of general goals or purposes, such as mastery or superiority (compare these two goals in Ford's 1992 taxonomy), as well as more specific criteria or targets by which performance will be judged (e.g., progress or self-improvement vs. higher grades than others). Beyond this type of integration across different levels of analysis, achievement goal constructs such as mastery and performance goals are assumed to reflect an organized system, theory, or schema for approaching, engaging, and evaluating one's performance in an achievement context. In this way, the term *goal orientation* is often used to represent the idea that achievement goals are not just simple target goals or more general goals but represent a general orientation to the task that includes a number of related beliefs about purposes, competence, success, ability, effort, errors, and standards. In some ways, this represents a merger of the purpose and target goals from Harackiewicz and Sansone (1991) into an integrated orientation to the task. From an achievement goal perspective, it is the integrated and organized nature of these different beliefs about competence and purpose that provides the theoretical utility and power of the achievement goal construct.

There are a number of different models of goal orientation that have been advanced by different achievement motivation researchers (cf. Ames, 1992; Dweck & Leggett, 1988; Harackiewicz et al., 1998; Maehr & Midgley, 1991; Nicholls, 1984; Wolters et al., 1996). These models vary somewhat in their definition of goal orientation and the use of different labels for similar constructs. They also differ on the proposed number of goal orientations. In this chapter, we attempt to present an synthesis of these different models. We are not proposing a new model but rather are building on the existing models to develop a integrated model that reflects the different perspectives.

Most models propose two general goal orientations that concern the reasons or purposes individuals are pursuing when approaching and engaging in a task. In Dweck's model, the two goal orientations are labeled *learning* and *performance goals* (Dweck & Leggett, 1988), with learning goals reflecting a focus on increasing competence and performance goals involving either the avoidance of negative judgments of competence or attainment of positive judgments of competence. Ames (1992) labeled them mastery and performance goals, with mastery goals orienting learners to "developing new skills, trying to understand their work, improving their level of competence, or achieving a sense of mastery based on self-referenced standards" (Ames, 1992, p. 262). In contrast, performance goals orient learners to focus on their ability and self-worth, to determine their ability in reference to besting other students, to surpassing others, and to receiving public recognition for their superior performance (Ames, 1992).

Maehr and Midgley and their colleagues (e.g., Kaplan & Midgley, 1997; Maehr & Midgley, 1991, 1996; Middleton & Midgley, 1997; Midgley, Arunkumar, & Urdan, 1996) have mainly used the terms *task goals* and *performance goals* in their research program, terms that parallel the two main goals from Dweck and Leggett (1988) and Ames (1992). Task-focused goals involve an orientation to mastery of the task, increasing one's competence, and progress in learning, which are similar to the learning and mastery goals of Dweck and Leggett and Ames. Performance goals involve a concern with doing better than others and demonstrating ability to one's teacher and peers, similar to the performance goals discussed by Dweck and Leggett and Ames. In a similar vein, Nicholls and his colleagues (Nicholls 1984, 1990; Nicholls, Cheung, Lauer, & Patashnick, 1989) have used the terms *task involved* and *ego involved* to represent the goals of focusing on the task and task involvement in contrast to a concern with the self and one's performance relative to others.

Finally, Harackiewicz and Elliot and their colleagues (e.g., Elliot, 1997; Elliot & Church, 1997; Elliot & Harackiewicz, 1996; Harackiewicz et al., 1997; Harackiewicz et al., 1998) have proposed two general goal orientations, a mastery orientation and a performance orientation. In their work, a mastery-goal orientation reflects a focus on the development of knowledge, skill, and competence relative to one's own previous performance and is thus self-referential. Performance goals concern a striving for demonstrating competence by trying to outperform peers on academic tasks. These two general orientations are in line with the other definitions of goals used by other researchers.

However, Elliot and his colleagues (Elliot, 1997; Elliot & Church, 1997; Elliot & Harackiewicz, 1996) also have made a distinction between two different types of performance goals, a performance approach goal and a performance avoidance goal. They suggest that individuals can be positively motivated to try to outperform others, to demonstrate their competence and superiority, reflecting an approach orientation to the general performance goal. In contrast, individuals also can be negatively motivated to try to avoid failure, to avoid looking dumb or stupid or incompetent, what they label an avoidance orientation to the performance goal. Midgley and her colleagues (e.g., Middleton & Midgley, 1997; Midgley et al., 1998) have made this distinction as well. Finally, Skaalvik and his colleagues (Skaalvik, 1997; Skaalvik, Valas, & Sletta, 1994) have proposed two dimensions of performance or ego goals, what they have labeled self-enhancing ego orientation, where the emphasis is on besting others and demonstrating superior ability, as in the approach performance goal, and self-defeating ego orientation, where the goal is to avoid looking dumb or to avoid negative judgments, as in the avoidance-performance orientation.

Given all these different goals and orientations that have some similar and some different features, it seems helpful to propose a general framework that allows for the classification and organization of these different goals. Table 8.1 represents one attempt at such a taxonomy. The columns in Table 8.1 reflect the general approach/avoidance distinction that has been a hallmark of achievement motivation research (Atkinson, 1957; Elliot, 1997; McClelland, Atkinson, Clark, & Lowell, 1953) since its inception, as well as more recent social cognitive perspectives on approaching and avoiding a task (e.g., Covington & Roberts, 1994; Elliot, 1997; Harackiewicz et al., 1998; Higgins, 1997). For instance, Higgins' (1997) social cognitive model of self-

TABLE 8.1
Two Goal Orientations and Their Approach and Avoidance States

	Approach state (promotion focus)	Avoidance state (prevention focus)
Mastery orientation	Focus on mastering task, learning, understanding	Focus on avoiding misunderstanding, not learning, not mastering task
	Use of standards of self-improvement, progress, deep understanding of task	Use of standards of not being wrong, not doing it incorrectly relative to task
Performance orientation	Focus on being superior, besting others, being the smartest, best at task in comparison to others	Focus on avoiding inferiority, not looking stupid or dumb in comparison to others
	Use of normative standards such as getting best or highest grades, being top or best performer in class	Use of normative standards of not getting the worst grades, not being lowest performer in class

regulation explicitly used this distinction of approach/avoidance (or *promotion-prevention focus*, in his terms) to discuss different self-regulatory processes. An approach or promotion focus leads individuals to move toward positive or desired end states, to try to promote them to occur, whereas an avoidance or prevention focus leads individuals to move away from negative or undesired end states, to prevent them from occurring (Higgins, 1997). As such, there should be some important distinctions between approaching and avoiding certain goals, with concomitant influences on learning and behavior. For example, a promotion or approach orientation might be expected to have some generally positive relations with cognition, motivation, and behavior, whereas a prevention or avoidance orientation may be negatively related to these same outcomes.

The rows in Table 8.1 reflect the two general goals toward which students might be striving and parallel the two general goals of mastery and performance that have been proposed by the different models discussed here. The entries in Table 8.1 include the general-purpose goal as well specific standards under which an individual might be operating for that particular goal orientation. For example, an approach mastery goal orientation reflects a general goal of learning and understanding, and the standards or criteria used to evaluate goal progress include self-standards of improvement, as in all the different models of mastery, task, or learning goals. The two performance goals, approach and avoid, reflect the distinction made by Elliot and his colleagues (Elliot, 1997; Elliot & Church, 1997; Elliot & Harackiewicz, 1996) regarding attempting to best others using normative, comparative standards (approach performance goal) and attempting to not look stupid using normative, comparative standards (avoid performance goal).

The entry in Table 8.1 for avoid mastery goals has not been formally proposed in previous models, but it is possible on logical grounds, as well as theoretical symmetry, to hypothesize that there may exist an avoid mastery goal orientation (see Elliot, 1999; Pintrich, 2000a, 2000b). All the previous models agree that mastery goals are represented by attempts to improve or promote competence, knowledge, skills, and learning and that standards are self-set or self-referential. Paralleling the "syntax" of the other table entries, it may be that some individuals also want to avoid the demonstration of incompetence or misunderstanding relative to their own self-set standards. In more colloquial terms, approach mastery goal students want to get it "correct" relative to the task or to their own standards and avoid mastery goal students want to avoid being "wrong" relative to the task or their own standards. Students who are "perfectionistic" and never want to be wrong or incorrect relevant to their own high self-standards may be working from an avoid mastery goal more than from an approach mastery goal. In this way, avoid mastery goals could be indexed by examining the focus of a student's goals in terms of avoiding doing classwork incorrectly or getting the wrong answer relative to the task, whereas approach mastery goals entail a focus on learning and improving. This avoid mastery goal is also distinct from an avoid performance goal, where the focus is on not demonstrating low ability compared with others rather than on one's own self-set standards regarding task performance.

For example, a niece of the second author was in a whole-language reading class in elementary school. She wanted to never write her spelling words incorrectly and she got quite frustrated with the constant encouragement of invented and idiosyncratic spellings by the teacher. It seemed that she was motivated to "not be wrong" in spelling the words, which did generate a great deal of effort as well as good performance in terms of the use of normative spelling conventions, but her affect was less positive and included anxiety, worry, and frustration. It seemed that her standards or criteria were not norm-referenced because she was not concerned with the other students in the class. In fact, given the emphasis on invented spellings in the whole-language class, comparisons with other students were not relevant because the teacher allowed the use of many diverse spellings. It seems that she was focused on not getting it "wrong" or not mastering the task, not because she was concerned about competing with others or looking dumb but because of her own self-set standards for avoiding spelling words incorrectly.

There is other anecdotal evidence regarding a focus on mastery avoidance goals when individuals, especially older adults, come to learn how to use computers. They often are afraid to make mistakes and they limit their use of the computer because they do not want to do something wrong. In addition, Elliot (1999) has argued that avoid mastery goals may be especially relevant for older individuals as they lose some of their skills for performance, such as does an athlete with increasing age. In all these cases, the individual is motivated to avoid certain types of judgments and may limit his or her engagement in the task. Alternatively, as in the spelling example, performance may be fairly good (at least in terms of spelling words correctly), but the accompanying affect may not be particularly adaptive.

Of course, this type of anecdotal evidence is only suggestive; proof of the validity of the existence and separation of the avoid mastery orientation from the other three established goals awaits actual empirical evidence. In addition, the functional relations of this goal with other mediators and outcomes also must be demonstrated empirically. This is clearly one direction for future research in goal theory. However, it is important to note that in our model, this proposed avoid mastery goal is distinct from a third goal, work-avoidant or academic alienation, examined in some empirical research (e.g., Meece, Blumenfeld, & Hoyle, 1988; Nicholls et al., 1989). Students with a work-avoidant orientation try to avoid work and putting forth effort and probably do not do well in general. In contrast, students operating with an avoid mastery goal are less concerned with the amount of work exerted and more concerned with not meeting their self-set level of performance, which could lead to good performance, albeit less positive affect and more anxiety, as in the spelling anecdote.

ACHIEVEMENT GOALS, MEDIATORS, AND OUTCOMES

The role of different goal orientations in achievement dynamics has been examined in numerous studies since the 1990s. All of the models assume that these goals influence the ways individuals approach a task, how they engage in the task, their actual achievement, and how they evaluate their performance when the task is complete. Figure 8.1 displays the general model that guides our work at the University of Michigan, Ann Arbor, and serves as an organizer for this chapter. As can be seen in Figure 8.1, the model assumes that goals can give rise to different motivational and affective processes. For example, goals can influence motivational beliefs, such as self-efficacy and task-value judgments, as well as the affect that is generated and experienced. In turn, both goals and these motivational and affective processes are related to various cognitive and behavioral processes. Cognitive processes include the operation of working memory and attention as well as general cognitive and self-regulatory strategy use. Behavioral processes involve the traditional motivational outcomes, such as effort exerted during the task, persistence at the task, and choice of the task. Finally, it is assumed that these cognitive and behavioral processes lead to actual learning by the student.

It also should be stressed that we believe these processes are reciprocal. We assume that the different motivational, affective, cognitive, behavioral, and actual learning processes can and do feed back into a student's goal orientation, although for the purpose of clarity, we did not show this in Figure 8.1. For example, actual performance and outcomes can influence the ongoing goals adopted by students, just as different affective experiences or efficacy judgments may subsequently influence goal adoption. In some ways, this is a problem for all motivational models—how to represent the reciprocal relations of a dynamic process such as motivation. We assume, as for all motivation models, that the relations are reciprocal, but we begin our model and discussion with goals, given the importance of goals in guiding and directing subsequent behavior.

Table 8.2 summarizes how the four different goals may be related to various motivational, affective, cognitive, and behavioral mediators of the goal–outcome link as well as actual achievement and performance outcomes. If there is to be theoretical and practical significance to the postulation of four different goals, then there should be different functional relations between these goals and the various mediators and outcomes. Table 8.2 is based on the findings in the extant literature as well as extrapolation and hypotheses for conditions not yet investigated (i.e., the role of avoid mastery goals) or mediators and outcomes not yet examined for all four goals. In the following sections, we describe how the four goals relate to these various mediators as well as the paths through which these goals may have their influence. In our discussion of these relations, we do make comparative statements about how different goals may be related to the different mediators (e.g., approach mastery goals should lead to higher levels of X; avoid mastery goals should result in lower levels of Y). However, at this point in the development of the model and given that the extant research has not always generated consistent findings, it is not possible to provide definitive rank orderings of the four goals relative to different mediators.

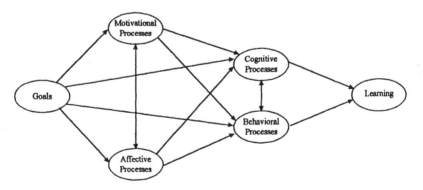

FIGURE 8.1
Proposed process model relating achievement goals to outcomes via motivational, affective, cognitive, and behavioral mediators.

TABLE 8.2

Four Type of Approach and Avoidance Achievement Goals and Their Hypothesized Differential Links to Mediators and Outcomes

	Approach mastery	Avoid mastery	Approach performance	Avoid performance
Motivational processes				
Beliefs about effort/ability	Strong belief in role of effort	Effort or ability attributions	More ability focused, positive ability attributions	Ability focused, negative ability attributions
Self-efficacy	Adaptive efficacy judgments	Lower efficacy	High efficacy when successful	Low efficacy
Interest/value	High interest and task value, high competence value	Lower interest and task value, lower competence value	High interest when successful, low task value, high competence value	Low interest and task value, high competence value
Affective processes				
Positive affect	High elation	Low elation	Mixed; high elation when successful	Low elation
Negative affect	Low anxiety	Moderate anxiety	Moderate anxiety	High anxiety
Cognitive processes				
Use of strategies	Deeper processing	More surface	Expedient processing	More surface
Metacognition/regulation	Regulation oriented to the task	Regulation oriented to not being wrong	Regulation oriented to besting others	Regulation oriented to not looking dumb
Working memory and attentional processes	More available, task focused	Less available, concerns about being wrong	Less available, concerns about others	Less available, concerns about looking dumb
Behavioral processes				
Actual effort	High	Moderate/high	High when successful	Low/moderate
Persistence	High	Moderate/high	High when successful	Low/moderate
Achievement outcomes				
Performance	Moderate/high	Moderate	Moderate/high	Low
Learning/conceptual change	High	Low	Moderate/low	Low

Accordingly, we make general comparative statements about the four goals, and most of the comparisons are in reference to approach mastery goals, which does provide a good anchor for comparisons because the findings are most consistent regarding the role of approach mastery goals.

Goals and Motivational Mediators

Table 8.2 shows how different motivational beliefs may be linked to the four different goal orientations. Attributions and beliefs about effort and ability have been linked in consistent ways with mastery and performance goals (Ames, 1992; Dweck & Leggett, 1988), albeit there may be some differences regarding approach and avoidance states that still need to be explored. In particular, students who are focused on approaching mastery attribute success or failure to effort because mastery goals are associated with incremental beliefs about intelligence (Dweck & Leggett, 1988; Elliott & Dweck, 1988; see Table 8.2). It follows that avoid mastery goals are also likely to be associated with attributions to effort rather than ability, given the emphasis on self-set standards, although in the case of older individuals, lack of ability may come to play a role. In contrast, approach performance goals are associated with attributions, after success or failure, to internal, stable causes, such as ability, given the focus on entity views of intelligence (Dweck & Leggett, 1988; Elliott & Dweck, 1988). As with approach performance goals, we would expect avoid performance goals to be associated with attributions to ability rather than to effort.

Another important motivational component to consider is self-efficacy, or one's confidence in one's ability to perform a given task. Of course, self-efficacy judgments can be independent of goals (Bandura, 1997), but research examining the relation between self-efficacy and goals has generally taken two distinct paths: one concerned with mediational relations and the other with moderating relations. In the mediational perspective, self-efficacy is thought to mediate the relation between goals and performance, and in this model, goals would predict self-efficacy. For instance, survey research has demonstrated that students with an approach mastery goal generally have high ratings of self-efficacy (Pintrich & DeGroot, 1990; Wolters et al., 1996). The general assumption is that students focused on approaching mastery in terms of self-improvement and progress will feel efficacious as they compare their current performance with their own past performance. The use of self-set standards can foster an increase in self-efficacy as the individual makes progress in meeting these standards.

In contrast, the relation of approach performance goals to self-efficacy is not as clear. For instance, some researchers have found no relation between approach performance goals and efficacy (Middleton & Midgley, 1997), whereas others have found a positive relation between approach performance goals and efficacy (Elliot & Church, 1997; Wolters et al., 1996) and still others have found a negative relation between approach performance goals and self-efficacy (Anderman & Young, 1994). These varied findings in the relation of approach performance goals and self-efficacy may be due in part to the fact that researchers have not considered whether students are meeting their goal of outperforming others. One would expect that if they are successful in outperforming others, they should have higher ratings of efficacy, similar to the levels experienced by mastery-oriented students. If they are not successful in outperforming others, they should have lower levels of efficacy, more similar to those of students with avoid mastery goals and avoid performance goals.

In contrast to approach goals, avoid performance goals are associated with lower levels of self-efficacy (Elliot & Church, 1997; Middleton & Midgley, 1997). Students who are afraid of looking dumb probably focus on their poor performance relative to others, with a resulting drop in efficacy. Although there is no research examining efficacy and avoid mastery goals, we would expect that these students would have lower levels of efficacy than would approach mastery students. These lower levels of efficacy for avoid mastery students may stem from the lowering of expectations associated with avoidance goals. That is, both avoid mastery and avoid performance students are focused on trying not to fail or be incorrect. With this orientation on avoiding failure, they will likely be more focused on their inadequacies that make completing the task difficult, rather than on their skills that will aid them in completing the task. A focus on one's inadequacies may result in lower levels of self-efficacy.

It is important to note that although we are suggesting that a student's goal orientation predicts his or her feelings of self-efficacy, much of this research is based on correlational data. Therefore, it is conceivable that efficacy may predict the adoption of goals rather than that goals predict one's feelings of efficacy, and the relation is undoubtedly reciprocal. In particular, low levels of efficacy may be associated with the adoption of an avoidance goal, whereas high levels of efficacy may be associated with adopting approach goals. Whether or not one adopts a mastery goal or performance goal may be based on environmental and contextual cues. Thus, in a mastery environment, a person with high efficacy may adopt an approach mastery goal and a person with low efficacy may adopt an avoid mastery goal. A premise of this argument is that the environment itself is without cues that would promote the adoption of an approach or avoidance orientation. Experimental or microgenetic longitudinal research examining the causal order of efficacy beliefs and personal goal orientation as well as the role of environmental cues would help to clarify this relation.

A second approach to thinking about achievement goals and efficacy is to view efficacy beliefs as a moderator of performance goals and other outcomes (Dweck & Leggett, 1988). In Dweck's model, self-efficacy moderates the negative effect of performance goals for those who are high in self-efficacy. In other words, if a student has a performance goal of besting others but has high self-efficacy for accomplishing the task and doing better than others, then he or she will not show the maladaptive pattern of cognition, motivation, or behavior that usually operates under a performance goal. In contrast, those with a performance goal and low self-efficacy should show the debilitating pattern of cognition, motivation, and behavior that leads to general helplessness (Dweck & Leggett, 1988). However, there is conflicting empirical evidence that suggests that efficacy may not moderate the effects of goals on other mediators and outcomes (see Harackiewicz et al., 1998; Kaplan & Midgley, 1997). Some of the discrepancies in this research may be due to the confounding of approach and avoid performance goals in some of the studies. It may be that efficacy plays a different role under approach performance than under avoid performance goals, but there is a clear need for more research on the mediating or moderating role of self-efficacy with different goals.

In addition to attributions and self-efficacy, students' interest and value are also important mediators to consider in our proposed process model. Numerous studies have shown that interest and task value are high when students adopt an approach mastery goal (see Harackiewicz et al., 1998; Pintrich & Schunk, 1996). As students are focused on approaching mastery and using self-set standards, not only should their efficacy increase but their interest and value for the task should increase as well. Positive feelings of personal or situational interest should be associated with making progress and learning how to do a task. Under this goal, students should be "attracted" to the task as well as more involved in the task, and this type of situational interest and involvement should foster personal interest.

Harackiewicz and Sansone's (1991) process model of intrinsic motivation further suggests that the relation between goals and interest should be mediated by efficacy, competence valuation, and task involvement. Experimental studies support the notion that competence valuation and increased task involvement, but not efficacy, mediate the relation of approach mastery goals to interest (Elliot & Harackiewicz, 1996; Harackiewicz & Elliot, 1994). That is, as students are focused on approaching mastery and using self-set standards, the degree to which they value being competent and their involvement in the task increases. As students become more involved in the task and increase their perceptions of the value of the task, they are more likely to "get into" the activity and discover the interesting or enjoyable aspects of the activity (Harackiewicz et al., 1998). These effects, however, may be attenuated by the match between general purpose goals (of developing competence) and specific target goals for the situation (Sansone, Sachau, & Weir, 1989). A mismatch in these goals can lessen the high levels of interest generally associated with approach mastery goals (Harackiewicz & Elliot, 1998). Further, some studies have found that approach mastery goals result in enhanced interest for those low in need for achievement but not for those who are high in need for achievement (Harackiewicz & Elliot, 1993). In general, however, the pattern that approach mastery goals are related to increased interest in the activity is fairly robust and holds in both experimental and classroom settings (see Harackiewicz et al., 1998).

Although there is no existing research documenting the relation of avoid mastery goals to interest, it is likely that these students would value the task less and be less involved, resulting in decreased interest and enjoyment. That is, as students try to avoid being wrong or incorrect, the general anxiety and worry that can accompany this type of avoid mastery goal might attenuate any positive feelings of personal or situational interest. This avoidance goal might "drive" students away from the task, limiting the development of situational or personal interest.

The findings relating approach performance goals to interest are somewhat mixed (see Harackiewicz et al., 1998). In their experimental work, Harackiewicz and her colleagues (Elliot & Harackiewicz, 1996; Harackiewicz & Elliot, 1998) have documented that approach performance goals relate to competence valuation and task involvement, which relate to increased enjoyment and likelihood to continue to engage in the activity. As with approach mastery goals, these effects may be moderated by both personality (Harackiewicz & Elliot, 1993) and the match between purpose and target goals (Harackiewicz & Elliot, 1998). In classroom studies, however, approach performance goals were unrelated to interest (Elliot & Church, 1997; Harackiewicz et al., 1997). The inconsistency of these classroom findings with the experimental work may be because all students are able to meet their goal of besting others in the experimental studies (i.e., they receive positive feedback about performance), whereas students in the college classroom may or may not meet their goal of doing better than others. Thus, the positive effects of approach performance goals on interest may occur only when students are successful at meeting their goals. It is important to note that although approach performance goals are related to high levels of competence valuation, it is not likely that they would be related to high levels of task value, as an approach performance student is more concerned about doing well compared to others (i.e., demonstrating competence) and less concerned with the task itself.

In contrast to approach performance goals, avoid performance goals are associated with decreased interest both in the college classroom (Elliot & Church, 1997) and in experimental settings (Elliot & Harackiewicz, 1996). Further, Elliot and Harackiewicz (1996) documented that this detrimental effect of avoid performance goals on interest was mediated by task involvement. That is, students in the avoid performance goal condition were less involved in the task and were also less likely to report enjoying the task and less likely to engage in the task during free time. The general anxiety associated with avoid performance goals may be the reason that these students were less involved. Because these students were so concerned with not performing poorly, they were unable to become engaged in the activity and subsequently enjoyed it less and were less interested in it. As with approach performance goals, it is unlikely that avoid performance–oriented students would value the task itself; they would be more concerned with avoiding the appearance of incompetence.

Goals and Affective Mediators

In addition to motivational variables, it is also apparent that affect is differentially related to the various goal orientations (Diener & Dweck, 1978; Dweck & Leggett, 1988; Elliott & Dweck, 1988; Kaplan & Bos, 1995; Roeser, Midgley, & Urdan, 1996) and is also an important mediator of goals to various cognitive and achievement outcomes (Linnenbrink, Ryan, & Pintrich, 1998; Pintrich, Linnenbrink, & Ryan, 1998). The role of affect in motivational models and self-regulated learning models has not been explored to the same extent as some of the other motivational and cognitive mediators; there is a clear need for more research in this area. In addition, the literature on affect and emotions is exceedingly complex and there is not even complete agreement on a basic taxonomy of emotions or the underlying theoretical models (cf. Carver & Scheier, 1998; Diener, 1999; Russell & Feldman Barrett, 1999; Watson, Wiese, Vaidya, & Tellegen, 1999). Nevertheless, in this section we briefly describe how achievement goals may relate to affect with a focus on two general dimensions of affect, a pleasant–unpleasant dimension (e.g., happy–sad) and an activation–deactivation dimension (arousal–relaxation or engagement–disengagement (see Russell & Feldman Barrett, 1999; cf. Watson et al., 1999). In particular, we focus on positive affect in terms of general feelings of happiness and positive arousal, such as elation, and negative affect, including feelings of sadness and anxiety.

In making predictions, we draw from both achievement goal theory and Carver and Scheier's general model of self-regulation (Carver & Scheier, 1998; Carver, Lawrence, & Scheier, 1996). This model describes affect associated with self-regulation toward (approaching) or away from (avoiding) a particular goal. According to this model, students could experience feelings ranging from elation to sadness as they adopt approach goals and move toward them at different rates. Elation would be experienced when students are approaching a goal at a rate equal or above the rate they view as standard; failure to approach the goal at this rate would result in sadness or depression. In contrast, students who adopt avoidance goals would experience anxiety when they are not progressing away from the goal at a sufficient rate; when students are making sufficient progress at avoiding the undesired goal, they would experience relief (Carver & Scheier, 1998; Carver et al., 1996).

The relation of approach mastery goals to affect is fairly straightforward and consistent. Approach mastery goals are related to general positive affect and the absence of negative affect or anxiety (Dweck & Leggett, 1988; Roeser et al., 1996; see Table 8.2). That is, approach mastery–oriented students are likely to perceive difficult tasks as an opportunity for learning and mastery and thus experience less anxiety or depression and increased pleasure or pride at the opportunity to challenge themselves. This is also consistent with the model of Carver et al. (1996) that approach goals should be associated with positive affect, including elation and positive arousal. Presumably, failure to meet one's goal of mastery would be associated with sadness; however, it seems likely that approach mastery goals are often met because they are self-set and based on improvement.

In contrast, avoid mastery goals should generate some anxiety because the individual is concerned with being "wrong." Further, a person with an avoid mastery goal would likely experience less positive affect because he or she would not be engaged in the interesting aspects of the activity owing to his or her focus on avoiding, not mastering, the activity. This is consistent with a self-regulation model suggesting that avoidance goals are associated with moods ranging from relief to anxiety. That is, if a student is not able to avoid being "incorrect" at a sufficient rate, that student will experience this as doing poorly and will feel anxiety and frustration, as in the spelling anecdote. In contrast, if the student is able to do well and avoid being "incorrect" at a reasonable rate, then he or she will not feel happy or elated but will most likely feel relief (Carver & Scheier, 1998).

The relation of approach performance goals to affect is less clear. Studies have found mixed reports of affect, ranging from low levels of positive affect (Elliott & Dweck, 1988) to no relation (Roeser et al., 1996) to high levels of positive affect (Elliott & Dweck, 1988). These differences may be dependent on levels of efficacy (as in Dweck's work on the moderating role of efficacy) or on whether a person is reaching his or her goal to perform better than others. On the basis of a self-regulation model, it is conceivable that those who are successful at besting others will experience positive feelings, such as elation and arousal, whereas those not successful will experience feelings of sadness, depression, or perhaps disengagement. At the same time, students with approach performance goals may be more anxious, given their concerns about doing better than others (Wolters et al., 1996). Although this is inconsistent with Carver and Scheier's model that doing poorly at approach goals is associated with sadness and not anxiety, the idea of external evaluation and competition is linked to feelings of anxiety (Hill & Wigfield, 1984). Thus, it seems plausible that approach performance–oriented students could also experience feelings of anxiety (at least relative to those of approach mastery–oriented students). It is likely that approach performance students would be more anxious than would avoid mastery students because approach performance students would be concerned with how others were viewing them regardless of whether they were successfully approaching their goal and thus would feel anxiety more often than would avoid mastery students (who experience anxiety only when not avoiding their goal at a sufficient self-set rate).

Finally, avoid performance goals are related to high levels of anxiety (Elliot & McGregor, 1999). This is consistent with a self-regulation model, which suggests that avoidance goals are associated with feelings ranging from relief to anxiety (similar to those feelings of avoid mastery–oriented students). It is likely that these reports of anxiety stem both from anxiety associated with not avoiding their goal at a sufficient rate and from concern about being compared with other students. Thus, because avoid performance students experience anxiety in general as well as when they are not meeting their avoidance goal, these students should experience the highest levels of anxiety.

In addition to the relation between goals and affect, we propose that affect and the motivational variables discussed earlier are reciprocally related (as shown in Figure 8.1). For instance, positive mood has been related to increased feelings of efficacy, whereas negative mood has been related to decreased feelings of efficacy (Wright & Mischel, 1982). Further, high efficacy can also lead to lowered anxiety, suggesting that people who are confident in their ability to do a task will experience lower levels of anxiety while completing the task than will those who are not confident in their abilities (Meece, Wigfield, & Eccles, 1990). The types of attributions that students make are also related to the types of emotions that students experience (Weiner, 1985), although they are not necessarily linked to mood per se. In particular, when a person does not succeed and attributes the failure to an internal, controllable state such as effort, he or she will experience feelings of guilt. Attributions to stable, uncontrollable factors, such as ability, after failure will likely result in helplessness.

Finally, it is also likely that goals relate to interest via affect. Although there is no empirical evidence to date documenting this link, there is evidence suggesting that positive affect is associated with increased interest (Hirt, Melton, McDonald, & Harackiewicz, 1996; Sansone et al., 1989; Tauer & Harackiewicz, 1999) and that approach mastery and approach performance goals are associated with positive affect, at least in some cases (e.g., Dweck & Leggett, 1988; Elliott & Dweck, 1988). This association between goals and interest via affect could also help to explain why approach performance goals were associated with interest in experimental settings in which students' goals were met but not in classroom settings (see Harackiewicz et al., 1998). That is, if students meet their goal of developing understanding or outperforming others, they should experience positive affect, which will in turn enhance their interest. Because approach performance goals are more difficult to meet (*everyone* cannot meet his or her goal of doing better than others in a class), it is plausible that enough students did not meet their goal of besting others and therefore did not experience positive affect about the class; therefore, their interest in the class was not enhanced. This relation between interest and affect may be bidirectional; students who are interested in a task may also feel positively about it and therefore experience increased levels of positive affect.

Goals and Cognitive Mediators

There are two general hypotheses regarding how goals are linked to cognition. First, there is the "strategic or self-regulated learning" hypothesis that suggests that goals give rise to the use of different cognitive or self-regulation strategies. The second general hypothesis is the "changes in working memory" proposal that predicts that goals influence the content and operation of working memory. These two cognitive hypotheses are not mutually exclusive but can operate simultaneously. For example, if working memory is overloaded, then certain types of cognitive or metacognitive strategies can be invoked to compensate for memory difficulties (Schneider & Pressley, 1997). We first examine the links between goals and strategies and then turn to the working memory hypothesis.

There are a number of different potential cognitive mediators of goals, with the most often examined being the use of various cognitive and self-regulatory strategies (see Pintrich, 2000b; Pintrich & Schrauben, 1992). Almost all of the research has found that approach mastery goals are positively related to the use of deeper processing strategies as well as to more metacognitive control, monitoring, and regulating of learning (Pintrich, 2000b). This seems to be a fairly stable and reliable generalization. On the other hand, it is not clear what avoid mastery goals might predict, but if students operating under this goal are less concerned with mastery for its own sake, it is likely that they will not engage in deep processing unless it is essential to meet their goal of avoiding not meeting their self-set performance level. Further, rather than focusing on regulating their progress toward mastering the task (as in approach mastery goals), they will regulate toward not being wrong. Thus, under avoid mastery goals, the regulatory focus is not on the task itself but rather on the avoidance of being wrong. This could lead to the use of less adaptive cognitive and self-regulatory strategies.

In contrast to the findings for approach mastery goals, the research on approach performance goals and strategy use and self-regulation is mixed, partially because many of the studies have not empirically separated out approach and avoidance goals. Some studies (e.g., Meece et al., 1988; Nolen, 1988) have found negative relations with strategy use and regulation, other studies have found no relation (Kaplan & Midgley, 1997; Middleton & Midgley, 1997), and yet others have found a positive relation of approach performance goals to strategy use and regulation (e.g., Wolters et al., 1996).

It seems clear that more research is needed to clarify these relations between approach performance and avoidance performance goals, but there also may be contextual factors that moderate these relations. For example, Wolters et al. (1996) suggested that in cases in which the students are asked to do fairly routine and overlearned tasks (as in their data), then an approach performance orientation, where they are regulating toward besting others (see Table 8.2), may lead them to engage in self-regulation because they have external criteria by which to judge their progress (doing better than others). This type of motivation stemming from outside of the task may be necessary when regulating toward the completion of boring or uninteresting tasks (Sansone, Weir, Harpster, & Morgan, 1992; Wolters, 1998). Further, when completing tasks where deep processing is required in order to do better than others, approach performance–oriented students might be more likely to engage in deep rather than superficial processing. However, in many classroom tasks, students can succeed at fairly high levels in terms of performance or grades without much cognitive engagement. As noted in Table 8.2, approach performance students might be expedient in their processing in these cases, determining that they can succeed in besting others without using deeper strategies, which do involve more time and effort. Clearly, future research is necessary to document under what circumstances approach performance goals are adaptive in terms of self-regulation and strategy use.

The relation of avoid performance goals to strategy use and self-regulation is not thoroughly documented; however, one study found that avoid performance goals were unrelated to self-regulation (Middleton & Midgley, 1997). This lack of a relation may be because students adopt a variety of strategies in their attempts to meet their goal of not looking stupid. It is clear, however, that under an avoid performance goal, the focus is not on the task itself (as it is with approach mastery goals) but on regulating toward not looking dumb. The strategies employed to meet these goals are likely to be superficial unless the task demands deep processing. Additional research documenting the relation of both avoid mastery and avoid performance goals is needed.

Another important cognitive mediator is working memory and attentional focus (see Table 8.2). Working memory refers to the short-term storage of information as well as the allocation of cognitive resources and attention (Baddeley, 1986). There is assumed to be some upper limit to working memory resources—that is, working memory cannot be ever expanding—and these limits place constraints on the operation of the cognitive system. If working memory is crowded with many different thoughts regarding how others are doing (under performance goals) or not getting it wrong (under avoid mastery goals), then there will be fewer resources available to focus on the task. In contrast, approach mastery goals should result in more resources devoted to the task, because the general goal is to master and understand the task. Indeed, two recent studies examining the relation between approach goals and working memory found that approach mastery goals were associated with increased levels of working memory functioning (DiCintio & Parks, 1997; Linnenbrink et al., 1998). Future research should focus on clearly documenting this relation for all four goal orientations.

In addition to the direct relations of goals to self-regulation and working memory, it is also likely that there are indirect relations via motivational, affective, and behavioral mediators (see Figure 8.1). For instance, high feelings of competence or efficacy are related to increased use of deep processing strategies and metacognitive self-regulation (Pintrich & DeGroot, 1990). Given that goals are related to efficacy beliefs, it seems plausible that the relation of goals to cognitive processes is partially mediated by self-efficacy. In contrast, interest and value are generally associated with more behavioral processes than cognitive processes (Wigfield & Eccles, 1992). However, Pintrich and DeGroot (1990) did find that intrinsic value predicted both strategy use and self-regulation and Sansone and Harackiewicz (1996) have suggested that interest is important for self-regulation.

In terms of affective processes, there seems to be no dispute that affect relates to cognitive processes; however, the nature of this relation is unclear, owing to the plethora of contradictory findings. In an attempt to simplify this discussion, we focus here on how mood relates to cognitive processing separately for self-regulation and working memory. We begin by providing a brief review of how mood relates to self-regulation.

Most research relating mood and self-regulation has focused on the informational aspects that positive or negative mood tells a person about his or her progress toward a goal (see Aspinwall, 1998). That is, a positive mood provides a signal that a goal has been met and that there is no need to continue to self-regulate. In contrast, a negative mood signals failure to reach the goal and thus self-regulation continues until the goal is met. It follows that positive moods should result in decreased self-regulation whereas negative moods should result in increased self-regulation. This traditional approach to understanding the relation between mood and self-regulation, however, does not adequately account for findings suggesting that positive moods can result in enhanced self-regulation and that negative moods can be detrimental to self-regulation (see Aspinwall, 1998).

To help reconcile these disparate findings, Aspinwall (1998) proposed that the relation between mood and self-regulation may be based on a number of factors, including a person's goals, his or her current needs and resources, and features of the task context. For instance, Martin and Stoner (1996) suggested that it is the goal that the person adopts that determines whether positive mood signals completion of the task. Thus, if a person is focused on enjoying the task, a positive mood would indicate that the person should continue to work on the task, whereas a negative mood would indicate that the person should stop working. In contrast, if one's goal was to process information thoroughly, a positive mood might signal the completion of a task, whereas a negative mood would suggest that one's goal was not reached and thus the person would continue to engage in deep processing. This is in line with Carver and Scheier's (1998) suggestions about different affects being generated by approach goals versus avoidance goals. That is, doing well on an approach goal should lead to positive affects, such as elation or happiness, which might signal to the individual to continue engagement and self-regulation. In contrast, doing poorly on an approach goal can lead to sadness or depression and could cue less self-regulation. In the same manner, doing well at an avoidance goal is usually accompanied by relief, which could lead to less self-regulation, whereas doing poorly at an avoidance goal leads to anxiety and tension, which could foster more or less self-regulation. This line of argument suggests that depending on the goal of the activity and whether it is an approach- or avoidance-type goal, affect and mood could have a variety of effects on self-regulation.

In addition to a direct effect of mood on self-regulation, which could vary on the basis of the goal one has, Aspinwall (1998) also suggested that there may be indirect paths via a person's current psychological resources and needs. A person in a positive mood may feel that he or she has more "resources" to deal with negative information because he or she will not need to engage in mood repair. Further, a positive mood may signal to a person that he or she can afford to attend to negative feedback without experiencing unacceptably high negative feelings, and thus a person in a positive mood can attend to negative information, which may help that person reach his or her ultimate goal.

Finally, mood may also trigger different types of processing strategies that could influence the types of strategies students use to self-regulate (Aspinwall, 1998). In particular, Isen's research (see Isen, 1984; Isen, Daubman, & Nowicki, 1987) suggests that positive affect is associated with more flexible and efficient processing. This type of flexibility may be especially beneficial with certain types of tasks (especially those requiring creativity); thus, positive mood may enhance rather than hinder the types of strategies students use to self-regulate.

As is apparent by this brief review, the relation between mood and self-regulation is complex and warrants future research. Although we include it in our model, the way in which mood and affect mediate the relation between goals and self-regulation is unclear. Future research should investigate this relation across a variety of tasks to allow a better understanding of it.

The relation between mood and working memory functioning is also somewhat complicated. One predominant theory suggests that mood of any type (either positive or negative) results in increased task-irrelevant thoughts, which overload working memory functioning (Ellis, Seibert, & Varner, 1995). The picture, however, may not be as clear as this model suggests. For instance, Schwarz (1990) proposed that a positive mood results in heuristic processing, whereas a negative mood results in more detail-oriented processing. Although Schwarz did not link this to differences in working memory, we can extend this to suggest that people in a positive mood might have greater capacity available in working memory because they use schemes to help clump information, thus freeing working memory resources. With a positive mood, even an increase in task-irrelevant thoughts might not have detrimental effects on working memory because the use of more holistic processing associated with positive affect would free capacity. That is, the increase in processing demands associated with task-irrelevant thoughts would be offset by the increase in available space because of the use of efficient schemas. In terms of negative mood, a focus on details would likely overload working memory; this, in combination with increased task-irrelevant thoughts, would likely have an enhanced detrimental effect on working memory.

A study in our laboratory provides preliminary evidence of the importance of affect as a mediator of the relation between goals and working memory functioning. In particular, we found that the positive relation between approach mastery goals and working memory functioning was mediated by negative affect (Linnenbrink et al., 1998). In contrast, approach performance goals were related positively to working memory for men, but only after controlling for negative affect, suggesting that the detrimental effects that are generally associated with approach performance goals occur because performance goals increase negative affect. Performance goals were unrelated to working memory functioning for women. Although approach mastery goals were related positively to positive affect and approach performance goals were related negatively to positive affect, positive affect did not relate to working memory functioning. This suggests that negative affect, but not positive affect, impairs working memory. As this study was correlational in nature, future research should further examine whether positive and negative affect mediate the relation between achievement goals and working memory functioning.

We also should point out that an aspect of mood that is missing from much of the research relating affect to both self-regulation and working memory is the consideration of both the direction (positive/negative) and activation (low arousal/high arousal) components of mood and affect. This distinction between direction and activation seems especially important when considering approach goals and avoidance goals, given the proposed differential relations of approach goals versus avoidance goals to affect. As noted previously, approach goals are thought to be related to positive arousal (elation) and sadness and avoidance goals are thought to be related to negative arousal (anxiety) and feeling relaxed (Carver et al., 1996; Carver & Scheier, 1998). Given that the various goals are expected to relate to these different types of mood, it is especially important to consider how a more fine-grained level of mood relates to various cognitive processes as moderated by the types of approach or avoidance goals adopted by the individual.

Further, consideration of both the direction and activation components of mood may also help to clarify some of the contradictory findings relating mood to cognitive processing (Revelle & Loftus, 1990).

In addition to the direct relation between mood and cognitive processing, mood may also affect cognition via motivational processes, such as self-efficacy and interest (see Figure 8.1). For instance, Bandura (1993) suggested that one's feelings of efficacy might relate to one's ability to regulate emotions during a given task. Thus, regardless of the affect one is currently experiencing, an efficacious person will be better able to cope with various feelings and continue to work on a given activity. In this way, the effect of mood on cognitive processing may also be moderated by self-efficacy. Interest can also play an important role in whether a person continues to self-regulate toward a goal (Sansone & Harackiewicz, 1996). Given the positive relation of positive mood to interest (Hirt et al., 1996; Sansone et al., 1989; Tauer & Harackiewicz, 1999), it seems plausible that positive mood may relate to self-regulation via interest. Consideration of these various motivational variables in the relation of mood to cognitive processing may also help to explain some of the contradictory findings and should therefore be investigated further.

Finally, we should note that cognitive processes such as self-regulation and behavioral processes such as effort and persistence are inextricably linked. Given the effortful nature of deep-processing strategies, it is necessary that a person put forth effort to engage in deep processing. Further, self-regulation requires persistence in that a person must continue to work on a task until his or her goals are met. Self-regulation involves the regulation of persistence and effort; therefore, increased self-regulation should result in increased persistence and effort.

Goals and Behavioral Mediators

As shown in Table 8.2, the four different goal orientations should result in different levels of effort and persistence. Consistent with normative goal theory, approach mastery goals have been related to high levels of effort and persistence (Ames, 1992, Elliott & Dweck, 1988). It is likely that under an avoid mastery goal, students may actually try hard to not do the task incorrectly, as in the spelling anecdote. This may work well for tasks like spelling or mathematics where it is relatively clear what are correct and incorrect answers. Given these types of tasks, students with avoid mastery goals can regulate their effort to "succeed" at these tasks with obvious correct and incorrect answers. In contrast, for tasks where it is not necessarily clear what criteria might be used to judge correctness, students with avoid mastery goals may try less hard for fear of doing something incorrectly. More research is needed to examine how task characteristics might moderate the relations between both types of mastery goals and effort and persistence.

The relation of approach performance goals to effort and persistence is mixed. In some circumstances, such as when students have confidence in their ability to do the task, approach performance goals lead to high levels of persistence and effort (Elliott & Dweck, 1988). However, studies have also found that effort and persistence are low when students report approach performance goals (see Ames, 1992). The relation of approach performance goals to effort and persistence may be moderated by both efficacy and actual success and failure, with failure producing low levels of effort and persistence. Finally, although there is no empirical evidence linking avoid performance goals to effort and persistence, these students would likely exert low levels of effort. Avoid performance–oriented students want to avoid poor grades or comparisons with others, so they may exert some effort, but not as much as under an approach mastery or approach performance goal.

It is likely that goals have an indirect influence on these behavioral mediators via affect and motivation (see Figure 8.1). In particular, although anxiety might initially lead to increased persistence and effort to overcome anxious feelings, students may have difficulty performing under high anxiety conditions for prolonged periods and therefore would not persist in the task (Hill & Wigfield, 1984). Motivational variables may also play an important role. For instance, high levels of efficacy are associated with increased persistence and effort, especially in the face of a challenging task (Schunk, 1991). Generally, low levels of efficacy are related to decreased persistence and effort when faced with difficulty; however, sometimes low levels of efficacy can trigger increased persistence and effort because they serve as a cue that increased effort is needed to enhance understanding. In addition to efficacy, high interest and value of the task are also related to increased effort and persistence (Hirt et al., 1996; Wigfield & Eccles, 1992). Students who find a task interesting or perceive the task to be valuable are likely to engage in the task for longer periods of time and to put forth higher levels of effort during this engagement.

Goals, Mediators, and Achievement Outcomes

The final rows in Table 8.2 summarize the relations of goals to performance and learning, such as conceptual change. These relations should be mediated by the motivational, affective, cognitive, and behavioral variables discussed in the previous four sections and depicted in Figure 8.1. Accordingly, the goals–achievement links will vary depending on the multiple pathways taken by individuals as they use different cognitive and motivational resources and act differently under different goals. Nevertheless, there should be some consistency and prediction to actual performance and achievement from the four different goals.

If approach mastery goals generally result in positive and adaptive cognition and motivation as well as high levels of effort and persistence, then it would be expected that students with these goals should perform at fairly high levels. In some research, this has been the case (e.g., Dweck & Leggett, 1988); however, in other studies, mastery goals did not relate strongly to grades or test performance (Elliot & Church, 1997; Elliot & McGregor, 1999; Harackiewicz et al., 1997). Interestingly, although Elliot and McGregor (1999) found that mastery goals were unrelated to examination performance, they did find that mastery goals were related to long-term retention of the material.

In contrast, research examining approach performance goals has found these goals are related, at least in college classrooms, to high levels of performance in terms of grades and test scores (Elliot & Church, 1997; Elliot & McGregor, 1999; Harackiewicz et al., 1997). The relation may vary owing to contextual factors such as the nature of the achievement task and assessment procedures. In cases in which the achievement task requires knowledge recall or memorization (e.g., multiple-choice tests) and the assessment procedures include norm-referenced grading or competitive criteria, then approach performance goals may be useful to motivate the students to try hard, even if they do not gain deep conceptual understanding. Indeed, one study suggests that although approach performance goals do result in higher test scores, they are not linked to outcomes associated with deep-level processing and elaboration, such as long-term retention of the material (Elliot & McGregor, 1999).

Both types of avoidance goals should be linked to lower levels of achievement. The existing research relating avoid performance goals to achievement suggests that students who adopt avoid performance goals do not perform well in college classrooms (Elliot & Church, 1997; Elliot & McGregor, 1999). Although there is no research examining how avoid mastery goals relate to performance, it would be expected that avoid mastery goals would reduce achievement on some types of tasks, especially in cases in which deep understanding or conceptual reorganization is required. However, as noted previously, for some tasks, such as spelling or mathematics tests, avoid mastery goals could foster increased effort and persistence, which could lead to better performance.

In addition to actual performance, it is also important to consider how goals relate to learning. By examining conceptual change as an outcome, we hope to demonstrate one way in which our understanding of goals and cognition can be applied to a specific learning situation in schools. Conceptual change involves the change or integration of prior knowledge concepts with new concepts (Dole & Sinatra, 1998; Pintrich, Marx, & Boyle, 1993; Strike & Posner, 1992). This process differs from general learning in that a prior conception must exist that is then replaced or modified to form a new conceptual understanding; in contrast to learning that does not assume that a prior concept needs to be changed (i.e., acquisition of new facts or knowledge). Conceptual change is most often used to describe learning in science, where students have naive conceptions or misconceptions about natural phenomena that do not conform to scientifically acceptable definitions and models of the phenomena. This type of learning is most often described as involving a change in deep levels of conceptual understanding and is usually one of the most desired goals in education, in comparison with performance on simple multiple-choice tests.

The conceptual change process is fairly time consuming, difficult, and long term and requires a high level of cognitive and metacognitive engagement as well as persistence. Given these qualities, it is likely that the motivational, affective, cognitive, and behavioral processes described earlier (see Figure 8.1) would serve as important mediators in the relation between goals and conceptual change. In particular, there may be indirect relations of motivational variables, such as efficacy and interest, and affective variables, such as elation and anxiety, via cognitive and behavioral mediators. Further, cognitive mediators such as deep processing have been linked to increased conceptual change (Pintrich et al., 1998), and it is likely that high levels of self-regulation would result in increased conceptual change because of the importance of monitoring of one's understanding of new information. Because new information must be compared with prior beliefs, working memory should also play a role as the student attempts to reconcile new information with prior knowledge and beliefs, and this process is generally assumed to occur in conscious working memory. Finally, behavioral mediators are important in that conceptual change requires persistence and effort to reconcile new information with prior beliefs.

Although the research linking achievement goals to conceptual change is by no means extensive, the existing research suggests that there is indeed a relation and that the relation is mediated by motivational, affective, cognitive, and behavioral processes (Lee & Anderson, 1993; Pintrich et al., 1998). In particular, approach-mastery goals seem to be adaptive for conceptual reorganization (Lee & Anderson, 1993; Pintrich et al., 1998). That is, students who are focused on learning and understanding are more likely to undergo drastic changes in their ways of thinking through the course of instruction. There is preliminary evidence suggesting that this relation is mediated by the absence of negative affect and task-irrelevant thoughts as well as the use of deep-processing strategies (Pintrich et al., 1998). Further, a qualitative study conducted by Lee and Anderson (1993) suggested that behavioral mediators are important in that approach mastery students were more engaged in the task, persisting even when the task was difficult, which resulted in higher levels of conceptual change. Although it has not been empirically examined, high levels of interest and self-efficacy associated with approach mastery goals would also serve as likely mediators of conceptual change via cognitive and behavioral processes. Further, enhanced self-regulatory and working memory functioning associated with approach mastery goals should also result in higher levels of conceptual change, but this awaits empirical validation.

Although there is no research examining how avoid mastery goals relate to conceptual change, it is likely that avoid mastery goals would be associated with lower levels of conceptual reorganization. Given avoid mastery students focus on trying to avoid being wrong, it may be more difficult for them to relinquish prior conceptions because this would signal that they were incorrect in their way of thinking and this is the very thing they are trying to avoid. This focus on not being wrong may lead avoid mastery students to seek cognitive closure quickly, thus "freezing" their cognition (Kruglanski, 1989), which would result in no change in their thinking or conceptions. We also can make predictions about the relation between avoid mastery goals and conceptual change via the mediators proposed in Figure 8.1. First, the anxiety that avoid mastery students would likely experience would interfere with conceptual change, causing students to cling to their prior beliefs. Second, the low levels of self-regulation and diminished working memory functioning as well as decreased persistence and effort that are likely to be associated with avoid mastery goals would all lead to lower levels of conceptual change.

The relation of approach performance goals to conceptual change is less straightforward. One study found that approach performance goals were unrelated (Pintrich et al., 1998), whereas another study found a negative relation of approach performance goals to conceptual change (Lee & Anderson, 1993). Lee and Anderson's research (1993) suggested that the negative relation occurred because approach performance students were more distracted during the task and did not seem to exert as much effort as did approach mastery students, suggesting that this negative relation between approach performance goals and conceptual change was at least partially mediated by behavioral processes.

The inconsistency in the way that approach performance goals relate to conceptual change may occur because the relation of approach performance goals to motivational, affective, cognitive, and behavioral processes is unclear. For instance, approach performance students' cognitive processing ranges from being adaptive to maladaptive (e.g., Meece et al., 1988; Middleton & Midgley, 1997; Wolters et al., 1996). It may be that if a student can do well compared with others without engaging in deep processing, he or she would be less likely to use strategies that would result in conceptual change. That is, if simply memorizing answers for a test is sufficient and a clear conceptual understanding is not emphasized, approach performance students would be more likely than approach mastery students to use superficial processing strategies, which are less likely to lead to conceptual change. Research examining how approach performance goals relate to the proposed mediators and conceptual change may help us to better understand when approach performance goals are adaptive.

There is no research to date examining the relation of avoid performance goals to conceptual change; however, it is expected that, similar to avoid mastery goals, students with avoid performance goals will not experience much conceptual reorganization because they would be more likely to ignore contradictory evidence. Preliminary evidence about the relation of avoid performance goals to a number of detrimental motivational, affective, cognitive, and behavioral processes (Elliot & Church, 1997; Elliot & Harackiewicz, 1996; Elliot & McGregor, 1999; Middleton & Midgley, 1997) also supports the idea that avoid performance goals should be negatively related to conceptual change.

In summary, these initial studies examining conceptual change and achievement goals suggest that achievement goals and their motivational, affective, cognitive, and behavioral mediators are important to consider when studying conceptual change. Future research examining how achievement goals relate to a variety of achievement outcomes, including performance in classrooms and specific instances of conceptual change learning, would help to increase our understanding of the adaptiveness and maladaptiveness of the four proposed goal orientations.

CONCLUSIONS AND FUTURE DIRECTIONS

The conceptual framework presented in this chapter suggests that approach mastery goals are generally related to positive cognitive, motivational, affective, and learning outcomes. This generalization seems to be very reliable and robust across different studies with diverse populations and domains of learning and achievement. At the same time, the model and findings from previous research suggests that approach performance goals can have some positive effects on cognition, motivation, and performance (e.g., Harackiewicz et al., 1998). The model assumes that avoid mastery and avoid performance goals will generally give rise to less adaptive patterns of cognition, motivation, affect, and achievement, but there is a clear need for more research on the avoidance state for both mastery and performance goals. However, the most important conclusion generated by the mediational model proposed here is that future theory and research needs to investigate how different goals give rise to different patterns of cognitive, motivational, behavioral, and affective processes and, in turn, how these mediators are related to achievement outcomes. This perspective will lead to a more complex but perhaps more realistic and ecologically valid view of the role of different goal orientations in learning and achievement rather than the simple dichotomous and oppositional views that have plagued research on intrinsic motivation.

Beyond this general conclusion, it is clear that there are a number of important directions for future research. First, there is a need for the validation of the avoid mastery goal orientation and the tracing of the hypothesized links with cognition, motivation, affect, and behavior. Moreover, there is a need for research that examines all the various linkages proposed in Table 8.2 and Figure 8.1 for all the goals. Many of these are supported in the literature, but many are hypotheses based on general theoretical assumptions. The issue of multiple goals is also important to consider, as it seems likely that students may operate with more than one orientation at a time. The issues of how these multiple goals are represented and how they lead to differential patterns of cognition, motivation, and behavior are important to clarify in future research.

Finally, as we develop the general model and linkages, we will need to place boundary conditions on our generalizations as we come to understand how various contextual factors might moderate the basic relations among goals, mediators, and outcomes. These contextual conditions would include not just classroom factors, such as the testing and evaluation systems used in the classroom, but also personal factors, such as gender and ethnicity. In addition, the generalization of the model to different cross-cultural contexts would provide opportunities for refining and extending the model.

The general model also has implications for classroom practice and instruction. It seems clear that an approach mastery orientation can have beneficial effects for student learning. However, this does not imply that an approach performance orientation cannot also be used in some classrooms. Given that many classrooms already have some version of an approach performance orientation in place, the issue becomes one of how to move the classroom toward the inclusion of an approach mastery orientation in a context where normative comparisons of performance are inherent. The mediational model proposed here also suggests that if classrooms are approach performance oriented, then the teacher needs to be aware of the potential negative affect and anxiety that could be generated and have strategies for how to lessen the impact of anxiety. It seems clear that more research is needed on how these different goal orientations are created and maintained in different classroom contexts and how they influence the adoption of different goals by students. At the same time, the mediational model proposed here suggests that this classroom-based research should attend to the potential positive and negative aspects of the different goal orientations rather than just assume that an approach mastery goal orientation is the only orientation that should be encouraged in the classroom context. This more nuanced and complex view of classrooms not only should prove to be more useful in capturing the effect of classrooms on student goals but also should be more useful to teachers as they struggle with issues of how to motivate their students in the classroom context.

Acknowledgments

We thank the editors of this book for their very helpful comments on an earlier version of this chapter, which have improved it immeasurably, but, of course, we take full responsibility for the ideas presented in this chapter.

224

Elizabeth A. Linnenbrink and Paul R. Pintrich

References

Ames, C. (1992). Classrooms: Goals, structures, and student motivation. *Journal of Educational Psychology, 84,* 261–271.

Anderman, E., & Young, A. (1994). Motivation and strategy use in science: Individual differences and classroom effects. *Journal of Educational Psychology, 80,* 260–267.

Aspinwall, L. (1998). Rethinking the role of positive affect in self-regulation. *Motivation and Emotion, 22,* 1–32.

Atkinson, J. (1957). Motivational determinants of risk-taking behavior. *Psychological Review, 64,* 359–372.

Baddeley, A. (1986). *Working memory.* Oxford, UK: Clarendon Press.

Bandura, A. (1993). Perceived self-efficacy in cognitive development and functioning. *Educational Psychologist, 28,* 117–148.

Bandura, A. (1997). *Self-efficacy: The exercise of control.* New York: Freeman.

Cameron, J., & Pierce, W. D. (1994). Reinforcement, reward, and intrinsic motivation: A meta-analysis. *Review of Educational Research, 64,* 363–423.

Carver, C. S., Lawrence, J. W., & Scheier, M. F. (1996). In L. L. Martin & A. Tesser (Eds.), *Striving and feeling: Interactions among goals, affect, and self-regulation* (pp. 11–52). Mahwah, NJ: Erlbaum.

Carver, C. S., & Scheier, M. F. (1998). *On the self-regulation of behavior.* New York: Cambridge University Press.

Covington, M., & Roberts, B. (1994). Self-worth and college achievement: Motivational and personality correlates. In P. R. Pintrich, D. R. Brown, and C. E. Weinstein (Eds.), *Student motivation, cognition, and learning: Essays in honor of Wilbert J. McKeachie* (pp. 157–187). Hillsdale, NJ: Erlbaum.

Deci, E., Koestner, R., & Ryan, R. (1999). A meta-analytic review of experiments examining the effects of extrinsic rewards on intrinsic motivation. *Psychological Bulletin, 125,* 627–688.

Deci, E., & Ryan, R. (1985). *Intrinsic motivation and self-determination in human behavior.* New York: Plenum.

DiCintio, M., & Parkes, J. (1997, August). *The influence of goal orientation on working memory capacity.* Paper presented at the annual meeting of the American Psychological Association, Chicago.

Diener, E. (1999). Introduction to the special section on the structure of emotions. *Journal of Personality and Social Psychology, 76,* 803–804.

Diener, C., & Dweck, C. (1978). An analysis of learned helplessness: Continuous changes in performance, strategy and achievement cognitions following failure. *Journal of Personality and Social Psychology, 36,* 451–462.

Dole, J., & Sinatra, G. (1998). Reconceptualizing change in the cognitive construction of knowledge. *Educational Psychologist, 33,* 109–128.

Dweck, C., & Leggett, E. (1988). A social cognitive approach to motivation and personality. *Psychological Review, 95,* 256–273.

Eisenberger, R., & Cameron, J. (1996). Detrimental effects of reward: Reality or myth? *American Psychologist, 51,* 1153–1166.

Elliot, A. (1997). Integrating the "classic" and "contemporary" approaches to achievement motivation: A hierarchical model of approach and avoidance achievement motivation. In M. L. Maehr & P. R. Pintrich (Eds.), *Advances in motivation and achievement* (Vol. 10., pp. 143–179). Greenwich, CT: JAI Press.

Elliot, A. (1999). Approach and avoidance motivation and achievement goals. *Educational Psychologist, 34,* 169–189.

Elliot, A., & Church, M. (1997). A hierarchical model of approach and avoidance achievement motivation. *Journal of Personality and Social Psychology, 72,* 218–232.

Elliot, A., & Harackiewicz, J. (1996). Approach and avoidance achievement goals and intrinsic motivation: A mediational analysis. *Journal of Personality and Social Psychology, 70,* 968–980.

Elliot, A., & McGregor, H. (1999). Test anxiety and the hierarchical model of approach and avoidance achievement motivation. *Journal of Personality and Social Psychology*, 70, 968–980.

Elliott, E., & Dweck, C. (1988). Goals: An approach to motivation and achievement. *Journal of Personality and Social Psychology*, 54, 5–12.

Ellis, H. C., Seibert, P., & Varner, L. (1995). Emotion and memory: Effects of mood states on immediate and unexpected delayed recall. *Journal of Social Behavior and Personality*, 10, 349–362.

Ford, M. (1992). *Motivating humans: Goals, emotions, and personal agency beliefs*. Newbury Park, CA: Sage Publications.

Harackiewicz, J., Barron, K. E., Carter, S., Lehto, A., & Elliot, A. (1997). Predictors and consequences of achievement goals in the college classroom: Maintaining interest and making the grade. *Journal of Personality and Social Psychology*, 73, 1284–1295.

Harackiewicz, J., Barron, K. E., & Elliot, A. J. (1998). Rethinking achievement goals: When are they adaptive for college students and why? *Educational Psychologist*, 33, 1–21.

Harackiewicz, J., & Elliot, A. (1993). Achievement goals and intrinsic motivation. *Journal of Personality and Social Psychology*, 65, 904–915.

Harackiewicz, J., & Elliot, A. (1994). Goal setting, achievement orientation, and intrinsic motivation: A mediational analysis. *Journal of Personality and Social Psychology*, 66, 968–980.

Harackiewicz, J., & Elliot, A. (1998). The joint effects of target and purpose goals on intrinsic motivation: A mediational analysis. *Personality and Social Psychology Bulletin*, 24, 675–689.

Harackiewicz, J., & Sansone, C. (1991). Goals and intrinsic motivation: You can get there from here. In M. L. Maehr & P. R. Pintrich (Eds.), *Advances in motivation and achievement* (Vol. 7., pp. 21–49). Greenwich, CT: JAI Press.

Higgins, E. T. (1997). Beyond pleasure and pain. *American Psychologist*, 52, 1280–1300.

Hill, K. T., & Wigfield, A. (1984). Test anxiety: A major educational problem and what can be done about it. *Elementary School Journal*, 85, 105–126.

Hirt, E. R., Melton, R. J., McDonald, H. E., & Harackiewicz, J. M. (1996). Processing goals, task interest, and the mood–performance relationship: A mediational analysis. *Journal of Personality and Social Psychology*, 71, 245–261.

Isen, A. (1984). Toward understanding the role of affect in cognition. In R. Wyer & T. Srull (Eds.), *Handbook of social cognition* (pp. 174–236). Hillsdale, NJ: Erlbaum.

Isen, A., Daubman, K., & Nowicki, G. (1987). Positive affect facilitates creative problem solving. *Journal of Personality and Social Psychology*, 52, 1122–1131.

Kaplan, A., & Bos, N. (1995, April). *Patterns of achievement goals and psychological well-being in young adolescents*. Paper presented at the annual meeting of the American Educational Research Association, San Francisco.

Kaplan, A., & Midgley, C. (1997). The effect of achievement goals: Does level of perceived academic competence make a difference? *Contemporary Educational Psychology*, 22, 415–435.

Kohn, A. (1996). By all available means: Cameron and Pierce's defense of extrinsic motivators. *Review of Educational Research*, 66, 1–4.

Kruglanski, A. (1989). *Lay epistemics and human knowledge: Cognitive and motivational bases*. New York: Plenum.

Lee, O., & Anderson, C. W. (1993). Task engagement and conceptual change in middle school science classrooms. *American Educational Research Journal*, 30, 585–610.

Lepper, M. R., Keavney, M., & Drake, M. (1996). Intrinsic motivation and extrinsic rewards: A commentary on Cameron and Pierce's meta-analysis. *Review of Educational Research*, 66, 5–32.

Linnenbrink, E. A., Ryan, A. M., & Pintrich, P. R. (1998, April). *The role of goals and affect in working memory functioning*. Paper presented at the annual meeting of the American Educational Research Association, San Diego.

Locke, E., & Latham, G. (1990). *A theory of goal setting and task performance*. Englewood Cliffs, NJ: Prentice-Hall.

Maehr, M. L., & Midgley, C. (1991). Enhancing student motivation: A schoolwide approach. *Educational Psychologist*, 26, 399–427.

Maehr, M. L., & Midgley, C. (1996). *Transforming school cultures.* Boulder, CO: Westview Press.

Martin, L. L., & Stoner, P. (1996). Mood as input: What we think about how we feel determines how we think. In L. L. Martin & A. Tesser (Eds.), *Striving and feeling: Interactions among goals, affect, and self-regulation* (pp. 279–301). Mahwah, NJ: Erlbaum.

McClelland, D., Atkinson, J., Clark, R., & Lowell, E. (1953). *The achievement motive.* New York: Appleton-Century-Crofts.

Meece, J. L., Blumenfeld, P. C., & Hoyle, R. H. (1988). Students' goal orientations and cognitive engagement in classroom activities. *Journal of Educational Psychology, 80,* 514–523.

Meece, J., Wigfield, A., & Eccles, J. (1990). Predictors of math anxiety and its influence on young adolescents' course enrollment intentions and performance in mathematics. *Journal of Educational Psychology, 82,* 60–70.

Middleton, M., & Midgley, C. (1997). Avoiding the demonstration of lack of ability: An underexplored aspect of goal theory. *Journal of Educational Psychology, 89,* 710–718.

Midgley, C., Arunkumar, R., & Urdan, T. (1996). "If I don't do well tomorrow, there's a reason": Predictors of adolescents' use of academic self-handicapping behavior. *Journal of Educational Psychology, 88,* 423–434.

Midgley, M., Kaplan, A., Middleton, M., Maehr, M. L., Urdan, T., Anderman, L., Anderman, E., & Roeser, R. (1998). The development and validation of scales assessing students' achievement goal orientations. *Contemporary Educational Psychology, 23,* 113–131.

Nicholls, J. (1984). Achievement motivation: Conceptions of ability, subjective experience, task choice, and performance. *Psychological Review, 91,* 328–346.

Nicholls, J. (1990). What is ability and why are we mindful of it? A developmental perspective. In R. Sternberg & J. Kolligian (Eds.), *Competence considered* (pp. 11–40). New Haven, CT: Yale University Press.

Nicholls, J., Cheung, P., Lauer, J., & Patashnick, M. (1989). Individual differences in academic motivation: Perceived ability, goals, beliefs, and values. *Learning and Individual Differences, 1,* 63–84.

Nolen, S. B. (1988). Reasons for studying: Motivational orientations and study strategies. *Cognition and Instruction, 5,* 269–287.

Pintrich, P. R. (2000a). An achievement goal theory perspective on issues in motivation terminology, theory, and research. *Contemporary Educational Psychology, 25,* 92–104.

Pintrich, P. R. (2000b). The role of goal orientation in self-regulated learning. In M. Boekaerts, P. R. Pintrich, & M. Zeidner (Eds.), *Handbook of self-regulation* (pp. 451–502). San Diego: Academic Press.

Pintrich, P. R., & DeGroot, E. (1990). Motivational and self-regulated learning components of classroom academic performance. *Journal of Educational Psychology, 82,* 33–40.

Pintrich, P. R., Linnenbrink, E., & Ryan, A. (1998, November). *The role of motivational beliefs in conceptual change.* Paper presented at the Second European Symposium on Conceptual Change, Madrid.

Pintrich, P. R., Marx, R. W., & Boyle, R. B. (1993). Beyond cold conceptual change: The role of motivational beliefs and classroom contextual factors in the process of conceptual change. *Review of Educational Research, 63,* 167–199.

Pintrich, P., & Schrauben, B. (1992). Students' motivational beliefs and their cognitive engagement in the classroom academic tasks. In D. Schunk & J. Meece (Eds.), *Student perceptions in the classroom* (pp. 149–183). Hillsdale, NJ: Erlbaum.

Pintrich, P. R., & Schunk, D. H. (1996). *Motivation in education: Theory, research, and applications.* Englewood Cliffs, NJ: Merrill.

Revelle, W., & Loftus, D. A. (1990). Individual differences and arousal: Implications for the study of mood and memory. *Cognition and Emotion, 4,* 209–237.

Roeser, R., Midgley, C., & Urdan, T. (1996). Perceptions of the school psychological environment and early adolescents' psychological and behavioral functioning in school: The mediating role of goals and belonging. *Journal of Educational Psychology, 88,* 408–422.

Russell, J. A., Feldman Barrett, L. (1999). Core affect, prototypical emotional episodes, and other things called emotion: Dissecting the elephant. *Journal of Personality and Social Psychology*, 76, 805–819.

Ryan, R. M., & Deci, E. L. (1996). When paradigms clash: Comments on Cameron and Pierce's claim that rewards to not undermine intrinsic motivation. *Review of Educational Research*, 66, 33–38.

Sansone, C., & Harackiewicz, J. M. (1996). "I don't feel like it": The function of interest in self-regulation. In L. L. Martin & A. Tesser (Eds.), *Striving and feeling: Interactions among goals, affect, and self-regulation* (pp. 203–228). Mahwah, NJ: Erlbaum.

Sansone, C., Sachau, D. A., & Weir, C. (1989). Effects of instruction on intrinsic interest: The importance of context. *Journal of Personality and Social Psychology*, 57, 819–829.

Sansone, C., Weir, C., Harpster, L., & Morgan, C. (1992). Once a boring task, always a boring task? The role of interest as a self-regulatory mechanism. *Journal of Personality and Social Psychology*, 63, 379–390.

Schneider, W., & Pressley, M. (1997). *Memory development between 2 and 20*. Mahweh, NJ: Erlbaum.

Schunk, D. H. (1991). Self-efficacy and academic motivation. *Educational Psychologist*, 26, 207–231.

Schwarz, N. (1990). Feelings as information: Informational and motivational functions of affective states. In E. T. Higgins & R. M. Sorrentino (Eds.), *Handbook of motivation and cognition: Foundations of social behavior* (Vol. 2, pp. 528–561). New York: Guilford Press.

Skaalvik, E. (1997). Self-enhancing and self-defeating ego orientation: Relations with task avoidance orientation, achievement, self-perceptions, and anxiety. *Journal of Educational Psychology*, 89, 71–81.

Skaalvik, E., Valas, H., & Sletta, O. (1994). Task involvement and ego involvement: Relations with academic achievement, academic self-concept and self-esteem. *Scandinavian Journal of Educational Research*, 38, 231–243.

Strike, K. A., & Posner, G. J. (1992). A revisionist theory of conceptual change. In R. A. Duschl & R. J. Hamilton (Eds.), *Philosophy of science, cognitive psychology, and educational theory and practice* (pp. 147–176). Albany, NY: State University of New York Press.

Tauer, J. M., & Harackiewicz, J. M. (1999). Winning isn't everything: Competition, achievement orientation, and intrinsic motivation. *Journal of Experimental Social Psychology*, 35, 209–238.

Urdan, T. (1997). Achievement goal theory: Past results, future directions. In M. L. Maehr & P. R. Pintrich (Eds.), *Advances in motivation and achievement* (Vol. 10., pp. 99–141). Greenwich, CT: JAI Press.

Watson, D., Wiese, D., Vaidya, J., & Tellegen, A. (1999). Two general activation systems of affect: Structural findings, evolutionary considerations, and psychobiological evidence. *Journal of Personality and Social Psychology*, 76, 820–838.

Weiner, B. (1985). An attributional theory of achievement motivation and emotion. *Psychological Review*, 92, 548–573.

Wigfield, A., & Eccles, J. (1992). The development of achievement task values: A theoretical analysis. *Developmental Review*, 12, 265–310.

Wolters, C. A. (1998). Self-regulated learning and college students' regulation of motivation. *Journal of Educational Psychology*, 90, 224–235.

Wolters, C. A., Yu, S. L., & Pintrich, P. R. (1996). The relation between goal orientation and students' motivational beliefs and self-regulated learning. *Learning and Individual Differences*, 6, 211–238.

Wright, J., & Mischel, W. (1982). Influence of affect on cognitive social learning person variables. *Journal of Personality and Social Psychology*, 43, 901–914.

Achievement Goals
and Optimal Motivation:
A Multiple Goals Approach

KENNETH E. BARRON
JUDITH M. HARACKIEWICZ
Department of Psychology
University of Wisconsin

We would like to share the first author's experience with two students, Mark and Sam, in an undergraduate psychology course on research methods. Right before each examination, Mark was sure to attend office hours to go over material he needed to know for the upcoming test. During the rest of the semester, Mark sat quietly in lecture taking notes. He demonstrated little interest in learning anything beyond what was required, but he did master the necessary material and earned the highest grade in the class. In contrast, Sam actively participated in class and frequently came up after lecture to talk in greater depth about topics introduced that day. In addition, he regularly stopped by office hours to find out how he could learn more about particular subjects. In short, he demonstrated genuine curiosity and interest in the material. Surprisingly, he received only a C in the course. When asked about his graded performance, Sam remarked that grades held little importance for him. He was more interested in learning the material for himself.

Mark and Sam serve as good examples of students who display different types of motivation for their coursework. Mark's motivation seemed to be predominately extrinsic (to receive a high grade), whereas Sam's seemed more intrinsic (to learn about the subject matter). Thinking about these two students and different types of motivation raises important questions about motivation in education. For example, which student would we say had the more successful semester, and which type of motivation is optimal in education?

We live in a competitive culture that often defines success in terms of how well a person performs relative to others. In an educational context, the most obvious indicator of success is a student's grade. From this perspective, Mark was successful because he obtained an A in the class. However, another important indicator of success in education is whether students develop interest in course material and continue to pursue further learning (Maehr, 1976; Nicholls, 1979). From this perspective, Sam was successful because he developed great interest in the material and demonstrated a desire to learn more about it. When the definition of educational success is broadened to include both performance and intrinsic motivation, Mark and Sam both achieved some degree of success, but neither seemed totally successful.

Along with other authors in this book, we believe that developing intrinsic motivation in learning is critical to education, and indeed, most of our own research has focused on factors that increase or undermine intrinsic motivation. However, to consider students' interest as the *only* indicator of success may be idealistic or naive. In reality, grades are frequently used as our best indicator of learning, and we are all probably guilty of rewarding and placing greater value on students' academic performance. After all, when we select students for admission into our graduate programs or for fellowship offers, we frequently rely on objective markers of performance, such as students' undergraduate grade point averages. Furthermore, if Mark and Sam each asked to join your research laboratory, who would you be more likely to select, especially on finding out their grades in a research methods course? We suspect that most readers would choose Mark, and we know that we probably would, too. If we weigh grades this heavily, should we really fault Mark for his emphasis on grades? Should we applaud Sam for developing interest without displaying competence? The obvious question, of course, concerns how students can succeed in *both* domains.

In the case of Mark and Sam, different types of motivation led to distinct, positive outcomes in the course. Mark's extrinsic orientation seemed to help him to achieve a high level of academic performance. In contrast, Sam's intrinsic orientation seemed to foster interest and continued involvement in the material. However, each student's motivational orientation also appears to have a cost. Mark's lack of deeper interest in the course material may prevent him from learning more, whereas Sam's poorer academic performance may shut him out of additional educational opportunities. Optimal motivation may therefore require *both* types of motivation.

THE ROLE OF ACHIEVEMENT GOALS
IN OPTIMAL MOTIVATION

In this chapter, we address the question of optimal motivation using an achievement goal approach. In general, goals can be defined as cognitive representations of what we hope to accomplish, and they give direction and energy to our behavior. They also can vary in their level of specificity, ranging from concrete and task-specific goals to more general and broad goals. One particular class of goals, achievement goals, has emerged as the dominant framework for studying achievement motivation (Midgley et al., 1998; Nicholls, 1984; Pintrich & Schunk, 1996). Achievement goals reflect the purpose or reason for an individual's achievement pursuits in a particular situation (Dweck & Leggett, 1988; Maehr, 1989), and theorists have converged on two general types of achievement goals (Ames & Archer, 1988; Dweck & Leggett, 1988): mastery goals and performance goals.[1]

When pursuing mastery goals, an individual's reason for engaging in an achievement activity is to *develop* his or her competence in the activity. In contrast, when pursuing performance goals, an individual's reason for engagement is to *demonstrate* his or her competence relative to others. Thus, an individual's achievement pursuits can be motivated for two very different reasons: the aim to "improve" one's competence by learning as much as one can about a topic (as in the case of Sam) or to "prove" one's competence by trying to outperform peers (as in the case of Mark). Theorists argue that achievement goals create a framework for how individuals approach, experience, and react to a particular achievement situation (see chapters 6 through 8, this book). For example, Dweck and Leggett (1988) proposed that each goal sets into motion a "program" with distinct affective, behavioral, and cognitive consequences, where mastery goals are more likely to foster an adaptive pattern of achievement, and performance goals, a maladaptive pattern.

In an early review of the achievement goal literature, Ames (1992) championed the advantages of pursuing mastery goals *over* performance goals. For example, initial goal research suggested that when students pursued mastery goals, they used deeper, more elaborate study strategies, selected more challenging tasks, persisted in the face of difficulty, and held more positive attitudes toward learning. Conversely, students pursuing

---

[1] A variety of labels have been used to differentiate between these two general classes of goals. For example, mastery goals also have been called task goals (Nicholls, 1984), learning goals (Dweck & Leggett, 1988), and intrinsic goals (Pintrich & Garcia, 1991). Performance goals have also been called ego goals (Nicholls, 1984), ability goals (Ames & Ames, 1984), relative ability goals (Midgley et al., 1998), and extrinsic goals (Pintrich & Garcia, 1991). Following the convention of others (Ames, 1992; Ames & Archer, 1988; Pintrich & Schunk, 1996), we use *mastery* and *performance* as labels throughout this chapter.

performance goals engaged in more superficial or strategic learning strategies, chose easier tasks, and withdrew effort when difficulty was encountered (Ames & Archer, 1988; Elliott & Dweck, 1988; Meece, Blumenfeld, &
Hoyle, 1988; Nolen, 1988). Thus, Ames (1992) concluded that "it is a mastery
goal orientation that promotes a motivational pattern likely to promote
long-term and high-quality involvement in learning" (p. 263) and argued for
creating classroom environments that would encourage students' adoption
of mastery goals and minimize their adoption of performance goals. The
idea that mastery goals are adaptive and performance goals are maladaptive
for learning is referred to in this chapter as the *mastery goal perspective* because
it implies that only mastery goals can have positive consequences and that
performance goals will have deleterious consequences.

Although little debate exists about the positive effects of mastery goals,
others disagree with the second component of the mastery goal perspective.
More recent reviews of the achievement goal literature suggest that strong
conclusions about the negative effects of performance goals may be premature (Harackiewicz, Barron, & Elliot, 1998; Hidi & Harackiewicz, 2000; Urdan,
1997). Some theorists have argued that performance goals can have positive
effects because they also orient individuals toward competence and can
promote adaptive achievement behaviors (Dweck, 1986; Harackiewicz &
Sansone, 1991). In fact, a number of studies suggest that performance goals
can have positive effects in some situations and for certain individuals (e.g.,
Bouffard, Vezeau, & Bordeleau, 1998; Harackiewicz & Elliot, 1993; Urdan,
1997). Later in this chapter, we review experimental work that reveals some
of the conditions under which performance goals promote intrinsic motivation, as well as correlational work that reveals a positive association
between performance goals and academic performance. We therefore
endorse a multiple goal perspective in which mastery goals and performance goals are both adaptive (Butler & Winne, 1995; Harackiewicz et al.,
1998; Pintrich & Garcia, 1991; Wentzel, 1991).

Moreover, achievement goal theorists have reexamined the performance
goal construct and argued that it confounds theoretically distinct components (Elliot & Harackiewicz, 1996; Middleton & Midgley, 1997; Skaalvik,
1997; Wolters, Yu, & Pintrich, 1996). For example, Elliot and Church (1997)
separated the performance goal construct into *performance-approach* goals, in
which an individual is focused on attaining favorable judgments of competence relative to others, and *performance-avoidance* goals, in which an individual is focused on avoiding unfavorable judgements of competence. Wolters
et al. (1996) separated performance goals into *relative ability* goals, in which
an individual is focused on outperforming others, and *extrinsic* goals, in
which an individual is focused on seeking extrinsic rewards or avoiding
external sanctions. When separated, maladaptive learning patterns have
been more closely associated with performance-avoidance goals and
extrinsic goals, whereas adaptive learning patterns have been associated

with performance-approach goals and relative ability goals. The use of general measures of performance goals that confound multiple components may mask the potential benefits (and disadvantages) of particular types of performance goals. Thus, for the remainder of this chapter, we constrain our use of the term *performance goals* to performance-approach goals, because it is this type of performance goal that we believe can contribute to optimal motivation.

Armed with a more refined understanding of performance goals, we now consider how mastery goals as well as performance-approach goals can promote adaptive achievement behavior. Research on achievement goals has been pursued using both experimental and correlational methods. Our review is divided to reflect these separate research traditions. First, we describe a theoretical model that has guided our own experimental work on this topic and then present experimental results that support the model. Second, we present some of our recent correlational work in classroom settings. We then demonstrate how our findings, whether experimental or correlational, support a multiple goal perspective rather than the mastery goal perspective. Finally, we describe a set of studies designed to bridge existing experimental and correlational work and outline four ways in which mastery and performance goals can work in concert to promote optimal motivation.

A MODEL OF GOAL EFFECTS
ON INTRINSIC MOTIVATION

Our work has been guided by Harackiewicz and Sansone's process model of intrinsic motivation (1991; Sansone & Harackiewicz, 1996). We have extended the model to consider the effects of goals on intrinsic motivation in achievement contexts (Harackiewicz et al., 1998). In this model, we draw an important distinction between the goals that are suggested or implied by external factors and the goals that are actually adopted by an individual in a particular situation (the perceived purpose and target goal; see Figure 9.1). Rather than assume a one-to-one correspondence between an assigned goal and a personally adopted goal, we suggest that the goals an individual adopts in a given situation can have multiple determinants. These effects are represented as A paths in Figure 9.1. One determinant involves situational factors, such as an experimental manipulation in a laboratory setting or a particular characteristic of a classroom setting. A second important determinant involves personality factors, such as individual differences in achievement orientation.

In this model, we focus on two levels of goals: purpose goals and target goals. Purpose goals reflect the reason for engaging in a task and represent what an individual hopes to accomplish in a particular situation. Achieve-

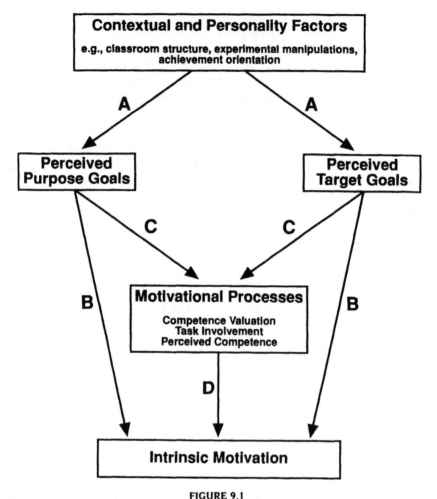

FIGURE 9.1
Schematic model of Harackiewicz and Sansone's (1991) process model.
(See text for explanation of paths A through D.)

ment goals (e.g., trying to develop or demonstrate one's competence) would be examples of purpose goals, but it is important to note that purpose goals can encompass other reasons for engaging in an activity that do not involve competence and achievement (e.g., trying to relax or have fun; see chapter 12, this book). Target goals, on the other hand, reflect more specific goals (or standards) for how an individual might achieve their overarching purpose goal (Bandura, 1986; Locke & Latham, 1990). For example, students may set a target goal of reading a chapter of their textbook each week. This specific standard (or target) serves as a more proximal mechanism to help the students achieve their higher-level purpose, which might be to develop competence in the subject (see chapter 5, this book).

To better understand *when* and *why* achievement goals have particular effects, two types of "third variables" (Baron & Kenny, 1986) have been incorporated in the model: moderator variables and mediator variables. The question of *when* achievement goals have particular effects is addressed with an analysis of moderator variables. First, we consider the possibility that achievement goals may have different effects in different setting and/or for different types of individuals. In other words, the effects of goals on intrinsic motivation can be moderated by personality and situational factors, such that the direct effect of goals on intrinsic motivation (the B path in Figure 9.1) can vary as a function of personality and/or the situation. Second, Harackiewicz and Sansone (1991) argued that goals at different levels of specificity can also interact such that higher-order goals moderate the effects of lower-order goals. Specifically, they suggested that the direct effect of target goals can be moderated by purpose goals (the higher-order goals). In other words, the direct effect of a target goal on intrinsic motivation can vary as a function of higher-order purpose goals.

The question of *why* achievement goals have particular effects is addressed with mediation analysis. The inclusion of mediator variables allows us to examine the underlying process through which goals affect intrinsic motivation. When mediation is established, the direct effect of a predictor on an outcome (the B paths of goals to intrinsic motivation) can be better understood through the predictor's effect on process variables (the C paths), which in turn influences the outcome (the D path). In particular, three key mediators of goals are shown in Figure 9.1: competence valuation, task involvement, and perceived competence. In other words, individuals are more likely to experience intrinsic interest in an activity to the extent that they value doing well in the activity (competence valuation), become absorbed and engrossed in the activity while engaged in it (task involvement), or feel proficient at the activity (perceived competence). Incorporating moderator variables and mediator variables into our theoretical analysis and our experimental designs has provided a richer understanding of when mastery and performance goals are likely to enhance intrinsic motivation and why they have these effects.

EVIDENCE FOR POSITIVE EFFECTS OF BOTH MASTERY GOALS AND PERFORMANCE GOALS FROM THE LABORATORY

In a series of experimental studies, Harackiewicz and Elliot (1993, 1998; Elliot & Harackiewicz, 1994) provided empirical support for a number of the assumptions of the Harackiewicz and Sansone model (1991). Because these studies all used a similar paradigm, we briefly describe it here. The experimental activity in each of these studies involved playing an enjoyable pinball game. Before the start of the session, a mastery goal or performance goal was suggested to participants, who were all college students. Within each condition, participants were blocked on achievement orientation (a hypothesized moderator variable), using Jackson's achievement orientation subscale from the Personality Research Form (1974). Participants played two games, and performance was experimentally controlled to ensure that each participant's performance improved and that each achieved a similar level of overall performance. After the second game, intrinsic motivation for the activity was measured with both self-report and behavioral measures of intrinsic motivation.

Moderator Effects

In their first study, Harackiewicz and Elliot (1993) investigated the effects of purpose goals on intrinsic motivation. Their mastery purpose goal highlighted development and improvement of pinball skills and their performance purpose goal highlighted normative comparisons and demonstration of pinball ability. (Table 9.1 provides a summary of the specific purpose goal manipulations used in this study as well as target goal manipulations used in later studies.) In addition, they included a neutral condition in which neither achievement goal was assigned to evaluate whether either achievement goal increased (or decreased) intrinsic motivation in the activity relative to the interest generated by the activity itself in this neutral control condition. The results revealed no main effects of purpose goals. Instead, the effects of assigned achievement goals were moderated by achievement motivation. Specifically, individuals low in achievement motivation (LAMs) showed higher levels of intrinsic motivation when assigned mastery goals, whereas individuals high in achievement motivation (HAMs) became more interested when assigned performance goals.

In explaining this pattern, Harackiewicz and Elliot (1993) noted that HAMs characteristically enter activities with a desire to increase their competence (Atkinson, 1974; McClelland, 1961). Assigning a mastery goal may not add much to what they normally bring into the situation. A performance goal, however, provides HAMs the additional challenge of outperforming others and demonstrating competence and thus may make the game more exciting and interesting (Tauer & Harackiewicz, 1999). In contrast, LAMs characteristically avoid normative comparisons and experience performance anxiety in achievement settings (Atkinson, 1974), and assigning a performance goal can undermine their interest. A mastery goal, however, may help LAMs to better appreciate their development of competence in the activity, increasing their interest in the game. In sum, neither achievement goal proved optimal for all participants. Instead, the optimal goal to assign depended on individual differences in achievement orientation.

TABLE 9.1
Experimental Manipulations of Goals

Purpose goal manipulations

Performance
   What we are interested in is how well some students play pinball compared to others...
We're collecting data on how well students play compared with others.

Mastery
   What we are interested in is how students develop their pinball skills on our pinball
machines... We're collecting data on how students learn to play and improve on our machine.

Neutral
   What we are interested in is students' reactions to games and leisure activities... We're
collecting data on what students think of our pinball machine.

Target goal manipulations

Performance
   We'd like you to pursue a performance goal for each game. We have selected these goals
on the basis of prior testing of students with your level of pinball experience, so these goals
can give you a good sense of your pinball-playing ability. The goals represent the 65th
percentile score for students with your level of pinball experience. For the first game, your
goal is 29,750 points. Only 35% of students were able to attain this score on their first game
of pinball on this machine. Your goal for the second game is 31,430 points.

Mastery
   We'd like you to pursue a moderately challenging goal for each game. We have selected
these goals on the basis of prior testing of this particular pinball machine. These goals have
been selected for students with your level of pinball experience, so these goals can help you
develop your skills on this pinball machine and gauge your progress. For the first game, your
goal is 29,750 points. For someone with your level of pinball experience, this score represents a
moderately challenging goal for this machine. Your goal for the second game is 31,430 points.

In a second study, Elliot and Harackiewicz (1994) investigated the effects of
the mastery–performance goal distinction at the target-goal level. Like purpose
goals, even more specific target goals can be framed in reference to developing
ability or demonstrating ability. The same objective standard or target (to
reach a particular score for each pinball game) was provided with each goal;
the only difference involved the framing of the standard (whether it was self-
referential or normative; see Table 9.1). The results revealed that personality
differences in achievement motivation once again moderated goal effects on
intrinsic motivation. Specifically, LAMs showed higher levels of intrinsic motivation when assigned mastery target goals, whereas HAMs showed higher levels of intrinsic motivation when assigned performance target goals.

   Earlier, we suggested that goals can be pursued at various levels of specificity, ranging from task-specific goals (e.g., target goals described above) to
more general goals (e.g., purpose goals). Harackiewicz and Elliot's first two
studies examined the effects of different goals at one particular level in this

hierarchy (either at the purpose or target level). However, target and performance goals can be construed hierarchically, such that lower-order goals
can help individuals achieve higher-order goals. Harackiewicz and Sansone
(1991) argued that congruence between an individual's higher- and lower-
order goals is another key determinant of intrinsic motivation. Goals are
congruent (or match) when they orient an individual to the same end. This
matching hypothesis suggests that the specific type of goal pursued is less
important than the congruence between goals and is in line with other theories that suggest behavior is optimally regulated when lower-order standards facilitate the attainment of higher-level standards (see also Carver,
Lawrence, & Scheier, 1996; chapter 5, this book). Thus, target goals that help
individuals achieve their purpose goal (e.g., when goals at the purpose and
target levels are both oriented toward improving skills and task mastery *or*
when both are oriented toward demonstrating ability compared to others)
should optimize intrinsic motivation.

A study by Sansone, Sachau, and Weir (1989) provided initial support for
the importance of goal congruence. They manipulated the presence or
absence of instructional tips for playing a computer fantasy game. These
tips (which can be considered a target goal) were provided in the context of
either a competence purpose goal (the activity was described as a test of
puzzle-solving skills) or a fantasy purpose goal (the activity was described as
exploring a fantasy world). Sansone et al. found that the highest levels of
interest resulted when the competence purpose goal was paired with
instructional tips and when the fantasy purpose goal was unaccompanied
by tips. In other words, interest in the activity was highest when the target
goals and purpose goals were congruent.

Harackiewicz and Elliot (1998) tested the matching hypothesis with mastery goal and performance goal manipulations in a third pinball study. Participants were provided a mastery target goal or a performance target goal
(as in the Elliot and Harackiewicz [1994] study) in the context of either a performance goal or a neutral purpose goal (as in the Harackiewicz and Elliot
[1993] study). In this study, the beneficial effects of a particular target goal
depended on the situational context established by the higher-order purpose goal for the session. In other words, the effects of target goals on
intrinsic motivation were moderated by purpose goals. Performance target
goals enhanced intrinsic motivation more than did mastery target goals
when participants were given a performance purpose goal, whereas mastery
goals enhanced intrinsic motivation more than did performance target goals
in the neutral control condition.

The findings from all three pinball studies clearly suggest that mastery
goals are not the only route to increasing intrinsic motivation. Performance
goals can promote interest above baseline levels for some people (i.e., HAMs)
and in some situations (i.e., when they match higher-order goals), and they
are *more* effective than mastery goals in these cases. Clearly, these results are

inconsistent with the mastery goal perspective that mastery goals are always more adaptive than performance goals. Rather, these findings indicate that both goals can promote interest and that performance goals are sometimes superior to mastery goals. Inclusion of important third variables (personality and situational moderators of goal effects) revealed the conditions under which mastery goals and performance goals can each enhance interest.

Mediator Effects

These findings raise the question of *why* both types of goals can increase interest in an activity. To address this question, we consider another type of third variable, mediators. Mediators represent the more proximal mechanism underlying the relationship between a predictor and outcome. In our work, we have identified three variables as mediators of intrinsic motivation: competence valuation, task involvement, and perceived competence. As noted earlier, our model suggests that intrinsic motivation can develop from placing greater importance on one's competence in an activity (i.e., competence valuation), from becoming absorbed while engaged in an activity (i.e., task involvement), and from feeling competent in the activity (i.e., perceived competence). For example, in the research methods course that Mark and Sam took, students' intrinsic motivation would depend on whether they valued the skills and knowledge that they were learning, whether they became absorbed in lectures and involved in class activities, and whether they developed a sense of competence in the material. However, in the research described below, we focus on the role of competence valuation and task involvement as mediators. Although we consider all three mediators important, our research has concentrated on the two processes initiated earlier in the motivational process (competence valuation and task involvement), because we have found these processes most relevant to goal effects. Specifically, goals can make individuals care more about doing well, and they can promote involvement in activities.

To establish mediation, three criteria must be met (Judd & Kenny, 1981). First, one needs to establish a significant effect between the predictor and outcome (the B paths in Figure 9.1). Second, one needs to establish that the predictor affects the hypothesized mediator (the C paths). Third, the hypothesized mediator must affect the outcome variable when tested simultaneously with the predictor (the D path). Mediation occurs when the direct effect between the predictor and outcome is substantially reduced when the mediator is included.

Harackiewicz and Elliot (1993) found that mastery and performance purpose goals raised competence valuation and task involvement relative to the neutral goal control condition; thus, both types of achievement goals were linked to individuals' commitment to pursuing competence as well as to their involvement in the activity. Elliot and Harackiewicz (1994) found that performance target goals raised competence valuation for HAMs and that mastery target goals raised competence valuation and task involvement for LAMs. Furthermore, competence valuation mediated the positive effects of performance goals for HAMs and task involvement mediated the positive effects of mastery goals for LAMs.

In the goal-matching study, Harackiewicz and Elliot (1998) found that performance target goals were especially effective in promoting competence valuation and task involvement in the performance purpose goal condition, whereas mastery target goals had similar positive effects in the neutral purpose goal condition. They also documented that competence valuation and task involvement mediated the direct effects of goals on intrinsic motivation. Participants who cared more about doing well in the beginning of the activity reported higher levels of task involvement while playing pinball. In turn, higher levels of task involvement during the game promoted intrinsic interest in pinball and mediated the goal-matching effect. These results revealed a process in which participants first became affectively committed to attaining competence and then cognitively involved in the pinball game, resulting in increased intrinsic motivation.

In sum, the experimental work by Harackiewicz and Elliot revealed that both achievement goals could promote intrinsic motivation. Specifically, positive mastery achievement and performance achievement goal effects depended on personality differences (e.g., whether an individual was characteristically high or low in achievement motivation) or on characteristics of the situation (e.g., the match with other goals in the situation). Furthermore, by examining the underlying motivational process, Harackiewicz and Elliot found that mastery goals and performance goals facilitated interest through the same key mechanisms (competence valuation and task involvement). What proved more critical than the type of goal pursued was whether the goal fostered competence valuation and task involvement. Only by including third variables were we able to understand this complex motivational process. These experimental results provide clear evidence that performance goals are not always maladaptive and reveal that mastery goals and performance goals can both initiate positive motivational processes. Thus, rather than supporting a strict mastery goal perspective, this initial experimental work led us to consider a multiple goal perspective in which both goals could have positive consequences.

EXPERIMENTAL VERSUS CORRELATIONAL APPROACHES TO TESTING THE MULTIPLE GOAL PERSPECTIVE

Even though Harackiewicz and Elliot (1998) examined multiple goal pursuit in their matching study (in which participants were assigned both a target goal and a purpose goal), these goals were manipulated at very different levels, and participants only pursued one goal at each level. Recall that proponents of the multiple goal perspective discuss how pursuing both types of achievement goals (at the purpose goal level) can be more advantageous than pursuing a single mastery goal or performance goal. Thus, a limitation of experimental studies conducted to date is that participants have typically been asked to work on some activity under a mastery goal *or* a performance goal. Experimental conditions in which both goals are assigned to participants have gone untested, and this methodological shortcoming has limited the conclusions that can be drawn from experimental work. Such designs force us into either-or inferences that compare one goal to the other, and they may have prematurely biased us toward accepting the mastery goal perspective. Current investigations tell us nothing about the additional benefits or disadvantages of pursuing a performance goal in conjunction with a mastery goal.

In contrast, in correlational studies, students are typically surveyed in actual classroom settings and asked to indicate the extent to which they pursue each type of goal in their coursework. Instead of finding mastery goals and performance goals to be negatively correlated (which would support the assumption that students do in fact pursue one goal to the exclusion of the other), survey studies consistently find that measures of mastery goals and performance goals are either uncorrelated (e.g., Ames & Archer, 1988; Bouffard, Boisvert, Vezeau, & Larouche, 1995; Harackiewicz, Barron, Carter, Lehto, & Elliot, 1997; Middleton & Midgley, 1997) or even positively correlated (e.g., Archer, 1994; Meece et al., 1988; Midgley et al., 1998; Nolen, 1988; Wolters et al., 1996). Mastery goals and performance goals are therefore more appropriately construed as relatively independent motivational orientations. Given the clear possibility that students can pursue multiple goals, it becomes important and necessary to test for the simultaneous effects of mastery goals and performance goals, as well as test whether mastery goals and performance goals interact to predict important educational outcomes (Ames & Archer, 1988; Harackiewicz et al., 1997; Meece & Holt, 1993). This led us to conduct our own series of survey studies in college classrooms to examine the joint effects of achievement goals on optimal motivation.

EVIDENCE FOR POSITIVE EFFECTS OF BOTH MASTERY GOALS AND PERFORMANCE GOALS FROM THE CLASSROOM

The basic paradigm for each study involved measuring goals, interest, and performance in college classes at different points in a 15-week academic semester. First, we collected self-report measures of students' mastery goals and performance goals for the class at the outset of the semester (2 to 3 weeks into the term). We then collected self-report measures of students' interest in the course near the end of the term and then obtained students' final course grades at the end of the term.

In our first study, we followed college students enrolled in introductory psychology classes (Harackiewicz et al., 1997). We evaluated both the independent and interactive effects of mastery goals and performance goals on interest and performance in the class using multiple regression. We found no evidence that goals interacted in predicting either interest or performance; rather, our results revealed a simple pattern of main effects. Students who endorsed mastery goals at the beginning of the course were more likely to report interest in the course at the end to the semester, but performance goals were unrelated to students' interest. In contrast, students who endorsed performance goals at the beginning of the course were more likely to achieve higher grades in the course, but mastery goals were unrelated to students' final grades. Thus, mastery goals and performance goals each had independent, positive effects on interest and performance, respectively.

Although we documented a clear and important advantage of adopting mastery goals, our classroom findings also qualify the position that performance goals are maladaptive in a number of ways. First, we found no evidence that pursuing performance goals negatively affected students' interest. Second, we found a direct, positive effect of performance goals on grades. Because mastery goals and performance goals were each linked to a different educational outcome, adopting both goals would appear to be an optimal strategy. The student who adopts mastery goals is more likely to develop interest in the course and the student who adopts performance goals is more likely to do well, but the student who adopts both goals is more likely to achieve both outcomes. Returning to our opening example, Mark and Sam seem to illustrate these results nicely. Sam appeared to pursue mastery goals, and he developed greater interest in the class, whereas Mark appeared to pursue performance goals, and he achieved a higher grade in the class. Neither student was completely successful. However, a third (hypothetical) student, Esmerelda, who was both mastery oriented and performance oriented could perform well *and* develop interest.

In a second classroom study (Harackiewicz, Barron, Tauer, Carter, & Elliot, 2000), we again tracked introductory psychology students during the course of the semester, but we also extended the study in time to examine longer-term consequences. Once again, students' achievement goals measured at the beginning of the semester were linked to their interest and final grades in the course, replicating the identical pattern we found in our first study (Harackiewicz et al., 1997). To determine whether the consequences of mastery goals and performance goals observed in the short term (over the course of a semester) changed over the long term (over the course of several semesters), we tracked students' course choices and academic performance in the three semesters following the semester in which they took introductory psychology. We computed a measure of continuing interest in psychology by counting the number of course credits taken in psychology over subsequent semesters. Our long-term measure of interest reflects continuing motivation in the field of psychology (Maehr, 1976) and is conceptually similar to behavioral measures of intrinsic motivation employed in laboratory research. Our long-term measure of academic performance was more complex. For students who enrolled in additional psychology courses, we computed a grade point average for their subsequent psychology courses. However, because a large number of students did not enroll in additional psychology courses, we also computed a grade point average for all courses taken in subsequent semesters to examine long-term academic performance for all students.

We found that the goals adopted in an introductory course continued to predict students' interest in psychology and academic performance and that these effects were comparable to those observed in the short term. Specifically, mastery goals were positively linked to continued interest in psychology and performance goals were positively linked to subsequent grades in psychology courses (for those students who actually enrolled in additional psychology courses) and subsequent academic performance (for all students in our sample). Thus, the same pattern of goal effects obtained in the short term was also observed on behavioral measures of continued interest and performance collected over additional semesters. These results suggest that *both* mastery goals and performance goals continue to have positive consequences on different indicators of academic success and that the goals adopted by students in introductory classes may have far-ranging implications for their subsequent academic work.

One explanation for the positive performance goal effects found in our classroom research concerns the type of classroom environment that we studied. Introductory psychology classes at our university represent a fairly typical college environment in which performance goals may be particularly adaptive. These classes are taught as large lecture courses (300 to 400 students), and instructors rely on multiple-choice examinations to evaluate students' learning. Grades are based on normative curves, and students must therefore outperform others to obtain particular grades. Competence is clearly defined in terms of relative ability and normative comparisons. Thus, a performance goal orientation may be well matched to this type of context. This idea is consistent with the matching hypothesis advanced by Harackiewicz and Sansone (1991) that goal effects depend on the general context in which goals are pursued. In other words, students who are striving to outperform other students may be optimally motivated in a university context in which excellence is defined in terms of an individual's achievement relative to others and in which grades are typically assigned on normative curves.

Although this type of classroom environment is quite common at the college level, not all college courses are taught in this way. We therefore conducted a third classroom study to evaluate the generalizability of this pattern beyond the introductory psychology classroom (Barron, Schwab, & Harackiewicz, 1999). Specifically, we followed students enrolled in upper-level psychology seminars to evaluate the consequences of achievement goals for interest and performance in a classroom environment in which normative comparisons between students were less salient. These upper-level seminars were small (approximately 20 to 30 students), discussion-oriented classes on specialized topics in psychology. Evaluation was based on papers, projects, and essay examinations rather than on "curved" multi-ple-choice examinations. In other words, this classroom environment appeared to be less performance oriented, and it seemed possible that a mastery goal orientation would promote performance in this educational context. However, our results revealed the same relationships between achievement goals and end-of-semester outcomes as in our previous two investigations. Mastery goals were positively linked to students' interest in the course, and performance goals were positively linked to final grades. Thus, the pattern observed in introductory psychology courses generalized to this less performance oriented context where good grades no longer depended on having to outperform other students on multiple-choice examinations. Although we thought that mastery goals might have been better matched to this type of class, our guess is that the more general con-text of university education is still quite performance oriented. Even if a particular class is relatively less performance oriented than are other courses, it is important to consider the overall educational context. In other words, any particular college class is taught in the context of a larger university environment that may play the most critical role in shaping the motivational climate (Maehr & Midgley, 1991).

In sum, when we examined the consequences of mastery goals and per-formance goals in college classes, we continued to find that both types of achievement goals promote important educational outcomes. Across all three of our classroom studies, students who adopted mastery goals reported more interest in the class. However, mastery goals had no effect on any measure of academic performance. Instead, we documented a clear advantage of performance goals on academic performance measures. These benefits were documented both cross-sectionally (for a group of students enrolled in an introductory course and for another group enrolled in advanced college courses) as well as longitudinally (for a subset of students tracked over multiple semesters). Success in college and university contexts depends on both performance and interest, and our results demonstrate the independent contributions of mastery goals and performance goals in pro-moting these two outcomes. Moreover, because neither type of goal pro-moted both outcomes, our results suggest that in this college environment the optimal pattern of goal adoption would include both mastery goals and performance goals.

INTEGRATING EXPERIMENTAL
AND CLASSROOM FINDINGS

The findings from our experimental and correlational research provide different kinds of support for a multiple goal perspective. However, it is difficult to integrate findings across these diverse methodologies for a number of reasons. First, although the experimental findings reviewed have indicated that both types of achievement goals can have positive effects on intrinsic motivation, they are silent regarding the effects of multiple goals. The experimental work reviewed so far tells us nothing about the additional benefits or disadvantages of pursuing a performance goal *in conjunction* with a mastery goal, because conditions in which *both* mastery goals and performance goals are assigned at the purpose goal level have gone untested.

Moreover, a number of other factors also make it difficult to reconcile experimental and classroom findings. Consider the following passage from Middleton and Midgley (1997):

> The results from our study in the field lead us to some different conclusions than those of Elliot and Harackiewicz (1996) in the laboratory. Contrasting methodologies may account for the differences. Elliot and Harackiewicz conducted experimental studies with college-aged students using puzzle-like tasks; whereas our study focuses on an academic setting, specifically the mathematics classroom, with middle school students. (p. 715)

Any one or some combination of these factors (field vs laboratory setting, age of participants, or academic task vs nonacademic task) could further moderate the effects of mastery goals and performance goals. Concluding that "contrasting methodologies" may account for the difference between studies is not terribly satisfying when evaluating research findings, but it is a necessary caution when methodologies vary so widely. As a better test of contrasting theoretical perspectives, continued research is needed that systematically varies each of these variables while holding the others constant.

For example, one factor that makes comparisons between studies particularly difficult is that the results from a certain age group (e.g., elementary school students) cannot be generalized to other age groups (e.g., high school or college students). Our work has focused on college-aged students and of course this limits the generalizability of our findings to earlier age groups (cf. Sears, 1986). Research by Eccles and Midgley (1989) suggested that the transition from elementary to junior high school is marked by a shift to a more performance oriented and competitive school climate. They argued that this new climate is mismatched with students' developmental stage, resulting in a number of negative effects on students' motivation and performance, and that performance goals have particularly negative consequences for this age group (see also Anderman & Maehr, 1994). Although research based on younger age groups may reveal a particular advantage for mastery goals, students may learn how to integrate both mastery goal and performance goal pursuits over time. In other words, we might expect to find more support for the mastery goal perspective with elementary and middle-school students but to find more support for a multiple goal perspective in high school and college students. Indeed, these ideas have been supported in a developmental study of middle school, junior high school, and high school students by Bouffard et al. (1998).

Another important factor that has yet to be fully considered is the origin of the goal. Specifically, experimental studies tend to externally assign goals, whereas correlational studies tend to assess self-set goals, thereby confounding goal origin with the type of research methodology adopted. It seems particularly important to examine whether goal effects vary as a function of their origin (assigned vs self-set). In fact, theorists differ in the extent to which they view achievement goals as contextually and situationally based versus stable and driven by personality differences (Pintrich & Schunk, 1996). If goals are malleable, it may be possible to induce optimal goals with interventions in classroom environments, and we would expect these goals to have effects comparable to the same goals when freely adopted by students. However, it is not clear whether situationally induced goals are directly comparable to self-set goals or what type of intervention would be sufficient to instantiate a particular goal with the same motivational power as a self-set goal. On the other hand, if goals are stable and resistant to change, then instructors will need to rely on students adopting (i.e., self-setting) optimal goals.

A CRITICAL TEST OF THE MASTERY VERSUS MULTIPLE GOAL PERSPECTIVES

We conducted two studies to offer a stronger test of the mastery goal versus multiple goal perspectives and to bridge existing experimental and class-room studies (Barron & Harackiewicz, 1999). First, to extend the ecological validity of the earlier pinball studies, we devised a laboratory version of an academic activity to simulate a classroom learning experience. Students were taught new methods for solving mathematics problems. These methods used simple strategies to add, subtract, multiply, and divide complex numbers mentally (as opposed to more traditional strategies of working out problems with paper and pencil). Second, we employed both experimental and correlational approaches to investigate goal effects on interest and performance for the activity. In Study 1, college students' self-set achievement goals for the learning session were measured and evaluated correlationally. In Study 2, college students' achievement goals for the learning session were assigned and evaluated experimentally. Furthermore, in Study 2, we created a multiple goal condition in which mastery goals and performance goals were both assigned and we compared the multiple goal condition to a mastery goal–only condition and a performance goal–only condition. Beyond the difference of measuring self-set achievement goals in Study 1 and manipulating achievement goals in Study 2, the procedure for both studies was virtually identical. In addition, the self-report and behavioral measures of intrinsic motivation were the same as those used in the pinball studies. However, the results of our classroom studies led us to consider the importance of assessing both interest and performance, so we collected a performance measure, which was the number of problems that participants could complete with the new method during a fixed time period.

In Study 1, when participants indicated their level of mastery goals and performance goals for the session, mastery goals and performance goals were each linked to distinct, positive outcomes. Mastery goals were the sole predictor of interest in the mathematics activity, and performance goals were the sole predictor of performance in the mathematics activity. Mastery goals had no effects on performance, and performance goals had no effects on intrinsic motivation. Furthermore, there were no interactions of mastery goals and performance goals on any outcome. This pattern of findings replicates the pattern found in each of the three classroom studies reported earlier (e.g., Harackiewicz et al., 1997) but also extends these previous findings by indicating that students' goals can shape their interest and performance even in a very short learning session. Thus, multiple goal adoption may reap benefits early in the educational process.

In Study 2, when participants' goals were assigned, a different pattern of effects emerged. On measures of intrinsic motivation, no one type of goal (or combination of goals) proved optimal for all participants. Instead, the effects of assigned goals were moderated by achievement orientation. When participants were low in achievement orientation (LAMs), assigning mastery goals promoted the highest levels of interest in the mathematics activity. In contrast, when participants were high in achievement orientation (HAMs), assigning performance goals promoted the highest levels of interest. This pattern of results replicates the experimental results reviewed earlier (Harackiewicz & Elliot, 1993). However, the current study offers a crucial extension by including a condition in which both goals were assigned. Interestingly, the multiple goal condition led to similar, moderate levels of interest for both LAMs and HAMs. Although the multiple goal condition did not promote the highest levels of interest, it appeared to at least offer some buffer to low achievers who least preferred the session when assigned only a performance goal, as well as to high achievers who least preferred the session when assigned only a mastery goal. These results once again suggest that mastery goals and performance goals can both promote intrinsic motivation. Moreover, a multiple goal manipulation may offer a compromise because it has elements that are effective for both HAMs and LAMs but may not be as effective as assigning the single preferred goal.

Finally, although self-set performance goals were associated with better mathematics scores in Study 1, assigning performance goals had no effect on mathematics performance in Study 2. In fact, there were no performance differences among the mastery goal–only, performance goal–only, and both goal conditions. These results suggest that assigned goals may not work in the same fashion as when goals are self-adopted.

In sum, rather than supporting a strict mastery goal perspective, the results of the mathematics studies revealed that mastery goals and performance goals can both promote important educational outcomes. However, the benefits of self-adopted goals observed in Study 1 could not be reproduced by simply assigning the same goals in Study 2. Assigning mastery goals did not promote interest for everyone, and assigning performance goals did not affect individuals' performance in the activity. Because careful steps were taken to control for other variables that have made systematic comparisons between previous studies difficult (e.g., differences in type of task, type of research environment, or age of population), we are in a good position to conclude that the difference in results observed between Study 1 and Study 2 involve the origin of the goal. Thus, in addition to the *content* of goals that students can pursue (mastery, performance, or a combination of the two), these two studies suggest that the *origin* of participants' achievement goals (self-adopted vs assigned) may be an important variable to consider when evaluating goal research.

CAPTURING THE COMPLEXITY OF THE MULTIPLE GOAL PERSPECTIVE

Our experimental and correlational work has led us to appreciate the complexity of multiple goal processes, and it has led us to carefully reconsider the pattern (or patterns) of evidence that would support a multiple goal perspective. Whereas the mastery goal perspective suggests that students who pursue single mastery goals will be best off, multiple goal theorists suggest that mastery goals and performance goals can work in concert to facilitate optimal educational outcomes. However, *how* goals might work together has not been clearly delineated in the literature. Thus, even when appropriate methodology is adopted, it is important to recognize that the potential benefits of multiple goals may be revealed in different ways. For example, the benefit of pursuing multiple goals might be revealed on one particular educational outcome (e.g., pursuing both goals leads to higher grades in a course) or, as in our own research, through the attainment of different educational outcomes (e.g., mastery goals lead to interest in coursework, but performance goals lead to higher grades). Therefore, a challenge in testing and evaluating the multiple goal perspective is providing a clear statement of how multiple goal effects might be revealed.

We believe that four different patterns of evidence should be evaluated in future goal research to test the potential benefits of multiple goals. An *additive goal hypothesis* proposes that mastery goals and performance goals both contribute independent, positive effects for achieving a particular educational outcome. Statistical support for this pattern would come in the form of positive main effects for both mastery goals and performance goals on the same educational outcome. Figure 9.2A presents a hypothetical pattern of data that would support the additive goal hypothesis on academic performance.

An *interactive goal hypothesis* proposes that above and beyond independent effects, mastery goals and performance goals interact, such that

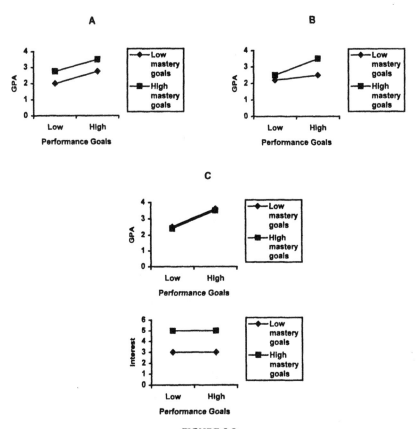

FIGURE 9.2

Hypothetical data supporting alternative versions of the multiple goal perspective: (A) An example of data supporting an additive goal hypothesis; (B) An example of data supporting an interactive goal hypothesis; (C) An example of data supporting a specialized goal hypothesis. GPA = grade point average.

individuals who strongly endorse both goals are notably advantaged in achieving a single educational outcome. Statistical support for this hypothesis would come in the form of a positive *Mastery Goal ×* *Performance Goal* interaction on an educational outcome. Figure 9.2B presents a hypothetical pattern of data that would support the interactive goal hypothesis.

A *specialized goal hypothesis* proposes that rather than promoting the same educational outcomes, mastery goals and performance goals have independent effects on different education outcomes. For example, in our own classroom work reviewed above, we found that mastery goals and performance goals were each associated with distinct, positive outcomes for students in college courses. Thus, the specialized goal hypothesis suggests an alternative benefit of pursuing multiple goals that is revealed only when multiple educational outcomes are assessed. Statistical support for this hypothesis would be represented by a positive main effect for mastery goals on one educational outcome (e.g., interest) and a positive main effect for performance goals on a different education outcome (e.g., final grade in a course). Figure 9.2C presents a hypothetical pattern of data that would support a specialized goal hypothesis.

Finally, a *selective goal hypothesis* proposes that when individuals have the option of pursuing multiple goals, they can better negotiate their learning experiences by focusing on the achievement goal that is most relevant for maintaining their motivation at a particular time. This version of the multiple goal perspective differs from the previous hypotheses because rather than assuming that individuals pursue mastery goals and performance goals simultaneously, it suggests that individuals may selectively focus on one particular goal at a time. In other words, different achievement goals may be better suited for different types of situations, and students who can selectively shift between goals depending on the situation may be particularly advantaged. For example, when students are required to take coursework that does not hold much appeal to them, adopting a performance goal may at least help students remain motivated and engaged in the course.

In addition, the selective goal hypothesis takes on added significance when goals are assigned externally. Under experimental conditions in which both goals are assigned (as in Study 2 of Barron & Harackiewicz, 1999), the selective goal hypothesis would predict that participants in the multiple goal condition would be particularly advantaged because they would have multiple goals to select from and could focus on the goal optimally suited for them. In other words, LAMs could focus on a mastery goal during the activity, whereas HAMs could focus on a performance goal. An overall benefit of assigning multiple goals would be revealed, not because both goals were simultaneously pursued but because different individuals focused on different goals.

CONCLUSIONS

We adopted an achievement goal approach to address the question of optimal motivation. In particular, we considered how two different types of goal orientations can shape achievement pursuits: a mastery goal, in which an individual is focused on developing his or her competence, and a performance goal, in which an individual is focused on demonstrating his or her competence relative to others. A number of theorists have likened the mastery–performance goal distinction to intrinsic–extrinsic motivation (see chapters 8 and 12, this book; Pintrich & Schunk, 1996; Utman, 1997). Thus, it may not be surprising that a mastery goal orientation (the more intrinsic orientation for learning) has taken center stage as the optimal motivation to hold and has been championed by a number of theorists. In this chapter, however, we challenged the notion that mastery goals are always adaptive and that performance goals are always maladaptive. We reviewed our program of research conducted in both laboratory and classroom settings that reveals a number of positive consequences for both mastery goals and performance goals. Specifically, in a series of laboratory studies designed to examine goal effects on intrinsic motivation, no one goal proved optimal for all participants. Rather, the optimal goal to assign depended on personality characteristics of the individual or on other contextual factors. In a series of classroom studies in which we measured participants' self-set goals, we found that mastery goals and performance goals were linked to distinct, positive outcomes. Students endorsing mastery goals reported higher levels of interest in the course, and students endorsing performance goals obtained higher grades in their coursework. Thus, instead of supporting the mastery goal perspective, in which optimal motivation stems from the exclusive pursuit of mastery goals, our findings offer strong support for a multiple goal perspective, in which mastery goals and performance goals can both promote optimal motivation.

Throughout this chapter, we also discussed limitations of previous research that have prevented fair tests of the multiple goal perspective and may have led to some premature conclusions. For example, theorists now recognize that the performance goal construct is multidimensional. Studies that fail to differentiate between types of performance goals may mask the potential benefits of approach-oriented performance goals (see chapter 8, this volume). Furthermore, very few studies to date have employed methodologies that allow an adequate test of the two perspectives. For example, experimental investigations are silent regarding multiple goal pursuit (which we have started to rectify in our own work). We also suggested that a number of additional factors may moderate when results might support the mastery goal versus multiple goal perspective (e.g., the benefits of multiple goals may be revealed only with older age groups). Finally, we argued that support for the multiple goal perspective may be revealed in a number of different ways. Specifically, we outlined four different hypotheses that should be tested when evaluating the effects of multiple goals (the additive, interactive, specialized, and selective goal hypotheses).

In sum, we believe that continued work is needed to examine how both mastery goals and performance goals may promote adaptive achievement behaviors before concluding that one particular type of motivation is optimal (Hidi & Harackiewicz, 2000; chapter 10, this book). In particular, we need to adopt methodologies that go beyond pitting one type of motivation against the other (e.g., mastery goals vs. performance goals or intrinsic motivation vs. extrinsic motivation) to understand how multiple sources of motivation may contribute to optimal functioning. Thus, in the case of achievement goals, instead of encouraging students to pursue mastery goals *in place of* performance goals, we may be better off trying to encourage students to adopt mastery goals *along with* performance goals. With this in mind, let us return to the dilemma of choosing a research assistant or a new graduate student. Mark (the performance oriented student) and Sam (the mastery oriented student) both have a lot to offer, but Esmerelda (who is both mastery oriented and performance oriented) may be the ideal candidate.

Acknowledgments

We thank Carol Sansone and Johnny Tauer for their helpful comments on earlier drafts of this chapter. Correspondence concerning this article should be addressed to Kenneth Barron or to Judith Harackiewicz, Department of Psychology, 1202 West Johnson Street, University of Wisconsin—Madison, Madison, WI 53706. E-mail: kebarron@facstaff.wisc.edu or jmharack@facstaff.wisc.edu.

References

Ames, C. (1992). Classrooms: Goals, structures, and student motivation. *Journal of Educational Psychology, 84*, 261–271.

Ames, C., & Ames, R. (1984). Systems of student and teacher motivation: Toward a qualitative definition. *Journal of Educational Psychology, 76*, 535–556.

Ames, C., & Archer, J. (1988). Achievement goals in the classroom: Students' learning strategies and motivation processes. *Journal of Educational Psychology, 80*, 260–267.

Anderman, E., & Maehr, M. (1994). Motivation and schooling in the middle grades. *Review of Educational Research, 64*, 287–309.

Archer, J. (1994). Achievement goals as a measure of motivation in university students. *Contemporary Educational Psychology, 19*, 430–446.

Atkinson, J. W. (1974). The mainsprings of achievement oriented activity. In J. W. Atkinson & J. O. Raynor (Eds.), *Motivation and achievement* (pp. 11–39). Washington, DC: Winston.

Bandura, A. (1986). *Social foundations of thought and action: A social cognitive theory.* Englewood Cliffs, NJ: Prentice-Hall.

Baron, R. M., & Kenny, D. A. (1986). The moderator–mediator variable distinction in social psychological research: Conceptual, strategic, and statistical considerations. *Journal of Personality and Social Psychology, 51*, 1173–1182.

Barron, K. E., & Harackiewicz, J. M. (1999). Achievement goals and optimal motivation: Testing multiple goal effects. Manuscript submitted for publication.

Barron, K. E., Schwab, C., & Harackiewicz, J. M. (1999, April). Achievement goals and classroom context: A comparison of different learning environments. Paper presented at the meeting of the Midwestern Psychological Association, Chicago.

Bouffard, T., Boisvert, J., Vezeau, C., & Larouche, C. (1995). The impact of goal orientation on self-regulation and performance among college students. *British Journal of Educational Psychology*, 65, 317–329.

Bouffard, T., Vezeau, C., & Bordeleau, L. (1998). A developmental study of the relation between combined learning and performance goals and students' self-regulated learning. *British Journal of Educational Psychology*, 68, 309–319.

Butler, D., & Winne, P. (1995). Feedback and self-regulated learning: A theoretical synthesis. *Review of Educational Research*, 65, 245–281.

Carver, C. S., Lawrence, J. W., & Scheier, M. F. (1996). A control-process perspective on the origins of affect. In L. L. Martin & A. Tesser (Eds.), *Striving and feeling: Interactions among goals, affect, and self-regulation* (pp. 11–52). Mahwah, NJ: Erlbaum.

Dweck, C. S. (1986). Motivational processes affecting learning. *American Psychologist*, 41, 1040–1048.

Dweck, C. S., & Leggett, E. L. (1988). A social-cognitive approach to motivation and personality. *Psychological Review*, 95, 256–273.

Eccles, J. S., & Midgley, C. (1989). Stage–environment fit: Developmentally appropriate classrooms for young adolescents. In C. Ames & R. Ames (Eds.), *Research on motivation in education: Goals and cognitions* (vol. 3, pp. 139–186). New York: Academic Press.

Elliot, A. J., & Church, M. A. (1997). A hierarchical model of approach and avoidance achievement motivation. *Journal of Personality and Social Psychology*, 72, 218–232.

Elliot, A. J., & Harackiewicz, J. M. (1994). Goal setting, achievement orientation, and intrinsic motivation: A mediational analysis. *Journal of Personality and Social Psychology*, 66, 968–980.

Elliot, A. J., & Harackiewicz, J. M. (1996). Approach and avoidance achievement goals and intrinsic motivation: A mediational analysis. *Journal of Personality and Social Psychology*, 70, 461–475.

Elliot, E. S., & Dweck, C. S. (1988). Goals: An approach to motivation and achievement. *Journal of Personality and Social Psychology*, 54, 5–12.

Harackiewicz, J. M., Barron, K. E., Carter, S. M., Lehto, A. T., & Elliot, A. J. (1997). Determinants and consequences of achievement goals in the college classroom: Maintaining interest and making the grade. *Journal of Personality and Social Psychology*, 73, 1284–1295.

Harackiewicz, J. M., Barron, K. E., & Elliott, A. J. (1998). Rethinking achievement goals: When are they adaptive for college students and why? *Educational Psychologist*, 33, 1–21.

Harackiewicz, J. M., Barron, K. E., Tauer, J. M., Carter, S. M., & Elliot, A. J. (2000). Short-term and long-term consequences of achievement goals in college: Predicting continued interest and performance over time. *Journal of Educational Psychology*.

Harackiewicz, J. M., & Elliot, A. J. (1993). Achievement goals and intrinsic motivation. *Journal of Personality and Social Psychology*, 65, 904–915.

Harackiewicz, J. M., & Elliot, A. J. (1998). The joint effects of target and purpose goals on intrinsic motivation: A mediational analysis. *Personality and Social Psychology Bulletin*, 24, 675–689.

Harackiewicz, J. M., & Sansone, C. (1991). Goals and intrinsic motivation: You can get there from here. In M. L. Maehr, & P. R. Pintrich (Eds.), *Advances in motivation and achievement* (vol. 7, pp. 21–49). Greenwich, CT: JAI Press.

Hidi, S., & Harackiewicz, J. M. (2000). Motivating the academically unmotivated: A critical issue for the 21st century. *Review of Educational Research*.

Jackson, D. N. (1974). *Personality Research Form Manual*. Goshen, NY: Research Psychologists Press.

Judd, C. M., & Kenny, D. A. (1981). Process analysis: Estimating mediation in treatment evaluations. *Evaluation Review*, 5, 602–619.

Locke, E. A., & Latham, G. P. (1990). *A theory of goal setting and task performance*. Englewood Cliffs, NJ: Prentice-Hall.

Maehr, M. L. (1976). Continuing motivation: An analysis of a seldom considered educational outcome. *Review of Educational Research, 46,* 443–462.

Maehr, M. L. (1989). Thoughts about motivation. In C. Ames & R. Ames (Eds.), *Research on motivation in education: Goals and cognitions* (vol 3., pp. 299–315). New York: Academic Press.

Maehr, M. L., & Midgley, C. (1991). Enhancing student motivation: A schoolwide approach. *Educational Psychologist, 26,* 399–427.

McClelland, D. C. (1961). *The achieving society.* Princeton, NJ: Van Nostrand.

Meece, J. L., Blumenfeld, P. C., & Hoyle, R. H. (1988). Students' goal orientations and cognitive engagement in classroom activities. *Journal of Educational Psychology, 80,* 514–523.

Meece, J. L., & Holt, K. (1993). A pattern analysis of students' achievement goals. *Journal of Educational Psychology, 85,* 582–590.

Middleton, M., & Midgley, C. (1997). Avoiding the demonstration of lack of ability: An under-explored aspect of goal theory. *Journal of Educational Psychology, 89,* 710–718.

Midgley, C., Kaplan, A., Middleton, M., Maehr, M., Urdan, T., Anderman, L., Anderman, E., & Roeser, R. (1998). The development and validation of scales assessing students' achievement goal orientations. *Contemporary Educational Psychology, 23,* 113–131.

Nicholls, J. G. (1979). Quality and equality in intellectual development. *American Psychologist, 34,* 1071–1084.

Nicholls, J. G. (1984). Achievement motivation: Conceptions of ability, subjective experience, task choice, and performance. *Psychological Review, 91,* 328–346.

Nolen, S. B. (1988). Reasons for studying: Motivation orientations and study strategies. *Cognition and Instruction, 5,* 269–287.

Pintrich, P. R., & Garcia, T. (1991). Student goal orientation and self-regulation in the college classroom. In M. L. Maehr & P. R. Pintrich (Eds.), *Advances in motivation and achievement* (vol. 7, pp. 371–402). Greenwich, CT: JAI Press.

Pintrich, P. R., & Schunk, D. H. (1996). *Motivation in education: Theory, research, and applications.* Englewood Cliffs, NJ: Merrill.

Sansone, C., & Harackiewicz, J. M. (1996). "I don't feel like it": The function of interest in self-regulation. In Martin, L. L. & Tesser, A. (Eds.), *Striving and feeling: Interactions among goals, affect, and self-regulation* (pp. 203–228). Mahwah, NJ: Erlbaum.

Sansone, C., Sachau, D. A., & Weir, C. (1989). The effects of instruction on intrinsic interest: The importance of context. *Journal of Personality and Social Psychology, 57,* 819–829.

Sears, D. (1986). College sophomores in the laboratory: Influences of a narrow database in social psychology's view of human nature. *Journal of Personality and Social Psychology, 44,* 515–530.

Skaalvick, E. M. (1997). Self-enhancing and self-defeating ego orientation: Relations with task and avoidance orientation, achievement, self-perceptions, and anxiety. *Journal of Educational Psychology, 89,* 71–81.

Tauer, J. M., & Harackiewicz, J. M. (1999). Winning isn't everything: Competition, achievement orientation, and intrinsic motivation. Special issue on intrinsic motivation of the *Journal of Experimental Social Psychology, 35,* 209–238.

Urdan, T. C. (1997). Examining the relations among early adolescent students' goals and friends' orientation toward effort and achievement in school. *Contemporary Educational Psychology, 22,* 165–191.

Wentzel, K. R. (1991). Social and academic goals at school: Motivation and achievement in context. In M. L. Maehr, & P. R. Pintrich (Eds.), *Advances in motivation and achievement* (vol. 7, pp. 185–212). Greenwich, CT: JAI Press.

Wolters, C. A., Yu, S. L., & Pintrich, P. R. (1996). The relation between goal orientation and students' motivational beliefs and self-regulated learning. *Learning and Individual Differences, 8,* 211–238.

PART

III

The Role of Interest in Learning and Self-Regulation

"Extrinsic" versus "Intrinsic"
Motivation Reconsidered

Turning "Play" into "Work" and "Work" into "Play": 25 Years of Research on Intrinsic Versus Extrinsic Motivation

MARK R. LEPPER
JENNIFER HENDERLONG
Stanford University
Department of Psychology

> [Tom] had discovered a great law of human action ... namely, that Work consists of whatever a body is *obliged* to do, and that Play consists of whatever a body is not obliged to do. And this would help him to understand why constructing artificial flowers or performing on a treadmill is work, while rolling ten-pins or climbing Mont Blanc is only amusement.
>
> — Mark Twain, in *The Adventures of Tom Sawyer* (1876)

INTRODUCTION

For the first half of the 20th century, the study of motivation was dominated by a focus on instrumental learning and extrinsic motivation. From Thorndike's early studies of problem solving in cats (Thorndike, 1911) to the extensive work of Skinner and his students on elementary learning in rats and pigeons (Skinner, 1938, 1953), psychologists interested in motivation were concerned primarily with the effects of externally imposed instrumental contingencies that linked the receipt of some seemingly arbitrary reinforcer to the performance of some equally arbitrary response. Thus, in this tradition, rats/cats/pigeons could be taught to press bars/nudge panels/peck keys in order to obtain food/water/relief from pain.

From the outset, the power of this approach was evident. By defining reinforcers solely in terms of their demonstrated effectiveness in altering subsequent response probabilities, these theorists were able to finesse an array of problematic conceptual and definitional issues. More important, given this definition, reinforcement procedures frequently produced dramatic effects, and investigators were able to teach animals to perform surprisingly complex sequences of actions. Indeed, in the heyday of these approaches, students in introductory psychology might be shown a film of a white rat, irreverently nicknamed Rodent E. Lee, turning a wheel to raise a miniature Confederate flag, pushing a button to turn on a recording of "Dixie," and rising on its hind paws with one front paw touching its head, as if standing at attention and saluting the flag.

Beginning in the second half of the 20th century, however, psychology began to see the emergence of a variety of challenges to this model. These challenges came from theorists who sought to illustrate and champion various forms of allegedly "intrinsic" motivation—motivations that seemed inherent to engagement in many activities, regardless of the subsequent "extrinsic" rewards or punishments to which those activities might lead in particular situations. We may go bowling, play bridge, read novels, listen to Mozart, or even, as Mark Twain suggested, climb Mont Blanc, for the sheer fun of it—without thought, or so it seemed, of the subsequent instrumental value of these activities.

Indeed, within a short period of time, a number of different types of seemingly intrinsic motivation were independently identified. Four of these that have remained of interest since the 1950s include what we might call the "4 C's" of intrinsic motivation—challenge, curiosity, control, and context. In one very early and influential analysis, for example, White (1959, 1960) described an effectance or mastery motive, suggesting that people deliberately seek out challenges to overcome and new skills to master, simply to experience the pleasure of accomplishment itself. Young children, he noted, routinely invest extraordinary amounts of time and effort in learning to walk, to talk, and to interact to others, and they seem to do so without a great deal of direct instruction or extensive extrinsic reinforcement. About this same time, Berlyne (1960, 1966) began to describe curiosity and related forms of epistemic motivation as inherent to people's constant struggles to make sense of the world around them and as intrinsically rewarding, independent of any additional extrinsic rewards or punishments. Ostentatiously hiding something from a child, he would note, will usually produce a very strong motive in that child to discover what has been hidden.

Similarly, Hunt (1961, 1965)—perhaps the first of these theorists to use the precise term *intrinsic motivation*—focused on what we might now call the motivational value of a sense of control. Elaborating on Piaget's earlier observations of the systematic experimentation and exploration that even infants seem to engage in time after time, Hunt suggested that humans find the exercise of control over their environment to be inherently motivating. Finally, during this same period, Bruner (1961, 1966) wrote of the importance of the contextualization of learning—of students' being able to see, for example, the relevance and utility of the skills they are being taught in school for solving problems or accomplishing goals of their own, objectives they would find of inherent personal interest, in the larger world outside of their classrooms.

Once people had begun to contrast these sorts of intrinsic motivations with the kinds of extrinsic motivations that had been central to the Skinnerians and the early social-learning theorists, it was not long before the field of motivation saw the emergence of various hypotheses that these two types of motivation might not always complement one another. Indeed, in the early 1970s, in three different laboratories in three different parts of the world, results were obtained—using different activities, procedures, rewards, contingencies, and subject populations—showing that offering people functionally superfluous extrinsic rewards for engagement in activities of initial inherent interest could undermine their subsequent intrinsic interest in those activities when extrinsic incentives were no longer available or contingent on those activities.

In the present chapter, we review some of the major themes that characterize the quarter century of research on these issues since these early studies. The three major issues we examine involve three potential relationships between intrinsic and extrinsic motivation. First, we examine the experimental literature that has shown that the two may be opposed to one another—in which the imposition of unnecessarily powerful extrinsic contingencies may undermine prior intrinsic interest. We begin, in short, with the study of "intrinsic *versus* extrinsic motivation." Next, we turn to some more recent literature that has examined real-world situations in which intrinsic and extrinsic motivation may coexist—in which one may assess independently an individual's levels of "intrinsic *and/or* extrinsic motivation." Last, we will turn to the final logical possibility—that intrinsic and extrinsic motivation may enhance or complement one another—the case of "intrinsic *plus* extrinsic motivation."

INTRINSIC VERSUS EXTRINSIC MOTIVATION

Consider, first, the experimental literature that seems to demonstrate the inherent opposition of intrinsic and extrinsic motivation. In the early 1970s,

Deci (1971, 1972), Kruglanski, Friedman, and Zeevi (1971), and Lepper, Greene, and Nisbett (1973) each independently demonstrated a detrimental effect of the imposition of extrinsic incentives on participants' subsequent intrinsic interest in the activities for which extrinsic incentives had been, but were no longer, available.

The Original Experiments

Interestingly, in these three early studies, comparable findings were obtained despite striking variations in the specific tasks, rewards, and procedures used in these different investigations. Deci (1971, Experiment 1) offered Carnegie Mellon University undergraduates $1 for each three-dimensional manipulative puzzle that they correctly solved. Later he covertly observed the amount of time these students chose to spend continuing to work with this same activity, the SOMA Cube, when the experimenter had seemingly left the laboratory and there was no longer any money contingent upon engagement in this activity. Compared with students who had not received payment for working on the same puzzles (or students who had received payment not contingent upon their successful solutions of the problems [Deci, 1972]), students in this extrinsic incentive condition subsequently chose to spend less time with these puzzles once these puzzles no longer had instrumental value. In addition, in a further experiment using this same general paradigm, Deci (1971, Experiment 3) also examined the effects of "verbal rewards" for performance on the SOMA Cube task on subsequent intrinsic motivation. In this condition, after each puzzle solved, students were given (false) feedback that their time to solution was "much better than average" for their peers at Carnegie Mellon. In contrast to the receipt of the tangible reward of money, the receipt of such purely verbal rewards, compared to a no-feedback condition, served to increase, rather than decrease, later intrinsic motivation.

At the same time, halfway around the world, Kruglanski and his collaborators (Kruglanski et al., 1971) offered half of a sample of Israeli high school students an extrinsic incentive, in the form of a personal tour of the research laboratories at nearby Tel Aviv University, for engaging in a series of experimental tasks in the laboratory. Again, compared with students not offered such a contingent reward for their efforts, students in the extrinsic incentive condition described themselves as less interested in the activities. In addition, their performance on the various experimental tasks suffered in several respects. They showed less creativity in listing unusual uses for everyday objects, they displayed lower incidental recall of the activities they had just undertaken, and they proved less likely to show significant "Zeigarnik effects" (i.e., heightened recall for uncompleted or interrupted tasks, indicative of high task involvement).

Finally, in yet a third quite different context, Lepper and his colleagues (Lepper et al., 1973) examined the effects of a superfluous extrinsic incentive on the intrinsic motivation of nursery school children. These children were specifically selected on the basis of their initial high levels of intrinsic interest in drawing pictures with special Magic Marker pens, as determined during baseline free-play periods in their regular preschool classrooms. Subsequently, these children were asked, in individual experimental sessions apart from their classrooms, to engage in the same art activity under one of three conditions. In an expected-award condition, children were first shown a fancy "good player award" and were asked if they would be willing to work on the art activity in order to win one of these awards. In a second, unexpected-award condition, the children received exactly the same award and the same feedback unexpectedly at the end of the experimental session; and in a third, no-award condition, the children received the same verbal feedback but neither expected nor obtained any tangible reward. Two weeks later, the children's intrinsic interest in the Magic Markers was again assessed covertly in their regular classrooms. As predicted, intrinsic motivation decreased only in the expected-award condition, in which the children had explicitly contracted to engage in the activity in order to obtain a tangible prize.

Given the convergent, comparable results from the tangible-reward conditions of these three initial studies—obtained across quite different procedures, extrinsic incentives, dependent measures, subject populations, and the like—one might have expected these early studies to have produced some consensus that superfluous extrinsic incentives can indeed undermine prior intrinsic motivation. Instead, these early findings were met with considerable resistance and have led to an extensive and continuing controversy, since the mid-1970s, concerning the exact conditions under which extrinsic rewards and punishments will have either positive or negative effects on intrinsic motivation.

Later Experimental Literature

Since the mid-1970s, more than 100 additional experiments have been reported in this area—extending, qualifying, and sometimes challenging the results from the first studies in this field. Nonetheless, these initial three studies alone presage most of the important distinctions and conclusions that characterize the decades of research that followed them. Thus, these early experiments explicitly demonstrated the importance of reward contingency, of expectation of reward, and of tangibility of reward in determining whether a particular reward manipulation will be likely to undermine, enhance, or have no effect on subsequent intrinsic motivation—each of which has been borne out as an important variable in subsequent research.

That is, virtually every review of this literature seems to have agreed—all else being held constant—on three basic propositions:

- That noncontingent extrinsic rewards will be less likely to produce detrimental effects and more likely to produce beneficial effects on later intrinsic motivation than otherwise identical rewards that are contingent on task engagement or task completion (and under some conditions, on task performance)
- That unexpected extrinsic rewards will be less likely to produce negative and more likely to produce positive effects on intrinsic motivation than otherwise identical rewards that are expected
- That extrinsic rewards that are intangible (e.g., diffuse, implicit, social, verbal) will be less likely to produce adverse effects and more likely to produce facilitative effects than otherwise comparable rewards that are more tangible.[1]

Also more implicit in these early studies was a fourth proposition—that rewards that provide salient evidence of one's competence or ability at an activity will have more positive (or less negative) effects on intrinsic motivation than will rewards that do not provide such information. Consider the comparison between the monetary reward Deci employed in Experiment 1 (i.e., $1 for each correctly completed design) and the "verbal reward" he employed in Experiment 3 (i.e., being given highly positive feedback, such as "That's very good. That's much better than average for this configuration" after each correctly completed design). In later writings, many authors, including Deci himself, have focused on the additional informational value of the positive feedback in the verbal reward condition concerning the participant's competence at the activity as a critical factor in the greater intrinsic motivation shown by this group (e.g., Condry, 1977; Deci & Ryan, 1985; Lepper & Greene, 1978; chapter 4, this book).

Finally, although shortly after the initial studies, a number of different investigators explicitly demonstrated the importance of high initial task interest that had been presumed in the deliberate selection of activities of high intrinsic interest to participants in the original experiments. Thus, a number of subsequent studies—once again using different participants, activities, rewards, and specific procedures—have supported a fifth proposi-

---

[1] In fact, it may be worth noting that it is virtually impossible to create an ecologically valid version of a purely verbal "expected reward" that would have the same degree of specificity as a comparable tangible expected reward. To learn that one will be paid precisely $5 is potentially quite different than to learn that some other person will be "quite pleased" with one, in that the latter remains significantly more ambiguous. *How pleased?* or *With what effect?* one might still wonder. Were a person actually told that the other person will "tell you that you are 'very smart,'" the procedure would be somewhat more comparable, but this would be extremely unusual in everyday discourse.

tion, that identical expected tangible rewards can both undermine participants' intrinsic motivation in tasks designed or selected to be of high initial interest yet enhance participants' interest in tasks designed or selected to be of little or no initial interest (e.g., Calder & Staw, 1975; Danner & Lonky, 1981; Loveland & Olley, 1979; McLoyd, 1979; Newman & Layton, 1984).

In more explicitly theoretical terms, we believe that it is possible to summarize most of the existing literature on the effects of rewards on later motivation in terms of three potentially distinct conceptual variables (Lepper & Gilovich, 1981; Lepper & Greene, 1978), as illustrated schematically in Figure 10.1.

Perceptions of Continued Instrumental Value

First, as shown in the upper one third of Figure 10.1, the receipt of extrinsic rewards may convey information about the likelihood of further tangible or social extrinsic rewards in related situations in the future. Having received a tangible reward for some particular activity or accomplishment in one setting, one may often come to expect some comparable instrumental payoff for a similar activity or accomplishment in the future, at least in psychologically similar situations. Moreover, even if tangible rewards may no longer be available, the receipt of such a reward from some particular individual, group, or institution may convey information that that same individual, group, or institution (and perhaps related others) would be pleased by, and likely to approve of, one's engagement in similar tasks or achievement of similar goals in the future. Such expectations of continued extrinsic tangible or social payoffs in the future, then, may provide continued extrinsic motivation for the individual to continue to engage in a previously rewarded activity, whether or not that activity is of any intrinsic interest to the person.

Perceptions of Personal Competence

Second, as depicted in the middle one third of Figure 10.1, extrinsic rewards may also convey information about one's level of mastery of, or ability at, a particular task, or one's more general personal competence. The receipt of rewards or other feedback that enhances an individual's perceptions of competence may influence both that person's later intrinsic and later extrinsic motivation. On the one hand, other things being equal, increases in perceived competence at an activity will generally lead to corresponding increases in intrinsic motivation, at least when doing well is salient or important (Sansone, 1986)—that is, people tend to like things they think they are good at. On the other hand, increases in perceived competence may also make a person more likely to attempt or persevere at activities for which extrinsic rewards are anticipated to be available only for specific lev-

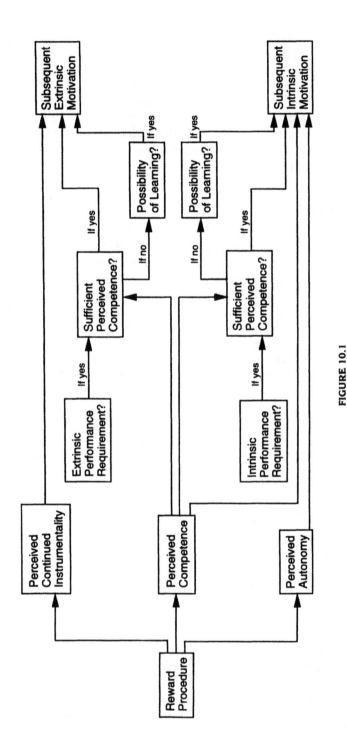

FIGURE 10.1

A schematic view of how rewards may affect subsequent intrinsic and extrinsic motivation via the conceptual variables of perceived continued instrumentality, perceived competence, and perceived autonomy.

els of performance. Both such effects should, of course, be especially likely when later intrinsic, or extrinsic, rewards are seen as requiring high levels of performance or success relative to others. Such perceptions, in turn, are more likely if prior rewards had been made contingent upon some criterion of excellence than if those rewards had depended merely on task engagement or task completion.

Perceptions of External Control

Finally, the receipt of extrinsic rewards may, in addition, convey information about one's level of personal control or autonomy in that setting, as illustrated in the lower one third of Figure 10.1. All else held constant, the receipt of rewards that lead people to view their actions as having been extrinsically motivated—that lead people to feel like "pawns" rather than "origins" of their own actions (deCharms, 1968)—may undermine subsequent intrinsic motivation. This should be particularly likely when rewards are expected, tangible, salient, and superfluous, as well as when rewards are accompanied by other forms of extrinsic constraint that may heighten perceptions of external control, such as close surveillance (Lepper & Greene, 1975), temporal deadlines (Amabile, DeJong, & Lepper, 1976), or statements of obligation (Pittman, Davey, Alafat, Wetherill, & Kramer, 1980; Ryan, 1982). Under such circumstances, people will be less likely to engage in similar activities in future situations in which they no longer expect further tangible or social extrinsic rewards to be contingent upon those actions.

With these three factors, one can derive the central findings of the literature outlined above, as has been described in greater detail elsewhere (e.g., Lepper, 1981; Lepper & Gilovich, 1981). In addition, one can predict that the effects of expected tangible rewards will be most variable when the receipt of a reward simultaneously increases both perceptions of personal competence (thereby, *ceteris paribus*, increasing later intrinsic motivation) and perceptions of external control (thereby, *ceteris paribus*, decreasing later intrinsic motivation). In such situations, the net effect of the reward procedure will depend on the relative magnitudes of these two competing effects. Certainly, this prediction concerning the potential variability of the effects of such rewards seems to us borne out by the conflicting findings concerning such procedures since the 1970s (e.g., Boggiano & Ruble, 1979; Deci, Koestner, & Ryan, 1999; Greene & Lepper, 1974; Harackiewicz, 1979; Harackiewicz, Manderlink, & Sansone, 1984).

It is worth explicitly noting, however, the contrast between "relative" versus "absolute" predictions that can be derived from this model, as well as other related analyses (e.g., Deci, 1975; Deci & Ryan, 1985). Whereas it is easy to generate clear predictions, under controlled conditions, about the relative effects of different reward procedures—for example, expected versus unexpected, contingent versus noncontingent, or highly informative versus uninformative rewards—it is much more difficult to generate unequivocal predictions concerning the absolute effects of any particular reward procedure (compared, for instance, to a no-reward control group or to baseline levels). This is because a single reward manipulation may produce explicitly opposing effects via our three conceptual variables.

Moreover, other factors may also determine the absolute level of motivation among previously rewarded subjects, compared with others who received no rewards at all. For example, if a particular reward procedure produces an increase in the amount of time spent with the activity, that increase in sheer time on task may have at least short-term positive (via mere exposure and enhanced familiarity) or negative (via boredom or satiation) motivational consequences. Similarly, if a specific reward procedure has either a positive or a negative effect on the quality of immediate task performance, such differences in task performance may themselves exert corresponding influences on later motivation. Finally, and most important, if a given reward procedure leads to changes in either the quality or the amount of task engagement that prove sufficient to produce an improvement in task-relevant skills or knowledge, such increases in actual capabilities would be expected to have long-term beneficial effects on both later intrinsic and later extrinsic motivation. (See Lepper and Gilovich [1981] for a more extended analysis of these sorts of "task performance" effects.)

Finally, a consideration of these three determinants of the effects of extrinsic rewards on later intrinsic and extrinsic motivation also permits us to predict and understand a variety of other theoretically significant findings that appear in the later literature on this topic. Such an analysis would predict, first, that extrinsic rewards or feedback presented in a manner that highlights their use as external controls or constraints can decrease later intrinsic motivation, whereas identical extrinsic rewards or feedback presented as indicators of personal competence can instead increase later intrinsic motivation (e.g., Pittman et al., 1980; Ryan, Mims, & Koestner, 1983). This analysis would also predict that even highly controlling extrinsic rewards may not have the otherwise predicted negative effects on intrinsic motivation if participants are explicitly reminded of (Fazio, 1981) or are given false feedback about (Pittman, Cooper, & Smith, 1977) their actual initial intrinsic motivation. Similarly, an objectively unexpected reward should have the same detrimental effect as its expected counterpart, if people are (falsely) persuaded that the reward had been offered earlier and they had been expecting it all along (Kruglanski, Alon, & Lewis, 1972). Finally, this model would also account for an array of experiments showing comparable detrimental effects on subsequent intrinsic motivation of a variety of other forms of external constraint not involving the use of rewards per se, such as temporal deadlines (Amabile et al., 1976), threats of punishment (Deci & Cascio, 1972), unnecessarily close adult surveillance (Lepper & Greene,

1975), or the mere presentation of some activities as "means" and others as "ends" (Lepper, Sagotsky, Dafoe, & Greene, 1982).[2]

In summary, it seems to us, as it did to Deci and colleagues (1999), that the experimental literature on the potentially deleterious effects of superfluous extrinsic rewards on subsequent intrinsic motivation does indeed provide a reasonably "clear and reliable" set of findings. As shown schematically in Figure 10.1, there are a number of processes by which rewards may influence a person's later intrinsic, and extrinsic, motivation (Lepper, 1988; Lepper & Gilovich, 1981; chapters 1 and 2, this book). Hence, the detrimental effects of decreases in perceived autonomy should be most evident when one has controlled both for the effects of potential differences in perceptions of continued instrumentality (e.g., by observing later behavior in settings in which it is clear that the previously rewarded activity will no longer yield further tangible, or social, rewards) and for the effects of potential differences in perceptions of personal competence (e.g., by examining the effects of reward procedures that do not convey differential information about a person's ability). Under these conditions, the imposition of superfluous and tangible extrinsic rewards will produce decreases in subsequent intrinsic motivation, as first shown in the early studies by Deci (1971), Kruglanski and associates (1971), and Lepper and colleagues (1973).

Meta-analytical Analyses

Despite the apparent consistency of most of the findings in this literature, particularly the results of studies involving children (Deci & Ryan, 1985, 1991; Lepper & Gilovich, 1981; Lepper & Hodell, 1989; Quattrone, 1985),[3]

---

[2] In particular, in what might be viewed as a paradigmatic demonstration of the effects of perceptions of external control per se, Lepper et al. (1982) examined the differential effects of the imposition of a purely nominal contingency on children's engagement in two activities of high and identical initial interest. Thus, in a "means–end" condition, children were confronted with two activities deliberately selected to be of equally high initial intrinsic interest to them and were told that they could "win a chance" to engage in one of these activities (i.e., the end) only if they first engaged in the other of these activities (i.e., the means). The nominal "reward" in this procedure, in short, was of no greater value than the activity required to obtain that "reward." In a control condition, by contrast, the children simply engaged in the two activities without any stated contingency between the two. Two weeks later, these two activities were again presented during scheduled free-play periods in the children's regular classrooms, to assess the effects on children's subsequent intrinsic motivation. As predicted, children in the means–end condition, relative to their counterparts in the control condition, showed decreased interest in the activity that had been presented as a means but increased interest in the activity that had been presented as an end—a pattern of results that has been replicated by a number of investigators in different domains (e.g., Birch, Birch, Marlin, & Kramer, 1982; Birch, Marlin, & Rotter, 1984; Newman & Taylor, 1992).

[3] It may be of some interest to note that the detrimental effects of superfluous extrinsic rewards seem significantly greater with children than with adult subjects (Deci et al., 1999). Whether this is due to differences in the interpretations these two populations characteristically place on the offer of tangible rewards, differences in the normative expectations of these two groups, or other differences in experimental procedures remains to be studied.

it is hard to present any review of this work without considering the recent plethora of meta-analyses of this literature (Cameron & Pierce, 1994; Deci, Koestner, & Ryan, 1999; Eisenberger & Cameron, 1996; Rummel & Feinberg, 1988; Tang & Hall, 1995) that have evoked such substantial controversy and concern (Hennessey & Amabile, 1998; Kohn, 1996; Lepper, 1995, 1998; Lepper, Henderlong, & Gingras, 1999; Lepper, Keavney, & Drake, 1996; Ryan & Deci, 1996; Sansone & Harackiewicz, 1998). As with the original empirical studies in this field, the idea of using meta-analytical techniques in reviewing this literature seems to have independently occurred to a number of different authors at approximately the same time. In sharp contrast to the original experimental studies in this area, however, there has been considerably less agreement in the conclusions reached by these different meta-analyses.

Basically, these more recent statistical summaries fall into two camps. On the one hand, several of these meta-analyses (Deci et al., 1999; Rummel & Feinberg, 1988; Tang & Hall, 1995) provided general support for the conclusions reported above and in previous narrative reviews of this literature. Thus, Deci et al. (1999) described the detrimental effects of extrinsic rewards on intrinsic motivation, under the conditions discussed earlier, as displaying "clear and reliable" effects, and Tang and Hall (1995) concluded that such detrimental effects appear "when they should," as predicted by the factors described above. By contrast, "two" other closely related meta-analyses (Cameron & Pierce, 1994; Eisenberger & Cameron, 1996) reported similar conclusions regarding a number of specific questions but continually emphasize a simple "summary" of their findings as indicating that there are no systematic "general" or "overall" effects of rewards on intrinsic motivation. Specifically, these authors argued that rewards have detrimental effects only under very limited conditions that rarely occur and can easily be avoided in the real world, and therefore that conclusions about real-world detrimental effects of rewards on intrinsic motivation are merely a "myth."[4]

Our response to these meta-analyses, and especially to the assertions of these latter reviewers, is twofold (Lepper et al., 1999). First, we believe that this literature has a number of characteristics that make the use of *any* meta-analytical procedure problematic and suspect. Second, we believe that the specific meta-analytical procedures used by Cameron and her colleagues further exacerbate the inherent general difficulties of applying meta-analysis to this particular research domain.

Consider, then, some of the more general arguments against the possibility of using meta-analytical procedures effectively on this particular

---

[4] Our discussion here focuses more on the earlier Cameron and Pierce article (1994) than the later Eisenberger and Cameron article (1996), simply because the former provides details on the analyses employed with different individual studies and the latter does not.

research literature (Lepper, 1995). In the first place, it makes almost no sense to consider the set of studies that have been performed and published to constitute a random or representative sample of any meaningful larger population of reward procedures in the real world. Because of the theoretical nature of this literature and the early recognition by most researchers that rewards could have both positive and negative effects on motivation—depending on the situation—virtually every relevant study was deliberately designed to test some statistical interaction prediction. In some cases, researchers sought to illustrate explicitly that rewards would produce opposite effects (i.e., a full crossover interaction design) under different specified conditions; in other cases, they sought to show that rewards would produce a particular effect under specified conditions but would not produce any difference when some theoretically critical ingredient had been changed (i.e., an experimental-versus-control interaction design). Staw, Calder, Hess, and Sandelands (1980), to take but one example, showed that the same extrinsic reward could enhance intrinsic motivation in situations in which rewards were seen as normative but could undermine intrinsic motivation in situations in which rewards were seen as non-normative. Hence, any main-effect analysis that fails to separate such cases and instead averages across different findings within an experiment to summarize crossover interactions as "no" overall effects or experimental/control interactions as "weak" or "nonsignificant" overall effects will necessarily yield misleading and generally meaningless results.

Similarly, in this literature, there are many "singular" studies—studies that employ procedures of particular theoretical significance that neither mirror any real-world situation nor warrant further investigation once an initial demonstration has been reported. In some studies, as noted earlier, various "false feedback" techniques have been used to test a range of theoretical assertions. Thus, in one study, children receiving an objectively unexpected reward were falsely told that this reward was one that had been promised to them earlier—to show that the mere perception of having engaged in an interesting activity in order to obtain that reward would result in the sorts of negative effects normally produced only by expected awards (Kruglanski et al., 1972). Likewise, in another study, students promised a salient extrinsic reward for engaging in a task of initial intrinsic interest were hooked up to an alleged physiological monitoring device that showed them to be displaying either high levels of interest in the activity itself or high levels of interest in the reward to which engagement in the activity would lead (Pittman et al., 1977). Because of their singularity, such studies can be entered into traditional meta-analyses only as additional instances of the very conditions from which they were explicitly designed to differ.

There are other problematic aspects to this literature as well. There happen to be, for instance, many strong correlations across the available studies among theoretically relevant independent variables, dependent measures, subject populations, and specific procedures. Virtually all studies involving "verbal rewards," for example, also happen to involve highly informative rewards, unexpected rewards, adult subjects, and short-term measures of choice. In addition, the substantial variations in the measures of intrinsic motivation used in this literature tend to ensure that there will be a negative correlation between the actual practical significance or "functional effect size" of a finding and its "statistical effect size" (Lepper, 1995), because measures that involve more consequential behaviors, which occur days or weeks later and which take place in real-world settings in which many competing pressures are present, will, all else being equal, tend to produce effects that are both more practically important and less statistically significant than simple self-reports obtained in laboratory settings immediately afterward. In general, then, there is no reason to assume—and there is good reason to reject the assumption—that the studies that comprise this literature involve a representative or random sampling of the ways or contexts or forms in which rewards are likely to be used in any class of real-world settings to which the results of any meta-analysis might be appropriately generalized.

Moreover, these general problems are multiplied exponentially by a number of the specific techniques employed in the meta-analyses by Cameron and associates (Cameron & Pierce, 1994; Eisenberger & Cameron, 1996)—particularly their practices of averaging both across demonstrably opposite and competing effects and across deliberately designed experimental and control groups within studies and then averaging yet again across different types of studies that have been shown to produce different outcomes. Thus, in nearly three quarters of the articles cited by Cameron and Pierce (1994), their meta-analytical summaries of the studies averaged across either opposing effects or experimental and control groups. To take but one salient illustration, four different studies (by different researchers) reviewed by Cameron and Pierce showed identical crossover interactions between expectation of reward and the initial interest value of the task—that the same reward manipulation may decrease subsequent motivation for initially interesting tasks but increase subsequent motivation for initially uninteresting tasks (Calder & Staw, 1975; Danner & Lonky, 1981; Loveland & Olley, 1979; McLoyd, 1979). In each case, Cameron and Pierce ignored these competing effects, averaged across the positive versus negative effects of rewards under the different interest conditions, and argued that each of these studies showed no "overall" effect of rewards.

The magnitude of these difficulties can perhaps be illustrated by a simple analogy. Imagine a pharmaceuticals company with a highly promising new drug to sell—one that grows hair, perhaps, or removes wrinkles. However, the company must first do the requisite literature review to determine whether there are any untoward or dangerous side effects. Were the company to try to summarize a literature in which strong and replicable interactions had been shown (e.g., in which the risks of heart attacks were increased for men or for patients with hypertension but were decreased for women or for those without hypertension—or vice versa) as showing no evidence of negative side effects "overall," the government would have strong cause for legal action against the company for fraudulent claims. Conversely, the company would itself have legal recourse were the government to try to summarize studies that had been specifically designed to examine the mechanism of the drug's operation and in which theoretically designed control conditions were employed to show that the drug's effects could be effectively blocked by some relevant inhibitory chemical, as evidence that the drug did not "in general" produce significant benefits for patients.

Other specific problems with the Cameron reviews (Cameron & Pierce, 1994; Eisenberger & Cameron, 1996) have been detailed elsewhere (Deci et al., 1999; Hennessey & Amabile, 1998; Kohn, 1996; Lepper, 1995, 1998; Lepper et al., 1999; Lepper et al., 1996; Ryan & Deci, 1996; Sansone & Harackiewicz, 1998) and are not discussed further here. Suffice it to say that we do not believe that the grand general conclusions that have been drawn from these reviews, and that provide so clear a contrast with the conclusions of other meta-analytical and traditional reviews, have any merit.

Nonetheless, one general caution about any summary of this literature may be in order. At the same time that the research concerning the potential detrimental effects of extrinsic rewards and constraints on intrinsic motivation has failed to impress behavioristically oriented opponents of this literature, such as Cameron and her colleagues, it has clearly overimpressed others. Certainly, a number of misleadingly broad claims about the strength and ubiquity of the negative effects of rewards have been made, particularly in the popular press. In our view, grand and sweeping claims on *either* side of the issue fail to recognize the demonstrated existence of both positive and negative effects of rewards, under appropriate circumstances, and thus fail to provide a fair and accurate summary of this literature.

Scales of Intrinsic versus Extrinsic Motivation

Indeed, in quite a different sense, the more recent literature concerning the development of scales to measure people's general levels of intrinsic and extrinsic motivation might be viewed as tending to overgeneralize the experimental findings that extrinsic rewards may sometimes undermine intrinsic motivation. Consider, for example, the design of individual-difference scales that require individuals to identify themselves as *either* intrinsically or extrinsically motivated.

Of the various scales of intrinsic motivation that have been developed, by far the most prominent has been that designed by Harter (1980, 1981). In this scale, children are presented with a series of items, each of which contrasts two "types" of pupils facing some common school-related situation—one of whom is intrinsically motivated and the other of whom is extrinsically motivated. For each item, respondents are asked to indicate which type of person they most closely resemble and how much they feel they resemble that type. For example, children are asked to consider that "Some kids ask questions in class because they want to learn new things" but "Other kids ask questions because they want the teacher to notice them." They are then asked which type of child is most like them and, once they have made this choice, whether they think that their choice is "really true of me" or only "sort of true of me."

Three subscales, each addressing a different source of intrinsic motivation, comprise the motivational aspect of Harter's (1980, 1981) instrument. A first component contrasts a preference for challenging but difficult tasks with a preference for unchallenging assignments at which it is easy to succeed. The second component contrasts a focus on curiosity and interest in the material itself with a focus on teacher approval and good grades. The third and final component pits a desire for independent mastery against a tendency to depend on the teacher to define goals and identify accomplishments. Across a variety of these sorts of items, a student's answers are taken as a measure of his or her general intrinsic versus extrinsic motivational orientation in school.

With such a scale, of course, it is simply not possible for children to report themselves to be both intrinsically and extrinsically motivated in a given situation. A child cannot, on this measure, want to do further readings on a topic both out of curiosity about the topic and out of a desire to please the teacher. One cannot separately assess a person's intrinsic motivation and extrinsic motivation because the scale has built into it a perfect negative correlation between the two.

Nonetheless, Harter (1980, 1981) and others using her pioneering scale with elementary and middle-school children (e.g., Newman, 1990; Tzuriel, 1989) have uncovered some findings of both theoretical interest and potential practical importance, especially concerning changes in students' motivation that appear to occur, at least in our country, as children progress through school. Specifically, in the United States, as children move from the third through the eighth or ninth grade, they appear progressively less likely to describe themselves as intrinsically motivated about their schoolwork. It seems that the more time children spend in schools in our country, the less interest they have in learning for its own sake.

Because of related findings to which we will shortly turn, it seems likely that a steady decrease in intrinsic motivation as children progress through school is indeed the best interpretation of these findings. In principle, however, this same pattern of results using this measure could be equally well interpreted as showing a steady *increase* in *extrinsic* motivation as children progress through these grades. Hence, an analysis of these questions that would permit independent assessments of intrinsic and extrinsic motivation, without forcing a strictly inverse relationship between the two, might uncover important new areas for investigation.

INTRINSIC AND/OR EXTRINSIC MOTIVATION

Consider, then, the possibility that intrinsic and extrinsic motivation may coexist. Most academicians, for example, can easily remember cases in which they may have read books both because of the inherent pleasure in doing so (intrinsic motivation) and out of a desire to gain a teacher's or a parent's approval (extrinsic motivation). Obviously, it would be inappropriate to label such behaviors as either exclusively intrinsically or exclusively extrinsically motivated; both forces are clearly at work. Indeed, one actually may read more books or do so more carefully precisely *because* these forces are operating in tandem. Thus, like a number of other contributors to this book (e.g., Sansone & Harackiewicz [chapter 1], this book; Linnenbrink & Pintrich [chapter 8], this book), we think—despite the experimental demonstrations that superfluous extrinsic contingencies *can* undermine intrinsic interest in controlled experimental contexts—that intrinsic and extrinsic motivation may, in many real-world settings, exert simultaneous positive influences on behavior.

In fact, even the experimental literature on overjustification suggests that intrinsic and extrinsic motivation *ought* frequently to coexist. As noted earlier, we know from this research that extrinsic rewards that provide salient information about one's competence at an activity or are presented in a manner that highlights their informational value can actually enhance intrinsic motivation (e.g., chapter 4, this book). Likewise, we know that extrinsic rewards that are verbal, less tangible, unexpected, or noncontingent will not typically undermine intrinsic interest (e.g., chapter 2, this book). Thus, many common real-world extrinsic rewards, such as grades or teacher approval in school, may not necessarily undermine (or may even facilitate) intrinsic motivation, depending on the specifics of the rewards, contingencies, manner of administration, and the like used in any particular classroom situation.

Interestingly, although Harter's scale did not allow for an independent assessment of intrinsic and extrinsic motivation, Harter herself acknowledged the possibility of "situations in which intrinsic interest and extrinsic rewards might collaborate, as it were, to motivate learning" (1981, p. 311; see also Harter & Jackson, 1992). In fact, although Harter's scale was specifically designed to assess intrinsic *versus* extrinsic motivation, one can imagine using an adaptation of her scale to assess whether a child is intrinsically *and/or* extrinsically motivated in school. That is, if Harter's own scale were simply recast so that children's responses to her intrinsic and extrinsic items were made independent of one another, one could determine the degree to which these sources of motivation empirically coexist in common school settings.

There are, of course, some potential theoretical pitfalls to such an approach. Given the particular way in which Harter devised her scale, some of its three specific components seem much more amenable to this coexistence argument than others. One might have a fairly difficult time, for example, reconciling a simultaneous preference both for challenge and for easy work, unless the situations and tasks involved were more highly specified. On the other hand, it seems quite possible that a child may act out of curiosity or interest while concurrently hoping to please the teacher or receive a good grade. To take one example from Harter's "curiosity" scale, children might choose to do extra projects both "because they learn about things that interest them" and "so they can get better grades." One also can make a fairly easy coexistence argument for the dimension of independent mastery versus dependence on the teacher. For example, Harter asked children whether, when faced with a difficult problem, they would "keep trying to figure out the problem on their own" or to "ask the teacher for help." It is not difficult to imagine children who have a desire to master a task on their own but are wise enough to turn to the teacher when their own efforts are no longer fruitful. Such children might persist in the name of independent mastery only for so long before seeking outside assistance, and their doing so would not then necessarily connote an exclusively extrinsic orientation (cf. Butler & Neuman, 1995).[5]

---

[5] Moreover, it may be important to recognize several additional characteristics of Harter's (1980, 1981) scale. First, her conceptual definition of *challenge* might be expanded to recognize that tasks that are "too hard" as well as "too easy" may not be intrinsically motivating (e.g., Csikszentmihalyi, 1975; Hunt, 1961; McClelland, Atkinson, Clark, & Lowell, 1953; Malone & Lepper, 1987). That is, in Harter's scale, a desire for challenge is contrasted only with a desire for easy work, and not also with a desire for tasks that are so impossibly difficult that they would not be diagnostic of competence or mastery. An ideal assessment tool might include both ends of this spectrum. Second, although Harter's category of *curiosity* jibes with classic motivational theory (e.g., Berlyne, 1960, 1966; Hunt, 1961, 1965), the "contrasting half" of this dimension may be problematic. In Harter's scale, it is assumed not only that curiosity or interest and a desire to please the teacher or receive good grades are inversely related but also that these latter desires are necessarily extrinsic in nature. In fact, desiring good grades could be either extrinsic (if children seek good marks only to satisfy their parents or to please their teachers) or intrinsic (if children seek them not to post proudly on the refrigerator but simply as evidence concerning their level of competence and accomplishment in a given domain). In this latter sense, even less-than-perfect grades may affect intrinsic motivation by serving to indicate the areas of study that may need improvement. Third, in Harter's category of "independent mastery," although there are hints of classic motivational theories about the effectiveness of personal control and self-determination (e.g., Condry, 1977; Deci, 1981; Deci & Ryan, 1985), such a "desire for autonomy" may not be fully instantiated in the actual questionnaire. Rather than asking children about a desire to make their own choices or to control their academic outcomes, Harter's questions ask primarily about a desire to persist at and complete assignments without help. However, it is not at all clear that intrinsic motivation requires such complete independence. Presumably children could be intrinsically motivated but still recognize a need for assistance when problems become too complex for them.

New Empirical Findings

In view of these considerations, Lepper, Sethi, Dialdin, and Drake (1997) have sought to examine whether Harter's (1980, 1981) scale could indeed be sensibly decomposed to yield separate measures of children's intrinsic motivation and extrinsic motivation. In their study, several hundred third-grade through eighth-grade children were administered a version of Harter's scale that, rather than forcing them to make a choice, allowed them to answer intrinsic and extrinsic items independently of one another. For example, Harter's original item that asked children to choose whether they were more like kids "who do extra projects because they learn about things that interest them" or more like kids "who do extra projects so they can get better grades" was transformed into two separate items, each with a five-point Likert scale. This modification of Harter's scale, as shown in Figure 10.2, allowed for the possibility that children might be simultaneously intrinsically and extrinsically motivated.

Using this modified scale, Lepper and colleagues (1997) indeed found that intrinsic and extrinsic motivation, when assessed with separate items, proved far from perfectly negatively correlated. Summing across subscales, they found a statistically significant but relatively weak negative correlation between overall intrinsic and overall extrinsic motivation ($r = -.14$; $p < .01$.). Clearly, the general assumption that these two constructs must be mutually exclusive proved unfounded. Furthermore, the relationship between intrinsic and extrinsic motivation varied for the three components of the general scale. Thus, there was indeed a fairly strong negative correlation between a preference for challenge and a preference for easy work ($r = -.53$; $p < .0001$), as speculated above. There was, however, a highly significant *positive* correlation between curiosity/interest and attempting to please the teacher or receive a good grade ($r = .22$; $p < .001$), and only a slight negative correlation between independent mastery and dependence on the teacher ($r = -.16$; $p < .01$). In short, only the contrast between the intrinsic component of preference for challenge and the extrinsic component of preference for easy work even comes close to approaching mutual exclusivity.

More recently, we have attempted to replicate these findings with a sample of 337 third- through eighth-grade children from two large parochial schools in the San Francisco Bay area (Henderlong & Lepper, 1997, 2000). As before, Harter's items were decomposed and both halves of each item were presented separately, with a 5-point Likert scale on which to indicate agreement. Again, the results were consistent with the coexistence argument. Overall, the correlation between intrinsic and extrinsic motivation was negative and significant, but again, it accounted for only a small fraction of the variance ($r = -.17$; $p < .01$). The relationship between intrinsic and extrinsic motivation was also examined separately for the three component measures. In this new sample, once again there was a significant negative correlation between a preference for challenge and a preference for easy

Sample Item from Harter's (1980) Scale of Intrinsic vs. Extrinsic Motivational Orientation:

Really True for Me	Sort of True for Me			Really True for Me	Sort of True for Me
☐	☐	Some kids do extra projects because they can learn about things that interest them	**BUT** Other kids do extra projects so they can get better grades	☐	☐

Sample Item Above Decomposed into Separate Scales for Intrinsic and Extrinsic Motivation:

Intrinsic Item:

I do extra projects because I can learn about things that interest me.

☐ ☐ ☐ ☐ ☐

Extrinsic Item:

I do extra projects so I can get better grades.

☐ ☐ ☐ ☐ ☐

FIGURE 10.2

Sample item from scale of intrinsic versus extrinsic motivational orientation, from Harter (1980). (Copyright © 1980 by Susan Harter, University of Denver. Adapted with permission.) Below a decomposition of this item, from Lepper et al. (1997).

work ($r = -.35$, $p < .001$). The relationship between curiosity/interest and desire for teacher approval was again positive ($r = .10$), but this time was only marginally significant ($p < .06$). Finally, the correlation between independent mastery and dependence on the teacher was again negative but also quite small ($r = -.12$; $p < .05$). Intrinsic and extrinsic motivation, in short, can clearly coexist in the real world outside the laboratory.

Developmental Trends

Both of these studies, moreover, were designed not only to assess the correlations between independent measures of intrinsic and extrinsic motivation but also to revisit the strong and provocative developmental findings from Harter's initial study (1980, 1981)—namely, that intrinsic motivation seemed to decrease steadily as children progressed from third grade through eighth or ninth grade, as portrayed in Figure 10.3. These developmental comparisons, in turn, provided yet another opportunity to explore the complementary or oppositional nature of these two constructs. If intrinsic and extrinsic motivation are truly mutually exclusive, a developmental increase in one would necessarily lead to a developmental decrease in the other. If the two can coexist in the classroom, however, the developmental trajectories of the two may be separate and, in a sense, doubly informative.

As noted earlier, Harter's original scale could not rule out an obvious potential alternative interpretation for the apparent decrease in intrinsic

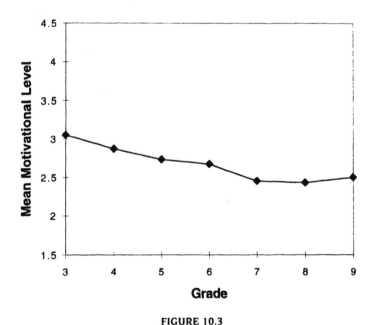

FIGURE 10.3

Overall intrinsic versus extrinsic motivation, by grade, from Harter (1980). (Copyright © 1980 by Susan Harter, University of Denver. Adapted with permission.)

motivation as children progressed through the grades. The seeming developmental *decrease* in intrinsic motivation could also have been produced by
a developmental *increase* in extrinsic motivation. Perhaps, as children
progress through school, there is an increasing emphasis on external
contingencies, such as performing well to receive good grades, achieving to
please one's parents, and memorizing material merely to do well on
examinations. Such an explanation would, of course, have quite different
implications than one that emphasized an increasingly severe lack of internal motivation as children progress through school. Clearly, then, there
seemed to be considerable value in looking separately at the development
of intrinsic and extrinsic motivation across this grade range.

Examining these issues using the decomposed version of Harter's scale,
Lepper and his colleagues (1997) found a strong developmental decrease
over grades three through eight, both on the composite measure of students' overall intrinsic motivation and on each of the three component measures, just as Harter's original analysis had suggested. On the other hand, in
contrast to Harter's original analysis, these students' extrinsic motivation
remained roughly constant across this same age range. The only extrinsic
component measure that showed any significant developmental change was
that of desire for teacher approval, which actually *decreased* from third to
eighth grade. Thus, these findings both replicate Harter's original conclusion that intrinsic motivation steadily decreases as children progress
through school and eliminate the alternative explanation that an increase in
extrinsic motivation could be driving this effect. In addition, they provide
further evidence that intrinsic and extrinsic motivation can and do coexist,
at least in American elementary-school and middle-school classrooms.

Similar developmental trends also emerged in our more recent replication of this study (Henderlong & Lepper, 1997, 2000). Once again in this new
sample, there was a significant although less dramatic decrease in intrinsic
motivation from third through eighth grade. This decline in intrinsic motivation also was reflected in the component measures for both
curiosity/interest and independent mastery, though not in the component
measure of preference for challenge. Moreover, in this sample, even more
dramatically than in the results of Lepper et al. (1997), extrinsic motivation
showed a significant overall developmental decline over grades three
through eight. Indeed, this decline was reflected in each of the three component measures of preference for easy work, desire for teacher approval,
and dependence on the teacher.

Taken together, these findings suggest a clear developmental decrease in
children's intrinsic motivation and something of a developmental decrease in
children's extrinsic motivation as well, as displayed in Figure 10.4. Moreover,
Henderlong and Lepper's study (1997, 2000) also provided one further line of
evidence indicative of the conceptual independence of intrinsic and extrinsic
motivation. When children's scores on the two separate scales of intrinsic and

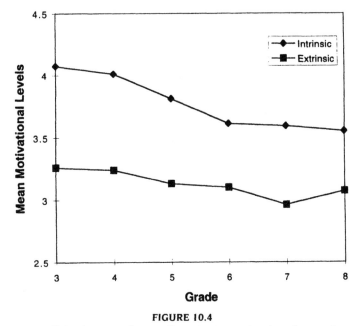

FIGURE 10.4
Overall intrinsic and overall extrinsic motivation, by grade,
from Lepper et al. (1997) and Henderlong and Lepper (1997).

extrinsic motivation were correlated with their actual classroom grade averages, the two scales showed opposite relationships to this standard measure of actual classroom performance. Although both effects were relatively small, they were both significant: Higher levels of reported overall intrinsic motivation were associated with better grades in school ($r = .17$; $p < .01$), whereas higher levels of reported overall extrinsic motivation were actually associated, by contrast, with lower classroom grades ($r = -.16$; $p < .01$).

Sadly, these findings are not the only ones to suggest significant motivational problems in our schools that appear to increase, rather than decrease, as children progress through the grade-school and middle-school years (e.g., Anderman & Maehr, 1994; Eccles & Midgley, 1990). For example, Epstein and McPartland (1976) examined the reported quality of school life for children from grades 4 through 12. They defined quality of life in terms of the three dimensions of general satisfaction, commitment to classwork, and reactions to teachers. Both cross-sectional and longitudinal data indicated that as the years progressed, the reported quality of children's lives in school decreased, especially on the dimension of commitment to classwork. They suggested that this effect was partly driven by schools' inability to meet the needs of their students as the variance in their abilities increased with age. In another study, Sansone and Morgan

(1992) used a cross-sectional approach to document the academic and nonacademic activities that kindergarten and first graders, fifth and sixth graders, and undergraduates found intrinsically interesting. With increasing age, they found a progressive decline in intrinsic motivation, both in terms of enjoyment and willingness to repeat an activity for school-based—but not for non–school-based—activities.[6]

Likewise, other research has documented negative developmental changes in constructs theoretically linked to intrinsic motivation. For example, Nicholls (1978) found that 5 through 13 year-old children became increasingly pessimistic about their own abilities in reading as they progressed through school. Covington and colleagues showed that children decreasingly value effort as they grow older, because they come to view the exertion of effort as a sign of low ability (e.g., Covington, 1984; Harari & Covington, 1981). Intrinsic motivation can hardly be facilitated by situations in which children constantly feel a need to try to disguise their expenditure of effort. Finally, there is also evidence of a developmental increase in learned helplessness (Rholes, Blackwell, Jordan, & Walters, 1980) and of an increased focus on self-evaluation, rather than on task mastery, in various achievement settings (Anderman & Midgley, 1997; Maehr & Anderman, 1993; Midgley, Anderman, & Hicks, 1995).[7]

[6] It is important to point out that with all of these negative changes in academic motivation, it appears that children do remain intrinsically motivated in other domains of their lives, such as their relationships with peers or their involvement in sports (e.g., Sansone & Morgan, 1992). Indeed, although there seem to be few relevant findings at present, it might be hypothesized that students who come to be particularly demotivated in school will also come to disidentify with academic success and may, as a consequence, be motivated to seek out other sources of self-esteem and affirmation (e.g., Steele, 1988, 1992).

[7] Despite the array of evidence illustrating developmental decreases in intrinsic motivation, it is also important to note that not every study finds such a motivational decline. Specifically, Gottfried examined children's academic intrinsic motivation, both in general and for the specific content areas of reading, mathematics, social studies, and science, using her Children's Academic Intrinsic Motivation Inventory (e.g., Gottfried, 1985). In one study of fourth- through seventh-grade students, she found a developmental *decrease* in intrinsic motivation for reading but a developmental *increase* in intrinsic motivation for social studies (Gottfried, 1985). There were no significant developmental changes either for overall intrinsic motivation or for the specific content areas of mathematics and science. The differences between these findings and those of the research programs described in this chapter may be due in part to a more restricted age range, and, unfortunately, mean levels of intrinsic motivation in each of the areas by grade are not reported, so the data cannot be examined for possible trends. An alternative explanation might be that, in contrast to reading, there is a focus on new subjects each year in the content areas of mathematics, social studies, and science. For example, the tasks associated with reading are likely very similar in third, sixth, and ninth grades, but the tasks associated with mathematics may very greatly from multiplication in third grade to pre-algebra in sixth grade to geometry in ninth grade.

Understanding Developmental Declines
in Motivation

In some sense, these developmental data merely reinforce an age-old impression of schools as citadels of boredom and alienation. Certainly, many Western thinkers who have written or spoken about schools—from William Blake (1794), Charles Dickens (1838–1839), and Mark Twain (1876) to George Orwell (1933) and Albert Einstein (1949)—have portrayed them as places of drudgery, ennui, and misery for many children. More recent and more professional critics of U.S. schools have also been frequently impressed with the lack of motivation that students seem so often to display in American classrooms (e.g., Bruner, 1962, 1966; Csikszentmihalyi, 1975; Dreeben, 1968; Holt, 1964; Jackson, 1968; Silberman, 1970).

Plainly, the availability of persuasive empirical evidence consistent with these claims should give us significant pause. If children, on average, are becoming less and less motivated each year they remain in our schools, it suggests that U.S. schools may be doing something wrong. Coupled with the array of recent findings attesting to the relatively poor performance of American students in various cross-national comparisons of academic accomplishment (e.g., Stevenson, Chen, & Lee, 1993; Stevenson, Lee, & Stigler, 1986; Stevenson & Stigler, 1992), these results point to a potentially significant problem—an education system in which many students are not learning or performing up to their potential. Consequently, it is of considerable practical significance, as well as some theoretical interest, to understand why these developmental decreases in motivation are occurring in American schools.

Before turning to potential substantive explanations for the reported developmental declines in intrinsic motivation, however, it is important to rule out the possibility that these differences are simple artifacts of the use of self-report measures and reflect merely developmental changes in children's perceptions of relevant social norms, their willingness to admit to an interest in their schoolwork, or the standards by which they judge their motivation (Lepper et al., 1997). Thus, it is worth noting several sources of evidence that suggest the basic validity of these measures. First, there is evidence that children's self-reports on these sorts of measures are highly correlated with reports made about those children by their teachers (Gottfried, 1985; Harter, 1981; Lepper et al., 1997) and their parents (Dollinger & Seiters, 1988). Second, there is also evidence that children's reports on these sorts of measures are correlated with other more objective indices of school performance, such as achievement-test scores (Boggiano et al., 1992; Gottfried, 1985), classroom grades (Gottfried, 1985; Henderlong & Lepper, 1997, 2000), and retainment in grade (Dollinger & Seiters, 1988). Finally, these sorts of measures have also been shown to predict behavioral indicators of at least some aspects of intrinsic motivation, such as a preference for challenging academic tasks (Boggiano et al., 1992; Harter, 1980, 1981).

Undermining Effects of Extrinsic Incentives and Constraints

One set of possible explanations for the decline in children's intrinsic motivation is, of course, implicit in the literature on the potential undermining effects of salient extrinsic incentives, external constraints, and other forms of social control just reviewed. As thoughtful classroom observers (e.g., Deci, Schwartz, Scheinman, & Ryan, 1981; Dweck, Davidson, Nelson, & Enna, 1978; Jackson, 1968; Kohn, 1993; Silberman, 1970) have long noted, a great deal of what goes on in typical American classrooms revolves around issues of overt social control. Indeed, Winnett and Winkler's systematic analysis (1972) of the goals of token economies and related contingency programs in schools clearly revealed a chilling preponderance of teachers' attention and effort devoted to the goals of making pupils be "quiet," "still," and "docile." Perhaps being subject to these powerful extrinsic forces in the classroom year after year may contribute to the observed decreases in intrinsic motivation. Moreover, some authors have argued, this emphasis on social control may well increase as children progress through school (Condry, 1978; Kohn, 1988; 1993).

In fact, Eccles and her colleagues (e.g., Eccles & Midgley, 1989; Eccles et al., 1993) took this basic argument one step further. These authors discussed the decline in intrinsic motivation in terms of a progressively greater mismatch between children's developing needs for autonomy and the demands of the classroom environment. On the basis of this "stage–environment fit" model, Eccles and her colleagues (1993) documented a number of developmentally inappropriate changes that occur, especially during early adolescence, as children make the transition to middle school. That is, just as students begin to thirst for increased autonomy and personal growth, schools seem to increase their focus on discipline, provide fewer opportunities for decision making, and assign less cognitively challenging coursework.[8]

Decontextualization of Learning

A second general class of factors that may also contribute to the reported developmental declines in intrinsic motivation may involve what Bruner (1962, 1966) first referred to as the "decontextualization" of learning—that is, the attempt to teach skills and impart information in a highly abstract

---

[8] Eccles et al. (1993) have also suggested that parents may play a role in the developmental decrease in intrinsic motivation. As with teachers, parents often begin to tighten controls over their adolescents' behaviors just as adolescents are desiring increased autonomy. Indeed, they have found that excessive parental control is positively correlated with a decrease in intrinsic motivation. Eccles et al. concluded that parents need to find the right balance between excessive control and excessive leniency to match their adolescents' developing needs.

form, independent of any particular context of learning. Such instructional methods were presumably first developed in the hope of producing more generalizable, less situation-specific learning, although it is not clear from extant data that they regularly succeed in achieving even this goal (e.g., Ginsberg, 1977; Lave, 1988; Perkins, 1992). What does seem clear, however, is that deliberately divorcing the learning of academic skills from the real-world contexts in which their intrinsic utility might be obvious to students can have significant motivational costs (Condry & Chambers, 1978; Cordova & Lepper, 1996). If there is no "natural" value for students in learning about some particular topic that has been assigned to them, no "natural" curiosity about the topic, then learning can easily become little more than an exercise in memorization, aimed solely at improving performance on abstract classroom tests on the material.

Moreover, such pedagogical practices appear to be increasingly common as children progress through school. In the early grades, it appears, teachers are more likely to see their task as involving, in part, making the material more intrinsically interesting for students and showing them the way that what is learned in school may be relevant in their own lives. In later grades, however, teachers seem to presume that students *ought* to be already motivated to achieve, independent of their intrinsic interest in an activity or topic. Hence, any lack of motivation in the classroom comes to be seen as the student's, rather than the teacher's, problem. Indeed, teachers working with older students will often dismiss attempts to make tasks more interesting or more relevant for students as counterproductive "sugar-coating."

Shifts in Students' Goal Orientations

A third set of reasons for the developmental decrease in intrinsic motivation may be a potentially maladaptive shift in children's classrooms goals. In general, it has been argued that children often tend to adopt one of two competing goals in achievement situations: namely, (1) what have been termed *learning, mastery,* or *task* goals, where the focus is on increasing knowledge and task mastery, or (2) what have been termed *performance* or *ego* goals, where the focus is instead on gaining positive judgments of competence and avoiding negative judgments of competence (e.g., Ames, 1992; Dweck, 1986; Elliott & Dweck, 1988; Nicholls, 1984). Learning goals have been associated with a wide variety of positive achievement outcomes, such as cognitive engagement (Meece, Blumenfeld, & Hoyle, 1988), challenge-seeking (Ames & Archer, 1988; Elliott & Dweck, 1988), and persistence in the face of failure (Dweck & Leggett, 1988; Elliott & Dweck, 1988), as well as positive attitudes toward learning, stronger beliefs that effort leads to success, and more effective use of strategies (Ames, 1992; Ames & Archer, 1988). Performance goals, on the other hand, have often been associated with negative achievement outcomes, such as a focus on ability rather than effort (Ames & Archer, 1988), decreased cognitive engagement (Meece et al., 1988), challenge avoidance, and learned help-lessness when coupled with low perceived competence (Dweck, 1986; Dweck & Leggett, 1988; Elliott & Dweck, 1988). Thus, it has been argued, learning goals will typically have positive consequences whereas perfor-mance goals will often have negative consequences—especially for chil-dren who have low perceptions of their own competence.

However, much like the traditional assumption of a perfect negative corre-lation between intrinsic and extrinsic motivation discussed earlier, research on classroom goals may have created something of a false dichotomy. Thus, like Harter's measure of intrinsic versus extrinsic motivational orientations, Dweck's standard measure (Dweck, 1999; Dweck & Henderson, 1988) of goal choice requires the child to select one option or the other but not both. Yet there are obviously many classroom contexts in which students may hold both learning goals and performance goals simultaneously, truly hoping to master the material but also striving to outperform their classmates and demonstrate their competence relative to others. Holding these two goals simultaneously, we suggest, is likely a familiar experience for many high-achieving students, as well as for most readers of this chapter. Indeed, recent empirical work has shown that when measured separately, learning goals and performance goals can even be positively correlated (e.g., Harackiewicz, Bar-ron, Carter, Lehto, & Elliot, 1997; Meece et al., 1988).

Once we treat learning and performance goals as potentially indepen-dent constructs, however, it is necessary to examine their effects on achieve-ment and motivation more carefully. Ample evidence suggests that learning goals do indeed have positive consequences for achievement and motiva-tion (Ames, 1992; Dweck, 1986; Elliott & Dweck, 1988; Meece et al., 1988; Molden & Dweck, chapter 6 and Limenbrink & Pintrich, chapter 8, this book). It is the "negative" consequences of performance goals that have been called into question. Most notably, a program of research by Harackiewicz and her colleagues (Harackiewicz et al., 1997; Harackiewicz, Barron, & Elliot, 1998; Harackiewicz & Sansone, chapter 4, this book) has shown that the effects of performance goals tend to be varied and complex—sometimes negative and sometimes positive—at least in college classrooms. Although it is not yet as clear that the positive consequences of performance goals would be as apparent or widespread in the elementary school classroom, our argument is not that performance goals are necessarily harmful but rather that learning goals are adaptive and should therefore be encouraged.

Given that learning goals have such clear and positive consequences, it is unfortunate that children appear to value them less and less as they progress through school. Midgley et al. (1995) found that compared with elementary school students and teachers, middle-school students and teachers perceived a greater emphasis on performance goals relative to learning goals. Further, these same authors also found that middle-school teachers actually used instructional practices that reflected a performance-goal orientation more than did elementary school teachers. Similarly, in terms of teacher behavior, the increasing emphasis placed on zero-sum competitive activities as children progress through our school system may also serve to focus classrooms less on learning goals and more on performance goals (Aronson, Blaney, Stephan, Sikes, & Snapp, 1978; Kohn, 1988; Nicholls, 1989).

Likewise from the students' perspective, Anderman and Midgley (1997) found, in a longitudinal investigation, that fifth-grade pupils became less learning-goal oriented and perceived the school culture to be more performance-goal oriented as they progressed into middle school. Other related research has shown developmental increases in anxiety about performance (Eccles & Midgley, 1989) and in learned helplessness (Rholes et al., 1980), both of which are thought to be negatively correlated with learning goals. Thus, several lines of research suggest that learning goals tend to decrease across the school years.

Though it is clear that learning goals are generally adaptive and that they may decrease developmentally, are they necessarily related to intrinsic motivation? The literature suggests that although the mapping may not be precise, the answer is yes (e.g., Dweck, 1986; Harackiewicz et al., 1997, 1998; Henderlong & Lepper, 1997; Heyman & Dweck, 1992; Sansone & Harackiewicz, 1996; chapter 8, this book). Such a suggestion is consistent both with general speculations about the possible links between these two research areas and with several specific empirical findings. For example, Harackiewicz and her colleagues (1997) found that college students who adopted mastery goals tended to be more interested in the course than those who did not adopt these goals, and Elliot and Harackiewicz (1994) showed that specific mastery goals enhanced intrinsic motivation in a context with neutral higher-order goals.

Changing Levels of Challenge

Finally, although this is the area in which there is the least direct evidence, a number of authors have suggested that the level of challenge offered by schoolwork may also change as children progress through the grades. On the one hand as the curriculum becomes more highly regimented and regulated in the later grades, some authors have argued simply that it may become increasingly difficult for teachers to provide the sort of individualization of instruction to students that would ensure that each student is being given tasks that are at an appropriate level of challenge—that is, classroom tasks that are neither trivially easy nor impossibly hard for each student, given his or her current level of ability and performance (Csikszentmihalyi, 1975; Dreeben, 1968). Other authors have argued more directly that the average level of cognitive challenge provided for students by their assigned coursework steadily decreases as children go through elementary and middle school (Deci, 1975; Eccles et al., 1993). Finally, still other authors have suggested that classrooms place greater emphasis on zero-sum competition at higher grade levels. If so, the very nature of such competitions—that success by some students must imply failure for others—may ensure that the proportion of students in a class who will find the material optimally challenging will necessarily decrease with increases in grade level (Aronson et al., 1978; Kohn, 1988).

Summary

In reality, of course, the sources of the developmental decrease in intrinsic motivation are almost certainly overdetermined. Nevertheless, it does seem clear that simply increasing the number of salient extrinsic rewards is not likely to reverse this developmental trend. If anything, the data suggest that at least in American schools, extrinsic motivation may also decline as children progress through the grades. In the next section, therefore, we examine some less controlling, and potentially more effective, strategies for addressing the motivational problems indicated by the developmental data.

INTRINSIC PLUS EXTRINSIC MOTIVATION

How, then, might we best design learning environments, to make judicious and effective use of both intrinsic motivation and extrinsic motivation? Can a social-psychological approach help us promote and sustain children's motivation to learn as they progress through school?

Promoting Intrinsic Motivation

We first consider this problem in terms of strategies for promoting intrinsic motivation—as it might be approached from the perspective of the four classes of factors outlined above as potential causes of the current developmental decline in intrinsic motivation.

Promoting Perceptions of Autonomy and Personal Control

One obvious approach, derived directly from the literature on the potential undermining effects of superfluous extrinsic incentives and constraints, would focus on increasing children's sense of personal autonomy and self-determination in the classroom (deCharms, 1968, 1984; Deci, 1981; Deci & Ryan, 1985; Nuttin, 1973), particularly as children approach adolescence and their need for autonomy increases (Eccles et al., 1993). Thus, in deCharms's terms, children should be treated in the classroom as "origins" of their behaviors, rather than "pawns" simply carrying out the instructions and desires of others.

Indeed, Ryan and Grolnick (1986) found that the more children perceived their classrooms to be "origin focused," the greater their sense of self-worth, cognitive competence, internal control, and intrinsic motivation. Interestingly, it was not primarily the objective classroom climate that guided children's perceptions, but rather their differing construals of this climate. Even the same classroom environment was experienced differently by different children, suggesting that both the individual and the environment interact to determine children's perceptions of autonomy.

There are a number of strategies one might employ to increase feelings of autonomy. Thus, teachers who are autonomy oriented have been shown to have more intrinsically motivated students with higher levels of self-esteem, compared with students of teachers who are control oriented (Deci et al., 1981). This suggests that training teachers to become more autonomy oriented may have benefits for their students. Indeed, in one 4-year longitudinal study, teachers who were trained in "origin promotion" had students who showed greater academic achievement, more adaptive risk taking, and fewer absences and tardies compared to students in control classrooms (deCharms, 1984). The effectiveness of "origin promotion" training may be limited, however, by teachers' own feelings of control concerning the intervention. That is, teachers must feel ownership over an origin-promoting curriculum and must believe that they can help all students to become origins by providing an optimal amount of structure, in order for such a curriculum to be effective.

Another strategy for promoting a sense of self-determination is, of course, to avoid superfluous external controls. In many classrooms, rewards are used excessively, in situations where they are not needed to produce task engagement. Consider, for example, programs that offer highly salient extrinsic incentives (e.g., fast food, candy, or cash) for reading books (e.g., Kohn, 1995). In such programs, rewards are often given simply on the basis of the number of books read, without taking account of differences in ability levels, effort, or the difficulty of the various books. For the many children who actually enjoy reading books *before* such systems are implemented, reading for the sake of earning rewards may send a very confusing message. Are they reading books because they enjoy them, or because they want to earn the rewards? More important, what happens when the reward program ends? Rather than relying on such nondescriptive rewards, teachers might give children more informational feedback about their strengths and weaknesses. As noted earlier, rewards tend to enhance motivation when they provide positive information regarding competence but undermine it when they serve only to control behavior (Deci, 1975; Deci & Ryan, 1980; 1985; Lepper, 1981).

Public systems of recognition, such as honor rolls, gold stars, and bulletin boards displaying the "best papers," may also be harmful to the motivation of many children. For every student given the opportunity to bask in glory, there are often 10 to 20 whose feelings of competence may be lessened. Moreover, even for the most successful students, such forms of recognition may encourage children to think about the task as a means to an end rather than an end in itself (Kruglanski, 1978; Malone & Lepper, 1987)—a situation that can lead even young children to devalue the activity per se (Lepper et al., 1982). Such controlling tactics may produce compliance in the short run, but the message they send is that academic tasks are done to please the teacher and to earn public recognition rather than because of interest in or enjoyment of the material.

In addition, it may also be possible to help "inoculate" children against the potential detrimental effects of superfluous tangible rewards. Hennessey, Amabile, and Martinage (1989), for instance, designed an "immunization" procedure to help children to focus on their intrinsic motivation and to distance themselves psychologically from superfluous extrinsic incentives. Students exposed to this procedure proved both more creative when they were rewarded than when they were not and more creative than students who had not received this training. Similarly, Cordova, Christensen, and Lepper (2000) showed that comparable immunization techniques could eliminate the negative effects of salient extrinsic incentives on children's problem solving and learning of new concepts.

Yet another general method for enhancing children's feelings of self-determination is to provide them with choices. Thus, many experiments have illustrated the potential motivational and educational benefits of the provision of choice (Cordova & Lepper, 1996; Iyengar & Lepper, 1999; Langer, 1989; Nuttin, 1973; Perlmutter & Monty, 1977; Zuckerman, Porac, Lathin, Smith, & Deci, 1978). Of course, in typical classroom settings, the provision of unfettered student choice runs the significant risk that at least some students may select only the least effortful options or may otherwise make pedagogically dysfunctional decisions (Malone & Lepper, 1987; Steinberg, 1989). Hence, it is important to note that even seemingly trivial (e.g., Cordova & Lepper, 1996; Iyengar & Lepper, 1999) or purely illusory (e.g., Langer, 1975, 1989) choices can still have significant benefits.[9]

[9] Interestingly, although Iyengar and Lepper's (1999) studies do illustrate the motivational and instructional benefits of choice in general, they also point to a potentially critical cultural difference in the importance of personal choice, with choice proving more important for students from highly individualistic than from highly collectivistic societies. In particular, both Asian American and Anglo American children performed and learned better when they made small instructionally irrelevant choices for themselves than when those choices were made for them by strangers—although this effect appeared somewhat stronger among the Anglo American children. By contrast, Asian American students performed best of all when these same small choices were made for them by people with whom they had ongoing personal relationships (i.e., parents and classmates), whereas Anglo American students performed just as poorly when the choices were made for them by significant in-group members as by total strangers.

Cordova and Lepper (1996) and Iyengar and Lepper (1999), for instance, both showed that permitting grade-school children to make even a small set of seemingly trivial and instructionally irrelevant choices in using an educational computer program substantially increased their learning from that program and their subsequent intrinsic interest in the material taught. Similarly, in a series of studies of the motivational strategies of especially effective human tutors, Lepper, Woolverton, Mumme, and Gurtner (1993) showed that expert tutors will frequently offer small choices, or will create the illusion of offering such choices, to their pupils. Finally, deCharms (1984) noted that teachers can provide carefully designed choices to students, in which the alternatives are fixed so that any option is acceptable, and Eccles et al. (1993) have suggested that children should be allowed to participate in classroom rule making to enhance feelings of autonomy.[10]

In summary, one way to enhance children's intrinsic motivation is for teachers and administrators to promote autonomy and self-determination. This can involve encouraging an origin orientation, using extrinsic rewards more sparingly and informatively, and providing choices when possible. However, if teachers and administrators are wedded to the idea of widespread reward systems, one inventive approach is to use learning activities themselves as the rewards. In one illustrative study, children who were rewarded for completing routine mathematics problems with the opportunity to engage in special mathematics activities showed enhanced subsequent motivation, in terms of the number of problems completed and time spent working (Taffel & O'Leary, 1976). Thus if means–end contingencies are to be employed, making the end an academic task may help both motivation and learning.

Increasing Contextualization and Curiosity

A second general approach for combating the current developmental decline in motivation in U.S. classrooms would involve attempts to promote children's sense of curiosity by placing learning in meaningful and exciting contexts that would illustrate its inherent utility and would capitalize on

---

[10] Just as teachers must give students choices and treat them as origins, so, too, must administrators promote teacher autonomy and personal control over their classroom practices (deCharms, 1984; Eccles et al., 1993). As noted, origin-promotion teacher training is not effective if teachers do not themselves feel like origins with respect to the intervention curriculum. More generally, if teachers are subjected to stringent controls and minimal opportunities to make decisions about their own classrooms, it will likely be very difficult for them to promote feelings of autonomy in their students. As Deci, Spiegel, Ryan, Koestner, and Kauffman (1982) and Garbarino (1975) showed experimentally, when teachers or tutors are held responsible for their students' performing above a given standard, they become more control oriented toward their students, whereas when this performance pressure is removed, these teachers promote more student autonomy by giving more choices, issuing fewer commands, and being less critical of their students.

students' prior interests (see also Jacobs & Eccles, chapter 14, this book). Strategies of this sort might include the contextualization and personalization of instruction and a focus on topics and projects that make contact with children's existing interests.

Studies by Parker and Lepper (1992) and Cordova and Lepper (1996), for example, compared the responses of grade-school students working on educational computer programs that presented elementary mathematics problems either in a purely abstract numerical form or in a meaningful and interesting fantasy context in which correct problem solutions were facilitative of larger role-playing goals. In both studies, students who worked with contextualized programs showed greater learning, better transfer, and more subsequent interest in the topic than did their peers who worked with more abstract versions of these programs.[11]

In similar fashion, Cordova and Lepper (1996) also examined the effects of "personalizing" educational computer programs on students' learning and subsequent motivation. In the relevant conditions of their study, students were presented with problems and instruction embedded either in generic fantasy contexts or in personalized fantasy contexts in which various specific bits of information about the child's own friends, hobbies, preferences, and the like were included to heighten the relevance and interest of the context for each individual student. As in previous investigations along these same lines (e.g., Anand & Ross, 1987; Ross, 1983), students presented with more personalized material learned more effectively and showed greater subsequent interest in the material than did those exposed to the more generic presentation.

There is also evidence that learning is most effective when it is linked to topics about which students have high levels of interest outside the classroom. Asher and his colleagues (e.g., Asher, 1981; Asher, Hymel, & Wigfield, 1978), for instance, showed that students' recall of material from educational essays was highly correlated with prior measures of their interest in the topics of these essays. In comparable fashion, Anderson, Shirey, Wilson, and Fielding (1987) demonstrated that grade-school children's memory for sentences they had read earlier was better predicted by independent ratings of the interest value of the sentences than by standard student reading comprehension scores or text "readability" indices. More generally, the potential value (and possible pitfalls) of capitalizing on children's existing interests have been examined by Renninger, Hidi, and Krapp (1992; see also chapters 11 and 13, this book).

---

[11] In both these cases, it is important to note that the fantasies were integrated with, or endogenous to, the material to be learned. Malone and Lepper (1987) have suggested that the use of more arbitrary, exogenous fantasy contexts, like more tangible extrinsic rewards, might undermine learning and subsequent intrinsic motivation.

Finally, at the classroom level, the sorts of motivational and instructional advantages outlined in this section are often a central ingredient in what have been called "project-based" or "integrated" curricula. As discussed in more detail elsewhere (e.g., Bruner, 1962, 1996; Edwards, Gandini, & Foreman, 1993; Katz & Chard, 1989), these approaches involve the embedding of instruction in specific meaningful and interesting contexts. Such programs may be expected both to increase student motivation and to illustrate the utility of the material being presented outside of the classroom.

Emphasizing Learning Goals

A third potential response to the developmental decrease in intrinsic motivation is to encourage children to adopt learning goals in the classroom. How might this be accomplished? Findings from laboratory studies and classroom observations indicate that although some aspects of goal orientation may be relatively stable within individuals (e.g., Dweck, 1990; Dweck & Leggett, 1988), teachers and parents also play a critical role. Because children within the very same classroom may possess vastly different constellations of goals and achievement-related beliefs (e.g., Dweck, 1986; 1990; Dweck & Leggett, 1988; Elliott & Dweck, 1988), however, it is important that interventions be targeted not only at the classroom as a whole but also at particular children who may harbor strong and exclusive performance goals.

In considering how children's individual goal orientations might be altered, it is useful to examine how performance and learning goals have been experimentally induced in past research. For example, Elliott and Dweck (1988) experimentally induced either a performance-goal orientation or a learning-goal orientation by emphasizing different aspects of the situation. In the performance-goal condition, children were told that their performance would be filmed and evaluated by experts. In the learning-goal condition, children were told that what they learned might be helpful in school, that mistakes were a necessary part of the learning process, and that the task would "sharpen the mind." Compared to children in the learning-goal condition, children in the performance-goal condition showed strategy deterioration, maladaptive attributions for failure, and negative affect, illustrating the importance of the framing of educational tasks for children. Perhaps if learning goals are to be fostered, educators should explicitly emphasize the natural process of learning through one's mistakes rather than the process of testing and performance evaluation (e.g., Lampert, 1986; Papert, 1980, 1993).

Similarly, learning goals may also be induced by encouraging children to view intelligence as a malleable quality rather than a fixed entity. Research by Dweck and her colleagues (e.g., Dweck, 1986, 1999; Dweck & Bempechat, 1983; Dweck & Leggett, 1988) has demonstrated that children who believe intelligence is malleable (incremental theorists) tend to adopt learning goals in the classroom whereas children who believe intelligence is immutable (entity theorists) tend to adopt performance goals in the classroom. Therefore, encouraging children to adopt incremental theories may encourage learning goals and intrinsic motivation. Attribution "retraining," in which attributions of failure to controllable factors like effort expenditure or strategy employed are modeled and reinforced, provides one example of such a procedure (e.g., Dweck, 1975; Foersterling, 1985). Again, however, children within the same classroom may vary widely in their beliefs about the malleability of intelligence, so that interventions may be most effective when adapted for individuals with different types of beliefs.

Finally, at the classroom level, Ames and her colleagues (Ames, 1992; Ames & Archer, 1988) demonstrated that different classroom contexts can create different goals for children. Thus, the negative and positive behaviors that are typically associated with performance goals and learning goals, respectively, can be predicted on the basis of student perceptions of whether their classroom teacher focuses more on performance or on learning. Ames (1992), for example, outlined in some detail the steps required for a successful classroom intervention to promote learning goals, which may need to include changing both teachers' perceptions about the advisability of a preoccupation with performance and their own personal theories about the malleability of intelligence (Dweck & Bempechat, 1983).

Promoting Challenging Learning Environments

A final potential ameliorative for the developmental decrease in intrinsic motivation is to focus on creating appropriately challenging learning activities and environments. Given that there are clearly not resources available to provide individualized instruction and materials for each student, educators are typically forced to settle on common tasks and assignments that are likely to prove too easy for some and too difficult for other children in a given class. This can lead to motivational problems, such as boredom on the one hand and frustration on the other. There are, however, several possible strategies that might help educators to address these motivational needs of individual students.

One current approach is to take advantage of modern technology, such as computers in the classroom (e.g., Lajoie & Derry, 1993; Larkin & Chabay, 1992; Lepper, 1985; Lepper et al., 1993). If students are given the opportunity to work individually at the computer, it is possible in most domains to create tasks with graded levels of difficulty that will allow each student to begin at an appropriate level and to progress at an appropriate pace. On the one hand, for children who have fallen behind their classmates, computerized instruction can allow them to work at their own pace and gain small-scale mastery experiences rather than be consumed by worries about being behind the rest of the class. On the other hand, computerized instruction would also allow more advanced children to push their limits rather than be "held back," bored by the seemingly slow pace of the standard curriculum. Further, not only do computerized tasks afford several levels of difficulty but they also allow for immediate feedback. In contrast to typical classwork—where feedback is given days or even weeks after the work has been completed—computers are capable of immediately explaining to children both their strengths and weaknesses. Such timely feedback about performance is surely beneficial in terms of both motivation and achievement, because immediate feedback can be given while students can still remember the details of the task, the particular problems they encountered, and/or the questions that had occurred to them. Indeed, the individualization of instruction in terms of the appropriate match of task difficulty and student ability has been one of the earliest and most sustained hopes of proponents of computer-based instruction (e.g., Lajoie & Derry, 1993; Larkin & Chabay, 1992; Suppes, 1966).

A second way to address students' individual motivational needs is through human tutors. Research suggests that individualized instruction through tutoring is consistently superior to whole-class instruction, even when classrooms adopt a mastery-oriented approach (Bloom, 1984). Because tutors are concerned with only one student—rather than with an entire class—they can, and do, continuously adjust the level of challenge to the current cognitive and motivational needs of that student (Lepper et al., 1993; Lepper, Drake, & O'Donnell-Johnson, 1997). Clearly, hiring personal tutors for each child is prohibitively costly, but there may be less "expensive" yet still mutually beneficial solutions. For example, cross-age peer-tutoring programs, in which older children learn to teach and sharpen their own skills by providing individualized tutoring for younger children, have been shown to increase the motivation and performance of both the tutors and the tutees in a wide variety of educational settings (e.g., Foster-Harrison, 1997; Goodlad & Hirst, 1990).

Finally, at the classroom level, a number of techniques for encouraging cooperative learning seem to maximize the likelihood of an appropriate level of challenge while minimizing perceptions of a zero-sum atmosphere. In general, research has shown that children working in cooperative groups demonstrate superior problem solving compared with children working either individually or in competitive groups (Johnson, Skon, & Johnson, 1980; Qin, Johnson, & Johnson, 1995; Slavin, 1996). Further, it is not only the low-ability and average students who show improvement; even high-ability students show enhanced performance in cooperative learning situations (Johnson et al., 1980).

Although they differ in the specifics of the programs they recommend, many educators have shown the motivational benefits of the introduction of specific cooperative learning programs into U.S. schools. Slavin's (1983, 1996) procedures for offering group rewards based on the average of independent measures of the success of each group member and Aronson's "jig-saw classroom" (Aronson et al., 1978), for instance, represent two models of cooperative learning that seem to have produced substantial cognitive and motivational benefits. Likewise, studies of Palincsar and Brown's (1984) "reciprocal teaching" procedures and Dansereau's cooperative learning strategies (1988) have demonstrated the effectiveness of pedagogical techniques based on the use of small cooperative learning groups within classrooms. Similarly, though at a slightly higher level of analysis, Brown and Campione's (1994) attempts to transform traditionally individualistic U.S. classrooms into "communities of learners," and similar initiatives by others (Brown, Collins, & Duguid, 1989: Scardamalia & Bereiter, 1991), seek to promote cooperative learning across even larger groups in school.

Summary

In short, if we accept the evidence that children show less and less intrinsic motivation as they progress through school, there are interventions available that might help to ameliorate this problem. By promoting a sense of control and self-determination in students, by situating learning activities in meaningful and interesting contexts, by emphasizing learning goals, and by seeking to provide an appropriate level of challenge and difficulty for individual students, we may begin to address this problem more effectively.

Promoting Other Motivations

Although we believe that the promotion of intrinsic motivation is an important and highly desirable educational goal, it is not the only factor to deserve consideration. In closing this chapter, we examine two additional issues of substantial importance in understanding children's motivation in school.

Promoting Extrinsic Motivation?

A first additional consideration concerns the necessity and indeed the value, under appropriate conditions, of extrinsic motivation in U.S. schools. Although the utopian goal of a school system in which students are constantly motivated by a purely intrinsic desire to learn new topics and master new skills has been a persistent and appealing vision to some (e.g., Kleiman, 1984; Leonard, 1968; Neill, 1960; Rousseau, 1762; Schank, 1984), it seems to us to be both an unattainable and perhaps even an undesirable goal.

In the first place, not all activities we want children to undertake in school are naturally—or even can be made—intrinsically motivating. In many cases in the early stages of learning, the intrinsic value of a given activity may not even be apparent until the individual has acquired some minimal level of competence. A child first learning to sound out single words, for instance, will not be able to experience many of the inherent pleasures of reading. At the other end of the continuum, real mastery of most significant domains of learning may require thousands of hours of repetition and practice (Ericsson, Krampe, & Tesch-Roemer, 1993)—substantially more than many students would choose to invest in even the most interesting of educational activities. In both cases, the judicious use of extrinsic incentives may be entirely appropriate, to encourage the level of task engagement needed to produce learning. Moreover, if the level of initial interest in the task is sufficiently low, the use of extrinsic rewards may even have positive effects on later motivation, as noted in our earlier review. Extrinsic rewards delivered in an informative manner may likewise help focus students' attention on their strengths and weaknesses, in ways that may help them improve their performance and identify more general skills and strategies that will continue to have value and to earn approbation throughout school and beyond.

More generally, as long as we retain the practice of "compulsory" education and the idea of a general curriculum of material that we expect all students to master, some use of extrinsic rewards may be inevitable. At the same time, there may also be techniques that could be used, as we have suggested, to minimize the possible detrimental effects of such rewards. A start would be to avoid the use of truly superfluous extrinsic rewards. Arbitrary tangible rewards used to produce initial task engagement, for instance, may later be gradually "faded out" as students achieve levels of competence that permit them to enjoy the inherent values of the task (e.g., Turkewitz, O'Leary, & Ironsmith, 1975). Similarly, making extrinsic rewards contingent on individual mastery of material rather than on comparative performance standards may permit all students to experience a sense of competence and progress in their schoolwork (Bandura & Schunk, 1981), and using higher-interest academic activities as "rewards" for low-interest activities may limit or eliminate potential negative effects (e.g., Taffel & O'Leary, 1976).

In short, success in school, as in many areas of life outside of school, may require us to attend simultaneously to both intrinsic and extrinsic sources of motivation (Heyman & Dweck, 1992; Jackson, 1968; Lepper, 1983; Nisan, 1992). If there is too exclusive a preoccupation with intrinsic motivation on the one hand, students are likely to shortchange or ignore areas of the curriculum that happen not to appeal to their personal interests and proclivities. If there is too exclusive a preoccupation with extrinsic motivation on the other hand, students are likely to suffer from a lack of motivation and a sense of helplessness outside of the specific situations in which extrinsic rewards are available. Our challenge as educators is, therefore, to make use of extrinsic rewards in a manner that supports rather than undermines students' intrinsic interest.

Promoting Internalized Motivation?

A second and final additional consideration takes these issues one step further, by focusing on the process by which students come to internalize initially external and imposed goals into their own system of goals and values. Although internalization has long been a central concept in developmental theories (e.g., Aronfreed, 1968; Freud, 1930; Hoffman, 1970; Kelman, 1958; Lepper, 1983), it has proved remarkably difficult to study with precision in the laboratory or in the classroom. Clearly, we do often undertake tasks that require great effort or persist at tasks in the face of substantial difficulties—not just to meet others' expectations or for the sake of immediate tangible rewards but also to meet our own expectations for ourselves or to achieve our own long-term goals. Yet, understanding how these sorts of longer-term internalized motivations are derived from their more clearly external precursors has proved particularly resistant to direct empirical study.

In part because there are a number of mechanisms that may contribute to this process of internalization, various investigators have focused on somewhat different aspects of this phenomenon. On the one hand, Deci and his colleagues (Deci, Eghrari, Patrick, & Leone, 1994; Grolnick, Deci, & Ryan, 1997; Rigby, Deci, Patrick, & Ryan, 1992) have delineated a continuum of internalized responses ranging between purely extrinsic and purely intrinsic motivations. They have begun to examine the antecedents of the introjection of, and identification with, adult values by studying the regulatory and disciplinary practices of parents and teachers. Similarly, although in a somewhat more limited context, Lepper (1981, 1983) proposed a "minimal sufficiency" model to describe the conditions under which initial compliance with external requests and prohibitions may lead to later internalization of those standards in the absence of continued external pressures.

On the other hand, Harackiewicz and her associates (Harackiewicz & Elliot, 1998; Harackiewicz & Sansone, 1991) have stressed the complex interplay between people's immediate and longer-term goals, as well as the ways in which the larger social and cultural context may influence both the general expected value of an activity and the specific manner in which it is undertaken, experienced, and continued by an individual. In a related vein, Sansone and her collaborators (Sansone & Harackiewicz, 1996; Sansone, Weir, Harpster, & Morgan, 1992) have sought to situate these processes within the larger context of the multiple self-regulation strategies that people may use to cope and to persist when faced with initially unpleasant but required tasks.

Still others have focused more on the specific content and characteristics of activities, and on the match between these features and the particular abilities and proclivities of individuals, as determinants of the development of longer-term values and interests (e.g., Berlyne, 1960; Cordova & Lepper,

1996; Csikszentmihalyi, 1975; Malone & Lepper, 1987, Jacobs & Eccles, chapter 14, this book). These authors have stressed factors such as the extent to which a particular activity provides a continuing series of challenging goals at an appropriate level of difficulty for the person, the degree to which an activity supports a sustained sense of self-efficacy and personal control, and the variety of ways that an activity is associatively linked with other tasks and topics of intrinsic interest to the individual.

Despite these many different approaches to this problem, however, there seems to be substantial implicit agreement that such internalized motivations become prominent only rather late developmentally. Hence, in terms of our discussion of the decreases in motivation that characterize children's progression through schools in the United States, the explicit developmental findings of Chandler and Connell (1987) seem of particular interest. In this interview study, children between the ages of 5 and 15 years were asked to tell why they engaged in an array of different activities. On the one hand, across this entire age range, when the activities in question were those the children had said they liked, children gave primarily "intrinsic" reasons for task engagement. On the other hand, when children were queried about why they engaged in activities they said they did not like, clear developmental trends were apparent. As age increased, purely "extrinsic" reasons (e.g., "I study hard to please my parents") were progressively supplanted by more "internalized" reasons (e.g., "I study hard because I want to get into a good college"). This phenomenon, we trust, is not unfamiliar to most academicians. Coupled with our prior evidence of the developmental decline of other sources of motivation in the classroom, these findings illustrate the importance of including internalized motives in future investigations of academic motivation.

Moreover, once more abstract and long-term goals and more internalized principles and interests have come to the fore developmentally, we believe that two additional processes may gain increased importance. First, the person is likely to be faced with more situations in which there are multiple acceptable alternatives, all of which would suffice to produce some extrinsic reward (e.g., many ways of completing one's college requirements or making a living). In these cases, feelings of personal choice may easily outweigh feelings of external control—thus promoting, rather than undermining, subsequent intrinsic motivation. Second, once engagement with particular activities has become integrated into a person's basic self-definition (e.g., that one is a teacher, a researcher, a professor, and/or a psychologist), we believe that the offer of extrinsic rewards contingent upon those activities will be more likely to produce positive effects on later motivation than would comparable rewards contingent upon equally interesting activities that are not a part of the person's self-concept.

In any case, it seems certain that a better understanding of this "missing link" in the study of motivation should help the field to move beyond its traditional focus on purely "intrinsic" or "extrinsic" motivations. As Thomas Huxley (1897) argued long ago: "Perhaps the most valuable result of all education is the ability to make yourself do the thing you have to do, when it ought to be done, whether you like it or not..."

CONCLUSIONS

The first experimental studies demonstrating that the misuse of superfluous extrinsic rewards and constraints to control behavior can undermine intrinsic motivation were done in the 1970s. Since then, as illustrated in this book, more than 100 additional experiments and dozens of research reviews have been added to this literature, which certainly seems to have generated more than its fair share of controversy.

Nonetheless, as we look back at the research and rhetoric on this topic, it seems to us time for the field to cast aside extreme views of this literature on both sides of this debate. The effects of rewards on subsequent motivation are neither all positive nor all negative; detrimental effects are neither "ubiquitous" nor "mythical." Instead, the effects depend on the particulars of the situation—for example, the nature of the activity and its initial value to the individual; the timing, informativeness, controllingness, and salience of the reward; the precise contingency between the activity and the reward; and often the larger context in which the reward is provided. Perhaps it is time to devote our efforts more explicitly to clarifying the conditions under which both positive and negative outcomes are likely.

Equally important, it also seems to us time for the field to move beyond an exclusive focus on those settings in which intrinsic and extrinsic motivation may be in conflict with each other to a fuller consideration of the ways in which the two may, in many real-world contexts, operate independently or in tandem with one another. To do so, we will need to pay increased attention to the ways in which rewards are most commonly used in concrete real-world settings, like children's classrooms, as well as to the multiple messages that rewards may convey in those settings.

In both cases, the larger message for researchers is the same: As Einstein is said to have remarked about the goal of theory in science more generally, we should aim to keep our analyses "as simple as possible—but no simpler."

Acknowledgments

Preparation of this chapter was supported in part by research grant MH-44321 from the National Institute of Mental Health to the first author and a National Science Foundation graduate research fellowship to the second author. The authors are greatly indebted to Bonny Brown, Judith Harackiewicz, Carol Sansone, and Paul Whitmore for their insightful and extensive comments on an earlier draft of this chapter.

References

Amabile, T. M., DeJong, W., & Lepper, M. R. (1976). Effects of externally imposed deadlines on subsequent intrinsic motivation. *Journal of Personality and Social Psychology, 34*, 92–98.

Ames, C. (1992). Classrooms: Goals, structures, and student motivation. *Journal of Educational Psychology, 84*, 261–271.

Ames, C., & Archer, J. (1988). Achievement goals in the classroom: Students' learning strategies and motivational processes. *Journal of Educational Psychology, 80*, 260–267.

Anand, P., & Ross, S. M. (1987). A computer-based strategy for personalizing verbal problems in teaching mathematics. *Educational Communication and Technology Journal, 35*, 151–162.

Anderman, E. M., & Maehr, M. L. (1994). Motivation and schooling in the middle grades. *Review of Educational Research, 64*, 287–309.

Anderman, E. M., & Midgley, C. (1997). Changes in achievement goal orientations, perceived academic competence, and grades across the transition to middle-level schools. *Contemporary Educational Psychology, 22*, 269–298.

Anderson, R. C., Shirey, L. L., Wilson, P. T., & Fielding, L. G. (1987). Interestingness of children's reading material. In R. E. Snow & M. C. Farr (Eds.), *Aptitude, learning, and instruction: III. Conative and affective process analyses* (pp. 287–299). Hillsdale, NJ: Erlbaum.

Aronfreed, J. (1968). *Conduct and conscience.* New York: Academic Press.

Aronson, E., Blaney, N., Stephan, C., Sikes, J., & Snapp, M. (1978). *The jigsaw classroom.* Beverly Hills: Sage Publications.

Asher, S. R. (1981). Topic interest and children's reading comprehension. In R. J. Spiro, B. C. Bruce, & W. F. Brewer (Eds.), *Theoretical issues in reading comprehension* (pp. 525–534). Hillsdale, NJ: Erlbaum.

Asher, S. R., Hymel, S., & Wigfield, A. (1978). Influence of topic interest on children's reading comprehension. *Journal of Reading Behavior, 10*, 35–47.

Bandura, A. (1977a). *Social learning theory.* Englewood Cliffs, NJ: Prentice Hall.

Bandura, A. (1977b). Self-efficacy: Toward a unifying theory of behavioral change. *Psychological Review, 84*, 191–215.

Bandura, A., & Schunk, D. (1981). Cultivating competence, self-efficacy, and intrinsic interest through proximal self-motivation. *Journal of Personality and Social Psychology, 41*, 586–598.

Berlyne, D. E. (1960). *Conflict, arousal, and curiosity.* New York: McGraw-Hill.

Berlyne, D. E. (1966). Curiosity and exploration. *Science, 153*, 25–33.

Birch, L. L., Birch, D., Marlin, D. W., & Kramer, L. (1982). Effects of instrumental consumption on children's food preference. *Appetite: Journal for Intake Research, 3*, 125–134.

Birch, L. L., Marlin, D. W., & Rotter, J. (1984). Eating as the "means" activity in a contingency: Effects on young children's food preference. *Child Development, 55*, 431–439.

Blake, W. (1794). *Songs of Experience.* London.

Bloom, B. S. (1984). The 2-sigma problem: The search for methods of group instruction as effective as one-to-one tutoring. *Educational Researcher, 13*, 4–16.

Boggiano, A. K., & Ruble, D. N. (1979). Competence and overjustification effect: A developmental study. *Journal of Personality and Social Psychology, 37*, 1426–1468.

Boggiano, A. K., Shields, A., Barrett, M., Kellam, T., Thompson, E., Simons, J., & Katz, P. (1992). Helplessness deficits in students: The role of motivational orientation. *Motivation and Emotion, 16*, 271–296.

Brown, A. L., & Campione, J. C. (1994). Guided discovery in a community of learners. In K. McGilly (Ed.), *Classroom lessons: Integrating cognitive theory and classroom practice* (pp. 229–270). Cambridge, MA: MIT Press/Bradford Books.

Brown, J. S., Collins, A., & Duguid, P. (1989). Situated cognition and the culture of learning. *Educational Researcher*, 32–42.

Bruner, J. S. (1961). The act of discovery. *Harvard Educational Review, 31*, 21–32.

Bruner, J. S. (1962). *On knowing: Essays for the left hand.* Cambridge, MA: Harvard University Press.

Bruner, J. S. (1966). *Toward a theory of instruction.* Cambridge, MA: Harvard University Press.

Bruner, J. S. (1996). *The culture of education*. Cambridge, MA: Harvard University Press.

Butler, R., & Neuman, O. (1995). Effects of task and ego achievement goals on help-seeking behaviors and attitudes. *Journal of Educational Psychology, 87*, 261–271.

Calder, B. J., & Staw, B. M. (1975). Self-perception of intrinsic and extrinsic motivation. *Journal of Personality and Social Psychology, 31*, 599–605.

Cameron, J., & Pierce, W. D. (1994). Reinforcement, reward, and intrinsic motivation: A meta-analysis. *Review of Educational Research, 64*, 363–423.

Chandler, C. L., & Connell, J. P. (1987). Children's intrinsic, extrinsic, and internalized motivation: A developmental study of children's reasons for liked and disliked behaviours. *British Journal of Developmental Psychology, 5*, 357–365.

Clemens, S. L. (1876). *The adventures of Tom Sawyer*. Hartford, CT: American Publishing Co.

Condry, J. (1977). Enemies of exploration: Self-initiated versus other initiated-learning. *Journal of Personality and Social Psychology, 35*, 459–477.

Condry, J. (1978). The role of incentives in socialization. In M. R. Lepper & D. Greene (Eds.), *The hidden costs of reward* (pp. 179–192). Hillsdale, NJ: Erlbaum.

Condry, J., & Chambers, J. (1978). Intrinsic motivation and the process of learning. In M. R. Lepper, & D. Greene (Eds.), *The hidden costs of reward* (pp. 61–84). Hillsdale, NJ: Erlbaum.

Cordova, D. I., Christensen, D., & Lepper, M. R. (2000). The effects of intrinsic versus extrinsic rewards on the process of learning. Manuscript in preparation, Stanford University, Stanford, CA.

Cordova, D. I., & Lepper, M. R. (1996). Intrinsic motivation and the process of learning: Beneficial effects of contextualization, personalization, and choice. *Journal of Educational Psychology, 88*, 715–730.

Covington, M. V. (1984). The self-worth theory of achievement motivation: Findings and implications. *The Elementary School Journal, 85*, 5–20.

Csikszentmihalyi, M. (1975). *Beyond boredom and anxiety*. San Francisco: Jossey-Bass.

Danner, F. W., & Lonky, E. (1981). A cognitive-developmental approach to the effects of rewards on intrinsic motivation. *Child Development, 52*, 1043–1052.

Dansereau, D. F. (1988). Cooperative learning strategies. In C. E. Weinstein, E. T. Goetz, & P. A. Alexander (Eds.), *Learning and study strategies: Issues in assessment, instruction, and evaluation* (pp. 103–120). San Diego: Academic Press.

deCharms, R. (1968). *Personal causation*. New York: Academic Press.

deCharms, R. (1984). Motivation enhancement in educational settings. In R. E. Ames & C. Ames (Eds.), *Research on motivation in education* (Vol. 1, pp. 275–310). Orlando, FL: Academic Press.

Deci, E. L. (1971). Effects of externally mediated rewards on intrinsic motivation. *Journal of Personality and Social Psychology, 18*, 105–155.

Deci, E. L. (1972). The effects of contingent and non-contingent rewards and controls on intrinsic motivation. *Organizational Behavior and Human Performance, 8*, 217–229.

Deci, E. L. (1975). *Intrinsic motivation*. New York: Plenum.

Deci, E. L. (1981). *The psychology of self-determination*. Lexington, MA: Heath.

Deci, E. L., & Cascio, W. F. (1972, April). Changes in intrinsic motivation as a function of negative feedback and threats. Paper presented at the meeting of the Eastern Psychological Association, Boston.

Deci, E. L., Eghrari, H., Patrick, B. C., & Leone, D. R. (1994). Facilitating internalization: The self-determination theory perspective. *Journal of Personality, 62*, 119–142.

Deci, E. L., Koestner, R., & Ryan, R. M. (1999). A meta-analytic review of experiments examining the effects of extrinsic rewards on intrinsic motivation. *Psychological Bulletin, 125*, 627–668.

Deci, E. L. & Ryan, R. M. (1980). The empirical exploration of intrinsic motivational process. In L. Berkowitz (Ed.), *Advances in Experimental Social Psychology* (Vol. 13, pp. 39–80). New York: Academic Press.

Deci, E. L., & Ryan, R. M. (1985). *Intrinsic motivation and self-determination in human behavior*. New York: Plenum.

Deci, E. L., & Ryan, R. M. (1991). A motivational approach to self: Integration in personality. In R. Dienstbier (Ed.), *Nebraska Symposium on Motivation: Vol. 38. Perspectives on motivation* (pp. 237–288). Lincoln: University of Nebraska Press.

Deci, E. L., Schwartz, A. J., Sheinman, L., & Ryan, R. M. (1981). An instrument to assess adults' orientations toward control versus autonomy with children: Reflections on intrinsic motivation and perceived competence. *Journal of Educational Psychology, 73*, 642–650.

Deci, E. L., Spiegel, N. H., Ryan, R. M., Koestner, R., & Kauffman, M. (1982). Effects of performance standards on teaching styles: Behavior of controlling teachers. *Journal of Educational Psychology, 74*, 852–859.

Dickens, C. (1838–1839). *Nicholas Nickleby.* Monthly magazine serialization.

Dollinger, S. J., & Seiters, J. A. (1988). Intrinsic motivation among clinic-referred children. *Bulletin of the Psychonomic Society, 26*, 449–451.

Dreeben, R. (1968). *On what is learned in school.* Reading, MA: Addison-Wesley.

Dweck, C. S. (1975). The role of expectations and attributions in the alleviation of learned helplessness. *Journal of Personality and Social Psychology, 31*, 674–685.

Dweck, C. S. (1986). Motivational processes affecting learning. *American Psychologist, 41,* 1040–1048.

Dweck, C. S. (1990). Self-theories and goals: Their role in motivation, personality, and development. In R. A. Dienstbier (Ed.), *Nebraska Symposium on Motivation: Vol. 38. Perspectives on motivation.* (pp. 199–235). Lincoln: University of Nebraska Press.

Dweck, C. S. (1999). *Self-theories: Their role in motivation, personality, and development.* Philadelphia: Psychology Press.

Dweck, C. S., & Bempechat, J. (1983). Children's theories of intelligence: Consequences for learning. In S. G. Paris, G. M. Olson, & H. W. Stevenson (Eds.), *Learning and motivation in the classroom* (pp. 239–256). Hillsdale, NJ: Erlbaum.

Dweck, C. S., Davidson, W., Nelson, S., & Enna, B. (1978). Sex differences in learned helplessness: II. The contingencies of evaluative feedback in the classroom; III. An experimental analysis. *Developmental Psychology, 14*, 268–276.

Dweck, C. S., & Henderson, V. L. (1988). Theories of intelligence: Background and measures. Unpublished manuscript, University of Illinois, Champaign-Urbana.

Dweck, C. S., & Leggett, E. L. (1988). A social-cognitive approach to motivation and personality. *Psychological Review, 95*, 256–273.

Eccles, J. S., & Midgley, C. (1989). Stage/environment fit: Developmentally appropriate classrooms for early adolescents. In R. E. Ames & C. Ames (Eds.), *Research on motivation in education* (Vol. 3, pp. 139–186). San Diego: Academic Press.

Eccles, J. S., & Midgley, C. (1990). Changes in academic motivation and self-perceptions during early adolescence. In R. Montemayor, G. R. Adams, & T. P. Gullotta (Eds.), *Advances in adolescent development: From childhood to adolescence* (Vol. 2, pp. 134–155). Newbury Park, CA: Sage Publications.

Eccles, J. S., Midgley, C., Wigfield, A., Buchanan, C. M., Reuman, D., Flanagan, C., & MacIver D. (1993). Development during adolescence: The impact of stage–environment fit on young adolescents' experiences in school and in families. *American Psychologist, 48*, 90–101.

Edwards, C., Gandini, L., & Forman, G. (1993). *The hundred languages of children: The Reggio Emilia approach to early childhood education.* Norwood, NJ: Ablex.

Einstein, A. (1949). Autobiography. In P. Schilpp, *Albert Einstein: Philosopher-Scientist* (pp. 2–95). Evanston, IL: Library of Living Philosophers.

Eisenberger, R., & Cameron, J. (1996). Detrimental effects of reward: Reality or myth? *American Psychologist, 51*, 1153–1166.

Elliot, A. J., & Harackiewicz, J. M. (1994). Goal setting, achievement orientation and intrinsic motivation: A mediational analysis. *Journal of Personality and Social Psychology, 66*, 968–980.

Elliott, E. S., & Dweck, C. S. (1988). Goals: An approach to motivation and achievement. *Journal of Personality and Social Psychology, 54*, 5–12.

Epstein, J. L., & McPartland, J. M. (1976). The concept and measurement of the quality of school life. *American Educational Research Journal*, 13, 15–30.

Ericsson, K. A., Krampe, R. T., & Tesch-Roemer, C. (1993). The role of deliberate practice in the acquisition of expert performance. *Psychological Review*, 100, 363–406.

Fazio, R. H. (1981). On the self-perception explanation of the overjustification effect: The role of the salience of initial attitude. *Journal of Experimental Social Psychology*, 17, 417–426.

Foersterling, F. (1985). Attributional retraining: A review. *Psychological Bulletin*, 98, 495–512.

Foster-Harrison, E. S. (1997). *Peer-tutoring for K–12 success*. Bloomington, IN: Phi Delta Kappa Educational Foundation.

Freud, S. (1930). *Civilization and its discontents*. London: Hogarth.

Garbarino, J. (1975). The impact of anticipated rewards on cross-age tutoring. *Journal of Personality and Social Psychology*, 32, 421–428.

Ginsberg, H. (1977). *Children's arithmetic: The learning process*. New York: Van Nostrand.

Goodlad, S., & Hirst, B. (Eds.). (1990). *Explorations in peer tutoring*. Oxford, UK: Blackwell Education.

Gottfried, A. E. (1985). Academic intrinsic motivation in elementary and junior high school students. *Journal of Educational Psychology*, 77, 631–645.

Greene, D., & Lepper, M. R. (1974). Effects of extrinsic rewards on children's subsequent intrinsic interest. *Child Development*, 45, 1141–1145.

Grolnick, W. S., Deci, E. L., & Ryan, R. M. (1997). Internalization within the family: The self-determination theory perspective. In J. E. Grusec & L. Kuczynski (Eds.), *Parenting and children's internalization of values: A handbook of contemporary theory* (pp. 135–161). New York: John Wiley & Sons.

Harackiewicz, J. M. (1979). The effects of reward contingency and performance feedback on intrinsic motivation. *Journal of Personality and Social Psychology*, 37, 1352–1361.

Harackiewicz, J. M. (1979). The effects of reward contingency and performance feedback on intrinsic motivation. *Journal of Personality and Social Psychology*, 37, 1352–1361.

Harackiewicz, J. M., Barron, K. E., Carter, S. M., Lehto, A. T., & Elliot, A. J. (1997). Predictors and consequences of achievement goals in the college classroom: Maintaining interest and making the grade. *Journal of Personality and Social Psychology*, 73, 1284–1295.

Harackiewicz, J. M., Barron, K. E., & Elliot, A. J. (1998). Rethinking achievement goals: When are they adaptive for college students and why? *Educational Psychologist*, 33, 1–21.

Harackiewicz, J. M., & Elliot, A. J. (1998). The joint effects of target and purpose goals on intrinsic motivation: A mediational analysis. *Personality and Social Psychology Bulletin*, 24, 675–689.

Harackiewicz, J. M., Manderlink, G., & Sansone, C. (1984). Rewarding pinball wizardry: The effects of evaluation on intrinsic interest. *Journal of Personality and Social Psychology*, 47, 287–300.

Harackiewicz, J. M., & Sansone, C. (1991). Goals and intrinsic motivation: You *can* get there from here. In M. L. Maehr & P. R. Pintrich (Eds.), *Advances in motivation and achievement* (Vol. 7, pp. 21–49). Greenwich, CT: JAI.

Harari, O., & Covington, M. V. (1981). Reactions to achievement behavior from a teacher and student perspective: A developmental analysis. *American Educational Research Journal*, 18, 15–28.

Harter, S. (1980). *A scale of intrinsic versus extrinsic orientation in the classroom* (Manual available from Susan Harter, Department of Psychology, University of Denver, Denver, CO 80208).

Harter, S. (1981). A new self-report scale of intrinsic versus extrinsic orientation in the classroom: Motivational and informational components. *Developmental Psychology*, 17, 300–312.

Harter, S., & Jackson, B. K. (1992). Trait vs. nontrait conceptualizations of intrinsic/extrinsic motivational orientation. *Motivation and Emotion*, 16, 209–230.

Henderlong, J., & Lepper, M. R. (1997, April). *Conceptions of intelligence and children's motivational orientations: A developmental perspective*. Poster presented at the biennial meeting of the Society for Research in Child Development, Washington, DC.

Henderlong, J., & Lepper, M. R. (2000). A developmental perspective on children's intrinsic and extrinsic motivation. Manuscript in preparation, Stanford University, Stanford, CA.

Hennessey, B. A., & Amabile, T. M. (1998). Reward, intrinsic motivation, and creativity. *American Psychologist*, 53, 674–675.

Hennessey, B. A., Amabile, T. M., & Martinage, M. (1989). Immunizing children against the negative effects of reward. *Contemporary Educational Psychology*, 14, 212–227.

Heyman, G. D., & Dweck, C. S. (1992). Achievement goals and intrinsic motivation: Their relation and their role in adaptive motivation. *Motivation and Emotion*, 16, 231–247.

Hoffman, M. L. (1970). Moral development. In P. H. Mussen (Ed.), *Carmichael's manual of child psychology* (Vol. 2, pp. 261–360). New York: Wiley.

Holt, J. (1964). *How children fail*. New York: Holt, Rinehart & Winston.

Hunt, J. M. V. (1961). *Intelligence and experience*. New York: Ronald Press.

Hunt, J. M. V. (1965). Intrinsic motivation and its role in psychological development. In D. Levine (Ed.), *Nebraska Symposium on Motivation: Vol. 13.* (pp. 189–282). Lincoln: University of Nebraska Press.

Huxley, T. H. (1897). *Collected Essays: Vol. III. Science and Education*. New York: Appleton.

Iyengar, S. S., & Lepper, M. R. (1999). Rethinking the role of choice: A cultural perspective on intrinsic motivation. *Journal of Personality and Social Psychology*, 76, 349–366.

Jackson, P. (1968). *Life in classrooms*. New York: Holt, Rinehart & Winston.

Johnson, D. W., Skon, L., & Johnson, R. (1980). Effects of cooperative, competitive, and individualistic conditions on children's problem-solving performance. *American Educational Research Journal*, 17, 83–93.

Karniol, R., & Ross, M. (1977). The effect of performance-relevant and performance-irrelevant rewards on children's intrinsic motivation. *Child Development*, 48, 482–487.

Katz, L. G., & Chard, S. C. (1989). *Engaging children's minds: The project approach*. Norwood, NJ: Ablex.

Kelman, H. L. (1958). Compliance, identification, and internalization: Three processes of opinion change. *Journal of Conflict Resolution*, 2, 51–60.

Kohn, A. (1988). *No contest*. New York: Houghton Mifflin.

Kohn, A. (1993). *Punished by rewards: The trouble with gold stars, incentive plans, A's, praise, and other bribes*. New York: Houghton Mifflin.

Kohn, A. (1995, April 19). Newt Gingrich's reading plan: Money is the wrong motivator for kids. *Education Week*, pp. 42, 52.

Kohn, A. (1996). By all available means: Cameron and Pierce's defense of extrinsic motivators. *Review of Educational Research*, 66, 1–4.

Kruglanski, A. W. (1978). Endogenous attribution and intrinsic motivation. In M. R. Lepper & D. Greene (Eds.), *The hidden costs of reward: New perspectives on the psychology of human motivation* (pp. 85–107). Hillsdale, NJ: Erlbaum.

Kruglanski, A. W., Alon, S., & Lewis, T. (1972). Retrospective misattribution and task enjoyment. *Journal of Experimental Social Psychology*, 8, 493–501.

Kruglanski, A. W., Friedman, I., & Zeevi, G. (1971). The effects of extrinsic incentives on some qualitative aspects of task performance. *Journal of Personality*, 39, 606–617.

Lajoie, S. P., & Derry, S. J. (Eds.). (1993). *Computers as cognitive tools*. Hillsdale, NJ: Erlbaum.

Lampert, M. (1986). Knowing, doing, and teaching multiplication. *Cognition and Instruction*, 3, 305–342.

Langer, E. J. (1975). The illusion of control. *Journal of Personality and Social Psychology*, 32, 311–328.

Langer, E. J. (1989). *Mindfulness*. Reading, MA: Addison-Wesley.

Larkin, J. H., & Chabay, R. W. (Eds.). (1992). *Computer-assisted instruction and intelligent tutoring systems: Shared goals and complementary approaches*. Hillsdale, NJ: Erlbaum.

Lave, J. (1988). *Cognition in practice: Mind, mathematics and culture in everyday life*. Cambridge, MA: Cambridge University Press.

Leonard, G. B. (1968). *Education and ecstasy*. New York: Dell Publishing Company.

Lepper, M. R. (1981). Intrinsic and extrinsic motivation in children: Detrimental effects of superfluous social controls. In W. A. Collins (Ed.), *Minnesota Symposium on Child Psychology: Vol. 14. Aspects of the development of competence* (pp. 155–213). Hillsdale, NJ: Erlbaum.

Lepper, M. R. (1983). Social-control processes and the internalization of social values: An attributional perspective. In E. T. Higgins, D. N. Ruble, & W. W. Hartup (Eds.), *Social cognition and social development* (pp. 294–330). New York: Cambridge University Press.

Lepper, M. R. (1985). Microcomputers in education: Motivational and social issues. *American Psychologist*, 40, 1–18.

Lepper, M. R. (1988). Motivational considerations in the study of instruction. *Cognition and Instruction*, 5, 289–310.

Lepper, M. R. (1995). Theory by the numbers? Some concerns about meta-analysis as a theoretical tool. *Applied Cognitive Psychology*, 8, 1–12.

Lepper, M. R. (1998). A whole much less than the sum of its parts. *American Psychologist*, 53, 675–676.

Lepper, M. R., Drake, M., & O'Donnell-Johnson, T. M. (1997). Scaffolding techniques of expert human tutors. In K. Hogan & M. Pressley (Eds.), *Scaffolding student learning: Instructional approaches and issues* (pp. 108–144). New York: Brookline Books.

Lepper, M. R., & Gilovich, T. J. (1981). The multiple functions of reward: A social-developmental perspective. In S. S. Brehm, S. M. Kassin, & F. X. Gibbons (Eds.), *Developmental social psychology: Theory and research* (pp. 5–31). New York: Oxford University Press.

Lepper, M. R., & Greene, D. (1975). Turning play into work: Effects of adult surveillance and extrinsic rewards on children's intrinsic motivation. *Journal of Personality and Social Psychology*, 31, 479–486.

Lepper, M. R., & Greene, D. (1978). Overjustification research and beyond: Toward a means–end analysis of intrinsic and extrinsic motivation. In M. R. Lepper & D. Greene (Eds.), *The hidden costs of reward* (pp. 109–148). Hillsdale, NJ: Erlbaum.

Lepper, M. R., Greene, D., & Nisbett, R. E. (1973). Undermining children's intrinsic interest with extrinsic rewards: A test of the "overjustification" hypothesis. *Journal of Personality and Social Psychology*, 28, 129–137.

Lepper, M. R., Henderlong, J., & Gingras, I. (1999). Understanding the effects of extrinsic rewards on intrinsic motivation: Uses and abuses of meta-analysis. *Psychological Bulletin*, 125, 669–675.

Lepper, M. R., & Hodell, M. (1989). Intrinsic motivation in the classroom. In C. Ames & R. E. Ames (Eds.), *Research on motivation in education* (Vol. 3, pp. 73–105). New York: Academic Press.

Lepper, M. R., Keavney, M., & Drake, M. (1996). Intrinsic motivation and extrinsic rewards: A commentary on Cameron and Pierce's meta-analysis. *Review of Educational Research*, 66, 5–32.

Lepper, M. R., Sagotsky, G., Dafoe, J. L., & Greene, D. (1982). Consequences of superfluous social constraints: Effects on young children's social inferences and subsequent intrinsic interest. *Journal of Personality and Social Psychology*, 42, 51–64.

Lepper, M. R., Sethi, S., Dialdin, D., & Drake, M. (1997). Intrinsic and extrinsic motivation: A developmental perspective. In S. S. Luthar, J. A. Burack, D. Cicchetti, & J. R. Weisz (Eds.), *Developmental psychopathology: Perspectives on adjustment, risk, and disorder* (pp. 23–50). New York: Cambridge University Press.

Lepper, M. R., Woolverton, M., Mumme, D. L., & Gurtner, J. (1993). Motivational techniques of expert human tutors: Lessons for the design of computer-based tutors. In S. P. Lajoie & S. J. Derry (Eds.), *Computers as cognitive tools* (pp. 75–105). Hillsdale, NJ: Erlbaum.

Loveland, K. K., & Olley, J. G. (1979). The effect of external reward on interest and quality of task performance in children of high and low intrinsic motivation. *Child Development*, 50, 1207–1210.

Maehr, M. L., & Anderman, E. M. (1993). Reinventing schools for early adolescents: Emphasizing task goals. *Elementary School Journal*, 93, 593–610.

Malone, T. W., & Lepper, M. R. (1987). Making learning fun: A taxonomy of intrinsic motivations for learning. In R. E. Snow & M. J. Farr (Eds.), *Aptitude, learning, and instruction: III. Conative and affective process analyses* (pp. 223–253). Hillsdale, NJ: Erlbaum.

McClelland, D. C., Atkinson, J. W., Clark, R. W., & Lowell, E. L. (1953). *The achievement motive*. New York: Appleton-Century-Crofts.

McLoyd, V. C. (1979). The effects of extrinsic rewards of differential value on high and low intrinsic interest. *Child Development*, 50, 1010–1019.

Meece, J. L., Blumenfeld, P. C., & Hoyle, R. H. (1988). Students' goal orientations and cognitive engagement in classroom activities. *Journal of Educational Psychology*, 80, 514–523.

Midgley, C., Anderman, E. M., & Hicks, L. (1995). Differences between elementary and middle school teachers and students: A goal theory approach. *Journal of Early Adolescence*, 15, 90–113.

Neill, A. S. (1960). *Summerhill: A radical approach to child rearing*. New York: Hart Publishing Company.

Newman, J., & Layton, B. D. (1984). Overjustification: A self-perception perspective. *Personality and Social Psychology Bulletin*, 10, 419–425.

Newman, J., & Taylor, A. (1992). Effect of a means–end contingency on young children's food preferences. *Journal of Experimental Child Psychology*, 64, 200–216.

Newman, R. S. (1990). Children's help-seeking in the classroom. The role of motivational factors and attitudes. *Journal of Educational Psychology*, 82, 71–80.

Nicholls, J. G. (1978). The development of the concepts of effort and ability, perception of academic attainment, and the understanding that difficult tasks require more ability. *Child Development*, 49, 800–814.

Nicholls, J. G. (1984). Achievement motivation: Conceptions of ability, subjective experience, task choice, and performance. *Psychological Review*, 91, 328–346.

Nicholls, J. G. (1989). *The competitive ethos and democratic education*. Cambridge, MA: Harvard University Press.

Nisan, M. (1992). Beyond intrinsic motivation: Cultivating a "sense of the desirable." In F. K. Oser, A. Dick, & J.-L. Patry (Eds.), *Effective and responsible teaching: The new synthesis* (pp. 126–138). San Francisco: Jossey-Bass.

Nuttin, J. R. (1973). Pleasure and reward in human motivation and learning. In D. E. Berlyne & K. B. Madsen (Eds.), *Pleasure, reward, preference* (pp. 243–274). New York: Academic Press.

Orwell, G. (1993). *Down and out in Paris and London*. London: Victor Gollancz Ltd.

Palincsar, A. S., & Brown, A. L. (1984). Reciprocal teaching of comprehension-fostering and monitoring activities. *Cognition and Instruction*, 1, 117–175.

Papert, S. (1980). *Mindstorms: Children, computers, and powerful ideas*. New York: Basic Books.

Papert, S. (1993). *The children's machine: Rethinking school in the age of the computer*. New York: Basic Books.

Parker, L. E., & Lepper, M. R. (1992). Effects of fantasy contexts on children's learning and motivation: Making learning more fun. *Journal of Personality and Social Psychology*, 62, 625–633.

Perkins, D. (1992). *Smart schools: From educating memories to educating minds*. New York: Free Press.

Perlmutter, L. C., & Monty, R. A. (1977). The importance of perceived control: Fact or fantasy? *American Scientist*, 65, 759–765.

Pittman, T. S., Cooper, E. E., & Smith, T. W. (1977). Attribution of causality and the overjustification effect. *Personality and Social Psychology Bulletin*, 3, 280–283.

Pittman, T. S., Davey, M. E., Alafat, K. A., Wetherill, K. V., & Kramer, N. A. (1980). Informational versus controlling verbal rewards. *Personality and Social Psychology Bulletin*, 6, 228–233.

Qin, Z., Johnson, D. W., & Johnson, R. T. (1995). Cooperative versus competitive efforts and problem solving. *Review of Educational Research*, 65, 129–143.

Quattrone, G. (1985). On the congruity between internal states and action. *Psychological Bulletin*, 98, 3–40.

Renninger, K. A., Hidi, S., & Krapp, A. (1992). *The role of interest in learning and development*. Hillsdale, NJ: Erlbaum.

Rholes, W. S., Blackwell, J., Jordan, C., & Walters, C. (1980). A developmental study of learned helplessness. *Developmental Psychology*, 16, 616–624.

Rigby, C. S., Deci, E. L., Patrick, B. C., & Ryan, R. M. (1992). Beyond the intrinsic–extrinsic dichotomy: Self-determination in motivation and learning. *Motivation and Emotion*, 16, 165–185.

Ross, S. M. (1983). Increasing the meaningfulness of quantitative material by adapting context to student background. *Journal of Educational Psychology, 75,* 519–529.

Rousseau, J. -J. (1979). *Emile or On education.* (A. Bloom, Trans.). New York: Basic Books, Inc. (Original work published in 1762).

Rummel, A., & Feinberg, R. (1988). Cognitive evaluation theory: A meta-analytic review of the literature. *Social Behavior and Personality, 16,* 147–164.

Ryan, R. M. (1982). Control and information in the intrapersonal sphere: An extension of cognitive evaluation theory. *Journal of Personality and Social Psychology, 43,* 450–461.

Ryan, R. M., & Deci, E. L. (1996). When paradigms clash: Comments on Cameron and Pierce's claim that rewards do not undermine intrinsic motivation. *Review of Educational Research, 66,* 33–38.

Ryan, R. M., & Grolnick, W. S. (1986). Origins and pawns in the classroom: Self-report and projective assessment of individual differences in children's perceptions. *Journal of Personality and Social Psychology, 50,* 550–558.

Ryan, R. M., Mims, V., & Koestner, R. (1983). Relation of reward contingency and interpersonal context to intrinsic motivation: A review and test using cognitive evaluation theory. *Journal of Personality and Social Psychology, 45,* 736–750.

Sansone, C. (1986). A question of competence: The effects of competence and task feedback on intrinsic interest. *Journal of Personality and Social Psychology, 51,* 918–931.

Sansone, C., & Harackiewicz, J. M. (1996). "I don't feel like it": The function of interest in self-regulation. In L. L. Martin & A. Tesser (Eds.), *Striving and feeling: interactions among goals, affects, and self-regulation* (pp. 203–228). Hillsdale, NJ: Erlbaum.

Sansone, C., & Harackiewicz, J. M. (1998). "Reality" is complicated. *American Psychologist, 53,* 673–674.

Sansone, C., & Morgan, C. (1992). Intrinsic motivation and education: Competence in context. *Motivation and Emotion, 16,* 249–270.

Sansone, C., Weir, C., Harpster, L., & Morgan, C. (1992). Once a boring task always a boring task? Interest as a self-regulatory mechanism. *Journal of Personality and Social Psychology, 63,* 379–390.

Scardamalia, M., & Bereiter, C. (1991). Higher levels of agency for children in knowledge building: A challenge for the design of new knowledge media. *The Journal of the Learning Sciences, 1,* 36–67.

Schank, R. (1984). *The cognitive computer: On language, learning, and artificial intelligence.* Menlo Park, CA: Addison-Wesley.

Silberman, C. (1970). *Crisis in the classroom.* New York: Random House.

Skinner, B. F. (1938). *The behavior of organisms: An experimental analysis.* New York: Appleton-Century-Crofts.

Skinner, B. F. (1953). *Science and human behavior.* New York: Macmillan.

Slavin, R. E. (1983). When does cooperative learning increase student achievement? *Psychological Bulletin, 94,* 429–445.

Slavin, R. E. (1996). Research on cooperative learning and achievement: What we know, what we need to know. *Contemporary Educational Psychology, 21,* 43–69.

Staw, B. M., Calder, B. J., Hess, R. K., & Sandelands, L. E. (1980). Intrinsic motivation and norms about payment. *Journal of Personality, 48,* 1–14.

Steele, C. M. (1988). The psychology of self-affirmation: Sustaining the integrity of the self. In L. Berkowitz (Ed.), *Advances in experimental social psychology* (Vol. 21, pp. 261–302). New York: Academic Press.

Steele, C. M. (1992, April). Race and the schooling of black Americans. *Atlantic Monthly, 269,* 68–78.

Steinberg, E. R. (1989). Cognition and learner control: A literature review, 1977–1988. *Journal of Computer-Based Instruction, 16,* 117–121.

Stevenson, H. W., Chen, C., & Lee, S. Y. (1993). Mathematics achievement of Chinese, Japanese, and American children: Ten years later. *Science, 259,* 53–58.

Stevenson, H. W., Lee, S. Y., & Stigler, J. W. (1986). Mathematics achievement of Chinese, Japanese, and American children. *Science, 231*, 693–699.

Stevenson, H. W., & Stigler, J. (1992). *The learning gap: Why our schools are failing and what we can learn from Japanese and Chinese education.* New York: Summit.

Suppes, P. (1966). The uses of computers in education. *Scientific American, 215*, 206–221.

Taffel, S. J., & O'Leary, K. D. (1976). Reinforcing math with more math: Choosing special academic activities as a reward for academic performance. *Journal of Educational Psychology, 68,* 579–587.

Tang, S-H., & Hall, V. C. (1995). The overjustification effect. A meta-analysis. *Applied Cognitive Psychology, 9,* 365–404.

Thorndike, E. L. (1911). *Animal intelligence.* New York: Macmillan.

Turkewitz, J., O'Leary, K. D., & Ironsmith, M. (1975). Producing generalization of appropriate behavior through self-control. *Journal of Consulting and Clinical Psychology, 43,* 577–583.

Tzuriel, D. (1989). Development of motivational and cognitive-informational orientations from third to ninth grades. *Journal of Applied Developmental Psychology, 10,* 107–121.

White, R. W. (1959). Motivation reconsidered: The concept of competence. *Psychological Review, 66,* 297–333.

White, R. W. (1960). Competence and the psychosexual stages of development. *Nebraska Symposium on Motivation: Vol. 8.* (pp. 97–141). Lincoln: University of Nebraska Press.

Winnett, R. A., & Winkler, R. C. (1972). Current behavior modification in the classroom: Be still, be quiet, be docile. *Journal of Applied Behavior Analysis, 5,* 499–504.

Zuckerman, M., Porac, J., Lathin, D., Smith, R., & Deci, E. L. (1978). On the importance of self-determination for intrinsically-motivated behavior. *Personality and Social Psychology Bulletin, 4,* 443–446.

An Interest Researcher's Perspective: The Effects of Extrinsic and Intrinsic Factors on Motivation

SUZANNE HIDI

Ontario Institute for Studies in Education
University of Toronto

My work since the early 1980s has focused on the role of interest in learning and development. Much of the motivational research during this period can be characterized as clustered rather than integrated across different approaches (Bergin, 1999; Murphy & Alexander, 2000). The areas of goal orientation (Ames, 1992; Dweck & Leggett, 1988), self-efficacy (Bandura 1977a, 1986; Zimmerman, 1985, 1995), task value (Wigfield & Eccles 1992), intrinsic/extrinsic motivation (Deci, 1975; Deci & Ryan 1985; Lepper, 1985; Lepper & Greene 1978; Lepper, Greene & Nisbett, 1973), and interest (Hidi, 1990; Hidi & Baird, 1986; Renninger, Hidi and Krapp, 1992; Schiefele, 1992) were studied in detail separately and with little overlap across some of the clusters. My own interest research was no exception to the singular focus, as it has been only since the mid-1990s that I started to consider how interest fits in with other motivational variables. When I attempted to integrate interest research with other findings in the motivational literature, I could not help but get involved and try to make sense out of the large and controversial literature on how rewards affect individuals' intrinsic motivation. As I read first the early articles, and then the ensuing debates and meta-analyses, I became focused, persistent, and emotionally involved. In other words, I became interested in the topic.

When I reviewed the early literature, what struck me as remarkable was the singular focus that seemed apparent in both the behavioristic and the intrinsic-motivation researchers' perspectives on the operations and roles of rewards in learning. Behaviorists, who explained behavior in terms of externally controlled rewards and reinforcements, tended to consider only their positive effects and ignored any potential negative outcome of these same rewards. In contrast, many motivational theorists who focused on intrinsic factors were inclined to ignore the importance and/or potential benefits of extrinsic rewards and acknowledged only their negative, controlling aspects. This view first emerged from research conducted in the 1970s that indicated that extrinsic and intrinsic factors were not additive and that rewards might interfere with individuals' interested engagements (see Calder & Staw, 1975, for a review of this early literature). There were some exceptions to the singularly negative attitude of motivational researchers toward rewards. For example, Lepper and colleagues (Lepper, 1985; Lepper and Green 1978; etc.) called for examining ways in which reward programs could enhance rather than undermine intrinsic motivation. Calder and Staw (1975) cautioned that rewards may have negative effects only under some conditions and suggested that external motives and interest in activity may not be mutually exclusive. Others have suggested that tangible rewards may be effective for inducing poorly motivated children to engage in learning activities (Bandura, 1977b; Zimmerman, 1985) and that rewards that convey clear standards of competence may not have adverse effects on intrinsic motivation (Harackiewicz, 1979; Karniol & Ross, 1977).

As this book demonstrates, most motivational researchers have, by now, rejected the view that human motivation should or could be considered as resulting from purely extrinsic or intrinsic factors and now acknowledge the potential benefits of a more balanced view that allows for a combination of intrinsic and extrinsic factors (Deci, 1992; Harackiewicz, Barron, & Elliot, 1998; Harackiewicz & Sansone, chapter 4, this book; Hidi & Harackiewicz, 2000; Lepper & Henderlong, chapter 10, this book; Rigby, Deci, Patrick & Ryan, 1992; Sansone & Morgan, 1992, etc.). Although in these new theoretical orientations researchers acknowledge that rewards providing informational feedback might not be detrimental to intrinsic motivation, a generally negative attitude toward rewards in the literature still prevails (e.g., Anderman & Maehr, 1994; Kohn, 1993). Deci, Koestner, and Ryan (1999) have argued that the primary negative effect of rewards is that they tend to forestall self-regulation and they have warned that the use of extrinsic rewards runs a serious risk of diminishing intrinsic motivation. Moreover, many researchers continue to view learning that is an outcome of intrinsic motivation as superior and more desirable than learning that is fostered through use of extrinsic rewards (Hidi & Harackiewicz, 2000).

Although intrinsic motivation researchers investigated the relation between rewards and interest, rewards have not been central to interest research and/or to interest theory. In fact there is no relevant literature in this field of which I am aware that has considered the association between rewards and interest. Neither have attempts been made by interest researchers to evaluate from their perspective the motivational literature indicating that rewards may have negative effects on individuals engaged in interesting, intrinsically motivating tasks. The primary objective of this chapter is to provide such a consideration. In the first part of the chapter, I discuss interest researchers' conceptualization of interest and how interest relates to intrinsic motivation. In the second part of the chapter, I review changes in motivational aspects of school activities and suggest that extrinsic factors may play an inevitable and increasingly more important role in motivating students as they progress through their education. In the third and final part of the chapter, I consider research examining how rewards affect individuals' behavior and motivation, and the relation of this literature to research on interest. Specifically, it is argued that the questions raised, the research conducted, and the conclusions reached in the intrinsic-motivation literature have not taken into account critical issues, some of which are implicit in interest research, and therefore the studies may not sufficiently inform us about how rewards affect individuals' interests and real-life academic performance.

CONCEPTUALIZATIONS OF INTEREST

Interest has been conceptualized in a variety of ways. As Renninger, Hoffmann, and Krapp (1998) noted, interest recently has been studied as a habitual tendency, a motivational belief, trait, a component of personality, and as being elicited by text characteristics. Most frequently, however, interest has been defined as a psychological state and/or as an individual disposition (e.g., Krapp, Hidi, & Renninger, 1992; Todt & Schreiber, 1998). The psychological state of interest has also been referred to as the actualized state of individual interest (e.g., Krapp et al., 1992). However, because I believe that this state can be the outcome of various forms of interests, I prefer to use the term psychological state of interest.

Interest as a psychological state involves focused attention, increased cognitive functioning, persistence, and affective involvement. Although focusing attention and continuing cognitive engagements normally requires increased effort, when interest is high, these activities feel relatively effortless. Rheinberg (1998) suggested that because interest has evolutionary profit, it causes individuals to concentrate their cognitive, emotional, and motor processes on a certain part of their environment, for a continuous period. Hidi (1995) argued that automatic attention is an aspect of interest that contributes to the facilitative effect that interest has on cognitive functioning. Increased affective functioning is also associated with experiencing interest, and many researchers consider mainly positive affect, such as enjoyment or liking, when they refer to the affective component of interest (Prenzel, 1992; Todt and Schreiber, 1998). Others have acknowledged that even though interest-based activities tend to be associated with positive emotional experiences, negative emotions can also be involved with experiencing interest (e.g., Bergin, 1999; Hidi & Harackiewicz, 2000; Iran-Nejad, 1987; Krapp & Fink, 1992). Two types of interest have been most commonly associated with experiencing the psychological state of interest: *situational* and *individual*; these are reviewed briefly here.[1]

Situational interest is generated by particular conditions and/or objects in the environment that focus attention; and it represents an affective reaction that may or may not last (Hidi, 1990; Hidi & Anderson, 1992; Krapp, et al 1992; Murphy & Alexander, 2000). This initial affective reaction may be positive or negative in tone (Hidi & Harackiewicz, 2000; Iran-Nejad, 1987). For example, a student who is not interested in science may watch an engaging television show one day that demonstrates how black holes can "suck up" things. Fascinated and somewhat frightened, the student's interest is *triggered*. Her attention is focused. She experiences excitement mixed with some negative emotions, driven by apprehension or even by fear as to what might happen in her lifetime. If the student's situational interest is short term, she will stop watching the show and go on to other activities. On the other hand, if her situational interest is *maintained*, the student will continue watching the show. That is, the student continues to experience the psychological state of interest. The student is fully engaged and is riveted to the show.

Acknowledging these two possibilities, Hidi & Baird (1986) suggested that situational interest should be conceptualized as having two potential stages, one in which interest is triggered and a subsequent stage in which interest is further maintained. Mitchell (1993) experimentally investigated this distinction and found support for the two-stage model. Rather than using the terminology of triggering interest and maintaining interest, Mitchell adopted Dewey's (1913) phrases of *catching* interest and *holding* interest. More recently, several researchers have referred to these two stages of situational interest and have used the terms interchangeably (e.g., Bergin, 1999; Harackiewicz, Barron, Tauer, Carter, & Elliot, 2000). It should be

---

[1] In 1980, Kintsch made a distinction between cognitive interest and emotional interest. A similar categorization was suggested by Schank in 1979. More recently, Harp and Mayer (1997) further substantiated these categories. I consider emotional interest and cognitive interest to be two instances of situational interest.

noted, however, that *trigger* and *catch* are not synonymous verbs. Triggering interest describes an initial beginning phase of the psychological state of interest in which attention is increased and arousal is generated in disengaged individuals. On the other hand, catching interest suggests that the interest that individuals already experience is being diverted toward the situation. For this reason, I recommend referring to triggering as the first stage of situational interest.

Situational interest, once maintained, may contribute to the development of the early stages of long-term individual interest (Hidi & Anderson, 1992; Krapp, 1998; Renninger, chapter 13, this book). That is, when situational interest continues over time, it may lead to increased knowledge, value, and positive feelings. Considering the various stages of situational interest, Hidi and Harackiewicz (2000) have argued that it is only when situational interest is triggered and maintained that it should be considered as intrinsically motivated behavior.

Individual interest has been described as an individual's relatively enduring predisposition to attend to certain objects, stimuli, and events, and to engage in certain activities (e.g., Ainley, 1998; Krapp, et al., 1992; Renninger, chapter 13, this book; Renninger and Wozniak, 1985). Through repeated engagements over time, individuals build related knowledge structures, experience positive affects, and come to value highly the object of their individual interests. For example, a person with an individual interest in science values and seeks out opportunities to engage in scientific activities that he or she finds stimulating and enjoyable, continues through such engagements to accumulate scientific knowledge, and, most important, experiences the psychological state of interest. Investigations focused on individual interest show that it is an important determinant of academic motivation and learning (e.g., Ainley 1994, 1998; Prenzel, 1988; Renninger, 1992, 1998; Schiefele, 1998). Renninger (chapter 13, this book) discusses the pervasive influence of individual interest in detail.

Several researchers have pointed out that although situational interests and individual interests are distinct, they are not dichotomous phenomena, and they can be expected to interact and influence each other's development (Alexander, 1997; Alexander, Jetton, & Kulikowich, 1995; Bergin, 1999; Hidi, 1990; Hidi & Anderson, 1992). It is of particular relevance to this chapter that individual interest can influence situational interest by moderating the impact of environmental factors on the psychological state of interest (Bergin, 1999; Murphy & Alexander, 2000; Pintrich, 2000). For instance, having individual interest in science would predispose a student to want to watch a science video. If the video turns out to be a basic introduction to black holes and reiterates information that the student knows well – even if the video is interesting to novices – she will turn to something else. If the information turns out to be new and extends what the student already knows, she will likely find it interesting and continue to watch the whole video. Furthermore, as I argue later in this chapter, individual interest may also moderate the effect of extrinsic rewards on situationally interesting activities.

Another form of interest that has been investigated in the literature is *topic interest*. Unfortunately, the meaning that has been ascribed to the term topic interest is ambiguous. As Ainley, Hidi, and Berndorff (1999) pointed out, some researchers have considered topic interest to be a form of individual interest (e.g., Schiefele, 1996; Schiefele & Krapp, 1996), but others have treated topic interest more like a form of situational interest (e.g., Hidi & McLaren, 1990, 1991). To demonstrate the ambiguity of topic interest, consider presenting students with the title "Black Holes and Quasars." For our student with her now well-developed individual interest in astronomy, topic interest generated by the title will be closely linked to her individual interest. In contrast, students who do not have an individual interest in astronomy may also report strong topic interest. In such cases, this is the outcome of situational interest factors like novelty or incongruity of the information conveyed by the title.

A study by Jacobs, Finken, Lindsley Griffin, and Wright (1998) further illustrates how the ambiguity inherent in the definition and measurement of topic interest can influence the interpretation of empirical findings. These researchers reported that among several variables, "current intrinsic interest" was the most powerful influence on adolescent girls' career choices in science. In the study, what was referred to as intrinsic interest in biology was measured by individuals' ratings of biology assignments as interesting versus boring, and by how much they liked doing biology. Parallel questions were used to measure interest in physical science. Jacobs et al.'s measures assessed topic interest, but they did not assess how well developed were individuals' interests in biology and in physical science.

It would be of significant practical importance to know how situational and individual factors contributed to the topic interest subjects experience. In fact, Ainley et al. (1999) investigated the relation between the various forms of interest and found that both situational and individual factors contribute to topic interest. They also reported that the arousal of topic interest initiated processes contributing to student persistence with reading and increased learning. They have concluded that situational interest and individual interest overlap in specific instances, such as in individuals' reactions to topics, or topic interest.

Common to the conceptualizations of situational, individual, and even topic interest is the interactive relation between an individual and her or his environment. This conceptualization goes back to Dewey (1913), who said that "self and world are engaged with each other in a developing situation" (p. 126), and has been adopted by most interest researchers (e.g., Bergin, 1999; Hidi, 1990; Krapp et al., 1992; Renninger, 1989; H. Schiefele, Hausser, & Schneider, 1979). More specifically, Krapp et al. (1992) suggested that interest always refers to a person's interaction with a specific class of objects, events, and so forth, and that its strong focus on specificity distinguishes it from other psychological concepts such as curiosity.

Viewing interest as object-specific, and acknowledging that it results from people's interactions with specific objects, has implications for understanding the origins or development of interest, as it suggests that such development may include both intrinsic and extrinsic motivational components. Given that interest both as a psychological state and as a disposition is object specific, it is inappropriate to describe it as either intrinsic or extrinsic. Object specificity implies that interest cannot be seen as purely intrinsic to the person nor as purely extrinsic to the object. Thus, reference to *intrinsic interest*—a term widely used in the intrinsic-motivation literature – seems questionable. Clearly, *extrinsic interest* would also be a misnomer.[2]

INTEREST AND INTRINSIC MOTIVATION

Various definitions of intrinsic motivation have been proposed since the mid-1970s (see Lepper, 1985, for an earlier review) and several chapters of this book provide overviews of these definitions (see Shah & Kruglanski, chapter 5, this book). Rather than review them here in detail, I focus on how interest relates to the basic concept of *intrinsic motivation*. The most common definition of intrinsic motivation involves performing an activity for its own sake rather than as a means to an end. This definition has been interpreted to mean that intrinsically motivated behavior occurs independently of any forms of reinforcement or reward. As Kruglanski (1975) pointed out, however, some activities such as playing poker or performing a business transaction have inherent rewards, in which case rewards may well enhance intrinsic motivation.[3] The origins of intrinsic motivation were explained by various factors such as individuals experiencing pleasure by overcoming challenges and achieving competence (White, 1959), or their need to exer-

---

[2] The term *intrinsic interest* sets up an expectation of extrinsic interest. However, not only is such a concept an oxymoron but nobody in the literature has actually referred to extrinsic interest. Furthermore, I could not find a definition as to what exactly intrinsic-motivation researchers mean when they refer to intrinsic interest.

[3] Kruglanski (1975) proposed that attributing external causes versus internal causes to actions should be replaced by a distinction between exogenous factors and endogenous factors. He defined *exogenous* as action that is "means" to a further goal, and *endogenous* as an "end" in itself. A major issue in Kruglanski's argument was that both external causes and internal causes can be endogenous. More specifically, contingent monetary rewards that have been considered external causes of actions could also be endogenous to an activity, in which case they would enhance rather than suppress intrinsic motivation. For example, Kruglanski argued that activities to which monetary rewards are inherent, such as playing poker, performing a business transaction, or receiving a pay-check, are pleasurable and do not fit the usual descriptions of activities performed for external causes.

cise control over their environment (Hunt, 1965; Deci, 1975). Lepper and Henderlong (chapter 10, this book) provide a detailed discussion of the theoretical background of intrinsic motivation.

Interest has been considered to be an implicit aspect of intrinsic motivation (Deci, 1992). For example, Deci (1998) argued that "intrinsically motivated behavior is done because it is interesting" (p. 149) and concluded that to read a book just because it interests one is to be intrinsically motivated. From this standpoint, therefore, interest and intrinsic motivation are practically synonymous terms (Tobias, 1994). They are both contrasted with extrinsic motivation that is defined as doing something for separable consequence, either provided by the environment or oneself. Nothing illustrates more clearly how ingrained the view of treating interest and intrinsic motivation as identical concepts is in the literature than the way in which motivational researchers measure intrinsic motivation. In the majority of studies investigating the relationship between intrinsic motivation and rewards, participants' self-reported levels of interest served as one of the direct measures of intrinsic motivation. The other most commonly used measure was behavioral, focusing on the length of time subjects choose to reengage with tasks.

To evaluate how intrinsic motivation and interest are related, it is necessary to look more closely at these two concepts.[4] The same action can be classified as intrinsically or as extrinsically motivated behavior. Reading a book is intrinsically motivated behavior when the motive is interest. Reading the book because it was given as homework would be extrinsically motivated behavior. Intrinsically motivated actions can be based on such motives as need, desire, situational interest, and self-influence (Green-Demers, Pelletier, Stewart, & Gushue, 1998). Once individual interest in a given activity has developed, these motives are in a more interrelated, complex relation (see Renninger, chapter 13, this book). Thus, when one is describing specific actions, intrinsic motivation is one of the two general classes (i.e., intrinsically motivated and extrinsically motivated behavior) and interest is one of a set of motives that may result in intrinsically motivated behavior. Similarly when one is dealing with motivational orientations, individual interest can be viewed as a specific case of intrinsic motivation.

Other researchers have also suggested that intrinsic motivation may be best viewed as a broader concept. Bandura (1977b), considering what he viewed as problems with the concept of intrinsic motivation, proposed that intrinsic motivation should be treated as a response class. Guthrie and Wigfield (1999) suggested that intrinsic motivation is a more general concept than interest. Similarly, Schiefele (1992) argued that motivational orienta-

---

[4] Mary Ainley (personal communication, 1999) made a significant contribution to developing and conceptualizing the following distinction between interest and intrinsic motivation.

tions are usually general concepts that can affect individuals' learning behavior across different subject areas. In contrast, interest in educational research is conceptualized as a domain-specific motivational variable that can inform us about why some students are motivated to learn specific subject matter over others. For example, some students may be motivated to learn mathematics, whereas they dislike chemistry. The concept of interest helps explain such choices. Bergin (1999) concluded that interest theory, as opposed to other motivational theories, is concerned with explaining why individuals choose one activity over another when they ostensibly perceive each as having the same value and providing the same challenge. That is, among many challenging activities only some become interests.

Rheinberg (1998) has contrasted object indifference of achievement motivation with the object specificity inherent in the theoretical conceptualization of and research on interest (e.g., H. Schiefele et al., 1979; Krapp & Fink, 1992). Rheinberg argued that achievement motivation can occur in relation to nearly any kind of activity, as it is "object indifferent" (p. 127). For example, a person within this framework could be equally proud of his or her competence in painting an excellent watercolor and the skillful way in which he or she can break into a car. On the other hand, interest is "object specific." It is not only the outcome of general, inner personal processes but also the result of a specific interaction between a person and an object. The distinction drawn by Rheinberg between achievement motivation and interest may be analogous to the distinction between intrinsic motivation and interest. Whereas both intrinsic motivation and interest result in self-intentional, autotelic activities, the former is a broader concept and is less focused on object specificity than interest. Because of object specificity, interest in subject areas can inspire and enthuse, certain things can become irresistible, and individuals may come to view topics in a positive light for longer periods of time (Rheinberg, 1998).

Schiefele (1999) argued that individual interest may be an antecedent to cognition that determines the strength of individuals' intrinsic motivation or extrinsic motivation to act in a particular situation. If interest is considered to be one of several motives within the general class of intrinsic motivation, situational interests and topic interests might also be best understood as antecedents of specific cognitions that, in turn, determine the strength of arousal in a particular situation. The level of arousal then determines activity. When sufficient interest of this type is aroused for action to follow, the activity can be described as being intrinsically motivated (see Sansone & Smith, chapter 12, this book). Renninger (chapter 13, this book) argues that individual interest (a relatively stable orientation to specific objects) drives the activation of the motives that characterize intrinsic motivation. Whether one is referring to individual interest or to situational interest, the general class is intrinsic motivation, and one of the specific motives within that class is interest.

A further complication in the relationship between the concepts of intrinsic motivation and individual interest as disposition arises when exploring them from the perspective of their origins. Whereas the origins of intrinsic motivation have been assumed to be rooted in basic human needs for competence, challenge, and control, individual interest is seen as developing from internal sources in concert with external influences. In particular, viewing individual interest as object-specific and acknowledging that it develops from people's interactions with specific objects implies that individual interests have their origins in both intrinsically motivated and extrinsically motivated experiences. It appears, then, that content-specific individual interests that develop from a combination of situational and individual factors contribute at the more general level to the development of intrinsic motivation.

An example that has been used to demonstrate how situational interest can affect both cognitive and motivational functioning and contribute to the development of individual interest also has implications for the development of intrinsic motivation. Hidi & Berndorff (1998) and Hidi and Harackiewicz (2000) considered the case of a student with no prior background in psychology who hears an exciting lecture about Freud and then does the assigned readings on the topic. First, she reads about Freud's life and personality theory only because it is required for the course. However, as the student continues to read, her situational interest is maintained, and eventually she becomes fascinated with Freud's ideas. She reflects and relates aspects of the theory to her personal experiences. She becomes excited, and as she continues to read, she develops her own interpretations about the behavior of significant people in her life. She develops an individual interest in the topic.

Hidi and colleagues argued that several aspects of this type of engagement are important. From a cognitive point of view, a broad range of knowledge patterns have been activated. As the student continues to read about Freud's theory, changes can be expected to occur across her declarative, conceptual, and logical knowledge structures (Farnham-Diggory, 1994). From a motivational point of view, although interest originally has been triggered by external factors (the professor's lecture and reading assignment), it results in continued and persistent activity that becomes self-initiated. Thus, as the activity proceeds, it is no longer externally imposed on the student but becomes enjoyable, autonomous, and self-determined. In short, the person develops an individual interest and her motivation can now be considered intrinsic (Deci, 1992; Rigby et al., 1992).

Finally, from a combined cognitive and motivational point of view, the ongoing changes can be characterized by an affective-cognitive synthesis. Rathunde and colleagues (Rathunde, 1993, 1998; Rathunde & Csikszentmihalyi, 1993) have called such synthesis an integral part of "undivided interest." This type of interest will likely be maintained over time and combines positive affective qualities (such as feelings of enjoyment) with cognitive qualities of focused attention, perceptions of value or importance, and meaningful thoughts. Hidi and colleagues proposed that once the affective-cognitive synthesis occurs and situational interest is maintained, these factors can contribute to the development of individual interest, or, described at the more general level, to intrinsic motivation. This analysis suggests that creating environments that stimulate situational interest is one way for schools to trigger student motivation (Mitchell, 1993; Schraw & Dennison, 1994) and help students make cognitive gains in areas that initially hold little interest for them. Furthermore, adjusting instruction to build an individual interest is a way to facilitate the development of motivation (see Renninger, chapter 13, this book).

We can also consider how intrinsic motivation driven by other motives than interest (needs or desires) can influence the development of specific activities. On the one hand, specialized interests such as interest in mathematics cannot be explained exclusively in terms of intrinsic motivation and the related concepts of competence and autonomy (Bergin, 1999). On the other hand, intrinsic motivation can sustain individuals performing and/or learning complex activities with inherent value. These activities may vary in how interesting they are. Some may be interesting, stimulating, and exciting; others, boring or even painful. Once intrinsically motivated, individuals persevere toward the inherent goals of such motivation. For example, learning Greek can be an intrinsically motivated activity for an individual with Greek ancestors. However, studying the vocabulary and the conjugation of verbs can be boring and tedious. In self-determination theory, these tasks represent integrated external motivation. Because there are no external controls involved, the person is self-determined and autonomous in performing them but not intrinsically motivated. From the perspective of interest research, regardless of the autonomy, the individual may find an activity time-consuming, painful, boring, and something that creates negative affect (Krapp and Fink, 1992). However, the intrinsically motivated person may persist, in spite of these negative feelings, because of the strength of an overriding desire to achieve her superordinate goal, being able to speak Greek fluently.

This conceptualization of *intrinsic motivation* is different from the conventional usage of the term. It considers intrinsic motivation to be a more general concept than interest and it has the advantage of not using the term interchangeably with *interest*. In addition, it may help to explain why some people persevere in complex activities against bad odds, boredom, and painful experiences whereas others do not have the motivation to do so. Neumann (1999) has argued that passionate thought is far more complex than it is in the "flow"-derived view alone. Passionate thought is "detachment in as much as heightened awareness – one clearing a space for the other, one conditioning the possibility of the other's existence" (p. 32). Neumann concluded that to have peak experiences requires experiences that are "not so peak," each pushing the other. The above more general view of intrinsic motivation includes the forces that propel individuals through the set of experiences Neumann talked about.

FROM PLAY TO SCHOOL ACTIVITIES: CHANGES IN TASKS AND IN MOTIVATION

Psychologists and educators have frequently noted young children's intrinsic motivation and boundless energy to explore, their joy in untutored learning of new skills, and their continuing efforts to satisfy their own curiosity (e.g., Berlyne, 1960, 1966; Cordova & Lepper, 1996; Lepper & Cordova, 1992; Piaget, 1940; Renninger, 1989). It has also been argued that making sense of one's own environment, overcoming challenges, exercising control, and enjoying individual competence are intrinsic human desires or needs (e.g., Deci and Ryan, 1985; Heckhausen, 1968; Hunt, 1965; White, 1959).

Unfortunately, as they get older, many children find that learning becomes more a chore than a challenging, exciting, and rewarding activity (e.g., Hidi and Harackiewicz, 2000; Lepper and Cordova, 1992). A plethora of recent research has demonstrated that as children age, their motivation, interests, and attitudes toward school in general and toward learning in specific subject areas tend to deteriorate (see Eccles & Midgley, 1990; Fay, 1998; Haladyna & Thomas, 1979; Hoffmann & Haussler, 1998; Sansone & Morgan, 1992; Wigfield & Eccles, 1992). Some investigators suggest that these motivational changes may start as early as between grades 3 and 6 and continue over the course of secondary school (e.g., Baumert and Koller, 1998; Graber, 1998; Harter, 1981; Koller, 1998; Murphy & Alexander, 2000; Shernoff, Schneider & Csikszentmihalyi, 1999). Lepper, Sethi, Dialdin, and Drake (1977) reported a strong developmental decrease of students' intrinsic motivation between grades 3 and 8, but no change in their extrinsic motivation.

In their influential article, Anderman & Maehr (1994) reviewed the literature on children's and adolescents' motivation and concluded that overall, the literature shows that student motivation in the middle grades decreases for academic activities and increases in nonacademic areas. Follings-Albers and Hartinger (1998) investigated children's interest, studying 676 children between the ages of 8 and 11 years, and found that sports activities were the overwhelming choices of the participants as their favorite activities. Ainley et al. (1999) found that when Australian and Canadian students (around 14 years of age) were asked to name their areas of interest, 79% of the students included one or more recreational/sports activities. The corresponding figures for school activities were 47% for music and 42% for art. Eccles and colleagues (Eccles and Midgley, 1990; Wigfield & Eccles, 1992; etc.) also reported that whereas children's valuing of academic subjects decreases across these ages,

their valuing of sports at the same time increases. One aspect of the conceptualization of value in these investigations was "intrinsic interest."

Some investigators have proposed that instruction is increasingly routine and repetitive in nature and that if learning tasks were more like play
or recreational activities, external controls could be reduced and motivation in academic activities would increase (Shernoff et al., 1999). For example, Lepper & Cordova (1992) reported a series of studies that suggested
that making learning more fun resulted in increased interest and learning.
In these studies, two or more educational activities with identical instructional content and varying motivational appeal were compared. Using fantasy as a motivational embellisher of computer-based learning activities,
Lepper and Cordova demonstrated how subjects' interest and retention of
information can be increased. One important educational principle that
Lepper and Cordova have emphasized in their work is the design of activities in which motivational and educational goals are congruent. They maintained that the success of their program rested on content in which the
goals of learning the material and winning a game correspond. More specifically, the enjoyment of activities depended on the students' learning of the
subject matter presented.

Lepper and Cordova developed the type of novel and creative educational
program that must be supported and encouraged. However, even with the best
of intentions and unlimited resources, educators can not change all academic
learning into play or recreational activities. Nor can all activities be intrinsically motivated (Lepper & Henderlong, chapter 10, this book; Miller, Greene,
Montalvo, Ravindran, & Nichols, 1996). Unfortunately, when educational
researchers decried the loss of children's academic motivation, they tended to
attach blame for this loss to the educational system. For example, it has been
suggested that as students move through grades, instruction becomes
increasingly routine (Goodlad, 1984). In the meantime, intrinsic-motivation
researchers have paid little attention to the changes in learning tasks that children experience as they get older, and to the increasing demands these tasks
place on them. It is likely that these increasing demands make it inevitable
that some young children's intrinsic motivation to play and explore does not
carry on to their schoolwork and to their academic performance.

In their now classic book, Deci & Ryan (1985) suggested that an optimal
"educational environment provides optimal challenges, right sources of stimulation, and a context of autonomy" (p.245). They acknowledged, however,
that most school environments are not optimal, and in fact our culture
requires children to pursue goals that are not interesting or engaging. Such
goals include routine homework assignments, an emphasis on order, and so
forth. As a result, children require extrinsic supports and structures. Eccles
and colleagues (Eccles & Midgley, 1990; Wigfield & Eccles, 1992; etc.) also
suggested that there may be a mismatch between early adolescents' goals
and psychological needs and the type of environments schools provide.

It is important to note that it is not only the societal or cultural influences or pressures that result in the reduction of intrinsic motivation. As children advance in school, the content they are trying to learn gets more complex and harder to master. More information needs to be retained and reviewed. Students need to further develop reflective thought and an ability to integrate new information into existing knowledge structures. Engagements get longer and students must develop strategies to deal with tasks that are not necessarily interesting.

An example of the complex tasks that require knowledge acquisition that is not always intrinsically motivating or engaging is learning to speak a second language. Language acquisition requires the kind of hard work, drills, learning of grammatical rules, and so forth, that is based on perseverance and effort and can hardly be called "spontaneously compelling". Another good example of a complex academic task is the learning of various aspects of expository writing. Zimmerman and Kitsantas (1999) recently examined one aspect of expository writing, the acquisition of writing revision skills. They have argued that such acquisition is a long-term process requiring many hours of solitary practice, high levels of personal discipline, and varied techniques of self-regulation. Learning a second language and acquiring writing skills are only two examples of the many academic skills that require focused attention, serious effort, long-term commitment, and self-discipline. However, they illustrate the long distance children have to travel from a state of natural curiosity and joyful discovery of the world through sometimes painful efforts to acquire complex academic skills.

In addition to the increased complexity of academic tasks, another significant difference between younger children's play activities and older children's academic engagements relates to their social relationships. These may contribute to the undermining of older children's motivation to study. Younger children's play activities, exploration, and learning most frequently subsume social relations. With increasing age, academic and social activities start to be separated and, by adolescence, these activities compete for students' interests, preferences, goals, and choices (Shernoff et al., 1999; Urdan & Maehr, 1995). In fact, social activities frequently focus on sports and recreation and may well explain why so many students' interests are in these areas rather than in academia (see Sansone & Smith, chapter 12, this book).

There is a further developmental issue that needs to be considered to explain adolescents' changing motivational orientations. Theory from developmental psychology suggests that a key developmental task in adolescence is the consolidation of a clear sense of self (see Harter, 1990) or identity (Erikson, 1968). This task has been described for adolescents as developing a sense of who they are; identifying their own strengths, abilities, and interests; and making some active synthesis of these in the form of lifestyle and occupational choices.

From this general developmental perspective, school learning that has clear connections with students' broader sense of themselves and their future has important motivational implications (Ainley, 1998; Eccles, Wigfield, & Schiefele, 1998). Some of the motivational significance of students' views about their own future can be seen in findings reported by Ainley (1998). Groups of students who were identified as having contrasting motivational orientations to their schooling (committed versus disengaged) were compared on their responses to a satisfaction with schooling questionnaire. One of the main differences between these groups of students was that committed students were more likely than were disengaged students to report seeing schooling as important for their future. Miller et al. (1996) also reported that when students perceive performance in their math classes as being related to future goals or desirable consequences, their efforts and persistence are significantly increased.

These findings suggest that although the novel, creative, and fantasy elements in learning that appeal to young children's delight in play may not disappear from the motivational strategies at the adolescent level, they need to be supported with strategies that acknowledge connections between current learning and students' future. The strategies should not only focus on students' connection with their future in an extrinsic sense, such as instructing students that they need to do well at school to move into prestigious, well-paid careers. These strategies should also encourage students to experience the challenges of mastering academic skills that build toward the self they wish to become. For example, encouraging a student to identify with her future career as a novelist involves having her apply herself to do well in English classes, to spend time learning the structure of English, to learn how to use a computer for writing and editing, and to confer with classmates to gain a sense of the impact of writing for an audience. This type of intention involves both intrinsic and extrinsic components.

The above considerations suggest that some of the changes observed between young children's play interests and older students' academic interests may be inevitable. Rather than denying this disturbing possibility and attaching all the blame for bored children to educators and parents for not making learning more interesting, more enjoyable, and less externally controlled, we need to consider what can be done to motivate the academically unmotivated. Hidi and Harackiewicz (2000) have argued that only by acknowledging the multidimensional nature of motivational forces and by utilising both extrinsic and intrinsic factors, will we be able to help our academically unmotivated children. More specifically, whereas these researchers recognized the positive effects of individual interest, intrinsic motivation, and mastery goals, they urged educators to utilise the additional benefits of externally triggered situational interest, extrinsic motivation, and performance goals to complement approaches based on mastery goals and self-determination (see Barron & Harackiewicz, chapter 9, this book). Nobody wants to deny that curiosity is an important energizer of human functioning and that the desire to explore, comprehend, and discover is as basic to human nature as Deci and Ryan (1985) argued. But the suggestion that intrinsic motivation, even in an ideal world, would lead to the type of hard work that a student needs, for example, to become a successful writer, without any external reinforcement or rewards is highly debatable. Positive outcomes of rewards, however, have been neglected in the literature. Therefore, I now focus on the issue of rewards.

REWARDS, INTRINSIC MOTIVATION, AND INTEREST

The accumulation of data in the early 1970s suggesting that extrinsic rewards under certain conditions have negative effects on individuals' intrinsic motivation generated a great deal of interest and a large number of experimental investigations. The question of how external controls applied through various forms of rewards affect individuals' behavior and feelings (measured by free-choice task engagements and self-rated interest) was so controversial that it fueled decades of research, over 150 studies, and at least 6 meta-analyses. Several chapters in this book deal with the various theoretical and experimental aspects of this substantial literature.

Literature on Rewards and Intrinsic Motivation

Rather than reviewing the vast material on rewards and intrinsic motivation, I take as my starting point the results of the meticulously conducted meta-analyses by Deci, Koestner, and Ryan (1999) (see also Ryan & Deci, chapter 2, this book). After a brief summary of their conclusions, I discuss some methodological and theoretical issues related to the investigations reviewed and examine their implications about the place of intrinsic and extrinsic motivation in student learning.

The major focus of the studies included in the Deci et al. meta-analyses is the various types of reward conditions that served as independent variables in these studies. In particular, Deci et al. distinguished between tangible rewards and verbal rewards and subdivided tangible rewards into expected rewards and unexpected rewards. Finally, they identified four subcategories of expected tangible rewards. These included the contingent rewards of engagement, of completion, and of performance, as well as task-noncontingent rewards. Dependent variables in the studies were two measures of intrinsic motivation: free-choice reengagements and/or self-reported interest. Deci et al. conducted separate analyses for these two dependent measures.

The studies included in the Deci et al. meta-analyses were experiments conducted in the laboratory or under well controlled, "laboratory-like" conditions that explored reward effects. Regarding initial task interest, the activities employed in the studies ranged from not being explicitly defined as interesting versus uninteresting, to tasks that were established as being one or the other. It is noteworthy that the self-reported measures of pretest interest were usually based on one or two questions, such as these: Are you interested in the activity? Do you like it? As Deci et al. were primarily concerned with how rewards affect people's intrinsic motivation for interesting activities, they excluded from their primary meta-analysis 13 studies that experimentally manipulated task interest. They subsequently performed a supplementary meta-analysis on these studies.

In sum, three major conclusions of the meta-analyses that are critical to my discussion are as follows:

1. Most tangible rewards were found to significantly undermine the free-choice behavioral measure of intrinsic motivation for interesting activities, but performance-contingent rewards did not undermine self-reported interest. In addition, unexpected rewards and those that were not contingent on task behavior had no undermining effect on either of the two measures.
2. Verbal rewards (i.e., positive feedback) had a significant positive effect on intrinsic motivation, although the results were stronger for college students than for children.
3. On the basis of their supplementary meta-analysis, Deci et al. concluded that tangible rewards did not undermine intrinsic motivation of people engaged in uninteresting activities.

Deci et al. interpreted the results of their two meta-analyses in terms of their cognitive evaluation theory (Deci & Ryan, 1985). That is, they argued that the informational and/or controlling aspects of rewards determine whether undermining of intrinsic motivation occurs. For example, the findings that unexpected and task-noncontingent, tangible rewards did not have detrimental effects was attributed to the fact that participants did not perform the tasks to get rewards in the first place and therefore did not feel controlled by these rewards. Positive effects of verbal rewards were also considered to be in line with the predictions of the theory, in part because verbal rewards are not typically expected. Moreover, Deci et al. attributed their positive effects to the informational aspects of verbal rewards, which provide positive feedback and affirm competence. Deci et al. further qualified these conclusions because a) verbal rewards seem to enhance only college students' intrinsic motivation but did not affect younger children's behavioral display of intrinsic motivation; b) controlling administration of positive feedback moderated the positive effect; and c) verbal rewards may not be equally effective for males and females. They suggested that authors of previous meta-analyses were premature in advocating the widespread use of verbal rewards in educational settings. Finally, the findings that tangible rewards have no effect on the way people perform boring tasks were also in line with the predictions of the cognitive evaluation theory, because the theory does not prescribe that rewards undermine intrinsic motivation for boring, dull tasks.

Methodological and Theoretical Issues Related to the Literature on Rewards and Intrinsic Motivation

The above conclusions are well supported by the extensive literature carefully reviewed by Deci et al. However, there are several methodological issues that suggest the importance of being cautious in directly mapping findings from experimental settings to real-life educational activities. These include evaluation of subjects' initial task interest, the types of activities and the timing of rewards, absence of rewards, and rewards and affect. I now discuss each of these issues in turn.

Evaluation of Subjects' Initial Task Interest

Although researchers emphasized that they were evaluating the effect of rewards on individuals' intrinsic motivation for interesting activities, in most studies participants 'initial task interests were only superficially examined. For example, as far as I could ascertain, only in a few of the 128 investigations did researchers distinguish between participants' situational interest and their individual interest in relation to the experimental tasks. The lack of emphasis on subjects' level and type of interest is especially puzzling, as researchers paid meticulous attention to the various reward conditions. By not distinguishing between different types of interests, motivational researchers have neglected to consider that the effects of rewards may depend on the type of interest individuals experience.

To be more specific, there is a critical difference between whether participants found a task situationally interesting or whether they brought their individual interests to the task (see Renninger, chapter 13, this book). The essence of situational interest is that it may be short-term and easily terminated (Alexander et al. 1995; Hidi, 1990; Hidi & Berndorff, 1998; Hidi & Harackiewicz, 2000; Krapp, et al., 1992; Mitchell, 1993). Thus, individuals who are engaged in activities that they find situationally interesting may be more vulnerable to the negative effects of tangible rewards than are individuals engaged in tasks that represent their long-term interest and possibly their passion. Individual interests reflect high levels of knowledge, value, and positive feelings for a given activity (Hidi, 1990; Krapp, 1998; Renninger, 1990; Schiefele, 1991). This type of interest may be less susceptible than situational interest to the detrimental effects of tangible rewards.

A tangible reward given to a chess player whose passion is solving chess puzzles, for example, may not be the same as that given to an individual who is working on an experimental task of solving puzzles and for whom the puzzles hold no personal relevance or commitment. A reward for a chess victory might reaffirm competence for a grand master, but a reward for performing a novel task may change a participant's experience and change the goal structure of the activity. Thus, rewards may disrupt intrinsic motivation when the activity involves situational interest, but they may enhance it when it is based on individual interest. Along the same lines, Harackiewicz, Manderlink, and Sansone (1984) suggested that rewarding a pinball wizard for his or her competence may enhance subsequent intrinsic motivation (see Harackiewicz & Sansone, chapter 4, this book). Underlying these differences may be different goal structures that are associated with various stages of situational interest and individual interest. Thus, well-developed individual interest may yield different reactions to rewards than would situations without such interests (Renninger, 1998).

It should be noted that there were attempts in the literature to acknowledge that the levels of initial interest experienced in a particular activity may influence the effect of rewards. Zimmerman (1985) suggested that children's initial interest in their engagements may affect the outcome of rewards. Lepper et al. (1973) measured young children's initial interest in drawing pictures with markers during three 1-hour (baseline) free-play periods. Whereas these procedures give a good demonstration of maintained situational interest, they tell us nothing about children's well-developed individual interests.

The fact that most of the research concentrated on interesting, novel tasks and/or on individuals who did not have well-developed interest indicates that researchers focused on situational interest and had not considered or were not interested in studying individual interest. In 1976, Arnold foreshadowed the argument that the level of a person's initial task interest and the levels of situational interest aroused by a given task both are critical variables in the investigation of extrinsic rewards. Arnold (1976) had taken into consideration these two variables. However, as interest research and terminology appeared only in the late 1980s in the North American literature, Arnold had no access to the terms *individual interest* and *situational interest*. He referred to both types of interest as high levels of intrinsic motivation.

Using current terminology, Arnold's investigation can be described as follows: He examined how external rewards and competence feedback affected the performance of college students who had individual interest in a task that was also situationally interesting. Only those subjects (college students) who expressed interest in computer games and volunteered were participants in his study. Thus, at least some level of individual interest was a prerequisite for participation. The experimental task was a highly interesting, complex, cognitively stimulating computer game. The results indicated that extrinsic rewards did not affect or enhance intrinsic motivation under these conditions. Arnold proposed that high levels of interest produce stable cognitive states and therefore the introduction of extrinsic rewards would not initiate a process of cognitive reevaluation of the reasons for or causes of the highly interested students' behavior. Although Arnold clearly warned his colleagues that the hypothesis of extrinsic rewards undermining intrinsic motivation might not be valid in situations where individuals were highly interested (here again, Arnold used the term *intrinsically motivated*), his argument has not been heeded, nor, to the best of my knowledge, have motivational researchers replicated Arnold's study. It would be especially important to conduct such an investigation with a control group of students without preexisting interests in the experimental activity.

Another study that suggests that individual interest may influence the effect of rewards on performance was done by Fazio (1981). When young children in this study were reminded about how much they liked an activity initially, rewards did not have detrimental effects on their intrinsic motivation or on their performance. Such reminding could serve as an instantiation of individual interest and exclude cognitive reevaluation. Other research by Hennessey (chapter 3, this book) has documented similar "immunization" effects that might work through the same mechanism.

It is noteworthy that Deci et al. (1999) criticized two previous meta-analyses (Cameron and Pierce, 1994; and Eisenberger and Cameron, 1996) for collapsing studies across both interesting and boring task conditions, and this is indeed an important theoretical distinction. Deci et al. suggested that these meta-analyses were conducted from a behavioristic perspective in which initial task interest had no theoretical meaning. However, from my point of view, neither behaviorists nor intrinsic-motivation researchers have examined participants' initial interest in sufficient detail. More specifically, if educational activities involve only situational interest, as often is the case, tangible rewards may indeed be as detrimental to intrinsic motivation as the literature suggests. However, when individuals' well-established individual interests are involved, the effect of rewards may not be detrimental to intrinsic motivation, and overgeneralizing from the results of the meta-analyses may be a problem. Thus, it seems critical to determine if the detrimental influence of tangible rewards applies only to interest aroused by and limited to specific experimental tasks or also to activities that represent more enduring individual interests.

Types of Activities Included in the Studies

In the studies included in the meta-analyses, activities were far from real-life academic tasks. They were interesting, relatively short-term, simple engagements, such as playing pinball or solving puzzles, and were performed in the laboratory or in laboratory-like situations. One characteristic of such tasks is that individuals' goals as well as their rewards are inherent in the activity. Rheinberg (1989, 1998) pointed out that "activity related motivations" are characteristic of tasks in which the impulse to perform a certain activity lies in the very activity itself. The tasks involved in many studies seem to have such built-in motivations. In addition, as Harackiewicz et al. (1984) noted, games like pinball provide ongoing performance feedback. These tasks are clearly different from the complex learning required in academic settings. Thus, as Zimmerman (1985) suggested, the literature on intrinsic motivation focused on children who were engaged in interesting activities and does not speak to the most significant problem facing educators of how to motivate children who are distracted or uninterested.

The role of choice is another area of research that suggests general caution for assuming that results of studies conducted with relatively simple short-term activities also apply to complex educational tasks. Self-determination theory states that choice is an essential component of intrinsic motivation and has a positive impact on cognitive and affective functioning of individuals. Zuckerman, Porac, Lathin, Smith, & Deci (1978) found that when compared with no-choice subjects and controls, college students who had choices about the puzzles on which they could work reported a greater feeling of control, indicated they would be more willing to return for another session of puzzle solving, and spent work time in a free-choice period solving similar puzzles. Many other investigators (e.g., Gambell, 1993; Gambrell & Marinak, 1997; Kohn, 1993) suggested that choice increases cognitive engagements during academic activities.

Schraw, Flowerdale, and Reisetter (1998) recently reviewed the literature and have questioned whether choice increases cognitive engagement at all. They conducted two experiments on the effect of choice on cognitive and affective engagement during reading. In both experiments, college students who selected what they read were compared to students who were assigned their reading material. Essentially, both studies found that unrestricted choice increased positive affective reactions and self-reported interest in the reading experience but had no effect on various cognitive measures of engagement. The results suggest that the effect of choice may depend on what types of tasks are investigated. Even when positive affective reactions are recorded, cognitive outcomes may vary across tasks.

The important implication to be drawn from the above discussion is that caution needs to be exercised when we generalize about individuals' motivation from the short-term, simple tasks frequently used in experimental studies to the longer term, more complex tasks students are required to perform in educational settings.

Timing of Rewards

Providing superfluous tangible rewards (Lepper & Henderlong, chapter 10, this book), either while subjects perform interesting activities or immediately after such performance, creates difficulties from the perspective of both behavioristic and interest research. Supplying a second set of rewards to activities that have their own built-in rewards requires a restructuring and a reordering of reward priorities. Sometimes these will be conflicting priorities. For this conflict to be resolved, the value weightings of different reinforcements or rewards require some changes. Expected tangible rewards may be especially prone to result in forming close associations in the course of changing goals with activities and result in changing existing reward structures. Delayed, unexpected, or verbal rewards may compete with the built-in rewards of activities to a lesser degree and as a result are less likely to change individuals' goals. The very fact that they are "delayed," "unexpected," or "verbal" may provide these rewards with structures that are less likely to generate conflict and consequent change in the valuing of the within-task rewards.

From the perspective of interest research, it is especially problematic to offer tangible rewards during or immediately after short-term interesting activities. Interest theory specifies that when individuals are engaged in tasks that they find interesting, their attention is focused, their cognitive resources are utilised, and they are likely to experience positive affect. The introduction of tangible rewards during such activities is likely to interrupt both the cognitive and the affective processes, divert attention from the task, and introduce a new set of goals to the participants. Rewards given after some time, as opposed to during or immediately following the initial activities, however, might encourage rather than interrupt and/or interfere with individuals performing interesting tasks.

No literature seems to be available on the effect of delayed tangible rewards (Deci, personal communication, 1999), even though the above discussion suggests that delayed tangible rewards may not have the same detrimental effects on intrinsic motivation for performing interesting activities as rewards given concurrently or immediately after task engagements. Future investigations of the effect of delayed tangible rewards on intrinsic motivation to continue activities seem especially important, because in real-life situations such delays are common when individuals get rewarded for their efforts.

Absence of Rewards

On the basis of finding detrimental effects of tangible rewards on individuals performing interesting, short-term, and relatively simple tasks, researchers inferred that in general, the absence of such rewards would positively influence task performance. However, with different types of activities, the lack of rewards may have a different effect on individuals' performance. For example, more complex activities that require focused attention and sustained effort over time may be detrimentally affected by the absence of rewards. Only by examining both the presence and absence of rewards can we understand how they affect individuals' academic motivation and performance.

Although motivational researchers have acknowledged that rewards can have informational aspects with respect to individual competence (see Harackiewicz & Sansone, chapter 4, this book), they have focused on the controlling aspects of rewards. More specifically, the basically negative evaluations of rewards were related to viewing the motivations of the givers of rewards as controlling and manipulating, and to viewing recipients as fully pressured and coerced. However, rewards can be provided for many other reasons. They can be given as demonstrations of appreciation for effort (Deci et al., 1999), hard work, or kindness; they can be provided to elicit momentary excitement and joy or to cause longer-term happiness; and most important, rewards can indicate positive feelings of the giver toward the recipient. These various motivations of individuals who provide rewards may influence the recipients in as yet unexplored ways, beyond control and/or informational feedback. For example, rewards may contribute to individuals' sense of accomplishment.

At the conclusion of their article, Deci et al. (1999) made recommendations as to when and how rewards should be used in real-world settings. They made several important suggestions regarding how rewards could be made more informational and less controlling. Although they acknowledged that through such procedures negative effects of tangible rewards may be reduced, they warned of the unintended consequences of rewards. Specifically, they consider the problem of individuals who do not qualify for rewards. They caution that in the real world, rewards are used to signify competence. People who do not perform up to special standards may consider their failure to receive maximum rewards as highly punishing. Thus rewards may convey not only control but also negative feedback about competence. Lepper and Henderlong (chapter 10, this book) also propose that such rewards as external recognition and grades may be harmful to the motivation of children. They suggest that informational feedback regarding children's strength and weaknesses could be more appropriate than other rewards.

However, there may also be problems involved in not rewarding individuals who work hard, persist in activities that require effort, and expect and qualify for rewards. Negative reactions to the absence of expected and deserved rewards may constitute serious problems for society, as it may diminish the effort and work of some of its most industrious and contributing members. What happens when rewards are withheld? Take an academic—a self-determined, autonomous professor—who has been working on a theory for several years. What kinds of rewards are important to such a person? I propose that the expected rewards include students who seek out opportunities to attend the professor's lectures and to work with him or her on their research project, grant money (which may or may not mean personal financial gains), colleagues who come to hear and applaud his or her conference presentation, and most important, the acceptance of his or her article for publication in a prestigious journal in the field. These rewards are combinations of tangible and intangible rewards and go beyond simply providing competence feedback. What happens if some of these rewards are not forthcoming? In some cases, there are serious negative effects. We all know of a professor who lost his or her enthusiasm, changed research topics, and eventually applied for a job in industry, leaving academia behind. The reality is that academics may not continue working hard, putting in countless hours, and making large sacrifices without being rewarded. Why should we assume that our children will produce high level schoolwork without expecting and receiving rewards?

Rewards and Affect

It has become increasingly more evident that learning cannot be explained by purely rational cognitive factors and that affective variables also play a critical role in knowledge acquisition (e.g., Alexander, 1997; Alexander et al., 1995; Hidi & Baird, 1986, 1988; Pintrich, Marx, & Boyle, 1993). It is therefore puzzling how few studies considered the role of affect in the investigations of the undermining effects of rewards. For example, it is conceivable that rewards that have positive affective outcomes are more likely to have positive effects on motivation than are rewards without such outcomes.

Harackiewicz et al. (1984) proposed that performance-contingent rewards can serve as a symbol of excellence with "cue values" to individuals. They further suggested that such cue value may affect interest directly (i.e., independently of the feedback) by making the evaluative outcome more salient and intensifying the affective significance and the importance of the accomplishment. They have also shown that rewards can promote intrinsic motivation to the extent that they lead individuals to value competence and become emotionally involved in the pursuit of competence (Harackiewicz & Manderlink, 1984; Harackiewicz, Abrahams & Wageman, 1987; Harackiewicz & Sansone, chapter 4, this book)

Pretty and Seligman (1984) considered the role of affect in how rewards influence intrinsic motivation. They proposed that when rewards decrease intrinsic motivation, increased negative affect may have been created. Their results demonstrated that positive affect can alter the way students respond to rewards. More specifically, Pretty and Seligman suggested that only when rewards and feedback are associated with negative affective reactions will the result be a decrease in intrinsic motivation. They further proposed that affect can be created at least in two ways. First, affect might be a direct outcome of the form of reinforcement received, as when positive feedback makes one feel good. Second, the cues used in the experimental treatment may contain strong negative or positive affective elements. Pretty and Seligman concluded that affect may be a basic determinant of intrinsic motivation, one that might be more critical than specific cognitions about self-determination and competency. To investigate this proposition seems critical for motivational research in the 21st century. Harackiewicz and Manderlink (1984) have also shown that rewards can promote intrinsic motivation to the extent that they lead individuals to value competence and become emotionally involved in the pursuit of competence.

The findings of the literature demonstrated that verbal rewards tend to enhance intrinsic motivation. The explanation for this finding has been that verbal rewards provide salient information about individuals' competencies. In other words, the informational value of verbal rewards is seen as the key to their positive effect. The affective reactions of individuals to such rewards, however, may be entirely different than to tangible external rewards such as a dollar. Affective reactions are automatic and individuals may not even be consciously registering them as they occur. If future research were to demonstrate that verbal rewards can indeed generate joy or excitement, or reduce anxiety, more so than tangible rewards, these findings could have far reaching consequences that intrinsic-motivation researchers would need to take into consideration.

CONCLUSIONS

Motivational researchers have criticized behaviorally oriented theorists, such as Eisenberger and Cameron, for advocating the widespread use of performance-contingent and completion-contingent rewards. For example, Deci et al. (1999) argued that on the basis of their meta-analyses "this advocacy is inconsistent with the empirical results indicating clearly that, for interesting activities, performance-contingent rewards have a detrimental effect on free-choice persistence and that completion-contingent rewards have a detrimental effect on both measures of intrinsic motivation" (p. 657). Deci et al. then went on to suggest that their results further indicate that the use of such rewards in schools could be very detrimental to intrinsic motivation. However, the studies included in the metaanalyses may have limited implications for learning in academic settings.

Therefore, it is my contention that recommending the withholding of rewards in schools on the basis of the 128 motivational studies included in the Deci et al. meta-analyses is premature.

Since the 1970s, there has been a momentous shift in the research agenda. The behaviorist model with learning tightly controlled through external rewards is no longer the dominant paradigm. Significant research attention has been given to the rich contribution to learning that comes from personal strivings, and from intrinsic motivation. The same studies have drawn attention to the controlling and negative effects that dependence on external rewards may have for learning. Maybe it is time to shift the agenda toward finding the syntheses of intrinsic and extrinsic motivation that will engage students, especially adolescents, in learning the broad-ranging skills and competencies they need for creative and productive futures.

Acknowledgments

The preparation of this manuscript was partially supported by a grant from the Social Sciences and Humanities Research Council of Canada. I am grateful to Mary Ainley and Ann Renninger for their significant contributions to this manuscript. In addition, my thanks go to Pietro Boscolo, Judith Harackiewicz, and Carole Sansone for their helpful comments. Finally, I acknowledge Dagmar Berndorff, Barbara Dyce, and Maria Medved for their editorial assistance and express my appreciation for their patience in the preparation of this paper.

References

Ainley, M. D. (1994). *Motivation and learning: Psychology and you* (3rd ed.). Victoria, Australia: Hawker Brownlow Education.

Ainley, M. D. (1998). Interest in learning in the disposition of curiosity in secondary students: Investigating process and context. In L. Hoffmann, A. Krapp, K. Renninger, & J. Baumert (Eds.), *Interest and learning: Proceedings of the Seeon Conference on Interest and Gender* (pp. 257–266). Kiel, Germany: IPN.

Ainley, M. D., Hidi, S., & Berndorff, D. (1999). Towards identification of processes mediating the relationship between interest and learning: Individual, situational, and topic interest. *Manuscript submitted for publication.*

Alexander, P. A. (1997). Mapping the multidimensional nature of domain learning: The interplay of cognitive, motivational, and strategic forces. In M. L. Maehr & P. R. Pintrich (Eds.), *Advances in motivation and achievement: Vol. 10.* (pp. 213–250). Greenwich, CT: JAI Press.

Alexander, P. A., Jetton, T. L., & Kulikowich, J. M. (1995). Interrelationship of knowledge, interest, and recall: Assessing a model of domain learning. *Journal of Educational Psychology, 87,* 559–575.

Ames, C. (1992). Classrooms: Goals, structures, and student motivation. *Journal of Educational Psychology, 84,* 261–271.

Anderman, E. M., & Maehr, M. L. (1994). Motivation and schooling in the middle grades. *Review of Educational Research, 64,* 287–309.

Arnold, H. J. (1976). Effects of performance feedback and extrinsic reward upon high intrinsic motivation. *Organizational behavior and human performance, 17,* 275–288.

Bandura, A. (1977a). Self-efficacy: Toward a unifying theory of behavior change. *Psychological Review, 84,* 191–215.

Bandura, A. (1977b). *Social learning theory.* Englewood Cliffs, NJ: Prentice-Hall.

Bandura, A. (1986). *Social foundations of thought and action: A social cognitive theory.* Englewood Cliffs, NJ: Prentice-Hall.

Baumert, J. & Koller, O. (1998). Interest research in secondary level I: An overview. In L. Hoffmann, A. Krapp, K. Renninger, & J. Baumert (Eds.), *Interest and learning: Proceedings of the Seeon Conference on Interest and Gender* (pp. 241–256). Kiel, Germany: IPN.

Bergin, D. A. (1999). Influences on classroom interest. *Educational Psychologist, 34,* 87–98.

Berlyne, D. E. (1960). *Conflict, arousal, and curiosity.* New York: McGraw-Hill.

Berlyne, D. E. (1966). Curiosity and exploration. *Science, 153,* 25–33.

Calder, B. J., & Staw, B. M. (1975). Self-perception of intrinsic and extrinsic motivation. *Journal of Personality and Social Psychology, 31,* 599–605.

Cameron, J., & Pierce, W. D. (1994). Reinforcement, reward, and intrinsic motivation: A meta-analysis. *Review of Educational Research, 64*(3), 363–423.

Cordova, D. I., & Lepper, M. R. (1996). Intrinsic motivation and the process of learning: Beneficial effects of contextualization, personalization, and choice. *Journal of Educational Psychology, 88,* 715–730.

Deci, E. L. (1975). *Intrinsic motivation.* New York: Plenum.

Deci, E. L. (1992). The relation of interest to the motivation of behavior: A self-determination of theory perspective. In K. A. Renninger, S. Hidi, & A. Krapp (Eds.), *The role of interest in learning and development* (pp. 43–70). Hillsdale, NJ: Erlbaum.

Deci, E. L. (1998). The relation of interest to motivation and human needs—the self-determination theory viewpoint. In L. Hoffmann, A. Krapp, K. Renninger, & J. Baumert (Eds.), *Interest and learning: Proceedings of the Seeon Conference on Interest and Gender* (pp. 146–163). Kiel, Germany: IPN.

Deci, E. L., Koestner, R., & Ryan, R. M. (1999). A meta-analytic review of experiments examining the effects of extrinsic rewards on intrinsic motivation. *Psychological Bulletin, 125,* 627–668.

Deci, E. L., & Ryan, R. M. (1985). *Intrinsic motivation and self-determination in human behavior.* New York: Plenum Press.

Dewey, J. (1913). *Interest and effort in education.* Boston: Riverside Press.

Dweck, C. S., & Leggett, E. L. (1988). A social-cognitive approach to motivation and personality. *Psychological Review, 95,* 256–273.

Eccles, J. S., & Midgley, C. (1990). Changes in academic motivation and self-perceptions during early adolescence. In R. Montemayor, G. R. Adams, & T. P. Gullotta (Eds.), *Advances in adolescent development: Vol. 2. From childhood to adolescence* (pp. 134–155). Newbury Park, CA: Sage Publications.

Eccles, J. S., Wigfield, A., & Schiefele, U. (1998). Motivation to succeed. In N. Eisenberg (Ed.), *Social, emotional, and personality development in handbook of child psychology* (Vol. III, pp. 1017–1095). New York: Wiley.

Eisenberger, R., & Cameron, J. (1996). Detrimental effects of reward: Reality or myth? *American Psychologist, 51,* 1153–1166.

Erikson, E. H. (1968). *Identity, youth, and crisis.* New York: Norton.

Farnham-Diggory, S. (1994). Paradigms of knowledge and instruction. *Review of Educational Research, 64,* 463–477.

Fay, A. L. (1998). The impact of CRO on children's interest in and comprehension of science and technology. In L. Hoffmann, A. Krapp, K. Renninger, & J. Baumert (Eds.), *Interest and learning: Proceedings of the Seeon Conference on interest and gender* (pp. 205–214). Kiel, Germany: IPN.

Fazio, R. H. (1981). On the self-perception explanation of the overjustification effect: The role of the salience of initial attitude. *Journal of Experimental Social Psychology, 17,* 417–426.

Follings-Albers, M., & Hartinger, A. (1998). Interest of girls and boys in elementary school. In L. Hoffmann, A. Krapp, K. Renninger, & J. Baumert (Eds.), *Interest and learning: Proceedings of the Seeon Conference on Interest and Gender* (pp. 175–183). Kiel, Germany: IPN.

Gambell, T. J. (1993). From experience to literary response: Actualizing readers through the response process. In S. Straw & D. Bogdan (Eds.), *Constructive reading: Teaching beyond communication* (pp. 30–45). Portsmouth, NH: Heinemann.

Gambrell, L. B. & Marinak, B. A. (1997). Incentives and intrinsic motivation to read. In J. T. Guthrie & A. Wigfield (Eds.), *Reading engagement: Motivating readers through integrated instruction* (pp. 205–217). Newark, DE: International Reading Association.

Goodlad, J. I. (1984). *A place called school: Prospects for the future.* New York: McGraw-Hill Book Co.

Graber, W. (1998). Schooling for lifelong attention to chemistry issues: The role of interest and achievement. In L. Hoffmann, A. Krapp, K. Renninger, & J. Baumert (Eds.), *Interest and learning: Proceedings of the Seeon Conference on Interest and Gender* (pp. 290–300). Kiel, Germany: IPN.

Green-Demers, I., Pelletier, L. G., Stewart, D. G., & Gushue, N. R. (1998). Coping with the less interesting aspects of training: Toward a model of interest and motivation enhancement in individual sports. *Basic and Applied Social Psychology, 20*(4), 251–261.

Guthrie, J. T., & Wigfield, A. (in press). Engagement and motivation in reading. *Handbook of reading research.* III.

Haladyna, T., & Thomas, G. (1979). The attitudes of elementary school children toward school and subject matters. *Journal of Experimental Education, 48,* 18–23.

Harackiewicz, J. M., Abrahams, S., & Wageman, R. (1987). Performance evaluation and intrinsic motivation: The effects of evaluative focus, rewards, and achievement orientation. *Journal of Personality and Social Psychology, 53,* 1015–1023.

Harackiewicz, J. M., Barron, K. E., & Elliot, A. J. (1998). Rethinking achievement goals: When are they adaptive for college students and why? *Educational Psychologist, 33,* 1–21.

Harackiewicz, J. M., Barron, K. E., Tauer, J. M., Carter, S. M. & Elliot, A. J. (in press). Short-term and long-term consequences of achievement goals: Predicting interest and performance over time. *Journal of Educational Psychology.*

Harackiewicz, J. M., & Manderlink, G. (1984). A process analysis of the effects of performance-contingent rewards on intrinsic motivation. *Journal of Experimental Social Psychology*, 20, 531–551.

Harackiewicz, J. M., Manderlink, G., & Sansone, C. (1984). Rewarding pinball wizardry: Effects of evaluation and cue value on intrinsic interest. *Journal of Personality and Social Psychology*, 47(2), 287–300.

Harp, S. F., & Mayer, R. E. (1997). The role of interest in learning from scientific text and illustrations: On the distinction between emotional interest and cognitive interest. *Journal of Educational Psychology*, 89(1), 92–102.

Harter, S. (1981). A new self-report scale of intrinsic versus extrinsic orientation in the classroom: Motivational and informational components. *Developmental Psychology*, 17, 300–312.

Harter, S. (1990). Causes, correlates and the functional role of global self-worth. A life-span perspective. In J. Kolligian & R. Sternberg (Eds.), *Perceptions of competence and incompetence across the life-span* (pp. 67–98). New Haven, CT: Yale University Press.

Heckhausen, H. (1968). Achievement motive research: Current problems and some contributions towards a general theory of motivation. In W. J. Arnold (Ed.), *Nebraska Symposium on Motivation: Vol.* (pp. 103–174). Lincoln: University of Nebraska Press.

Hidi, S. (1990). Interest and its contribution as a mental resource for learning. *Review of Educational Research*, 60, 549–571.

Hidi, S. (1995). A re-examination of the role of attention in learning from text. *Educational Psychology Review*, 7, 323–350.

Hidi, S., & Anderson, V. (1992). Situational interest and its impact on reading and expository writing. In K. A. Renninger, S. Hidi, & A. Krapp (Eds.), *The role of interest in learning and development* (pp. 215–238). Hillsdale, NJ: Erlbaum.

Hidi, S., & Baird, W. (1986). Interestingness—a neglected variable in discourse processing. *Cognitive Science*, 10, 179–194.

Hidi, S., & Baird, W. (1988). Strategies for increasing text-based interest and students' recall of expository texts. *Reading Research Quarterly*, 23, 465–483.

Hidi, S., & Berndorff, D. (1998). Situational interest and learning. In L. Hoffmann, A. Krapp, K. Renninger, & J. Baumert (Eds.), *Interest and learning: Proceedings of the Seeon Conference on Interest and Gender* (pp. 74–90). Kiel, Germany: IPN.

Hidi, S., & Harackiewicz, J. (2000). Motivating the academically unmotivated: A critical issue for the 21st century. *Review of Educational Research*.

Hidi, S., & McLaren J. (1990). The effect of topic and theme interestingness on the production of school expositions. In H. Mandl, E. De Corte, N. Bennet, & H. F. Friedrich (Eds.), *Learning and instruction: European research in an international context* (vol. 2.2). Oxford, UK: Pergamon Press.

Hidi, S., & McLaren J. (1991). Motivational factors and writing: The role of topic interestingness. *European Journal of Psychology of Education*, 6(2), 187–197.

Hoffmann, L., & Haussler, P. (1998). An intervention project promoting girls' and boys' interest in physics. In L. Hoffmann, A. Krapp, K. Renninger, & J. Baumert (Eds.), *Interest and learning: Proceedings of the Seeon Conference on Interest and Gender* (pp. 301–316). Kiel, Germany: IPN.

Hunt, J. M. V. (1965). Intrinsic motivation and its role in psychological development. In D. Levine (Ed.), *Nebraska Symposium on Motivation: Vol.* 13. (pp. 189–282). Lincoln: University of Nebraska Press.

Iran-Nejad, A. (1987). Cognitive and affective causes of interest and liking. *Journal of Educational Psychology*, 7, 120–130.

Jacobs, J. E., Finken, L. L., Lindsley Griffin, L. N., & Wright, J. D. (1998). The career plans of science-talented rural adolescent girls. *American Educational Research Journal*, 35(4), 681–704.

Karniol, R., & Ross, M. (1977). The effects of performance-relevant and performance-irrelevant rewards on motivation. *Child Development*, 48, 482–487.

Kintsch, W. (1980). Learning from text, levels of comprehension, or: Why anyone would read a story anyway. *Poetics*, 9, 87–98.

Kohn, A. (1993). *Punished by rewards*. Boston: Houghton Mifflin.

Koller, O. (1998). Different aspects of learning motivation: The impact of interest and goal orientation on scholastic learning. In L. Hoffmann, A. Krapp, K. Renninger, & J. Baumert (Eds.) 1998. *Interest and learning: Proceedings of the Seeon Conference on Interest and Gender* (pp. 317–326). Kiel, Germany: IPN.

Krapp, A. (1998). Interest, motivation and learning: An educational-psychological perspective. *European Journal of Psychology of Education, 14*, 23–40.

Krapp, A., & Fink, B. (1992). The development and function of interests during the critical transition from home to preschool. In R. A. Renninger, S. Hidi, & A. Krapp (Eds.), *The role of interest in learning and development* (pp. 397–429). Hillsdale, NJ: Erlbaum.

Krapp, A., Hidi, S., & Renninger, A. (1992). Interest, learning and development. In R. A. Renninger, S. Hidi, & A. Krapp (Eds.), *The role of interest in learning and development* (pp. 3–25). Hillsdale, NJ: Erlbaum.

Kruglanski, A. W. (1975). The endogenous–exogenous partition in attribution theory. *Psychological Review, 82*(6), 387–406.

Lepper, M. R. (1985). Microcomputers in education: Motivational and social issues. *American Psychologist, 40*, 1–18.

Lepper, M. R., & Cordova, D. I. (1992). A desire to be taught: Instructional consequences of intrinsic motivation. *Motivation and Emotion, 16*, 187–208.

Lepper, M. R., & Greene, D. (Eds.) (1978). *The hidden costs of reward.* Hillsdale, NJ: Erlbaum.

Lepper, M. R., Greene, D., & Nisbett, R. E. (1973). Undermining children's intrinsic interest with extrinsic rewards: A test of the "overjustification" hypothesis. *Journal of Personality and Social Psychology, 28*, 129–137.

Lepper, M. R., Sethi, S., Dialdin, D., & Drake, M. (1997). Intrinsic and extrinsic motivation: A developmental perspective. In S. S. Luthar, J. A. Burack, D. Cicchetti, & J. R. Weisz (Eds.), *Developmental psychopathology: Perspectives on adjustment, risk, and disorder* (pp. 23–50). New York: Cambridge University Press.

Miller, R. B., Greene, B. A., Montalvo, G. P., Ravindran, B., & Nichols, J. D. (1996). Engagement in academic work: The role of learning goals, future consequences, pleasing others, and perceived ability. *Contemporary Educational Psychology, 21*, 388–422.

Mitchell, M. (1993). Situational interest: Its multifaceted structure in the secondary school mathematics classroom. *Journal of Educational Psychology, 85*, 424–436.

Murphy, P. K., & Alexander, P. A. (2000). A motivated exploration of motivation terminology. *Contemporary Educational Psychology, 25*(1), 3–53.

Neumann, A. (1999, April). *Passionate talk about passionate thought: The view from professors at early midcareer.* Paper presented at the annual meeting of the American Educational Research Association, Montreal, Canada.

Piaget, J. (1940). The mental development of the child. In D. Elkind (Ed.), *Six psychological studies.* New York: Random House.

Pintrich, R. (2000). An achievement goal theory perspective on issues in motivation terminology, theory, and research. *Contemporary Educational Psychology, 25*(1), 92–104.

Pintrich, P. R., Marx, R. W., & Boyle, R. A. (1993). Beyond cold conceptual change: The role of motivational beliefs and classroom contextual factors in the process of conceptual change. *Review of Educational Research, 63*, 167–199.

Prenzel, M. (1988, April). *Task persistence and interest.* In U. Schiefele (Chair), Content and interest as motivated factors in learning. Symposium conducted at the annual meeting of the American Educational Research Association, New Orleans.

Prenzel, M. (1992). The selective persistence of interest. In R. A. Renninger, S. Hidi, & A. Krapp (Eds.), *The role of interest in learning and development* (pp. 71–98). Hillsdale, NJ: Erlbaum.

Pretty, G. H., & Seligman, C. (1984). Affect and the overjustification effect. *Journal of Personality and Social Psychology, 46*(6), 1241–1253.

Rathunde, K. (1993). The experience of interest: A theoretical and empirical look at its role in adolescent talent development. In P. Pintrich & M. Maehr (Eds.), *Advances in motivation and achievement* (vol. 8, pp. 59–98), Greenwich, CT: JAI Press.

Rathunde, K. (1998). Undivided and abiding interest: Comparisons across studies of talented adolescents and creative adults. In L. Hoffmann, A., Krapp, K. Renninger, & J. Baumert (Eds.), *Interest and learning: Proceedings of the Seeon Conference on Interest and Gender* (pp. 367–376). Kiel, Germany: IPN.

Rathunde, K., & Csikszentmihalyi, M. (1993). Undivided interest and the growth of talent: A longitudinal study of adolescents. *Journal of Youth and Adolescence, 22*, 1–21.

Renninger, A. (1989). Individual patterns in children's play interests. In L. T. Winegar (Ed.), *Social interaction and the development of children's understanding* (pp. 147–172). Norwood, NJ: Ablex.

Renninger, K. A. (1990). Children's play interests, representation, and activity. In R. Fivush & J. Hudson (Eds.), *Knowing and remembering in young children* (pp. 127–165). Emory Cognition Series (Vol. III). Cambridge, MA: Cambridge University Press.

Renninger, A. (1992). Individual interest and development: Implications for theory and practice. In A. Renninger, S. Hidi, & A. Krapp (Eds.), *The role of interest in learning and development* (pp. 361–395). Hillsdale, NJ: Erlbaum.

Renninger, K. A. (1998). The roles of individual interest(s) and gender in learning: An overview of research on preschool and elementary school–aged children/students. In L. Hoffmann, A., Krapp, K. Renninger, & J. Baumert (Eds.), *Interest and learning: Proceedings of the Seeon Conference on Interest and Gender* (pp. 165–175). Kiel, Germany: IPN.

Renninger, A., Hidi, S., & Krapp, A. (Eds.). (1992). *The role of interest in learning and development.* Hillsdale, NJ: Erlbaum.

Renninger, K. A., Hoffmann, L., & Krapp, A. (1998). Interest and gender: Issues of development and learning. In L. Hoffmann, A. Krapp, K. Renninger, & J. Baumert (Eds.), *Interest and learning: Proceedings of the Seeon Conference on Interest and Gender* (pp. 9–21). Kiel, Germany: IPN.

Renninger, K. A., & Wozniak, R. H. (1985). Effect of interest on attention shift, recognition, and recall in young children. *Developmental Psychology, 21*, 624–632.

Rheinberg (1989). *Zweck Und Tätigkeit.* Gottingen: Hogrefe.

Rheinberg, F. (1998). Theory of interest and research on motivation to learn. In L. Hoffmann, A. Krapp, K. Renninger, & J. Baumert (Eds.), *Interest and learning: Proceedings of the Seeon Conference on Interest and Gender* (pp. 126–145). Kiel, Germany: IPN.

Rigby, C. S., Deci, E. L., Patrick, B. C., & Ryan, R. M. (1992). Beyond the intrinsic–extrinsic dichotomy: Self-determination in motivation and learning. *Motivation and Emotion, 16*, 165–185.

Sansone, C., & Morgan, C. (1992). Intrinsic motivation and education: Competence in context. *Motivation and Emotion, 16*, 249–270.

Schank, R. C. (1979). Interestingness: Controlling inferences. *Artificial Intelligence, 12*, 273–297.

Schiefele, U. (1991). Interest, learning, and motivation. *Educational Psychologist, 26*, 299–323.

Schiefele, U. (1992). Topic interest and levels of text comprehension. In R. A. Renninger, S. Hidi, & A. Krapp (Eds.), *The role of interest in learning and development* (pp. 151–182). Hillsdale, NJ: Erlbaum.

Schiefele, U. (1996). Topic interest, text representation, and quality of experience. *Contemporary Educational Psychology, 12*, 3–18.

Schiefele, U. (1998). Individual interest and learning, what we know and what we don't know. In L. Hoffmann, A. Krapp, K. Renninger, and J. Baumert (Eds.), *Interest and learning: Proceedings of the Seeon Conference on Interest and Gender* (pp. 91–104). Kiel, Germany: IPN.

Schiefele, U. (1999). Interest and learning from text. *Scientific Studies of Reading, 3*, 257–279.

Schiefele, H., Hausser, K., & Schneider, G. (1979). "Interesse" als Ziel und Weg der Erziehung. Überlegungen zu einem vernachläßigten padagogischen Konzept. *Zeitschrift fur Padagogik, 25*, 1–20.

Schiefele, U., & Krapp, A. (1996). Topic interest and free recall of expository text. *Learning and Individual Differences, 8*, 141–160.

Schraw, G., & Dennison, R. S. (1994). The effect of reader purpose on interest and recall. *Journal of Reading Behavior, 26*, 1–18.

Schraw, G., Flowerdale, T., & Reisetter, M. F. (1998). The role of choice in reader engagement. *Journal of Educational Psychology, 90*(4), 705–714.

Shernoff, D., Schneider, B., & Csikszentmihalyi, M. (1999, April). *The quality of learning experiences in American classrooms: Toward a phenomenology of student engagement.* Paper presented at the annual meeting of the American Educational Research Association, Montreal, Canada.

Tobias, S. (1994). Interest, prior knowledge, and learning. *Review of Educational Research, 64,* 37–54.

Todt, E., & Schreiber, S. (1998). Development of interests. In L. Hoffmann, A. Krapp, K. Renninger, & J. Baumert (Eds.), *Interest and learning: Proceedings of the Seeon Conference on Interest and Gender* (pp. 25–40). Kiel, Germany: IPN.

Urdan, T. C., & Maehr, M. L. (1995). Beyond a two-goal theory of motivation and achievement: A case for social goals. *Review of Educational Research, 65*(3), 213–243.

White, R. W. (1959). Motivation reconsidered: The concept of competence. *Psychological Review, 66,* 297–333.

Wigfield, A., & Eccles, J. S. (1992). The development of achievement task values: A theoretical analysis. *Developmental Review, 12,* 265–310.

Zimmerman, B. J. (1985). The development of "intrinsic" motivation: A social learning analysis. *Annals of Child Development, 2,* 117–160.

Zimmerman, B. J. (1995). Self-efficacy and educational development. In A. Bandura (Ed.), *Self-efficacy in changing societies* (pp. 202–231). New York: Cambridge University Press.

Zimmerman, B. J., & Kitsantas, A. (1999). Acquiring writing revision skill: Shifting from process to outcome self-regulatory goals. *Journal of Educational Psychology, 91,* 1–10.

Zuckerman, M., Porac, J., Lathin, D., Smith, R., & Deci, E. L. (1978). On the importance of self-determination for intrinsically-motivated behavior. *Personality and Social Psychology Bulletin, 4,* 443–446.

chapter 12

Interest and Self-Regulation: The Relation between Having To and Wanting To

CAROL SANSONE
JESSI L. SMITH
Department of Psychology
University of Utah

Mary, Tony, and Robert are taking an English literature class on British writers. They have an essay due the next day on the topic of John Donne's influence as a metaphysical poet. That evening, Mary sits in her room and stares at the blank page in front of her. She flips on the television and starts watching Jerry Springer instead. Across the hall, Tony reminds himself that to maintain his grade point average (GPA), he needs to do a good job on his essay. He sits down and immediately begins working on the assignment. In the meantime, Robert arranges to meet up with a friend from the class at the student union. Over hamburgers, Robert and his friend talk about what a lame assignment it is, the meaning of *metaphysical*, John Donne's influence, and how much they like the class instructor. They then spend the next several hours alternating between writing their essays and continuing to talk.

Mary, Tony, and Robert are faced with the same ostensible activity: an essay due on John Donne. However, their responses to that assignment are very different. According to traditional approaches, none of these students would be considered to be intrinsically motivated to perform the activity. Whether and how they do the assignment, therefore, depends on their level of extrinsic motivation. On the basis of their behavior, we would infer that Tony's is high, Mary's is low, and Robert's is somewhere in the middle.

Rather than considering behavior as either intrinsically or extrinsically motivated, however, we consider the behavior of these three students to demonstrate the alternatives when attempting to regulate motivation in day-to-day life. Self-regulatory perspectives typically focus on performance of an activity as a means to achieve some goal or end. In contrast, to qualify as intrinsic motivation, many researchers propose that performance of the activity needs to be an end in and of itself. As a result, intrinsic motivation is often discussed in terms of a particular class of activities, restricted to optimal conditions that are relatively rare in everyday life.

We consider intrinsic motivation to be a process as well as an outcome, however, and propose that it is a process embedded in our everyday regulation of behavior. Motivation to perform goal-directed actions at a given point in time may depend on whether we "feel like it"—that is, on the degree to which we experience interest and enjoyment. We expect that this phenomenological experience may become the more proximal motivator for persistence and subsequent engagement, particularly for activities that take place over the long term (Harackiewicz, Barron, Tauer, Carter, & Elliot, in press; Jacobs, Finken, Griffin, & Wright, 1998; Morgan, Isaac, & Sansone, 1999; Rathunde & Csikszentmihalyi, 1993). For example, although Tony is sufficiently motivated by the goal of maintaining his GPA to start work on the essay, will this motivation be sufficient to keep him reading, thinking, and writing about John Donne's poetry beyond this assignment, class, or degree?

Our perspective suggests that to maintain performance, we need to regulate both outcome-oriented motivation and process-oriented motivation. For example, Mary does not appear to be sufficiently motivated by either the potential outcome (her grade) or by interest in John Donne's poetry to work on her assignment. Tony is sufficiently motivated by his GPA to work on his essay but appears to have no interest in the topic. In contrast, of the three, Robert may in fact experience the greatest interest, because he has chosen to perform the activity in a way that makes the experience more interesting for him (discussing the essay and other topics with a friend). Robert may thus be the only one who is likely to voluntarily read John Donne, or other poets, in the future.

Our example illustrates several important points. First, it suggests that being motivated by the experience of interest can be important even when individuals see the activity as a means to some outcome. Moreover, interest may depend on aspects of the "activity" that are not an ostensible part of the task and that do not involve feelings of efficacy and control over the environment (e.g., White, 1959)—for example, discussing the essay and other topics with a classmate.

In this chapter, we describe our model that attempts to bridge research on self-regulation and intrinsic motivation. From our perspective, it is difficult to identify an intrinsically motivated "activity" or "person," because in addition to being an important outcome, intrinsic motivation can be part of the *process* of pursuing another goal, or multiple goals, over time. In contrast to definitions that focus on underlying needs (e.g., Ryan & Deci, chapter 2, this book) or a unitary relationship between a goal and activity (Shah & Kruglanski, chapter 5, this book), we consider individuals to be intrinsically motivated when their behavior is motivated by the *actual, anticipated, or sought experience of interest.* In our research, we examine how this motivation can be embedded in goal striving over time.

MODEL OF THE SELF-REGULATION OF MOTIVATION PROCESS

Figure 12.1 represents a schematic drawing of the theoretical model that has continued to evolve (Harackiewicz & Sansone, chapter 4, this book; Harackiewicz & Sansone, 1991; Sansone & Harackiewicz, 1996; Sansone, Sachau & Weir, 1989). In this model, we portray interest as an inherent and critical component of the self-regulation process.

The left-hand side of the figure illustrates the part of the self-regulation process that occurs within the individual. The right-hand side of the figure illustrates the potential impact of the context at various points in the process. In the middle lies the "activity," which encompasses an individual's actions over time (Vygotsky, 1978). As we have attempted to illustrate, we believe that the activity is composed of the actions resulting from the transactions among an individual's goals, task characteristics, and the context in which the person performs the activity at a particular point in time (e.g., Higgins, Lee, Kwon & Trope, 1995; Higgins, Trope & Kwon, 1999; Sansone, Sachau, & Weir, 1989). Thus, the "activity" is only partially defined by objective task characteristics.

Moreover, we propose that the nature of the activity can change over time, to incorporate individuals' subsequent actions that result from intentional strategies, emotional responses, feedback, and so on. The ostensible same activity can thus differ because of both the particular context and goals of the individual going into the activity, as well as because of processes that emerge once the activity has begun. To understand Mary's, Tony's, and Robert's motivation to write about John Donne, therefore, we need to locate the external demand of the essay assignment within their larger self-regulation process.

Characteristics of the individual and of the context are proposed to influence the goals that individuals bring to an activity. As first defined in Harackiewicz and Sansone (1991), the level of goals that are most proximal to performance of an activity are target goals and purpose goals. Target goals include behavioral referents specific to that activity at a given point in time (e.g., complete the essay on John Donne). Purpose goals operate at a higher level, representing the reasons for behavior (e.g., to achieve a good

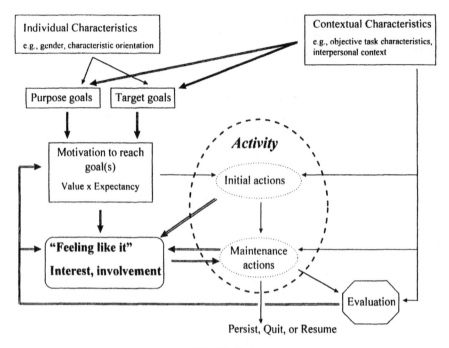

FIGURE 12.1
Self-regulation model. The left-hand side of the figure illustrates the part
of the process that occurs within the individual; the right-hand side of the
figure illustrates the role of the context at various points in the process. In
the middle lies the "activity," which is composed of the actions resulting
from the transaction among an individual's goals, task characteristics, and
the context in which the person performs the activity at a particular point
in time. Double lines indicate relationships that may be moderated by
individual characteristics.

grade). Purpose goals can be relevant to multiple activities. These purpose
goals could be different kinds of achievement goals (e.g., to master a skill,
to outperform others) but can also include non–competence-related goals
(e.g., to have fun, to connect to another person).

Higher-level individual differences such as personality characteristics
(e.g., conscientiousness [Costa & McCrae, 1991]), characteristic motivational
orientations (e.g., approach- and avoidance achievement orientation [Elliot
& Church, 1997]), cognitive beliefs (e.g., entity or malleable theories of intelligence [Molden & Dweck, chapter 6, this book]), and individual interests
(Renninger, chapter 13, this book), contribute to the purpose and target goals
adopted in a particular situation. Similarly, broad, higher-level contextual
factors, such as culture and socioeconomic status, as well as lower-level contextual variables, such as a class assignment or the presence of other people,

can prompt adoption of particular purpose goals and target goals at a given point in time. Mary, Tony, and Robert may thus have different goals even though they face the same situation (an essay due in their class).

Even if they do have similar goals, however, whether these goals motivate behavior depends on the degree to which the individuals value the goals and believe that it is possible to reach these goals. Like other expectancy–value formulations (e.g., Bandura, 1986; Eccles, 1983; Jacobs & Eccles, chapter 14, this book), therefore, this level of the model suggests that goals may differ in their motivating potential across individuals or within individuals across time. In our example, Mary and Tony may both have the goal of getting a good grade in their class, but the goal is more important to Tony. Thus, the motivation to reach this goal was of sufficient magnitude for Tony but not for Mary to begin work on the essay.

A critical difference from other self-regulation perspectives is our hypotheses about the process once the activity has begun. As noted in our initial example, we expect that the experience of interest and enjoyment may become the more proximal motivator for persistence and subsequent engagement, particularly for activities that take place over the long term. Like many researchers, we define *interest* as a phenomenological experience involving both cognitive and affective components. Attention is directed and focused, and the general affective tone is positive. At its extreme, this may be experienced as "flow" (Csikszentmihalyi, 1975). As such, our definition of interest is closer to "situational" (see Hidi, chapter 11, this book) than "individual" (see Renninger, chapter 13, this book) interest.

The motivation to reach the goals is one factor that can directly contribute to this experience of interest (Renninger, chapter 13, this volume). For example, Tony may actually find thinking about John Donne's poetry more interesting because his concern about the assignment led him to become more involved in the task. The experience of interest also arises from the actions associated with performance of the activity. As illustrated in the figure, these actions are influenced by contextual characteristics, such as objective task demands. However, these actions are also influenced by the individual's goals, which can lead an individual to perform the activity in goal congruent ways.[1]

---

[1] Although we have focused on the case of approaching a desired outcome, we would expect a similar process to work when individuals are striving to avoid a negative outcome (e.g., Elliot & Church, 1997; Higgins, 1997). For example, greater motivation to reach the goal of avoiding a negative outcome could negatively affect interest both directly (because of greater anxiety [e.g, Elliot & McGregor, 1999]) and indirectly (through actions that correspond to an avoidance regulatory focus [e.g., Shah, Higgins, & Friedman, 1998]). Moreover, for clarity's sake we have illustrated only the goal-mediated effects for individual characteristics. However, these characteristics could affect actions directly (e.g., people may engage in habitual behaviors in a given situation that are not specifically or consciously goal directed. See Bargh and Chartrand, 1999). Even when initial actions are not goal directed, however, we suggest that they can affect the phenomenological experience and, thereby, the self-regulation process.

The degree of interest experienced while performing can influence subsequent actions ("maintenance actions"). For example, if interest level is not sufficient, individuals may actively engage in strategies that make performance more interesting (Sansone, Weir, Harpster & Morgan, 1992), even if they are not required by the task. In our example, Robert's decision to meet with a classmate might have made performing the assignment more interesting. However, Robert might not have been as thorough or as quick in completing the essay as he would have if he were working alone. Individuals may thus engage in strategies to regulate interest even when they come at a cost to immediate performance (Sansone et al., 1992). On the other hand, had Robert *not* chosen to meet with his classmate, he might have been more likely to choose Mary's option and watched Jerry Springer instead.

Figure 12.1 also illustrates the multiple points at which the context can affect this process. In addition to influencing individuals' goals, the context can directly constrain or shape individuals' initial actions as well as their maintenance actions. In our example, the instructor's assignment created the initial demand and defined the task as an analytical approach to understanding John Donne's poetry (i.e., his influence as a metaphysical poet). The instructor might also monitor progress (e.g., have students meet with him or her weekly) and provide evaluative feedback on the essay once it is completed.

Evaluation is illustrated in the lower right-hand corner of Figure 12.1. We suggest that whether evaluation comes from the context (e.g., the instructor's feedback) or through the person's own behaviors, the evaluation outcome can feed back into both the motivation to reach the goal as well as the phenomenological experience. This cycle can continue until the person decides to quit, continue, or resume the activity. This cyclic process contributes to the situational and individual characteristics that operate at a later time, including potential individual interest in the activity. For example, although Robert might have begun with no interest in John Donne's poetry, after discussing the poetry with his classmate he might develop both sufficient knowledge and value of the subject matter to develop a more enduring individual interest in John Donne's poetry or in poetry more generally (Renninger, chapter 13, this volume).

The double lines in Figure 12.1 illustrate another important dimension that accounts for variability in the process. Specifically, these lines indicate relationships among these variables that may be moderated by individual differences. For example, individuals with an incremental theory of intelligence may respond to feedback that they had received a grade of B on the essay with an increase in motivation to do well in the subject, whereas individuals with an entity theory may respond to the same feedback with lowered motivation. These students may consequently experience different interest and engage in different motivational strategies in response to the same competence feedback.

Our model thus suggests that motivation to reach some outcome goal and motivation to experience interest may both be necessary for an activity to be performed on a regular basis. The prototypic "extrinsically motivated" activity may be one entirely motivated by the desire to achieve some outcome goal; in contrast, the prototypic "intrinsically motivated" activity may be one motivated entirely by interest. In reality, however, most of our everyday activities are motivated by both kinds of motivation, and these motivations can work together or in opposing ways to direct and energize our behavior. We thus believe it is essential to understand the relation between outcome-focused and process-focused motivation over time.

GOAL CONGRUENCE AND INTEREST

Goals direct individuals' orientation toward the activity. In our perspective, intrinsic motivation can potentially occur with a variety of goals and is not necessarily limited to those times when individuals approach an activity with the process goal of experiencing interest (Csikszentmihalyi, 1975) or to satisfy needs for autonomy (deCharms, 1968; Deci & Ryan, 1985a) or competence (Bandura, 1982; Deci & Ryan, 1985a; White, 1959). The key to a particular goal's effect is whether it is associated with performing the activity in a way that is involving and interesting for the person.

There is a potential motivational dilemma implied by this orienting feature of goals, however. If goals are not congruent with each other, or if goal-relevant actions are constrained by the environment, interest may be reduced (e.g., Harackiewicz & Elliot, 1998; Sansone et al., 1989). We next review evidence for the role of goal congruence when goals are defined in terms of achievement and when goals are defined in terms of other people.

Empirical Support for Goal Congruence and Interest: The Case of Competence Goals

Many theories about intrinsic motivation propose that positive competence feedback will enhance interest in the activity because feeling competent is an important basis of intrinsic motivation (e.g., Bandura, 1982; Deci & Ryan, 1985a; White, 1959). Sansone and colleagues suggested that being and feeling competent at an activity might be a necessary but not sufficient factor to create or enhance interest in an activity. That is, although incompetence may make an activity uninteresting, being or feeling competent may enhance interest only if attaining competence was the primary goal of the person's engagement.

For example, in several studies Sansone and colleagues employed activities that could be interesting because they allow satisfaction of skill goals *and/or* because they allow satisfaction of other goals (satisfying curiosity, becoming involved in fantasy adventures). They then systematically varied whether the skill component was highlighted and whether individuals received competence-related feedback (e.g., normative standards showing good performance, tips on how to score more points). They found that competence-related feedback was associated with greater interest primarily when skill goals were emphasized at the outset. When nonskill goals were salient (e.g., getting involved in a computer fantasy adventure), the same competence-related feedback could have no effect or even a negative effect compared with receiving no feedback (Sansone, 1986; 1989; Sansone et al., 1989).

These results suggested that the match between individuals' primary activity goals and the feedback they received from the context was a better predictor of interest than was the nature of the goals themselves. Sansone et al. (1989) also found that this matching effect on subsequent intrinsic motivation was mediated by the degree of positive affect (e.g., excitement) experienced while performing the task. These studies did not examine whether match or mismatch affected individuals' actions as they performed the activity, though Sansone et al. (1989) found that individuals became more likely to define the activity in terms of competence-related dimensions when the context emphasized skill goals. These findings suggest that the "activity" can change even when presumably objective task demands remain constant. Moreover, they imply that what is "intrinsic" to an activity can change as a function of individuals' goals as they approach and begin to perform the activity.

Rather than focus on the presence or absence of competence-related goals, research by Harackiewicz, Elliot, and colleagues examined goal congruence among different kinds of achievement goals (performance goals and mastery goals), and as moderated by individual differences in achievement orientation (Elliot & Harackiewicz, 1994; Harackiewicz & Elliot, 1993; 1998). In contrast to research suggesting that mastery goals are associated with intrinsic and performance goals are associated with extrinsic motivation, they found that congruence among achievement goals was a more important predictor of interest in the activity than was the type of achievement goal. For example, Harackiewicz and Elliot (1998) examined the effects of match between performance purpose goals and performance target goals on intrinsic motivation. They found that mastery target goals enhanced interest relative to performance target goals in a neutral achievement context (playing pinball, with no additional information). When the context cued performance purpose goals for playing pinball, however, performance target goals were associated with greater interest than were mastery target goals. Moreover, this matching effect on interest was mediated by participants' degree of competence valuation and task involvement while playing.

Empirical Support for Goal Congruence and
Interest: The Case of Interpersonal Goals

Given the emphasis on competence and effectance in many motivation theories (Harter, 1981; White, 1959), a number of rich models have developed that describe the complex motivational processes associated with different kinds of competence or achievement goals (e.g., Butler, chapter 7, and Linnenbrink & Pintrich, chapter 8, this book; Dweck & Leggett, 1988; Elliot & Church, 1997; Harackiewicz, Barron, & Elliot, 1998; Thorkildsen & Nicholls, 1998). In contrast, relatively little is known about how interpersonal goals may affect motivational processes in achievement situations (Urdan & Maehr, 1995), although our model suggests that interpersonal goals could be just as relevant to interest in achievement-related activities.

In the education literature, interpersonal goals have been examined primarily in terms of a domain of competence that parallels achievement (i.e., interpersonal competence; see Pintrich & Garcia, 1991; Wentzel, 1991) or in terms of strategies in the service of achievement (e.g., help seeking [Butler & Neuman, 1995]) or collaborative problem solving (e.g., Ames, 1992; Brown, 1985). In the intrinsic-motivation literature, the interpersonal context is typically considered extrinsic to achievement activities. The role of other people has been examined primarily in terms of the context they establish for the activity. For example, research examines whether the interpersonal context interferes with or facilitates the processes that are proposed to be more directly related to interest (e.g., whether others provide competence feedback in a controlling or autonomy-supportive way, whether achieving competence is defined in terms of outperforming another person). In addition, other researchers have discussed "social" motivation as involving similar but parallel processes to intrinsic motivation for an activity (e.g., Boggiano, Klinger, & Main, 1986; Kunda & Schwartz, 1983; Pittman, Boggiano, & Main, 1992; Vallerand, 1997).

Because in our perspective the "activity" is fluid, we proposed that interpersonal factors may become part of any achievement activity, depending on the characteristics of the individual and the context. For example, in a cross-sectional life span study, we found that when individuals described their everyday experiences and problems in achievement domains (school and/or work), they spontaneously cited *both* interpersonal goals and competence goals to a significant degree (Morgan & Sansone, 1995; Sansone & Berg, 1993; Sansone & Morgan, 1992; Strough, Berg, & Sansone, 1996). Moreover, these interpersonal goals were not always parallel to competence goals, or in service of competence goals. In some cases, the competence goals appeared to be in service of interpersonal goals (e.g., wanting to achieve in a particular career so as to be able to help people). In other cases, the goals that individuals described as their own goals were in fact goals for other people (e.g., a daughter's matriculation; see Strough et al., 1996). This

suggested that interpersonal goals are often inextricably bound to competence goals and that the relation between them and the context can be complex. Furthermore, though the importance of interpersonal goals was true
for everyone in our sample, certain individuals (females) were even more
likely to have this interpersonal focus in their achievement domains.

We thus proposed that individuals may approach achievement activities
with interpersonal goals *and* competence goals. According to our model,
therefore, match with interpersonal goals should influence interest while
performing the activity, as well as the subsequent likelihood of performing
the same or similar activity. Moreover, we expected that match might have
this effect at least partially through the effect on how individuals performed
the activity.

To start to examine this possibility, Isaac, Sansone, and Smith (1999) first
identified individuals who should be most likely to approach activities with
an interpersonal focus and then operationalized potential "match" by
manipulating the actual presence of other people. To separate gender from
interpersonal focus, we used Swap and Rubin's (1983) interpersonal orientation scale in a mass testing session at the beginning of the term. Previous
research suggested that women tend to score higher on this scale than do
men but that both men and women are represented at all points along the
distribution. Individuals who score higher on this scale are particularly sensitive to others and demonstrate an affective involvement with others
(Rubin & Brown, 1975). Moreover, in pilot testing (Isaac, 1998), these individuals were more likely to spontaneously cite interpersonal goals when
describing their personal strivings (Emmons, 1989). Blocking on gender,
therefore, participants whose interpersonal orientation (IO) scores were in
the upper and lower one third of the distribution were selected to represent
individuals more likely and less likely, respectively, to approach achievement activities with interpersonal goals.

All participants were assigned the same objective competence goal: to
design and calculate the infrastructures budget for a satellite college cam-
pus. They performed this task in one of three contexts: alone, with another
person (same-sex confederate) present and collaborating on the task, or
with another person (same-sex confederate) present but working independently on the task. Thus, the achievement requirements were similar across
the three conditions, but the degree of match between having an interpersonal goal (i.e., higher in IO) and the interpersonal context (i.e., another
person present) varied accordingly.

Isaac et al. (1999) assessed the occurrence of math errors in performance
as well as task interest and likelihood of engaging in similar activities in the
future. Furthermore, each session with a confederate was also unobtrusively
videotaped, to begin to examine *how* match with the interpersonal context
might influence interest. Even though the objective achievement demands
were the same across condition, the "activity" might change as the result of

potential interpersonal interactions when another person was present. Confederates were not allowed to initiate conversation with participants, but once participants had initiated conversation, the confederates were free to initiate follow-up exchanges as they would in normal conversation.

In support of our model, we found that individuals higher in IO enjoyed the task more and were more likely to engage in a future similar task when the confederate was present, no matter whether they were working with or alongside the confederate. Interestingly, the results for individuals lower in IO were more mixed: When they worked in the presence of another person, individuals lower in IO expressed greater task interest but were *less* likely to engage in future similar activities.

Importantly, Isaac et al. (1999) were able to examine participants' interpersonal interactions when the confederate was present to begin to understand how the context led to different motivational outcomes for higher versus lower IO individuals. Using a coding scheme derived from an initial study and others' research (deCharms, 1976; Ryan & Grolnick, 1986), we first coded participants' conversation in terms of their style of interactive behaviors (e.g., the degree to which they tried to maintain harmony, sought input). We also coded the interactions in terms of the quantity of on-task (e.g, "Do you think I should put a building here?") and off-task (e.g., "Have you had any classes with Dr. Smith?") exchanges initiated by the participant and by the confederate.

We found that although there were no differences in the total number of exchanges as a function of IO level, there were differences in the quality of the interactions. As predicted, relative to lower IO individuals, individuals higher in IO displayed a more interpersonally involving interaction style (e.g., expressing thoughts and information to a greater degree). Moreover, this interaction style of higher IO individuals was not directly related to their interest but instead seemed to draw behavior out of the confederate (more off-task interactions) that did predict their interest.

Indeed, a major difference between higher and lower IO individuals was in how off-task interactions were related to participants' interest and performance. Lower IO individuals appeared to identify off-task conversation as extrinsic to the task. For example, when lower IO individuals worked in the presence of a confederate, the only predictor of the number of confederate-initiated off-task exchanges was the number of off-task exchanges initiated by the participants. Moreover, off-task exchanges were associated with lower IO participants' being more likely to commit mathematical errors while performing.

In contrast, higher IO individuals did not appear to distinguish between on-task and off-task interactions. When higher IO individuals worked in the presence of a confederate, the number of confederate-initiated off-task exchanges was predicted by the number of both on-task and off-task exchanges initiated by participants, as well as by the quality of their exchanges. In addition, higher IO individuals were *not* more likely to commit mathematical errors when there were off-task exchanges. In terms of our model, this pattern suggests that for higher IO individuals, interpersonal interactions were "intrinsic" to the activity and helped to make the task more interesting. Interest, in turn, predicted their likelihood of engaging in a similar activity in the future. For lower IO individuals, interpersonal exchanges were both intrinsic (when on task) and extrinsic (when off task), such that the presence of others was associated with a mixed motivational payoff.

In another study (Sansone, Morgan, & Smith, 1999), we examined match with interpersonal goals in a different way. To measure whether individuals were likely to approach achievement tasks with interpersonal goals, we measured whether individuals spontaneously cited interpersonal goals (to help and work with other people) when describing their reasons for their future work plans (Morgan et al., 1999). We also varied the context of the task to match or not match this type of interpersonal work goal. Rather than varying the actual presence of other people, therefore, in this case we varied the knowledge that their actions would affect others, although performance itself would occur alone. All participants performed the same computer-based achievement task, involving planning and mathematics. In the baseline condition, participants received no other information about the task. In contrast, individuals in the constructive impact condition were told that their responses would help the researchers to develop jobs for disadvantaged others.

Preliminary results indicated that the context condition interacted with whether individuals spontaneously cited interpersonal work goals to affect how interesting they found working on the computer-based achievement task. Specifically, individuals who cited interpersonal work goals reported greater interest in the computer planning task when told that their performance would have a constructive impact on others, relative to the baseline condition (baseline, $M = 13.60$; constructive impact, $M = 15.26$). Conversely, individuals who did not cite interpersonal work goals reported less task interest in the constructive impact condition than in the baseline condition (baseline, $M = 15.26$; constructive impact, $M = 14.04$).

Interestingly, although women and higher IO individuals were significantly more likely to spontaneously cite interpersonal work goals than were men and individuals scoring lower on IO, gender and IO did not work identically to interpersonal work goals in this study. This potential diversity in the meaning of interpersonal goals suggests a parallel to achievement-goal research, which continues to identify distinct effects of different types of achievement goals on both the process and outcome of task engagement (Butler, chapter 7; Linnenbrink & Pintrich, chapter 8; Barron and Harackiewicz, chapter 9 this book).

In ongoing research, we are attempting to systematically distinguish among different meanings of interpersonal focus and interpersonal goals.

For example, Smith, Ruiz, and Isaac (1999) found that there may be several distinct meanings that underlie the construct of interpersonal orientation and that these different meanings (i.e., sensitivity and responsiveness to others' reactions, warmth and nurturance toward others, strategic use of others) could have distinct implications for self-regulation. For example, the response to conflict may be very different depending on whether the individual was primarily concerned with helping others or with being liked by others. It is clear that future research is needed to more completely understand how the social world can be integrated into the motivational self-regulation process. If we do not recognize the role that other people might play, however, we may miss or unintentionally interfere with an important source of interest for some people. For example, if the instructor in English literature had forbidden students to work together on the assignment, Robert might never have completed the essay.

Together these studies support the model's suggestion that characteristics of the individual and the context can create different purpose goals and target goals as individuals approach and begin to perform a particular activity. These studies also suggest that rather than particular kinds of goals' being automatically associated with intrinsic or extrinsic motivation, the same goals can be associated with greater or lesser interest depending on the match among goals and between goals and the context. In our laboratory, we have now documented this "matching effect" across a variety of types of goals and activities, and other researchers have begun to find support using other individual and contextual variables (e.g., narcissism and ego goals; see Morf et al., 2000).

Moreover, the studies support the model's suggestion that the "activity" itself can change as a function of individuals' goals and the resultant goal-related actions. Thus, "activity" characteristics affect interest, but these characteristics may not remain the same as the individual and the surrounding context changes. When possible, individuals appear to regulate their actions to make the activity compatible with their goals, and, as a result, enhance or maintain interest. In fact, because the experience of interest is critical to maintaining motivation, in the next section we suggest that the experience of interest may itself be an implicit process goal that emerges even if it was not one of the initial goals held by individuals. Moreover, we suggest that individuals may actively regulate their behavior in the service of this implicit goal.

WHAT IF IT IS NOT INTERESTING?

If interest is critical to maintaining motivation, particularly over the longer term, what happens when the individual does not find the activity interesting? As our initial example illustrated, we believe that individuals have several options when faced with this decision, and we propose that this decision is part of the self-regulation process. Figure 12.2 is a closeup of the relevant part of the self-regulation process that focuses on the transactions among the phenomenological experience and maintenance behaviors.

The model suggests that once begun, the experience of interest while performing can serve as the most proximal motivator for continued performance (illustrated on the far left of Figure 12.2). When performance is not interesting, therefore, individuals may respond in one of several ways.

First, the individual might quit the activity (e.g., Mary's decision to watch Jerry Springer). Whether individuals choose this option, we propose, depends on whether they believe there is sufficient reason to perform the uninteresting activity. If the individual is highly motivated to maintain performance, he or she may persist for a time regardless of the experience (e.g., Tony's choice to sit down and immediately work on the essay). Experiencing boredom can be stressful (Berlyne, 1960), however, and may be part of the daily hassles and chronic strain of everyday life. For example, Csikzentmihayli (1975) found that when individuals were "flow-deprived," they reported feeling "...more tired and sleepy and less healthy and relaxed" (p. 177). The continued experience of everyday stressors can result in detrimental effects on psychological and physical well-being (e.g., DeLongis, Coyne, Dakof, Folkman, & Lazarus, 1982; Lazarus & Folkman, 1984; Selye, 1956).

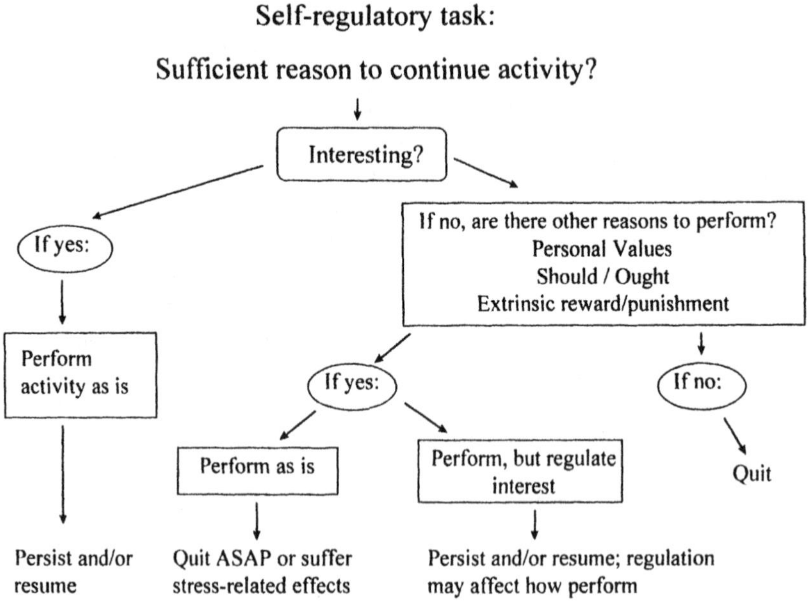

Self-regulatory task:

Sufficient reason to continue activity?

FIGURE 12.2
Self-regulatory task.

This suggests that individuals who persist at an uninteresting activity over time may be more likely to suffer stress-related psychological and physical health effects. Thus, another option is that the individual may change the activity into something more positive to perform through real or psychological transformations of the activity (Mischel, 1984; Sansone et al., 1992). For example, individuals may change their repetitive job by setting goals that make the task more challenging, reconstruing the task to focus primarily on its more interesting properties, using the time to socialize with other workers, and so on (e.g., Robert's meeting a friend to work on the essay).

At least for some people and/or in some situations, therefore, we suggest that individuals may adopt an implicit process goal of creating or maintaining interest level to reach their outcome goal. In control-theory language (Carver & Scheier, 1990; Powers, 1973), this would be a subroutine in service of a higher-level regulatory loop. In our model, we are in essence suggesting that individuals may strive to avoid this unpleasant state to approach a desired outcome.

As an initial test of this possibility, Sansone et al. (1992) compared an initially interesting activity (i.e., finding words in a matrix of letters) and an initially uninteresting activity (i.e., copying the identical matrix of letters). In the first study, college students were asked after some experience with one of the tasks to generate strategies that would make performing the task more interesting. In the second study, Sansone et al. (1992) tested whether individuals actually used the strategies primarily in conditions consistent with a self-regulation process. Individuals performed either the hidden-words task or the copying task. Within copying-task conditions, half of the participants were told that there were health benefits from performing the task on a regular basis.

To support a self-regulation interpretation, Sansone et al. (1992) predicted that individuals performing the copying task with knowledge of potential health benefits should be most likely to engage in the interest-enhancing strategies, because they had the need (the task was boring) and a reason to expend the effort (the potential health benefit). Individuals performing the hidden-words task should be least likely to engage in strategies to enhance interest, because there was no need (i.e., the task was already interesting). Individuals performing the copying task without knowledge of health benefits were predicted to fall in between the other two conditions, because they had a need to enhance interest (compared to the hidden-words condition) but not a good reason to expend the effort (compared to the copying task–health benefit condition).

Sansone et al. (1992) found this predicted linear pattern in strategy use. Moreover, strategy use was positively correlated with subsequent likelihood of performing the copying task (as assessed by the number of matrices individuals requested to take with them). Strategy use was also reflected in how individuals defined the activity (e.g., when the available strategy was reading incidental text, the topic of this text became part of the activity definition). The results that Sansone et al. (1992) obtained thus indicate that individuals may strategically attempt to enhance interest as a way to regulate and maintain motivation.

In a more recent study, Sansone, Wiebe, and Morgan (1999) directly tested the hypothesized mediating role of strategy use when another option (stopping) was available. A second purpose of the study was to contrast individual differences that should reflect differential weighing of the costs and benefits associated with deciding to regulate interest. The potential stress associated with performing an uninteresting activity may be one important cost. However, there can be other costs. As a case in point, Sansone et al. (1992) found that individuals who used the strategies in the limited time allowed also ended up copying less, suggesting that in the short term, regulating interest came at the cost to performance. More generally, actively coping with the uninteresting task (or any stressor) requires the use of limited resources in time, attention, and effort (e.g., Hobfoll, 1989; Kahneman, 1973).

One benefit of regulating interest, in contrast, is that it may make it possible to maintain motivation to perform activities over the long term, allowing individuals to reach long-term goals. For example, even though individuals who engaged in interest-enhancing strategies copied less during the experimental session in Sansone et al. (1992), they requested more matrices to take with them, suggesting that their motivation would extend beyond the session. On the other hand, a potential benefit to *not* regulating interest is that individuals may be more likely to try other alternatives (e.g., an individual may seek a new job that turns out to be better than the current job). Moreover, if limited resources are not allocated to regulating interest, these resources may be spent in service of other activities or domains in one's life.

Sansone et al. (1999) measured two individual differences—conscientiousness and hardiness—that they expected to maximize the differential weighing of possible costs and benefits. Individuals high in conscientiousness (Costa & McCrae, 1991) were expected to be more concerned about the achievement outcome and, as a consequence, to be more likely to persist without using interest-enhancing strategies that may interfere with performance. In contrast, individuals high in hardiness (Kobasa, 1979; Wiebe & Williams, 1992) were expected to weigh the quality of their subjective experience more heavily and to be more likely either to quit the activity (if there was not a sufficient reason to persist) or to engage in interest-enhancing actions.

Undergraduates performed the same boring copying activity used in Sansone et al. (1992). Instead of having a set number of matrices to copy, however, individuals were instructed to stop when they felt they could evaluate the task. Half were given a reason to value their performance: They were told that their evaluations would help researchers develop good jobs for others.

As expected, highly conscientious individuals persisted longer than did individuals lower in conscientiousness, independent of the benefit manipulation or strategy use. In contrast, individuals high in hardiness persisted primarily when they were provided the additional benefit information, and this effect was mediated by their attempt to make copying more interesting.

Internal analyses suggested that individuals' reasons for deciding to stop performing the activity differed as a function of strategy use. This was particularly true for individuals high in hardiness. Interestingly, one of the reasons affected by strategy use was the belief that it was senseless to continue. Individuals who used the interest-enhancing strategy were *less* likely to cite this as a reason for stopping. These results suggest that the externally provided benefit information gave individuals an important reason to do the activity in the first place. However, individuals' own attempts to make performance more interesting affected whether they perceived a reason to continue. This pattern supports a potentially alternating influence between value and interest over time, as suggested by our model (see also Renninger, chapter 13, this book).

Believing that the activity is meaningful and valuable appears to be an important part of self-regulation. Although in our model we suggest that valuation can affect interest directly as well as indirectly, in our research the reason to value the task had its effect on interest primarily by motivating the use of other interest-enhancing strategies (i.e., we typically do not find direct effects on interest). When asking high school students to report on their academic behaviors, Wolters and Rosenthal (in press) similarly found that the more students viewed the academic task as important and valuable, the greater reported use of interest-enhancing strategies. In contrast, Werner and Makela (1998) and Green-Demers, Pelletier, Stewart, and Gushue (1998) found significant, direct relationships between finding value and meaning in the activities of recycling (Werner & Makela, 1998) and sports training (Green-Demers et al., 1998) and the report of interest in these activities. They suggest that actively creating or seeking meaning for an activity may be an important strategy that individuals use to make everyday activities more interesting and involving and thereby more likely to be maintained.

DOES THE TYPE OF REASON MATTER?

In our previous studies, we used two different reasons, one that had conveyed a reward to the participant (better health) and one that conveyed aid to others (what Deci, Ryan, and colleagues termed a "meaningful rationale"). We found self-regulation using both kinds of reasons, which suggests that the type of reason may not matter as long as it conveys that performance is valued. According to some approaches, however, the type of reason should matter.

Traditionally, the reasons for engaging in a behavior have been dichotomized as originating from within the person or from an external source (e.g., Heider, 1958), and this dichotomy helped to shape early definitions of intrinsic and extrinsic motivation. However, Ryan (1982) demonstrated that when intrinsic motivation is defined as performing an activity for its own sake, some internal reasons (e.g., to preserve self-esteem) can instead create a controlling set toward that task that decreases intrinsic motivation (Deci & Ryan, 1985a). Deci and Ryan (1987; see also Ryan & Connell, 1989) went on to extend this thinking to "extrinsic" motivation, which they define as whenever individuals are motivated by reasons external to the activity (but not necessarily to the self). They proposed different "stages" of extrinsic motivation that fall along a continuum ranging from very low to very high levels of self-determination: external, introjection, identification, and integration. External regulation (a reward or another external constraint, such as money or praise) ranks as the most blatant form of control. Introjected regulation occurs when individuals experience pressure to perform a task, but in this case the pressure arises from within the individual (e.g., feeling shame for not doing an activity). In contrast, identified regulation occurs when the activity is perceived as being important and chosen by the individual. Identified regulation is self-determined, though still extrinsic to the activity. Finally, with the greatest degree of self-determination, integrated regulation may occur. Here, the activity is perceived as part of the self, freely chosen, and consistent with the individual's values and beliefs.

Deci and Ryan (1987, 1991) hypothesized that individuals may progress through these stages developmentally, although most empirical tests have used cross-sectional methods or an individual difference approach. Overall, the empirical work supports the relative distinction between more or less self-determined reasons along this continuum and has shown effects across a number of outcome measures (learning, self-esteem, affect, psychological well-being; see, for example, Deci et al. 1981; Grolnick & Ryan, 1987.

Because this approach focuses on the relative difference in self-determination, exact distinctions among these different kinds of reasons have not been consistently made in the empirical literature. For example, in many studies researchers create a dichotomy between more and less controlling, rather than keeping the reasons distinct (e.g., Williams & Deci, 1996). For our purposes, however, these reasons may be worth examining separately. In our research, we focus on how "extrinsic" motivation may lead to greater "intrinsic" motivation by motivating individuals to transform the activity into something more interesting. It is possible that reasons that emphasize self-determination, such as a meaningful rationale in accord with internalized values, lead to greater self-regulation, as Deci and Ryan suggested (e.g., Deci, Eghrari, Patrick & Leone, 1994). However, the degree to which reasons are autonomy supportive may not be the only dimension that influences self-regulation of interest.

For example, in addition to a difference in controllingness, the distinction between external and internal reasons may be important because individuals may be less likely to monitor their internal states when their attention is focused outward. Alternatively, an introjected reason may create a set toward the task that makes people less likely to deviate from what they "should" do as part of the task instructions, with the result that they are less likely to engage in an interest-enhancing strategy unless it is compatible with the task instructions.

The effects of different types of reasons may also be moderated by individual differences. For example, Deci and Ryan (1985b) suggested that through cumulative experience, individuals can develop a characteristic orientation toward autonomy-supportive, controlling, or amotivational features of the environment. Individuals characteristically oriented toward autonomy-supportive features may be particularly likely to regulate their motivation when the reason to perform the task maximizes autonomy (e.g., a meaningful rationale). In contrast, individuals characteristically oriented toward controlling features of the environment may be particularly likely to regulate interest in response to offers of a reward.

A final possibility that may encompass the previous possibilities is that a given type of reason may have distinct effects at different points in the process. For example, the incentive value created by the offer of an extrinsic reward may be effective in getting people to initiate an activity that they think will be boring (Lepper & Gilovich, 1981; chapter 10, this book). Once they have begun an activity, however, people performing the activity to receive the reward may be less likely to regulate interest because the reward cues an extrinsic focus that makes them less likely to monitor their subjective experience.

In a series of studies, we attempted to compare the effects of different types of reasons on both initiating behavior and maintaining the behavior within the self-regulation paradigm (Sansone & Smith, 1999; Smith & Sansone, 1999). Figure 12.3A illustrates the theoretical continuum as proposed by Deci and Ryan (1987), and Figure 12.3B illustrates our operationalizations as they map onto that continuum.

In the first study, we examined college students' willingness to volunteer for a study that involved performing a repetitive copying task. A graduate student went into several undergraduate classes presumably to recruit for participants for a study. The graduate student distributed to all students a written description of the study and asked each student to rate on a scale of −5 to +5 how willing he or she was to volunteer.

Keeping the description of the task constant, we systematically varied reasons to perform the activity. In the control condition, no additional reason was provided. In the three other conditions, we provided reasons that would vary according to the continuum specified by Deci and Ryan. Thus, in the most extrinsic condition, students were offered a reward (a free pass to

A. Theoretical continuum (Deci & Ryan, 1987):

	Amotivation		Extrinsic Motivation		Intrinsic Motivation
Task Type		*Boring*			*Interesting*

Additional Reasons	None	External	Internal-Controlling (Introjected)	Internal-Autonomy Supportive (Identified)	None

B. Operationalization (Sansone & Smith, 1999):

Task Type	Copying	Copying	Copying	Copying	Finding Hidden Words

Additional Reasons	None	Movie Pass	Should Help Others	Will Help Others	None

FIGURE 12.3

Juxtaposition of (A) the theoretical motivational continuum of Deci and Ryan (1987) and (B) the operationalizations of Sansone and Smith.

a local movie theater) if they volunteered and completed the task (task-contingent reward). In the other two conditions, we used a similar internal reason but varied the degree of controllingness and pressure. In the identi-fied-regulation condition, individuals were simply provided the meaningful rationale used in Sansone, Morgan, and Smith (1999): they were told that by participating and completing the task they would allow researchers to develop good jobs for other people. In the more controlling (or introjected) condition, we added the modifiers employed in other studies (e.g., Ryan, 1982) that have been shown to create an internal but controlling state. Thus, individuals were told that they "should" and "ought to" participate and com-plete the task because their participation would help the researchers develop jobs for others.

Preliminary results are presented in Table 12.1. As illustrated, there was a significant effect of the reason condition on students' willingness to volun-teer. Specifically, students were significantly more willing to volunteer when offered the movie pass than in any of the other conditions. These results suggested that the offer of a task-contingent reward might be the most effective reason for initial engagement in a task when individuals know that the task will be boring (Calder & Staw, 1975; Loveland & Olley, 1979).

In a second study, however, we examined the effects of these different reasons on the self-regulation process once students had already agreed to

TABLE 12.1

Means for Likelihood of Initiating Task (Study 1) and for Regulating Interest Once Begun (Study 2) as Function of Task Type and Additional Reason for Performing

Dependent measure	Task/reason condition				
	Copying/ none	Copying/ movie pass	Copying/ should help others	Copying/ will help others	Hidden word/none
Study 1					
Willingness to volunteer	$-.41^a$	1.83^b	$-.59^a$	$.00^a$	—
Study 2					
Interest-enhancing strategies	1.76^a	$2.33^{a,\,b}$	1.68^a	3.23^b	0^c
Interest	9.45^a	9.17^a	8.89^a	10.54^a	14.41^b
Percent who requested matrices	27^a	$38^{a,\,b}$	22^a	$41^{a,\,b}$	54^b

For willingness to volunteer, possible range is −5 to +5; for number of interest-enhancing strategies, possible range is 0 to 12; for interest, possible range is 3 to 21; for percent requested matrices, possible range is 0 to 100. Means not sharing superscripts within rows differ at $p < .06$. (Data adapted from Sansone and Smith, 1999 and Smith and Sansone, 1999.)

participate to fulfill requirements in their introductory psychology classes. When they reported for the study, students were randomly assigned to perform either the interesting hidden-words task or the uninteresting copying task used in previous studies (Sansone et al., 1992; Sansone Wiebe, & Morgan, 1999). Within copying-task conditions, individuals were also randomly assigned to one of the reason conditions used in the first study: no additional reason, receiving a movie pass (external reward), should be helping others (internal—introjected), will be helping others (internal—identified).

We used a procedure similar to that used in Sansone et al. (1992). After completing a practice session and three matrices in the experimental session, students rated how interesting they thought their task was and had the opportunity to (anonymously) request additional matrices to take with them. At the end of the session, individuals completed the General Causality Orientation (GCO) scale, designed by Deci and Ryan (1985b), as one of a number of personality and individual difference measures presented in counterbalanced order. We subsequently coded the matrices that participants used (and ostensibly discarded) in terms of the number of matrices on which participants used the previously identified interest-enhancing strategy. (For a more detailed description of these methods, see Sansone et al., 1992.)

We hypothesized that the type of reason provided to perform the copying task could affect the degree to which individuals engaged in interest-enhancing strategies and that the use of interest-enhancing strategies could attenuate the difference in motivation to perform the copying task and the hidden-words task. To test these hypotheses, we used orthogonal contrast coding to correspond to specific comparisons among the five conditions and conducted a series of hierarchical regression equations (Judd & Kenny, 1981).

The first contrast tested the effect of task type (Hidden Words vs Copying). To replicate Sansone et al. (1992), we expected the copying task to be rated as less interesting than the hidden-words task. Strategy use, therefore, should be more likely when individuals performed the copying task. The other contrasts compared the relative effects of different reasons to perform the uninteresting copying task: Any vs No Reason, Internal vs External Reason, Identified vs Introjected Internal Reason. In the multiple-regression equations, we included these four main effect contrasts, the three GCO subscale scores (autonomy, control, and impersonal), and their interactions. Because there were no significant interactions in any of the analyses, the final basic model included only the seven main effect terms (Cohen & Cohen, 1983).

We first regressed interest on this seven-term basic model. The overall model was significant, and there were two individually significant effects. The Hidden Words vs Copying contrast indicated, as expected, that individuals performing the copying task reported lower interest than did individuals performing the hidden-words task. The Identified vs Introjected Internal Reason contrast indicated that when given an internal reason to perform the copying task, individuals provided the more autonomy-supportive version reported greater task interest than did individuals provided the more controlling version. The Internal vs External Reason and Any vs No Reason contrasts were not significant, nor were the measures of motivational orientation. Condition means for interest are reported in Table 12.1.

These results confirmed that there were effects on interest involving both the initial interest level of the task and the reason provided to perform the boring task. In contrast to the results of Study 1, however, the key difference in reasons was not between the external reward and the other reasons. Rather, the critical difference appeared to be between the identified and introjected internal reasons. We next tested whether these effects on interest were mediated by the use of interest-enhancing strategies. We regressed strategy use on the seven-term model and then regressed interest on the basic model plus strategy use (Judd & Kenny, 1981). As expected, the Hidden Words vs Copying contrast significantly predicted strategy use, such that individuals used more strategies when performing the copying task than when performing the hidden-words task.

More critically, the results of these regression equations clearly show that strategy use mediated the effect of the Identified vs Introjected Internal Reason on interest. Mirroring the effect on interest, the Identified vs Introjected Internal Reason contrast significantly predicted individuals' attempt to regulate interest while performing. As can be seen in Figure 12.4, individuals

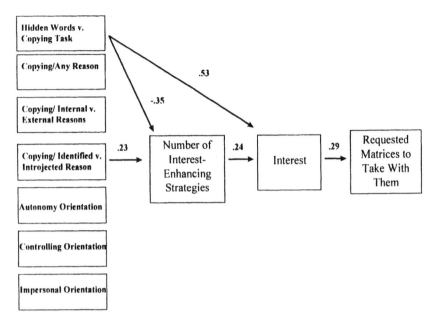

FIGURE 12.4

Mediation path model from Smith and Sansone (1999). Only significant paths are shown. Path coefficients are betas from hierarchical multiple-regression equations.

who were provided the identified internal reason engaged in more strategies than did individuals who were provided the introjected internal reason. There were no significant effects either for the Any Reason or Internal vs External Reason contrasts or for the motivational orientation measures. Condition means for strategy use appear in Table 12.1.

In addition to showing that task type and type of internal reason predicted strategy use, Figure 12.4 shows that greater use of interest-enhancing strategies was associated with greater interest. Moreover, the previously significant effect of the Identified vs Introjected Internal Reason contrast on interest was no longer significant once strategy use was controlled. Interestingly, the effect of the Hidden Words vs Copying contrast on interest became stronger once strategy use was controlled, suggesting that the difference in interest that emerged from the initial task characteristics became stronger once the variance due to strategy use was partialled out.

The degree of interest, in turn, significantly predicted whether individuals requested matrices to take with them, and this was true no matter the task or reason for performing. (Condition means for requested matrices appear in Table 12.1.) We found no significant main effects or interactions involving the GCO subscales, suggesting that the contextual factors similarly affected the self-regulatory process regardless of individuals' characteristic motivational orientation.

Together, the results from Studies 1 and 2 suggest that the type of reason to perform a boring activity may matter but that its impact on the self-regulation of interest may not depend solely on where the reason falls along a continuum of self-determination. The results from Study 1 suggested that only the offer of the external reward was sufficient to motivate individuals to be willing to initiate performance of the boring task. (All other means were at or below zero.) The results from Study 2 suggested, in contrast, that once individuals had agreed to perform the boring task, the identified reason or rationale promoted the greatest self-regulation of interest.

The Any Reason contrast tested the hypothesis of Sansone et al. (1992) that any good reason may be sufficient to regulate interest. This contrast was not significant, and it confirmed instead that the type of reason may matter. In contrast, the Internal vs External Reason comparison tested the hypothesis of Deci and Ryan (1987) that the external reward would be the most clearly controlling reason and would be associated with the least self-regulation. Our results suggest that in terms of interest regulation, the effects for the offer of a task-contingent reward were actually closer to the effects of the internal-identified reason condition than were the effects of the internal-introjected reason condition.

Together, the results from this pair of studies suggest that "extrinsic" rewards can be good for motivating initial performance when the activity is not one that is likely to be interesting. Moreover, extrinsic rewards may not be detrimental for maintaining behavior if they induce individuals to regulate interest while performing. The introjected reason appeared to be most detrimental to self-regulation of interest. According to Deci and Ryan's (1987) framework, this suggests that the experience of being controlled might have been greater in the internal-introjected reason condition than the external-reward condition, although there was no reason to make this prediction a priori. An alternative explanation is that in the presence of an emphasis on what individuals ought to and should do, individuals might have been less likely to stray from their task instructions by varying the procedure (the available interest-enhancing strategy).

Overall, our results suggest that when one is attempting to understand the self-regulation of interest, it may be best to consider different kinds of reasons in terms of whether and how they lead the individual to approach and perform the activity, rather than in terms of where they fall along a single continuum. Our results also suggest that the predictions based on the earlier work from both Sansone et al. (1992) and Deci and Ryan (1987) may need to be revised as we continue to explore the self-regulation process.

REGULATING INTEREST AND PERFORMANCE

Our model and research have come from the perspective of highlighting and documenting the importance of interest in maintaining motivation and suggesting that it is an important and overlooked dimension of self-regulation. One issue that has emerged is the relationship between attempting to enhance interest and "performance" as defined by external standards. When we used the copying activity in the laboratory, we found strategy use to negatively affect performance in the short term but predict greater persistence over the longer term. For this paradigm, we purposely created a task that was unambiguously repetitive and boring, and the available interest-enhancing strategy was purposely unrelated to task demands. Performance in this case was defined in terms of the quantity produced in a given time period. In this context, time spent on the strategy was "off task" and took away from attention to performance. In other contexts, in contrast, we found that off-task behavior can be related to interest and *not* interfere with performance, at least for some individuals (Isaac et al., 1999).

Research by Wolters (in press) has more systematically examined the relationship between the reported use of interest-enhancing strategies and academic performance among high school students. He found that the reported frequency of using interest-enhancing strategies did not predict GPA. However, use of these strategies was related to a general learning orientation, as well as to the reported degree of effort expended and some specific cognitive and regulation strategies (organization, monitoring, and regulation).

We wish to make two points about the relationship between performance and interest regulation. First, this relationship depends on whether the relevant strategies interfere with or facilitate other task demands. Lepper and Cordova (1992) have made a similar point about external interventions to enhance interest. When there is potential detrimental effect on performance, it may be something that is more important for some people (e.g., people high in conscientiousness) than others, or at certain times or in certain situations than others. If individuals are primarily concerned with regulating interest, they may not notice or place priority on potential detrimental effects on performance.

Research by Wolters (1998) suggested that individuals use different types of strategies to regulate motivation depending on why they feel unmotivated. He asked college students to report strategies they would use to regulate motivation for academic tasks under three different circumstances: when the tasks were irrelevant, when the tasks were difficult, and when the tasks were uninteresting. Wolters (1998) found that students' reported frequency of use of interest-enhancing strategies was greatest when they were unmotivated because the academic task was uninteresting. If they were unmotivated because the material was difficult, they reported a greater frequency of use of information processing and help-seeking strategies. If they were unmotivated because they did not find the task to be personally relevant, in contrast, they reported a greater frequency of use of strategies that entailed reminding oneself of performance goals (e.g., grades) or other reasons to value the task. This suggests that students are sensitive to the situation when they regulate motivation, limiting the use of interest-enhancing strategies to those situations in which they feel unmotivated because the task is boring.

However, enhancing the perceived importance of the task could also make the task more interesting, either directly (Green-Demers et al., 1998; Werner & Makela, 1998) or indirectly by motivating the use of interest-enhancing strategies. The second point that we wish to make, therefore, is that some strategies may fulfill dual purposes. For example, one type of interest-enhancing strategy cited in the first study in Sansone et al. (1992) was to make the task more challenging (e.g., set goals, compete with someone else). Although these strategies, if possible to implement, might have in fact served to make performance more interesting, they would also probably have enhanced individuals' achievement. The potential positive effect on achievement may be unintended initially but may become intentional with experience or time. Alternatively, individuals could purposely select interest-enhancing strategies that they believe will also benefit achievement or, at least, will not interfere with achievement. Thus, the frequency with which individuals attempt to regulate interest could be underestimated in everyday life, because these efforts are embedded in individuals' efforts to achieve the desired outcome. The relationship between regulating interest and performance can be obscured under these circumstances.

IMPLICATIONS AND CONCLUSION

As has been illustrated in other chapters in this book, researchers have often been more successful in identifying factors that decrease interest than factors that can increase interest. Recommendations for promoting "intrinsic" motivation in school, home, or the workplace are thus often described in terms of what to avoid doing. More recently, researchers have begun to emphasize interventions that may enhance interest either by increasing value, importance, and meaning of the activity (Cordova & Lepper, 1996; Renninger and Jacobs & Eccles, chapters 13 and 14, this book) or by embellishing the structure of the task (e.g., Csikszentmihalyi, 1978; Malone & Lepper, 1987; Lepper & Henderlong, chapter 10, this book). One implication of our approach, however, is that individuals are not passive recipients of others' attempts to motivate. Individuals appear to take an active role in promoting their own motivation.

This realization does not provide easy solutions to the problem of creating settings that will maximize individuals' intrinsic motivation. Consistent with a self-regulatory framework, our research suggests that there can be variability in terms of who is likely to regulate interest and under what circumstances. Moreover, the factors that may make something interesting to one person may not make it interesting to another person, or even to the same person at different points in time. For example, creating a context that promotes competence but at the expense of interpersonal interactions may work to enhance interest for males or individuals lower in interpersonal orientation (e.g., Tony) but decrease interest for females or individuals higher in interpersonal orientation (e.g., Robert).

Perhaps the best option is to create a context that allows some variability in the *process* of performance while monitoring the impact on performance outcomes. This may maximize the ability of individuals to regulate their interest and promote subsequent motivation. One implication of this suggestion is that autonomy and choice in performance may not affect interest only directly by allowing individuals to feel more self-determining (deCharms, 1968; Deci & Ryan, 1987). Rather, autonomy and choice may affect interest indirectly by allowing individuals the flexibility to perform the activity in a way that will maintain his or her motivation. In this case, interventions may be more likely to take the form of providing opportunities and encouragement for individuals to self-regulate interest. Our recommendation, then, is to recognize and try to work with the motivational self-regulation process, because individuals may engage in this process anyway (even if it comes at the expense of immediate performance).

Our research also suggests that setting up a dichotomy of intrinsic motivation "versus" extrinsic motivation may be unnecessarily simplistic. As others have suggested (e.g., Lepper and Henderlong, in chapter 10, and Hidi, in chapter 11 this of book), both kinds of motivation may be necessary for motivation to be maintained over time. In our example at the beginning of this chapter, Tony was sufficiently motivated by the thought of his grade to write the essay without engaging in any additional strategies to make the experience more interesting. Robert was sufficiently motivated by the thought of his grade to exert the effort to make the essay assignment more interesting by meeting with a classmate. In contrast, Mary was *not* sufficiently motivated by the thought of her grade to choose either Tony's or Robert's option, and, as a result, she did not write the essay. Without some level of extrinsic motivation, therefore, these students may not begin what they perceive to be a boring assignment. Even if these students had found John Donne's poetry to be interesting initially, their enjoyment could ebb over time and during prolonged analysis. Thus, even if initially unnecessary, some level of "extrinsic" motivation may become necessary over time for the activity to be continued or resumed.

We also suggest, however, that if the experience of performing a boring activity is prolonged, individuals can suffer stress-related effects on physical and psychological well-being. Thus, over the long term it will be important to find a way to make the activity interesting or "intrinsically" motivated, at least some of the time. Individuals may be more likely to find a way to be "intrinsically" motivated if they believe it is important to continue performing the activity and the strategies that would make the activity more interesting are available and encouraged by the environment.

Conversely, it may not always be in someone's best interest to make an uninteresting activity more interesting. Rather, it may be best to quit the activity and find another activity that is more interesting. For example, rather than persisting in English literature, it may be better for Mary to focus her studies in an area that she finds more inherently interesting (e.g., working with dysfunctional families). It may also not be worth the effort to try to regulate interest if the activity is short lived or temporary. In those cases, it may be more cost-effective to have a strong extrinsic motive to complete the task. For example, if Tony is taking only one English literature class to fulfill his general core requirements, the short-lived motivation of maintaining his GPA may be all he needs.

We suggest, therefore, that decisions whether to promote intrinsic motivation or extrinsic motivation, or both, depend on the person, the nature of the activity, and the circumstances in which the person performs the activity at a given point in time. Rather than argue about intrinsic motivation "versus" extrinsic motivation, therefore, we suggest that the distinction between "intrinsic" and "extrinsic" can lose its meaning as the activity itself changes over individuals, situations, and time. Our model and program of research suggest that *having to* and *wanting to* perform an activity are distinct but related motivational constructs. To understand motivation as it occurs in everyday life, therefore, we must understand the potential complexities of this relationship as well as individuals' own roles in creating and maintaining that complexity.

Acknowledgements

Jessi L. Smith was supported by a Marriner S. Eccles Graduate Fellowship during preparation of this chapter. The authors thank Kenneth Barron, Judy Harackiewicz, and Carolyn Morgan for their very helpful comments on earlier versions of this chapter. The authors also thank Robyn Lemon, Doug Alderman, Crystal Fox, and Alisha Shiffer for their excellent assistance in data collection and coding for a number of the studies described in the chapter.

References

Ames, C. (1992). Classrooms: Goals, structures, and student motivation. *Journal of Educational Psychology, 84*, 261–271.
Bandura, A. (1982). Self-efficacy mechanism in human agency. *American Psychologist, 37*, 122–147.
Bandura, A. (1986). *Social foundations of thought and action: A social cognitive theory.* Englewood Cliffs, NJ: Prentice-Hall.
Bargh, J. A., & Chartrand, T. L. (1999). The unbearable automaticity of being. *American Psychologist, 54*, 462–479.
Berlyne, D. N. (1960). *Conflict, arousal, and curiosity.* New York: McGraw-Hill.

Boggiano, A. K., Klinger, C., & Main, D. S. (1986). Enhancing interest in peer interaction: A developmental analysis. *Child Development*, 57, 852–861.

Brown, A. L. (1985). Motivation to learn and understand: On taking charge of one's own learning. *Cognition and Instruction*, 5, 311–321.

Butler, R., & Neuman, O. (1995). Effects of task and ego achievement goals on help-seeking behaviors and attitudes. *Journal of Educational Psychology*, 87, 261–271.

Calder, B. J., & Staw, B. M. (1975). Self-perception of intrinsic and extrinsic motivation. *Journal of Personality and Social Psychology*, 31, 599–605.

Carver, C. S., & Scheier, M. F. (1990). Origins and functions of positive and negative affect: A control-process view. *Psychological Review*, 97, 19–35.

Cohen, J., & Cohen, P. (1983). Applied Multiple Regression/Correlation Analysis for the Behavioral Sciences. (2nd ed.) Hillsdale, NJ: Erlbaum.

Cordova, D. I., & Lepper, M. R. (1996). Intrinsic motivation and the process of learning: Beneficial effects of contextualization, personalization, and choice. *Journal of Educational Psychology*, 88, 715–730.

Costa, P. T., Jr., & McCrae, R. R. (1991). *Revised NEO Personality Inventory*. Odessa, FL: Psychological Assessment Resources Inc.

Csikszentmihalyi, M. (1975). *Beyond boredom and anxiety*. San Francisco: Jossey-Bass.

Csikszentmihalyi, M. (1978). Intrinsic rewards and emergent motivation. In M. R. Lepper & D. Greene (Eds.), *The hidden costs of reward* (pp. 205–216). Hillsdale, NJ: Erlbaum.

deCharms, R. (1968). *Personal causation: The internal affective determinants of behavior*. New York: Academic Press.

deCharms, R. (1976). *Enhancing motivation: Change in the classroom*. New York: Irvington.

Deci, E. L., Eghrari, H., Patrick, B. C., & Leone, D. R. (1994). Facilitating internalization: The self-determination theory perspective. *Journal of Personality*, 62, 119–142.

Deci, E. L., & Ryan, R. M. (1985a). *Intrinsic motivation and self-determination in human behavior*. New York: Plenum Press.

Deci, E. L., & Ryan, R. M. (1985b). The general causality orientations scale: Self-determination in personality. *Journal of Research in Personality*, 19, 109–134.

Deci, E. L., & Ryan, R. M. (1987). The support of autonomy and the control of behavior. *Journal of Personality and Social Psychology*, 53, 1024–1037.

Deci, E. L., & Ryan, R. M. (1991). A motivational approach to self: Integration in personality. In R. Dienstbier (Ed.), *Nebraska Symposium on Motivation*: Vol. 38. *Perspectives on motivation* (pp. 237–288). Lincoln: University of Nebraska Press.

Deci, E. L., Schwartz, A. J., Sheinman, L., & Ryan, R. M. (1981). An instrument to assess adults' orientations toward control versus autonomy with children: Reflections on intrinsic motivation and perceived competence. *Journal of Educational Psychology*, 73, 642–650.

DeLongis, A., Coyne, J. C., Dakof, G., Folkman, S., & Lazarus, R. S. (1982). Relationship of daily hassles, uplifts, and major life events to health status. *Health Psychology*, 1, 119–136.

Dweck, C. S., & Leggett, E. L. (1988). A social-cognitive approach to motivation and personality. *Psychological Review*, 95, 256–273.

Eccles, J. (1983). Expectancies, values and academic behaviors. In J. T. Spence (Ed.), *Achievement and achievement motives: Psychological and sociological approaches* (pp. 75–146). San Francisco: W. H. Freeman.

Elliot, A. J., & Church, M. A. (1997). A hierarchical model of approach and avoidance achievement motivation. *Journal of Personality and Social Psychology*, 72, 218–232.

Elliot, A. J., & Harackiewicz, J. M. (1994). Goal setting, achievement orientation, and intrinsic motivation: A mediational analysis. *Journal of Personality and Social Psychology*, 66, 968–980.

Elliot, A., & McGregor, H. (1999). Test anxiety and the hierarchical model of approach and avoidance motivation. *Journal of Personality and Social Psychology*. 76, 628–644.

Emmons, R. A. (1989). The personal striving approach to personality. In L. A. Pervin (Ed.), *Goal concepts in personality and social psychology* (pp. 87–126). Hillsdale, NJ: Erlbaum.

Green-Demers, I., Pelletier, L. G., Stewart, D. G., & Gushue, N. R. (1998). Coping with the less interesting aspects of training: Toward a model of interest and motivation enhancement in individual sports. *Basic and Applied Social Psychology, 20*, 251–261.

Grolnick, W. S., & Ryan, R. M. (1987). Autonomy in children's learning: An experimental and individual difference investigation. *Journal of Personality and Social Psychology, 52*, 890–898.

Harackiewicz, J. M., Barron, K. E., & Elliot, A. J. (1998). Rethinking achievement goals: When are they adaptive for college students and why? *Educational Psychologist, 33*, 1–21.

Harackiewicz, J. M., Barron, K. E., Tauer, J. M., Carter, S. M., & Elliot, A. J. (in press). Short-term and long-term consequences of achievement goals: Predicting interest and performance over time. *Journal of Educational Psychology.*

Harackiewicz, J. M., & Elliot, A. J. (1993). Achievement goals and intrinsic motivation. *Journal of Personality and Social Psychology, 65*, 904–915.

Harackiewicz, J. M., & Elliot, A. J. (1998). The joint effects of target and purpose goals on intrinsic motivation: A mediational analysis. *Personality and Social Psychology Bulletin, 24*, 675–689.

Harackiewicz, J. M., & Sansone, C. (1991). Goals and intrinsic motivation: You can get there from here. *Advances in Motivation and Achievement, 7*, 21–49.

Harter, S. (1981). A new self-report scale of intrinsic versus extrinsic orientation in the classroom: Motivation and informational components. *Developmental Psychology, 17*, 300–312.

Heider, F. (1958). *The psychology of interpersonal relationships.* New York: Wiley.

Higgins, E. T. (1997). Beyond pleasure and pain. *American Psychologist, 52*, 1280–1300.

Higgins, E. T., Lee, J., Kwon, J., & Trope, Y. (1995). When combining intrinsic motivations undermines interest: A test of activity engagement theory. *Journal of Personality and Social Psychology, 68*, 749–767.

Higgins, E. T., Trope, Y., & Kwon, J. (1999). Augmentation and undermining from combining activities: The role of choice in Activity Engagement Theory. *Journal of Experimental Social Psychology, 35*, 285–307.

Hobfoll, S. E. (1989). Conservation of resources: A new attempt at conceptualizing stress. *American Psychologist, 44*, 513–524.

Isaac, J. (1998). *Interpersonal orientation differences in college student's appraisals of tasks.* Unpublished master's thesis, University of Utah, Salt Lake City.

Isaac, J. D., Sansone, C., & Smith, J. L. (1999). Other people as a source of interest in an activity. *Journal of Experimental Social Psychology, 35*, 239–265.

Jacobs, J. E., Finken, L. L., Griffen, N. L., & Wright, J. D. (1998). The career plans of science-talented rural adolescent girls. *American Educational Research Journal, 35*, 681–704.

Judd, C. M., & Kenny, D. A. (1981). Process analysis: Estimating mediation in treatment evaluations. *Evaluation Review, 5*, 602–619.

Kahneman, D. (1973). *Attention and effort.* Englewood Cliffs, NJ: Prentice-Hall.

Kobasa, S. C. (1979). Stressful life events, personality, and health: An inquiry into hardiness. *Journal of Personality and Social Psychology, 37*, 1–11.

Kunda, Z., & Schwartz, S. H. (1983). Undermining intrinsic moral motivation: External reward and self-presentation. *Journal of Personality and Social Psychology, 45*, 763–771.

Lazarus, R. S., & Folkman, S. (1984). *Stress, appraisal, and coping.* New York: Springer.

Lepper, M. R., & Cordova, D. I. (1992). A desire to be taught: Instructional consequences of intrinsic motivation. *Motivation and Emotion, 16*, 187–208.

Lepper, M. R., & Gilovich, T. J. (1981). The multiple functions of reward: A social developmental perspective. In S. S. Brehm, S. M. Kassin, & F. X. Gibbons (Eds.), *Developmental social psychology: Theory and research* (pp. 5–31). New York: Oxford University Press.

Loveland, K. K., & Olley, J. G. (1979). The effect of external reward on interest and quality of task performance in children of high and low intrinsic motivation. *Child Development, 50*, 1207–1210.

Malone, T. W., & Lepper, M. R. (1987). Making learning fun: A taxonomy of intrinsic motivations for learning. In R. E. Snow & M. J. Farr (Eds.), *Aptitude, learning, and instruction: III. Conative and affective process analyses* (pp. 223–253). Hillsdale, NJ: Erlbaum.

Mischel, W. (1984). Convergences and challenges in the search for consistency. *American Psychologist*, 39, 351–364.

Morf, CC., Weir, C. R., & Davidor, M. (2000). Narcissism and intrinsic motivation: The role of goal congruence. *Journal of Experimental Social Psychology*, 36.

Morgan, C., Isaac, J., & Sansone, C. (1999). *The role of interest in predicting college students' career choice.* Manuscript under review.

Morgan, C., & Sansone, C. (1995). *Achievement and interpersonal concerns in everyday problems: Gender differences and similarities.* Unpublished manuscript.

Pintrich, P. R., & Garcia, T. (1991). Student goal orientation and self-regulation in the college classroom. In M. L. Maehr & P. R. Pintrich (Eds.), *Advances in motivation and achievement* (vol. 7, pp. 371–402). Greenwich, CT: JAI Press.

Pittman T. S., Boggiano, A. K., & Main, D. S. (1992). Intrinsic and extrinsic motivational orientations in peer interactions. In A. K. Boggiano & T. S. Pittman (Eds.), *Achievement and motivation: A social-developmental perspective* (pp. 37–53). New York: Cambridge University Press.

Powers, W. T. (1973). *Behavior: The control of perception.* Chicago: Aldine.

Rathunde, K., & Csikszentmihalyi, M. (1993). Undivided interest and the growth of talent: A longitudinal study of adolescents. *Journal of Youth and Adolescence*, 22, 385–405.

Rubin, J. Z., & Brown, B. R. (1975). In *The social Psychology of bargaining and negotiation.* New York: Academic Press.

Ryan, R. M. (1982). Control and information in the intrapersonal sphere: An extension of cognitive evaluation theory. *Journal of Personality and Social Psychology*, 43, 450–461.

Ryan, R. M., & Connell, J. P. (1989). Perceived locus of causality and internalization: Examining reasons for acting in two domains. *Journal of Personality and Social Psychology*, 57, 749–761.

Ryan, R. M., & Grolnick, W. S. (1986). Origins and pawns in the classroom: Self-report and projective assessments of children's perceptions. *Journal of Personality and Social Psychology*, 50, 550–558.

Sansone, C. (1986). A question of competence: The effects of competence and task feedback on intrinsic interest. *Journal of Personality and Social Psychology*, 51, 918–931.

Sansone, C. (1989). Competence feedback, task feedback, and intrinsic interest: An examination of process and context. *Journal of Experimental Social Psychology*, 25, 343–361.

Sansone, C., & Berg, C. (1993). Adapting to the environment across the lifespan: Different process or different inputs? *International Journal of Behavioral Development*, 16, 215–241.

Sansone, C., & Harackiewicz, J. M. (1996). "I don't feel like it": The function of interest in self-regulation. In L. Martin and A. Tesser (Eds.), *Striving and feeling: Interactions between goals and affect.* Hillsdale, NJ: Erlbaum.

Sansone, C., & Morgan, C. (1992). Intrinsic motivation and education: Competence in context. *Motivation and Emotion*, 16, 249–270.

Sansone, C., Morgan, C. L., & Smith, J. L. (1999). The effects of match between interpersonal work goals and interpersonal purpose goals on interest. Unpublished data.

Sansone, C., Sachau, D. A., & Weir, C. (1989). Effects of instruction on intrinsic interest: The importance of context. *Journal of Personality and Social Psychology*, 57, 819–829.

Sansone, C., & Smith, J. L. (1999). Reasons for performing a boring activity: Effects on initial engagement and regulation of interest. Manuscript in preparation.

Sansone, C., Wiebe, D. J., & Morgan, C. (1999). Self-regulating interest: The moderating role of hardiness and conscientiousness. *Journal of Personality*, 67, 701–733.

Sansone, C., Weir, C., Harpster, L., & Morgan, C. (1992). Once a boring task always a boring task? interest as a self-regulatory mechanism. *Journal of Personality and Social Psychology*, 63, 379–390.

Selye, H. (1956). *The stress of life.* New York: McGraw-Hill.

Shah, J. Y., Higgins, E. T., & Friedman, R. (1998). Performance incentives and means: How regulatory focus influences goal attainment. *Journal of Personality and Social Psychology*, 74, 285–293.

Smith, J. L., Ruiz, J. M., & Isaac, J. D. (1999). Interpersonal orientation in the interpersonal circumplex and FFM: Reducing three conceptualizations to a common denominator. Manuscript under review.

Smith, J. L., & Sansone, C. (1999 August). *Reasons for self-regulating interest: Does it matter?* Paper presented at the 107th meeting of the American Psychological Association, Boston.

Strough, J., Berg, C. A., & Sansone, C. (1996). Goals for solving everyday problems across the life span: Age and gender differences in the salience of interpersonal concerns. *Developmental Psychology, 32*, 1106–1115.

Swap, W., & Rubin, J. (1983). Measurement of interpersonal orientation. *Journal of Personality and Social Psychology, 44*(1), 208–219.

Thorkildsen, T. A., & Nicholls, J. G. (1998). Fifth graders' achievement orientations and beliefs: Individual and classroom differences. *Journal of Educational Psychology, 90*, 179–201.

Urdan, T. C., & Maehr, M. L. (1995). Beyond a two-goal theory of motivation and achievement: A case for social goals. *Review of Educational Research, 65*, 213–243.

Vallerand, R. J. (1997). Toward a hierarchical model of intrinsic and extrinsic motivation. In M. Zanna (Ed.), *Advances in Experimental Social Psychology* (vol. 29, pp. 271–360). San Diego: Academic Press.

Vygotsky, L. S. (1978). *Mind in society: The development of higher psychological processes* (M. Cole, V. John-Steiner, S. Scribner, & E. Souberman, Eds.). Cambridge, MA: Harvard University Press.

Wentzel, K. R. (1991). Social and academic goals at school: Motivation and achievement in context. In M. L. Maehr & P. R. Pintrich (Eds.), *Advances in motivation and achievement* (vol. 7, pp. 185–212). Greenwich, CT: JAI Press.

Werner, C. M., & Makela, E. (1998). Motivations and behaviors that support recycling. *Journal of Environmental Psychology, 18*, 373–386.

White, R. W. (1959). Motivation reconsidered: The concept of competence. *Psychological Review, 66*, 297–333.

Wiebe, D. J., & Williams, P. G. (1992). Hardiness and health: A social psychophysiological perspective on stress and adaptation. *Journal of Social and Clinical Psychology, 11*, 238–262.

Williams, G. C., & Deci, E. L. (1996). Internalization of biopsychosocial values by medical students: A test of self-determination theory. *Journal of Personality and Social Psychology, 70*, 767–779.

Wolters, C. A. (1998). Self-regulated learning and college students' regulation of motivation. *Journal of Educational Psychology, 90*, 224–235.

Wolters, C. A. (in press). The relation between high school students' motivational regulation and their use of learning strategies, effort, and classroom performance. *Learning and Individual Differences.*

Wolters, C. A., & Rosenthal, H. (in press). The relation between students' motivational beliefs and their use of motivational regulation strategies. *International Journal of Educational Research.*

CHAPTER 13

Individual Interest and Its Implications for Understanding Intrinsic Motivation

K. ANN RENNINGER

Program in Education
Swarthmore College

Although there is an overlap in the outcomes of intrinsic motivation and well-developed individual interest—namely, the behaviors of intrinsically motivated individuals and people engaged with content that is of individual interest are positive, fully engaged, and appear to be focused on a given task for the sake of the task itself—there are also important differences between these concepts. Study of intrinsic motivation (including what has been called intrinsic interest) appears to have subsumed study of two types of interest: situational interest and individual interest. *Situational interest* refers to the likelihood that particular subject content or events will trigger a response in the moment, which may or may not "hold" over time (Hidi & Baird, 1986; Mitchell, 1993). Thus, it refers to elicited attention for content in the sense of enjoyment, curiosity, and so forth, but no assumption can be made about the level of content knowledge. *Individual interest*, on the other hand, refers to an ongoing and deepening relation of a person to particular subject content that does, in fact, have qualities of full engagement and task orientation. It includes a more enriched kind of value than does situational interest, as well as an increasingly consolidated base of discourse knowledge (Renninger, 1990).

One reason that there are controversies regarding the role of intrinsic motivation in learning may be directly related to the fact that no distinction has been made between these two qualitatively different types of interest in the literature on intrinsic motivation. The distinction between these types of interest refers to whether a particular content captures attention (situational interest) and continues to hold attention (sometimes situational interest, always individual interest). It also refers to the particular relation between interest and motives. Situational interest can be considered to be one type of motive, distinct from other motives such as needs and desires (see Hidi, chapter 11, this book), individual interest co-occurs with and can appear to be conflated with needs and desires but also is a distinct concept.

Research on individual interest is a literature that has examined particular person–subject content relations over time and in terms of both the knowledge and value that each person brings to his or her engagement with contents of individual interest. As such, it provides a contrast to studies of intrinsic motivation that have typically focused on the process and affect involved in reengagement with tasks.

Individual interest is the kind of involvement teachers love to see in their students. In fact, teachers often appeal to what they think will be interesting in their efforts to motivate students to do schoolwork. They choose topics they expect will trigger students' attention (Hidi, 1990) or use instructional methods to increase individual interest (Goldman, Mayfield-Stewart, Bateman, Pellegrino, and the Cognition and Technology Group at Vanderbilt, 1998; Hidi, Weiss, Berndorff, & Nolan, 1998; Hoffmann & Häussler, 1998; Schank & Joseph, 1998). Teachers may also use what students know and the questions they ask to inform the specific focus of the content covered and the order of the skills introduced in class (Renninger, 1998a). These efforts can meet with varying success, however, because individual interests may affect learning differently than do situational interests. In everyday language, there is no clear use of the term *interest* (Valsiner, 1992), and this may account for confusion about what it means and how it is applied.

Students working with contents of individual interest are typically focused, relaxed, and engaged in comparison with the way they work with subject content that does not interest them (Prenzel, 1992; Renninger, 1989, 1990; Renninger & Leckrone, 1991). They also are likely to achieve better grades and do well on tests (see Csikszentmihalyi, Rathunde, & Whalen, 1993; U. Schiefele & Csikszentmihalyi, 1995). In fact, when contexts of individual interest are inserted in expository passages and contrasted with contexts that are of less well-developed interest, for example, students are likely to recall more points, recall information from more paragraphs, recall more topic sentences, write more sentences, provide more detailed information about topics read, make fewer errors in written recall, and provide additional topic-relevant information (Renninger, 1998c).

In this chapter, some background for thinking further about individual interest and its bearing on what a student is motivated to learn is overviewed. Following this, discussion focuses on the relation of differing levels of knowledge and value to what and how students learn. Finally, some implications of this information for thinking about how the development of individual interest contributes to the conceptualization of intrinsic motivation are considered.

BACKGROUND

Individual interest has been variously discussed as a psychological state; a relatively enduring predisposition to engage a class of objects, events, or ideas; and as an identified class of objects (subject content) to which a student predictably will attend (see discussions in Alexander, Kulikowich, & Jetton, 1994; Gardner, 1998; Krapp, 1999; Krapp & B. Fink, 1992; Krapp, Hidi, & Renninger, 1992; Krapp, Renninger, & Hoffmann, 1998; Renninger, 1990, 1998b; U. Schiefele, 1991; Tobias, 1994; Todt & Schrieber, 1998). In this chapter, discussion centers specifically on well-developed individual interest as a psychological state and also refers to the effect that this state has on the relation between a person and particular subject content over time.[1]

On the basis of the work of Baldwin (1897, 1906, 1911), Dewey (1913, 1916), James (1890), Mandler (1984/1975), Piaget (1966) H. Schiefele (1986), and H. Schiefele, Krapp, Prenzel, Heiland & Kasten (1983), individual interest is conceptualized as a continually evolving relation of a person and particular subject content that is at once a somewhat idiosyncratic psychological state of being interested and also a process of internalization through which a person comes to identify and be identified with the content. As such, the term *interest* is also used to refer to the subject content of interest.[2] Although individual interest is linked to several motivational concepts such as flow, intrinsic interest, intrinsic motivation, personal interest, topic interest, situa-

---

[1] In my own work, I have been careful to study individual interest for each student relative to that student's other engagements. In this way, identification reflects high levels of both stored knowledge and stored value relative to other classes of subject content. Moreover, I do not ask students directly about their interest for particular subject content, because the term interest is used to refer to both preferences and attractions in everyday language, and neither preferences nor attraction involves much stored knowledge (see Renninger & Leckrone, 1991). For further information about these decisions, see Renninger, 1998c.

[2] Although *individual interest* (or *situational interest*, for that matter) is used interchangeably with *interest* (e.g., a person's interest is mathematics), it is important to emphasize that when interest is linked to a particular content as it is in everyday use, this could be interpreted as suggesting that mathematics, the domain, is responsible for the emergence of interest. Instead, individual interest is both a psychological state and a relatively enduring predisposition of the person to engage this content and grow through his or her work with it.

tional interest, and task value,[3] it can be distinguished from each in that it is specific to each individual and it includes two interrelated components: stored knowledge and stored value—where stored value includes both feelings of competence and positive and negative feelings related to the particular engagement (see also H. Schiefele et al., 1983).

The stored-knowledge component of individual interest refers to a person's developing understanding of the procedures and discourse (structural) knowledge of subject content (see Renninger, 1989, 1990). For individual interest to emerge, a person needs to have enough knowledge to begin to organize this information in ways that raise what have been called curiosity questions (Lindfors, 1987). Thus, a child working with multiplication might ask, "Why isn't six times seven the same as five times eight?" The ability to pose questions that are rooted both in what is known and in what still needs to be figured out is the basis for a person's developing knowledge about what he or she could do or might eventually be able to undertake in pursuing particular subject content. Not only does this knowledge about possible actions lead a person to challenging himself or herself to seek answers, but it also informs his or her developing sense of possible selves (Markus & Nurius, 1986; see related discussions in Eccles, Barber, Upde-

---

[3] For purposes of clarity, working definitions of related motivational concepts are listed below.

1. *Flow* refers to the inherent enjoyment in being totally immersed in activity. It has both a cognitive component (focused attention) and an affective component (feelings of enjoyment) and occurs when abilities are exactly matched to task demands (Csikszentmihalyi, 1975).
2. *Intrinsic interest* refers to intrinsic motivation for particular engagement.
3. *Intrinsic motivation* typically refers to engagement in an activity because it is enjoyable and is rewarding (see Ryan & Deci, chapter 2, this book; Vallerand, 1997), although optimal challenge, piqued curiosity, autonomy, and the opportunity to engage fantasy are identified as sources of motivation (Lepper & Hodell, 1989; see discussion in Pintrich & Schunk, 1996). Harackiewicz, Barron, Tauer, & Carter (in press) have reported that interestingness, usefuless, meaningfulness, and importance predicted reengagement in classes, whereas enjoyment in a particular class did not.
4. *Personal interest* has been used to refer to topic interest, or positive feelings about particular subject content (see U. Schiefele, 1999).
5. *Situational interest* refers to the triggering of a person's attention by characteristics of the environment (typically features of text). This form of interest refers to a short-term involvement with a class of objects or events, although as Hidi and Anderson (1992; see also Krapp, 1999) have pointed out, it is also possible for a situational interest to grow into an individual interest.
6. *Task value* refers to cognitive and positive affective influences on a person's beliefs or self-concept, which in turn influence his or her decision making, and includes perceptions of importance and utility (see Jacob & Eccles, chapter 14, this book; Boekarts, 1999).
7. *Topic interest* has been used in both the situational interest and the individual interest literatures to refer to the likelihood of attending to particular subject content (see Hidi & Baird, 1986) or positive feelings for content (U. Schiefele & Krapp, 1996).

graff, & O'Brien, 1998; Gisbert, 1998; Hannover, 1998; Renninger & Lehman, 1999; Schick, 2000; H. Schiefele, 1986).

The stored-value component of individual interest works in tandem with the stored-knowledge component. It refers both to a person's developing feelings of competence (White, 1959; see Renninger, 1989, 1990) and the corresponding positive and negative emotions that derive from the effort to impose order and consistency on newly acquired understanding. The process of problem posing and problem solving that generates this understanding involves working to figure out something that is not known. Because the problems are curiosity questions, they are not simply answered and they involve some reorganization of what has been understood to date. Thus, even though the outcome of new understanding is ostensibly self-rewarding, the process can also lead to feelings of frustration (see Krapp & Fink, 1992; Neumann, 1999).

Individual interest enables a person to persist in the face of frustration and feelings of failure, to answer questions, and to resolve difficulty[4] (Csikszentmihalyi et. al., 1993; Prenzel, 1992; Renninger & Leckrone, 1991). It sets him or her up to take risks and be resourceful as a problem solver (Renninger & Shumar, 2001). It also means that the processes of problem posing and problem solving might never exactly be completed. This is a critical feature of individual interest. Its value (including concomitant feelings) is enhanced by the challenges it represents as long as the stored knowledge about this content continues to be consolidated, deepened, and extended (see also discussions in H. Schiefele, 1986; Voss & Schauble, 1992).

Individual interest presumes changed—typically deepened—involvement over time. A person picks up on the affordances of particular subject content and uses these to further inform what he or she knows. If his or her base of knowledge is substantive, then this permits the kind of curiosity questions that result in enhanced value of the subject content.

Like motivation, individual interest is generally used to describe people's choices and their activity (Bergin, 1999). Unlike achievement-goal orientation, which has been considered basic to motivation, however, a person is often unaware of his or her goal setting with respect to contents of individual interest. Individual interest may not typically be characterized by specific or articulated goals, because of its flowlike quality (Czikszentmihalyi & Rathunde, 1998[5]) and/or its propensity to shape individual cognition. Individual interest refers to a more fluid process of goal setting and goal adjust-

---

[4] It should be noted, too, that people may persist in activity that is not an individual interest. Prior to the development of individual interest, intrinsic or even extrinsic factors may also result in persistence (see Green-Demers, Pelletier, Stewart, & Gushue, 1998; Sansone, Weir, Harpster, & Morgan, 1992; chapter 11, this book).

[5] Although Czikszentmihalyi & Rathunde (1998) referred to flow as its own goal, they also suggested that a person is clear about goals and feedback. This differs from the present suggestion that a person may be unaware of the process of goal setting with individual interest(s).

ment than that typically discussed in the literature on goals. Even though experts asked about their problem solving can talk about the process of their work (Pintrich, 1999), this is different from spontaneous problem posing and problem solving. People working with content that is of individual interest are addressing questions (through manipulating or exploring, continuing to read, and so forth) that they have posed to themselves. It is the quality of this engagement that presumably fuels their efforts to persist in refining and shaping what they understand.

In fact, individual interest is not necessarily something of which a person is always reflectively aware (Fazio, 1981; Nisbett & Wilson, 1977; Renninger, 1989, 1990, 1998c). In piloting methods to identify contents of individual interest with 10- to 12-year-old students, we found that they could identify a broad spectrum of activity[6] that attracted them, but they were not reliable in their ability to either recount contents of individual interest or evaluate activity as being of individual interest unless their responses were juxtaposed with other possible activities. Young children, for example, may need to be reminded about the nature of their engagements in order to appreciate their interest for them (Fazio, 1981). Older individuals may have a sense of their attraction or preference for a content but have little or no understanding of the contribution knowledge makes to enriching the value of an individual interest. Thus, for them, interest may be equated with attraction, or positive feelings.

Individual interest could be said to describe *the intersection of cognitive and affective functioning*. It appears to be associated with a person's activity, (B. Fink, 1991; Krapp & B. Fink, 1992; Renninger, 1989; Renninger & Leckrone, 1991; Wigfield & Eccles, 1992). It has been said to "school" attention (James, 1890; see also Hidi, 1995; Renninger, 1990; Renninger & Wozniak, 1985), and, although universal, it is individually varying (Renninger, 1990). This means that although all neurologically intact individuals can be identified as having individual interest (Travers, 1978), the content of these interests may differ even when they are identified as being the same (Fink, 1991; Häussler, Hoffmann, Langeheine, Rost, & Sievers, 1998; Krapp & Fink, 1992; Renninger, 1990). The next section of this chapter describes each of these characteristics of individual interest.

INDIVIDUAL INTEREST DEVELOPS IN RELATION TO ACTIVITY

Individual interest at any given point in time describes an individual's consolidated knowledge of and value for particular subject content and the

---

[6] The use of *activity* instead of *topic* here follows in the tradition of activity theorists (see discussion in Lompscher, 1999). It underscores the relational nature of individual interest.

process of further consolidation. Consider the case of Max, an 11-year-old student with a well-developed individual interest in mathematics, who reliably focuses on numbers in stories and jokes even if these are irrelevant; chooses to focus his research project on the economics of baseball (one can buy six hot dogs for $2.99 at a store, but at a ballpark one hot dog costs $3.00; owners and teams angle for new stadiums and drive up the cost of tickets, and so on); and asks his parents for tutoring so that he can do more work in mathematics. Not surprisingly, he has very solid mathematics skills for a child of his age. Max's individual interest in mathematics continues to develop because he is in a position to deepen his knowledge and value for mathematics. He sets mathematical challenges for himself, is supported by a teacher who allows him to pursue his interest, and by a family that can follow through to offer him enrichment work in mathematics.

Although interest can be thought of as propelling a child to seek out particular information or texts—see R. P. Fink's description (1998a, 1998b) of dyslexic students who at ages 10 to 12 read volumes about a content of individual interest—the role of others and objects (i.e. stories, jokes) in helping to support or shape particular contents of interest is an important, perhaps obvious, and yet subtly complex phenomenon (Wigfield & Eccles, 1992). For an individual interest to continue to develop, a person needs opportunities for cognitive challenge. As Feldman (1980) pointed out, the reason that chess prodigies in the United States are concentrated in two cities (New York and Albuquerque) is directly related to the availability of others (masters) who are in a position to challenge these children's knowledge of chess. Although children who are chess prodigies have both strong intrinsic motivation for playing chess and the approval of others such as parents to support them (extrinsic motivation), they need people with whom to play who will enable them to continue to develop their knowledge (people whose questions, challenges, or modeling enable them to further organize what they do know, in turn further enhancing its value and readying them for the next sets of questions). They are not in a position to do this for themselves.

Individual interest, even in the most extreme example of the ability of a prodigy, requires opportunities to identify and work on interest-specific questions. Thus, Max recognizes that he wants more interactions with mathematics than he is getting in school, and he chooses a research topic that allows him to continue to think and work on mathematics. He even overgeneralizes from his individual interest to stories and jokes in which the numbers are not relevant.

Engagement with a content of individual interest, then, refers to *a deepening of interest over time* where the individual continues to question and is encouraged to do so and where there are models and tasks or opportunities available that facilitate its development. As a result, individual interest at Time 1 is not exactly the same as individual interest at Time 2. By Time 2, it is elaborated or more nuanced (B. Fink, 1991, Krapp & B. Fink,

1992; Renninger, 1990; Renninger & Leckrone, 1991). Max continues to have an individual interest for mathematics because his knowledge and value for mathematics continue to deepen.

INDIVIDUAL INTEREST SCHOOLS ATTENTION

Although a person may be attracted to mathematics, poetry, or science and set some goals to learn more about these subjects, one does not simply sit down and *decide* to have an individual interest for mathematics, poetry, science, or the like. Instead, a person with an individual interest for, say, science has in some sense already come to see and question like a scientist and thus has already been asking questions that are similar to those addressed by scientists: A leaf falling from a tree raises a question about momentum; pulling onto the highway leads to marveling at acceleration. Observations and questions specific to a subject emerge in interaction with its particular content and in conjunction with others who see and question in similar ways.

Even though a person is not always reflectively aware of individual interest, it does direct his or her attention toward some subject contents and not others. As such, individual interest might be said to serve as a filter for information to which a person really pays attention (Renninger & Wozniak, 1985). Thus, even though Max knows that he likes doing mathematics, he seems to be unaware that he pays attention to the numbers in stories or jokes whereas others do not, and he does not appear to notice that his research project is the only one that is explicitly mathematical. Moreover, he does not appear concerned about what others will think about his desire to do extra work in mathematics.

The process of perceiving, representing, and acting on information involves continual accommodation to and/or assimilation of information (see discussions in Case, 1998; Fischer & Bidell, 1998; Karmiloff-Smith, 1992; Piaget, 1966; and Rogoff, 1998). Individual interest can acts as a mediator for this process. It influences to what a person pays attention and his or her recognition and recall memory (Renninger & Wozniak, 1985). It helps to form the foundation on which subsequent learning is built. As such, individual interest is always in the process of being further developed, and its focus may be shifted as a function of newly acquired knowledge.

The valuing of knowledge can be said to drive interest development: Value emerges in relation to the quality of understanding and the challenge that a subject content affords. Value serves to maintain a person's attention to interest-related content, in turn leading to a deepened understanding, to more content-specific questions, and so on. Thus, the attention of a person is schooled both by individual interest and by the possibilities of particular contexts for extending and/or constraining its development. These include support to grow a particular individual interest, interaction with expert others, and tasks that permit use of individual interest as context.

ALTHOUGH IT IS UNIVERSAL, INDIVIDUAL INTEREST IS INDIVIDUALLY VARYING

A person's knowledge and value system evolves in relation to environmental constraints and opportunities, the structure or affordances of particular subject areas, and biological predisposition. It develops in relation to all of the activity in which a person is engaged. This means that for each person, there exists a particular configuration of knowledge and value for every subject content. It also means that there are some content areas for which each person can be identified as having more stored knowledge and more stored value (well-developed individual interest), others for which there may be knowledge but less value (less well-developed individual interest),[7] and yet others for which there is low knowledge and high potential value (attraction) (Renninger & Leckrone, 1991).

Because the process of representing information is specific to an individual, two people who share an identified individual interest may not set the same challenges or ask the same questions about subject matter content (Renninger, 1990). The interaction between the subject content (the domain of mathematics, for example) and the possibilities for action that a person understands it to include is unique. People may appreciate the same things and appear to have similar contents of individual interest, but each person has had experiences that preclude the possibility that the contents of individual interests of any two people could be identical (Krapp & B. Fink, 1992; Schick, 2000). The reason for this is that the specific character of an individual interest is influenced by the questions a person generates on the basis of the knowledge he or she has and the way in which this has been organized, his or her sense of possible selves, and his or her feelings of competence. These, in turn, are informed by support from others, interaction with expert others, and the nature of the tasks with which they engage. Thus, even if the mechanisms governing the way in which information is perceived function similarly for most people, the way in which a person represents and subsequently engages with particular subject content is informed by what he or she has come to know and value in interactions with it (Renninger, 1990).

A person is in a qualitatively different position to act on the information gathered about an individual interest, than that about either an attraction or a less well-developed individual interest, however, owing to the knowl-

---

[7] In previous papers, less well-developed individual interest has been labeled noninterest.

edge he or she has garnered and the valuing that comes from posing and acting on curiosity questions. It is possible that with time an attraction will develop into an individual interest. This has been suggested with respect to situational interest (see B. Fink, 1991; Krapp, 1999; Hidi & Anderson, 1992; Hidi & Berndorff, 1998).[8] It is also possible that a less well-developed individual interest will develop into a well-developed individual interest.

Given that a person's process of representing information is developed over time, the nature of the knowledge developed needs to be recognized as being informed by both his or her shared cultural milieu (see Lotman, 1988; Rogoff, 1998) and biological predisposition. Thus, even though individual interests are truly individual, group-based patterns in individual interests can be identified for gender, age, and change over time. These patterns are overviewed here in terms of their effects on both the content of individual interest and its impact on learning.

Individual Interest and Gender

The contents of girls' and boys' individual interest typically match gender stereotypes (Folling-Albers & Hartinger 1998; Hidi, McLaren, & Renninger, 1993). They also influence the ways in which girls and boys work with tasks that are and are not of individual interest (Renninger, 1998c; Renninger, Ewen, & Lasher, in press).

At the risk of stating the obvious, it is useful to keep in mind that although it is likely that the content of individual interest will be gender typical, there is also a possibility that for any particular child this will not be the case. In addition, some subject matter is not gender typical, whereas other subject matter is. Given differences in school culture, child rearing, and so on, it is also possible that the gender typicality or gender atypicality of an individual interest can be context specific. Thus, in one school, for example, girls may not spend a lot of time on computers, whereas in another school they do because a MOO[9] has been set up that provides them with relational opportunities not afforded by their regular classwork (see Davidson & Schofield, 2001).

Gender and the Content of Individual Interest

At 3 years of age, children are sometimes identified as having contents of individual interest that might be considered more typical of the opposite sex (e.g., a boy might be interested in a doll). By 4 years of age, however,

---

[8] On the other hand, an attraction is not synonymous with situational interest; it refers to the triggering stage of situational interest (see Hidi, chapter 11, this book).

[9] A MOO, or multiuser object-oriented, environment, is a an online text-based environment that enables a number of users to converse with each other.

these interests generally shift to or merge with gender-typical play objects (Renninger & Leckrone, 1991). It appears that when a child reengages in play, the challenges are twofold: They include opportunities for him or her to generate and answer questions, and forms of implicit and explicit feedback provided by other children, teachers, and/or parents, about things they could or should do with this subject content (Wigfield & Eccles, 1992).

With age, students' individual interests are increasingly likely to be matched to gender-neutral or gender-typical content. For an older person to maintain an individual interest in a gender-atypical subject, it is likely that (1) he or she is intensely invested in it, (2) this investment is supported by feedback received from others (Hanson, 1996), and (3) opportunities to engage and develop further understanding are available (Jacobs, Finken, Griffin, & Wright, 1998). Not surprisingly, then, the individual interest of a 10- to 12-year-old girl for football, which is gender atypical at this age, is likely to be more intense than that of boys of the same age who share an interest in football (Renninger, 1992).

It may be that girls with an identified individual interest in football are supported in their interest, much as Max was when he sought additional work in mathematics. On the other hand, the constraint of not receiving support from others can also contribute to the development of individual interest. Thwarted efforts to pursue an interest have been identified as contributors to later achievement for some individuals (Coren, 1997). It appears that the role of others is a critical factor in development of individual interest even if their response is not always intended as support.

Gender and Contents of Individual Interest

The content of individual interest influences the types of questions younger girls and boys pose for themselves in play, work undertaken by older children and their sense of the effort this requires.

At 3 and 4 years of age, girls are more likely than boys are to engage an object[10] of individual interest in investigative play, operational play (exploring relations such as balance), and transformational play (substituting something else for the actual object; e.g., wrapping a truck in a blanket and rocking it as a doll), whereas boys are more likely than girls are to engage with an object of individual interest in functional play (using the object as it is used in the real world—a truck is used as a truck) (Renninger, 1990). Such differences suggest that gender influences these children's understanding of possibilities for play with objects of individual interest.

---

[10] Here, *object*, or *play object*, is used to refer to the classes of objects or play areas in which young children play, such as dolls, trucks, scene play, and books.

One might question whether gender-typical contents of individual interest afford only particular types of play; however, study of play actions in each of 16 play areas in a nursery school indicates that 4 types of play (investigative, functional, operational, and transformational) can be identified for any given play object or area (Renninger, 1990). Thus, it seems likely that rather than promoting gender-typical interests, children's play affords opportunities for different types of play and that their activity reflects differences in the nature of the questions they ask (or with which they choose to challenge themselves in play) as a function of both gender and their perceptions of possible activity with objects of individual interest.

Interestingly, the work of 10- to 12-year-old students with expository text and mathematical word problems into which contexts of well-developed and less well-developed individual interest are inserted also reveal some consistent patterns in strategy selection as a function of gender and individual interest (Renninger & Stavis, 1995a, 1995b). For example, when students have difficulty with comprehension, girls are most likely to have difficulty with problems with contexts of well-developed individual interest, whereas boys are more likely to have difficulty with comprehension for problems with contexts of less well-developed individual interest (Renninger, Ewen, & Lasher, in press). When students have difficulty setting up problems, girls are most likely to have difficulty with problems with contexts of well-developed individual interest, whereas boys are more likely to have difficulty setting up problems with contexts of less well-developed individual interest. When students employ keywords as a strategy, girls are more likely to employ them with problems in which the context is a less well-developed individual interest, whereas boys are more likely to employ keywords as a strategy with problems in which a well-developed individual interest is the context.

Although the presence of individual interests as a context improves students' work with expository text and word problems generally, such findings suggest that when students have difficulty, gender and level of individual interest together influence their work. It further suggests that boys may be benefited most by the presence of contexts of well-developed individual interest in school tasks. It may be that because the organization of school tasks is so often geared to the individual interests of boys, girls who confront their own individual interests as isolated contexts for problems and passages either are overstimulated or overconfident in their approach to them (Renninger, 1992).

Regardless of what the explanation is for interactions between gender and contexts of individual interest, the overall impact of gender appears to be substantially more limited for older girls and boys than for younger children. No gender differences emerged, for example, when students in science classes were asked to choose one of three tasks and to describe how they would work with it. Students with a well-developed individual interest for science, however, were more likely than those who were identified as having a less well-developed individual interest for science to need fewer probes, to generate more different strategies, and to explain their choice of solution paths (Renninger & Lehman, 1999). Because middle-school and high school students are at an age when they begin to recognize the depth and complexity of their activity (Todt & Schreiber, 1998), it may also be the case that at these ages they are expanding their repertoire of strategies at least with respect to their work with contents of individual interest. If students do expand their repertoire of strategies with age, this would also account for fewer gender differences with respect to the difficulties they encounter and to the strategies available for working with contents of individual interest. It is consistent with descriptions of individual interest as increasingly consolidated knowledge about and value for particular subject content.

Individual Interest, Age, and Change over Time

Patterns of variation in individual interest have also been identified as a function of both age and typicality—in other words, they change over time and also in relation to a student's neurological profile. In particular, it appears that individual interest serves a somewhat different role in learning as children move from preschool into elementary school and on into adulthood. This role might even be said to be exaggerated in the case of students with atypical profiles.

Individual Interest and Age

At 3 and 4 years of age for most children, approximately two contents of well-developed individual interest can be identified, and because it is a pervasive influence on all facets of their activity, it is described as leading development (Renninger, 1992). Compared to their activity with other play objects, children playing with objects of well-developed individual interest are likely to have more attention, exhibit higher levels of recall and recognition, employ a wider range of play types, carry out more different types of actions, experience more conflict with others who share the same individual interest, show more tenacity in developing skills in order to play with another identified as having the same object of individual interest, and demonstrate more ability to reorganize their activity under conditions requiring persistence. (For an overview, see Renninger, 1992.)

Individual interest leads the development of older children like Max as well. By 10 to 12 years of age, the number of contents for which individual interest can be identified expands to approximately six. These contents of individual interest tend to be strong and to hold across the high school years, although some shifts do occur, especially during middle school (Renninger & Lehman, 1999; Wigfield & Eccles, 1992), suggesting that the occurrence of such shifts reflects a developing sense of competence in engaging with contents of individual interest (Gisbert, 1998; Hannover, 1998).

In fact, when identified as having a well-developed individual interest for science at 10 to 12 years of age, students are most likely to describe science as hard; it is not until 14 to 16 years of age that they are likely to describe it as easy (Renninger & Lehman, 1999). Although seemingly counterintuitive, these findings corroborate points made by Todt and Schreiber (1998), who suggested that by 10 to 12 years of age, students are generally concerned about their competence and ability and, with time, about the prestige or social relevance of possible and preferred engagements. That students who have a well-developed individual interest for science initially rate science as harder than other subjects suggests that they are grappling with the nature of the questions that can be set in science. It is almost as though they need to identify science as being difficult because this is the challenge that they are taking on. It may also be the case that because they have a deeper understanding/appreciation of science, they are more likely to foresee complexities (and thus the level of difficulty) that this content entails.

It appears that by 14 to 16 years of age, students understand that part of developing an understanding of a subject's content involves not having all the answers and working to figure them out (Renninger & Lehman, 1999). Presumably, confidence in their ability to continue to work through challenges provides a basis for their perception that the problem solving required for working with subject matter that is of individual interest is easier for them than it is for others.

With age, students become more cognizant of their questions and more clear about the information they need, so it is not surprising that students' contents of well-developed individual interest also become progressively more focused with age. A well-developed individual interest for physics, for example, might more appropriately be identified as an individual interest for momentum (Häussler et. al., 1998). The questions that form the basis of a student's individual interest, however, are always undergoing increasing consolidation, and new interests do emerge. Thus, a student new to an interest for physics is likely to have an undifferentiated or broad individual interest in physical science, whereas a student whose individual interest has existed and is more developed has been setting challenges for himself or herself and is likely to be more focused about the nature of the questions he or she undertakes (Renninger, 1998b).

Regardless of its particular content, individual interest has been found to influence the way in which students engage and perform on tasks including those in: business education (Wild, Krapp, Schreyer, & Lewalter, 1998; Wild & Krapp, 1998), educational psychology (Alexander, Murphy, Woods, Duhon, & Parker, 1997; U. Schiefele, Wild, & Krapp, 1995), mathematics (see Baumert & Koeller, 1998; Eccles et. al., 1998; Mitchell, 1993; Renninger, 1998c), music (O'Neill, 1997), reading (Ainley, Hillman, & Hidi, in press; Alexander, Kulikowich, & Jetton, 1994; R. P. Fink, 1998a, 1998b; Renninger,

1998c; U. Schiefele, 1991, 1999; U. Schiefele & Krapp, 1996; Wade, Buxton, & Kelly, 1999), science (Alexander, Kulikowich, & Schulze, 1994; Hoffmann & Häussler, 1998; Renninger & Lehman 1999; Schick, 2000; see review in Gardner, 1998), sports (Eccles et. al., 1998; Green-Demers et al., 1998; Rheinberg & U. Schiefele, 1997), vocational education (Athanasou, 1994), and writing (Albin, Benton, & Khramtsova, 1996; Benton, Corkill, Sharp, Downey, & Khramtsova, 1995).

Often, however, students' contents of well-developed individual interest are not a good fit with academic content (Follings-Albers & Hartinger, 1998; Hidi & Anderson, 1992; Hidi & Harackiewicz, 2000, Hidi, Krapp, & Renninger, 1992). Furthermore, contents of well-developed individual interest may or may not be challenged and developed in the context of schools, depending largely on what the content is, the pedagogy, whether there are after-school clubs, and so on. Outside of school, a student might seek a chess master, find challenging problems on the Internet, or read books to continue learning. It is outside of school that many students pursue a content of well-developed individual interest (see Bergin, 1999).

Students spend much of their time in school working with subjects that are contents of less well-developed individual interest,[11] and they need to learn to work with such content if they are to be successful. To do so, however, they need to be able to develop the ability to connect to and develop strategies for working with such content. Because they do not have as developed a knowledge base on which to draw, such ability needs to be set up and supported by an expert other (teacher, parent, caretaker, or possibly a more skilled peer). It is not likely to be generated independently. They also need to begin to see possibilities for their own engagement in content areas of less well-developed individual interest even if, relative to contents of more well-developed individual interest, they never develop as deep a level of knowledge or value.

Over time, a content of less well-developed individual interest might become well-developed. When a person is able to connect to and develop strategies for working with a content such as mathematics, he or she can accurately identify (1) what the problem being discussed requires beyond specifying an algorithm, (2) real-world connections for the mathematics that is being covered in class, and/or (3) alternate solution paths (Renninger,

---

[11] *Interest*, like *individual interest*, refers to levels of stored knowledge and value that an individual brings to his or her engagement with subject content. Low interest refers to subject content about which a person has knowledge, but low value. The terms *boring* and *uninteresting* are not used here because they refer to an interpretation of a student's judgment about value. They do not necessarily refer to the *levels* of stored knowledge and stored value that an individual brings to his or her engagement with subject content. Similarly, the term *disinterest* is not used because it refers to judgment about a person's valuing and, as such, may not refer to an individual's levels of stored knowledge and value for subject content.

Farra, & Feldman-Riordan, 2000). This kind of knowledge is the basis of the kind of curiosity questions that characterize work with a well-developed individual interest.

Without the ability to generate curiosity questions about the mathematics being covered in a class, it is likely that a student will have low value for mathematics and that mathematics will continue to be a content of less well-developed individual interest. With the capacity to ask such questions, the student begins to develop a sense of possibility about the content to be learned. The value component of interest is enabled to deepen and fuels the questioning and challenge seeking that characterizes well-developed individual interest.

Unlike the flowlike quality of work with contents of well-developed individual interest, however, contents of less well-developed individual interest require students to spend time working on tasks they are not likely to choose for themselves. Some students may set themselves mastery goals of identifying what is interesting to them in an assignment, and enable themselves to make connections that, in turn, lead to the kind of reorganization and ownership necessary to an enriched or deep valuing. Such students might be said to fit the description of the performance-oriented students and may even be task oriented as well (Ames & Archer, 1988; Dweck, 1986; Nicholls, 1989). Others students may do only as much as they have to do. They may develop enough knowledge to do the task but typically hold little value for it and it makes little impact on their developing knowledge base. Still others appear to have chosen not to engage, but it may also be the case that they really *cannot*—at least not without assistance. They seem to have little or no knowledge and to hold no value for a task.

When teachers, parents, and researchers think about students, interests, and schooling, they may identify these three types of students, even if they do not give them these labels. A critical and often overlooked aspect of such classification is that even though students are not resourceful with respect to one content area, they too have contents of well-developed individual interest. These may not be considered desirable by teachers, parents, and so forth, but when observed in an arcade, the so-called disinterested student can look like a task-oriented learner. Because of their specific concern for particular subject content, teachers (and researchers) often do not know what the contents of students' well-developed individual interest are or whether their genetic makeup predisposes them to need substantial amounts of support to work with contents of less well-developed individual interest.

Individual Interest and Atypical Developmental Profiles

Studies of students with atypical developmental profiles suggest that individual interest can have such a dominant effect on learning that it overshadows the resources they need to be able to work with contents of less well-developed individual interest. Students with dyslexia, Asperger's syndrome (AS), and Williams syndrome (WS), in particular, raise questions about the relation between individual interest and the resourcefulness of those considered to be typical students.

Briefly, R. P. Fink (1998a, 1998b) reported that for extremely bright but dyslexic individuals, readiness was critical to their perseverance with reading for which they had a less well-developed individual interest, as was the association of content of a well-developed individual interest to reading. At 11 to 12 years of age, they were not new to the process of learning to read; however, they had not thought that they could read very well and only somewhat suddenly realized that reading well was a possibility, presumably because they had the tools for decoding and found that these enbaled them to extend their knowledge.

Similarly, people with AS, a pervasive developmental disorder, read and learn more effectively if working with contents of individual interest (K. Kalwaic, personal communication, June 28, 1999); in fact, they are invested in these contents to the exclusion of almost everything else (O'Neil, 1999). Typically, students with AS are quite verbal and have average intelligence. Like autistic children, they also have almost no social skills or intuition and need support to take care of themselves (Siegel, 1996). Although individual interest appears to play an exaggerated role in the lives of these students, the characteristics of their contents of individual interest are not so different from those of more typical populations. They allow for deepening understanding of a particular (although sometimes arcane) subject content (e.g., authoritarian control in political systems) that includes opportunities for the kind of manipulation and reorganization that contribute to personal valuing (Siegel, 1996). Students with AS can also learn to work with contents of less well-developed individual interest such as daily living skills, but specific plans for training and support are necessary (Siegel, 1996).

Children with WS also have unusual strengths in a content of well-developed individual interest (often music), strong verbal abilities, and social skills, although they are poor readers and writers and obtain low scores on standard IQ tests (Lenhoff, Wang, Greenberg, & Bellugi, 1997). In fact, as Lenhoff et al. (1997) pointed out, the verbal abilities of WS children often obscure their difficulty with reasoning. As a result, they sometimes do not get the kind of academic support they really need because they look more capable than they are.

A parallel can be drawn between the pervasive influence of well-developed individual interest on the functioning of young children and its role in the learning of students with the atypicalities described. Both groups of students appear goal directed although they are likely to be unaware of the process of their goal setting. The content of their individual interest is exceptionally well developed and influences their knowledge acquisition, strategy use, and performance. They appear to have few resources for working with less well-developed individaul interest, however, unless these are organized for them.

More typical older populations develop an expanded number of individual interests and an ability to work with contents of less well-developed individual interest. In fact, it appears that in the course of problem posing, the content of well-developed individual interest merges with other subject matter, providing them with natural scaffolds for learning in related areas (Renninger & Shumar, 2001). Even if knowledge and value for other subject content does not develop to the point of being a well-developed individual interest, the basis for learning about these contents is established in a way that it may not be for younger children (because of age, experience, and so forth) or for students who because of their neurological profiles are either developmentally delayed or are prodigies.

Descriptions of the role of individual interest in the learning of young children, older children, and atypical children underscore the universal yet individually varying role of individual interest in development, and its impact on learning. They also call attention to the importance of seriously examining the particular contribution of well-developed and less well-developed individual interest to discussions of motivation and learning. Although students working with individual interest can always be understood to be motivated, all motivated behavior does not necessarily reflect well-developed individual interest.

Individual Interest, Motivation, and Learning

Although a kind of ongoing shifting takes place over time in terms of what is understood and how much it is valued, at any given time it is possible to identify subject content for which a person has well-developed and less well-developed individual interest. People working with contents of well-developed individual interest are motivated learners, in the sense that their activity appears purposeful, sustained, and ever deepening. Because their learning of this content tends to be ongoing, they also are likely to be unreflective about the learning in which they are engaged. For them, learning is not necessarily the product of specific or articulated goals. Instead, their understanding of contents for which they have well-developed individual interest continues to develop because they seize opportunities to learn and seek to work with others and/or texts that provide models for and feedback that supports their curiosity questioning and challenge seeking and serves as a kind of scaffold to more complex aspects of the subject content. People do not really need to make a choice to learn subject matter that is of well-developed individual interest; choice in this instance is largely an effortless process (Hidi, 1995; Schraw, Flowerday, & Lehman, in press).

Learning the skills and discourse knowledge of content of less well-developed individual interest, however, is not so easy. Students are less likely to organize and work on developing the knowledge they have about such content. They also are generally unable to ask any but procedural questions of others (or the texts with which they work)—unless they set a goal to learn it.

Most people can set goals to master content of less well-developed individual interest, and they can learn to do so (Sansone & Morgan, 1992; Sansone et al., 1992; Werner & Makela, 1998; Wolters, 1998). They can reorganize what they understand a task to involve using interest-enhancing strategies that call attention to previously unappreciated aspects of the task and/or change the way in which they approach and follow through in their work with it (Sansone et al., 1992; see also Green-Demers et al., 1998). Interestingly, each of these interest-enhancing strategies requires increased knowledge about a given content to enable individuals to reorganize and, in turn, deepen their value for it.

Of note in this regard are findings from Werner and Makela's (1998) study of intervention methods for involving a neighborhood in recycling. Individuals identified as having prorecycling attitudes developed a way to organize recycling and they reported that their efforts felt "interesting and worthwhile" (p. 381), whereas those who did not have these attitudes remained poor recyclers. Although the achievement of the prorecyclers was discussed in terms of their positive prorecycling attitudes, using the lens of well-developed and less well-developed individual interest it seems likely that they could not have had such positive attitudes without having some understanding of what recycling was. This group had knowledge but low value for recycling relative to the other things that they were doing. Interest-enhancing strategies facilitated the development of their knowledge and value for this knowledge such that by the end of the study, their understanding about what recycling involved was no longer the same as it had been at the outset of the study (Sansone, Sachau, & Weir, 1989). Whether these maintained behaviors would be identified as a well-developed individual interest is an open question. Those in the prorecycling group had been able to reorganize their knowledge of recycling and were, as a result, in a position to maintain recycling behaviors (see related discussion in Yarlas, 1999).

It seems likely that in the case of the prorecyclers, positive feelings provided the trigger that enabled their knowledge and value to develop. Their less well-developed individual interest for recycling might or might not have shifted to being a well-developed individual interest. Regardless of the extent of the shift, they sustained their recycling behaviors because of the reciprocal relation between the knowledge generated by the interest-enhancing strategies and the preferences or feelings that provided the prorecyclers with a reason for engagement (Sansone et. al., 1992; Werner & Makela, 1998). Such findings provide support for a thesis that it is in conjunction with the development of knowledge that people develop habits that enable them to deepen their value for a content. In addition to the positive regard that positive feelings invoke, the ability to use a strategy that results in effective work with a content of less well-developed individual interest such as recycling is the product of what a person's knowledge/value system allows. To be able to organize information, make a decision to learn it, and come to "own" questions about it, a person must (1) know enough to organize what he or she knows, (2) seek resources to figure out what is not known, (3) come to enjoy the facts of understanding and developing competence, and (4) be clear about what he or she still wants to understand/work out.

In fact, it seems likely that those with less well-developed individual interest for particular subject content are more dependent on direct instruction from others than are those with well-developed individual interest, precisely because they are less resourceful about generating their own questions and challenges (Renninger, 1998a; Roehler, Duffy, & Meloth, 1986). Although Max seeks additional work in mathematics to grow his well-developed individual interest, another child may need a tremendous amount of support to move from a few memorized multiplication facts to a conceptual understanding of what x means. Still another child may need feedback before he or she can do anything at all mathematical.

Individual motivation for working with both well-developed and less well-developed individual interest content over time can appear to occur spontaneously, such as when a person discovers that technology parallels his or her well-developed individual interest in, say, mathematics. In such a situation, the skills, discourse knowledge, and questioning that characterize well-developed individual interest could be said to provide a scaffold to the content to be mastered (Renninger & Shumar, 2001).

More typically, developing the kind of knowledge and value that leads to well-developed individual interest needs to be facilitated by more than available texts. This requires planful effort on the part of a teacher or an expert other. Students need enough of a knowledge base that they become curious and begin generating their own questions about a given content and begin to develop the depth of value for it that will lead to reengagement. Facilitating such knowledge development is not a discrete task, however. It involves working to support students, their habits, and their potential: their self-perceptions (Bandura, 1986; Schunk, 1991; Zimmerman, 1989), attributions (Weiner, 1992), goals (Ames, 1992; Harackiewicz, Barron, & Elliot, 1998), and task value (Wigfield & Eccles, 1992). More particularly, it means working to shift school, peer, and even family culture to provide them with opportunities to change and enable them to self-regulate (Schunk & Zimmerman, 1994). Supporting the development of knowledge, then, catalyzes questioning about content of less well-developed individual interest and shifts both in value—including concomitant feelings about self-worth and possibility—and in habits such as questioning and reflection that are requisite to effective learning.[12] On the basis of what we know about the relation between well-developed and less well-developed individual interest as a reflection of the knowledge/value system, it seems likely that any attempt to facilitate a person's continued involvement with a less well-developed individual interest requires identifying (1) the nature of students' present activity, (2) what draws their attention, and (3) how to help them learn to use the resources they have to develop the knowledge and ultimately the value necessary for working with these tasks. This means figuring out what students understand about a given subject and what they still need to understand. On the basis of this information, the teacher (parent, expert other) can adjust instruction (information and expectations) to meet student's strengths and needs as learners[13] (see Renninger, 1998a).

Even if a less well-developed individaul interest never becomes well-developed, teachers are in a position to facilitate the expansion of students' sense of possibility and to organize instruction to meet their strengths and needs. Given that students already have contents of well-developed individual interest and that new ones develop over time, teachers can work with students to develop their knowledge and value for other content and they can communicate the possibility of learning it. They can provide students with opportunities that increase levels of confidence and competence (Maehr & Midgley, 1991). They can help them to learn to work effectively with a less well-developed individual interest—to evaluate

---

[12] It is likely that such shifts are gradual and that they occur in relation to the strengths and needs of the person and his or her circumstances (see Sansone & Smith, chapter 12, this book).

[13] A further complication for teachers as they endeavor to work with students to learn content involves their own content(s) of well-developed individual interest. Teachers who have a well-developed individual interest for the content they teach see connections between subject matter and the real world or other subject content to be learned; they may generate alternative strategies for solutions to problems without having to really think about how they did so; and they may make leaps in the way they talk about the subject matter because to them the links are obvious. On the other hand, their comfort with the subject also means they need to learn how to chunk or model thinking about each of these dimensions of the subject content to be learned so that those with less well-developed individual interest for content can begin to ask the kind of questions that will enable them to have the resources with which to pursue it further.

It takes work to recognize what it is that students do not understand about a problem—but teachers who have content knowledge are in a position to think about what the student does not understand (see Carpenter, Fennema, & Franke, 1996; Stigler, Fernandez, & Yoshida, 1996). They need to figure out how to organize information so that connections between the content to be learned and the real world or other known contents can be made, strategies can be modeled, and explanations can be offered. This also involves being aware that having a well-developed individual interest in a subject matter could lead one to make assumptions about the ways in which others learn.

accurately what a problem/task involves, to generate ideas about problem solution, and to apply a strategy to meet the demands of the task (see Polya, 1945/88; Schoenfeld, 1992; Sternberg, 1985).

When well orchestrated, group work and project-based learning enable students to connect to subject matter and to do so through thinking together with others[14] (see effective examples in Ball, 1993; Cobb, 1995; Lampert, 1986; Springer, 1994; also see discussions in Blumenfeld, Soloway, Marx, Krajcik, Guzdial, & Palincsar, 1991, and in Bransford, Brown, & Cocking, 1999). Tasks of this type enable students to begin experimenting with knowledge and can position them for asking curiosity questions. They also result in better performance[15] (Goldman et al., 1998; Hidi et al., 1998; Hoffmann & Häussler, 1998). In fact, the process of talking together about contents of less well-developed individual interest presumably positions students to begin developing the habit of talking through content and to use others as a resource for thinking through (and reflecting on) content in the future. The provision of time and a context within which to reflect on and revise what they think they understand enables students to discard the irrelevant and correct what has been misunderstood (see examples in Cobb, 1995). It also affords the teacher an opportunity to observe where a student is in the process of developing his or her understanding, in turn allowing facilitation of subsequent instruction to be tailored to what the student knows.

Inserting contexts of well-developed individual interest into tasks that are of less well-developed individual interest (e.g., making ice hockey the context of a word problem) increases the likelihood that all students will try to do a given problem, and it may even influence the accuracy of their problem solution (Renninger 1992; 1998c). Such insertions are not likely, however, to cause the student to be resourceful about work with contents of less well-developed individual interest or to develop their skills over time—unless this effort is organized systematically to meet students' content-specific strengths and needs. What insertion of a context of well-developed individual interest into a task does provide is an opportunity for the student to (1) ask questions, (2) make connections between contents of well-developed and less well-developed individual interest (Renninger, et. al., in press) and (3) make choices about goals for activity that may be qualitatively different from those possible when the context of the word problem refers to content of less well-developed individual interest.

---

[14] Well-orchestrated group work includes tasks that are adjusted to the strengths and weaknesses of students and includes both clear role assignments and goals (see Renninger, 1998a).

[15] This is not to suggest that all of the students' time should be spent in group work or on projects but rather that opportunities to further consolidate learning through such activities (assuming they are well executed) provide a useful complement to more direct instruction (see discussion in Renninger, 1998a).

Given a learning environment in which another (teacher, expert other, etc.) supports the development of knowledge about and valuing for content, it is possible for individuals to experience changed motivation, including increased value for subject matter and the development of habits such as questioning and reflection that are necessary for effective learning. Without a knowledge base from which to ask curiosity questions and begin to set challenges for oneself that lead to valuing, however, there is little to understand or value, and changed motivation is unlikely.

Individual Interest and Intrinsic Motivation

Individual interest and *intrinsic motivation* do appear to describe similar outcomes. These include the enjoyment of focused and continued engagement in a task for the sake of the task itself, the pursuit of challenge, and the desire for mastery. For individual interest, these outcomes are linked to particular person–subject content relations. For intrinsic motivation, these outcomes apply more generally to human behavior, in the moment (situational interest) and over time (individual interest). As such, individual interest might be considered to provide a developmental context for thinking about intrinsic motivation. It focuses on the relations between each person and particular subject content over time and the impact of these on behavior.

Individual interest has characteristics that map onto each of the three independent conceptualizations of intrinsic motivation identified by Lepper (1985): (1) a focus on problem solving (studies of challenge, competence, effectance, mastery motivation), (2) a focus on information processing (studies of complexity, curiosity, discrepancy, and incongruity), and (3) a focus on control (studies of autonomy, choice, contingencies, responsiveness of the environment).

For a content of well-developed individual interest to emerge, a person needs to have enough knowledge about a particular subject content to begin asking curiosity questions and setting the kinds of challenges that involve reorganizing what he or she has understood previously. This reorganization provides the basis for deepening value, including feelings of competence and effectance. It is an ongoing process that permits the working and reworking of questions over time, or mastery. Because of its interrelation with knowledge, such value can manifest itself as enjoyment and pleasure but cannot simply be equated with enjoyment (see Harackiewiz et al., in press). Instead, the value component of individual interest evolves over time in relation to knowledge. It includes both the pleasure that comes from figuring something out and the commitment to work through frustration.

Well-developed and less well-developed individual interest specify predictable qualitites of engagement with subject content (provided that these are assessed in relation to the rest of a person's activity). They are conceptualized as reflecting the knowledge/value system that informs activity. They regulate to what a person pays attention, including the lens with which a person is then in a position to engage content of less well-developed individual interest. A person is more likely to shift attention to, recognize, and recall subject contents of well-developed rather than less well-developed individual interest (Renninger & Wozniak, 1985) and will overgeneralize on the basis of his or her content of well-developed individual interest (Renninger, 1989). Furthermore, it appears that well-developed individual interest affords more complexity and more options for activity than does less well-developed individual interest, because it involves ongoing efforts to grapple with discrepancy and incongruity (Renninger, 1990, Renninger & Leckrone, 1991).

Research on the effects of well-developed individual interest on young children's learning suggest that it is a pervasive influence on what and how children learn (Renninger, 1992). With age, students can learn to work with contents of less well-developed interest if provided with interest-enhancing strategies (see Hoffmann & Häussler, 1998; Sansone et al., 1992) that involve making connections to, developing strategies for, and increasing levels of autonomy in working with tasks. They also can maintain focused and continued engagement with a task of well-developed individual interest for the sake of the task itself, the pursuit of challenge, and the desire for mastery.

It appears that individual interest provides a particular kind of wide-angle lens for thinking about intrinsic motivation because it addresses problem solving, information processing, and control with respect to particular engagement over time. Furthermore, both internal and external factors contribute to its development. Well-developed individual interest cannot develop without the continued challenges that stem from modeling, opportunities to apprentice, and interaction with others and text. It will not emerge unless a person owns the curiosity questions on which he or she is working. Knowledge about possibilities for activity derive from the process of problem posing and problem solving, and this, in turn, informs a person's valuing, including his or her developing sense of possible selves (Markus & Nurius, 1986). At this level of analysis, the contribution of both internal and external factors to behavior is salient.

Furthermore, because individual interest does not reside solely in the task or in the person but in the possibilities for activity with a task that are perceived by the individual (Renninger, 1990), it needs to be recognized as a specified type of intrinsic motivation that differs from that on which intrinsic motivation has typically focused. Methodologically, research on well-developed individual interests has focused on individual engagement with identified individual interests (where for one person this may be mathematics and for the other person it is skiing) or has focused specifically on a knowledgeable group such as figure skaters in training, assessing value-related feelings (Green-Demers et al., 1998)—always considering the particular person-content relation relative to other such relations. It has been assessed using (1) naturalistic observation over extended periods of time in which knowledge and value are operationalized in terms of play activity (Renninger, 1989, 1990; Renninger & Leckrone, 1991; see discussion in Renninger, 1992), (2) ratings of knowledge, feelings, and activity (Ainley, et. al., in press; Benton et al., 1995; Renninger, 1992, 1998c), or the dimensions of a student's interest for the subject content, its context, and a particular activity (Gräber, 1998; Häussler, 1987; Häussler & Hoffmann, 1998; see also Alexander et al., 1997).

Accounting for the differing levels of knowledge *and* value that each person brings to his or her engagement with tasks provides a context for revisiting conceptualizations of intrinsic motivation in terms of problem solving, information processing, and control. Furthermore, appreciating that motives such as needs and desire are interrelated with individual interest distinguishes them from their relation to contents of less well-developed individual interest or even situational interest. Given this, there are a host of open questions that remain concerning the role of individual interest, low interest, and situational interest in conceptualizations of intrinsic motivation—for example: What distinctions are introduced into the definition of competence, the nature of rewards, and/or a person's goals by differences in a person's levels of knowledge and value for particular subject content (see Hidi, chapter 11, this book)? What is the impact of interest-enhancing strategies on students' work with academic tasks that are of individual interest? Does self-regulation differ if a person has a well-developed rather than a less well-developed individual interest or a situational interest for a task? Do definitions of mastery change if a person has a well-developed rather than a less well-developed individual interest or a situational interest for a task? What does it mean to be interested in a task for the sake of the task itself, if in fact the task keeps changing because it raises new questions?

It appears that by focusing on issues of context, individual motivation, and change over time, research on the development of individual interest might extend current conceptualizations of intrinsic motivation (see related discussion in Eccles, Wigfield, & Schiefele, 1998). In particular, this research underscores the effect of differing levels of both knowledge and value on what and how students learn. It also illustrates the usefulness of moving beyond the laboratory and away from novel tasks to examine the ongoing learning in which an individual is engaged over time.

Acknowledgments

I acknowledge the many contributions that my students, fellow researchers, and colleagues have made to my thinking about the development of individual interest and its relation to both intrinsic motivation and learning. I also appreciate the thoughtful reviews of earlier drafts of this manuscript by Mary Ainley, Judy Harackiewicz, Lore Hoffmann, Suzanne Hidi, Carol Sansone, and Irving Sigel. I would like to thank Sarah Seastone, Claire Feldman-Riordan, and Alecia Magnifico for their help in preparing this chapter for publication. Support from Swarthmore College's Faculty Research Fund and Sabbatical Leave Program is also gratefully acknowledged.

References

Ainley, M., Hillman, K., & Hidi, S. (in press). Gender and interest processes in response to English texts: Situational and individual interest. *Learning and Instruction*.

Albin, M. L., Benton, S. L., & Khramtsova, I. (1996). Individual differences in interest and narrative writing. *Contemporary Educational Psychology*, 21, 305–324.

Alexander, P. A., Kulikowich, J. M., & Jetton, T. L. (1994). The role of subject-matter knowledge and interest in the processing of linear and non-linear texts. *Review of Educational Research*, 64, 201–252.

Alexander, P. A., Kulikowich, J. M., & Schulze, S. K. (1994). The influence of knowledge, domain knowledge, and interest on the comprehension of scientific exposition. *Learning and Individual Differences*, 6, 379–397.

Alexander, P. A., Murphy, P. K., Woods, B. S., Duhon, K. E., & Parker, D. (1997). College instruction and concomitant changes in students' knowledge, interest, and strategy use: A study of domain learning. *Contemporary Educational Psychology*, 22, 125–146.

Ames, C. (1992). Classrooms: Goals, structures, and student motivation. *Journal of Educational Psychology*, 84, 261–271.

Ames, C., & Archer, J. (1988). Achievement goals in the classroom: Students' learning strategies and motivation processes. *Journal of Educational Psychology*, 80, 260–267.

Athanasou, J. A. (1994). Some effects of career interests, subject preferences and quality of teaching on the educational achievement of Australian technical and further education students. *Journal of Vocational Education Research*, 19, 23–38.

Baldwin, J. M. (1897). *Social and ethical interpretations in mental development: A study in social psychology*. London: Cambridge University Press.

Baldwin, J. M. (1906). *Thought and things: A study of the development and meaning of thought* (vol. 1). New York: Macmillan.

Baldwin, J. M. (1911). *Thought and things: A study of the development and meaning of thought* (vol. 3). New York: Macmillan.

Ball, D. L. (1993). With an eye on the mathematical horizon: Dilemmas of teaching elementary school mathematics. *Elementary School Journal*, 93(4), 373–397.

Bandura, A. (1986). *Social foundations of thought and action: A social cognitive theory*. Englewood Cliffs, NJ: Prentice-Hall.

Baumert, J., & Koeller, O. (1998). Interest research in secondary level I: An overview. In L. Hoffmann, A. Krapp, K. A. Renninger, & J. Baumert (Eds.), *Interest and learning: Proceedings of the Seeon Conference on Interest and Gender* (pp. 241–257). Kiel, Germany: IPN.

Benton, S. L., Corkill, A. J., Sharp, J. M., Downey, R. G., & Khramtsova, I. (1995). Knowledge, interest, and narrative writing. *Journal of Educational Psychology*, 87(1), 66–79.

Bergin, D. A. (1999). Influences on classroom interest. *Educational Psychologist*, 34(2), 87–98.

Blumenfeld, P., Soloway, E., Marx, R., Krajcik, J., Guzdial, M., & Palinscar, A. (1991). Motivating project-based learning: Sustaining the doing, supporting the learning. *Educational Psychologist*, 26(3&4), 369–398.

Boekaerts, M. (1999). Motivated learning: Studying student–situation transactional units. *Learning and Instruction*, 14(1), 41–55.

Bransford, J. D., Brown, A. L., & Cocking, R. R. (1999). *How people learn: Brain, mind, experience, and school*. Washington, DC: National Academy Press.

Carpenter, T. P., Fennema, E., & Franke, M. L. (1996). Cognitively-guided instruction: A knowledge base for reform in primary mathematics instruction. *Elementary School Journal*, 97(1), 3–20.

Case, R. (1998). The development of conceptual structures. In D. Kuhn & R. S. Siegler (Vol. Eds.), *Cognition, perception, and language* (vol. 2). In W. Damon (Gen. Ed.), *Handbook of child psychology* (pp. 745–801). New York: Wiley.

Cobb, P. (1995). Mathematical learning and small-group interaction: Four case studies. In P. Cobb & H. Bauersfeld (Eds.), *The emergence of mathematical meaning: Interaction in classroom cultures* (pp. 25–131). Hillsdale, NJ: Erlbaum.

Coren, A. (1997). A psychodynamic approach to education. London: Sheldon Press.

Csikszentmihalyi, M. (1975). Beyond boredom and anxiety. San Francisco: Jossey-Bass.

Csikszentmihalyi, M., & Rathunde, K. (1998). The development of the person: An experimental perspective on the ontogenesis of psychological complexity. In W. Damon (Ed.) & R. Lerner (Vol. Ed.), Handbook of Child Psychology (vol. 1, pp. 635–685). New York: Wiley.

Csikszentmihalyi, M., Rathunde, K., & Whalen, S. (1993). Talented teenagers: The roots of success and failure. New York: Cambridge University Press.

Davidson, A. L., & Schofield, J. W. (in press). Female voices in virtual reality: Drawing young girls into an online world. In K. A. Renninger, & W. Shumar (Eds.), Building virtual communities: Learning and change in cyberspace. New York: Cambridge University Press.

Dewey, J. (1913). Interest and effort in education. New York: Houghton Mifflin.

Dewey, J. (1916). Democracy and education: An introduction to the philosophy of education. New York: Macmillan.

Dweck, C. S. (1986). Motivational processes affecting learning. American Psychologist, 41, 1040–1048.

Eccles, J. S., Barber, B. L., Updegraff, K., & O'Brien, K. M. (1998). An expectancy-value model of achievement choices: The role of ability self-concepts, perceived task utility and interest in predicting activity choice and course enrollment. In L. Hoffmann, A. Krapp, K. A. Renninger, & J. Baumert (Eds.), Interest and learning: Proceedings of the Seeon Conference on Interest and Gender (pp. 267–280). Kiel, Germany: IPN.

Eccles, J. S., Wigfield, A., & Schiefele, U. (1998). Motivation to succeed. In N. Eisenberg (Ed.), Social, emotional, and personality development (vol. 3). In W. Damon (Gen. Ed.), Handbook of child psychology (pp. 1017–1095). New York: Wiley.

Fazio, R. H. (1981). On the self-perception explanation of the overjustification effect: The role of the salience of initial attitude. Journal of Experimental Social Psychology, 17, 417–426.

Feldman, D. H. (1980). Beyond universals in cognitive development. Norwood, NJ: Ablex.

Fink, B. (1991). Interest development as structural change in person–object relationships. In L. Oppenheimer & J. Valsiner (Eds.), The origins of action: Interdisciplinary and international perspectives. New York: Springer-Verlag.

Fink, R. P. (1998a). Interest, gender, and literacy development in successful dyslexics. In L. Hoffmann, A. Krapp, K. A. Renninger, & J. Baumert (Eds.), Interest and learning: Proceedings of the Seeon Conference on Interest and Gender (pp. 402–408). Kiel, Germany: IPN.

Fink, R. P. (1998b). Literacy development in successful men and women with dyslexia. Annals of Dyslexia, 48, 311–347.

Fischer, K. W., & Bidell, T. R. (1998). Dynamic development of psychological structures in action and thought. In R. Lerner (Vol. Ed.), Theoretical models of human development (vol. 1). In W. Damon (Gen. Ed.), Handbook of child psychology (pp. 467–563). New York: Wiley.

Folling-Albers, M., & Hartinger, A. (1998). Interest of girls and boys in elementary school. In L. Hoffmann, A. Krapp, K. A. Renninger, & J. Baumert (Eds.), Interest and learning: Proceedings of the Seeon Conference on Interest and Gender (pp. 175–184). Kiel, Germany: IPN.

Gardner, P. L. (1998). The development of males' and females' interests in science and technology. In L. Hoffmann, A. Krapp, K. A. Renninger, & J. Baumert (Eds.), Interest and learning: Proceedings of the Seeon Conference on Interest and Gender (pp. 41–58). Kiel, Germany: IPN.

Gisbert, K. (1998). Individual interest in mathematics and female gender identity: Biographical case studies. In L. Hoffmann, A. Krapp, K. A. Renninger, & J. Baumert (Eds.), Interest and learning: Proceedings of the Seeon Conference on Interest and Gender (pp. 387–402). Kiel, Germany: IPN.

Green-Demers, I., Pelletier, L. G., Stewart, D. G., & Gushue, N. R. (1998). Coping with the less interesting aspects of training: Toward a model of interest and motivation enhancement in individual sports. Basic and Applied Social Psychology, 20(4), 251–261.

Goldman, S. R., Mayfield-Stewart, C., Bateman, H. V., Pellegrino, J. W., & the Cognition and Technology Group at Vanderbilt (1998). Environments that support meaningful learning. In L. Hoffmann, A. Krapp, K. A. Renninger, & J. Baumert (Eds.), Interest and learning: Proceedings of the Seeon Conference on Interest and Gender (pp. 184–197). Kiel, Germany: IPN.

Gräber, W. (1998). Schooling for lifelong attention to chemistry issues: The role of interest and achievement. In L. Hoffmann, A. Krapp, K. A. Renninger, & J. Baumert (Eds.), *Interest and learning: Proceedings of the Seeon Conference on Interest and Gender* (pp. 290–300). Kiel, Germany: IPN.

Hannover, B. (1998). The development of self-concept and interests. In L. Hoffmann, A. Krapp, K. A. Renninger, & J. Baumert (Eds.), *Interest and learning: Proceedings of the Seeon Conference on Interest and Gender* (pp. 105–126). Kiel, Germany: IPN.

Hanson, S. L. (1996). *Lost talent: Women in the sciences*. Philadelphia: Temple University Press.

Harackiewicz, J. M., Barron, K. E., & Elliot, A. J. (1998). Rethinking achievement goals: When are they adaptive for college students and why? *Educational Psychologist*, 33(1), 1–21.

Harackiewicz, J. M., Barron, K. E., Tauer, J. M., & Carter, S. M. (in press). Short-term and long-term consequences of achievement goals: Predicting interest and performance over time. *Journal of Educational Psychology.*

Häussler, P. (1987). Measuring students' interest in physics-design and results of a cross-sectional study in the Federal Republic of Germany. *International Journal of Science Education* 9(1), 79–92.

Häussler, P., & Hoffmann, L. (1998). Qualitative differences in students' interest in physics and the dependence on gender and age. In L. Hoffmann, A. Krapp, K. A. Renninger, & J. Baumert (Eds.), *Interest and learning: Proceedings of the Seeon Conference on Interest and Gender* (pp. 280–290). Kiel, Germany: IPN.

Häussler, P., Hoffmann, L., Langeheine, R., Rost, J., & Sievers, K. (1998). A typology of students' interest in physics and the distribution of gender and age within each type. *International Journal of Science Education*, 20(2), 223–238.

Hidi, S. (1990). Interest and its contribution as a mental resource for learning. *Review of Educational Research*, 60(4), 549–571.

Hidi, S. (1995). A reexamination of the role of attention in learning from text. *Educational Psychology Review*, 7(4), 323–350.

Hidi, S., & Harackiewicz, J. M. (2000). Motivating the academically unmotivated: A critical issue for the 21st century. *Review of Educational Research.*

Hidi, S., & Anderson, V. (1992). Situational interest and its impact on reading and expository writing. In K. A. Renninger, S. Hidi, & A. Krapp (Eds.), *The role of interest in learning and development* (pp. 215–239). Hillsdale, NJ: Erlbaum.

Hidi, S., & Baird, W. (1986). Interestingness—a neglected variable in discourse processing. *Cognitive Science*, 10, 179–194.

Hidi, S., & Berndorff, D. (1998). Situational interest and learning. In L. Hoffmann, A. Krapp, K. A. Renninger, & J. Baumert (Eds.), *Interest and learning: Proceedings of the Seeon Conference on Interest and Gender* (pp. 74–90). Kiel, Germany: IPN.

Hidi, S., Krapp, A., & Renninger, K. A. (1992). The present state of interest research. In K. A. Renninger, S. Hidi, & A. Krapp (Eds.), *The role of interest in learning and development* (pp. 433–446). Hillsdale, NJ: Erlbaum.

Hidi, S. E., McLaren J., & Renninger, K. A. (April, 1993). Individual interest and gender differences: A cross-cultural study. Poster displayed at the 74th annual meeting of the American Educational Research Association, Atlanta.

Hidi, S. E., Weiss, J., Berndorff, D., & Nolan, J. (1998). The role of gender, instruction and a cooperative learning technique in science education across formal and informal settings. In L. Hoffmann, A. Krapp, K. A. Renninger, & J. Baumert (Eds.), *Interest and learning: Proceedings of the Seeon Conference on Interest and Gender* (pp. 215–228). Kiel, Germany: IPN.

Hoffmann, L., & Häussler, P. (1998). An intervention project promoting girls' and boys' interest in physics. In L. Hoffmann, A. Krapp, K. A. Renninger, & J. Baumert (Eds.), *Interest and learning: Proceedings of the Seeon Conference on Interest and Gender* (pp. 301–317). Kiel, Germany: IPN.

Jacobs, J. E., Finken, L. L., Griffen, N. L., & Wright, J. D. (1998). The career plans of science-talented rural adolescent girls. *American Educational Research Journal*, 35(4), 681–704.

James, W. (1890). *The principles of psychology*. London: Macmillan.

Karmiloff-Smith, A. (1992). *Beyond modularity.* Cambridge, MA: MIT Press.

Krapp, A. (1999). Interest, motivation, and learning: An educational-psychological perspective. *Learning and Instruction,* 14(1), 23–40.

Krapp, A., & Fink, B. (1992). The development and function of interests during the critical transition from home to preschool. In K. A. Renninger, S. Hidi, & A. Krapp (Eds.), *The role of interest in learning and development* (pp. 397–431). Hillsdale, NJ: Erlbaum.

Krapp, A., Hidi, S., & Renninger, K. A. (1992). Interest, learning and development. In K. A. Renninger, S. Hidi, & A. Krapp (Eds.), *The role of interest in learning and development* (pp. 3–25). Hillsdale, NJ: Erlbaum.

Krapp, A., Renninger, K. A., & Hoffmann, L. (1998). Some thoughts on the development of a unifying framework for the study of interest. In L. Hoffmann, A. Krapp, K. A. Renninger, & J. Baumert (Eds.), *Interest and learning: Proceedings of the Seeon Conference on Interest and Gender* (pp. 455–464). Kiel, Germany: IPN.

Lampert, M. (1986). Knowing, doing, and teaching multiplication. *Cognition and Instruction,* 3(4), 305–342.

Lenhoff, H. M., Wang, P. P., Greenberg, F., & Bellugi, U. (1997). Williams Syndrome and the brain. *Scientific American,* December, 68–73.

Lepper, M. R. (1985). Microcomputers in education: Motivational and social issues. *American Psychologist,* 40(1), 1–18.

Lepper, M. R., & Hodell, M. (1989). Intrinsic motivation in the classroom. In C. Ames & R. Ames (Eds.), Research on motivation in education (vol. 3, pp. 73–105). San Diego: Academic Press.

Lindfors, J. (1987). *Children's language and learning* (2nd ed.). Englewood Cliffs, NJ: Prentice-Hall.

Lompscher, J. (1999). Motivation and activity. *European Journal of Psychology of Education,* 14(1), 11–22.

Lotman, Y. M. (1988). Text within a text. *Soviet Psychology,* 26, 32–51.

Maehr, M. L., & Midgley, C. (1991). Enhancing student motivation: A schoolwide approach. *Educational Psychologist,* 26(3&4), 399–427.

Mandler, G. (1984/1975). *Mind and body: Psychology of emotion and stress.* New York: W. W. Norton.

Markus, H., and Nurius, P. (1986). Possible selves. *American Psychologist,* 4(9), 954–969.

Mitchell, M. (1993). Situational interest: Its multifaceted structure in the secondary school mathematics classroom. *Journal of Educational Psychology,* 85(3), 424–436.

Neumann, A. (1999, April). *Passionate talk about passionate thought: The view from professors at early mid-career.* Paper presented at the 80th-annual meeting of the American Educational Research Association, Montreal.

Nicholls, J. G. (1989). *The competitive ethos and democratic education.* Cambridge, MA: Harvard University Press.

Nisbett, R. E., & Wilson, T. D. (1977). Telling more than we can know: Verbal reports on mental processes. *Psychological Review,* 84(3), 231–259.

O'Neil, J. (1999, April 6). A syndrome with a mix of skills and deficits. *New York Times* (Science Section), pp. 1, 4.

O'Neill, S. A. (1997). The role of practice in children's early musical performance achievement. In H. Jorgensen & A. C. Lehmann (Eds.) *Does practice make perfect? Current theory and research on instrumental music practice* (pp. 53–68). Oslo: NMH-publikasjoner.

Piaget, J. (1966). *The psychology of intelligence.* Totowa, NJ: Littlefield, Adams.

Pintrich, P. R. (1999). The role of goal orientation in self-regulated learning. In M. Boekaerts, P. R. Pintrich, & M. Zeidner (Eds.), *Handbook of self-regulation: Theory, research, and applications.* San Diego: Academic Press.

Pintrich, P. R., & Schunk, D. H. (1996). *Motivation in education: Theory, research, and applications.* Englewood Cliffs, NJ: Prentice Hall.

Polya, G. (1988). *How to solve it.* Princeton, NJ: Princeton University Press. (Original worked published in 1945).

Prenzel, M. (1992). The selective persistence of interest. In K. A. Renninger, S. Hidi, & A. Krapp (Eds.), *The role of interest in learning and development* (pp. 71–98). Hillsdale, NJ: Erlbaum.

Renninger, K. A. (1989). Individual differences in children's play interests. In L. T. Winegar (Ed.), *Social interaction and the development of children's understanding* (pp. 147–172). Norwood, NJ: Ablex.

Renninger, K. A. (1990). Children's play interests, representation, and activity. In R. Fivush & J. Hudson (Eds.), *Knowing and remembering in young children* (pp. 127–165), Emory Cognition Series, vol. III. New York: Cambridge University Press.

Renninger, K. A. (1992). Individual interest and development: Implications for theory and practice. In K. A. Renninger, S. Hidi, & A. Krapp (Eds.), *The role of interest in learning and development*. Hillsdale, NJ: Erlbaum.

Renninger, K. A. (1998a). Developmental psychology and instruction: Issues from and for practice. In I. E. Sigel & K. A. Renninger (Vol. Eds.) *Child psychology in practice* (vol. 4). In W. Damon (Gen. Ed.), *Handbook of child psychology* (5th ed., pp. 211–274). New York: Wiley.

Renninger, K. A. (1998b). The role of interest and gender in learning: An overview of research on preschool and elementary-school-aged children. In L. Hoffmann, A. Krapp, K. A. Renninger, & J. Baumert (Eds.), *Interest and learning: Proceedings of the Seeon Conference on Interest and Gender* (pp. 165–174). Kiel, Germany: IPN.

Renninger, K. A. (1998c). What are the roles of individual interest, task difficulty, and gender in student comprehension? In L. Hoffmann, A. Krapp, K. A. Renninger, & J. Baumert (Eds.), *Interest and learning: Proceedings of the Seeon Conference on Interest and Gender* (pp. 228–238). Kiel, Germany: IPN.

Renninger, K. A. Ewen, L., & Lasher, A. K. (in press). Individual interests as context in expository text and mathematical word problems. *Learning and Instruction*.

Renninger, K. A., Farra, L., & Feldman-Riordan, C. (2000). *The impact of The Math Forum's Problems of the Week on students' mathematical thinking*. Proceedings of the International Conference on the Learning Sciences 2000, Mahwah, NJ: Erlbaum.

Renninger, K. A., & Leckrone, T. G. (1991). Continuity in young children's actions: A consideration of interest and temperament. In L. Oppenheimer & J. Valsiner (Eds.), *The origins of action: Interdisciplinary and international perspectives* (pp. 205–238). New York: Springer-Verlag.

Renninger, K. A., & Lehman, D. (April, 1999). *Some implications of interest, competence, and gender for understanding the development of self-concept*. Paper presented as part of the Cognitive and Contextual Influences on the Development of Motivation Symposium, Society for Research in Child Development, Albuquerque.

Renninger, K. A., & Shumar, W. (in press). Community building with and for teachers: The Math Forum. In K. A. Renninger & W. Shumar (Eds.), *Building virtual communities: Learning and change in cyberspace*. New York: Cambridge University Press.

Renninger, K. A., & Stavis, J. (1995a, March). *The roles of interest, task difficulty, and gender in the process of students' reconstructive recall of expository text*. Poster presented at the 61st biennel meeting of the Society for Research in Child Development, Indianapolis.

Renninger, K. A., & Stavis, J. (1995b, March). *The roles of interest, task difficulty, and gender in the process of students' work with mathematical word problems*. Poster, presented at the 61st biennial meeting of the Society for Research in Child Development, Indianapolis.

Renninger, K. A., & Wozniak, R. H. (1985). Effect of interest on attentional shift, recognition, and recall in young children. *Developmental Psychology, 21*(4), 624–632.

Rheinberg, F., & Schiefele, U. (1997). Motivation and knowledge acquisition: Searching for mediating processes. *Advances in Motivation and Achievement, 10*, 251–301.

Roehler, L., Duffy, G., & Meloth, M. (1986). What to be direct about in direct instruction in reading: Content-only versus process-into-content. In T. E. Raphael (Ed.), *The contexts of school-based literacy*. (pp. 79–93). New York: Random House.

Rogoff, B. (1998). Cognition as a collaborative process. In D. Kuhn & R. S. Siegler (Vol. Eds.), *Cognition, perception, and language* (vol. 2). In W. Damon (Gen. Ed.), *Handbook of child psychology* (pp. 679–745). New York: Wiley.

Sansone, C., & Morgan, C. (1992). Intrinsic motivation and education: Competence in context. *Motivation and Emotion, 16*, 249–270.

Sansone, C., Sachau, D. A., & Weir, C. (1989). The effects of instruction on intrinsic interest: The importance of context. *Journal of Personality and Social Psychology, 57*, 819–829.

Sansone, C., Weir, C., Harpster, L., & Morgan, C. (1992). Once a boring task always a boring task? Interest as a self-regulatory mechanism. *Journal of Personality and Social Psychology, 63*(3), 379–390.

Schank, R. C., & Joseph, D. M. (1998). Intelligent schooling. In R. J. Sternberg & W. M. Williams (Eds.), *Intelligence, instruction, and assessment* (pp. 43–65). Mahweh, NJ: Erlbaum.

Schick, A. (2000). Self-concept reflected in students' activities during physics instruction: The role of interest-oriented actions. *Psychology: The Journal of the Hellenic Psychological Society.*

Schiefele, H. (1986). Interest: New answers to an old problem. *Zeitschrift für Pädagogik, 32*(2), 153–162.

Schiefele, H., Krapp, A., Prenzel, M., Heiland, A., & Kasten, H. (July-August, 1983). *Principles of an educational theory of interest.* Paper presented at the 7th annual meeting of the International Society for the Study of Behavioral Development, Munich, West Germany.

Schiefele, U. (1991). Interest, learning, and motivation. *Educational Psychologist, 26*(3&4), 299–323.

Schiefele, U. (1999). Interest and learning from text. *Scientific Studies of Reading, 3*, 257–280.

Schiefele, U., & Csikszentmihalyi, M. (1995). Motivation and ability as factors in mathematics and achievement. *Journal for Research in Mathematics Education, 26*(2), 163–181.

Schiefele, U., & Krapp, A. (1996). Topic interest and free recall of expository test. *Learning and Individual Differences, 8*, 141–160.

Schiefele, U., Wild, K. P., & Krapp, A. (1995). *Course-specific interest and extrinsic motivation as predictors of specific learning strategies and course grades.* Paper presented at the meeting of the 6th European Conference for Research on Learning and Instruction, Nijmegen, the Netherlands.

Schoenfeld, A. H. (1992). Learning to think mathematically: Problem solving, metacognition, and sense making in mathematics. In D. A. Grouws (Ed.), *Handbook of research on mathematics teaching and learning: A project of the National Council of Teachers of Mathematics* (pp. 334–370). New York: Macmillan.

Schraw, G., Flowerday, T., & Lehman, S. (in press). Increasing situational interest in the classroom. In K. A. Renninger & S. E. Wade (Eds.) Engaging students in reading and writing: Implications from and for research on interest and motivation. *Educational Psychology Review.*

Schunk, D. H. (1991). Self-efficacy and academic motivation. *Educational Psychologist, 26*, 207–231.

Schunk, D. H., & Zimmerman, B. J. (1994). *Self-regulation of learning and performance: Issues and educational applications.* Hillsdale, NJ: Erlbaum.

Siegel, B. (1996). *The world of the autistic child: Understanding and treating autistic spectrum disorders.* New York: Oxford University Press.

Springer, M. (1994). *Watershed: A successful voyage into integrative learning.* Columbus, Ohio: National Middle School Association.

Sternberg, R. J. (1985). *Beyond IQ.* London: Cambridge University Press.

Stigler, J. W., Fernandez, C., & Yoshida, M. (1996). Traditions of school mathematics in Japanese and American elementary classrooms. In P. L. Steffe, P. Nesher, P. Cobb, G. A. Goldin, & B. Greer (Eds.) *Theories of mathematics Learning* (pp. 149–175). Mahweh, NJ: Erlbaum.

Tobias, S. (1994). Interest, prior knowledge, and learning. *Review of Educational Research, 64*, 37–54.

Todt, E., & Schreiber, S. (1998). Development of interests. In L. Hoffmann, A. Krapp, K. A. Renninger, & J. Baumert (Eds.), *Interest and learning: Proceedings of the Seeon Conference on Interest and Gender* (pp. 25–41). Kiel, Germany: IPN.

Travers, R. M. W. (1978). *Children's interests.* Kalamazoo, MI: Michigan State University, College of Education.

Vallerand, R. J. (1997). Toward a hierarchical model of intrinsic and extrinsic motivation. In M. P. Zanna, (Ed.), *Advances in experimental social psychology* (pp. 271–360). New York: Academic Press.

Valsiner, J. (1992). Interest: A metatheoretical perspective. In K. A. Renninger, S. Hidi, & A. Krapp (Eds.), *The role of interest in learning and development* (pp. 27–43). Hillsdale, NJ: Erlbaum.

Voss, J. F., & Schauble, L. (1992). Is interest educationally interesting? An interest-related model of learning. In K. A. Renninger, S. Hidi, & A. Krapp (Eds.), *The role of interest in learning and development* (pp. 101–120). Hillsdale, NJ: Erlbaum.

Wade, S. E., Buxton, W. M., & Kelly, M. (1999). (in press). Using think alouds to examine reader-text interest. *Reading Research Quarterly*, 34(2), 194–216.

Weiner, B. (1992). *Human motivation: Metaphors, theories, and research*. Newbury Park, CA: Sage.

White, R. W. (1959). Motivation reconsidered: The concept of competence. *Psychological Review*, 66, 297–333.

Wigfield, A., & Eccles, J. (1992). The development of achievement task values: A theoretical analysis. *Developmental Review*, 12, 265–310.

Werner, C. M., & Makela, E. (1998). Motivations and behaviors that support recycling. *Journal of Environmental Psychology*, 18, 373–386.

Wild, K. P., Krapp, A., Schreyer, I., & Lewalter, D. (1998). The development of interest and motivational orientations: Gender differences in vocational education. In L. Hoffmann, A. Krapp, K. A. Renninger, & J. Baumert (Eds.), *Interest and learning: Proceedings of the Seeon Conference on Interest and Gender* (pp. 441–455). Kiel, Germany: IPN.

Wolters, C. A. (1998). Self-regulated learning and college students' regulation of motivation. *Journal of Educational Psychology*, 90(2), 224–235.

Yarlas, A. S. (1999, April). *Schema modification and enhancement as predictors of interest: A test of the knowledge-schema theory of cognitive interest*. Paper presented at the 80th annual meeting of the American Educational Research Association, Montreal.

Zimmerman, B. J. (1989). A social cognitive view of self-regulated learning. *Journal of Educational Psychology*, 81, 329–339.

CHAPTER

14

Parents, Task Values, and Real-Life Achievement-Related Choices

JANIS E. JACOBS

Department of Psychology
Department of Human Development and Family Studies
Pennsylvania State University

JACQUELYNNE S. ECCLES

Department of Psychology
University of Michigan

Why does a child who is equally talented in mathematics and tennis decide to join the tennis team instead of the mathematics club? When time and resources are limited, what leads children to choose one activity instead of another? What role do parents play in children's activity choices? Numerous theories dealing with competence, expectancy, and control beliefs provide explanations for performance on different kinds of achievement tasks; however, many of these theories do not systematically address another important motivational question: What makes the individual *want* to do the task? Even if people are certain they can do a task, they may not want to engage in it. According to some of the modern expectancy-value theories (e.g., Eccles [Parsons] et al., 1983; Feather, 1982; Wigfield & Eccles, 1992), an individual's values for particular goals and tasks can help explain *why* a child chooses one activity over another.

Eccles (Parsons) and her colleagues have elaborated and tested an expectancy-value model of activity choice (e.g., Eccles, 1987; Eccles

[Parsons] et al., 1983; Eccles, Adler, & Meece, 1984; Eccles & Wigfield, 1995; Meece, Eccles-Parsons, Kaczala, Goff, & Futterman, 1982; Meece, Wigfield, & Eccles, 1990) that focuses on the social psychological influences on choice and persistence (Figure 14.1). According to this model, the key determinants of choice will be the relative value and - perceived probability of success of each available option. Expectancies and values are assumed to directly influence performance and task choice and to be influenced by task-specific beliefs such as self-perceptions of competence, perceptions of the task demands, and the child's goals (both short and long term) and self-schemas. These social cognitive variables, in turn, are influenced by the child's perceptions of other people's attitudes and expectations for them, by gender roles and activity stereotypes, and by their own interpretations of their previous experiences with achievement outcomes. Finally, the child's perceptions are influenced by the greater cultural milieu, socializers' beliefs, their own aptitudes or talents, and their previous achievement-related performances.

As can be seen by the arrows in Figure 14.1, socialization experiences and previous history are expected to influence children's perceptions and expectations of the world, which, in turn, inform their self-beliefs; these self-beliefs ultimately lead to future expectancies and task values that will guide their task choices. However, we are well aware that the relations between these constructs are not unidirectional, and we discuss bidirectional influences in some detail later in this chapter.

In the model, expectancies for success are defined as children's beliefs about how well they will do on upcoming tasks, either in the immediate or longer-term future. We have emphasized the distinctive contributions made by competence beliefs, expectations for success, and task values to achievement and choice in different domains (e.g., mathematics, English, sports). Various aspects of this model have been confirmed (e.g., Eccles, 1987; Eccles, Adler, & Meece, 1984; Eccles, Wigfield, Harold, & Blumenfeld, 1993; Meece et al., 1982; Wigfield, Eccles, Mac Iver, Reuman, & Midgley, 1991), and our findings make it clear that task values play an important role in future plans and activity choices. For example, we find that even after controlling for prior performance levels, task values predict course plans and enrollment decisions in mathematics, physics, and English and involvement in sport activities (Eccles [Parsons] et al., 1983; Eccles et al., 1984; Eccles & Harold, 1991; Eccles & Wigfield, 1995; Wigfield, 1994). In addition, we have found that parents' values and perceptions of their children's abilities play a role in socializing the children's self-perceptions and activity values (e.g., Eccles [Parsons] et al., 1983; Jacobs, 1991; Jacobs & Eccles, 1992). Thus, for the remainder of this chapter, we focus on the importance of subjective task values and the role parents play in shaping them.

General Model of Achievement Choices

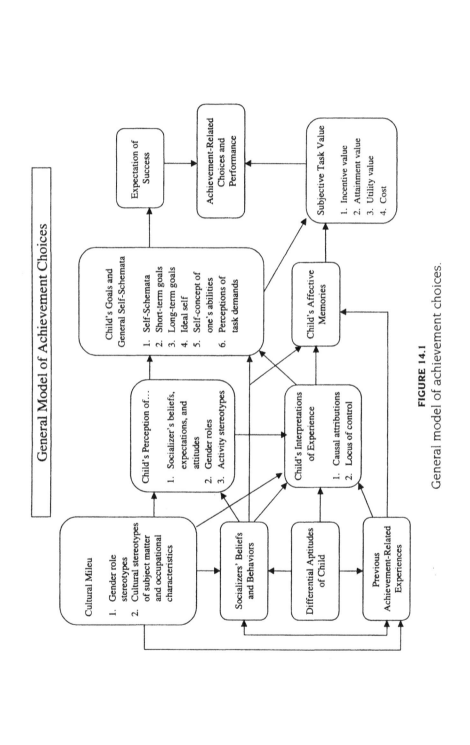

FIGURE 14.1

General model of achievement choices.

IMPORTANCE OF VALUES

Our empirical findings and those of others highlight the importance of values, interest, and engagement in activities, in addition to other constructs that are traditionally featured in theories of motivation, such as expectancies for success, attributions, or locus of control. This slight change in focus is tantamount to changing the question from "Can I do this task?" to "Do I want to do this task?" Several theorists have begun to expand the value construct to answer the second question.

Feather (e.g., 1988, 1992) broadened Atkinson's (1964) conceptualization of value by defining values as a set of stable, general beliefs about what is desirable. He integrated Rokeach's (1979) approach to values by arguing that they are a class of motives that affect behavior by influencing the attractiveness of different goals and, consequently, motivation to attain these goals. He confirmed these ideas by showing that values and expectancies are positively related for academic decisions and decisions to join political groups, suggesting that such decisions are influenced by more than the perceived difficulty of the task (Feather, 1982, 1988). However, his work was with college students and shed little light on the origins of task values.

Closely related to the work on values is the upsurge in the 1990s in research on the concept of *interest* (Alexander, Kulikovich, & Jetton, 1994; Hidi, 1990; Renninger, Hidi, & Krapp, 1992; Renninger & Wozniak, 1985; Schiefele, 1991; Tobias, 1994). These researchers differentiate individual and situational interest. Individual interest is a relatively stable evaluative orientation toward certain domains; situational interest is an emotional state aroused by specific features of an activity or a task. Two aspects or components of individual interest are distinguishable (Schiefele, 1991, 1996): feeling-related valences and value-related valences. *Feeling-related valences* refers to the feelings that are associated with an object or an activity itself—feelings such as involvement, stimulation, or flow (Csikszentmihalyi, 1988, 1990). *Value-related valences* refers to the attribution of personal significance or importance to an object.

We have included the concept of task value in our model by building on earlier work on attainment values (e.g., Battle, 1965, 1966), intrinsic motivation and extrinsic motivation (e.g., Deci, 1975), and Rokeach's view (1979) that values are shared beliefs about desired end states. We have outlined four motivational components of task value: attainment value, intrinsic value, utility value, and cost (Eccles [Parsons] et al., 1983). Like Battle (1965, 1966), we define *attainment value* as the personal importance of doing well on the task. We also link attainment value to the relevance of engaging in a task for confirming or disconfirming salient aspects of one's self-schema (see Eccles, 1984, 1987). This component is similar to the perspectives on values espoused by Feather (1982, 1988), Rokeach (1979), and Harackiewicz and Elliot (1998).

Intrinsic value is the enjoyment the individual gets from performing the activity, or the interest the individual has in the subject. This component of value is similar to the construct of intrinsic motivation as defined by Harter (1981) and by Deci and his colleagues (e.g., Deci & Ryan, 1985; Ryan, Connell, & Deci, 1985). It is also akin to the constructs of interest and flow as defined by Csiksentmihalyi (1988, 1990), Renninger (1990), and Schiefele (1991), although distinctions between interest and engagement while working on the task and general interest over time have since been discussed and tested by Sansone and her colleagues (Sansone & Harackiewicz, 1996; Sansone, Weir, Harpster, & Morgan, 1992). We have typically measured intrinsic value by using attitudinal items assessing general interest or liking for a task, similar to the "enjoyment scales" used to measure intrinsic motivation by others (e.g., Epstein & Harackiewicz, 1992; Harackiewicz & Elliot, 1993). However, it should be noted that although the measures are similar, intrinsic values in our model are considered a predictor of achievement outcomes (such as grades or activity choice), rather than the outcome measure of intrinsic motivation.

Utility value is determined by how well a task relates to current and future goals, such as career goals. A task can have positive value to a person because it facilitates important future career goals, even if she or he is not interested in the task for its own sake. For instance, students often take classes that they do not particularly enjoy but that they need in order to pursue other interests, to please their parents, or to be with their friends. In one sense, this component captures the more "extrinsic" reasons for engaging in a task. Indeed, Lepper and Gilovich (1982) suggested that the perceived instrumentality of a task can be a source of extrinsic motivation. An important question to explore, however, is how activity involvement that is extrinsically motivated in the beginning becomes intrinsically motivated over time.

Finally, we have identified *cost* as a critical component of value (Eccles [Parsons] et al., 1983; Eccles, 1987). Cost is conceptualized in terms of the negative aspects of engaging in the task, such as performance anxiety and fear of both failure and success, as well as the amount of effort that is needed to succeed and the lost opportunities that result from making one choice rather than another.

Before we proceed, it is important to discuss the relations among the four proposed components of task value, as well as developmental changes in task values. To determine whether the hypothesized components were empirically distinct, Eccles & Wigfied (1995) subjected responses from an adolescent sample representing all aspects of value (except cost) to a factor analysis. They were able to distinguish three clear task value factors: (1) perceived attainment value or importance, (2) intrinsic interest value, and (3) perceived utility value or usefulness. They also found no differences in the factor structure for younger (5th through 7th graders) versus older students

(8th through 12th graders), indicating that the distinctions between these dimensions of value exist at an early age and remain stable. In another study, however, Wigfield & Eccles (1992) found that children's subjective task values are less differentiated during early elementary school than later, with only two factors (interest and utility value) emerging for the younger children in mathematics, reading, and sports. This is consistent with Harter's proposition that children's achievement beliefs become more differentiated as they get older (Harter, 1990).

Wigfield and Eccles (1992) suggested that during the early elementary school grades, the subjective value of a task may be primarily characterized by children's interest in the task; thus, young children's choice of different activities may stem from their interest in those activities. At young ages, interests may shift fairly rapidly, so that children may try many different activities for a short time before deciding which activities they enjoy the most. During the early and middle elementary school grades, children's sense of the usefulness of different activities, especially for future goals, may not be very clear, and so this component may be understood only later. If such a shift in values for the same activity occurs, it would be tantamount to engaging in a task because of the intrinsic value of the task (interest) in childhood but staying engaged over time because of utility values (perceived usefulness). This might be seen as a shift from internal to external reasons for activity involvement. However, research with adults and with high school students suggests that interest or intrinsic value may continue to play an important and unique role in achievement choices and persistence (e.g., Jacobs, Finken, Griffin, & Wright, 1998; Sansone & Harackiewicz, 1996).

Despite the fact that these components of task value can be differentiated, the relations between each of them are not as easily distinguished. Eccles and Wigfield (1995) found that the correlations between intrinsic interest, importance, and utility values ranged between .51 and .79 in a sample of adolescents. They also found that the relations between each of the components of task values and self-perceptions of ability, effort required to succeed, and task difficulty were similar across constructs, although utility value had somewhat lower correlations with these constructs than did the other two. These findings suggest that although the components of task value are distinctive, they play similar predictive roles in our model.

In addition to the developmental changes in factor structure already noted, we have found that children value certain tasks less as they get older (see Eccles & Midgley, 1989, and Wigfield & Eccles, 1992, for reviews). For example, utility values (usefulness) and attainment values (importance) for mathematics, reading, instrumental music, and sports decrease across the elementary school years, and children's intrinsic values (interest) for reading and instrumental music show similar decreases over time whereas their intrinsic values for mathematics and sports do not

(Wigfield et al., 1997). In a follow-up study reporting on the same children but examining patterns for attainment values between 1st and 12th grades, we found that the declines for mathematics and sports values continued through high school. We also tracked similar declines in values for language arts through elementary school but found a slight leveling off or increase in attainment values for language arts in high school (Jacobs et al., 2000). These studies show the importance of examining children's subjective valuing of activities in different domains.

CONTEXTS IN WHICH CHILDREN LEARN TO VALUE ACTIVITIES

Task values can develop only within the contexts of children's lives; thus, as developmentalists, we believe that it is important to consider the conditions under which children begin to value one set of activities over another. For example, children are unlikely to begin to value activities that do not match either their social identities or their personal identities. Similarly, they are unlikely to develop task values in contexts in which they feel incompetent, have no control, or feel unsupported. Research on each of these contextual considerations, as well as the importance of a good "fit" between the child's developing values and the environment, is discussed in this section.

Social Identity

Examples of social identities that we know influence children's and adolescents' task values are gender, race, ethnicity, and peer group membership in adolescence. A major focus of our work has been gender differences in children's values in different domains. We have found gender-role stereotypic differences for sports, social activities, English, and music (Eccles et al., 1989; Eccles et al., 1993; Jacobs et al., 2000; Wigfield et al., 1991) across age groups. As a child, one of the ways to express one's gender identity is by participating in and valuing gender-appropriate activities. Data reported in 1999 from our longitudinal study on childhood and beyond (Altenburg-Caldwell, Jacobs, & Eccles, 1999) suggested that participation in activities during elementary school is highly gender typed. Girls participate significantly more than do boys in art activities, hobbies, clubs, and individual competitive sports; however, boys participate in team sports significantly more than do girls. Not surprisingly, this behavioral instantiation of their social identities is related to children's intrinsic values. For example, those children who participate the most in team sports not only value sports the most but also value the arts the least, and those who participate in the arts have the lowest values for sports.

Although little research on ethnic and racial differences in task values across a variety of domains is available, research on the value of education suggests that there are few differences between the values that minority and majority children place on education; everyone has high education aspirations (e.g., Stevenson, Chen, & Uttal, 1990). However, several researchers have suggested that when minority children are confronted with barriers within the schools, they protect their self-esteem by lowering the value of academic competence. For example, self-concept of academic ability has been found to be less predictive of general self-esteem for some African American children than for other groups (Bledsoe, 1967; Winston, Eccles, & Senior, in press). In addition, ethnic minority families may differ in how much they discuss or use the categories of ethnicity or race. In some families, ethnicity may be very salient and may form the backdrop for decisions and discussions, whereas in other families, such topics may seldom be raised. Okagaki, Frensch, and Dodson (1996) reported that Mexican American parents' beliefs about racial barriers to their children's success were related to children's perceptions of barriers. In turn, children's perceptions of barriers were related to their attitudes toward school. This work suggests that a number of "social address" variables, like gender, race, and social class, contribute to children's task values via their links to social identity.

Personal Identity

In addition to social identity, individuals are constructing their personal identities as they move through childhood and adolescence. Unlike social identity, which is based on ascribed social categories, this is the part of the self-system that is typically thought of as "earned" on the basis of competence and interests, and the competence component is often labeled *self-competence* or *self-esteem*. An important consideration is the way in which values are related to perceptions of self-competence. Building on the work of James (1982/1963), Harter (1998) has suggested that self-esteem and motivation are enhanced when one values those activities at which one is competent. Extending this idea to the choices made between activity domains suggests the importance of considering the hierarchy of individuals' subjective task values and competence perceptions. According to this view, the ability to form congruent hierarchies of task values and competence beliefs should lead to higher self-esteem and continuing motivation, whereas incongruent hierarchies of beliefs will lead to negative self-esteem and lowered motivation. For example, individuals may cope with being incompetent in baseball by lowering the value they attach to it and by enhancing the value they attach to another sport or another activity domain. Harter (1990) found support for this view. In her study, those who valued activities at which they did not feel competent had lower self-esteem than did those who showed congruent patterns of values and competence.

Our research has shown that children's competence and expectancy beliefs relate positively to their subjective task values (e.g., Eccles & Wigfield, 1995; Wigfield & Eccles, 1992). When Eccles and Wigfield (1995) examined the relations between competence beliefs and values in 5th through 12th graders, they found that children's beliefs about the importance and utility of different tasks correlated more highly with their competence beliefs as they got older. Wigfield (1994) asserted that children's competence beliefs may not relate to their valuing of different activities in the early years, leading children to pursue some activities in which they are interested, regardless of their competence during that period.

Universal Characteristics of Competence, Autonomy, and Relatedness

Although competence has been the focus of much research on the self-system, Connell and his colleagues (e.g., Connell, 1990; Connell & Wellborn, 1991) suggested that people have three universal and fundamental needs as they develop their self-systems: competence, autonomy, and relatedness. Their model defined *competence* as the need to experience oneself as capable of producing desired outcomes and avoiding negative outcomes, *autonomy* as the need to experience a choice in activities, and *relatedness* as the need to feel securely connected to the social world and to see oneself as worthy of love and respect. Connell suggested that the self-system will be organized around one's appraisal of these three components and that one's sense of self will lead to further engagement in a task or disaffection with a task.

We would echo the importance of these components, but we suggest that although they are necessary for long-term engagement in a task, they may not be sufficient. The child may feel competent, autonomous, and emotionally connected about a given task but not necessarily see the task as highly valued. We see competence, autonomy, and relatedness as critical for creating contexts in which task values might develop. The values, in turn, are related to self-perceptions and to long-term engagement in particular tasks.

Many researchers have emphasized the importance of the development of *autonomy* in adolescence (e.g., Hill & Holmbeck, 1986; Ryan & Lynch, 1989; Steinberg & Silverberg, 1986); however, it may be important for the development of task values at a much earlier age. Having the autonomy to choose some tasks and to discard others seems critical for the development of task values. Ryan and his colleagues have argued that one of the most important dimensions of autonomy is self-regulation (e.g., Ryan, 1991; Ryan, 1993; Ryan & Lynch, 1989). They defined *self-regulation* as the degree to which children feel that their actions are autonomous and self-initiated versus controlled by others (Ryan & Connell, 1989). Perceptions of autonomy related to regulating one's own behaviors to reach personal goals are expected to be related to higher value for the activity and greater engagement in it over time. This pattern has been found for academic achievement (e.g., Connell & Ryan, 1987; see Ryan, Connell, & Deci, 1985, for review), showing that children who experience clear expectations, feel that they have choices about how to reach their goals, and receive consistent feedback from teachers understand what it takes to be in successful in school and have higher perceived competence for academic tasks. When teachers do not provide support for students' needs for autonomy, interest and liking for the subject matter decline (Midgley, Feldlaufer, & Eccles, 1989); in addition, during the transition to junior high school, young adolescents are more likely to feel competent and to value schoolwork if they have some autonomy about choosing the activity (e.g., Midgley & Feldlaufer, 1987).

Another of the components listed as universal by Connell and colleagues and the one we have researched the most is perceived *competence*. Perceptions of competence have been linked to activity choice and achievement in numerous studies, so it is clear that a child who does not feel competent at an activity is not likely to want to continue to be involved in that activity. We know from our longitudinal analyses that children's beliefs about their own competence and the value they place on activities in most domains decrease with increasing grade level in school (Eccles et al., 1993; Jacobs et al., under review; Wigfield et al., 1997). In addition, stereotypic gender differences in competence beliefs and task-value perceptions are also apparent, but these neither interact with grade level nor change much over time. Thus, by the first grade, boys have a more positive view of their mathematics, computer, and sports abilities than do girls and girls rate their tumbling, social, and language arts abilities higher than do boys. Despite mean-level declines with age, children's self-perceptions of competence become more stable as they proceed through elementary school (Yoon, Wigfield, & Eccles, 1993) and their perceptions become more highly related to actual performance (Nicholls, 1979; Parsons & Ruble, 1977; Stipek, 1981).

The last part of the supportive context that we discuss here is the child's access to positive *relationships* with others. Researchers have often emphasized the importance of relatedness (Connell & Wellborn, 1991), emotional support (Deci & Ryan, 1985), or connectedness (Barber, Olsen & Shagle, 1994) for children's mental health, self-esteem, and achievement motivation. It is clear that most researchers find that an emotionally warm and caring tie to others is critical for healthy development, beginning in infancy with attachment to parents (Ainsworth, Blehar, Waters, & Wall, 1978) and continuing into older adulthood (Carstensen, 1992). Our work has focused on the nature of children's emotional relationships with their parents and how these connections may be related to developing values and activity choices. As might be expected, perceptions of high levels of connectedness and emotional support from parents are related positively to both psychological and behavioral indicators of successful development (Eccles, Early,

Frasier, Belansky, & McCarthy, 1996). This relationship holds in adolescence, even when children begin to establish other strong relationships with peers and to gain some independence from parents (Ladd & Le Sieur, 1995).

Person–Environment Fit

A major feature of contexts in which task values develop is the goodness of fit between the individual and the environment—children are likely to value tasks and to engage in them only when the opportunities found in their environments match their interests, competencies, and developmental level. The concept of person–environment fit has typically been used in the achievement literature to refer to the match between an individual's needs and talents and the particular education environment that is available. The concept has been refined further to focus on the importance of the education environment's match to the developmental needs of the child. For example, Hunt (1975) suggested that a teacher not only needs to take a student's current needs into account when providing classroom structure but should also view these needs on a "developmental continuum along which growth toward independence and less need for structure is the long-term objective" (Hunt, 1975, p. 221). Drawing on this work but focusing on the fit between changes in school organization and academic motivation, several researchers have used the term *stage–environment fit* to explain declines in motivation and performance that occur after the transition to middle school or junior high (e.g., Eccles, 1993; Eccles & Midgley, 1989; Simmons & Blyth, 1987). Eccles and Midgley (1989) have provided evidence on the importance of stage–environment fit during the transition to junior high school, showing that a mismatch between early adolescents' needs and the structure of junior high and middle schools affects their self-perceptions of competence and perceptions of the school environment.

Person–environment fit may also be applied to the child's fit within the family. Just as the school environment needs to be developmentally appropriate, the home environment needs to be structured to allow for developmental differences in the formation of activity choices and values. As children mature, parents' roles in activity choice may change and they may begin to "react" to children's ideas about activity involvement rather than to initiate all aspects of involvement. This means that the parent needs to be sensitive to developmental changes that may signal greater need for autonomy of choice but to continue to provide appropriate rules and guidance about how to make such choices. There may also be a mismatch if the child's values or abilities do not fit the expectations of the parents. For example, if the parents' activity value hierarchy is both rigid and inconsistent with the child's relative competencies, the child may be at risk of lowered self-esteem because she/he cannot lower the values for areas of less competence without encountering negative feedback from the parents.

SOCIALIZATION FOR TASK VALUES

We have just discussed a variety of features of contexts in which task values are likely to flourish. Although many experiences (e.g., teams, lessons, school) and a variety of socializers (e.g., parents, teachers, peers) help provide these contexts and shape children's values, here we focus primarily on the role of parents. Over the years, numerous studies have linked parenting practices to children's achievement motivation (see Eccles, Wigfield, & Schiefele, 1998, for review); however, few researchers have focused on how parents motivate their children to do different things or to value different activities.

The model of parent socialization set forth by Eccles (Parsons) et al. (1983) is presented in Figure 14.2. As indicated in the model, we believe that characteristics of the parents, family, and neighborhood and characteristics of the child will influence parents' behaviors and their general beliefs about the world, as well as their specific beliefs about the child. We expect these beliefs to then influence their parenting behaviors, which, in turn, will affect child outcomes. Examples of each of these constructs are given in the figure. Although the model is drawn in a linear fashion and the original model (Eccles [Parsons] et al., 1983) proposed a causal sequence, it is important to acknowledge that parents' and children's beliefs are likely to influence each other reciprocally and that different beliefs depicted as a single construct in the model are likely to influence each other (e.g., values and competence beliefs).

In this chapter, we focus on the three boxes in the middle of Figure 14.2, depicting parents' general beliefs and behaviors, parents' child-specific beliefs, and parenting behaviors. Although several examples of each construct are listed in the figure, here we focus on only the following four ways in which parents influence their children: (1) by the general social-emotional climate they offer and by their general child-rearing beliefs, (2) by providing specific experiences for the child (e.g., enrollment in lessons, involvement in religious activities), (3) by modeling involvement in valued activities, and (4) by communicating their perceptions of the child's abilities and expectations for performance.

The environment, role modeling, and messages that parents provide regarding the value they attach to various activities are expected to influence children's motivation to pursue any particular activity. Over time, children construct their own values for particular activities and integrate these values into their self-systems. Ultimately, the values that are incorporated into one's self-beliefs will affect future task choices. (It is important to remember, however, that the influence between self-beliefs and values is bidirectional.) Parent's roles may shift in this process from providing exposure, opportunities, and role modeling in the early phases of activity choice to providing encouragement and guidance for activities that continue to be supportive of the child's developing self-systems. We have tested and found support for each of the four components of parent influence (e.g., Eccles,

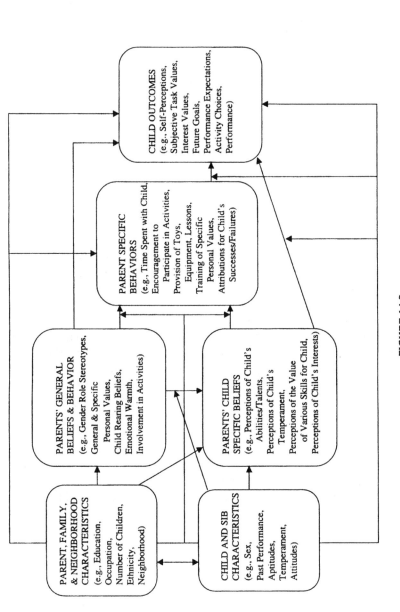

FIGURE 14.2

Parental socialization model.

1994; Eccles |Parsons| et al., 1983; Jacobs, 1991; Jacobs & Eccles, 1985, 1992). Our findings on each are briefly reviewed below.

Social-Emotional Climate and General Beliefs

Warmth and relatedness have often been connected with successful parental socialization. Although we have not emphasized this construct, Eccles et al. (1996) found that perceived high levels of connectedness and emotional support were positively related to both psychological and behavioral indicators of successful development during early adolescence, particularly for girls. We have also found support for the impact of parental emotional support during childhood on later adolescent behaviors and parent–adolescent relationships. For example, we found that parents' reports of perceived closeness to their elementary school–aged children are positively related to the children's perceptions of parent support, affection, and monitoring several years later during adolescence and negatively related to perceptions of parental strictness and involvement in problem behaviors (Jacobs, Hyatt, Tanner, & Eccles, 1998).

To test our hypotheses about general beliefs, we have considered gender stereotypes in several studies. For example, in two studies, we investigated the relationships among parents' gender-based stereotypes, their beliefs about their own children's abilities, and their children's self-perceptions and performance (Jacobs, 1991; Jacobs & Eccles, 1992). The first study focused on stereotypes, beliefs, and performance related to mathematical ability only. The second study involved three domains of ability (mathematics, sports, and social). Parents' gender stereotypes in both studies and in all domains directly influenced their perceptions of their children's abilities, resulting in more positive perceptions for children favored by the stereotypes (e.g., daughters for social skills, sons for mathematics and sports skills). Parents' perceptions, in turn, influenced their children's performance and their self-perceptions of their abilities in each domain, even after controlling for the child's previous performance. These findings suggest that parents hold general beliefs (stereotypes) that influence the way in which they interpret their children's performance, depending on individual characteristics of the children, such as gender. More important, their interpretations of that performance are conveyed to their children and tend to influence the children's self-perceptions and grades, ultimately carrying more weight than previous performance.

Provision of Specific Experiences for the Child

Parents structure children's experiences in a variety of ways that should affect self- and task values, skill acquisition, preferences, and choice. We have found that exogenous child and family characteristics (e.g., parents' income, education, child sex, age) influence the experiences parents provide for their children primarily through their impact on parents' perceptions of their children's abilities and interests and parents' valuing of the activity domain. For example, parents were more likely to provide extra sports experiences for their children if they believed that the children were interested in the activity and had sports ability (Fredericks, 1999). This is a good example of the reciprocal nature of parent–child attitudes: parents are using the feedback they receive from the child, as well as their own assessment of the child, to inform their decisions about which opportunities to provide. Not surprisingly, parents often provide experiences for their children that fit existing expectations for gender-appropriate activities. For example, in one study (Altenburg-Caldwell et al., 1999), we found that parents provide equal numbers of organized activities during early middle childhood for girls and for boys but that the activities provided differ by gender.

Modeling Involvement in Valued Activities

The importance of role models in socializing behavior has been well documented in the developmental literature (e.g., Bandura & Walters, 1963). According to this work, parents exhibit behaviors that children may later imitate and adopt as part of their own repertoire. Role models' influence may include the messages they provide about their beliefs regarding their own abilities and about their values in general, and previous work suggests that children perceive these messages accurately. The ways in which parents spend their time, the choices they make between available activities, and the sense of self-competence that they project send strong messages to their children about activities that are valued and about acceptable ways to spend time. To test this facet of parental influence, we have included numerous indicators of parents' practices and involvement in different types of activities. Our findings support the importance of modeling that has often been reported in experimental studies. For example, we have found that children's perceptions of their parents' enjoyment of mathematics are significantly correlated with the parents' self-reports of past and present mathematical ability, difficulty with mathematics, and the effort needed to do well in mathematics. In addition, children who see their parents do household mathematics (e.g., balancing a checkbook) believe that their parents like mathematics more than those whose parents do not engage in mathematical activities at home (Eccles-Parsons, Adler, & Kaczala, 1982).

Communicating Ability Perceptions
and Future Expectations

We have found that parents' perceptions of their children's abilities and their expectations for the children's future success have a large impact on children's developing perceptions of self-competence (e.g., Eccles-Parsons et al., 1982; Jacobs & Eccles, 1992). In these studies, parents' perceptions of their children's abilities, their expectations for their children's success, and their gender stereotypes predict children's self-perceptions of competence and their actual achievement, even after previous indicators of achievement are controlled. Although parents are clearly forming their opinions about the child's ability on the basis of such objective indicators as grades and performance in sports competitions, it appears that the direction of influence for perceptions of competence is from parents to children and that parents' views of their children's abilities are quite stable over time (Yoon et al., 1993).

PARENTAL CONTRIBUTIONS
TO THE DEVELOPMENT OF TASK VALUES:
DILEMMAS FOR PARENTS AND RESEARCHERS

Although it is clear that parents play a role in the socialization of activity engagement and values, it is not always clear exactly what the parameters of that role should be. As suggested earlier, parents may influence their children's values and choices in many ways; however, both researchers and parents have trouble defining the optimal levels of encouragement, reward, and guidance when trying to initiate or maintain a child's value for an activity. This was exemplified in the research community by an article questioning whether the detrimental effects of reward found in some research studies are myth or reality (Eisenberger & Cameron, 1996) and by the scholarly exchange that followed about the conditions under which either the myth or the reality (or both) might be true (Hennessey & Amabile, 1998; Lepper, 1998; Lepper, Keavney, & Drake, 1996; Sansone & Harackiewicz, 1998). Although researchers may phrase their questions in terms of intrinsic and extrinsic motivation, parents are posing the same questions when they ask: Should I reward my son to get him involved or to keep him involved in an activity I value? When do I let my daughter decide to stop practicing or attending an activity? Will I undermine his interest if I push too hard, seem to value it too much, or reward participation? When is she doing it for me rather than for herself?

At the heart of many of these questions is the notion that there is a clear dichotomy between the intrinsic rewards and extrinsic rewards of activity participation; if something is extrinsically rewarded, it cannot be intrinsically rewarding at the same time. Although this concept might be inferred from the early social psychological work on the topic (e.g., Deci, 1971; Lepper, Greene, & Nisbett, 1973) that found decreases in perceived intrinsic motivation when extrinsic rewards were introduced, the dichotomy is not an essential part of more recent thinking on the topic in either the developmental literature (e.g., Deci & Ryan, 1985) or in the adult literature (e.g., Harackiewicz, Abrahams, & Wageman, 1987; Lepper et al., 1996). Indeed, this issue is addressed in two chapters within this book (see chapters 2 and 10). Ryan, Deci, and their colleagues have suggested that the critical element is not whether external rewards are used but how they are used and how they are perceived by the child (Deci & Ryan, 1985; Grolnick, Ryan, & Deci, 1991). They have found that rewards undermine intrinsic motivation when they detract from the individual's sense of autonomy and initiative by attempting to control behavior. Autonomous behavior is initiated and regulated by actions that emanate from one's core sense of self, whereas controlled behavior is the result of yielding to pressure from some other force (this could be external pressure or intrapsychic pressure). They suggested that children are more likely to internalize parents' goals when parents provide support for autonomy versus using controlling techniques and that autonomy support facilitates persistence at a task when no external support is present (Deci & Ryan, 1985; Ryan, 1993). In support of this theory, they found that children whose parents used more "autonomy supportive" techniques versus controlling techniques had children who reported more internalized achievement values (Grolnick & Ryan, 1989) and that children's perceptions of parents' autonomy support predict both internalization of academic values and perceived competence (Grolnick et al., 1991). Thus, there is no clear distinction between intrinsic and extrinsic parenting techniques but a focus on the meaning of the parenting behavior and the potential for the motivational support to become internalized.

Even if some activities can be both internally and externally motivated or if some activities can make the transition from being extrinsic sources to intrinsic sources of motivation, there is still an inherent tension between socializers' external reinforcement of an activity and the child beginning to internalize a value for that activity. In addition, the parent still faces the dilemma of knowing how and when to provide and to withdraw the extrinsic supports that may initially engage or maintain the child's participation in the activity. Consider the following examples:

Parent A plays tennis and sees it as a great way to exercise and as a life-long kind of activity. She encourages her daughter to take tennis lessons, and her daughter complies because she can see how much her mother likes the sport and because she will get to spend time with her mother when they play together. However, after two lessons, the daughter hates it and does not want to return for more lessons. She tells her mother that she agreed to the lessons only to please her mother and now she does not want to continue. Her mother insists that she continue to take lessons until she has learned enough to be able to play. After 2 months of battling about lessons and practice, the mother tells her daughter that if she just keeps it up for 1 year, she will be rewarded by a trip to Disneyland. The daughter wants to go to Disneyland, so she quits complaining, but she does not enjoy tennis.

However, after she has taken lessons for a year (and hated most of it), the daughter's skills improve and she begins to really enjoy playing. The next year (after the trip to Disneyland), she chooses to continue to take lessons, she joins a tennis club, and she becomes very proficient. Eventually, tennis is one of the activities she values most and she is willing to give up other activities to pursue it.

The scenario is exactly the same for Parent B and his son; however, in this case, after a year of tennis lessons (and the trip to Disneyland), the son still does not really enjoy tennis. He has become quite good at it and he plays with his father sometimes, but he does not enjoy it and still says that the only reason he is doing it is because his father "makes him." The father sees that his son has the potential to be competitive at this sport, and he believes that if his son just plays enough, he will begin to love it (like his father). On this basis, he gets his son to agree to another year of tennis lessons by using another large incentive (like the trip to Disneyland). After taking lessons for another year, the son continues to hate tennis.

In situations such as these, parents may feel caught between a rock and hard place—they want to encourage their children to value an activity and they know that without enough experience, it will be impossible for their children to feel engaged or be intrinsically motivated; however, they do not want their efforts to backfire and undermine the intrinsic value of the activity for their children. Connell and Wellborn (1990) summarized the position well when they suggested that the "path to optimal engagement is difficult to find" (p. 70). Many parents are striving to find or to construct that "path" for their children, just as many researchers are trying to model it developmentally.

FINDING A MODEL OF OPTIMAL ENGAGEMENT

As social scientists, we are constantly asking a question that parallels the one facing parents—what model would best describe the path to optimal engagement in activities? It seems clear that the model must be one that is iterative, with the parent constantly reassessing and reacting to the child's needs, values, and interests and the child communicating about values and interests and reacting to the parent's signs of support. This process could begin with the parent (e.g., "Wouldn't you like to try Little League?") or with the child (e.g., "Can't I go to art camp?"). If it begins with the parent providing the initial impetus and support, the child may well be reacting and is likely to be externally motivated to engage in the activity. At some juncture, the parent must reassess the child's interest in the activity and decide whether to support continued engagement. At another point, however, the child begins to share responsibility for continued motivation (e.g., parental rewards become less tangible), and, ultimately, when the parent reassesses the child's value/interests, most of the external motivators drop out because the child has internalized values for the activity. This means not that there are not some external rewards that will continue to motivate the child (e.g., performances, competitions, friends, parents' praise) but that the child begins to value the activity for its own sake. Figure 14.3 is a simplified version of Eccles's socialization model. The emphasis in this model is on the feedback and interactions that take place between parents and children.

This kind of an iterative model has a long-standing tradition within behavioral analysis. For example, Herbst (1953) described a "co-directional situation pattern" as "one of the simpler types of learning processes" in which a person moves from not engaging in a disliked activity to being pressured to engage in the activity to liking the activity while being pressured to ultimately liking the activity once the pressure is withdrawn (pp.124–125). According to this view, external pressures and internal pressures coexist and determine an individual's behavior in a given situation, and "pressures" that begin externally can become internalized. Additionally, internal "pressures" are not deemed inherently more desirable than those originating externally, but a balance between the two is expected for optimum adjustment.

A relevant and more familiar model to developmentalists can be found in Vygotsky's sociocultural theory (Vygotsky, 1978/1934). In this theory of cognitive development, Vygotsky emphasized the social origins of cognition. He believed that children master activities and refine their thinking as a result of joint activities with more mature members of society. Most relevant for our discussion here are two features of his theory: intersubjectivity and

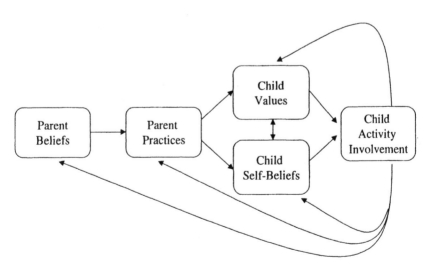

FIGURE 14.3
Codirectional model of parent–child influence.

scaffolding. *Intersubjectivity* refers to the process of two people who begin a task with different conceptualizations coming to a shared understanding of the task as each person adjusts to the perspective of the other (Newson & Newson, 1975; Vygotsky, 1978/1934). Parents (and other adults) try to promote shared meaning when they translate their own views into words that are within the child's grasp or when they point out the links between a new task and one that the child has done before (e.g., Rogoff, 1990). The concept of *scaffolding* refers to the social support provided by adults in any learning situation (Bruner, 1983; Wood, 1989). The idea is that adults offer enough support for a child to accomplish a task but that an effective scaffold is constantly being readjusted to fit the child's level of performance. If more assistance is needed, it is provided, but as the child exhibits independent mastery, the adult will withdraw support and let the child succeed alone. It is clear that Vygotsky saw the parents' role as both pushing and pulling development by adjusting communications and support to fit the child's understanding and ability to master a task. This theory highlights the need for ongoing assessment and adjustment of support to fit the child's needs and interests.

Thus far, we have focused on parents initiating and providing support for activity involvement, and this fits traditional social learning views, which described a unidirectional model that went from parents to children. Since the 1980s, however, attachment theories and life span views have placed the child in a more active and initiating role within the family (e.g., Baltes, 1987; Bretherton, 1985; Connell & Thompson, 1986). It is clear that much of what parents do is in response to their perceptions of the child and may be elicited by the child; thus, the process of activity involvement that results in a particular set of values may begin with the child. Although the process might be somewhat different if the child initiated it, we cannot assume that children who begin by valuing activities necessarily maintain that interest and involvement without some external support and/or pressure. Thus, the social context can still be regarded as either facilitating or inhibiting task interest and values.

IMPLICATIONS FOR THE SOCIALIZATION OF TASK VALUES AND ACTIVITY INVOLVEMENT

The conceptual models described earlier suggest that if parents want to foster task values, they will need to provide a context that will allow the child to begin to value an activity by supporting interest and task engagement. We believe that in general, parents want to create a supportive context; however, even the most well intentioned parents are not always successful and problems arise for a variety of reasons. In this section, we discuss what current research suggests parents can do to provide a supportive context for the development of achievement and activity values, and what might go wrong in these attempts. We discuss these in light of the major types of influence parents have at their disposal: (1) structuring opportunities, (2) interpreting reality, and (3) imparting their values. We conclude this section by reviewing potential parenting practices that might contribute to the development of contexts that will foster competence, autonomy, and relatedness.

Opportunity Structure

One of the main ways in which parents influence their children's developing activity values is by the opportunities they provide. Although it seems obvious that children need to be exposed to an activity if they are to become interested in it, the way in which such exposure affects preferences and activity choices is not clear. Theories of familiarity (Zajonc, 1968), and conditioning suggest that exposure should affect preference and skill acquisition and, therefore, perceived competence. Parents are in the position of choosing both the types and structures of the activities in which their children participate. (This is especially true at young ages.) As children pass into adolescence, parents may become as concerned with preventing their children from engaging in some activities as they are with getting their children to engage in particular activities.

The type of opportunities provided will depend on many factors—what is available in the community, economic resources (many activities and equipment for activities have high costs), time constraints (single parents, two-earner families, and families with many children have less time to devote to any given activity), and parents' values for a particular endeavor. Participation in extracurricular activities has been associated with socioeconomic class (e.g., Coleman, 1961; Hollingshead, 1949), but participation in activities can raise an individual's status within the school, extend the child's social network, and even serve as a protective factor against dropping out (e.g., Csikszentmihalyi, Rathunde, & Whalen, 1993; Eder & Parker, 1987; Kinney, 1993; Mahoney & Cairns, 1997). Therefore, parents' decisions to provide or to curtail particular opportunities may have an impact that reaches beyond the child's activity values and perceptions of competence.

The structure of the task will also play a large role. In this case, structure might be viewed as the overarching dimensions of the task. For example, dimensions that have been considered by researchers include infrequent versus daily activities (Crouter & Larson, 1998), leisure versus productive activities (Larson, 1990), organized versus informal activities (Kirshnit, Ham, & Richards, 1989), and obligatory versus nonobligatory activities (Shaw, Caldwell, & Kleiber, 1996). Parents may not consider these dimensions explicitly when they are choosing or allowing their children to choose how to spend their time; however, data from our recent study of elementary school–aged children suggest that most parents report that they involve their children in extracurricular activities for social reasons rather than for reasons related to competition or competence (Altenburg-Caldwell et al., 1999). At another level, task structure may involve the parents' support for the child's participation. Parents need to provide good scaffolding for any endeavor (Vygotsky, 1978/1934), giving a lot of structure and guidance in the beginning so that the child performs at a higher level than if left alone, but withdrawing the support as the child is ready to take on more responsibility for the task. The trick for any parent, coach, or teacher is to be able to provide the activity within the child's "zone of proximal development," defined by Vygotsky as the range of tasks that the child cannot yet handle alone but can do with the help of a more skilled partner.

Interpreters of Reality

Another way in which parents influence their children's task values is by acting as "interpreters of reality" through the messages they provide regarding their perceptions of their children's world and experiences (Eccles, Lord, Roeser, Barber, & Jozefowicz, 1997; Goodnow & Collins, 1990; Phillips, 1987). When children are young, they are not particularly good at assessing their own competence (Nicholls, 1978), so they must rely on their parents' interpretations of their performance as a major source of information about their competence. As mentioned earlier, parents' interpretations of their children's competence have been related to the children's self-perceptions and to their actual achievement (Eccles [Parsons] et al., 1983). In addition, parents' inappropriately low estimations of their children's competence are related to children's lower self-perceptions of their competence in the same areas. Owing to the links between self-competence and values, the accuracy of parents' interpretations is critical to children's continued interest, participation, and ultimate valuing of an activity. However, we know that parents' interpretations will be influenced by many things, including the values and expectations within their culture.

Although we know that parents play the "interpreter" role for their children, the precise behaviors that carry the messages are not well documented. It seems unlikely that parents tell their children outright that they are not competent at an activity, but the message may be conveyed in subtle ways. If the underlying message is "you aren't competent and you'd better change to increase your competence," the parents might try such strategies as providing extra help, tutoring, or lessons; threatening punishment if performance doesn't improve; structuring more time for the child to work on the activity; or comparing the child to others who are more competent. If the parents' underlying message is "You aren't competent at this task, so you shouldn't pursue it," the parents may try such strategies as refocusing the child's interests on a different activity, emphasizing other strengths, or lowering the value of the activity. The parents' strategy of choice is likely to depend on how much the parents value the activity themselves and whether they focus on performance or learning as the goal of involvement in the activity. (For more discussion of this point, see chapters 6 and 7 in this book). According to Dweck and her colleagues, a focus on performance may undermine intrinsic motivation to continue to be involved in the activity and it will certainly lower the intrinsic value of the activity for the child (Dweck & Leggett, 1988).

Provision of Values

As suggested several times in the preceding paragraphs, parents are providing messages about their own values through the opportunities they provide and the interpretations they give. In addition, their values may be imparted by their involvement in various activities (role modeling) and by direct instruction. The values in question may range from specific values for particular activities (e.g., the parent who plays tennis and makes it clear that tennis is valued by taking the child to Wimbledon) to general world beliefs and values (e.g., the parent who believes boys should not have dolls because they will become sissies). Children are likely to discern the parents' values by noticing how free time is spent; by comparing how much time, money, or effort goes into one activity versus another; and by participating in conversations with parents in which the parents convey enthusiasm or interest about one topic but little about another.

General beliefs or values may have an indirect effect by influencing what opportunities the parents provide (e.g., no dolls for boys) or how they respond to their children's performance (e.g., assuming greater effort was required for success in sports by girls than by boys), or they may be communicated directly (e.g., "Boys who take dance lessons are sissies and no son of mine is taking ballet"). We have documented the indirect effects of parents' general beliefs on the goals that they set for their children in the area of gender stereotyping (Jacobs, 1991; Jacobs & Eccles, 1992). It is likely that the messages provided and "received" change as children move into and through adolescence. For example, gender-role intensification theory (Hill & Lynch, 1983) suggests that the association of parents' gender-role beliefs to both their goals for their children and their socialization practices should increase as their children become adolescents.

Parenting Practices

We conclude by briefly discussing parenting practices that have been related to the development of competence, autonomy, and relatedness. Within each of these areas, we highlight the need for parents to use a developmental approach that takes into account individual and social identity as well as meets universal needs. Children and adolescents change rapidly and some-times leave their parents in the dust. Strategies and parenting practices that may have worked well last year or last month may no longer work. Several adolescence researchers have hypothesized that parent–child relationships change as children enter and move through adolescence (Eccles, 1993; Stein-berg, 1988). Numerous changes occur during this period of life: children experience physical maturation, their social roles change, parents and teach-ers may increase gender-role socialization pressures, parents may link their behaviors and choices to future adult roles, and the opportunity for partici-pating in unsupervised peer interactions increases (e.g., Jacobs & Osgood, 1994). Each of these types of changes should affect self and task beliefs, activity choices, and relative performance across a variety of activity domains. This means that parents have to be ready to adapt to the changing emotional, cognitive, and social needs of the child while still supporting (but not forcing) the development of internalized and autonomous task values.

Much of our work has looked at how parents' attitudes and practices are related to children's perceptions of *competence*. Parents' beliefs about their children's competence are likely to guide their decisions about which activ-ities to provide for their children (Sigel, 1982) and about how they interact with their children (Sigel, McGillicudy–Delisi, & Goodnow, 1992), making their actions into messages about their interpretations of reality. If children receive parental interactions and activity endorsements as messages about their abilities, it suggests that parents need to be careful about what mes-sages they are providing. For example, a decision to take a child out of swimming lessons may be interpreted by the child as an indication of lack of ability when the decision was made only to facilitate the parents' busy schedule. Parents' lack of involvement in academics may be interpreted as either lack of interest or perceptions of low academic ability. Many researchers have documented the relationship between parent involvement in schooling and increased achievement and positive school behaviors (e.g., Eccles & Harold, 1993; Epstein, 1992), and one of the mechanisms for these effects may be the messages sent to children about the importance of schooling and about the child's competence.

One way in which parents' messages about the child's ability may go awry is if the parents' estimates of the child's ability are inaccurate. Phillips (1987) found that parents differ in the accuracy of their estimates about their child's performance; those parents who underestimate their child's abilities have children who doubt their own abilities (Phillips & Zimmer-man, 1990). Although most studies show that feedback needs to be perfor-mance based to be believable to children and to be helpful, it also needs to be accurate. One of the ways in which parents may be inaccurate is by using old "data." We have found that parents' beliefs about their children's abili-ties are quite stable during the elementary school years; this is particularly true for reading and sports, areas in which they stick to perceptions of their children that are formed in kindergarten (Yoon et al., 1993). If children are late bloomers in a particular area and parents' perceptions remain stable, parents may underestimate their children's current abilities by relying on earlier beliefs.

Even if parents are accurate about their children's abilities and they are being supportive in an area at which their children excel, the messages may not always lead to greater intrinsic value for the domain. This may occur for a variety of reasons, but one of the ones we have documented is when parents become overly invested in one area. This may happen initially because the children are talented and interested, but as the focus narrows to that one domain, the children may feel increased pressure to perform or may begin to feel that they are participating to please their parents rather than because of intrinsic interest in the area. In one analysis of high school students, we found that all parents of gifted students professed a high value for academics but that the same parents differed in how much they valued social skills and social success. The parents who focused on academics alone had children who were more worried about school and had lower self-perceptions of their abilities than did those parents who had more balanced perceptions of the need for both academic and social skills (Tanner, Jacobs, & Eccles, 1998). It seems likely that parents who value more areas of competence encourage their children to participate in a broader array of activities. The provision of a larger range of opportunities may be particularly important as children move into adolescence.

As parents send messages about their children's competence, they need to be aware of their children's developmental needs and changing expertise. A child who is a star athlete at age 8 years may not continue on the same trajectory. Parents need to be able to respond to changes in their children's relative standing by being supportive but realistic. If the parent continues to focus on basketball prowess in the son who was tall for his age at 10 years but ended up short relative to age-mates after puberty, the son may continue to play basketball to please his parents but may be better off focusing on a different activity. We have found developmental trends in children's reasons for participating in activities; at younger ages, they say that they are involved because they "like" an activity, but ability or lack of ability at doing a task and task ease or difficulty became more salient reasons as children get older.

Most research suggests that parental support for *autonomy* is positively related to numerous indicators of successful development, such as achievement motivation (Deci & Ryan, 1985), self-esteem, connection to school, and academic achievement (Eccles et al., 1996). Parents provide support for autonomy primarily by giving children choices that will allow them to connect their behavior to their personal goals and values (Connell & Wellborn, 1991). For this to be successful, parents need to give children real choices that are within the child's "zone of proximal development" to carry out and that parents are willing to "live with." This can be contrasted with either making choices for the child or giving the appearance of allowing choice but overriding unpopular decisions.

Differences in the amount of autonomy that parents give may be due to parental beliefs or to differences in parents' responses to individual children. For example, we have some data suggesting that the amount of autonomy and decision making that parents afford their children may be a reaction to their perceptions of the child's personal characteristics (Hyatt, Jacobs, & Tanner, 1998), suggesting that parents may be assessing their children's readiness and then responding on the basis of their assessment. In addition, perceptions of the desirability of autonomy for children at different ages may vary by ethnicity or social class.

Although most of the research has focused on academic tasks, we expect the same dynamics between perceived autonomy and task values in any domain in which there is some choice; however, a problem that parents may experience is competitive dynamics between competence and autonomy (Connell & Wellborn, 1991). For example, a parent's goal may be for a child to like tennis and develop competence at it, but tactics that force the child's involvement may result in the child's feeling manipulated and controlled. Previous research suggests that perceptions of autonomy will decrease when others try to exercise too much control over an individual's behavior. This suggests that parents walk a very fine line between being supportive and being overcontrolling. The critical dimension seems to be perceived choice. If children believe that they are engaging in the activity because they like it or because they chose to be involved, they are more likely to continue to value it. Even if children make the choice to be involved, they may do it for a variety of reasons: (1) because performance on the activity is relevant to their self-concepts (e.g., "I have to practice violin because I will feel bad about myself if I don't"), (2) because they enjoy the activity (e.g., "Practicing violin is the best part of my day"), or (3) because they relate it to a higher self-chosen goal (e.g., "If I practice hard, I will be able to join the school orchestra"). Parents can facilitate their children's activity values by allowing the children to choose learning goals rather than performance goals and to develop realistic ways to meet those goals. The emphasis on choice does not mean that children are making decisions without adult guidance or that they may "choose" to change or quit activities on a whim. Parents must be able to create a scaffold for children's decisions that will allow the children to make choices within parental guidelines at earlier stages of involvement, with more flexibility and fewer constraints as the parent reassesses the child and is able to withdraw some of the scaffolding.

Another issue related to parental support of autonomy is that some parents may get their own identities involved in their children's achievements rather than see the children as separate from them. Parents' goals for their children are not independent of their own values, and their desires for their children to participate or excel at activities may be related to their perceptions of themselves as parents, coaches, and mentors. Although we often talk about parents' effects on their children, we keep coming back to the interactive nature of parent–child self-systems. Children's achievements, values, and task involvement also affect parents' perceptions of themselves and parents' values. For example, parents who may never have given a thought to the sport of soccer suddenly become very invested in soccer when their children show interest and talent for the sport. This may extend beyond children's soccer matches to include watching professional games on television or attending college matches.

Although the relationships between autonomy and successful outcomes have been found at different ages, support for autonomy may be particularly important at early adolescence because establishing oneself is the quintessential developmental task of the adolescent period (e.g., Eccles et al., 1993). The importance of autonomy during this period has already been demonstrated in school settings (e.g., Connell & Wellborn, 1991; Midgley et al. 1989). Families must respond to the same needs for autonomy that have been seen in education settings; however, it is very likely that parents provide greater support for autonomy to adolescents who are viewed as trustworthy and responsible than to those teens who are seen as likely to get into trouble if left on their own. For example, during the transition to junior high school, perceptions of one's parents as too controlling and intrusive are associated with a decline in self-esteem, whereas perceptions of involvement in family decision making are associated with increases in self-esteem (Eccles et al., 1997). In these families, the authority renegotiation process that accelerates in adolescence is more likely to proceed relatively smoothly than in families in which either the parents are incompetent, the parent–child relationship is already problematic, or the adolescent is already on a problematic developmental trajectory (Eccles et al., 1996). The extent to which parents adapt their general child-rearing strategies (particularly with regard to the support they provide for autonomous decision making and activity choice) to their children's increasing maturity should affect the parent–child relationship and the children's social development (see Eccles et al., 1993).

The importance of a warm and caring *relationship* between children and parents is clear in theories ranging from attachment (Ainsworth et al., 1978) to social learning (Bandura, 1994) to parenting styles (Baumrind, 1971); however, the question for parents is how to maintain a close emotional relationship with children as they develop. In one study, Eccles et al., (1996) found that perceived high levels of connectedness and emotional support were related positively to both psychological and behavioral indicators of successful development, particularly for girls. These results are consistent with theories hypothesizing that feeling connected and supported emotionally in both parent–child and school contexts has positive benefits (Connell & Wellborn, 1991; Goodnow, 1993).

One of the major ways in which parents seem to demonstrate their affection for their children is through involvement with them, defined by Connell and Wellborn (1991) as the "dedication of psychological resources," such as time and interest (p. 56). Positive correlations have been found between children's perceptions of their parents' involvement and their perceptions of their own abilities, academic success, and values for school (e.g., Epstein, 1989; Grolnick & Ryan, 1989; Roeser, Lord, & Eccles, 1994). Moreover, affective experiences during participation in activities with parents may influence subjective task value and participation (Skinner, 1991). It is clear that just spending time with children is not enough—the affect surrounding the parent–child involvement is important. If parents help children with homework but belittle the children and get angry if they do not understand a concept, both the affective relationship and value for the task are likely to suffer. Many parents report that monitoring homework drains their energy and patience (e.g., Corno, 1996; Hoover-Dempsy, Bassler, & Burow, 1995), suggesting that maintaining positive affect during interchanges about homework may be difficult. In a study comparing middle-school students who were highly alienated from school with those who reported low alienation, Roeser et al. (1994) found that alienated students experienced much more negative affect and less positive affect when doing schoolwork with their parents than did the other group.

Additionally, too much involvement or control may raise anxiety around activity involvement (Grolnick & Ryan, 1987). If children continue to participate in an activity to please their parents (as in the earlier tennis scenario), their intrinsic interest and eventual involvement with the activity are expected to decline (Deci & Ryan, 1985). For example, in one study, we found that when parental monitoring was perceived as reasonable rather than stifling, it was related to positive adolescent–parent affective relationships, but when it was perceived as overly strict and demanding, less positive adolescent–parent relationships resulted (Jacobs et al., 1998). These studies draw attention to the importance of children's *perceptions* of their parents' overtures at involvement and affection. Similar observed levels of involvement may have different meanings to different children, and it is the child's perception that will determine the effect.

Once again, developmental changes play a large role in the nature of parent–child affective relationships. Being "close" to parents during early elementary school may mean spending many hours together and sharing confidences, whereas during adolescence it may mean acknowledging parents' opinions and eating dinner together. This means not that adolescents have lower needs for affective relationships with their parents as they get older but that the fit between their needs and the expression of that relationship will be critical for maintaining close ties. It appears that one of the important tasks for parents is to maintain a supportive and close relationship as their children mature and develop their own values as they try out different activities. This may not always be easy; however, a close parent–child relationship is likely to lead the child to value activities that are important or at least acceptable to the parent.

CONCLUSION

We began this chapter by describing the importance of task values for intrinsic motivation, continued activity involvement, and achievement choices. We described the Eccles expectancy-value model and the role that parents play as socializers of their children's values. In the first section, we elaborated on the literature describing the ways in which values are developed within the contexts of social identity, individual identity, and the universal needs of competence, autonomy, and relatedness.

In the next section, we tried to elaborate the implications of models that emphasize task values for the socialization of activity involvement. We discussed the dilemmas facing both researchers and parents of trying to develop theoretical and practical models that specify optimal levels of support, so that intrinsic values are developed rather than undermined. The interactive and interative nature of the processes were emphasized. We then used our general model of parent influence to describe the potential avenues of influence on task values, including (1) the general social-emotional climate they provide and by their general child-rearing beliefs, (2) the provision of specific experiences for the child, (3) parental involvement in valued activities, and (4) communication of perceptions of the child's abilities and expectations for performance. We ended this section by talking about parenting practices that have been related to the development of autonomy, competence, and relatedness, highlighting the need for parents to be aware of changing needs as their children develop.

In conclusion, it is clear that parents play a large role in the development of task values across a variety of activity domains. Although some theoretical models (including Eccles's model) attempt to describe the relationships between the multifaceted contexts provided by parents, the interactions of parents and children, and what children bring to the mix, most empirical work has been piecemeal, emphasizing only one part of the picture at a time and often in only one domain or context. This is because it is a complex process that takes place over time and across many interactions that provide feedback and redirection for parents and children; it also varies by family and by domain. We are continuing to explore the processes that underlie both continuity and change across time in varied settings and across activities.

References

Ainsworth, M. D., Blehar, M., Waters, E., & Wall, S. (1978). *Patterns of attachment*. Hillsdale, NJ: Erlbaum.

Alexander, P. A., Kulikovich, J. M., & Jetton, T. L. (1994). The role of subject-matter knowledge and interest in the processing of linear and nonlinear texts. *Review of Educational Research, 64,* 201–252.

Altenburg-Caldwell, K., Jacobs, J. E., & Eccles, J. S. (1999, June). *Gender differences in activity involvement: Relations between activities, self-beliefs, and gender-typing.* Paper presented at the annual meeting of the American Psychological Society, Denver.

Atkinson, J. W. (1964). An introduction to motivation. Princeton, NJ: Van Nostrand.

Baltes, P. B. (1987). Theoretical propositions of life-span developmental psychology: On the dynamics between growth and decline. *Developmental Psychology, 23,* 611–626.

Bandura, A. (1994) *Self-efficacy: The exercise of control.* New York: W. H. Freeman.

Bandura, A., & Walters, R. H. (1963). *Social learning and personality development.* New York: Holt, Rinehart, & Winston.

Barber, B. K., Olsen J. E., & Shagle, S. C. (1994). Associations between parental psychological and behavioral control and youth internalized and externalized behaviors. *Child Development, 65,* 1120–1136.

Battle, E. (1965) Motivational determinants of academic task persistence. *Journal of Personality and Social Psychology, 2,* 209–218.

Battle, E. (1966). Motivational determinants of academic task persistence. *Journal of Personality and Social Psychology, 4,* 534–642.

Baumrind, D. (1971). Harmonious parents and their preschool children. *Developmental Psychology, 41,* 92–102.

Bledsoe, J. (1967). Self-concept of children and their intelligence, achievement, interests, and anxiety. *Childhood Education, 43,* 436–438.

Bretherton, I. (1985). Attachment theory: Retrospect and prospect. In I Bretherton & E. Waters (Eds.), Growing points of attachment theory and research. *Monographs of the Society for Research in Child Development, 50*(1–2, Serial No. 209), 3–35.

Bruner, J. S. (1983). *Child's talk: Learning to use language.* Oxford, UK: Oxford University Press.

Carstensen, L. L. (1992). Social emotional patterns in adulthood: Support for socioemotional selectivity theory. *Psychology and Aging, 7,* 331–338.

Coleman, J. S. (1961). *The adolescent society.* New York: Free Press.

Connell, J. P. (1990). Context, self, and action: A motivational analysis of self-system processes across the life-span. In D. Cicchetti (Ed.), *The self in transition: From infancy to childhood.* Chicago: University of Chicago Press.

Connell, J. P., & Ryan, R. (1987). A developmental theory of motivation in the classroom. *Teacher Education Quarterly, 11,* 64–77.

Connell, J. P., & Thompson, R. (1986). Emotion and social interaction in the strange situation: Consistencies and asymmetric influences in the second year. *Child Development, 57,* 733–745.

Connell, J. P., & Wellborn, J. G. (1991). Competence, autonomy, and relatedness: A motivational analysis of self-system processes. In M. R. Gunnar & L. A. Sroufe (Eds.), *Minnesota Symposia on Child Psychology: Vol. 23. Systems and development.* (pp. 43–77). Hillsdale, NJ: Erlbaum.

Corno, L. (1996). Homework is a complicated thing. *Educational Researcher, 25,* 27–29.

Crouter, A. C., & Larson, R. (1998). Temporal rhythms in adolescence: Clocks, calendars, and the coordination of daily life. *New Directions for Child and Adolescent Development, 82,* 1–6.

Csiksentmihalyi, M. (1988). The flow experience and its significance for human psychology. In M. Csikszentmihalyi & I. S. Csikszentmihalyi (Eds.), *Optimal experience* (pp. 15–35). Cambridge, MA: Cambridge University Press.

Csikszentimihalyi, M. (1990). *Flow: The psychology of optimal experience.* New York: Harper & Row.

Czikszentmihalyi, M., Rathunde, K., & Whalen, S. (1993). *Talented teenagers: The roots of success and failure.* New York: Cambridge University Press.

Deci, E. L. (1971). Effects of externally mediated rewards on intrinsic motivation. *Journal of Personality and Social Psychology, 18,* 105–115.

Deci, E. L. (1975). *Intrinsic Motivation.* New York: Plenum.

Deci, E. L., & Ryan, R. M. (1985). *Intrinsic motivation and self-determination in human behavior*. New York: Plenum.

Dweck, C. S., & Leggett, E. L. (1988). A social-cognitive approach to motivation and personality. *Psychological Review*, 95, 256–273.

Eccles, J. S. (1984). Sex differences in achievement patterns. In T. Sonderegger (Ed.), *Nebraska Symposium on Motivation: Vol. 32. Gender and Motivation.* (pp. 97–132). Lincoln: University of Nebraska Press.

Eccles, J. S. (1987). Gender roles and women's achievement-related decisions. *Psychology of Women Quarterly*, 11, 135–172.

Eccles, J. S. (1993). School and family effects on the ontogeny of adolescents' interests, self-perceptions, and activity choice. In J. Jacobs (Ed.), *Nebraska Symposium on Motivation: Vol. 40. Developmental perspectives on motivation* (pp. 145–208). Lincoln: University of Nebraska Press.

Eccles, J. S. (1994). Understanding women's educational and occupational choices: Applying the Eccles et al. model of achievement-related choices. *Psychology of Women Quarterly*, 18, 585–609.

Eccles, J. S., Adler, T. F., & Meece, J. L. (1984). Sex differences in achievement: A test of alternative theories. *Journal of Personality and Social Psychology*, 46, 26–43.

Eccles, J. S., Early, D., & Frasier, K., Belansky, E., & McCarthy, K. (1996). The relation of connection, regulation, and support for autonomy to adolescents' functioning. *Journal of Adolescent Research*, 12, 263–286.

Eccles, J. S. & Harold, R. D. (1991). Gender differences in sport involvement: Applying the Eccles' expectancy-value model. *Journal of Applied Sport Psychology*, 3, 7–35.

Eccles, J. S., & Harold, R. D. (1993). Parent-school involvement during the early adolescent years. *Teachers' College Record*, 94, 568–587.

Eccles, J. S., Lord, S. E., Roeser, R. W., Barber, B. L., & Jozefowicz, D. M. (1997). The association of school transitions in early adolescence with developmental trajectories through high school. In J. Schulenberg, J. L. Maggs, & K. Hurrelmann (Eds.), *Health risks and developmental transitions during adolescence*. New York: Cambridge University Press.

Eccles, J. S., & Midgley, C. (1989). Stage/environment fit: Developmentally appropriate classrooms for early adolescents. In R. Ames & C. Ames (Eds.), *Research on motivation in education* (vol. 3, pp. 139–181). New York: Academic Press.

Eccles, J. S., & Wigfield, A. (1995). In the mind of the achiever: The structure of adolescents' academic achievement related-beliefs and self-perceptions. *Personality and Social Psychology Bulletin*, 21, 215–225.

Eccles, J. S., Wigfield, A., Flanagan, C., Miller, C., Reuman, D., & Yee, D. (1989). Self-concepts, domain values, and self-esteem: Relations and changes at early adolescence. *Journal of Personality*, 57, 283–310.

Eccles, J. S., Wigfield, A., Harold, R., & Blumenfeld, P. (1993). Age and gender differences in children's achievement self-perceptions during the elementary school years. *Child Development*, 64, 830–847.

Eccles, J. S., Wigfield, A., Schiefele, U. (1998). Motivation to succeed. In W. Damon (Ed.), *Handbook of child psychology*: N. Eisenberg (Vol. Ed.), *Social, emotional, and personality development*. New York: Wiley.

Eccles-Parsons, J., Adler, T. F., & Kaczala, C. M. (1982) Socialization of achievement attitudes and beliefs: Parental influences. *Child Development*, 53, 322–339.

Eccles (Parsons), J., Adler, T. F., Futterman, R., Goff, S. B., Kaczala, C. M., Meece, J. L., & Midgley, C. (1983). Expectancies, values, and academic behaviors. In J. T. Spence (Ed.), *Achievement and achievement motivation* (pp. 75–146). San Francisco: W. H. Freeman.

Eder, D., & Parker, S. (1987). The cultural production and reproduction of gender: The effect of extracurricular activities on peer-group culture. *Sociology of Education*, 60, 200–214.

Eisenberger, R., & Cameron, J. (1996). Detrimental effects of reward: Reality or myth? *American Psychologist*, 51, 1153–1166.

Epstein, J. L. (1989). Family influence and student motivation. In R. E. Ames & C. Ames (Eds.), *Research on motivation in education* (vol. 3, pp. 132–157). New York: Academic Press.

Epstein, J. L. (1992). School and family partnerships. In M. Alkin (Ed.), *Encyclopedia of educational research* (pp. 1139–1151). New York: Macmillan.

Epstein, J. A., & Harackiewicz, J. M. (1992). Winning is not enough: The effects of competition and achievement orientation on intrinsic interest. *Personality and Social Psychology Bulletin, 18,* 128–138.

Feather, N. T. (1982). Expectancy-value approaches: Present status and future directions. In N. T. Feather (Ed.), *Expectations and actions: Expectancy-value models in psychology* (pp. 395–420). Hillsdale, NJ: Erlbaum.

Feather, N. T. (1988). Values, valences, and course enrollment: Testing the role of personal values within an expectancy–value framework. *Journal of Educational Psychology, 80,* 381–391.

Feather, N. T. (1992). Values, valences, expectations, and actions. *Journal of Social Issues, 48,* 109–124.

Fredericks, J. (1999). *"Girl-friendly" family contexts: Socialization into math and sports.* Unpublished doctoral dissertation, University of Michigan, Ann Arbor.

Goodnow. C. (1993). Classroom belonging among early adolescent students: Relationships to motivation and achievement. *Journal of Early Adolescence, 13*(1), 21–43.

Goodnow, J. J., & Collins, W. A. (1990). *Development according to parents: The nature, sources, and consequences of parents' ideas.* London: Erlbaum.

Grolnick, W. S., & Ryan, R. M. (1987). Autonomy in children's learning: An experimental and individual difference investigation. *Journal of Personality and Social Psychology, 52,* 891–898.

Grolnick, W. S., & Ryan, R. M. (1989). Parent styles associated with children's self-regulation and competence in school. *Journal of Educational Psychology, 81,* 143–154.

Grolnick, W. S., & Ryan, R. M., & Deci, E. L. (1991). The inner resources for school achievement: Motivational mediators of children's perceptions of their parents. *Journal of Educational Psychology, 83,* 508–517.

Harackiewicz, J. M., Abrahams, S., & Wageman, R. (1987). Performance evaluation and intrinsic motivation: The effects of evaluative focus, rewards, and achievement orientation. *Journal of Personality and Social Psychology, 53,* 1015–1023.

Harackiewicz, J. M., & Elliot, A. J. (1993). Achievement goals and intrinsic motivation. *Journal of Personality and Social Psychology, 65,* 904–915.

Harackiewicz, J. M & Elliot, A. J. The joint effects of target and purpose goals on intrinsic motivation: A mediational analysis. *Personality & Social Psychology Bulletin. Vol 24*(7), Jul 1998, 675–689.

Harter, S. (1981). A new self-report scale of intrinsic versus extrinsic orientation in the classroom: Motivational and informational components. *Developmental Psychology, 17,* 300–312.

Harter, S. (1990). Causes, correlates and the functional role of global self-worth: A life-span perspective. In J. Kolligan & R. Sternberg (Eds.), *Perceptions of competence and incompetence across the life-span* (pp. 67–98). New Haven, CT: Yale University Press.

Harter, S. (1998). The development of the self. In W. Damon (Ed.), *Handbook of child psychology:* N. Eisenberg (Vol. Ed.), *Social, emotional, and personality development.* New York: Wiley.

Hennessey, B. A., & Amabile, T. M. (1998). Reward, intrinsic motivation, and creativity. *American Psychologist, 53,* 674–675.

Herbst, P. G. (1953). Analysis and measurement of a situation. *Human Relations, VI* 113–140.

Hidi, S. (1990). Interest and its contributions as a mental resource for learning. *Review of Educational Research, 60,* 549–571.

Hill, J. P., & Holmbeck, G. N. (1986). Attachment and autonomy during adolescence. *Annals of Child Development, 3,* 145–189.

Hill, J. P., & Lynch, M. E. (1983). The intensification of gender-related role expectations during early adolescent. In J. Brooks-Gunn & A. C. Petersen (Eds.), *Girls at puberty: Biological and psychosocial perspectives* (pp. 15–62). New York: Cambridge University Press.

Hollingshead, A. B. (1949). *Elmstown's youth: The impact of social classes on adolescents.* New York: Wiley.

Hoover-Dempsey, K. V., Bassler, O. C., Burow, R. (1995). Parents' reported involvement in students' homework: Strategies and practices. *Elementary School Journal*, 95, 435–450.

Hunt, D. E. (1975). Person–environment interaction: A challenge found wanting before it was tried. *Review of Educational Research*, 45, 209–230.

Hyatt, S., Jacobs, J. E., & Tanner, J. (1998, March). *Explaining the decrease in adolescents' math and sports ability and interest: An example using hierarchical linear modeling.* Paper presented at the annual meeting of the American Educational Research Association, San Diego.

Jacobs, J. E. (1991). The influence of gender stereotypes on parent and child math attitudes: Differences across grade levels. *Journal of Educational Psychology*, 83, 518–527.

Jacobs, J. E., & Eccles, J. S. (1985). Gender differences in math ability: The impact of media reports on parents. *Educational Researcher*, 14, 20–25.

Jacobs, J. E., & Eccles, J. E. (1992). The influence of parent stereotypes on parent and child ability beliefs in three domains. *Journal of Personality and Social Psychology*, 63, 932–944.

Jacobs, J. E., Finken, L. L., Griffin, N. L., & Wright, J. D. (1998). The career plans of science-talented rural adolescent girls. *American Educational Research Journal*, 35, 681–704.

Jacobs, J. E., Hyatt, S., Eccles, J. E., Osgood, D. W., & Wigfield, A. (under review). The ontogeny of children's self-beliefs across domains: An examination of changes during grades one through twelve.

Jacobs, J. E., Hyatt, S., Tanner, J., & Eccles, J. (1998). *Lessons learned at home: Relations between parents' child-rearing practices and children's achievement perceptions.* Paper presented at the annual meeting of the American Educational Research Association, San Diego.

Jacobs, J. E., & Osgood, D. W. (1994, February). *Age trends in autonomy.* Paper presented at the biennial meeting of the Society for Research on Adolescence, San Diego.

James, W. (1982/1963). *Psychology.* New York: Fawcett.

Kinney, D. A. (1993). From nerds to normals: The recovery of identity among adolescents from middle school to high school. *Sociology of Education*, 66, 21–44.

Kirshnit, C. E., Ham, M., & Richards, M. H. (1989). The sporting life: Athletic activities during early adolescence. *Journal of Youth and Adolescence*, 18, 610–615.

Ladd, G. W., & Le Sieur, K. D. (1995). Parents and children's peer relationships. In M. H. Bornstein (Ed.), *Children and parenting* (vol. 4). Hillsdale, NJ: Erlbaum.

Larson, R. W. (1990). The solitary side of life: An examination of the time people spend alone from childhood to old age. *Developmental Review*, 10, 155–183.

Lepper, M. R. (1998). A whole much less than the sum of its parts. *American Psychologist*, 53, 675–676.

Lepper, M. R., Keavney, M., & Drake, M. (1996). Intrinsic motivation and extrinsic rewards: A commentary on Cameron and Pierce's meta-analyses. *Review of Educational Research*, 66, 5–23.

Lepper, M. R., Greene, D., & Nisbett, R. E. (1973). Undermining children's intrinsic interest with extrinsic rewards: A test of the "overjustification" hypothesis. *Journal of Personality and Social Psychology*, 28, 129–137.

Lepper, M. R. & Gilouich, T. (1982). Accentuating the positive: Eliciting generalized compliance from children through activity-oriented requests. *Journal of Personality & Social Psychology*, 42(2), 248–259.

Mahoney, J. L., & Cairns, R. B. (1997). Do extracurricular activities protect against early school dropout? *Developmental Psychologist*, 33, 241–253.

Meece, J. L., Eccles-Parsons, J., Kaczala, C. M., Goff, S. E., & Futterman, R. (1982). Sex differences in math achievement: Toward a model of academic choice. *Psychological Bulletin*, 91, 324–348.

Meece, J. L., Wigfield, A., & Eccles, J. S. (1990). Predictors of math anxiety and its consequences for young adolescents' course enrollment intentions and performances in mathematics. *Journal of Educational Psychology*, 82, 60–70.

Midgley, C., & Feldlaufer, H. (1987). Students' and teachers' decision-making fit before and after the transition to junior high school. *Journal of Early Adolescence*, 7, 225–241.

Midgley, C., Feldlaufer, H., & Eccles, J. S. (1989). Changes in teacher efficacy and student self- and task-related beliefs during the transition to junior high school. *Journal of Educational Psychology, 81,* 247–258.

Newson, J., & Newson, E. (1975). Intersubjectivity and the transmission of culture: On the social origins of symbolic functioning. *Bulletin of the British Psychological Society, 28,* 437–446.

Nicholls, J. G. (1978). The development of the concepts of effort and ability, perceptions of academic attainment, and the understanding that difficult tasks require more ability. *Child Development, 49,* 800–814.

Nicholls, J. G. (1979). Development of perception of own attainment and causal attributions for success and failure in reading. *Journal of Educational Psychology, 71,* 94–99.

Okagaki, L., Frensch, P. A., & Dodson, N. E. (1996). Mexican-American children's perceptions of self- and school achievement. *Hispanic Journal of Behavioral Sciences, 18,* 469–484.

Parsons, J. E., & Ruble, D. N. (1977). The development of achievement-related expectancies. *Child Development, 48,* 1075–1079.

Phillips, D. A. (1987). Socialization of perceived academic competence among highly competent children. *Child Development, 58,* 1308–1320.

Phillips, D., & Zimmerman, M. (1990). The developmental course of perceived competence and incompetence among competent children. In R. J. Sternberg & J. Kolligian, Jr. (Eds.), *Competence considered* (pp. 41–66). New Haven: Yale University Press.

Renninger, K. A. (1990). Children's play interests, representation, and activity. In R. Fivush & J. Hudson (Eds.), *Knowing and remembering young children* (pp. 127–165). Cambridge, MA: Cambridge University Press.

Renninger, K. A., Hidi, S., & Krapp, A. (Eds.). (1992). *The role of interest in learning and development.* Hillsdale, NJ: Erlbaum.

Renninger, K. A., & Wozniak, R. H. (1985). Effect of interest on attentional shift, recognition, and recall in young children. *Developmental Psychology, 21,* 624–632.

Roeser, R. W., Lord, S. E., & Eccles, J. (1994). A portrait of academic alienation in adolescence: Motivation, mental health, and family experience. Paper presented at the biennial meeting of the Society for Research on Adolescence, San Diego.

Rogoff, B. (1990). *Apprenticeship in thinking.* New York: Oxford University Press.

Rokeach, M. (1979). From individual to institutional values with special references to the values of science. In M. Rokeach (Ed.), *Understanding human values* (pp. 47–70). New York: Free Press.

Ryan, R. M. (1991). The nature of the self in autonomy and relatedness. In J. Strauss & G. R. Goethals (Eds.), *The self: Interdisciplinary approaches* (pp. 208–238). New York: Springer-Verlag.

Ryan, R. M. (1993). Agency and organization: Intrinsic motivation, autonomy, and the self in psychological development. In J. Jacobs (Ed.), *Nebraska Symposium on Motivation 1992.* Vol. 40. Lincoln: University of Nebraska Press.

Ryan, R. M., & Connell, J. P. (1989). Perceived locus of causality and internalization: Examining reasons for acting in two domains. *Journal of Personality and Social Psychology, 57,* 749–761.

Ryan, R. M., Connell, J. P., & Deci, E. L. (1985). A motivational analysis of self-determination and self-regulation in education. In C. Ames & R. E. Ames (Eds.), *Research on motivation in education: The classroom milieu* (pp. 13–51). New York: Academic Press.

Ryan, R. M., & Lynch, J. H. (1989). Emotional autonomy versus detachment: Revisiting the vicissitudes of adolescence and adulthood. *Child Development, 60,* 340–356.

Sansone, C., & Harackiewicz, J. M. (1996). "I don't feel like it": The function of interest in self-regulation. In L. Martin & A Tesser (Eds.), *Striving and feeling: Interactions between goals, affect, and self-regulation* (pp. 203–228). Hillsdale, NJ: Erlbaum.

Sansone, C., & Harackiewicz, J. M. (1998). "Reality" is complicated. *American Psychologist, 53,* 673–674.

Sansone, C., Weir, C., Harpster, L., & Morgan, C. (1992). Once a boring task, always a boring task? Interest as a self-regulatory mechanism. *Journal of Personality and Social Psychology, 63,* 379–390.

Schiefele, U. (1991). Interest, learning, and motivation. *Educational Psychologist, 26,* 299–323.

Schiefele, U. (1996). Topic interest, text representation, and quality of experience. *Contemporary Educational Psychology*, 21, 3–18.

Shaw, S., Caldwell, L., & Kleiber, D. (1996). Boredom, stress and social controls in the daily activities of adolescents. *Journal of Leisure Research*, 28, 274–292.

Sigel, I. E. (1982). The relationship between parental distancing strategies and the child's cognitive behavior. In L. M. Laosa & I. E. Sigel (Eds.), *Families as learning environments for children* (pp. 47–86). New York: Plenum Press.

Sigel, I. E., McGillicuddy-DeLisi, A. V., & Goodnow, J. J. (Eds.). (1992). *Parental belief systems* (2nd ed.). Hillsdale, NJ: Erlbaum.

Simmons, R. G., & Blyth, D. A. (1987). *Moving into adolescence: The impact of pubertal change and school context.* Hawthorn, NY: Aldine de Gruyter.

Skinner, E. A. (1991). Development and perceived control: A dynamic model of action in context. In M. Gunnar & L. A. Sroufe (Eds.), *Minnesota Symposa on Child Psychology: Vol. 23. Systems and development* (pp. 62–78). Hillsdale, NJ: Erlbaum.

Steinberg, L. D. (1988). Reciprocal relation between parent-child distance and pubertal maturation. *Developmental Psychology*, 24, 122–128.

Steinberg, L., & Silverberg, S. B. (1986). The vicissitudes of autonomy in early adolescence. *Child Development*, 57, 841–851.

Stevenson, H. W., Chen, C., & Uttal, D. H. (1990). Beliefs and achievement: A study of black, white, and Hispanic children. *Child Development*, 61, 508–523.

Stipek, D. J. (1981). *Children's use of past performance information in ability and expectancy judgments for self and other.* Paper presented at the meeting of the International Society for the Study of Behavioral Development, Toronto.

Tanner, J. L., Jacobs, J. E., & Eccles, J. S. (1998, April). *Putting it in a social context: High ability students' motivations to succeed.* Paper presented at the annual meeting of the American Educational Research Association, San Diego.

Tobias, S. (1994). Interest, prior knowledge, and learning. *Review of Educational Research*, 64, 37–54.

Vygotsky, L. S. (1978/1934). *Mind in society.* Cambridge, MA: Harvard University Press.

Wigfield, A. (1994). Expectancy-value theory of achievement motivation: A developmental perspective. *Educational Psychology Review*, 6, 49–78.

Wigfield, A., & Eccles, J. (1992). The development of achievement task values: A theoretical analysis. *Developmental Review*, 12, 265–310.

Wigfield, A., Eccles, J., Mac Iver, D., Reuman, D., & Midgley, C. (1991). Transitions at early adolescence: Changes in children's domain-specific self-perceptions and general self-esteem across the transition to junior high school. *Developmental Psychology*, 27, 552–565.

Wigfield, A., Eccles, J. S., Yoon, K. S., Harold, R. D., Arbreton, A. J., Freedman-Doan, C., & Blumenfeld, P. C. (1997). Change in children's competence beliefs and subjective task values across the elementary school years: A 3-year study. *Journal of Educational Psychology*, 89, 451–469.

Winston, C., Eccles, J. S., Senior, A. M. (in press). The utility of an expectancy/value model of achievement for understanding academic performance and self-esteem in African-American and European-American adolescents. *Zeitschrift Fur Padagogische Psychologie (German Journal of Educational Psychology).*

Wood, D. J. (1989). Social interaction as tutoring. In M. H. Bornstein & J. S. Bruner (Eds.), *Interaction in human development.* Hillsdale, NJ: Erlbaum.

Yoon, K. S., Wigfield, A., & Eccles, J. S. (1993, April). *Causal relations between mothers' and children's beliefs about math ability: A structural equation model.* Paper presented at the annual meeting of the American Educational Research Association,

Zajonc, R. B. (1968). Attitudinal effects of mere exposure. *Journal of Personality and Social Psychology*, 9, 1–27.

PART

IV

Conclusion

CHAPTER

15

Controversies and New Directions—Is It Déjà Vu All Over Again?

CAROL SANSONE

Department of Psychology
University of Utah

JUDITH M. HARACKIEWICZ

Department of Psychology
University of Wisconsin

As amply demonstrated by the collection of chapters in this book, we have learned much about intrinsic motivation since landmark books published in the 1970s (e.g., Deci, 1975; Lepper & Green, 1978). At the same time, the newer and evolving perspectives represented in this book show that we still have much to learn. There is a sense of déjà vu for some of the issues, but we believe this reflects the actual dynamics of the motivational process. In other words, understanding intrinsic motivation requires complex answers. Although we might wish for a simpler conclusion, whenever the "accepted wisdom" drifts toward a simple answer (e.g., rewards are good; rewards are bad; performance goals are bad; performance goals are good), researchers respond with a resounding "...*but*..."

One question that has reappeared is the question of whether rewards are "good" or "bad" for intrinsic motivation and creativity (Deci, Koestner, & Ryan, 1999; Eisenberger & Cameron, 1996; Hennessey & Amabile, 1998; Lepper, Henderlong, & Gingras, 1999; Sansone & Harackiewicz, 1998). We think

Intrinsic and Extrinsic Motivation
Copyright © 2000 by Academic Press. All rights of reproduction in any form reserved.

that all the contributors to this book would answer resoundingly, "It depends!" There is now a fair degree of consensus among the present contributors that rewards can have a variety of effects on intrinsic motivation and performance. There is also consensus that these reward effects depend on the nature of the activity, the reward contingency, the feedback obtained, the more general context for reward administration, and the people offering and receiving the reward.

Some disagreement arises, however, as we move from this general "it depends" conclusion toward specifying the precise nature of reward dynamics. There is perhaps the greatest divergence of opinion in terms of whether and how rewards can *positively* affect motivation. For example, Ryan and Deci (chapter 2) and Lepper and Henderlong (chapter 10) suggest that rewards can positively affect *extrinsic* motivation and thereby increase the probability of performing activities when the initial incentive to perform the activity is low (e.g., boring tasks). In contrast, Harackiewicz and Sansone (chapter 4), Hennessey (chapter 3), and Hidi (chapter 11) argue that rewards (particularly rewards for performing well) can positively impact *intrinsic* motivation and creativity through their effects on mediating processes such as competence valuation (e.g., chapter 4) or task valuation more generally (chapter 3).

Among this latter group of researchers, though, there is not consensus about the extent of this positive potential or the circumstances under which this positive potential of rewards is likely to outweigh negative effects. Although we may not yet have reached consensus on these issues, it is clear that researchers' understanding of the reward process has evolved far beyond the simple questions of whether external interventions are good or bad. And from these newer perspectives, the researchers who contributed to this book are also posing new and exciting questions that will drive important research in the future.

MAJOR THEMES AND NEW QUESTIONS

We would like to briefly highlight what we see as some of the major themes and newer issues and questions to arise in this book.

Definition of Intrinsic Motivation

One source of complexity in understanding intrinsic motivation is in defining the construct. In this book, a number of researchers define intrinsic motivation as occurring when an activity satisfies basic human needs for competence and control (e.g., Lepper & Henderlong, chapter 10 Ryan & Deci, chapter 2), which makes the activity interesting and likely to be performed for its own sake rather than as a means to an end. However, Shah and Kruglanski (chapter 5) point out that there may actually be two distinct ways to define *intrinsic motivation* that are embedded in the previous definition. That is, they suggest that *intrinsic motivation* can be defined in terms of structure (i.e., when an activity is associated with one and only one goal) and in terms of substance (i.e., when the content of the goals matters). They further suggest that when a person's relationship with an activity is considered "intrinsic" according to one definition, it may not be considered "intrinsic" according to the other, and that this has implications for understanding a person's choices, his or her degree of persistence, and his or her emotional experiences while working toward a given goal.

In contrast, Sansone & Smith (chapter 12) define intrinsic motivation as occurring when individuals are motivated to experience interest and suggest that a variety of goals may be associated with interest for different people and/or in different contexts (see also Barron & Harackiewicz, chapter 9). From a different perspective, Hidi (chapter 11) and Renninger (chapter 13) suggest that interest that results from a particular set of situational characteristics is not necessarily intrinsically motivated. Instead, intrinsic motivation occurs when the activity is central to the self (Hidi), or when it is associated with individual interest (Renninger); (i.e., more enduring interests that develop as knowledge and value increases).

These different definitions result in researchers asking different questions and interpreting results in different ways. Some of the disagreements between researchers may be more apparent than real, therefore, because of differences in starting definitions. One challenge for future researchers, therefore, is to clearly define the construct. At the very least, researchers should be cognizant of how their questions are shaped by the definition they are using.

Definition of Extrinsic Motivation

Researchers have also adopted different perspectives when defining *extrinsic motivation*. Two distinct definitions of *extrinsic motivation* appear to have emerged: (1) when motivation is based on something extrinsic to the activity and (2) when motivation is based on something extrinsic to the person. Endorsing the first definition of *extrinsic motivation*, Ryan and Deci (chapter 2) further suggest that individuals may have different kinds of extrinsic motivation, which differ in terms of the degree to which the person is self-determined. Self-determined extrinsic motivation, they suggest, can be sufficient to motivate individuals to select and persevere in activities that are not intrinsically motivated. Sansone and Smith (chapter 12), in contrast, agree with the first definition of *extrinsic motivation* but suggest an important caveat. Specifically, Sansone and Smith suggest that this criterion may be difficult to identify a priori because the individual can flexibly define the activity, and he or she can include factors that others would define as extrinsic.

Hidi (chapter 11) endorses the second definition, suggesting that individuals are extrinsically motivated when the source of the motivation is external to the person. She suggests, therefore, that individuals can be motivated by the degree of interest that is caused by characteristics of the activity but that this is extrinsic motivation. As with the definition of *intrinsic motivation*, therefore, these chapters suggest that researchers need to begin by carefully defining their constructs.

Relationship between Extrinsic Motivation and Intrinsic Motivation

As might be expected from the greater diversity in how researchers are defining *intrinsic motivation* and *extrinsic motivation*, conceptions of the relationship between them has also grown more complex. For example, although Ryan and Deci (chapter 2) keep intrinsic motivation and extrinsic motivation distinct, they suggest that the same factors that may enhance intrinsic motivation by promoting feelings of self-determination can also promote self-determined extrinsic motivation (and vice versa). Harackiewicz and Sansone (chapter 4) suggest that the same extrinsic motivator (performance-contingent reward) can simultaneously initiate processes that result in greater intrinsic motivation or extrinsic motivation, depending on the circumstances and the individuals. In contrast, Lepper and Henderlong (chapter 10) suggest that intrinsic motivation and extrinsic motivation can operate simultaneously and are not necessarily reciprocal. Rather than emphasizing parallel processes, Sansone and Smith (chapter 12) suggest that extrinsic motivation can actually enhance intrinsic motivation when it motivates the individual to engage in interest-enhancing strategies.

On the basis of these newer perspectives, researchers would not ask whether a particular extrinsic factor, such as a reward for performing an activity, enhances *or* detracts from intrinsic motivation but rather would ask how this factor affects both intrinsic motivation and extrinsic motivation. Thus, researchers need to directly examine the nature of the relationship between intrinsic motivation and extrinsic motivation for a given activity performed by a given individual in a given context rather than just assume it.

Intrinsic Motivation as an Outcome versus a Process

Researchers also differ in whether they examine intrinsic motivation as an outcome of performing an activity (i.e., the dependent measure) or as part of the process of performing the activity (i.e., as a predictor of some other dependent measure, such as quality of performance). With some exceptions (e.g., Kruglanski, Friedman, & Zeevi, 1971), much of the earlier research tended to examine intrinsic motivation as an outcome. This emphasis allowed researchers to systematically examine the effects of different kinds of extrinsic factors (e.g., different kinds of rewards, different kinds of feedback) on intrinsic motivation. By focusing on intrinsic motivation as an outcome, this perspective also helps to address the longer-term implications— that is, whether individuals are likely to continue to perform an activity over the long term (Barron & Harackiewicz, chapter 9; Renninger, chapter 13; Ryan & Deci, chapter 2).

One notable exception to the early emphasis on outcome was the work conducted by Amabile and colleagues (e.g., Amabile, Hennessey, & Grossman, 1986), which has been further developed by Hennessey and colleagues. In this work, they suggest that intrinsic motivation is necessary for individuals to perform tasks creatively, because an intrinsically motivated orientation to the task promotes characteristics essential for creativity (e.g., attention focused on the task rather than outcomes, willingness to take risks and explore alternatives (Hennessey, chapter 3). The role of intrinsic motivation as a process that contributes to optimal functioning can also be seen in the chapters that examine achievement goals (Barron & Harackiewicz, chapter 9; Butler, chapter 7; Molden & Dweck, chapter 6; Linnenbrink & Pintrich, chapter 8;).

An alternative perspective is offered by Sansone and Smith (chapter 12) and Lepper and Henderlong (chapter 10), who suggest that intrinsic motivation may not be associated with better performance if the aspects of the activity that make it interesting come at the expense of attention toward some performance outcome. In these cases, being intrinsically motivated could *negatively* affect performance. Before assuming that intrinsic motivation will positively affect performance, therefore, these researchers argue that we should first identify the relation between the factors that make performance interesting and the factors that make the individual do well on the specific performance outcome. When compatible, intrinsic motivation should be associated with better performance (Lepper & Henderlong, chapter 10).

The Nature of the Activity

Most of the original intrinsic-motivation research involved novel skill-based games and examined one-time reactions. As can be seen in this book, researchers have expanded their exploration of the process to include different kinds of activities and domains and to increasingly consider the process over time. For example, Ryan and Deci (chapter 2) discuss work guided by their theoretical framework that examines physical health and well-being over the long term.

As is evident in this book, education has been an important domain in which to examine intrinsic motivation and performance (Lepper & Henderlong, chapter 10; Molden & Dweck, chapter 6). An interesting trend reflected in this collection of chapters is that the bridge between traditional education research and traditional intrinsic-motivation research has been built by researchers on both sides. For example, researchers whose primary focus has been to understand intrinsic motivation have found it increasingly valuable to consider how the relevant motivational processes function in actual classroom contexts over time (e.g., Barron & Harackiewicz, chapter 9). Conversely, researchers who have worked to understand achievement motivation and behavior in the classroom have found it increasingly important to consider the role of intrinsic motivation (e.g., Butler, chapter 7; Linnenbrink & Pintrich, chapter 8).

As the scope of activities and domains has widened, results have continued to support many of the original insights (e.g., the importance of self-determination, the positive effects of mastery goals). On the other hand, casting this wider net has also resulted in some marked changes in thinking about motivational processes. For example, although *mastery* in achievement has been defined both by learning something new and by acquiring skills, most research has focused on the latter aspect: that is, on producing a "correct" product or level of output. By considering academic activities that emphasize reading and comprehending new material, however, Renninger (chapter 13) identifies an underexplored process in the study of intrinsic motivation: how increasing knowledge about a subject area can develop into a more enduring interest in that subject. By focusing on this different type of learning activity, Renninger (chapter 13) illustrates the need for researchers to examine the process by which momentary interest in an activity becomes integrated into more stable and enduring interests. In fact, Hidi (chapter 11) suggests that activities involving these more enduring interests may not be as vulnerable to any potential negative effects of rewards or other extrinsic constraints.

Another major change has been to consider the nature of the activity in light of individuals' goals and not just objective task characteristics (Barron & Harackiewicz, chapter 9; Harackiewicz & Sansone, chapter 4; Molden & Dweck, chapter 6; Ryan & Deci, chapter 2; Sansone & Smith, chapter 12; Shah & Kruglanski, chapter 5). There is an increasing recognition that there may be multiple goals for a given activity and that these goals may come from activity characteristics, individual characteristics, and the surrounding context. Some of these goals are competence related and some are not, and the processes that will enhance or detract from motivation can change as a function of these goals (Sansone & Smith, chapter 12; Shah & Kruglanski, chapter 5).

Furthermore, even when goals are competence related, the type of competence goal and its meaning to the individual can have different effects on short-term and on long-term motivational and performance outcomes (Barron & Harackiewicz, chapter 9; Butler, chapter 7; Linnenbrink & Pintrich, chapter 8; Molden & Dweck, chapter 6). For example, Molden and Dweck (chapter 6) propose that even when individuals have adopted similar goals for a given achievement activity (e.g., a performance goal), the tasks may functionally differ because some individuals believe that performance reflects "their fundamental and permanent intelligence" whereas other individuals believe that performance reflects "a more specific, acquirable skill (p. 138)." Finally, Sansone and Smith (chapter 12) suggest that the "activity" itself can change over time to incorporate goals and strategies that emerge once engagement has begun.

Thus, a number of dimensions of activities can affect the motivational process. Early research focused on whether an activity was initially interesting (e.g., Lepper, Green, & Nisbett, 1973) or whether problem solutions were algorithmic or heuristic (e.g., McGraw, 1978). The work presented in this book suggests that dimensions such as the salience of competence requirements, how competence is defined, and the time frame of the activity, among others, are also important. Moreover, the nature of the activity depends not solely on objective task characteristics but also on an individual's goals and their meaning to the individual. Thus, to understand how particular extrinsic factors will affect intrinsic motivation, extrinsic motivation and performance for a given activity, one must first understand what the individual defines as the "activity."

Goal Content versus Goal Congruence

In light of researchers' greater emphasis on goals, some new questions have been formulated. One critical issue has been goal content. Some researchers have argued that certain types of goals are, by definition, associated with intrinsic motivation and are also associated with better or deeper learning and greater well-being more generally. For example, Ryan and Deci (chapter 2) suggest that goals that satisfy intrinsic needs of competence and control define instances of intrinsically motivated behavior or completely integrated self-regulated behavior, and that these goals are associated with long-term health and well-being. Molden and Dweck (chapter 6) and Butler (chapter 7) suggest that in the context of achievement, goals defined in terms of mastery will be associated with greater intrinsic motivation to learn, greater cognitive elaboration, and less vulnerability to difficulties or failures. Goals defined in terms of demonstrating performance to others (performance goals), in contrast, are proposed to be associated with extrinsic motivation to learn, more shallow learning, and greater vulnerability in light of negative feedback.

In contrast, other researchers suggest that the same type of goal can be associated with different motivational and learning outcomes depending on the context and the individual. For example, in the context of achievement, Linnenbrink and Pintrich (chapter 8) and Barron and Harackiewicz (chapter 9) suggest that performance goals can be associated with both positive outcomes and negative outcomes, depending on whether the goal is defined in

terms of approaching success or avoiding failure and depending on whether
approach-performance goals are supported by the academic context. More
generally, Sansone and Smith (chapter 12) argue that rather than a particular goal content's being automatically associated with intrinsic motivation
and better performance, it is critical to know whether the experience of
working toward that goal is associated with the positive phenomenological
experience of interest and enjoyment.

Although some types of goals may be more likely to be associated with
intrinsic motivation, these latter perspectives suggest that the content of
goals may be less critical than their congruence with other goals, or their
congruence with features of the situation. Specifically, congruence among
the different goals individuals bring to an activity and the congruence of
those goals with the goals encouraged and facilitated by a particular context
may be more critical to the intrinsic-motivation process than goal content
is. Finally, as mentioned above, Shah and Kruglanski (chapter 5) suggest
that goal content or substance is orthogonal to goal structure (or the relation between the goal and the means) and that both dimensions are equally
important to consider when predicting effects on motivation and performance. Despite the different emphases, a common theme that emerges
from this work is the importance of goal dynamics. Furthering our understanding of these dynamics will continue to be one of the important directions for future research.

Relationship between Mastery Goals and Performance Goals

A second issue that has arisen in recent goals work is the relationship
between different goals. In the achievement literature, researchers have
explored relations between mastery goals and performance goals. Early the-
orizing suggested that these goals represented mutually exclusive orientations (much in the same way that intrinsic motivation and extrinsic motivation were originally conceptualized), but more recently, Barron and
Harackiewicz (chapter 9), Linnenbrink and Pintrich (chapter 8), Molden and
Dweck (chapter 6), and Butler (chapter 7) all suggest that individuals can be
motivated simultaneously to reach performance and mastery goals. The
challenge that confronts theorists now is to specify *how* individuals might
pursue more than one goal at a time and to detail the motivational dynamics of multiple goal pursuit. These four chapters highlight these challenges
and set the agenda for future goals research.

The Role of Affect and Subjective Experience

Researchers have also started to propose distinct roles for affect as a potential mediator of the relationships between goals and self-regulatory behav-

ior (e.g., Harackiewicz & Sansone, chapter 4; Linnenbrink & Pintrich, chapter 8; Sansone & Smith, chapter 12; Shah & Kruglanski, chapter 5). For example, Sansone and Smith (chapter 12) show that individuals can actively regulate behavior to enhance positive feelings of interest, which in turn serve to motivate persistence. Linnenbrink and Pintrich (chapter 8) propose instead that affective processes may parallel and influence motivational processes but are distinct from motivational processes.

Instead of focusing on the self-regulatory role of positive affective experiences, other researchers have focused on the role that negative affective experiences such as anxiety or worry can have as a mediator between external factors (e.g., evaluative situations) and motivational outcomes and performance outcomes (e.g., Harackiewicz & Sansone, chapter 4; Shah & Kruglanski, chapter 5). As these trends continue, researchers will be able to address increasingly more complex roles for affect. For example, when do particular experiences with an activity result in more or less positive affect, and when do they result in more or less negative affect?

The Role of the Social Context

Early research discussed the importance of the social context primarily in terms of how it moderated the effects of other factors on intrinsic motivation (e.g., whether a person provides feedback in a controlling manner, whether competence is defined in terms of social comparisons). Since then, other researchers have suggested that the social context can influence the goals adopted in a given situation (Barron & Harackiewicz, chapter 9; Butler, chapter 7; Harackiewicz & Sansone, chapter 4; Molden & Dweck, chapter 6), as well as create a more enduring climate that results in internalization of values (Ryan & Deci, chapter 2). For example, Jacobs & Eccles (chapter 14) suggest that socialization is critically important for the values adopted by individuals, which include values as to what is interesting and worth pursuing. Thus, in important ways and over the long term, the social context (particularly in the form of parents, teachers, and peers) has a cumulative influence on what people value, which ultimately affects what they find intrinsically motivating.

The previous perspectives describe a more distal role for the social context, in which the context affects or predicts motivational factors (e.g., goals, values) that are proposed to be more directly related to interest and intrinsic motivation. In addition to this more distal connection, Sansone and Smith (chapter 12) suggest that other people (whether real or implied) can affect interest (and intrinsic motivation) more proximally. That is, rather than being part of the context surrounding the activity, individuals may consider social factors to be *part* of the activity and a critical part of what makes performance interesting. In this case, factors such as interacting with others while working or knowing that one's work will affect others can create greater interest and enjoyment directly and can lead to greater subsequent intrinsic motivation to perform the activity.

The Role of Individual Differences

Since the earliest research on intrinsic motivation, researchers have increasingly recognized and incorporated individual differences in their understanding of the motivational process. How these are incorporated differs, however, according to the researcher. Several researchers have identified differences in characteristic motivational orientations (Hennessey, chapter 3; Ryan & Deci, chapter 2). From these perspectives, there are relatively stable and enduring differences between people in terms of whether they approach a variety of activities with an intrinsic and autonomous motivational orientation.

Rather than focusing on differences in an overall motivational orientation, in contrast, other researchers examine individual differences that are expected to influence the motivational process in particularly relevant situations. For example, differences in gender, age, theories of intelligence, achievement orientation, interpersonal orientation, and so on, are proposed to influence the goals individuals bring to a given activity in a given context, as well as to moderate the relationship between various processes and motivational outcomes and performance outcomes (Barron & Harackiewicz, chapter 9; Butler, in chapter 7; Harackiewicz & Sansone, chapter 4; Jacobs & Eccles, chapter 14; Molden & Dweck, chapter 6; Renninger, chapter 13; Sansone & Smith, chapter 12). In the context of achievement tasks, Molden and Dweck (chapter 6) further suggest that in addition to influencing the adoption of different goals, individual differences can influence the meaning of the same goal when individuals hold different theories about the malleability of the underlying attribute of intelligence.

SO WHAT HAVE WE LEARNED AND WHERE DO WE GO FROM HERE?

Despite our identification of some major theoretical differences, there are also many common themes and emphases across the collection of chapters in this book. Overall, the field has clearly evolved to focus more closely on process. As knowledge has accumulated from the pioneering efforts of the early research through newer voices in the field, it is no longer necessary or desirable to frame questions in terms of whether certain factors have positive or negative effects on motivation or performance. Instead, the greatest impact comes from asking *how* these effects occur. In so doing, researchers have developed more complex models that incorporate individuals' goals (both chronic and acute) and identify both cognitive and affective processes through which different factors can affect motivation and performance.

One of the strongest themes to emerge across chapters is that researchers no longer focus on mutually exclusive relationships between intrinsic motivation and extrinsic motivation. Instead, researchers have begun to investigate multiple ways that extrinsic motivation and intrinsic motivation can affect creativity, academic performance, and persistence, as well as affect activity choices both initially and over the long term throughout life. Thus, we have learned a lot since the mid-1970s, and it is clear that the contributors to this book will continue to pursue these important issues. These chapters provide exciting and fruitful directions on the path to further knowledge and progress in the field.

References

Amabile, T. M., Hennessey, B. M., & Grossman, B. S. (1986). Social influences on creativity: The effects of contracted for reward. *Journal of Personality and Social Psychology, 50*, 14–23.

Deci, E. L. (1975). *Intrinsic Motivation*. New York: Plenum.

Deci, E. L., Koestner, R., & Ryan, R. M. (1999). A meta-analytic review of experiments examining the effects of extrinsic rewards on intrinsic motivation. *Psychological Bulletin, 125*, 627–668.

Eisenberger, R., & Cameron, J. (1996). Detrimental effects of reward: Reality or myth? *American Psychologist, 51*, 1153–1166.

Hennessey, B. A., & Amabile, T. M. (1998). Reward, intrinsic motivation, and creativity. *American Psychologist, 53*, 674–675.

Kruglanski, A. W., Friedman, I., & Zeevi, G. (1971). The effects of extrinsic incentive on some qualitative aspects of task performance. *Journal of Personality, 39*, 606–617.

Lepper, M. R., Green, D., & Nisbett, R. E. (1973). Undermining children's intrinsic interest with extrinsic rewards: A test of the "overjustification" hypothesis. *Journal of Personality and Social Psychology, 28*, 129–137.

Lepper, M. R., & Green, D. (Eds.) (1978). *The hidden costs of rewards: New perspectives on the psychology of human motivation*. Hillsdale, NJ: Erlbaum.

Lepper, M. R., Henderlong, J., & Gingras, I. (1999). Understanding the effects of extrinsic rewards on intrinsic motivation—uses and abuses of meta-analysis: Comment on Deci, Koestner, and Ryan (1999). *Psychological Bulletin, 125*, 669–676.

McGraw, K. O. (1978). The detrimental effects of reward on performance: A literature review and a prediction model. In M. R. Lepper & D. Green (Eds.), *The hidden costs of rewards: New perspectives on the psychology of human motivation*. Hillsdale, NJ: Erlbaum.

Sansone, C., & Harackiewicz, J. M. (1998). "Reality" is complicated. *American Psychologist, 53*, 673–674.

Author Index

Subject Index

Autonomy (*continued*)
  in cognitive evaluation theory, 17
  competitive dynamics with compe-
    tence, 430
  individual orientations to, 42–43
  parental impact on, 420, 429–431
  in promoting intrinsic motivation,
    286–289
  psychological need for, 14
  rewards and, 15, 265
    verbal, 23
  support in education for, 39
Avoidance goals, affect and, 210, 345
Avoid mastery goals
  achievement outcomes, 219
  anecdotal evidence for, 202–203
  anxiety and, 210
  cognitive mediators, 212
  conceptual change and, 221
  generalizations regarding, 222
  interest and, 208
  logical existence of, 202
  self-efficacy and, 206
Avoid performance goals, 135, 184,
  232
  achievement outcomes, 219
  anxiety and, 211
  conceptual change and, 221–222
  effort and persistence in, 218
  generalizations regarding, 222
  in goal orientation models, 199
  interest and, 208–209
  intrinsic motivation and, 186
  self-efficacy and, 206
  strategy use and self-regulation,
    213

Behavior
  cognitive processes and, 217
  types of explanation for, 1
Behavioral activation systems, 46, 47
Behavioral inhibition systems, 46
Behavioral mediators, 217–218, 220
Behavioral regulation
  approach vs. avoidance systems, 46
  rewards and, 46, 47, 48

  self-regulation, 46–47, 48 (*see also*
    Self–regulation)
Behaviorism
  co-directional situation pattern, 423
  notions of reward and creativity,
    60–64, 74
Belief, achievement goals and, 205
Biological needs, 1
Blood donors, 36
Boredom, 354–355
Brain, stimulation experiments, 14–15

Catching interest, 312–313
Causality orientation, 42–43, 73
CET, *see* Cognitive evaluation theory
Challenge
  in Harter's scale, 274*n*
  in schoolwork, motivation and,
    285–286
Cheating, ability goals and, 177–178
Children, *see also* Students
  activity involvement
    model of optimal engagement,
      422–424
    provision of supportive contexts
      by parents, 420–433
    rewards and, dilemmas for par-
      ents, 420–422
  developmental contexts
    competence, autonomy, and
      relatedness needs, 413–415
    personal identity, 412–413
    person-environment fit, 415
    social identity, 411–412
  developmental declines in academic
    motivation, 272–273
    changing levels of challenge and,
      285–286
    decontextualization of learning
      and, 282–283
    goal orientation shifts and,
      283–285
    overview of, 272–273, 277–280,
      320–324
    significance of, 281
    undermining effect and, 282

Motivation (*continued*)
  behavior and, 1
  internalized, 296–298
  learning process and, 161–162
  orientations to, 73
  outcome- and process-oriented, 342
  promoting in education, 294–298
  studies in, historical perspective,
      257–259
Motivational synergy, 71–72
Multifinality, 112–114

Needs
  in achievement theories, 132
  in goal networks, 109
  psychological, 14
Negative affect, efficacy and, 211
Negative effects, 3, 4; *see also*
      Undermining effect of rewards
Negative feedback, response to, mood
      and, 215
Noncontrolling rewards, 33–35

Opportunity structure, 425–426
Optimal motivation
  achievement goals and, 231–233
  anecdotal example, 229–230
Outcome-oriented motivation, 342
Overjustification effect, 2, 65, 66–67,
      80; *see also* Undermining effect of
      rewards

Parent–child relationship, 431–433
Parenting practices, 427–433
Parents
  activity choices of children and, 415
  children's intrinsic motivation and,
      282n
  effects of children's achievements
      on, 430–431
  expectancy-value theory of activity
      choice and, 406

intersubjectivity and, 424
optimal activity engagement model
      and, 422–424
perception of child's competence
      and, 419–420, 426, 428–429
provision of supportive contexts,
      424–433
  interpreters of reality, 426–427
  opportunity structure, 425–426
  parenting practices in, 427–433
  presentation of values, 427
scaffolding and, 424
socialization for task values,
      416–420
student achievement goals and, 291
Parent socialization
  communicating ability perceptions,
      419–420
  model of, 416–418
  parental beliefs, 418
  provision of specific experiences,
      418–419
  role modeling, 419
  social-emotional climate, 418
Passionate thought, 319–320
Peak experiences, 320
Perceived competence, 153, 239, 263,
      265
  ability goals and, 184
  child development and, 414
Perceived goals, 98
Performance
  achievement motivation and,
      146–152
  effects of achievement goals and
      information seeking on,
      181–185
  positive feedback and, 187
  self-regulation and, 365–366, 367
Performance-contingent rewards, 3
  avoiding undermining effects, 33–34
  characteristics of, 81
  competence feedback and, 82
  cue value and, 34
  defined, 27, 80
  effects of, 27, 57
  evaluation conditions and, 34
  goal dissociation and, 114

Reward procedures
  applying to experimental results,
    266–267
  conceptual model, 263–265
  making predictions with, 265–266
Reward properties
  additivity in, 86
  competence feedback, 85–86
  empirical studies, 88–90
  evaluative threat, 84–85
  moderators of, 91–92
  overview of, 83–88
  process analysis of mediating
    effects, 92–95
  symbolic cue value, 83, 86–88
Rewards
  activity-related motivation and,
    328–329
  affect and, 332–333
  behavioral regulation and, 1, 46–47,
    48
  behaviorist notions of, 60–64, 74
  competence and, 79
  competence valuation and, 94–95
  controlling aspect, 17
  current debates on, 4–5
  delayed, 329–330
  electrical brain stimulation experi-
    ments, 14–15
  expectancy-value theory, 72
  expectation and, 25
  extrinsic motivation and, 444
  informational aspect, 17, 33, 34
  interest and, 324–332
  intrinsic motivation and, 16–17,
    56–57, 80
    avoiding reward effects, 32–35
    current debate in, 4–5, 55–57,
      443–444
    early studies on, 2–3
    limitations of concepts, 106
    meta-analytical studies, 4–5,
      18–32, 267–271, 324–332
    overjustification effects, 2, 65,
      66–67, 80
    overview of studies in, 310–311
  limitations of concepts, 106
  meta-analysis and, 4
  in modern society, 15–16

motivational additivity and, 2,
    67–68, 69, 71
motivational synergy model, 71–72
motivation and
  basic propositions regarding,
    262–263
  conceptual determinants, 263–265
  perceived autonomy and, 265
  perceived competence and, 263,
    265
  perceived continued instrumen-
    tality and, 263
nature and, 14–15
orientations to, 42–46
parental use of, dilemmas in,
    420–422
process analysis, 96–98
research history, trends, and issues,
    2–5, 55–57, 259–273, 310–311,
    443–444
  meta-analytical studies, 4–5,
    18–32, 267–271, 324–332
symbolic cue value and, 87–88
task interest and, 326–328, 359
timing of, 329–330
withholding of, 330–332
workplace performance and, 40–42

Sadness, 209
Scaffolding, 424
Schools
  decontextualization of learning and,
    282–283
  developmental declines in motiva-
    tion and, 281–286
  low interest tasks in, 387–388
  promoting intrinsic motivation in
    autonomy and self-determina-
      tion, 286–289
    contextualization and curiosity,
      289–291
    developing challenges, 292–294
    learning goals, 291–292
  promoting other motivations in,
    294–298
  shifts in student's goal orientations,
    283–285